Subseries on the History of
Japanese Business and Industry

Mitsubishi and the N.Y.K.,
1870–1914

HARVARD EAST ASIAN MONOGRAPHS
108

Subseries on the History of
Japanese Business and Industry

Japan's rise from the destruction and bitter defeat of World War II to its present eminence in world business and industry is perhaps the most striking development in recent world history. This did not occur in a vacuum. It was linked organically to at least a century of prior growth and transformation. To illuminate this growth a new kind of scholarship on Japan is needed: historical study *in the context of a company or industry* of the interrelations among entrepreneurs, managers, engineers, workers, stockholders, bankers, and bureaucrats, and of the institutions and policies they created. Only in such a context can the contribution of particular factors be weighed and understood. It is to promote and encourage such scholarship that this series is established, supported by the Japan Institute and published by the Council on East Asian Studies at Harvard.

Albert M. Craig
Cambridge, Massachusetts

MITSUBISHI AND THE N.Y.K., 1870–1914
Business Strategy in the Japanese Shipping Industry

WILLIAM D. WRAY

Published by COUNCIL ON EAST ASIAN STUDIES, HARVARD UNIVERSITY, and distributed by HARVARD UNIVERSITY PRESS, Cambridge (Massachusetts) and London   1984

The Council on East Asian Studies at Harvard University publishes a monograph series and, through the Fairbank Center for East Asian Research and the Japan Institute, administers research projects designed to further scholarly understanding of China, Japan, Korea, Vietnam, Inner Asia, and adjacent areas. Publication of this volume has been assisted by a grant from the Shell Companies Foundation.

Library of Congress Cataloging in Publication Data

Wray, William D., 1943–
   Mitsubishi and the N.Y.K., 1870–1914.

   (Harvard East Asian monographs ; 108)
   Bibliography: p.
   Includes index.
   1. Nippon Yūsen Kabushiki Kaisha—History.
2. Mitsubishi Zaibatsu—History.   I. Title.
II. Title: Mitsubishi and the NYK.   III. Series.
HE945.N72W7   1984   387.5'065'52   84–12114
ISBN 0–674–57665–9

To Tokuko,
with love

Acknowledgments

This study was first inspired in late 1970 by the works of William Lockwood and Kozo Yamamura on the Meiji economy and by J. H. Parry's lectures, which focused my interest in European expansion on shipping. In 1976 my dissertation, covering 1870–1894, was presented to the History Department of Harvard University. The dissertation was expertly guided by Professor Albert M. Craig, and its reader, Professor Edwin O. Reischauer, made many helpful suggestions and later provided valuable introductions for which I am grateful.

My dissertation thus marked the halfway point in the completion of the present study. Many personal debts have been accrued over such a long undertaking, the longest of which is to Professor Craig, whose catholicity of interests, careful questioning, and sage advice have immeasurably benefited this study.

I am deeply grateful to Professor Nakagawa Keiichirō for his enormous generosity in time, materials, introductions, and expert conversation throughout the past decade. I am also indebted to Professor Alfred D. Chandler, Jr. My first meeting with him was the turning point in the development of my thesis. Since then his astonishing capacity for rich ideas has continued to stimulate my work. Comments by Professors John Dower and Kozo Yamamura helped in my revisions, as did those of George Egerton, Bob Kubicek, Ed Wickberg, and Alex Woodside, colleagues at the University of British Columbia. Frank Langdon also shared material, and Andrew Fraser kindly offered suggestions.

Numerous Japanese scholars generously gave advice and materials: Professors Kita Masami, Kobayashi Masaaki, Kokaze Hidemasa, Miwa Ryōichi, Morikawa Hidemasa, Nakamura Masanori, Nakamura Seishi, Takatera Sadao, and Yui Tsunehiko. Professor Wakimura Yoshitarō provided valuable introductions. Professors Ishikawa Tsuneo, Tsuchiya Moriaki, and Uekusa Masu gave last-minute help. I owe special debts to Professor Ishida Takeshi for an extended sponsorship at Tōdai's Institute of Social Science, to Dr. Hata Ikuhiko for a productive two years in the Japanese Ministry of Finance's Postwar Financial History project, and to Tōdai's Economics Faculty for affiliation in 1982–1983.

I am grateful to Ishida Reiko for research assistance at an early stage of this work. For more recent help I would like to thank Steve Ericson, Pat Pringle, and especially Kumiko Terazawa. Questions raised by students in my course on Japanese business history at UBC have helped to clarify points. Valuable stylistic advice has been given by my good friend Bert Zelman and by Mary Ann Flood of Harvard's Council on East Asian Studies. My greatest debt by far is to my wife Tokuko. She helped me select the minutes of the N.Y.K. board meetings and then transcribed them into legible Japanese.

Among institutions, the N.Y.K. has been extraordinarily generous in providing material which survived earthquakes, fire bombing, floods, the American Occupation, and sheer neglect. Everyone who helped me deserves thanks, but for facilitating access to material I am especially grateful to Kawakubo Michiko, Mikami Ryōzō, and Yonesato Masaaki. In Britain, I would like to thank John Swire & Sons, Ltd., for the use of their well-organized archive in the School of Oriental and African Studies, University of London. I am grateful to Professor John Fairbank for urging me to examine the Swire papers. Mr. Stephen Rabson of the P. & O. provided useful introductions, kindly showed me material in the company library, and introduced me to the bulk of the firm's archives in Greenwich, where I enjoyed the company and advice of Campbell McMurray. For access to material there I thank The Trustees of the National Maritime Museum. Matheson & Co. Limited kindly permitted access to the archives of Jardine, Matheson & Co., Ltd., at Cambridge University and Mr. Alan Reid, director and honorary archivist for the firm, gave useful advice. I am also grateful to Mr. R. G. Sutton, Secretary of the Far Eastern Freight Conference. In Liverpool, Mr. G. T. Evans gave me access to the archives of Ocean Transport & Trading Limited (formerly The Ocean Steam Ship Company) and Miss Dora Hazelhurst facilitated my search. In North America, I was able to use the Great Northern Railway Company Records through the courtesy of the Minnesota Historial Society.

Space does not permit me to thank individually many librarians in Japan, North America, and Britain for their assistance. But I will always be grateful to Suzuki Hideo of Tōdai's Economics Library.

My thanks go to the Canada Council and Harvard's East Asian Research Center for financial aid at the beginning of this study. I am also grateful for grants received since then from Harvard's Japan Institute, UBC's Humanities and Social Science Awards and the President's Committee on Japanese Studies, the Donner Canadian Foundation, the Social Sciences and Humanities Research Council of Canada, and the Japan Foundation.

Finally, I would like to express my gratitude to my mother, Lilian Ellen Wray, who passed away in 1961. She would understand why accounting plays a major role in this study. Also indispensible in its preparation were lessons given over the years by my father, Frank C. Wray. I regret, though, that my daughter Sheila has had far too many summer vacations and other times interrupted by my writing. My wife Tokuko has endured years of waiting, but her knack for fixing things around the house prevented even further delays in this book.

Contents

Tables

Illustrations

Maps

1. *Dates* The Japanese adopted the Western calendar on January 1, 1873. In the Japanese lunar calendar that day was equivalent to the 3rd day of the 12th month of the 5th year of Meiji (1872). Thus January 1, 1873 would be rendered 12/3/1872. I have retained the Japanese dates for the years before 1873.

2. *Ship Tonnage* See Appendix A.

3. *Abbreviations of Company Names* Periods after the capital letters are retained if they were part of the company name; periods are not included in abbreviations that I have made myself. Main abbreviations are:

KUK	Kyōdō Un'yu Kaisha
N.Y.K.	Nippon Yūsen Kaisha
O. & O.	Occidental & Oriental Steamship Co.
O.S.K.	Osaka Shōsen Kaisha
P. & O.	Peninsular & Oriental Steam Navigation Co.
YJK	Nihon Koku Yūbin Jōkisen Kaisha

Also, the Ocean Steam Ship Company is sometimes referred to as the Blue Funnel, or A. Holt & Co.

4. *Company Administrative Terminology* See Appendix B.

5. *Term* That is, the "business term." See the description of *NYK-EH* in "Abbreviations Used in the Notes," p. 538.

6. *Use of Iwasaki Names* This study refers to four members of the Iwasaki family: Yatarō, his younger brother Yanosuke, Yatarō's son Hisaya, and Yanosuke's son Koyata. Following convenience and Japanese custom in this case, I refer to them by their personal names.

7. *Political Parties* For the sake of non-Japan specialists the names of Japanese parties are translated. Thus the nineteenth-century Jiyūtō and Kaishintō become the Liberal and Progressive parties. Japanese names of later parties like the Seiyūkai and Dōshikai have been retained since their translations have no meaningful political content.

8. *Macrons* Macrons have been omitted in common geographical or historical place names like Osaka, Tokyo, Hokkaido, Choshu, and Tokaido.

9. *Japanese Name Order* Japanese names, including those of Japanese scholars publishing in English, are rendered with the family name first.

10. *Money* ¥1 = 100 *sen*.   £1 = 20s. and 1s. = 12d.

*Mitsubishi and the N.Y.K.,
1870–1914*

Introduction

In 1867 a ship chartered from an English company embarked from
Nagasaki, bound for a small island off the east coast of Korea. In
charge of this expedition was Iwasaki Yatarō, a commercial official
of the Tosa domain, located on Shikoku, one of Japan's four main
islands, and facing the Pacific Ocean. Iwasaki's superiors in the Tosa
administration had heard that the small island had been used as an
entrepot for illegal trade between Japan and Korea earlier in the
nineteenth century and that the status of its sovereignty was in
doubt. Tosa decided to claim the island and use it as a new entrepot for trade with Korea. Bearing a signboard, "Iwasaki Yatarō,
by order of Tosa domain in Great Japan, discovered this island,"
Iwasaki reached his destination only to be chased away by the
Koreans living there. He returned to Japan to plan for another
day.[1]

On March 15, 1896, a Japanese ship embarked from Yokohama, bound for London on the first voyage of a regularly scheduled
shipping line between Japan and Europe operated by Japanese.[2]
The ship was the *Tosa Maru*, named for the domain of Iwasaki
Yatarō, builder of Japan's first modern steamship company, who
had died in 1885, more than a decade after he had established his
firm, Mitsubishi, with the slogan, "Encircle the globe with Japanese lines!" Several months after his death, Mitsubishi merged
with a government-sponsored concern to form a new company,

the Nippon Yūsen Kaisha (Japan Mail Steamship Company, or N.Y.K.). The N.Y.K., owner of the *Tosa Maru,* was now fulfilling Yatarō's exhortation to encircle the globe.

Following the Meiji Restoration of 1868 it took roughly a quarter century for Japan to establish its first regular line beyond the confines of East Asia. These were not years of unilinear progress. Success, when it came in the 1890s, was due to the interaction of several factors which brought tangible profits to those businessmen with visions of overseas expansion, including the financial strength of the Meiji government, the growth of the economy as a whole, the assimilation of Western corporate practices by Japanese business, and strategies of cooperation between different Japanese industries.

THE HISTORICAL SETTING

Overseas expansion has had an ambivalent tradition in Japanese history. Between the fourteenth and early seventeenth centuries the Japanese sent numerous commercial missions to China and Southeast Asia. These were sponsored by Buddhist temples, feudal lords, merchants in port towns, and even the Tokugawa bakufu, established in 1603. However, by 1640, for the sake of internal security—the need to prevent the rise of regional economic power which might disrupt the political and social structure upon which the Tokugawa order was based—and a new East Asian foreign policy, the bakufu suspended these overseas voyages and prohibited Europeans, except the Dutch, from trading in Japan. This "closed country" (*sakoku*) policy crippled Japanese maritime power through edicts against overseas travel, the purchase of foreign ships, and the construction of vessels with a capacity of more than 500 *koku*.[3] Though coastal shipping became a flourishing business over the next two centuries, with many vessels exceeding the proscribed limit, and though traditional Japanese ships continued to play an important role in coastal trade for several decades after the Restoration, they were unable to perform the services provided by the Western steamship after the country was reopened in the 1850s.

In the Meiji Restoration, western domains had overthrown the Tokugawa bakufu, established Japan's first truly national administration, and begun to abolish feudal regulations and customs. Even before their political power was fully secured, the new Meiji leaders had to confront an economic crisis caused as much by Japan's peculiar distribution of commercial and industrial enterprise as by any general lack of development. Tokugawa commercial activity is usually divided into two categories: first, urban merchant houses, through whom the bakufu tried to regulate the economy; and second, peasants, who were less subject to official controls, the result being that the wealthier among them, who sold their crops on the market, had in effect become rural entrepreneurs by the early nineteenth century, diversifying into such industrial activity as cloth production, sake brewing, and silk weaving.

By the 1850s this rural growth and the declining regulatory power of the bakufu had already undercut the urban merchants, who had relied on exclusive privileges granted by political authorities in exchange for their services. The opening of the country to trade with the West accelerated this structural change, as goods moved between rural Japan and foreign traders, by-passing urban merchants, many of whom went bankrupt. Yet even in the beginning, foreign trade proved a mixed blessing for rural areas. The heavy demand for Japanese raw silk brought wealth to some, but it drove the price beyond the means of domestic weavers. Furthermore, rural demand for foreign goods competed with cottage industries that the government could not protect, because the unequal treaties with the West had deprived Japan of tariff autonomy. Finally, the small size of rural enterprises, scattered throughout the country and hampered by the high cost and difficulty of transport, limited their competitiveness and increased the country's economic vulnerability.

The early Meiji government's response was twofold: first, industrial promotion programs emphasizing import substitution, or, failing that, the export of goods already in demand, especially raw silk and tea, to balance the inflow of foreign products; and second, the establishment of new services, like trading and shipping enterprises, and new communications, especially telegraphs and to a lesser extent railways.

As a prelude to these reforms, following the opening of the country the bakufu had repealed the restrictive edicts on shipping and shipbuilding. This led to rapid purchasing of ships and spurred maritime defense and commercial development agencies in many of the large domains. Iwasaki Yatarō first came to prominence through such an agency. Its vessels gave him valuable managerial experience, but in general, though Japan had purchased roughly 20,000 tons of Western shipping by the Restoration, these ships did not contribute directly to successful commercial shipping. Many were old and needed repair, their price was high, and they created a large burden on bakufu and domain finances. A competitive shipping industry was still too capital intensive for Japan's resources.[4] By the early 1870s, then, foreign shipping companies had established a thriving business in coastal routes.

The service sector of the early Meiji economy thus suffered from an institutional vacuum. Though dangerous to the nation as a whole, this provided rich opportunities for adroit entrepreneurs to exploit and establish their own fledging monopolies. They followed roughly four routes to wealth: (1) currency speculation—available to those with foreknowledge of the conversion of domain and bakufu currencies into the new national monetary unit, the yen (¥); (2) exclusive privileges—convenient for large merchant houses like Mitsui that survived the Restoration with emergency reserves, which they paid the Meiji government as forced loans but in return accepted official deposits; (3) acquisition of strategic information such as trading expertise—feasible for businessmen with experience in foreign firms, such as Masuda Takashi, first manager of Mitsui Bussan (the Mitsui Trading Company); and (4) government service contracts—invaluable to those whose bargaining position brought them advantageous terms. This final category included a deal for military transport that catapulted Yatarō to the top rank of the business world.

The businessmen who made fortunes during the 1870s by these methods are referred to as "political merchants" (*seishō*). Though often used as a pejorative, *seishō* aptly describes a particular institutional stage in the development of Japanese business, which lasted from the Restoration to the mid-1880s. During these years the privileged connections, the source of much business wealth, were essentially ad hoc relations with the government. While business greatly benefited from these special ties, its services, though expensive, helped stabilize the early Meiji government. The largest *seishō* of the 1870s, Mitsui and Mitsubishi, became strong in two general fields: services and financing. In services, Mitsui dominated trading and Mitsubishi, shipping. With its successful passage through the Restoration years Mitsui became strongest in the financial sector, exemplified by the establishment of the Mitsui Bank in 1876. For Mitsubishi financing became an essential subsidiary function for its shipping enterprise.

Trends in government policy during the 1880s transformed these *seishō* into a new form of business institution. First came the severance of exclusive privileges: the newly established Bank of Japan took over the official functions performed by the Mitsui Bank; government intervention in strategic industry led Mitsubishi to withdraw from shipping. Next came the government's sale of many of its enterprises to these same *seishō*. As a result of these policy trends, the leading business firms acquired a much greater degree of managerial autonomy, which they strengthened in the subsequent decade by accumulating enormous profits, especially through mining, an industry relatively free of government control even though the firms had originally purchased many of their mines from the government. As the fortunes of these concerns grew and as they became more diversified, *seishō* was gradually replaced by "zaibatsu," which came into popular usage after 1890 to describe business enterprises like Mitsui and Mitsubishi.[5] Zaibatsu literally means "financial clique" but actually refers to a large business concern, owned by a single family, of functionally related enterprises in commerce, mining, finance, and industry. Of these fields, the zaibatsu were slowest to move into industrial manufacturing. When they did so, it was usually through the planning and initiative of their managers rather than their owners,[6] and in Mitsubishi's case, it was also with government financial backing for shipbuilding. This aid, however, was given not through exclusive ad hoc arrangements, as had been the case in the 1870s, but according to specific laws which placed it on a longer-term basis. Despite the importance of subsidies in certain manufacturing fields, the institutional evolution of the zaibatsu after the mid-1880s was more the result of private business strategy than government ties.

Mitsui was the largest zaibatsu in the late nineteenth century, Mitsubishi the biggest of those born after the Restoration. This study will deal only with Mitsubishi's activities that relate to shipping. This will involve a detailed examination of Mitsubishi up until 1885, when shipping was its core enterprise, as well as a briefer look at the later connection between shipping and industries such as mining, railways, and shipbuilding, in which Mitsubishi became active either as an owner/manager or as an investor. The central thesis proposed in the first two parts of this study is that Mitsubishi began the institutional path toward zaibatsu formation only after it withdrew from direct management of shipping at the time of the N.Y.K.'s establishment in 1885. In the mid-1890s, this path converged again with shipping, which functioned as a trigger industry, stimulating demand for shipbuilding and steel, thereby initiating changes in Japan's industrial structure.[7]

While the zaibatsu were building business structures within Japan, many firms, including zaibatsu-related companies, were having an increasing impact in international business. By the 1890s some of these firms had become competitive well beyond East Asia. In this period the Big Four of Japanese international business were the N.Y.K., Mitsui Bussan, the Yokohama Specie Bank (a foreign exchange bank that promoted Japanese trade), and the Tokio Marine Insurance Company. These four performed essential service functions in importing raw materials and industrial equipment and in exporting light industrial products like cotton yarn and matches as well as raw silk. The cooperation of these service and financial firms with manufacturing industries facilitated the rise of Japanese economic power from the Restoration to World War I, which, in view of Japan's seclusion prior to the 1860s, can be termed an economic revolution. One of its most visible marks in the rest of the world was Japanese shipping, especially the N.Y.K., which by 1900 ranked among the world's largest shipping firms.

THEMES AND PROPOSITIONS

This book is a business history of a particular enterprise in its two forms: Mitsubishi before 1885 and the N.Y.K. thereafter. It takes an institutional approach and thus is not economic or quantitative history, though statistical data are presented that may benefit economic historians. My principal concern is business strategy, which Alfred Chandler defined as "the determination of the basic long-term goals and objectives of an enterprise, and the adoption of courses of action and the allocation of resources necessary for carrying out these goals."[8] Since the Meiji state considered shipping a strategic industry, the book also focuses on government-business relations. Although the Meiji government and the enterprises studied here often shared similar "long-term goals and objectives," this book views the history of Japanese shipping as institutional change through conflict. Themes illustrating tension and conflict were the struggle by managers to retain company autonomy, the role of the government in "guiding" private business, and internal company disputes between managers and stockholders over financial issues.

The first attribute of management strategy was its *autonomy*. This does not mean that companies operated in a laissez-faire environment. In the shipping industry, subsidies and other forms of government favor provided a framework that shaped company decisions. But innovative strategies leading to new operations created substantial room for autonomous managerial planning.

The assertion of autonomy was a major factor in the structural change of the economy. Mitsubishi, for example, helped to lay the basis for its growth into a zaibatsu by exploiting and resisting government policies. On the other hand, government backing was crucial both to the successful growth of the N.Y.K. and the diversification of Mitsubishi into heavy industry. Thus company autonomy and government planning interacted in the form of a dialectic leading to a coexistence that produced effects favorable to both the private firm and the state despite ongoing conflict between them.

It is often thought that the era between the early 1880s and the 1920s was an unusual period in modern Japanese history in that, unlike the 1870s or the years since the late 1920s, the government, in Chalmers Johnson's words, aided only "particular industries" instead of seeking "to organize a part of the whole economy." Though the government was relatively less active as an economic planner following the Matsukata deflation of the 1880s, one cannot characterize its policy as laissez-faire.[9] The principle of "designating" strategic industries became explicit during this period. Huge subsidies were given to shipping, for example, not just for its military importance but also for its ripple effects on the economy. In trade, lacking tariff autonomy, the government instituted various preferential measures that anticipated the later protectionism of non-tariff barriers. There also emerged in this period the distinction between direct industrial financing approved by the Diet and informal, non-legislative methods of government promotion and inducement. Finally, though his means were informal, even Matsukata Masayoshi, the finance minister who ushered in this allegedly non-interventionist age, viewed the developmental function of Imperial House assets much the way a Ministry of International Trade and Industry bureaucrat of the 1950s regarded the Japan Development Bank.

The Meiji period, then, set certain precedents for the kind of post-1920s industrial policy discussed in Johnson's work on MITI. His book, which emphasizes conflict within the government, analyzes the institutional evolution of the state's developmental role. Yet, to achieve a full picture of the changing economy, one would have to do an equally detailed study of private business strategy during the past half century. The present work treats the institutional beginnings of private strategy prior to World War I. The view here is that, at its most fundamental level, business history must focus on the strategy employed by management for *normal business operations.* This differs sharply from earlier historical monographs on Japanese business whose focus on the social origins of entrepreneurs and on ideology was closer to social and intellectual history than to business history.

Analysis of normal operations—in short, the basic function of the enterprise—reveals the second attribute of strategy to be *rationality.* Meiji businessmen were calculating men who made strategic decisions with the most careful attention to company finances. As early as the late 1870s, company practices such as imaginative depreciation, *minimum* observance of government directives, and long-term financial planning attest to this rationality. The first concerns of the entrepreneurs and managers studied here were expanding their market share, retaining the confidence of their business partners, securing *long*-term profits, jettisoning unprofitable operations, and, with a few exceptions, preparing for new ventures, especially where the burden of acquiring assets could be shared. These rational habits and goals defined the making of business strategy. In contrast to this view, the textbook-style presentation of Hirschmeier and Yui places more emphasis on distinct Japanese cultural and social patterns and perpetuates a value-oriented approach that constricts analysis at a time when many Japanese scholars are asking broader questions about strategy and business organization.[10]

Historical works which stress consensus, patriotism, and national character are similar in theme to recent books on postwar "Japanese-style management." During the period of high growth in the 1960s and early 1970s works on the contemporary Japanese economy focused on issues of strategy and finance, particularly the high debt/equity ratio of Japanese firms. At least in popular writing, in the past decade attention has shifted from growth to management techniques. One work typical of this trend contrasts what is called the "hard S's" (strategy, structure, and systems), which have been of central concern to Western managers, with the "soft S's" (staff, style, skills, and superordinate goals) in which the Japanese have excelled.[11] The present work contains information on Mitsubishi and N.Y.K. management "style" and "superordinate goals." Nevertheless, I have preferred to focus on strategy rather than style because most of the managerial techniques frequently noted in recent years as having a peculiarly Japanese style are in fact products of the 1937–1955 era. Furthermore, the fact that many scholarly works dealing with contemporary Japanese corporations have outdated historical perspectives makes all the more essential an examination of pre-World War I strategy.[12]

A third attribute of successful business strategy was *flexibility*. An enterprise like Mitsubishi was able to reallocate its resources according to its long-term profit projections and thus to change its structure. As an "organizer of the economy," Mitsui Bussan assembled companies from separate industries to create business networks competitive with foreign firms. This process of private diversification at the micro level has obvious parallels to MITI's more recent role in changing Japan's industrial structure. It also raises the question of the extent to which private diversification itself has contributed to structural changes at the macro level.[13] In this work I have examined private strategy and state policy together. Studying these separately perpetuates a common tendency of attributing too decisive a role to either one.

Rather than concentrating their resources—and risk—in one industry, the zaibatsu diversified into many fields. Japanese scholars, influenced by Chandler's models of organization and structure, have studied this strategic flexibility, and, since the mid-1970s, they have produced lengthy theoretical works on the zaibatsu, comparative studies, popular handbooks, scholarly essays in multivolume series, case studies of individual zaibatsu both in popular and textbook form (the latter containing exhaustive bibliographies),[14] and analyses of specific issues like the increasing power of professional managers, accounting, and stockholding. There is even a six-volume series on the history of the Japanese shipping business, though it deals only with the Inter-War period and thus does not overlap the present work.[15]

Despite this publishing boom there remains a lag in Japanese business historiography in two areas: in utilizing company archives (except Mitsui's) for independent research[16] and in using overseas archives to study Japan's international business. The present work makes contributions in these two areas: Part Three especially is based largely on archival materials from the N.Y.K. and from Britain. Though the N.Y.K.'s own material consists almost entirely of internal records, Western material on the company provides an external record. The two areas of data mix well, giving us the perspectives of both the principal and its competitors.

Apart from aggregate studies by economic historians like William Lockwood and Henry Rosovsky, the most useful work by Western scholars on Meiji business has been done by Gary Saxonhouse (on technology diffusion) and Kozo Yamamura (on entrepreneurship and banking).[17] In contrast to their focus on specific issues, I have analyzed strategy from the perspective of top management to determine why decisions were made. My explanations are on several levels: the external context of economic change and government policy and what pressures these exert on the firm; the internal dynamics of a firm's structure and how its various components affect management decisions; and the connection between market opportunities and the firm's economic needs and how that shapes the company's operational network. The substantial amount of factual detail in this work serves as the thread with which to weave together interpretations of government policy, company strategy, and market opportunities. The following basic propositions are an introduction to these interpretations.

(1) Leaders of Japanese shipping firms frequently made resolute, indeed sometimes visionary, statements favoring economic expansion through overseas lines.

(2) Companies, both those dependent on government aid and those which relied primarily on their own resources, went to great lengths to preserve their managerial autonomy.

(3) Shipping firms, as well as the zaibatsu, generally followed a strategy of risk avoidance.

(4) To limit risk, Japanese firms adopted effective strategies of risk sharing. The shipping industry achieved this in two ways: the government bore part of the risk by providing subsidies, and shipping firms established business alliances with shippers who gave them guarantees.

These propositions constitute a series of surface generalizations about the way Japanese business worked prior to 1914. To show what happened at a more complex level of activity, a second set of propositions about the consequences of the strategies outlined in the first four propositions must be constructed.

(5) Expansion was risky. Frequently, then, expansionist rhetoric (proposition 1) came into conflict with risk-avoidance strategy (proposition 3). In short, business often did the opposite of what it said. This puts a premium on acquiring primary material on decisions made by company boards. It is also a reason why studies of business ideology have limited value in explaining business operations.

(6) The aforementioned strategies contain a second potential conflict, namely, that between the desire for autonomy (proposition 2) and the strategy of risk sharing (proposition 4). For example, when the government provided subsidies it usually imposed conditions which eroded company autonomy.

(7) Many scholars argue that, although there is conflict in Japan between government and business, fundamentally companies have the same goals as the government and they are, furthermore, patriotic. Whatever the truth of this abstract argument, its proponents often evade important issues by drawing their conclusion only from statements and strategies such as those mentioned in my first set of propositions. By switching the analysis to a deeper level we can better understand the nature of conflict within the business world and between government and business. Historically, much of this conflict occurred over methods of sharing risks (as in propositions 5 and 6). This was not simply a disagreement over "means" to commonly accepted "ends." For example, the N.Y.K.

became a member of an international conference whose members shared risks. At the same time the Japanese government bore risk for the N.Y.K. by subsidizing it. But when the policy of the conference differed from that of the Japanese government, which acted as a public custodian trying to keep freight rates low, it was by no means clear that the N.Y.K. and the government shared the same goal.[18]

(8) In the case just described, the N.Y.K. could achieve immediate private gain through high freight rates. Yet even in this respect, the company's interest was ambiguous. The social gain from low rates, which was the government's goal, could also bring long-term benefit to the N.Y.K. by making exports more competitive, thereby providing more cargo for the company. In critical cases involving competition with foreigners the increasing competitiveness of Japanese products facilitated the strategy of risk sharing in which the N.Y.K. formed alliances with Japanese shippers.[19]

(9) The strategy of risk sharing was most effective in industries where Japan had a comparative advantage because long-term costs were declining, such as shipping and cotton spinning between the early 1890s and World War I. Business alliances adopting this strategy hastened the change in Japan's industrial structure toward more manufacturing at home.

(10) The strategy of risk sharing was least effective when it encroached upon company autonomy and when costs were not declining. Some Japanese firms have found themselves in such a disadvantageous situation after having made a successful start in a particular business. One strategic response has been for the firm to withdraw from the original business, taking whatever fortune it could to start a new enterprise in a different field. This is what Mitsubishi did in the 1880s.

COVERAGE

This work employs a chronological approach to periodize business strategy through the changing political and economic contexts of roughly forty-five years. A close reading of the chronology is essential for analyzing why decisions were made. My interpretation of Mitsubishi's motivation in 1885, for example, derives heavily from this approach. I have, however, included a topical analysis at the end of each of the three parts of the study.

The emergence of the N.Y.K. can be divided into two stages: a period of formation from 1870 to the mid-1890s and an era of expansion from the mid-1890s to 1914. Prior to the mid-1890s Japanese shipping was active primarily in coastal routes. During the era of expansion most N.Y.K. business was overseas. It is essential, however, that both of these eras be brought together to examine the process toward expansion.

Nineteen-fourteen and the beginning of World War I constitute an appropriate closing point to this work. Though the era of expansion that began in the 1890s lasted until about 1919, its World War I phase, with its extraordinary demand for goods and services from the West, is best regarded as distinct from the period of expansion up to 1914.[20] The 1893 to 1914 years can therefore be seen as a separate stage in modern Japanese economic expansion. In the early years of this period of growth (up to about 1904) the N.Y.K. adopted progressive and innovative strategies for expansion. From about 1907 to 1914, however, conservative tendencies characterize N.Y.K. decisions which anticipate managerial problems during World War I. I have attributed this loss of flexibility to increasing government intervention, competition, and certain features of the N.Y.K.'s internal structure.

Since N.Y.K. operations were far-flung, I have had to be selective in my treatment. Generally I have chosen those lines which best illustrate the mainstream of company strategy and offer the best opportunity for thematic discussion—the company's business to India, Europe, and China. I have given less attention to the American service, and little to the Australian line. N.Y.K. management viewed the prospects of the U.S. line pessimistically and allotted much less tonnage to it than to the more richly subsidized European line. Except for carrying raw silk, the country's largest export, Japanese shipping firms did not fully participate in the American trade until after the opening of the Panama Canal in 1914.

Since labor issues had little bearing on N.Y.K. strategy until about 1912, I have treated labor only briefly with regard to rising costs and changing employment patterns just prior to World War I. Labor relations did have a profound impact on N.Y.K. management decisions in the 1920s, but that will be the subject of a separate study.

Finally, a case study approach is employed not so much to write a comprehensive company history as to determine the reasons behind strategic decisions. Insofar as a context has been provided to these decisions, this work is more than a case study of a particular firm in the shipping industry, for it provides details of many related issues such as government economic policy, decision-making in the early Meiji government, the finances of the Imperial House, Japanese trading strategies (as exemplified by organized business alliances), international commercial diplomacy, imperialism, comparative shipping history (with regard to Japan and Britain), the adoption of Western accounting practices, and the diversification of a zaibatsu.

Through the turmoil and recovery from 1914 to the present, the N.Y.K. has remained within the Mitsubishi zaibatsu and the postwar Mitsubishi group. It continues today as Japan's leading shipping firm. Judging the size of shipping enterprises is a questionable undertaking because of the different measures used (tonnage owned or tonnage operated) and legal issues such as flags of convenience (for ships registered in countries like Liberia and Panama). The N.Y.K. is neither the world's largest shipowner nor its largest operator. Greek and Hong Kong firms like Onassis and Worldwide Shipping have peculiar legal structures in which each ship constitutes a company. Viewed as holding companies, these firms are the world's largest shipowners. On occasion, Japanese firms like the Japan Line, which charter heavily from Hong Kong, have been larger operators than the N.Y.K. The P. & O., the N.Y.K.'s oldest international competitor, is perhaps twice the size of the N.Y.K. in total sales, for this British firm holds substantial assets outside shipping. Nevertheless, in a composite index of tonnage owned and operated as well as income and profit from purely shipping business, the N.Y.K. is thought of as the world's largest shipping enterprise.[21] The diversity of the company's services (liners, tramps, tankers, specialized carriers) contrasts with the more conservative and specialized strategy the N.Y.K. followed between 1907 and World War II.

Part One
The Emergence of Mitsubishi: 1870–1880

In 1868 Japan's shipping services were in the hands of small transport agencies that had long served the country's feudal rulers. By 1880 Mitsubishi had emerged as the largest shipping company based in East Asia.

During the 1870s the Japanese shipping industry went through three phases of growth. The first, 1870–1873, was a period of origins when only the craftiest gambler survived. Shipping companies followed two radically different courses during these years. They could enter into a close relationship with the central government, accepting dependence on it, as well as on newly established financial institutions, for ships and capital; or they could operate independently of the government and rely on personal connections and opportunities within the domains to accumulate capital. Iwasaki Yatarō, founder of Mitsubishi, was the most successful entrepreneur who followed the latter course. Although his enterprise became a private one, Yatarō secured his original backing and capital from his own domain.

The decade's great transformation came in 1874 and 1875. During this short but decisive second phase a new government policy of massive subsidization to one private firm, Yatarō's Mitsubishi, defined a pattern of aid that continued into the 1880s, in the form of ships, initially given without charge, and annual operating subsidies. Yatarō won this favored position largely by building an effective company organization staffed by capable executives and by responding to the government's military needs. In promoting one firm the government opposed competition among Japanese shipowners and implicitly favored a private monopoly.

During the third phase, 1876–1880, Yatarō's organizational strength and government subsidies together made possible several business innovations. To consolidate its hold over the industry, Mitsubishi began to add new supporting functions like an office for financing shippers, a warehousing enterprise, and a repair works. Although the government had designated its subsidies for specific lines, by the early 1880s Mitsubishi's profits had grown so large that it could partially ignore these specifications and use its surplus funds to develop a more complex business structure.

These were the phases of growth. But what drove the government to subsidize shipping were two threats present through most of the decade: military emergencies and foreign competition. The Taiwan expedition of 1874 was the most decisive event of the decade for the shipping industry, the catalyst that transformed the confused, tentative moves of the first phase into the policy phase of 1874–1875, when ships purchased by the government were given to Mitsubishi. Similarly, during the Satsuma Rebellion of 1877 Mitsubishi received an influx of profits, enabling it to expand its business structure. Foreign shipping companies were a threat to Japan's economic security because they had: (1) exacerbated Japan's balance-of-payments deficits by carrying all of its foreign trade; and (2) taken an alarmingly high share of the country's coastal trade. The first major rollback of these companies occurred when Mitsubishi won two epic battles: in 1875 against an American firm; and in 1876 against a British firm. These victories gave Mitsubishi dominance on the Yokohama-Shanghai line, while the competition prompted it to develop supporting enterprises. Their growth eventually created tension between the company and the government, but in the 1870s, at least from the time of the Taiwan expedition, the prevailing theme was close cooperation between Mitsubishi and its government allies.

ONE

The First Shipping Companies: 1870–1874

THE FOUNDING OF MITSUBISHI

IWASAKI YATARŌ: TOSA ORIGINS. Iwasaki Yatarō was born in the Tosa domain in 1834 into a family of former rural-samurai status.[1] He was a diligent though mischievous student, and, unlike many contemporary samurai, he appears to have made a conscious decision to study business and eschew activist political movements. The most important influence on Yatarō was Yoshida Tōyō, a Tosa official in charge of trade and industry, who was the domain's leading proponent of Western learning. In the mid-1850s, during a period of forced retirement brought on by conservative opposition, Yoshida opened a private school, the Shōrinjuku, which Yatarō entered in his early twenties. The general thrust of Yatarō's later career clearly reflects Yoshida's ideas. Yoshida was an advocate of shipping development and viewed economic competition as a fierce struggle among nations. Reportedly he warned his students that "the countries of the world are now competing and expanding their territorial possessions and struggling to the death to build up their wealth." Japan, he went on, "must promote its industries, positively carry out trade with foreign countries, increase its wealth, and resist the countries of the world."[2]

After his return to the Tosa administration in 1858, Yoshida appointed Yatarō to several commercial posts. But Yoshida's assassination in 1862 forced Yatarō to withdraw from all official positions. He returned to favor in early 1866 under the sponsorship of Gotō Shōjirō, a former protégé of Yoshida. Gotō appointed Yatarō to the Kaiseikan (Industry Promotion Agency), newly established for supervising Tosa's enterprises. Over the next few years Yatarō took charge of the Nagasaki and Osaka branches, concentrating on trading and shipping. All was not smooth sailing, however. The firm ran a continuous deficit, and Yatarō was plagued by disagreement with Tosa officials. Activist samurai like Gotō and Sakamoto Ryōma wanted to use the agency for political purposes and sometimes clashed with Yatarō's business-first mentality. Conservatives like Sasaki Takayuki, on the other hand, found profit seeking suspect because it imitated foreigners. Nevertheless, as the Tosa leaders became more involved in the struggles of the Restoration and the new Meiji government, they needed Yatarō to handle the domain's enterprises and to support its defenses. In fulfilling these tasks Yatarō resorted to numerous questionable loans (some foreign) and various "unscrupulous practices." His biggest profits seem to have come from speculation in domain currency before it was converted to government notes.[3]

Yatarō was gradually able to transform the domain agency he managed into his own private business.[4] In 10/1870 part of the agency was detached from domain management and set up as a separate firm called Tsukumo Shōkai (Tsukumo Trading Firm), which operated with the permission of both the central government and the domain, but was not yet formally independent. Essentially it was still only a carrier for the domain. Yatarō began with three domain steamships, but soon acquired several more, some of which he used mainly for speculation.

Yatarō's own position at the time illustrates the continued link between the Shōkai and the domain. When the Shōkai was set up in 10/1870 Yatarō was promoted in the domain hierarchy to junior councillor and made head of the domain's Osaka residence. Here he was responsible for general domain business as well as the trade of the Kaiseikan, which had continued to exist as a domain agency even after the Tsukumo Shōkai was established.[5] In fact, until the abolition of the domains in 7/1871, Yatarō's primary role was that of a domain official. Although he may have been the most important figure in the Tsukumo Shōkai, he was not yet a private entrepreneur, a fact which leaves some ambiguity about the management of the Shōkai. Yatarō's official position with the domain prevented a formal connection with the firm. In reality, however, he did supervise it, though much of the everyday management seems to have been left to his subordinates. Yatarō's dual role gave him certain advantages. For example, in 5/1871 several subordinates in the Shōkai negotiated a fifteen-year lease of two mines of the Shingū domain in Kii Province. The lease contract contained the seals of both the Shōkai and "Iwasaki Yatarō of Tosa domain." Without the seal of a domain official, Shingū would not have agreed to the transaction.

In 7/1871 the domains were abolished, and in 11/1871 Tosa became Kōchi Prefecture. When the Tsukumo Shōkai finally became independent in 1/1872, it changed its name to Mitsukawa Shōkai to emphasize its separation from the prefecture. With the permission of the central government, the prefecture granted the Shōkai certain properties, principally ships the firm had been using but also camphor and silk-reeling enterprises. In exchange Yatarō agreed to incur part of the domain's debt. How he liquidated this is one of the most difficult puzzles to unravel. He appears to have managed it partly by currency speculation. But perhaps more important to him was the central government's assumption of the domain's entire foreign debt, a policy which seems to have covered at least some of the debt Yatarō previously incurred.[6]

In summary, Yatarō achieved his early success through adroit use of foreign loans, currency speculation, and reliance on the Kaiseikan's multiple functions. Backing from the domain's official institutions and its political leaders made this success possible and, in the process, set a precedent for close relations between the early Meiji government and Mitsubishi. The "government-business" relationship within the domains of the late 1860s, however, differed substantially from that between the bakufu and leading Tokugawa commerical institutions, especially in transport. Most importantly, although it did not become independent until 1872, the Tosa agency developed a more autonomous business strategy during its evolution from 1866 to 1871 than had these Tokugawa firms in earlier times; bakufu regulations, controls imposed by trade associations, and a rigid internal structure had greatly limited their flexibility. By contrast, Yatarō's experience had taught him to exploit opportunities offered by the government rather than to submit to its regulations. Prior to 1872 Yatarō had accumulated this experience as a domain official. Private business, however, was a new and riskier undertaking.

Contrary to many earlier perspectives of Yatarō simply utilizing the domain to set up his own private business, for him the most immediate effect of the domain's abolition was the loss of his official position. As a result, he temporarily withdrew from direct management of the Shōkai, entrusting it to subordinates. The firm's new name reflected this managerial situation: "Mitsukawa" (literally, "three rivers") was chosen because the firm's three leading representatives all had the character "*kawa*" (river) in their names. Under this new management the Shōkai for the first time began general freight and passenger business. In the meantime, Yatarō himself considered seeking a position in the central government. Consequently, the power relations inside the Shōkai were left unsettled, and remained so from the abolition of the domain to mid-1872, when Yatarō returned to the firm.

Although Yatarō had acted as a businessman before the domain's abolition, he had done so as an official accustomed to taking full advantage of that status. A government position, therefore, appeared to offer more continuity for his endeavors. He finally returned to the Shōkai partly through the persuasion of Gotō Shōjirō and Hayashi Yūzō, a Tosa samurai who had become the central government's main agent in supervising the transition of Tosa from domain to Kōchi Prefecture. Hayashi told Iwasaki that he would become a "great man" of the business world.[7]

YATARŌ'S LEADERSHIP. When Yatarō returned to the Shōkai he once again became its main figure because of his previous leadership, his superior managerial ability, and the influence he derived from the trust foreigners had in him. When Yatarō achieved the "one-man rule," which later became the hallmark of his management, is the subject of some debate. His official biography guesses that it was as late as 1875. Others date it from 1872. Certainly by early 1873 his personal stamp was upon the firm. In April 1873 he wrote to his younger brother Yanosuke, who had been studying in the United States since mid-1872, and explained his dislike of the name "Mitsukawa." A month earlier he had chosen a new name for the company: henceforth it would be known as "Mitsubishi" (three diamonds).[8] He assembled his employees to announce the new name, which symbolized his dominance over the three managers who had set up Mitsukawa. The speech Yatarō gave is sometimes referred to as the "Independence Declaration" of the new Mitsubishi Shōkai. He emphasized the transition from domain enterprise to private company:

> From now on I will resolutely suppress my ambitions in the official world and devote my undivided attention to the shipping industry. I am determined to make a success of myself in business. For a long time I have worked strenuously as an official of the domain. The fact that I have happily been able to avoid serious errors is due solely to everyone's hard work. [He then appealed to his employees] I hope with all my heart that you will serve under me, . . . but if there are things you do not like about engaging in business with me, by all means take this opportunity to resign. It is my hope, however, that our friendship will last forever.[9]

Yatarō demanded high standards of ability and loyalty from his employees, who were to be guided by the vision he expressed in an 1873 letter to Yanosuke: "In the whole of the Japanese Empire there shall be no other enterprise surpassing us in managerial ability."[10] He succeeded in this goal by bringing into the firm a group of immensely talented men, no mean achievement when the prospects of overseas study, the challenges of government reform, and the excitement of the popular political movements in the 1870s were attracting the attention of many bright young men. Yatarō paid his recruits well and gave them major responsibility.

Mitsubishi, like its arch-rival Mitsui, became an innovator in developing large-scale business enterprises through the use of professional managers. In fact, most of the key men Yatarō recruited in the 1870s became towering figures in their own right in the latter half of the Meiji era. This effective enlistment of personnel held true right up to the founding of the N.Y.K. in 1885.

The two main figures who had been with Yatarō since the days of the Tsukumo Shōkai were Ishikawa Shichizai, six years his elder, and Kawada Koichirō, two years his junior, both Tosa men. Kawada appears in most historical accounts as the "personification of feudal morality." Irimajiri Yoshinaga says that he consented to being beaten in the presence of customers to save Yatarō's face, but he neglects to point out that Kawada was a huge man for a Japanese and looked like a sumo wrestler.[11] He later served as president of the Bank of Japan from 1889 to 1896.[12] Ishikawa, a former domain official, was appointed to investigate Yatarō's finances in late 1870 when the latter was trying to run the Tsukumo Shōkai while also serving as a domain official. Showing Ishikawa his account book, Yatarō reportedly told him that "the first priority for Japan is to revive its shipping and trade. But if we keep up this hair-splitting as our domain is doing now, there will be no hope at all for the wealth and power of Tosa. Why don't you join with me and work for the good of the domain?"[13] Overwhelmed by these arguments, Ishikawa immediately abandoned his mission and entered the Shōkai. Later in the 1870s Ishikawa acquired primary managerial responsibility for Mitsubishi's shipping, and he unquestionably would have become a major business leader had he not died suddenly of cholera in 1882. Kawada and Ishikawa were two of the three "rivers" who had founded the Mitsukawa Shōkai.[14]

Two non-Tosa recruits later became the most important individuals in the development of Japanese shipping and shipbuilding. Kondō Renpei, from Tokushima Prefecture, entered the Mitsukawa Shōkai in 1872 and soon became head of the English school established in Yatarō's Osaka premises. Though he later served as N.Y.K. president (1895–1921), Kondō was engaged mainly in mining until

1883. Shōda Heigorō, of Inaba domain in eastern Kyushu, entered Mitsubishi in 1875 on the recommendation of Fukuzawa Yukichi. Shōda had previously taught at Fukuzawa's Keiō school, from which much of Yatarō's able staff came. Later, as Mitsubishi's general manager (*kanji*), Shōda's two major accomplishments were directing Mitsubishi into shipbuilding and recommending the purchase of the Marunouchi business center of Tokyo. Around 1900 he was probably the most influential leader in the Mitsubishi zaibatsu.[15]

Any account of key Mitsubishi personnel would be remiss without mention of Yatarō's younger brother Yanosuke. He had studied in the United States (1872–1873) and shortly after his return became the leader of the "modern" group within the company, for he was its only member with such foreign experience.[16] In contrast to the people who had followed Yatarō from Tosa, many members of this modern group, who entered the company after it became independent of Tosa, were graduates of Keiō or the Tōkyō Kaisei Gakkō, a forerunner of Tokyo University. Being better educated, these new members were quickly made local branch managers, and some, like Kondō in the case of mining, were assigned to new enterprises apart from shipping. Also, in later years Yatarō was frequently ill, and Yanosuke, though nominally vice-president, increasingly became acting president.

To his talented subordinates Yatarō brought the "worship of money." When calling on customers his employees had to wear the "uniforms of the merchant." He counseled Ishikawa as follows: "If you feel ashamed at bowing to the clerk or errand boy of a client firm, you will be angry and feel offended, but if you are aware that you are bowing to money, you will have patience."[17]

The relationship between patience and money is the basic theme of this study. Patience, after all, is a reflection of business strategy, and money is profit. The most important long-term strategic problem facing Yatarō was whether the shipping industry alone could provide sufficient profits to satisfy his "worship of money" or whether it would be necessary to allocate resources to other business activities. In the early 1870s shipping was

FIGURE 1 Iwasaki Yatarō and Mitsubishi Executives, ca. 1877

Front row, from left: Ishikawa Shichizai, Iwasaki Yatarō, Kawada Koichirō, Fredrick Krebs (a former employee of Walsh, Hall & Company who joined Mitsubishi in 1873).
Back row, from left: Asada Masabumi, Honda Masajirō, Iwasaki Yanosuke, Shōda Heigorō.
Courtesy of the Internal & Public Relations Chamber, NYK LINE.

Mitsubishi's largest enterprise, but the firm was also active in camphor distribution, silk reeling, and mining. By early 1873 shipping was becoming more profitable, but its long-term prospects were still clouded because of competition from government-sponsored companies and foreign concerns. Yatarō's response to this competition involved both short-term tactics and long-term strategy. Tactically, Yatarō fought vigorously, cutting his rates and skillfully soliciting business; strategically, he continued to employ resources outside shipping, which protected the firm as a whole from excessive risk, and was also a partial commitment to broaden the base of the firm. Some contradiction or tension existed between these tactical and strategic responses to competition. Mitsubishi waged frequent campaigns to cut salaries and reduce expenses to defeat its competitors, even though it was simultaneously investing its funds in other enterprises. For example, Mitsubishi made a major strategic move in October 1873 by buying the large Yoshioka copper mine for ¥10,000. At the time Mitsubishi was engaged in a fierce competitive struggle with a government-sponsored company. Employing capital in businesses outside shipping, however, enhanced rather than diminished the strength of the firm's shipping enterprise. Since these outside enterprises became profitable, they helped sustain the firm as a whole when it incurred losses in shipping competition. This made it possible for Yatarō to take greater competitive risks than if he had been the possessor only of ships. The Yoshioka mine in particular became profitable, partly because Mitsubishi utilized prisoners as mine workers. This success gave Yatarō high hopes for his mining enterprise, and he persuaded one of his top lieutenants, Kondō Renpei, to take over management of the Yoshioka mine.[18] From its beginnings, then, Mitsubishi was not exclusively a shipping company. However, during the 1870s, as long as it was able to better its shipping rivals, its other business interests either remained small or developed into supporting mechanisms for the main shipping enterprise.

COMPETITION AMONG SHIPPING COMPANIES

THE KAISŌ KAISHA. The Meiji government's initial attempts to promote shipping enterprises were dismal failures. In the bureaucratic confusion of the early 1870s, the departments responsible for the new shipping companies were often shuffled from one ministry to another, and reforms in accounting procedures prevented certain ministries from fulfilling their promises. Early government pronouncements on shipping were instructional in tone, affirming its preference for Western-style ships, but not supportive in content, at least in a financial sense. Two major proclamations of 1/1870 on merchant vessels and mail steamships contained endless minutiae about operating ships and establishing passenger services, but did not enunciate a concrete shipping policy.[19]

The government initially administered shipping through the Trade Bureau (Tsūshōshi) established by a Council of State (Dajōkan) decree of 2/1869. This bureau, which had broad authority to promote domestic trade, was responsible for establishing special new institutions, namely, exchange companies (*kawase kaisha*) and commercial companies (*tsūshō kaisha*). These were actually joint enterprises of the government and the leading merchant firms of the Tokugawa period and, in form, were modeled after the Western joint-stock company, though the main investors, the Mitsui, Ono, and Shimada, were traditional commercial houses and could not easily duplicate the Western model.[20]

The Trade Bureau's first official shipping company was the Kaisō Kaisha (Marine Transportation Company), organized in 12/1869 when the government combined several shipping and courier agencies and instructed them to transport cargo. A further initiative came from a manager of the Mitsuigumi, Suita Shirobē, who invested in the new company. It became, therefore, a "half public and half private" concern.[21]

There were two main reasons for establishing the Kaisō Kaisha. The land tax was still paid in rice, necessitating an authorized transportation agency to ship to Osaka and Tokyo the tax rice that was the financial base of the new Meiji government. The government also wanted to promote Japanese companies which could compete with foreign shipping. With thirteen ships chartered from the government and from several domains, the Kaisō Kaisha carried mail, passengers, and general freight, as well as tax rice. The fledgling enterprise, however, was faced with more problems than it could surmount. Its financing was shaky, for it relied on the *kawase kaisha,* themselves unstable institutions, seven of the eight established failing within two years. Poor equipment and managerial problems also contributed to the company's failure. The government could not find suitably experienced people to manage a technologically new enterprise like steamship operation, and the structure of the company's management was hopelessly unwieldy. Theoretically a government-appointed superintendent and manager jointly administered the company together with fifteen heads of the various private agencies. Since the government did not explicitly spell out its own role in day-to-day operations, authority tended to devolve upon the private agencies. By 12/1870 the government was complaining that the enterprise had been "reduced to a merchant undertaking." Even worse, much of the daily responsibility fell to inexperienced samurai who often behaved with impropriety, participating in "malpractices in the transport of tax rice."[22]

Throughout 1870 the government issued edicts to strengthen control of the tax-rice transport. One directive issued in 6/1870 reveals the type of corruption that the company leaders could not control.

> To lighten the hull in the event of a storm you must first throw your provisions overboard. Then, if it cannot be helped, you are permitted for the first time to discard the tax rice. But if you unreasonably throw tax rice overboard and keep your provisions, these will be confiscated . . . If you conceal the tax rice and submit a deceitful report that you met a storm and had to throw the tax rice overboard, you will be punished with a fine double the value of the stolen rice and 5 *ryō* for each *koku* of stolen rice. Thereafter, for a long period you will be prohibited from engaging in transport as an occupation.[23]

These irregularities and a debt of over ¥150,000 to the *kawase kaisha* led the government to attempt a reorganization of the Kaisō Kaisha, but the financial debacle was already too great.[24] As

Shibusawa Eiichi later wrote, "since funds were meager, there was virtually no hope of repaying the loans from the *kawase kaisha* and the [government] had to close down the business."[25]

The Kaisō Kaisha had also suffered from the intensified pressure of foreign shipping after the Restoration. After the company's dissolution the battle for supremacy in coastal transport became a triangular struggle among government-sponsored companies, Mitsubishi, and foreign firms. After the first commercial treaties were signed with the Western powers in the late 1850s, English companies quickly became the leading foreign shippers. But in the years immediately preceding the Restoration they were eclipsed by Americans when the Pacific Mail Steamship Company contracted with the U.S. Postmaster General in January 1867 to carry mail between San Francisco and Japanese and Chinese ports, specifically Yokohama and Hong Kong. The contract, motivated by the need for immigrant labor in the United States and by growing American commercial relations with Asia, was for ten years with an annual subsidy of $500,000. In August 1867 the company opened a Yokohama-Shanghai line, and in October 1873, under a second contract, another $500,000 was added to the annual subsidy to expand the service.[26] By the early Meiji period the Pacific Mail had achieved such dominance in passenger and freight transportation along the eastern coast of Japan that it ventured to petition the Meiji government for a special charter to serve Japan's coastal routes.[27] Such demands by foreign shipping companies were of serious concern to the government, and one objective of the Iwakura Mission, which went overseas to seek revision of the treaties, was to reserve coastal trade to Japanese ships.

The government soon ushered in a new stage by appointing members of the *kawase kaisha* to establish another shipping company. The *kawase kaisha* thus replaced the various private transport agencies as the executor of the government's policy when a new company, Kaisō Toriatsukaijo (Shipping Office), was set up in 4/1871, inheriting all the ships of the defunct Kaisō Kaisha.[28]

In 7/1871 when the government abolished the domains and took responsibility for their debts, it collected domain ships as payment. Bureaucratic shuffling, however, delayed the transfer of domain ships to the Kaisō Toriatsukaijo. Also, in the last half of 1871, establishment of prefectures and preparation for the Iwakura Mission to the West, which left in 11/1871 with Finance Minister Ōkubo Toshimichi among its members, set back the development of a shipping policy. Finally in 4/1872 a new Department of Ships (Senpaku-ka) was set up under the Bureau of Posts and Communications within the Finance Ministry to administer delivery of vessels from each domain.[29] The Bureau of Posts and Communications soon became the main office responsible for shipping under its new head, Maejima Hisoka, who had taken office in 8/1871. Maejima was an effective planner. He had earlier been involved in railway development, and in his new position he built Japan's first modern postal service. Though only a second-echelon official, Maejima gradually became the key government man in the formation of shipping policy between 1872 and 1875.

THE YŪBIN JŌKISEN KAISHA. Processing domain ships in mid-1872 provided the opportunity for the government to establish a new, larger company, the Japanese Government Mail Steamship Company (Nihon Seifu Yūbin Jōkisen Kaisha, or YJK).[30] The two previous companies had received Mitsui investment, but the sponsoring authorities in the government had not had as strong personal ties with Mitsui as in mid-1872. This more harmonious relation between the government sponsors and the new company's investors and managers developed indirectly from the Iwakura Mission, which sent many leading officials overseas. For example, Ōkubo Toshimichi, who had become finance minister in 6/1871, spent almost the entire period between 11/1871 and May 1873 in the West. In Ōkubo's absence Inoue Kaoru, the vice minister of finance, who had intimate ties with Mitsui, became acting minister. Another powerful associate of Inoue in the Finance Ministry, Shibusawa Eiichi, also had close ties with Mitsui and the Onogumi through his interest in banking. One colorful writer has commented that if "Inoue was the supreme advisor of the Mitsui House, we can correctly call Shibusawa its assistant advisor."

He concluded that "it would not be an exaggeration to say that the YJK was under their joint management."[31]

Miyamoto attributes expanded investment by Mitsui and other major commercial houses, the Ono, Shimada, and Kōnoike, to an attempt by Mitsui to "open fire on the newly risen financial power of the Mitsubishi Shōkai."[32] This assessment may be well founded, although Yatarō's Shōkai was, of course, still known by the name Mitsukawa at this time. Early in 1872 the Mitsukawa Shōkai had begun shipping general freight as a common carrier and, by 8/1872, had become a strong competitor to the government companies in domestic routes. The formation of the YJK may therefore be seen as the starting point in the struggle between Mitsui and Mitsubishi which has colored the history of modern Japanese business.

The YJK's business operations still concentrated on transport for the government, particularly mail and tax rice, though official policy initially seemed more supportive than it had been for the previous companies. In 10/1872, for example, the Finance Ministry ordered each prefecture to cooperate in this transport.[33] Government financial policy was more innovative. It granted the company ten Western-style ships collected from the domains, to be paid for in installments over fifteen years at no interest.[34] Later, the company received a ¥6,000 subsidy to open a route to Okinawa. The Finance Ministry also *promised* a ¥600,000 subsidy for ship-repair expenses. This subsidy, however, was never given, and the government promise led the company into an eventual financial disaster, which will be discussed below.

The YJK's management was not as unwieldy as the Kaisō Kaisha's, but its "cooperative" structure made for an excessive number of top officers from different commercial houses so the company did not have an identity of its own. This structure reflected Shibusawa's ideology of "cooperatism," an attempt, in part, to import Western joint-stock organization, and rather generously appraised by some Western observers.[35] Actually as a historical model, combining large investments and top executives from a few firms to form a new company under government control may be compared to the "national policy companies" (*koku-*

saku kaisha) that emerged as instruments of Japanese government policy in the 1930s.[36] Certainly this cooperative managerial structure provides a striking contrast between the YJK and Mitsubishi. While the YJK's leading officials were representatives of other firms, Mitsubishi was run by full-time managers serving under a single head, Yatarō, who was gradually moving toward one-man rule. Shibusawa regarded Yatarō's managerial style as dictatorial and a relic of the feudal past, and their conflicting philosophies were frequently debated in newspapers and journals later in the 1870s.

The early 1870s being a period of trial and error, it is perhaps dangerous to draw general conclusions from philosophical differences of that time. Nevertheless, Shibusawa's own forceful statement of his philosophy has led to an overly favorable bias toward him by both management historians and businessmen today. Much of Shibusawa's early success came in the 1880s with his sponsorship of new private joint-stock companies. Apart from banking his commercial policies for the early 1870s have been overrated. Essentially he tried to graft an imported idea (the joint-stock company) onto existing organizations (the Tokugawa commerical agencies), whose representatives were too concerned with their own firms to develop loyalty to the new enterprise.

In contrast, Yatarō transferred the traditional ideal of loyalty from the domain to the firm and grafted Western management techniques onto an existing institution (the domain agency) that was capable of a flexible response. One must also distinguish between Yatarō's rhetoric, style, and philosophy, which observers labeled dictatorial, and his actual management. Through their skills, business expertise, and commitment, the managers Yatarō recruited came to exercise considerable authority within the company. Their loyalty to Yatarō provided a more influential precedent than Shibusawa's ideas of the early 1870s for later Japanese corporate management.

As head of the Bureau of Posts and Communications, Maejima Hisoka had the ultimate responsibility for the YJK, but its managers from the commercial houses, primarily the Tokyo Kawase

Kaisha, and, to a lesser extent, Mitsui and the Onogumi, had no experience in running an industry like shipping. A logical step might have been to hire a foreigner as an agent, but instead they simply employed a certain Mr. Pfoundes as an interpreter. The directors of the YJK were, according to foreign observers, "deaf to all his representations," and they seemed aloof from the practical problems of the business. The English newspaperman John Black concluded: "It is impossible to conceive people more pigheaded, obtuse, slow, suspicious and blind to their own best interests, than the class of Japanese who belonged to this company."[37]

By late 1872 the YJK and Yatarō's enterprise had emerged as the two major Japanese shipping companies. Backed by government investment in its ships, the YJK occupied a stronger competitive position vis-à-vis Yatarō, and his line was very soon on the verge of crisis. Both companies, however, suffered from high personnel costs. Because of the inexperience of Japanese seamen, foreigners were still employed not only as captains but also as engineers and deck hands. The government companies had also undermined their advantages by their arrogant "bureaucratic mentality" toward the public. This contrasted with Yatarō's "passengers-first" policy, which won the favor of the public and enabled Mitsubishi to gain the upper hand in competition with the YJK.[38] The YJK's arrogance toward its passengers may have been paralleled in the freight business by the same kind of petty corruption and inefficiency that had plagued the Kaisō Kaisha. John Black observed: "From the president to the stokers, every native employed was watching for opportunities of helping himself. The foreign officers all tried to combat this universal pilfering until they found it hopeless."

Black also found "a great deal that was far from perfect" with the "native officers and men" on Mitsubishi vessels. Unlike the YJK, however, Mitsubishi overcame these problems; Black attributes this to Mitsubishi's good sense in hiring foreign agents to handle its business in Yokohama and Yatarō's "sagacity" in observing and profiting "by their honest management." As a result

Mitsubishi's trade was, on the whole, "conducted with so much regularity that it acquired a good name from the first."[39]

By the March 1873 "Independence Declaration," Yatarō had become optimistic about his business prospects. The Shōkai had expanded its fleet to seven steamships. Yatarō's ships, however, were even older and smaller than the YJK's, which were themselves in constant need of repairs. Once, when looking at the YJK's ships, Yatarō reportedly sighed, "Their ships may be old, but if our company only had one ship like theirs!"[40] In his letter to Yanosuke in April, Yatarō commented on the extent of the YJK's support from the Finance Ministry and told how the YJK and Mitsubishi were "locked in an unrelenting struggle." There were grounds for hope, he wrote, for with its popularity in Osaka and Tokyo, everyone was coming to rely on the Shōkai. As in many later business struggles, Yatarō saw this as a win-or-lose competition—with the winner achieving a monopoly. "If we crush the YJK," he told Yanosuke, "we will be able to control the shipping industry."[41]

The success Mitsubishi had achieved by mid-1873 can be attributed first to its more unified management. Second, Mitsubishi's public relations were more effective than the YJK's. Third, Mitsubishi's freedom in investment decisions enabled it to develop a business strategy more flexible than the government-controlled YJK. Yatarō perhaps could have bettered the YJK on business acumen alone; external forces more powerful than competition from Mitsubishi, however, were instrumental in bringing the YJK down. These forces were inseparable from the business advantages the YJK enjoyed—special patronage of the government and capital investment from the *kawase kaisha*.

The first privilege, bureaucratic protection received at the company's founding from Inoue and Shibusawa, was political and hence vulnerable. Both Inoue and Shibusawa left the Finance Ministry in May 1873, partly as a result of a dispute over a proposed military expedition to Taiwan, and in the same month Ōkubo, who lacked Inoue's personal commitment to the YJK, returned to Japan to resume his post as finance minister. The YJK's bureaucratic protection depended heavily on the favor of its government allies because the government itself had not yet developed a consistent policy toward shipping. Change in personnel was thus likely to bring with it a different policy.

Shipping was primarily a service, and the government's treatment of it differed from its handling of other new industries. Whereas shipping was under the jurisdiction of the Finance Ministry, the Meiji government's industrial policy was implemented mostly by the Ministry of Industry until 1873. The substance of policy formed another contrast. The government invested in and also operated railways, telegraphs, iron-foundries, mechanical silk-reeling plants, mines, and other industries, because it deemed private capital too weak for substantial investment and private entrepreneurs too inexperienced to operate new industries. In contrast, in the Finance Ministry, Inoue Kaoru and Shibusawa Eiichi had supported the joint investment of state and private capital in shipping companies initiated by the government, but operated mainly by private firms.[42] The government adopted this approach because it could not afford to give the strategic shipping industry a gestation period, as it did with numerous pilot factories under the Ministry of Industry program, but had to begin immediately with what was at hand. At first, this had not seemed a bad alternative. The traditional transport agencies surviving the economic changes of the Bakumatsu and the recently purchased Western-style sailing ships were available for service in government-sponsored shipping companies. Nevertheless, these ships were already old and in need of expensive repairs, and, furthermore, the traditional agencies lacked experience in providing the more rapid transport required by the new government as it sought to reinforce its authority over the whole country. Despite the larger scale of the YJK, by the time Inoue and Shibusawa resigned in mid-1873, little had been done by the government to improve the quality of shipping services.

By late 1873, then, the government was in search of a new policy. Though none was immediately forthcoming, the bureaucratic framework, through which policy was subsequently implemented in 1875, was established in late 1873 and 1874. The key event clearing the way for bureaucratic reform was the October 1873 resignations of many officials who had been demanding a military expedition to Korea. The government, heavily influenced by Ōkubo Toshimichi's arguments against the expedition, rejected their demands. In the wake of the resignations, Ōkubo became the most powerful figure in the government. Cooperating with him was Ōkuma Shigenobu, who became the new finance minister. In November 1873 a Home Ministry was created under Ōkubo's leadership, and in 1874 the administration of shipping was transferred from the Finance Ministry to the new Home Ministry. Also in 1874, functions hitherto scattered among several bureaus were consolidated in the Department of Ships under the Bureau of Posts and Communications, now in the Home Ministry. With Ōkubo the home minister, these bureaucratic changes meant that the YJK no longer enjoyed special patronage. Its future would depend solely on its business performance—or on regaining solid government support.

THE YJK AND MITSUBISHI: FINANCIAL CONTRASTS.   Unfortunately for the YJK, precisely at this time its business began to suffer a series of blows. First, rice shipments (the company's main freight) declined because of a bad harvest in 1873 and consequent price increases. Second, the Land Tax Reform, promulgated in July 1873 and implemented over the next few years, abolished the system of rice-tax transport for which the YJK had possessed an exclusive charter.[43]

The next problem arose more gradually but, in the long run, probably was the main cause of the YJK's eventual bankrupty—the financial imbroglio of the ¥600,000 repair subsidy promised by the government at the time of the company's establishment. The company had used this promise as collateral to borrow ¥400,000 from the Tokyo Kawase Kaisha. As 1872 and then 1873 passed, however, the government failed to produce the promised grant and the company's repair bills mounted. Though its operating deficit during the first ten months of 1874 came to only ¥35,209, repairs accounted for 30 percent of all expenses, cutting deeply into funds borrowed from the Tokyo Kawase Kaisha.[44] The backers of the *kawase kaisha* were also bankers to the government, that is, the government deposited its funds with them. Some of the main investors in the *kawase kaisha,* especially the Onogumi, used these deposits recklessly for their own purposes. In early 1874 the government began to exert more control over these commerical houses, which were acting as money-exchange brokers. In February it required official prefectural money-exchange brokers to deposit as security with the government about one-third of the funds in which they dealt. On October 22, 1874, it directed that these official deposits be fully secured and announced a December 15 deadline for compliance. Unable to meet this demand, the Onogumi found its property expropriated by the government and in November liquidated its business. As Ōkubo later wrote, "The Onogumi attempted so many things at one time in order to gain quick profits through its many branches spread all over the country, and in the end, owing to its mismanagement, it collapsed in bankruptcy."[45] The collapse of the Onogumi presented the Tokyo Kawase Kaisha with the prospect of immediate bankruptcy. It naturally turned to the YJK, demanding return of the ¥400,000 loan. The YJK, having already spent these funds, repeatedly appealed to the Finance Ministry to honor its earlier pledge and deliver the ¥600,000 repair grant. The Finance Ministry, however, was carrying out a reform in its accounting procedures and reneged on its promise.[46] As a result, the YJK was liquidated in June 1875, leaving a debt of ¥620,000 to the Tokyo Kawase Kaisha alone.[47]

Financing, then, played a major role in the YJK failure. Yatarō, by contrast, received most of his financing from foreigners. There has been a common perception that, since the Meiji government pursued a nationalist course of avoiding dependence on foreign aid, foreign capital did not play a decisive role in Japan's economic development in the nineteenth century. Nevertheless, in the disruption of the years immediately surrounding the Restoration, 1865 to 1870, individual entrepreneurs were inclined to take opportunistic risks with foreign capital. Yatarō's loan from Walsh,

Hall & Company, was a shrewd move, for the Finance Ministry bailed him out of the debts incurred prior to the abolition of the domain. Another major source of funds was the British firm of Alt & Company.[48] Yataro's extensive borrowing did not seem to harm his credit. A Mitsubishi employee commented that Yataro "won the confidence of foreigners because he always returned the money he borrowed on time." Yataro was often criticized for not borrowing from Japanese. The reason he did not, it was claimed, was that, if he did, the actual state of his debts would become known and he would lose his credit. More positive proof of foreign confidence may be adduced from his generally good reputation in the foreign press and especially from the fact that his business agent in Yokohama was none other than Walsh, Hall & Company.[49]

By the end of 1873 Yataro had purchased nine steamships and one Japanese-style sailing ship (*wasen*) for ¥245,000 and 47,000 Mexican silver dollars. These purchases generally included agreements for long-term payment so that no large immediate outlay was necessary.[50] Yataro operated one of the steamships as a joint investment with Ono Yoshimasa and Okamoto Kensaburo, two Finance Ministry officials of Tosa origin.[51] Earlier Yataro had sold one of his vessels to the Shingu domain for $75,000. However, when the domains were abolished, Shingu had yet to make full payment. Yataro then recovered the ship, which the government had expropriated from the domain and given to the Shokai. He also acquired two mines, earlier leased from Shingu, as partial payment for the ship.[52]

In addition to the return on these investments and from various speculative moves, Yataro relied on the profits of his other enterprises. Camphor production, silk reeling, and copper and coal mining, especially the Yoshioka copper mine, provided a large "dollar chest" that helped Yataro ride over the difficult period while he was establishing his shipping business.[53]

The Meiji government did not achieve real political or bureaucratic stability until 1874–1875, when Okubo consolidated his control over the Home Ministry. Financial institutions and business organizations were also unstable during this transition. In fact, various economic institutions—the private transport agenices, the *kawase kaisha,* the Onogumi—were less representative of the new economic order than of the merchant establishments of the Tokugawa period, and no more likely to survive. The ¥400,000 loan from the Tokyo Kawase Kaisha to the YJK was but one example of the comparatively large but elusive capital resources of these institutions tempting an ill-managed company into a disastrous financial arrangement. Once these houses fell, nothing could rescue the YJK but political will in high places, and that was missing. Yatarō, on the other hand, had an assorted patchwork of financial backers. If any failed or if he was tardy in paying his debts, the political support of his domain still gave him a certain leverage which often enabled him to extricate himself from difficulties. Yatarō was riding the political wave that was forcing the central government to bring the domains into the center of the nation.[54]

In the specific context of 1874, absence of a stable financial climate led to the Onogumi collapse that ultimately triggered the YJK's bankruptcy. But the Onogumi's failure in late 1874 was not the immediate cause of the YJK's defeat in its struggle with Mitsubishi. The reasons for Mitsubishi's triumph resided in another potent "external force" of 1874, the Meiji government's overseas military policy.

THE TAIWAN EXPEDITION OF 1874

In 12/1871 sailors from the Ryukyu Islands were shipwrecked on the southern coast of Taiwan and over fifty of them murdered by aborigines. This incident brought to the fore two problems which provided Japan with a pretext to invade Taiwan. The key issue was the sovereignty of the Ryukyus. China had traditional claims on them, but they had been incorporated into the administration of the Satsuma domain during the Tokugawa period. After the incident in 12/1871, the Meiji government took over their jurisdiction. The second issue was responsibility for controlling the Taiwan aborigines, in other words, who held sovereignty over the area they inhabited. China had not incorporated the areas where the aborigines lived into its administration. At the very least Japan wanted to pacify these areas in case of future shipwrecks and force China to accept responsibility for the incident. Japan's maximum goal was to exert sovereignty over the area and colonize it.[55]

During 1872 and 1873 several intelligence missions went to Taiwan, and calls for an expedition led to frequent conflicts inside the government. The Taiwan issue was eclipsed in 1873 by plans to invade Korea. When the proponents of this invasion resigned in October 1873, the new government, dominated by Home Minister Ōkubo and Finance Minister Ōkuma, made its own assessment of the Taiwan issue and on February 6, 1874, approved plans for an expedition.

GOVERNMENT MANAGEMENT OF TRANSPORT. Any overseas expedition would require supporting ships, and Japan conspicuously lacked these. The navy had approximately 3,700 sailors, but no transport facilities to move them overseas. In fact, even the steamships owned by Japanese shipping companies were incapable of making long sea voyages; of the 74 licensed mariners in the country in 1874, only 4 were Japanese.[56] Finding someone to undertake the transport was essential if the Meiji government was to accomplish its military objective. After many delays the government eventually awarded a transport contract to Mitsubishi, which was the critical turning point in Mitsubishi's development into a modern shipping enterprise. The government had to purchase numerous large steamships (over 1,000 tons), which were later entrusted to Mitsubishi. For the first time a Japanese shipping company had access to a substantial fleet of large steamers.[57] The consequent expansion in service marked a sudden departure from the relatively slow development of the mercantile marine during the Bakumatsu and early Meiji years. This much is generally accepted by scholars, but the precise sequence of events in 1874, which has not been studied, provides evidence on government-business relations and the evolution of commercial shipping policy. First, this suggests that Mitsubishi did not lobby intensively for the contract. Rather, the government itself turned to Mitsubishi out of necessity. Second, the government purchased ships during the early stages of the expedition, because it was faced with a military emergency. Policy considerations regarding commercial shipping arose gradually and became explicit only toward the expedition's end, in the autumn of 1874. Furthermore, no formal decision transferring the ships to Mitsubishi's ownership was made until mid-1875.

In early April 1874 the government set up the Bureau of Taiwan Aboriginal Affairs in Nagasaki. Several American advisers, particularly Charles LeGendre, former consul-general in Amoy, China, aided Ōkuma, the director of the bureau. Ōkuma's main responsibilities were acquiring ships and managing expedition finances. He planned to entrust ship operation to the Pacific Mail Company, which appears to have petitioned the government for a military transport contract. On April 19, however, the American ambassador, John Bingham, intervened with a letter of neutrality, which forced the removal of the American advisers as well as the *New York,* a Pacific Mail ship chartered by Ōkuma. The British ambassador, Sir Harry Parkes, also issued a warning against the use of British ships, but this did not deter the participation of several British advisers Ōkuma employed to purchase additional steamers.[58]

On May 3, Ōkubo and Ōkuma met with Saigō Tsugumichi, commander of the expedition and younger brother of Saigō Takamori, the Restoration hero, and confirmed the switch from the Pacific Mail to reliance on British advisers.[59] Several of them were long-term employees of the Japanese government. The activity of these foreigners has not been carefully integrated into most interpretations of transport policy during the expedition. Many scholars state, almost in the same breath, that the government received the neutrality declarations and decided to buy new vessels and entrust them to Mitsubishi. Shibusawa Eiichi, who did not participate in planning for the expedition, set the tone for this interpretation when he stated that after the neutrality letter, "the Mitsubishi Steamship Company came forward with great promptitude, offering to do any work required by the Government."[60] The United States, however, declared its neutrality on April 19, but no order for transport was issued to Mitsubishi until July 28. If Ōkuma, Ōkubo, and Yatarō were accustomed to going to the pleasure quarters of Yoshiwara together, as some writers suggest,[61] why did it take the government three months to complete an agreement with Mitsubishi? The meaning of the May discussions was that, Ōkuma, as director of the Taiwan Bureau, was content for the time being to follow a policy of government-managed transport. This, after all, had been the original policy, the only difference being the use of the American Pacific Mail. When that fell through, the government tried the nearest thing to it—employing foreigners familiar with East Asian shipping.

The most qualified was Captain Albert R. Brown, a former seaman and navigator of the British Peninsular & Oriental Steam Navigation Company (P. & O.), at the time one of the largest shipping companies in the world. Brown was a participant in Japan's lighthouse-building program and an instructor of Japanese mercantile marine officers. His work for the expedition began in May when he traveled to various East Asian ports to purchase more ships for Ōkuma. He and his associates equipped the ships, hired other foreigners to work in them, and in some cases operated them themselves. After Brown left the expedition in July, Ōkuma relied on an American merchant, J. M. Batchelder, to purchase the *New York* from the Pacific Mail and to carry out intelligence missions in China.[62]

MITSUBISHI AND THE TRANSPORT CONTRACT. By July Saigō's expeditionary force had achieved its immediate objective of subduing the aborigines. However, protracted negotiations with China, which would not take responsibility for the actions of the aborigines, obliged the government to maintain troops in Taiwan. As the troops were decimated by disease, the government faced a larger, more prolonged transport operation than it had anticipated. Two other events complicated the supply problem further. In late June, a warning from Parkes forced Brown to withdraw from the

expedition. Then, on July 8, the government decided to risk war
with China if satisfaction could not be obtained through negotiation. This decision, rather than the American and British neutrality declarations of April, marked the real critical point in the
government's transport policy. Five ships previously purchased by
Brown were too few to meet the expanded demand, and the services of the leading foreigners were no longer available. The government could no longer avoid more fundamental decisions.[63]
For the first time it had to rely on its own shipping companies.

At one point the navy asked the Council of State to let it manage the ships, but the navy was still too undeveloped to do so.[64]
The first company the government approached was the YJK, a
normal procedure, for in the agreement between the government
and that company at its formation was the stipulation that the
YJK would provide military transport.[65] But the standing of the
YJK had deteriorated considerably in the two years since its
founding. In this emergency of 1874 it stubbornly refused the government's request for transport services, a response usually attributed to the influence of Choshu faction leaders like Inoue Kaoru
and Kido Kōin, who opposed the expedition.[66] Inoue, of course,
was the main sponsor of the YJK, and his colleague Shibusawa,
though not from Choshu, also vigorously opposed the expedition.

It would be hard to deny the existence of political pressure on
the YJK, but its reasons for refusing the government appear to
have been more closely related to its own business operations.
Matsuo Shigeyoshi, later president of the Bank of Japan and in
1874 a Finance Ministry official in charge of national bonds, kept
records of conversations with YJK President Iwahashi Manzō.
These reveal the YJK's unwillingness to take risks. "I don't know
how this war will turn out," Iwahashi reportedly said. He examined
the government's request simply as a business proposition, asking
whether there would be more profit in engaging in military transport or in operating domestic lines. The primary motivation of the
YJK's refusal lay in its fear of competition with Mitsubishi. Yatarō
was the real "enemy." If the YJK undertook overseas transport
for the government, Iwahashi assumed that the domestic passenger

service would be snatched away by Mitsubishi. The YJK therefore judged it more profitable to keep the domestic lines and let Mitsubishi have the risky overseas business.[67]

The YJK's financial difficulties with the *kawase kaisha* may have limited its freedom of action at this time. The deluge from the Onogumi collapse did not come until October, however, and it seems unlikely that premonition of a financial panic was the main factor influencing management decisions in the spring and summer of 1874.[68]

The refusal of the YJK exasperated the government. Ōkubo and Ōkuma had earlier provoked the resignation of Saigō and his colleagues over the Korean issue. Now their own political lives depended on the successful outcome of the Taiwan expedition. Negotiations with the domestic shipping companies had probably begun sometime before the withdrawal of the British advisers in early July. However, there are several opinions about who in the government advocated Mitsubishi for the transport service.[69] According to one, Maejima Hisoka and Ono Yoshimasa made the recommendation. Most of Maejima's writing concerning Mitsubishi, however, relates to the post-expedition period, and seldom mentions the Taiwan problem. A second opinion attributes the recommendation to General LeGendre, and evidence bears this out. LeGendre criticized Ōkuma's transport policy of hiring foreigners and advised that it would be more efficient for a private shipping company, rather than the government, to undertake munitions transport. Ōkubo approved this and forwarded to Ōkuma his recommendation that Mitsubishi be awarded the contract.[70]

Most scholars assume that Mitsubishi petitioned the government for the transport contract,[71] but the evidence for this is sketchy. The secondary source which some scholars cite quotes a petition from Yatarō pledging to "use several ships in possession of our company" so that he could repay his debt of obligation to the country.[72] However, this appears to be Mitsubishi's response to the government order of July 28. Major documentary collections contain no reference to any Mitsubishi petition in advance of this order. Yatarō may have been reluctant to undertake the transport at the beginning of the expedition. Until then he had conducted his business outside of government channels, a not unwise policy in view of the YJK's experience.

All primary sources agree that Ōkuma had known Yatarō for several years before the expedition, though the origins and depth of their relationship are unclear. Ōkuma did, however, record a conversation with Yatarō during the critical period of mid-1874. After the YJK refused to operate ships for the expedition, Ōkuma said he "remembered" Yatarō. "Swindlers and adventurers," Ōkuma thought, "never maintain permanent enterprises. Generally they fail after two or three years. But several years had already passed since Iwasaki established his enterprise. We knew that he was not one of these [fly-by-night] speculators. So one day I summoned Iwasaki, asked him how his enterprise was going, and told him that we wanted him to undertake government business." Yatarō's response was that, though he realized the difficulty of the undertaking, "once begun, he would not stop in midcourse, for that would bring shame upon him." There was "no greater honor," Yatarō reportedly said, "than accomplishing the heavy duties delegated by the government."[73] If Ōkuma can be believed, this conversation suggests that the government, not Mitsubishi, took the initiative in beginning talks for the transport contract. Also, Ōkuma's account is not inconsistent with LeGendre's recommendation that the government employ a private shipping company.

Although Ōkubo, together with Ōkuma, persuaded the Council of State that the government should employ Mitsubishi's services,[74] he does not appear to have participated in the negotiations with Mitsubishi. Available evidence suggests that Ōkubo did not personally meet Yatarō until after the expedition. In writing about shipping policy at the end of 1874 and beginning of 1875 Maejima Hisoka mentioned several times that Ōkubo did not know Yatarō, and the context of his remarks is the post-expedition period.[75] Katsuta Magoya, Ōkubo's principal biographer, suggests that Ōkubo met Yatarō for the first time through an introduction from Matsukata Masayoshi. Katsuta's description of this meeting is also clearly post-expedition.[76] Kozo Yamamura, however, has quoted

Shiroyanagi's *Kaiun no kensetsusha* to demonstrate Yatarō's purported connection with Ōkubo and Ōkuma: "After a great deal of campaigning behind the scenes—mostly at famous inns and *geisha* houses—Iwasaki succeeded in talking these two [Ōkubo and Ōkuma] into giving him the contract on his terms." The context of Shiroyanagi's quotation is not the military transport contract, as Yamamura suggests, but rather the disposition of the ships used in the expedition, the competition with the American Pacific Mail, and specifically the demands of the YJK for the promised support from the Finance Ministry to cover its debts. These were problems that came to the fore in late 1874, after the expedition, not before it. The real implication of Shiroyanagi's statement is that, by winning the favor of Ōkubo and Ōkuma, Yatarō dissuaded them from giving the YJK the ¥600,000 repair subsidy promised by the Finance Ministry.[77]

The shortcoming of the popular prewar accounts, which most scholars have followed, is that they fail to differentiate between the government's purchase of ships, the military transport contract, the YJK repair subsidy issue, and the later aid to Mitsubishi. All are usually lumped together as one continuous process. Interpreting government policy, however, requires first seeing these problems as specific individual issues and then examining how they became intertwined.

POLICY CONSIDERATIONS AND THE EXPEDITION. The first policy considerations seem to have arisen, at least implicitly, from the transport contract itself. While Mitsubishi may not have had to lobby intensively to win the contract, there is no reason to doubt Yamamura's contention that Yatarō labored hard "to get the most favorable *terms.*"[78] On July 28 the Taiwan Bureau issued the transport order to Mitsubishi, and on August 10 the two parties signed a full agreement. The Taiwan Bureau laid down various "conditions" for Mitsubishi's use of the ships. Among these was the provision that Mitsubishi could freely use them for business other than that connected with the expedition. This was the most significant article for policy, because it involved the government in the expansion of commercial shipping, and use of the ships would give Mitsubishi a decided advantage after the expedition ended.[79]

Although Mitsubishi obtained considerable leeway in the use of the ships, it was not yet their owner. Instead the company had become a "purveyor to the government" (*goyō shōnin*), a function which places this contract in the "special privilege for special service" tradition of Tokugawa and even earlier times. In this tradition a daimyo—or shogun in the case of the bakufu—would seek economic objectives through a relationship with a selected merchant to whom the feudal lord would grant special rights to conduct private commercial operations. While Mitsubishi's contract followed this pattern, in the 1874 context there were some crucial differences. Arthur Tiedemann has described the traditional system as one in which "almost always the initiative lay with the government; and the merchant, although he might make suggestions which on occasion were adopted, was in a strictly subordinate position."[80] While the Meiji government may have taken the initiative in approaching Mitsubishi in this case, the objective, an overseas expedition, was totally unprecedented, at least for the previous 250 years of the Tokugawa period. Moreover, the government had already exhausted all other possible "initiatives," the American Pacific Mail, the British advisers, and the YJK. Mitsubishi was hardly in the traditional "subordinate position." The government had no choice but to employ Mitsubishi. This gave Yatarō the chance to drive a hard bargain, to expand his business, and to present the government with a *fait accompli* when the question of long-range policy was raised later.

The peak period of Mitsubishi's munitions and troop transport coincided with the most sensitive phase of negotiations in China. On August 6 Ōkubo had embarked for Peking as a special ambassador and minister plenipotentiary. He reached a settlement on October 31 through a combination of threats—which would not have been credible without Mitsubishi's cooperative efforts—and the mediation of Thomas Wade, the British ambassador to China. It took another six weeks for Mitsubsihi to complete all the transport. By the end of the year its ships had made 24 voyages, transported three battalions as well as 5,600 civilians, 45,000 bales of rice, large quantities of munitions, and currency, including the indemnity of 500,000 taels that Ōkubo had wrested from the Chinese.[81]

Yatarō thus fulfilled the expectations of the government. Ōkubo and Ōkuma had all the more reason to be grateful to him, because of the perilous political situation from which he had helped rescue them. The new faith in Mitsubishi, coming at the exact time that the Onogumi collapse was destroying the YJK's credit, completely overwhelmed the latter company.

The Taiwan expedition was a critical turning point in the development of the Japanese shipping industry, because it catapulted Mitsubishi into the dominant ranks of the shipping world and because it resulted in rapid purchase of ships. The expedition was not, despite the order to Mitsubishi, a time of explicit government policy making regarding shipping. The first ships were purchased as an emergency military measure, and policy considerations about management came up only in late 1874. Nevertheless, an examination of the purchase of the ships reveals gradual changes in the government's aims. Toward the end of the expedition these changes foreshadowed the type of policy that would later emerge.

N.Y.K. records state that during the expedition 13 ships were ordered totaling 17,828 tons and costing $1,576,800.[82] The major error made in most secondary accounts is the assumption that all 13 ships were used during the expedition. Shibagaki Kazuo's comment that the government "hurriedly purchased 13 foreign ships and entrusted their operation to Mitsubishi" is typical.[83] On the contrary, only 10 of the 13 ships even reached Japan before the end of 1874, and one of these arrived too late to be used in the expedition.[84] Also, the total number of ships is obscured somewhat in certain secondary accounts, because 5 warships were purchased in addition to the 13 transports.[85]

Three of the 13 ships, then, were not delivered until 1875. Two of these provide the best clue to the government's changing intentions. In August 1874 Ōkuma had instructed Captain Brown to

proceed to Britain on government business. He arrived in October
and soon received a supplementary order to purchase two steamers.
This instructed Brown to investigate Britain's shipping regulations and its method of training seamen, to engage crewmen, and
to dispatch the two new vessels to Yokohama for the Mitsubishi
Company. It is likely that these two ships were ordered for civilian
purposes unrelated to the Taiwan expedition.[86]

Two other matters testify to the government's, or at least Ōkuma's, concern about commercial shipping. On October 18, two
weeks before Ōkubo's accord with China, when Mitsubishi had
still only received six ships from the government, Iwasaki Yanosuke
petitioned the Taiwan Bureau for a ¥30,000 preparatory fund for
opening an overseas shipping line. Approval was granted the following day.[87] Such rapidity indicates that Yanosuke's request was
a formality and that the matter had probably been decided in
earlier discussions. This fund might be interpreted as simply the
logical extension of the transport contract, under which Mitsubishi
was permitted to use government ships in business unrelated to the
expedition, but the timing suggests the workings of a more positive
political favoritism. It was on October 22 that the government
issued its Deposit Increase Decree that quickly led to the bankruptcy of the Onogumi. While that decree was part of the government's overall banking policy that did not have any direct relation
to shipping, Ōkuma, as finance minister, could hardly have been
unaware of the effect it would have on the YJK, given that company's financial connections with the Onogumi and the Tokyo
Kawase Kaisha. The subsequent inability of the Finance Ministry
to grant the YJK its promised repair subsidy contrasts remarkably
with the preparatory fund granted Mitsubishi. Second, the ships
purchased by Brown in the spring of 1874 were entrusted to Mitsubishi by the Taiwan Bureau in December, that is, about the time
transport related to the expedition was coming to an end. Clearly
Ōkuma had made a political decision to aid Mitsubishi's commercial shipping enterprise.

In the course of the Taiwan expedition, then, the Meiji government had moved from an initial emergency purchase of transports

to a larger-scale build-up of naval vessels and transports under the threat of war. Finally, in the later stages of the transport, it had supplemented its ship purchases with measures for promoting a mercantile marine service that included an implied commitment to entrust ships and foreign lines to Mitsubishi. This evolution in ship purchasing was foreshadowed by the radical changes in the government's choice of a shipping contractor. It had moved from a foreign company to friendly foreign advisers, then to an unwilling government-sponsored company, and finally to a private concern. These changes were less deliberate than forced by the course of events. Despite the tentative measures favoring Mitsubishi, the rapid tempo of these changes left an unpreparedness for major decisions that would soon have to be made.

TWO

The Year of Decision: 1875

The accumulation of ships during the Taiwan expedition made possible the extension of coastal routes and the commission of steamers for overseas lines. The most immediate problem in the aftermath of the expedition, however, was the supervision of these vessels. Who would manage their operations—the government or Mitsubishi? If Mitsubishi, under what conditions and with what amount of government aid? And finally, what government department would have jurisdiction?

Opinions on these questions soon became entangled with other issues, delaying the process of decision but ensuring that the decision eventually taken was a firm and long-lasting one. Under the basic principles adopted in 1875 the government would provide financial aid to a private company that could meet certain qualitative standards and that would fulfill certain obligations to the state. In fact, the decisions of 1875 have lasted for over a century. Subsequent Japanese shipping policy has not deviated from these original principles, except between 1937 and 1949 when state controls temporarily transformed private shipping firms into virtual government organs. Prior to World War I, fluctuations in policy occurred within the general parameters set in 1875. During these policy changes the paramount issues for shipping companies were: (1) the amount of aid (and sometimes, the formula for determining it); and (2) the degree of managerial autonomy companies could exercise under the conditions set by the government.

POLICY DEBATE: BUREAUCRATIC RIVALRY

EARLY PROPOSALS OF MAEJIMA AND ŌKUMA. Bureaucratic rivalry played a central role in the development of shipping policy after the Taiwan expedition. Discussions on shipping in 1875 coincided with Ōkubo's formulation of the government's industrial promotion policy (*shokusan kōgyō seisaku*), and at the time various projects relating to this policy were still being shifted from the Ministry of Industry to the Home Ministry. Financial policy also impinged heavily on shipping policy, especially because of the balance-of-payments problems. Finally, disputes over extraterritoriality (involving the jurisdiction of Japan's postal service and foreign post offices on Japanese soil) brought Maejima Hisoka and the Bureau of Posts and Communications into the policy-making process because Mitsubishi had begun to carry mail. The subsequent proposals on shipping policy from Home Minister Ōkubo, Finance Minister Ōkuma, and Maejima, head of the Bureau of Posts and Communications, reflected the particular bureaucratic function of the ministry or agency concerned with each of the above issues. At the end of the Taiwan expedition, these issues had yet to be integrated into an overall policy for shipping.

One of the first steps taken after the agreement with China was a Council of State Proclamation on November 15 giving temporary jurisdiction of the ships under Taiwan Bureau control to the Finance Ministry pending further discussion. On the same day a Steamship Office (Kisen-gakari) was set up in the Finance Ministry to receive the ships.[1] At about this time Maejima sought a meeting with Yatarō. He started with "a feeling of uneasiness about Yatarō's character," but was soon won over by Yatarō's reference to the "founder of a dynasty who took talented people into his service and made his enterprise a success." Yatarō promised to do the same by employing talented Japanese and foreigners.

Commented Maejima, "I realized for the first time that we had a well-qualified person here, and I resolved to recommend to the Council members that we entrust him with our country's shipping industry."[2] While awaiting Ōkubo's return from China, Maejima drafted a memorandum on the supervision of the mercantile marine,[3] which he presented to Ōkubo in Tokyo on November 27.

Government leaders had been acutely aware of their dependence on foreign steamships in the Taiwan expedition, and Maejima emphasized this in the introduction to his proposal. He noted the desperate need to compete successfully with the foreigners and then to drive them out. To idly let events take their course would invite further losses from the competition of the American Pacific Mail. Most Japanese merchants, he said, were still indifferent to commercial shipping. Maejima listed three possible forms of business enterprise for the new venture: (1) government management; (2) a company (by which he meant a cooperative venture of several firms, as in the YJK); and (3) an individual, private businessman (*shijin*). Separate from these three he mentioned the idea of a combined government-private business operation (*kanshi konkō eigyō*), but he dismissed this as unworthy of consideration. Under plan one, he pointed out that operations under government management would alienate passengers and shippers because the right man could not be found among government officials. Under plan two, Maejima feared that no prominent people would care to risk organizing a new company. Even if they did, it would again be difficult to find the right man to head it; and if the company did not follow government directives, it would soon repeat the mistakes of the Kaisō Kaisha and the YJK and collapse. He therefore rejected another government attempt to underwrite a company. Under plan three, government aid to a talented and experienced private individual who showed signs of success would, said Maejima, later "give rise to monopolistic abuses and might hinder the progress of other companies." In view of the demands of the time, however, Maejima felt the government had no choice but to adopt this policy; he advocated Yatarō as the private individual to be favored. He further suggested a one-year trial period, after which the government would hand down a directive with "strict and just provisions."[4]

The second major proposal came from separate bureaucratic lines. In January 1875 Ōkuma presented a long memorandum on the economy to Chief Minister Sanjō Sanetomi of the Council of State,[5] which was written in the aftermath of the collapse of the Ono and Shimada houses and dealt with measures to combat the rising economic crisis of the mid-1870s. Central to this crisis were growing government deficits, rising prices, and a rapid outflow of hard currency. Throughout the 1870s Japan's trade balance had a chronic deficit, averaging ¥6.9 million annually between 1869 and 1880 (equivalent to 32 percent of exports). Only in 1876 did it have a surplus. Thomas Smith has pointed out that "the actual loss of specie was considerably greater than these figures suggest, for shipping, insurance, and other services not reflected in them were almost entirely in the hands of foreigners."[6] Ōkuma argued that the only way to relieve the economic crisis was to increase exports by promoting national industries. He attached special importance to the development of transportation, particularly shipping, as the basis for an improved distribution system that would stimulate domestic commerce.[7] Promoting exports would not itself reduce imports, but it would help balance trade by cutting the import surplus. Without a developed shipping industry, however, increased exports would simply mean increased payments for foreign services. Ōkuma regarded the resources of private capital as insufficient for such development,[8] and, in contrast to Maejima, advocated a system of government-managed shipping.[9]

Ōkuma wrote a separate memorandum to Sanjō in January clarifying this proposal,[10] and observing that the Finance Ministry now had ample capacity for transporting rice with the ships transferred from the Taiwan Bureau. Some vessels should be freed, he said, to open a steamship line to China. This memorandum favored government management of shipping. The government would operate the ships, build up domestic shipping lines, increase the shipping industry's capacity through lines to Chinese ports, and gradually extend sailings to Europe and America. To Ōkuma, at issue was the manner in which the government would manage shipping. If the industry were entrusted to the Finance Ministry or other government ministries which lacked experience, "it will fail and we will invite ridicule from our countrymen and from abroad." On the other hand, the Taiwan Bureau had accumulated experience and established a set of procedures. The best plan, therefore, would be to set up a Shipping Affairs Bureau (Kisen Jimukyoku) inside the Council of State, to choose able people from the Taiwan Bureau staff and from other ministries, and to put a qualified person in charge of the new bureau. This would have the advantage, Ōkuma claimed, of combining everything in one bureau. He briefly noted that the Home Ministry might be authorized to establish certain procedures for sea and land transport, but he opposed its having an operational function. Even in the largest aspect of land transportation, the railroads, said Ōkuma, the Ministry of Industry, not the Home Ministry, was in charge of operations. He therefore advocated a separate bureau for shipping.

Ōkuma's ideas on the economy in general were part of an emerging consensus within the government that had begun to place more emphasis on export promotion than on the program of import substitution favored earlier in the decade. But the separate shipping proposal raises questions about his motivation. His comments on the Home Ministry suggest that some bureaucratic competition lay behind the memorandum. Compared with Maejima's proposal, Ōkuma's plan seems unfavorable to Mitsubishi. Actually Yatarō appears to have sent a petition to Ōkuma shortly before the latter's memorandum on the Shipping Affairs Bureau which began by stating that "with, as always, Your Excellency's favor," he had come to operate his shipping enterprise. But now he had a grander vision. "Recently," he said, "the fortunes of the YJK have sunk and they have called on me for help." His investigation of the company revealed internal dissension and mounting debts which made repayment impossible. Yatarō therefore urged Ōkuma to merge the YJK with his company "for the promotion of the shipping industry."[11] Since Yatarō was trying to expand his own company, his petition does not seem to harmonize with Ōkuma's proposal. The problem is how to interpret Ōkuma's memorandum in the light of other measures favorable to Mitsubishi: the instructions to Brown; the preparatory fund for an overseas line; and three transports entrusted to Mitsubishi in December after the Taiwan expedition ended. The most credible inference is that Ōkuma's real purpose was to set up Mitsubishi as a privileged contract agent attached to the special bureau inside the Council of State. This would have perpetuated the same structural relationship that existed in Mitsubishi's link with the Taiwan Bureau.

THE SHANGHAI LINE AND THE RINGISEI. Whatever Ōkuma's underlying intentions, his memorandum was essentially abstract. It ignored the concrete issues of who actually would operate the ships, matters that involved government financing as well as ownership. Not surprisingly, then, Maejima appears to have made several indirect but critical comments on Ōkuma's ideas. In his autobiography he wrote that Ōkuma had tried to transform the temporary Steamship Office into a permanent bureau and in conjunction with this had attempted to open a combined government-private business operation (*kanshi konkō eigyō*), the same idea that Maejima scornfully denounced in his memorandum to Ōkubo as "foolish and unworthy of consideration."[12] Ōkuma's proposal, in short, was more a product of the Taiwan expedition than of the new issues concerning management that emerged in the 1875 debate. In fact, Maejima's objections echo LeGendre's criticism of Ōkuma's transport policy for the expedition. Ōkuma's proposal resembles his own government-managed shipping carried out through the employment of foreigners in the early stage of the expedition.[13]

Even though there were disputes over his policy, as finance minister, Ōkuma for the moment had authority over the ships that had belonged to the Taiwan Bureau. On January 18, 1875, he ordered Mitsubishi to open a weekly shipping service to Shanghai. Mitsubishi assigned four vessels to this, Japan's first overseas shipping line, and the first ship departed from Yokohama on February 3 with Iwasaki Yanosuke aboard.[14] In addition to Ōkuma's long-range plans for export promotion, there were more immediate reasons for the opening of the Shanghai line. The most important was to resist the American Pacific Mail's monopoly held on the line since the beginning of the 1870s. The Shanghai line was also an attempt to utilize excess cargo space resulting from ship purchases of the preceding six months.[15] As expected, the line did not fare well in the early months. It was also difficult for the Japanese to break into the profits from the China trade. Japan had had a trade deficit with China in 1874, with its exports only half the value of its imports. Later in the nineteenth century, shipping firms like the N.Y.K. increased their share of cargo on Asian lines by establishing business alliances with newly emergent Japanese industries like cotton spinning. In the mid-1870s, with these industries still in a primitive state and trading organizations that later buttressed Japanese shipping yet to be formed, profits from an undertaking like the Shanghai line flowed mostly to foreigners, especially to Chinese merchants, many of whom resided in Japan, and partly to British firms like the Oriental Banking Corporation and the Hong Kong and Shanghai Banking Corporation.[16]

At the time, the American Pacific Mail Company employed four vessels in the Yokohama-Shanghai service, each of which departed one day after a regular Mitsubishi sailing. The American firm also challenged Mitsubishi by drastically lowering passenger fares and freight rates. In the resulting competition both companies suffered great losses.

Despite the early problems of the Shanghai line, some scholars have regarded its opening as a decisive turning point. Ōe Shinobu comments that it inaugurated the government's promotion policy and that, when the debate on shipping policy reached its climax in mid-1875, the government's mandate had already effectively been transmitted to Mitsubishi in the opening of the Shanghai line.[17] This interpretation is premature in stressing the decisiveness of the line. The Shanghai line represented Ōkuma's unilateral action more than a full government commitment to Mitsubishi or even to a particular form of company. For example, when Ōkubo returned to Tokyo in late November 1874 and received Maejima's proposal, he soon became embroiled in political issues. On December 24 he left Tokyo again to attend the Osaka Conference on political reforms and did not return until February 18. Ōkuma's order for the opening of the Shanghai line, as well as his other memoranda of January 1875 by which he attempted to establish the Shipping Affairs Bureau, were sent while Ōkubo was away from Tokyo preoccupied with other matters. Presumably Ōkubo did not participate in these decisions. This was a crucial omission, for by 1875 Ōkubo was the most powerful man in the government, a virtual prime minister. Maejima had presented his proposal to Ōkubo not only because, as home minister, Ōkubo was his superior, but because Ōkubo was the "only one who could make a decision on the matter and then put it into effect."[18]

According to Maejima, in late 1874 Ōkubo knew Yatarō only by reputation, but he accepted Maejima's proposal to support Yatarō and decided to "leave everything to me."[19] In his memoirs Maejima frequently tries to credit himself with responsibility for major decisions. In the case of his proposal, even if Ōkubo did tentatively agree, a final resolution of the matter seems to have been left pending. The two plans of Maejima and Ōkuma not only differed substantially in content but also reflected a bureaucratic rivalry over which ministry or bureau should gain control of the ships. Maejima regarded Ōkuma's opening of the Shanghai line as a unilateral action and criticized it as a move "without the sanction of law."[20]

The main reason for Maejima's criticism of Ōkuma seems to have been his concern over the relationship between Mitsubishi and the Post Office. Since Mitsubishi was carrying mail, he wanted its activities supervised by the Bureau of Posts and Communications of which he was head; this wish stood opposed to Ōkuma's arrogation of authority to himself in the Finance Ministry. Until 1873 foreign post offices in Japan were under the jurisdiction of the respective consulates, which enjoyed extraterritorial status, and each country delivered its own mail. Maejima believed his Post Office was competent to handle foreign mail by itself and in 1873 signed a postal treaty to that effect with the United States. In

1875 he was still trying to work out a similar agreement with England when Mitsubishi, under the authority of Ōkuma's order to open the Shanghai line, began carrying mail at the request of the British Post Office. To Maejima this was illegal. Moreover, it seemed a special affront because, with the British Post Office enjoying extraterritorial status, Mitsubishi was in effect engaging in "third-country trade." Maejima censured the Finance Ministry and made Mitsubishi desist, but rather cleverly exonerated the powerful Ōkuma by blaming instead the "ignorance of lower officials" of his own bureau for the incident.[21]

To Maejima, the Shanghai line, Ōkuma's proposal for government-managed shipping, and his effort to transform the Steamship Office into a permanent shipping bureau were all part of a scheme to deprive the Bureau of Posts and Communications of jurisdiction over shipping. According to Maejima, Ōkuma had his proposal drafted and approved within his own ministry, and then attempted to have it ratified by the Council of State by presenting it as a *fait accompli.* To illuminate the dynamics of this conflict between Maejima and Ōkuma, a word must be said about the consensus or deliberative approach to decision making, the *ringi* system (*ringi-sei*), which, according to M. Y. Yoshino, "is believed to have been in use by the civil bureaucracy in the early Meiji era and to have been later adopted by private corporations." The basis of the system is the *ringisho,* a document prepared in proposal form by lower-echelon personnel and presented to superiors for approval. Before presentation, and in some cases before the drafting of the *ringisho,* prior consultations are held with bureaus and departments affected by the proposed decision. When a consensus is reached, the document is circulated for formal approval and presented to superiors where it receives virtually automatic acceptance. Reaching a consensus in this manner before formal approval ensures smooth and cooperative implementation.[22]

During Ōkubo's absence from Tokyo in the early weeks of 1875, Ōkuma attempted to circumvent this system by having the Finance Ministry's *ringisho* approved prior to full discussion. Maejima strongly protested Ōkuma's plans, however, and later claimed

that his opposition prevented the Finance Ministry from presenting the *ringisho* to the Council of State.[23] The events of the time
tend to bear out Maejima's contention. The basic purpose of
Ōkuma's January memorandum to Sanjō on shipping was the
establishment of a separate bureau for shipping affairs, but this bureau (the proposed Kisen Jimukyoku) was never instituted. Instead, the Steamship Office's provisional status was left unchanged,
a reminder that no basic decision had yet been made.[24] In short,
Ōkuma's memorandum incorporating plans for the Shanghai line
and a Shipping Affairs Bureau was a bureaucratically formulated
ringisho that was rejected before the views of the officials concerned were unified. In this sense, Ōkuma's actions represented
only the first stage in the debate over a shipping policy.[25]

POLICY DEBATE: ŌKUBO TOSHIMICHI'S ROLE

The acrimonious first stage of debate ended shortly after Ōkubo
returned to Tokyo in mid-February and turned his attention to
shipping policy. Ōkubo provided the institutional link between
shipping and the government's industrial promotion policy.[26] In
November 1873 he had established the Home Ministry to oversee
this policy. As home minister he outlined some of his basic economic views in a May 1874 memorandum. Ōkubo argued that no
country had succeeded in increasing its productive power without
the patronage of its government. Economic expansion required
cooperation between government and the people. The Japanese
people, lacking in technical knowledge of industry and unwilling
to take risks, needed institutions that would promote their industries. Establishing the foundations for a wealthy, powerful country
called for government leadership in encouraging the development
of manufacturing and trade. Ōkubo found a model for his policy
in the mercantilism of Great Britain's Navigation Acts, which had
restricted that country's imports to its own ships. These acts
aimed to expand the national mercantile marine so that it could
exercise total control over trade and thereby protect domestic industries. This type of protectionism seemed especially appropriate

for Japan, because the treaty system deprived Japan of the freedom to utilize tariffs to promote domestic industries.[27]

ŌKUBO'S MAY 18 MEMORANDUM. Ōkubo's May 1874 memorandum contained a statement of general principles. He did not
have time to formulate specific programs until the early spring of
1875. His economic policy emphasized government aid to private
industries in contrast to the government-managed enterprises begun under the Ministry of Industry. This change in policy and the
partial shift in jurisdiction of some industries to the Home Ministry
prompted criticism from the Ministry of Industry and put Ōkubo
under pressure to develop definite programs.[28] In response to this
pressure he began work on a shipping policy. By May 1875 he had
designated four categories of enterprise in which the government
would aid private industry. The emphasis was on agriculture and
light industry, but one category was reserved for shipping.[29]

Ōkubo's May recommendations on shipping were the product
of proposals by Maejima and Ōkuma and of private meetings held
during the spring. Ōkubo, Maejima (and apparently Ōkuma as
well) discussed but rejected Ōkuma's memorandum on the Shipping Affairs Bureau. Ōkubo agreed with Maejima's support of private management and concurred in his wish to have the Bureau of
Posts and Communications supervise the ships entrusted to Mitsubishi.[30] One immediate result of these meetings was a direct order
from Ōkubo to Mitsubishi on April 19 to carry mail under the
jurisdiction of the Bureau of Posts and Communications. Maejima
then issued detailed postal regulations to Mitsubishi.[31]

The Shanghai line had been a direct and (in view of the excess
of tonnage) expedient outgrowth of the Taiwan expedition. On
the other hand, mail transport by sea had been a more fixed and
long-term requirement of the government. The mail transport
orders to Mitsubishi were, therefore, a clearer expression of the
shift in the government's confidence from the YJK to Mitsubishi,
a death knell to an already bankrupt company.

Ōkubo's detailed memorandum on shipping policy was presented
to Chief Minister Sanjō on May 18, 1875. Seals on Mitsubishi's

copies of the original memorandum possessed by the Iwasaki Biographical Compilation Committee demonstrate that the company
was at least privy to the government's policy deliberations. Furthermore, that same month Mitsubishi put into effect numerous
company regulations and administrative changes, established partly
at the government's urging. Their detailed nature suggests that Mitsubishi consulted closely with government officials in their preparation.[32]

Ōkubo's memorandum was a list of three broad options for
government shipping policy, including a formal statement of their
advantages and disadvantages. These options are usually referred
to as: (1) noninterventionism, which would leave shipping to private capital; (2) government promotion and supervision of privately
owned and privately operated shipping; and (3) government-
owned and government-operated shipping.[33] In full they are:

1. If the government considers that our country's shipping industry can
   be managed entirely by private capital, the government must establish
   operating regulations for private management. The government will
   entrust these regulations to private management and confine itself to
   a protective role.
2. If the government considers that private management has not yet
   reached the point where it can establish itself independently, it can
   direct several shipowners to form a joint enterprise and then provide
   it with government-owned ships and operating funds. Also under this
   plan, the government will order the establishment of a private mercantile marine school for the education of seamen and will provide
   instruction so that the enterprise can observe the government's regulations.
3. If the government considers that private management has not yet attained a level where it can establish itself according to option two,
   the government can administer the marine transportation industry by
   itself. Utilizing government ships and others which it will purchase,
   the government will carry on shipping in the seas around Japan and
   between Japan and Shanghai, China. With government funds we will
   set up a state mercantile marine school for the education of seamen
   and instruct government officials to implement the regulations
   which the government itself has established.

Ōkubo noted that option one would require a clear distinction between government and private enterprise. Its main drawback, he said, would be enforcing the myriad rules and regulations the government would have to draw up to supervise private management. These were necessary, he wrote, to "eliminate the self-indulgence of our present shipowners and seamen, reject unskilled seamen, and prohibit unsound shipbuilding," but to enforce them would be like "exerting military discipline over unruly and untrained soldiers."

The establishment of one large shipping company, as envisaged in option two, would yield several immediate benefits. With one large company serving all areas of the country, the government could more easily set an appropriate range of freight rates. A single company would also eliminate cutthroat competition, which, according to Ōkubo, was the main thing troubling shipowners. The lowering of rates because of such competition, said Ōkubo, decreased freight income and rendered it impossible to make ship repairs. Measures would also have to be taken to reclaim the losses incurred through the competition with the American Pacific Mail Company.[34] More specifically, option two entailed granting to the new company the ships presently under the jurisdiction of the Finance Ministry and those previously sold to the YJK. The former YJK and Mitsubishi would be merged to form the new enterprise, which would be obliged to allow the government use of its ships in emergencies, to be attentive to ship repairs, and to transport mail. Under option two the government would not directly engage in operations, but, to avoid the mistakes committed by previous companies, it would carry out strict auditing of accounts. Despite these proposals, Ōkubo ended on a pessimistic note, lamenting the lack of skilled people who would "respond to the purposes of the government."

Option three, which would involve the opening of a government shipping agency, offered more immediate gains by giving the government a monopoly on the Shanghai service, achieved through the purchase of the four American Pacific Mail ships. In one clean sweep, then, the government could dispose of the obstacles in the coastal and Shanghai lines. All this, however, would yield only a small profit, Ōkubo noted. More importantly, the government's direct operation of the shipping industry would "produce monopolistic abuses and shift the losses onto the present domestic shipowners. It will thus frustrate the hard work of future shipowners and will have a harmful effect on the progress of the nation." The purchase of the Pacific Mail's Shanghai service would require over a million dollars; and, in any case, Ōkubo argued, "government enterprises generally tend to produce wasteful expenditures."

In transmitting the memorandum to Sanjō, Ōkubo requested a decision of the Council of State regarding the three options. He attached an estimate of annual financing for each option. A mere ¥20,000 would for the present suffice for option one, he said, but later developments would require many improvements. For option two, he estimated an annual outlay of ¥350,000, adding that the government would also "provide loans for ship repairs or funds which may be needed for such things as the liquidation of debts, as in the case of the YJK." An annual expenditure for option three was impossible to calculate, but in the long run it would probably exceed ¥500,000.

DECISION-MAKING AND POLICY. Of note in Ōkubo's memorandum was the seemingly offhand mention of Mitsubishi, referred to only as a member of the new enterprise to be formed under option two. This would suggest a degree of indecision regarding Mitsubishi. Scholarly consensus, however, holds that Ōkubo's comments on the financial estimates were tantamount to a recommendation for option two. Nakamura Naomi suggests that Ōkubo did not explicitly advocate aid to Mitsubishi because he wanted to "dilute the sense of personal bias" in the proposal by having the eventual recommendation issued in the shape of a cabinet decision. By this maneuvering Ōkubo hoped to avoid open conflict with political forces still opposing Mitsubishi.[35] Participants in the debate share a similar judgment of Ōkubo's motivation. Ōkuma later wrote that there was "great opposition from the public" at the decision to aid Mitsubishi. Ōkuma commented:

> Regardless of this Ōkubo resolved that by all means we had to choose Mitsubishi. Ōkubo was a man of extremely firm will. He was not a foolish kind of leader who could be deceived by other people or whose ideas changed easily. Nevertheless, since there was great public opposition at that time, if Maejima's opinion had changed, [the policy] would have been difficult to put into effect. [36]

Certainly the evidence is strong that the leading figures in the government might have jeopardized their positions had they identified themselves more closely with Mitsubishi. At the time there were rumors of Maejima being bribed by Mitsubishi, though he later claimed that "an investigation by the authorities clearly proved my innocence." [37]

Ōkuma's comments and the rumors of bribes both testify to Maejima's influence. Some scholars have even concluded that the greater part of Maejima's November proposal was virtually quoted in Ōkubo's memorandum. [38] This assessment, however, exaggerates Maejima's role and underestimates the importance of the private discussions in the spring of 1875. For example, several sections in Ōkubo's memorandum, apart from option three, are lifted directly from Ōkuma's January proposal. Ōkuma's true position, though, is something of a mystery. Nakamura Naomi implies that he too had been inhibited by political pressure from expressing explicit support for Mitsubishi but, once the discussion was out in the open and the results apparent, Ōkuma himself openly supported Mitsubishi. In a September 1875 memorandum on the economy, he seemed to advocate the Ōkubo-Maejima position in contrast to his earlier proposal for government management: "I have heard scarcely anything about capital to be used for a cooperative shipping undertaking between the government and private enterprise. Now there is Mitsubishi alone." [39]

Undeniably, much of the language and many of the key ideas in Ōkubo's memorandum came from Maejima. The latter's proposal that Mitsubishi receive government ships gratis was obviously the most fundamental point. No doubt recalling his earlier association with the YJK, Maejima argued that, even if the government sold the ships to a private company on lenient terms, the company's obligation to pay would put its business operations in the red. While not doubting Yatarō's ability, he believed that such a large financial burden would doom even an established company like Mitsubishi to the same fate as the YJK. He therefore proposed that the government favor Yatarō by granting him the ships outright. He later wrote that Ōkubo, "a man of clear thinking and broad vision, quickly indicated his approval."[40]

Maejima's more explicit comments highlight the contrast between Ōkubo's option two and the earlier shipping policy of the Finance Ministry under Inoue and Shibusawa. There were two main differences. First, the new policy promised much more generous government financing. The proposed outright grant of ships was an improvement over the long-term loan the YJK was to have paid for its ships. Furthermore, Ōkubo's option two explicitly provided for "operating funds." As seen in Chapter 1, the YJK had received a relatively small ¥6,000 subsidy for its Ryukyu line, and even the promised ¥600,000 that never materialized was earmarked for repairs, not operating expenses. Second, Ōkubo's reference in option two to directing "several shipowners to form a joint enterprise" was probably a euphemism to quiet the political backers of the YJK still opposed to Mitsubishi. The new enterprise, after all, was to be a union of the two companies' ships and equipment, not of their organizations. The management of the "joint enterprise" would come almost exclusively from Mitsubishi. The innovative aspect of Ōkubo's policy, in contrast to the YJK, was his utilization of one particular private company which would be allowed to retain considerable internal managerial autonomy.[41]

Along with the principle of large-scale aid, Ōkubo's recognition of managerial autonomy had the greatest impact in shaping the business structures that would accommodate private planning. Shipping, of course, was atypical in that it received more aid and government supervision than most industries. But, even within the shipping industry, companies usually gained considerable autonomy to shape their own strategies.

In 1875, however, government policy placed certain restrictions on company autonomy. Ōkubo's option two involved close state supervision, one consequence of which was a Mitsubishi management reform implemented partly to satisfy government accounting standards. Ōkubo's own policy suggestions seemed to necessitate this supervision, because he implicitly countenanced a monopoly. He pointed out the disadvantages of competition and favored one large company instead. In accepting the idea of heavy concentration in private industry he ignored Maejima's warning about the danger of monopolistic abuses arising from the dominant position of a private firm. Instead he, in effect, turned the warning around in option three, converting it into an admonition against the harmful effects of a state monopoly on private interests.

This policy orientation contained ambiguities which later became sources of tension between government and company. While tolerating a private monopoly, Ōkubo classified his options according to the "level" attained by private management. This language suggests that he saw development as being by stages. Since he also spoke of "shipowners of the future," it was not clear whether his recommendations actually provided Mitsubishi with a justification to preserve its monopoly in the face of future competition. Furthermore, the dual principles of state supervision and private autonomy, a kind of "coexistence of opposites," did not immediately lead to a harmonious balance. Usually the pendulum tended to swing too far in one direction, depending on the nature of political changes or the degree of company assertiveness.

The government's use of a single private company in shipping contrasts with its railway policy, for all the main railways constructed in the 1870s were government-owned. Nevertheless, the financing of railways early in the decade affords a parallel to the vicissitudes of the shipping industry before the policy debate of 1875. For example, in 1870 the Kansai Railway Company was established following a proposal by Maejima Hisoka that the government build the line with private investment. This joint venture was no more successful than the early government-sponsored shipping companies. The Kansai Railway Company could not attract sufficient investment, and soon had to be dissolved, with the government completing the line on its own. While the joint public-private investment pattern was unsuccessful, Japan's first railway, a short line between Tokyo and Yokohama completed in 1872, was built largely by a loan from Britain, a suggestive parallel to Yatarō's early reliance on foreign funds. Following these early experiments, the government itself constructed all other lines in the 1870s. These lines were only local in scale, connecting cities like Kobe, Osaka, and Kyoto. In the first decade of the Meiji period, then, shipping grew much more rapidly than railways. In addition to its great cost and technical difficulty, however, in the 1870s railway construction was less urgent than the development of a strong mercantile marine. The government had to develop shipping quickly to ward off the encroachment of foreign companies in Japanese coastal trade. The same threat did not imperil the country's railway development. In fact, the government, sensitive to the role railways had played in European imperialism, decided not to build any more railways with foreign loans; this kept ownership in Japanese hands, but meant that the pace of railway growth did not quicken until the 1880s.[42]

MITSUBISHI'S ABSORPTION OF THE YJK

MANAGEMENT REFORM. While awaiting a formal decision on the government subsidy policy, Yatarō carried out a thorough reform of Mitsubishi's management. On May 1, 1875, he changed the functions of company offices, provided detailed administrative regulations, and issued a company code. The most important articles of the code were:

(1) Although this enterprise assumes the name of a company and establishes company structure, in reality it is entirely a family enterprise and differs greatly therefore from companies which constitute themselves by collecting the funds of others. Accordingly, all things

that concern the company, praise and blame and all, are entirely up to the president.

(2) All profits of the company return to the person of the president, and the losses of the company likewise are borne entirely by the president. [43]

Mitsubishi's new administrative structure appears in Figure 2. This structure was highly centralized, which enabled the president "to give orders with respect to personal affairs and business operations, no matter how trivial the matter might be." The general manager, through whom the president operated, acted as chief of staff, summarizing all the business of the company for the president, but beyond that "neither his duties nor his authority were clearly specified." [44]

FIGURE 2 Mitsubishi Administrative Structure, 1875

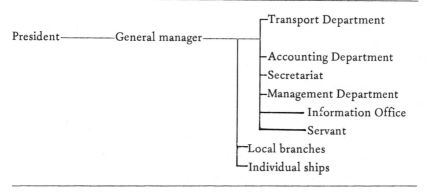

Sources: M Sha shi, II, 38–44; Takaura Tadahiko, "Mitsubishi no 'shasoku' ni tsuite," p. 116; Nagasawa Yasuaki, "Shoki Mitsubishi no keiei . . . kaiungyō," p. 32.

Before 1875 there had been perhaps as many as ten general managers. The reform changed the function of the office by centralizing its authority. After the start of the reform, on May 4, there appears to have been only two general managers, Ishikawa Shichizai and Kawada Koichirō. Both concurrently held positions as department heads—Ishikawa of transport and Kawada of management. Ishikawa's position gave him responsibility for the company's shipping affairs, whereas Kawada held additional duties in Mitsubishi's mining business.[45]

The new company code strengthened Yatarō's authority over the company. At the same time, the specification of department functions was partly a device for allowing the government more control. This was especially true of the Accounting Department, for Mitsubishi was soon obliged to submit annual business and accounting reports to the government.

Also in May, Yatarō issued a statement to his employees known as the "First Proclamation," a timely notice designed to win government approval.[46] Yatarō's rhetoric, nationalist as it was, did not affect the style of a mere "instrument" of government policy. Instead Yatarō asserted that he would take the initiative in reviving Japan's shipping fortunes and maintain his independence. This new impetus was possible, he said, because the government had recognized that shipping was indispensable to the nation. "Recovering for our country its navigation rights by eliminating the intrusion of the Pacific Mail" was the first step in this "national mission."

In this notice Yatarō also offered a moral treatise on freight rates and competition, which served to rationalize an attack on traditional shippers that he intensified over the next half decade. In contrast to the shifty expediency of the past, the present called for the path of righteousness, which meant maintaining appropriate (that is, high) freight rates. He admitted that, in his earlier competition with government-sponsored companies, "together we competed recklessly and were able neither to maintain set rules nor to determine fair freight rates." As a consequence, he claimed, shippers benefited and abuses became apparent.

ADMINISTRATIVE CENTRALIZATION AND THE YJK LIQUIDATION. During 1874 administration of shipping affairs had gradually been concentrated in the Department of Ships under the Bureau of Posts and Communications. However, after the Taiwan expedition an anomalous situation emerged in which Japan's best ships were under the jurisdiction of the Finance Ministry, headed by Ōkuma, while the Bureau of Posts and Communications, headed by Mae-jima, continued to exercise authority over shipping affairs. This division of bureaucratic functions underlay the disputes between Ōkuma and Maejima. During the spring 1875 discussions on ship-ping, the government decided to expand the functions of the Bureau of Posts and Communications. The British adviser Captain Brown was given a two-year contract to draw up plans for a marine bureau that would administer all matters connected with shipping and shipbuilding.[47] Then in June, the government transferred the ships in the Finance Ministry's Steamship Office to the Depart-ment of Ships in Maejima's bureau. The policy decisions of 1875, then, completed the gradual centralization of shipping affairs.

One reason for this centralization of administration was the anticipated purchase of the YJK's ships as part of that company's liquidation. In June the government bought up the company's 18 ships. This left the Department of Ships with 31 vessels, 13 of them operated by Mitsubishi.

In late May or early June the YJK had requested the govern-ment to purchase its assets for ¥500,000. The government regarded its counteroffer of ¥350,000 as exceptionally generous, but this was still not enough to satisfy the YJK, which presented a second petition, this time with detailed figures.[48] As the causes of the YJK's failure, the petition cited the repair expenses and conse-quent debts, the competition with Mitsubishi after it began using the Finance Ministry's ships, and the general decline in freight rates. As a company, it argued, "we could no longer compete with the government." Debts to the *kawase kaisha* had mounted to more than ¥800,000, while other obligations exceeded ¥100,000. The company this time requested ¥385,000 and provided a de-tailed liquidation statement, as shown in Table 1. Since the gov-ernment refused to increase its initial offer, the difference between the company's request and the government's offer was ¥35,000, while the company owed its stockholders, ¥34,000, virtually the same amount. It is not clear whether this was merely a coincidence or whether the government was trying to prevent the company from squeezing out a little extra money for its stockholders.

*but what
were YJK's worth??.
were assets*

TABLE 1 Proposed YJK Liquidation Settlement

Amount (¥)	Description
101,000	*Company loans:* represents the category of "other debts," including ¥5,000 to be returned to the Onogumi.
34,000	*Depreciated shares:* Original shares worth ¥188,000 had declined in value to less than 20%; the value of other stock had declined to one-third its original amount.
250,000	*Debts to kawase kaisha:* amount agreed upon to pay to the Dai Ichi Kokuritsu Ginkō, successor to the *kawase kaisha,* to eliminate its debt of over ¥800,000.
385,000	Total requested from the government.

Source: Matsukata ke monjo, vol. 61, Kōtsū, no. 31.

The petition's tone also provides a clear contrast to the initiative and independence Yatarō spoke of in his May proclamation. The company president's apologia stresses his dependence on being chosen as the "instrument" of government: "Having no ability, I could not really take charge of the company's business. Without aiming for success myself, I merely relied on the government's protection."

Following its liquidation many of the YJK's land employees and seamen transferred to Mitsubishi. The most capable of these was Kawasaki Shōzō, who briefly became an executive under Yatarō. Within Mitsubishi, however, "the two great men could not exist together," and in 1878 Kawasaki resigned to start his own company.[49] Mitsubishi also acquired 17 ships as well as warehouses and other facilities which the government had purchased from the YJK. The ships, transferred to Mitsubishi after the government's formal decision on shipping policy later in the year, totaled only about 8,000 tons, less than half the tonnage of the 13 ships Mitsubishi was operating for the government.[50]

THE FIRST DIRECTIVE

Mitsubishi's reforms, the centralization of administration in the Department of Ships, and the liquidation of the YJK smoothed the way for the government to move beyond policy debate to a formal decision. To expedite this process, in June 1875 Ōkubo appears to have had his first personal interview with Yatarō, arranged through the offices of Matsukata Masayoshi. Ōkubo, it is said, realized "at a glance" that Yatarō was the man "to challenge the foreign enemy."[51] Accordingly, he sent a short memorandum to Chief Minister Sanjō indicating his preference for option two of his May memorandum.[52] Approval was then transmitted to Ōkubo in an order from Sanjō to "reduce the budget as much as possible" and to report on methods of implementing option two.[53] In sharp contrast to his May memorandum, Ōkubo gave a strong and explicit recommendation of Mitsubishi in his report presented to Sanjō on July 29. Using the language of the YJK's liquidation petition, he criticized the YJK for having been excessively dependent on the government without any thought of becoming self-supporting. On the other hand, Mitsubishi's Iwasaki Yatarō, wrote Ōkubo,

> operates a completely self-reliant enterprise. Though he is president, he uses the financial resources of his own house mainly for this enterprise. He is also one who knows enough about business and who is sufficiently experienced to persevere in the shipping industry. From the beginning we have entrusted to him the 13 ships which belong under the jurisdiction of this ministry; and if we think together about the way he has used these ships and the great service he has rendered, it is my opinion that we should entrust this enterprise to him.[54]

With his report Ōkubo submitted a note to Sanjō about another accounting problem in the Finance Ministry. Ōkubo had planned to begin the subsidy to Mitsubishi as quickly as possible, but the Finance Ministry wanted "all new enterprises to hold up their commencement until [the Ministry] adjusts this year's financial accounts." In response Ōkubo had decreased the projected subsidy slightly and had made special arrangements with Ōkuma for Sanjō to sanction the extraordinary request and grant the subsidy quickly.[55] On August 10 Sanjō notified Ōkubo that a ¥300,000 subsidy would be authorized from the Finance Ministry.[56] Like other examples of favoritism to Mitsubishi, Ōkubo's intervention contrasts sharply with the negative response given to the YJK during the earlier period of accounting reform.

In his August 10 note Sanjō requested Ōkubo to change the form of the agreement with Mitsubishi from a contract (*yaku-jōsho*) to a directive (*meireisho*). Later that month Ōkubo produced a draft directive[57] and, following Sanjō's approval, on September 15 the First Directive was issued to Mitsubishi under Maejima's name.[58]

TERMS OF THE FIRST DIRECTIVE. The First Directive's preamble set forth its basic terms. The government granted to Mitsubishi without charge the thirteen steamships under the jurisdiction of the Bureau of Posts and Communications and an annual ¥250,000 operating subsidy. Following the preamble were seventeen articles. Scholarly opinions differ over the issue of government control as expressed in these articles. Kozo Yamamura, for example, calls the government directives on shipping "loosely worded."[59] Japanese scholars have been more inclined to find strict controls in the directive. One terms the articles "the codification of the government's intention to be serviced according to its own purposes."[60] A brief examination of the relevant articles may resolve this debate.

Article 1 placed limitations on the ownership of the vessels— prohibiting Mitsubishi from selling or using the ships or subsidies as collateral without advance permission, making more difficult the kind of speculative borrowing Yatarō had conducted during his Tosa years. After the First Directive almost all of Mitsubishi's loans were from the government. In late 1875 Yatarō did experience some inconvenience in borrowing from the government, for several smaller loans were delayed despite Maejima's intervention.[61] Still, loans were much less necessary now that the company was being subsidized. Between October 1874 and mid-1875 Mitsubishi received six special grants from the government totaling ¥320,000.[62] At least during the 1870s article 1 did not act as a restrictive measure.

Article 7 required Mitsubishi to present regular business reports and to submit to government audits, thereby stimulating Mitsubishi management reform, especially in accounting. Also regarding government supervision, Ōkubo had stipulated in his July 29 report that Mitsubishi's name should be changed to the Mail Steamship Mitsubishi Company (Yūbin Kisen Mitsubishi Kaisha).[63] As yet Japan had no corporation law, and changing a company's name was a common way of indicating a specific legal intent that in later years would have been expressed by a change in the articles of incorporation.[64] Mitsubishi's name change, effected on September 18, signified the combining of company business with certain state functions like carrying mail, handled earlier by the YJK. The new name was also an attempt to define the boundaries of the company's business activity. Article 12 forbade Mitsubishi from engaging in business other than shipping "under the name of this company."

Article 12 eventually exercised great restraint on Mitsubishi and contributed to the crisis in the 1880s that ended with the formation of the N.Y.K. and the splitting away of Mitsubishi from direct management of the shipping business. In the 1870s the government recognized Mitsubishi's coal mining as falling within the limits of article 12 because of the use of coal in ships. Mitsubishi was able to enter certain enterprises like exchange financing for shippers through special government permission. In the late 1870s and early 1880s Mitsubishi's expansion into subsidiary enterprises created a legal problem over whether these conformed to the requirements of article 12. Eventually Mitsubishi's activities provoked widespread critcism from both the government and the public, largely as a response to Mitsubishi's monopolistic position, but article 12 placed the critics on the side of legitimacy. The anti-Mitsubishi reaction put a brake on the company's expansion and demonstrated that a fully diversified concern, one that would later grow into a mature zaibatsu, could not use as its base an enterprise like shipping, which was too closely supervised by the government and tied to the requirements of national security.[65] The basic "control" articles thus either failed to recognize the potential conflicts in future business expansion or were highly ambiguous.

A similar ambiguity is present in article 13, which defined Mitsubishi's responsibility to national defense: "Regardless of whether it is peacetime or wartime and regardless of the state of company business, if the government has need, even though these ships are the property of Mitsubishi, the government shall be able to use them. However, on these occasions the government shall pay an appropriate amount for freight rates." The last part of this article became at times the equivalent of a massive and profitable defense contract; at other times, when the obligation to support the military efforts of the government conflicted with normal business, the "defense contract" became an unwanted burden.

Many scholars have emphasized the government's military motives in aiding Mitsubishi. Nakamura Naomi, for example, has commented on the urgency with which Ōkubo regarded the building of armaments and the consolidation of a network to transport them. Yatarō thus gave tangible shape to Ōkubo's vision of a "rich country and a strong military" (*fukoku kyōhei*).[66] As Thomas Smith points out, however, and I believe correctly, in the early Meiji period "the challenge of the West was not primarily military, but social and economic; and it was this challenge that industrial policy had to meet." In fact, notes Smith, the Meiji government "shifted the Tokugawa emphasis away from" military power.[67]

The First Directive itself says remarkably little about military matters. Yatarō, though, appears to have exploited military concerns in his appeal for aid. In his late 1874 meeting with Maejima, Yatarō claimed that "if the shipping industry does not succeed, the wealth and power of Japan will not grow; and without such growth, neither will we be able to achieve sufficient development of our naval power."[68] Later, during the policy discussions in the spring of 1875, Maejima proposed the establishment of a strong "merchant fleet that would in peacetime be commissioned to coastal routes and to the Shanghai line and in wartime be offered for the use of the navy."[69] These military considerations had become an important issue in the Ōkuma-Maejima debate over public or private operation of shipping. The opponents of a government-owned military transport system, which was supported by Ōkuma, believed that in peacetime the government would have "to tie up its transport fleet or to directly operate it commercially for profit." Instead they favored a private fleet designed to "meet both the commercial and military needs of the Government in an emergency."[70]

Less strategic articles concerned repairs, mail, hiring of foreigners (which was encouraged), and the establishment of a private merchant marine school. Finally, the directive was meant to cover a fifteen-year term, but Mitsubishi was given a one-year trial period, after which the government promised to extend its commitment another fourteen years provided that Mitsubishi had expanded the business.

VIEWS ON MITSUBISHI STRATEGY AND THE FIRST DIRECTIVE. The salient features of the First Directive were the ambiguities in its most important articles and the size of Mitsubishi's subsidy. Many Japanese scholars have viewed the directive as an example of the government's strong supervisory authority and the government's subsidy program as part of a carefully formulated industrial promotion policy. Saitō Yoshihisa, a representative of this view, has written that "Japan's modern shipping industry was established through a process of protective nurturing from above." This interpretation refers to the subsidized company as the "instrument" (*ninaite*) of the government's policy.[71] Some years ago Kozo Yamamura questioned this interpretation. He concluded that "It was Iwasaki who in effect forced the government to subsidize him after the government-favored company went bankrupt." Yamamura's research led him to see "more of a mixture of personal friendship, political accidents, and the desire on the part of government officials to protect the industry, rather than a conscious, carefully conceived plan to nurture an internationally competitive shipping industry with the least cost and maximum efficiency." [72] Furthermore, other Japanese scholars have differed with the emphasis on "protective nurturing." Kobayashi Masaaki views Mitsubishi as typical of "the large private enterprise in Japan which adroitly utilized the 'nationalism' of the government." [73] Mitsubishi's exploitation of government funds and the government's nurturing are regarded as complementary by Shibagaki Kazuo, who comments that Mitsubishi acted as "the real instrument of government policy while it continued to utilize to the limit government funds." [74]

Shibagaki's view leads to our principal consideration—Mitsubishi's use of government subsidies. Later in the 1870s Mitsubishi began to divert these subsidies into enterprises outside shipping. Yamamura argues that Mitsubishi was able to do this partly because of the ambiguities of the First Directive, which did not place an unequivocal ban on outside enterprises. He further implies that the ambiguities were the result of the successful terms achieved in the 1874 military transport contract and the subsequent way Mitsubishi "in effect forced" the government to subsidize it. On the contrary, the idea that Mitsubishi "in effect forced" the government to subsidize it, when the government had no "carefully conceived" policy, is an exaggeration which overlooks the deliberations of Ōkubo, Ōkuma, and Maejima in the spring of 1875 and the detailed memoranda they later considered. Certainly the timing of Mitsubishi's emergence—during the Taiwan expedition and on the eve of major policy decisions—was important. But in the context of 1875, Mitsubishi and the government had too many objectives in common for us to conclude that the company forced the government to subsidize it. Consider, for example, Ōkubo's support of concentration in the shipping industry. He expressly favored the dominance of a single firm, thereby countenancing a monopoly. The logic of Ōkubo's memorandum suggests that he reached this conclusion because he considered competition wasteful, not simply because the YJK had collapsed and the government was left with no one but Mitsubishi to turn to. A second qualification to Yamamura's view concerns the ambiguities in the directive. These should not be seen simply as a boon to Mitsubishi, that is, "loosely worded" articles that could easily be circumvented. A second perspective is that the prohibition against Mitsubishi using its name in businesses outside shipping became an impediment to later expansion. This indicates that the government did set certain conditions for the use of the subsidies.[75]

From the viewpoint of institutional development, the bargaining between Mitsubishi and the government over the first subsidization program may be characterized as a problem of "origins." More relevant to Mitsubishi's changing business structure were the effects of the subsidies. From its beginning Mitsubishi was not exclusively a shipping company and retained outside interests, especially in mining. This structure changed suddenly in 1874–1875. With government service in the Taiwan expedition and the beginning of the subsidy program, Mitsubishi had become predominantly a shipping concern. However, what kind of investment policy would Mitsubishi adopt now that it had access to a ¥250,000 annual subsidy? Would it concentrate solely on building up the strength of its shipping business? Would it make outside investments only in enterprises that were supporting mechanisms for the main shipping concern? Or, would it move into new ventures separate from shipping? Mitsubishi's strategic responses to these questions would shape the company's business structure and determine whether its relations with the government could be kept free of friction. For Mitsubishi, decisions on these issues became pressing matters as early as 1876.

In late 1875 the First Directive had temporarily brought all the threads of shipping policy together.[76] A mere fourteen months earlier Mitsubishi had, with 10 ships, been one of two major Japanese shipping firms. By international or even regional standards both were still inconsequential. But by September 1875, with 38 ships, Mitsubishi had gained predominance in Japanese shipping and was on the verge of international triumphs. The main obstacle in its way was the continued presence of the American Pacific Mail Line.

PURCHASE OF THE PACIFIC MAIL'S SHANGHAI LINE

Mitsubishi began the 1875 competition on the Shanghai line by slashing freight rates between Yokohama and Shanghai by one-third. More drastic cuts were made in domestic rates, with second-class passenger fares between Yokohama and Kobe falling from ten dollars to around two dollars.[77] Though both Mitsubishi and the Pacific Mail continued this severe rate cutting, there is evidence that the competition was not nearly the death struggle that some writers portrayed. The real issue was not who would emerge the "victor" or whether the "loser" would "collapse," but simply what was to be the price of the American company's withdrawal. Furthermore, it was assumed, in the short term at least, that the price would be borne by the government.

Some writers regard the January 18 order for the Shanghai line mainly as a strategy for creating advantageous conditions for the purchase of the Pacific Mail's service.[78] It is not known whether this was Ōkuma's primary intent, for he appears to have contemplated an even broader range of competition. In his January proposal for a Shipping Affairs Bureau he had referred to possible future lines to Europe and America. On January 23 the Steamship Office compiled a report on a possible trial run to San Francisco, though this was rejected as too costly.[79] On February 2, Maejima sent a proposal to Ōkuma for the government to purchase the American company's Shanghai line.[80] Maejima may have been responding to secret overtures from the Pacific Mail. Several times the previous year the company had proposed selling the line to the Japanese government, though it withdrew its proposals before action could be taken. Nevertheless, by the end of the year its asking price had declined considerably.[81]

On February 3, the day after Maejima's proposal and the same day Mitsubishi's first ship sailed on its Shanghai line, the Pacific

Mail made a new proposal for the sale of the line. In a letter from its agent, J. G. Walsh, to Hirai Yoshimasa of the Foreign Ministry, Walsh warned that the Pacific Mail "cannot be expected to give up the fruits of their enterprise without a struggle, even if their opponents have the support of the Japanese Government." The Pacific Mail, he claimed, "can also afford to lose a good deal of money as the Government and people of America would probably sympathise with them, and give them some assistance in their efforts."[82]

Walsh's assumptions were hollow. On March 3, 1875, the United States Congress passed a law abrogating the second Pacific Mail Company contract, which had gone into effect in October 1873. This slashed $500,000 from the company's annual million dollar subsidy. The first contract was scheduled to run till 1877, but had no chance of renewal, for the company had been attacked in Congress because it used Asian crews (a cost-cutting measure) and because its president had spent over a half million dollars "for bribes and fees."[83]

Quite possibly when Walsh wrote his February 3 letter, the Pacific Mail had already foreseen the impending congressional reaction against it. If so, it is not surprising that the second half of the letter abandons the hard line and virtually pleads with the Japanese government for a settlement. Walsh's offers of ships, facilities, and withdrawal from the line were similar to the terms of the solution eventually adopted. His letter raises the question of whether Mitsubishi actually knew about the abrogation of the American company's second contract. The likelihood that it knew is strong, for the Pacific Mail's agent was the ubiquitous Walsh, Hall & Company, the same firm that served as Mitsubishi's agent.[84] If the Japanese did know, it would account for their willingness to endure the competition and delay the settlement until the autumn.

While Mitsubishi was forced to forego its profits in the competition, the Pacific Mail apparently suffered more serious losses. Detailed negotiations began in June, and in September Yatarō secured the consent of Ōkubo and Ōkuma to borrow $810,000 for the purchase of the line. These were the terms reached in a purchase agreement between the two companies on October 16.[85]

TABLE 2 Ships Purchased from the American Pacific
         Mail Steamship Company

	Tonnage (GT)	Year Built
Golden Age *(Hiroshima Maru)*	1,869	1853
Costa Rica *(Genkai Maru)*	1,917	1863
Nevada *(Saikyō Maru)*	2,143	1864
Oregonian *(Nagoya Maru)*	1,914	1886

Source: *Yanosuke den,* I, 158-159.

Of the total, $780,000 went to the Pacific Mail and $30,000 to a
related company, the Occidental and Oriental S.N. Company, the
O. & O. One source says that $680,000 of the purchase price went
for the four ships (see Table 2) which Mitsubishi received from the
Pacific Mail and which John Black called "most commodious
steamers."[86] Based on (1) Ōkubo's May memorandum in which he
estimated a sum of more than one million dollars for the takeover
and on (2) selling prices of ¥250,000 and ¥275,000 which Batchelder had quoted to Ōkuma the previous year for two of these
same ships, it appears that Mitsubishi brought down the price by
several hundred thousand dollars, thereby justifying the nine-
month competition.[87] Mitsubishi, in short, had won its first international victory. "It at once gave not only the company, but Japan
itself, a standing among the trading nations in these seas. The Japa-.
nese flag was no longer confined to the coasts of Japan," wrote
Black, "but became familiar in the largest commercial emporium
in the Far East [that is, Shanghai]."[88]

THREE

Competition and Business Innovation: 1876–1880

COMPETITION WITH THE P. & O.

The subsidies begun in 1875 laid the financial basis for Mitsubishi's rapid growth over the next decade. However, the close state supervision accompanying this aid could potentially conflict with company desire for autonomy. Such conflict did not arise in 1876 because the supportive function of aid took precedence over its supervisory or regulatory dimension. In the face of competition from the P. & O., the powerful British firm, the Japanese government and Mitsubishi cooperated closely in employing new tactics and strategy in both the passenger and freight business. Also during 1876, Mitsubishi began to develop a more complex business structure through new investments: some supported by the government to buttress the company's shipping enterprise, and others, especially in mining, undertaken by Mitsubishi as a risk-avoidance strategy to free the company from exclusive dependence on its government connection. These ventures were still small in 1876, but the decisions initiating them set important precedents for a later, more autonomous investment strategy.

THE P. & O. THREAT AND YATARŌ'S STRATEGY. Early in 1876 Mitsubishi received a financial boost by providing eleven ships for a military venture off the Korean coast. Through this gunboat diplomacy Japan secured a commercial treaty with Korea which opened several ports and enabled Mitsubishi to begin a Nagasaki-Pusan service. For its part in the military operation Mitsubishi earned ¥139,000.[1]

The extra revenue from this Korean incident was extremely timely, for in February the P. & O. opened a Hong Kong-Shanghai-Yokohama line and before long ventured into Japanese coastal routes as well. Mitsubishi's dominance on the Shanghai line, achieved through the takeover of the American Pacific Mail's service, was thus short lived. The Pacific Mail had been essentially a special-purpose company serving American interests in the Pacific but was often beset by financial troubles. The P. & O., on the other hand, had far greater resources. In 1876 it was receiving an annual subsidy of about £400,000 from the British government to carry mail to China and South Asia. Moreover, its chairman, Thomas Sutherland, had played a leading role in the establishment of the Hong Kong and Shanghai Banking Corporation and had set up a shipping service to Japan earlier in 1864.[2]

Nevertheless, the initial threat the P. & O. posed to Mitsubishi was not as great as it seemed. Just as in 1875, when the Japanese may have had less than adequate intelligence about the Pacific Mail's domestic problems, so too in 1876 it appears that they exaggerated the P. & O. threat because they were unaware of the tentative nature of the British firm's decision to challenge Mitsubishi. P. & O. agents had reported on "general discontent" with Mitsubishi's Shanghai service, and on February 1 the P. & O. board accepted their recommendation to oppose Mitsubishi and placed one ship on the line "as an experiment."[3] Though it added a second ship two weeks later, this original tentative commitment helps to explain why the P. & O. withdrew from the line within six months instead of persevering after it began to lose business during the summer.

Virtually all accounts of this competition have assumed that the P. & O. had a greater resolve than that implied by the language of the aforementioned decision. Scholars have suggested that the P. & O. hoped to integrate Japan into its trading network, in which it paid for English imports of Chinese tea by exporting English manufactured products to India and shipping opium and raw cotton from India to China.[4] Similarly, the American adviser Batchelder warned the government of the P. & O. threat in a letter of February 24. Since the P. & O., he wrote, had "the confidence of English money and Foreign businessmen, the larger portion of Foreign and Chinese passengers, and freight will go with them. The Banks are foreign, and will give them their money to carry, the Insurance Cos. are foreign and will give them their lowest rates, many of your people will send cargoes, and travel with them." Because of the P. & O.'s connections with other European steamship lines and British trading houses, Batchelder regarded Japan's chance of retaining even half the business of the Shanghai line as "very doubtful," and predicted that before the end of the year "[Mitsubishi] will have lost more than the present market value of the P. & O. steamers." He then suggested purchasing the P. & O.'s Shanghai line, which he felt could be done for less than $300,000.[5]

Batchelder may have exaggerated the P. & O.'s commitment, but it was the *perceived* threat, evident in his alarmist tone, motivating Mitsubishi's vigorous response. For Mitsubishi the competition with the P. & O., while shorter than that of the previous year, was potentially more dangerous and in the end had a far greater impact on the Japanese firm's business organization.

The P. & O. threat forced Yatarō for the second time in a year into a rationalization of Mitsubishi's management. He introduced this in March by issuing a second "proclamation" to his employees, emphasizing both their responsibility and the epochal nature of the struggle. It is also an important document for Yatarō's concept of economic nationalism.[6] The first part of the notice concerned the effects of more than two centuries of isolation. According to Yatarō, the Japanese people had not yet come to regard as strange the monopolization of the coastal trade by foreign shipping companies. Some even debated the relative merits of having navigation rights for coastal trade in the hands of Japanese or foreigners. In doing so they failed to recognize that by surrendering these rights to foreigners Japan was endangering its own economic independence.

Yatarō attributed Japan's weak competitive position to an undeveloped sense of the relation among national consciousness, economic power, and entrepreneurship. He brushed aside as a secondary consideration the unequal treaties signed with the Western powers in the 1850s. "Even if the government revises the treaties and even if we change our former customs, all the endeavors of the government will come to naught," he claimed, unless a Japanese enterprise could recover the coastal trade. For this reason "the government is promoting our company, and our responsibilities are even greater than the full weight of Mt. Fuji thrust upon our shoulders. If we succeed it will not only mean benefits for one company, it will exalt the prestige of the Japanese Empire throughout the whole world." In a message that emphasized self-reliance and hard work he ended on an inspirational note: "whether or not we succeed in this depends, in part, on whether you gentlemen exert yourselves to the utmost."

A heavy price had to be paid for these "great efforts." Mitsubishi, said Yatarō, had been established only a short time before, while the "P. & O. has large capital resources and many ships, and its name is heard in countries throughout the East. What methods should we now employ to compete with this giant?" The answer: reduction of surplus personnel and elimination of wasteful expenditures. Cooperation was not long in coming. Company executives quickly petitioned for a reduction in salary. On April 1 Yatarō replied that their request had made a "deep impression" on him, and he announced a one-third reduction in their salaries, a 50 percent reduction in his own monthly salary from ¥800 to ¥400, and the release of sixteen company employees.[7]

Despite this apparent spontaneous support from the executives, cooperation with Yatarō's plans lacked unanimity. One company official opposing the idea of competing with the P. & O. was Kawamura Hisanao, former finance officer in the naval forces of Enomoto Takeaki, who had opposed the establishment of the Meiji government in 1868–1869. In a memorandum to Yatarō early in

1876, Kawamura had contrasted the massive resources of the P. & O. with Mitsubishi's precarious financial position in the wake of the competition with the American Pacific Mail Company. He advised Yatarō to concentrate on financial recovery and not to compete with the P. & O. until Mitsubishi had regained its strength.

Yatarō rejected this recommendation partly on the basis of a secret report from Kondō Renpei, manager of the Yoshioka Copper Mine. Kondō pointed out that after several years of lackluster results, the mine's production had rapidly increased in recent months. He urged Yatarō to commit additional funds to expand the mine's capacity. Yatarō agreed with Kondō, and reportedly hoped to use the mine profits to support the company's competition with the P. & O. In the meantime, unaware of Kondō's report, known only to Yatarō's closest associates, Kawamura resigned from Mitsubishi, predicting that the competition would drive the company into bankruptcy. As it was, the planned expansion of the mine was aborted by a June 1876 fire which destroyed all the equipment and buildings and seriously damaged the mine.[8] The mine, nevertheless, played an important role in decisions regarding the shipping competition. Just when his executives had come forward to volunteer one-third of their salaries for the struggle with the P. & O., Yatarō was preparing to expand his investments in mining. This illustrates the dual pattern of Mitsubishi's competitive response: strict retrenchment measures and simultaneous strategic investments outside shipping. Yatarō did not see this dual pattern as a contradiction. The profits from the mine, he hoped, would aid the competitive shipping struggle, and the planned expansion would strengthen the firm as a whole.

COMPETITION FOR PASSENGERS. After the P. & O. began competing in Japanese waters, shipping charges, which had been raised in the aftermath of the American Pacific Mail's withdrawal, quickly plummeted again. In the passenger business Mitsubishi did not feel the real brunt of the competition until early April. The P. & O. had employed two ships on the Yokohama-Shanghai line, and during their first round-trip sailing the competing Mitsubishi ships

carried more than twice as many passengers. A breakdown of these
passenger figures appears in a special report which Ōkuma commissioned from Batchelder (see Table 3).[9] By the inbound voyage
of April 6, the end of the first round of competition, Mitsubishi
had begun to fall behind the P. & O. Batchelder attributed this to
a stop made by the P. & O. at Tientsin on the way back from
Shanghai in which it took on more passengers. Accordingly the
P. & O. was able to pay almost all expenses incurred on this first
sailing. On the other hand, Mitsubishi had already drastically reduced its fares, and, with a decline in passengers, "was in a position which gave rise to enormous expenses."

TABLE 3 Passengers Carried on the Shanghai Line, 1876

Sailing & Date		P. & O. Ships		Mitsubishi Ships	
Outbound	February 26	Orissa	131	Tokyo Maru	525
Inbound	March 19	Orissa	54	Nagoya Maru	72
Outbound	March 13	Columbian	127	Genkai Maru	306
Inbound	April 6	Columbian	128	Genkai Maru	50
Total			440		953

Source: Batchelder to Ōkuma, Matsukata ke monjo, vol. 61, Kōtsū, no. 28.

The P. & O. threatened Mitsubishi's passenger business on both
the Shanghai line and coastal routes. In fact, in the mid-1870s
most Japanese traveling between Tokyo and Osaka still boarded
foreign vessels. To attract even more passengers following its first
sailing, the P. & O. intended to replace its ships, the *Columbian*
and *Orissa,* with two faster vessels that had larger capacities but
which were less expensive to maintain. To meet this challenge Mitsubishi initiated a movement to boycott foreign steamships
through a newspaper campaign.[10] Mitsubishi's strongest weapon in
the competition, however, was the government, which intervened
in 1876 to pass a control law requiring all Japanese traveling on
foreign steamships to purchase a pass costing 25 *sen,* without which

they would be subject to arrest upon reaching their destination. Foreign diplomats protested, for the law had immediate effect. Hardly any Japanese boarded the P. & O. ships during their second sailing on the Shanghai line.[11] It is reported that by July 12 Mitsubishi's Shanghai-bound ship was full, whereas a P. & O. ship on the same day carried only three passengers.[12]

The government's control law was an early example of Japanese "flag discrimination," that is, legislation or other forms of pressure employed by governments to direct passengers and cargoes to ships of their own flag. Most countries with developed merchant marines prohibit foreign flag vessels from shipping between their domestic ports. Japan could not enact this prohibition until the revised treaties with Western countries went into effect in 1899.[13] In the meantime this special boarding pass was an effective piece of protective legislation that helped to circumvent the restrictions of the treaties.

FREIGHT AND A NEW BUSINESS NETWORK. While Mitsubishi was able to gain the upper hand in the passenger business, the competition in freight was of more critical importance for two reasons: the relative quantity of freight in Mitsubishi's total business and the type of competition. During the 1870s and early 1880s, as shown in Table 4, the ratio of freight to passenger income was about 3 to 1. Furthermore, the freight competition centered predominantly on the coastal trade and exerted great pressure on domestic business institutions.

The distribution system of the time often led to difficulties between the transporter and the shipper regarding the consignment of freight. Once he had been entrusted with the freight, the transporter bore the entire responsibility for storage, transport, and security. On the other hand, the shipper had many liabilities because he had to wait until his goods had been delivered before he could receive full payment, usually through another agent. As an advance the transporter would sometimes pay the shipper a percentage of the freight's value.[14] Yatarō tried to reform this system by providing prompter payment to the shipper but at the same

TABLE 4 Freight and Passenger Income, 1876–1882
(¥)

	Freight	(%)	Passenger	(%)	Total
1876	1,321,165	(56.3)	489,711	(20.9)	2,344,976
1877	721,473	(16.2)	441,566	(9.9)	4,447,010
1878	1,922,513	(66.3)	620,465	(21.4)	2,899,534
1879	2,131,137	(64.8)	683,053	(20.8)	3,287,826
1880	2,887,207	(65.2)	803,178	(18.1)	4,430,628
1881	3,561,164	(60.5)	1,027,874	(17.5)	5,881,717
1882	3,074,456	(62.9)	907,298	(18.6)	4,889,616
Total	15,619,115	(55.4)	4,973,145	(17.7)	28,181,293

Source: Mitsubishi zaibatsu ni okeru shikin chōtatsu to shihai, ed., Mitsubishi Keizai Kenkyūjo, prepared for the Keizai Kikakuchō Chōsa-kyoku Chōsa-ka, no. 6 (April 12, 1959), pp. 18–19.

time levying interest charges for handling and storing freight. He also proposed to the government that Mitsubishi set up a full-scale business for handling insurance against sea damage. Since Mitsubishi already had the appearance of a monopoly in the shipping industry, this proposal met with vigorous opposition, especially from Shibusawa Eiichi. As a result Mitsubishi had to be content with a 17.5 percent share in the Tokio Marine Insurance Company, which was finally established as a joint-stock corporation with government permission in 1879.[15]

Yatarō's reforms clashed with the interests of a powerful group of commodity exchange traders in Osaka, collectively known as the Nine Shop Union (Kutana), who acted as agents for shippers. They vigorously opposed Mitsubishi's reforms and its shipping monopoly, because they believed Mitsubishi would impede the flow of domestic commodities and might break their tight grip over shippers and transporters. When the P. & O. began competing with Mitsubishi, this exchange traders association entered into an agreement with the P. & O. to refuse forwarding shipments to Mitsubishi. This challenge worried Yatarō even more than had earlier direct competition from foreign companies. "It is not necessarily difficult," he said, "to overwhelm other foreign steamship companies and to recover our navigation rights, but to reform the customs of more than 200 years and to build a commerce of enlightened companies by sweeping away the abuses of commerce and industry is truly burdensome."[16] Indeed, the alliance of the P. & O. and the Nine Shop Union provided the rationale for Yatarō's lament in his March Proclamation that the misconceptions of the people were the main obstacle to the growth of Japan's competitive power.

In response to this hostile alliance, on March 19 Yatarō petitioned the Finance Ministry for the establishment of an exchange bureau (*kawase kyoku*).[17] Through this bureau Mitsubishi hoped to finance shippers with exchange credits by using the freight to be forwarded as security. In his petition to Ōkuma, Yatarō claimed that the Nine Shop Union had allied with the P. & O. in "cleverly trying to monopolize the freight between Tokyo and Osaka and thus to drive our company into bankruptcy." The establishment of an exchange bureau, however, would give Mitsubishi victory in the struggle and "the benefits for the people would be unlimited."

Mitsubishi's Exchange Bureau was established in Osaka with government approval in June. Earlier, in May, Mitsubishi had received government loans of ¥50,000 for each Osaka-Tokyo voyage to finance the exchange business. The bureau operated with two transport departments (*unyō-ka*) and two exchange sections (*kawase-gata*), one each in Osaka and Tokyo. Since most trade went from Osaka to Tokyo, the Osaka transport department took charge of inspecting freight, warehousing, and consignments. It also reported the value of goods, market fluctuations, and the like. After receiving the transport department reports, the Osaka exchange section would determine the amount of exchange loans to be issued to shippers. The Tokyo transport department took charge of warehousing and contacted the consignee after freight arrived from the Osaka transport department. In addition, the Tokyo exchange section was responsible for collecting payments and issuing further loans when necessary. Yamamura has described this process as Mitsubishi's elimination of "middlemen in producing areas and wholesalers in consuming areas by means of forward-and-backward integration."[18]

That one company was able to manage this whole process from exchange credits to transport was of great benefit to shippers, and it soon placed Mitsubishi in a superior position in its competition with the P. & O. Also, the government aided Mitsubishi in the freight competition by placing limitations on transport by rail of P. & O.-carried goods, a move which paralleled the control pass requirement in the passenger business.[19] Having failed to win over the shippers, the Nine Shop Union broke its connections with the P. & O. This defeat in the domestic freight competition came just shortly after the P. & O.'s Japanese passenger service had collapsed. In August the company withdrew unconditionally from both the coastal and Shanghai lines, leaving Mitsubishi to enjoy the fruits of its dominance.[20] In conclusion, Mitsubishi's victory derived more from the freight than the passenger competition and the success in domestic shipping was of more decisive importance to the final victory than that in the highly publicized Shanghai trade. This assessment is borne out by statistics (see Table 5). Precisely because the competition was mainly domestic, the wider significance of the victory lay in Mitsubishi's utilization of the struggle to further integrate its growing number of enterprises.

Despite the competition Mitsubishi had a profit of ¥174,000 in the October 1875 to June 1876 business term. Subsidies, the support of the exchange business in the victory over the P. & O., Yataro's retrenchment, and the extra income from the Kanghwa Incident all made this possible. In a report to the government in late July, when the P. & O. withdrawal was imminent, Yataro expressed continued anxiety that renewed attempts by foreigners would be made to open a Japan-China route to service "English and French trade." For the time being, he reported, he had decided to maintain high freight rates (which had been raised again subsequent to the victory over the P. & O.) so that they could be lowered later in the event of competition.[21] These high rates testify to Mitsubishi's growing monopoly.

TABLE 5 Mitsubishi Income from Shipping Charges
by Port, October 1875–June 1876
(¥)

	Passenger	Freight	Total
Yokohama	72,404	67,617	140,021
Kobe	54,292	129,049	183,341
Osaka	20,331	142,061	162,392
Nagasaki	30,456	36,460	66,916
Hakodate	12,585	48,395	60,980
Niigata	407	1,090	1,497
Total for unopen ports	42,155	176,808	218,963
Shanghai	19,831	61,378	81,209
Other Chinese ports	89	492	581
Receipts onboard ship	11,733	18,527	30,260
Total	264,283	681,877	946,160

Sources: Yamaguchi Kazuo, "Gaikoku kaiun to Mitsubishi," p. 150; *M Sha shi*, III, 661–662.

MITSUBISHI'S SHARE IN THE SHIPPING INDUSTRY. In August Ya-tarō issued another proclamation to his employees that combined apprehensiveness about the future with grand visions of new business horizons and an implicit recognition of the value of business integration.[22] The struggle with the P. & O., he said, "had allowed the company to strengthen its base." For future business Yatarō envisaged more lines to the coast of China, a country whose "production is flourishing" and where "commodities are abundant," a new line between Hong Kong and San Francisco, and an even greater expansion of business "to encircle the earth."

As Yatarō was fond of repeating, the victory over the foreign companies was but a first step, for the great bulk of foreign trade was still carried by foreign ships.[23] Domestically, by the middle of the decade, many besides Mitsubishi were becoming owners of Western-style steamships, but most of the tonnage was going to Mitsubishi (see Tables 6 and 7). In fact, Mitsubishi's holdings put

TABLE 6 Western-style Steamships in Japan,
            1870–1877

	Number	Tonnage (NT)	Average NT per ship	Tonnage (GT)	Average GT per ship
1870	35	15,498	443	24,997	714
1871	71	20,934	295	33,765	476
1872	96	23,364	243	37,684	393
1873	110	26,088	237	42,077	383
1874	118	26,120	221	42,129	357
1875	149[a]	42,304	284	68,232	458
1876	159	40,248	253	64,916	408
1877	183[b]	49,105	268	79,202	433

Sources: Saitō Yoshihisa, "Meiji shonen no kaiun seisaku," pp. 65, 84; Miwa Ryōichi, "Suijō kōtsū," p. 481. The tables in these two works are taken from the *Nihon teikoku tōkei nenkan.*

Notes: The increases can be attributed to: [a]the Taiwan expedition and [b]the Satsuma Rebellion.

TABLE 7 Mitsubishi Steamship Holdings, 1876

	Number of Ships	Tonnage[b] (GT)	Average GT per Ship
Whole country	159	64,916	408
Mitsubishi	41 (26.8)[a]	36,852 (56.8)	899
Rest of the country	118 (74.2)	28,064 (43.2)	238

Sources: Figures for the entire country are from Table 6. Figures on Mitsubishi's holdings are from *M Sha shi,* III, 648–650; and *Yanosuke den,* I, 154–158.

Notes: [a]Figures in parentheses are percentages of national totals.

[b]Because of inconsistencies in the NT figures from *M Sha shi,* GT tonnages are used here (cf. Wray, p. 169). Mitsubishi's NT was probably about 23,000.

it among the largest steamship companies based in East Asia, with 36,852 tons in 1876 compared to the 27,002 tons owned in 1874 by an American firm, the Shanghai Steam Navigation Company, the largest steamship company operating out of Shanghai. The three largest foreign companies in Shanghai in 1873 possessed only 41,087 tons. By 1877 the Chinese-owned China Merchants' Steam Navigation Company had bought out its largest American rival, making its fleet of 23,967 net tons approximately equal to Mitsubishi's (see note b, Table 7).[24]

Mitsubishi's possession of almost all the large ships in Japan has led most scholars to argue that Mitsubishi occupied a monopolistic position in the domestic market. Table 7, showing Mitsubishi with 57 percent of the country's steamship tonnage, would appear to support this interpretation. Dissenting opinion has not denied Mitsubishi's monopoly among steamship holders, but has instead focused on the number of traditional Japanese-style sailing vessels (*wasen*). Yamaguchi Kazuo, a proponent of this counterargument, believes "it is rash to see in these figures a Mitsubishi monopoly, for at the time Japanese-style ships were still superior throughout the country." I would argue that though Mitsubishi did not have a monopoly throughout the country, the *wasen* being dominant in western Japan and part of the Japan Sea coast, it did occupy a monopolistic position in rapid long-distance transport. In 1876 the country's total *wasen* capacity was 3.4 million *koku* or 570,000 net tons. Measured against steamships (see Table 6), the ratio is 14.5 to 1 in favor of *wasen*.[25] But a simple numerical comparison of tonnage does not enable calculation of the relative power, reliability, or overall capacity of the two kinds of fleets. In measuring the power of early modern European fleets, Fernand Braudel commented that "around 1840, when the sailing ships and steam ships existed side by side, it was estimated that steam did the work of about five sailing ships for equal tonnage."[26] These estimates lower the *wasen*-steamship ratio to 2.8 to 1; hence, Yamaguchi's interpretation cannot be fully sustained.

Basically there are two ways of judging whether a monopoly exists in a shipping industry: to compare the share in a given market and to determine whether two or more separate markets exist. In the latter, a comparison simply of total capacity tells us little. Two other criteria are more important: the kind of goods carried and the type of transport employed. In the 1870s the country's basic agricultural products, such as rice, tea, beans, cotton, and lees, constituted the majority of freight carried by Mitsubishi. Since the *wasen* also carried these products, there was probably no great difference between Mitsubishi and the traditional ships in goods carried. The type of transport, however, differed greatly. The *wasen* were not fully national craft in the sense of providing regular services in all of the country's coastal routes. Some routes, especially in western Japan, were well developed. But until late in the Tokugawa period there were no regular sea communications down the Pacific coast of northeastern Japan to Edo. Navigational hazards like the powerful current in the Tsugaru Straits and the difficulty of rounding the Boso Peninsula and turning into Tokyo Bay made this a dangerous route for *wasen*.[27] (See Map 1.)

Despite the government's designation, later in 1876, of a Mitsubishi line to Hakodate, the company moved rather slowly into this northern market. The Satsuma Rebellion caused a temporary delay, but the fundamental obstacle was the lack of deep ports along the Pacific coast. *Wasen,* then, continued to flourish in local trade centered on shallow ports like Ishinomaki.[28] On the other hand, by the end of the 1870s the technical superiority of the steamship made Mitsubishi dominant in the inter-regional trade from the Japan Sea and Hokkaido to Tokyo. The steamship's greater carrying capacity and speed, regularity of service, and higher safety factor all made it more appropriate than the *wasen* for operating on a national scale and promoting the commercialization of regional products. Mitsubishi brought to Tokyo tea, indigo-ball, paper, and cotton from the Kansai; rice, lees, soybeans, and kelp from the Tohoku; and lees and many marine products from Hokkaido. It was also responding to a growing export market that the *wasen* could not meet. Finally, Mitsubishi's long-distance, domestic transport required the extension of credit on a far greater scale than could be provided by the *wasen* owners. Mitsubishi was rapidly adding new supportive functions to its main enterprise; other shipping competitors could not match its range of services and control mechanisms.[29]

MAP 1 Japan

Having "expanded the business," Mitsubishi was favored on September 15, 1876, with a brief Second Directive, which, in accordance with the First Directive, guaranteed continuance of the subsidy for a fourteen-year period.[30] Article 3 stated that the subsidy previously granted as an operating expense would henceforth be allotted in fixed amounts for specific mail routes as follows: (1) from Yokohama to Shanghai (¥200,000), Kobe (¥20,000), Hakodate (¥10,000), Niigata (¥10,000), and Yokkaichi (¥5,000); and (2) from Nagasaki to Pusan (¥5,000).[31] An accompanying instruction read: "The government will not hinder the company from diverting, according to its own convenience, funds specified for each line, but it must use these funds according to the directives of this bureau." It is hard to tell whether this was a word of caution or a note of approval regarding Mitsubishi's spreading activities, but it did increase the ambiguity of the First Directive.

THE SATSUMA REBELLION

MITSUBISHI AND THE POLITICS OF THE REBELLION. "Saigō is the tiger at the front gate, and Yatarō the wolf at the back door." This popular saying likened the government dilemma at the outbreak of the Satsuma Rebellion to being trapped between two wild animals—Saigō Takamori and his rebellious Kyushu samurai and Yatarō and his munitions transport monopoly.[32] Mitsubishi had become an indispensable naval support force and army transport service all in one; the government would now have to pay well for these services.

While the government found itself dangerously dependent upon Mitsubishi, Mitsubishi was caught in its own dilemma, a choice of loyalty between its principal benefactors. Since 1874 Mitsubishi had received many grants from the government, which had been either given during government emergencies or were sufficiently bureaucratic to have precluded personal bonds of obligation. On the other hand, Yatarō owed perhaps his greatest personal debt to Hayashi Yūzō, a former Tosa samurai who, as a government official, had assisted Yataro's fledging enterprise in its transition to independence during the abolition of the domains in 1871. Others who had helped Yataro, like Goto Shojiro and Okamoto Kensaburo, were now all active members of the Risshisha (Society to Establish One's Moral Will), a Tosa political organization led by Itagaki Taisuke and other Tosa samurai. Itagaki had resigned from the government for a second time in October 1875, and Goto in March 1876. When Saigo's rebellion began in February 1877, Risshisha members met to discuss strategy. Mitsubishi had to decide whether Tosa too would rise in revolt. Tosa never did rebel, but many Tosa samurai wanted to do so. There is no evidence that Yataro considered giving all-out support for a Tosa rebellion, nor is it likely that his former domain members ever expected him to, but he did try to play both sides of the fence.

The Risshisha was divided into two factions, one led by Itagaki and Goto favoring political action, and the other calling for an armed uprising. One of the leading advocates of rebellion was Hayashi Yuzo. In June, after the government rejected a Risshisha memorial advocating a national assembly, the rebels in the Risshisha came to the fore. At the time, the government's main supply base for the Satsuma campaign was in Osaka. Hayashi's plan to seize a Mitsubishi steamer to attack the Osaka arsenal proved abortive. But, he reportedly tried to persuade Ono Yoshimasa, now an adviser to Yataro acting as a liaison man with the government, to give Yataro ¥150,000 worth of government bonds in exchange for cash to buy weapons. It is not clear whether this exchange took place, but Yataro's biographer suggests that he probably gave some money to the Risshisha. Also, Hayashi once asked Yataro to operate ships for the society. Yataro replied "I cannot lend you ships, but if you should happen to seize one by force, there's nothing I could do about it." Before Hayashi could do anything, the plot was exposed by government spies and he was arrested on August 2. Among the Tosa rebels who received jail sentences were Okamoto, 2 years, and Hayashi, 10 years.[33]

Mitsubishi had actually been on the government's side since the beginning of the rebellion. In January 1877, in accordance with article 13 of the First Directive, the government requisitioned a Mitsubishi steamer to remove arms and ammunition from a Kagoshima arsenal. Early in February the Satsuma insurgents tried to interfere, and a full-scale rebellion soon followed. It was later said that the immediate cause was the government's decision to remove the military supplies.[34] Probably Mitsubishi had foreseen this. Unlike its role in the Taiwan expedition, which it joined only at the halfway point, in the Satsuma Rebellion Mitsubishi prepared in advance to play its expected part. After providing military transport for the suppression of the Hagi Rebellion in October 1876, Yatarō had sent Ishikawa Shichizai to Kyushu as a spy to investigate the condition of the army that Saigō was raising. Ishikawa correctly forecast the outbreak of the rebellion and apparently also foresaw what a profitable affair it would become for Mitsubishi.[35]

THE GOVERNMENT LOAN AND THE REPAYMENT ISSUE. During the rebellion almost all of Mitsubishi's ships engaged in military transport, carrying 60,000 soldiers as well as horses, munitions, and food supplies. Of the 40 ships that Mitsubishi possessed at the end of 1876, 32 were requisitioned. Twenty had been requisitioned by the end of February, and most continued operating for the government several months beyond the end of the rebellion in September.[36] As a result, coastal transport was totally disrupted. Only the 4 ships assigned to the Shanghai line maintained their usual services. Unable to meet its normal shipping schedule, Mitsubishi requested a loan of $800,000 from the government, which was approved on June 4. Mitsubishi then bought 7 large steamships totaling 12,725 tons and several small vessels.[37]

One of the government's major problems during the rebellion was raising sufficient funds. Generally, foreign financing was impracticable, partly because foreign bankers would not condone the large risk involved. Nevertheless, in order to finance its additional commitment to Mitsubishi, the government tried to negotiate a foreign loan from the Oriental Bank Corporation through the services of Minomura Rizaemon, head manager of the Mitsui House.

On June 6, the representative of the British firm refused, warning Minomura that "in the present disturbed state of the Country it would be a great pity for the Japanese Government to appear as borrowers of foreign money." Any money lent to Japan now, he said, "would of necessity bear a high rate of interest."[38]

According to the terms of Mitsubishi's $800,000 government loan, the company was to repay $100,000 between September and January 1878 in five installments. The remaining $700,000 was to be due in February at an annual interest rate of 8 percent.[39]

Huge profits were the most important feature of the rebellion for Mitsubishi. But the repayment schedule for this short-term loan was the first of several arrangements where Mitsubishi accepted a greater financial obligation to the government. By mid-1877 Mitsubishi's monopoly of military transport and its accompanying profits had, according to one writer, become an "obviously undisguised illicit union between the government and business world." To deflect such criticism, on July 21, at the height of the war, Yatarō presented the government with a petition that he be allowed to pay the government a "votive offering" (*myōgakin*):

> Our company's business has benefited from generous promotion...
> Now that our business has stabilized itself we feel uneasy about possessing the ships which have been given to us up to now...Many of the ships given to us have, however, already been scrapped. As the present value of the ones we are now using is about ¥1.2 million, we would like to pay the government this amount in annual payments over a 50-year period...but this will repay only one-ten thousandth of the favors hitherto bestowed upon us.[40]

The payment of the *myōgakin,* in effect, modified the protective clauses of the First Directive,[41] and it contradicted Maejima's conviction that Mitsubishi should not have to repay the value of the ships for fear that the financial burden would bankrupt the company. Such fears were now groundless. By the time of the N.Y.K.'s formation in 1885, Mitsubishi had repaid ¥513,000 of the ¥1.2 million. After deducting interest it had also repaid ¥1.5 million of ¥2.2 million received in loans from the government during this period.[42]

Since these repayment arrangements imposed new financial burdens on Mitsubishi, why did Yatarō "petition" the government to accept the *myōgakin*? Two factors shaped the content of Yatarō's petition: the build-up of increased political pressure against Mitsubishi because of its huge profits, and the reform of Mitsubishi's accounting system, which Shōda Heigorō was completing. New regulations went into effect on July 26.[43] Faced with demands for some form of repayment, Mitsubishi seems to have utilized this reform to assuage the political pressure and simultaneously to lighten its potential financial burden. Under its new regulations, for the first time Mitsubishi compiled a complete balance sheet of assets. In the first full-scale appraisal of all ships, which took place at about the same time as the *myōgakin* petition, the book value of the 29 ships relevant to the *myōgakin* appeared as ¥1,189,550. This served as the basis for Yatarō's round figure in his petition. An analysis of Mitsubishi's accounts subsequent to this petition indicates that these 29 ships were undervalued in July 1877. By undervaluing the ships, Mitsubishi lowered the amount it would be obliged to repay. The petition, then, was a tactical retreat in which Mitsubishi paid as little as possible and staved off potentially greater demands. It also acts as a good example of how analysis of accounting can unmask the surface meaning of business rhetoric and reveal the underlying financial concerns.[44]

Despite the emerging controversies surrounding him, following the rebellion Yatarō was given special merit awards for his service. The real gains were tangible profits, which came to ¥1.2 million, or 28 percent of the company's ¥4.4 million income during the 1877 business year. Government payments to Mitsubishi alone accounted for ¥3 million, or two-thirds of total income.[45] These large profits derived partly from the high rates Mitsubishi received from the government. Table 8 shows that 1877 was an exceptional year for its income; ship expenses did not increase proportionately.

This bonanza, which government service had provided, was partially canceled out by the immediate post-rebellion business slump. The rebellion itself had greatly disrupted trade. Furthermore, although the subsequent inflation would soon stimulate shipping

TABLE 8 Mitsubishi Ship Expenses and Income,
         1876–1879
         (1876 = 100)

	Expenses	Income
1876	100	100
1877	114	209
1878	97	131
1879	105	144

Source: Computed from *Mitsubishi zaibatsu ni okeru shikin chōtatsu to shihai,* p. 18.

demand, a surplus of tonnage, especially of Western-style sailing ships, led to a short-term recession in the shipping industry in 1878. One effect of this, the ¥ 505,700 deficit that Mitsubishi recorded in 1878, wiped out more than a third of the previous year's profit.[46] Yatarō expressed his disappointment in an April 1878 address to his employees: "Just when we had achieved victory over foreign companies and were planning to expand our lines across the Pacific and throughout the world, we were confronted by the enormous obstacles" of the Satsuma Rebellion and the subsequent business stagnation. For example, in the four months up to February 1878, the Shanghai line had had a deficit of ¥ 72,000. On a yearly basis that would exceed the subsidy specified for the line. In another case the domestic route from Osaka to Hakodate had lost ¥ 14,000 in one month.[47]

Despite Yatarō's lament Mitsubishi did not suffer unduly in this brief slump. Table 8, which shows a continued high income-to-expense ratio, suggests that, even with the surplus of tonnage in the country, Mitsubishi's monopoly of large steamships enabled it to maintain high rates. Moreover, with its now ample supply of ships, Mitsubishi did not have to use its accumulated profits to buy new vessels, as it had done by loans in 1875 and 1877. In fact, between 1878 and 1885 Mitsubishi purchased only 6,211 tons of shipping. Two ships accounted for 4,435 of the total, and they were not purchased until 1884–1885. In the meantime, between

1878 and 1884, Mitsubishi bought only three small ships, none more than 630 tons.[48] As a result it was able to plow its profits into its subsidiary enterprises. That was the main significance of the Satsuma Rebellion for Mitsubishi.

PROFITS AND COMPANY STRUCTURE

MITSUBISHI'S BUSINESS RECORD, 1876–1882. An assessment of Mitsubishi's business performance during its first decade must begin from its profit record. To obtain a meaningful series it is best to include all the years up to 1882; in other words until the competition with the government-sponsored Union Transport Company (Kyōdō Un'yu Kaisha, or KUK) began in 1883. Table 9 shows Mitsubishi's profit rate in terms of assets and income. These official figures have several unreliable features. First, Mitsubishi's mining enterprise results are not included.[49] Second, the Exchange Bureau profits are excluded from the company's general accounts beginning in the second half of 1881.[50] Nonetheless, in judging whether profits are "excessive" or "monopolistic," economists usually use a standard of 8 percent for profits in terms of assets.[51] With this standard Table 9 shows that the peak of Mitsubishi's monopoly occurred in 1880–1881, while 1879 and 1882 were more "normal." The significance of these profits depends upon how they were accumulated and what their utilization foretold for Mitsubishi's shipping future.

Shibagaki Kazuo has written that Mitsubishi's "sources of funds were above all government funds and also early monopoly profits."[52] Many scholars have contended that Mitsubishi was dependent on government subsidies. Hatade Isao, for example, concluded that Mitsubishi was not yet a mature enterprise because its business was unstable without government financing.[53] Scholars holding this interpretation have adopted the method of subtracting subsidies from Mitsubishi's stated profits to arrive at a "pure" or "net" profit. When this is done the pure profit for 1876–1885 comes to no more than about ¥370,000, only 11.9 percent of the

TABLE 9 Mitsubishi Profits as Percentage of Assets and Income,
1876–1882

(¥)

	Assets (A)	Income (B)	Profits (C)	% (C/A)	% (C/B)
1876	——	2,344,977	308,627	——	13.2
1877	6,325,980	4,447,010	1,217,975	19.3	27.4
1878	6,220,060	2,899,535	-505,722	-8.1	-17.5
1879	5,361,971	3,287,827	293,440	5.5	8.9
1880	6,358,429	4,430,628	691,674	10.9	15.6
1881	7,055,514	5,881,718	796,524	11.3	13.6
1882	7,462,342	4,889,616	560,509	7.5	11.5

Source: "Saimatsu zassai," in M Sha shi, III–IX.

stated profits (see Table 10). The problem with extrapolating significance from this low figure is that it obviously derives from the large deficits in the 1883–1885 period of competition with the government-sponsored KUK. If these three years are eliminated from Table 10, the pure profits for the period from 1876 to 1882 come to 41.2 percent of the stated profits. Shibagaki has recognized this point, and instead of concentrating on the "dependence" theory, emphasizes that the subsidies played the role of capital accumulation for Mitsubishi.[54]

From another angle we may question the validity of analyzing the subsidy rate to evaluate profit performance. The real question is how subsidies were employed. According to the specifications of the Second Directive, ¥200,000 of the basic ¥250,000 subsidy was for the Shanghai line. In the 1882 accounts the ¥200,000 amounted to 71.4 percent of all subsidies received that year.[55] The first detailed statistics on income are in the 1883 accounts, which give a breakdown of passenger and freight income according to the major line categories. Domestic lines generated 73.5 percent of shipping income, whereas only 18.6 percent came from the Shanghai line (see Table 11).[56]

TABLE 10 Mitsubishi Profit and Loss Account,
1876–1885

(¥ 1,000)

	Income	Expenditure	Profit (A)	Subsidy (B)	(A – B)
1876	2,345	2,037	308	321	–13
1877	4,447	3,229	1,218	263	995
1878	2,899	3,405	–506	267	–773
1879	3,288	2,994	294	280	14
1880	4,431	3,739	692	286	406
1881	5,882	5,085	797	281	516
1882	4,890	4,329	561	280	281
1883	3,736	3,781	–45	278	–323
1884	3,026	3,243	–217	269	–486
1885	2,297	2,303	–6	201	–207
Total	37,241	34,145	3,096	2,726	370

Sources: Shibagaki Kazuo, *Nihon kin'yū shihon bunseki,* p. 74; and his "The Early History of the Zaibatsu," p. 545.

Profits, however, are the key factor for analytical purposes. If the Shanghai line were operating at a deficit, then the function of the subsidy would have been the financing of an unprofitable line. As a corollary we could not claim that the subsidies contributed to capital accumulation, at least in the sense of producing immediate surplus funds. Since there are no figures for the expenses of the line as an entity, profits cannot be precisely determined, but an estimate can be made by drawing from the account books the individual expenses for the constituent parts of the line. Table 12 estimates the expenses at ¥682,875. Compared with income, this would leave a deficit of ¥113,056, about a third of Mitsubishi's 1883 deficit (calculated without subsidies). Probably certain indirect expenses, such as efforts by other branch offices to solicit business for the line, would not appear directly in the accounts but could also justifiably be charged against the line.[57] Although

TABLE 11 Income from Near-Seas and Domestic Lines,
          1883

(¥)

Line or Service	Freight Income	Passenger Income	Total Income	Percentage
Shanghai	291,239	278,580	569,819	18.6
Hong Kong	149,861	11,277	161,138	5.3
Vladivostok	39,191	11,787	50,978	1.7
Domestic	1,747,854	502,055	2,249,909	73.5
Others	14,723	14,380	29,003	0.9
Total	2,242,868	817,979	3,060,847	100

Source: M Sha shi, X, 262.

Note: I have not included ¥63,181 in income from government freight and ¥33,794 in supplemental freight income. The totals in Table 4 contain the supplemental income but not government freight income, though the latter first appeared as a separate item in the accounts in 1882. Mitsubishi had opened its Hong Kong line in October 1879 and its Vladivostok line in February 1881.

Table 12 is not precise, it is a workable estimate because there were no major relevant categories of expense other than those listed in the table and hinted at here.

If the Shanghai line's operating deficits equaled its subsidy, then Mitsubishi would have secured its monopoly profits mainly, if not solely, from its domestic routes, or, in other words, from the lines that were lightly subsidized. On the contrary, my estimate of the Shanghai line's deficit in 1883 leaves a profit of ¥86,944 if the subsidy is included. Furthermore, in 1883, when Mitsubishi's deficit was ¥45,324, shipping income was lower than usual because of the competition with the KUK. As for earlier years, we can speculate that from 1875 to 1878 initial efforts of building up the line may have produced larger deficits, but there is no hard evidence for this. Comparing the 1883 figures with the high profits in 1880–1882 suggests that in those three years the line's deficit would have consumed a small enough portion of its subsidy that Mitsubishi would have had little need to allot the ¥200,000

TABLE 12 Estimated Expenses of the Shanghai Line,
1883

	Expenses (¥)	
Ships		
Nagoya Maru	95,627	
Genkai Maru	96,512	
Tokyo Maru	105,093	
Takasago Maru[a] (17/24 x 97,216)	69,023	
Hiroshima Maru[a] (7/24 x 85,463)	24,784	
Total ship expenses	391,039 [21.4%][c]	391,039
Office Expenses		
Shanghai	26,554	
Tokyo (19% of total)[b]	37,022	
Yokohama (25%)	13,537	
Kobe (19%)	4,426	
Nagasaki (33%)	3,746	
Total office expenses	85,285 [17.4%]	85,285
Freight & Passenger Handling Expenses		
Shanghai	9,591	
Tokyo (19%)	17,872	
Yokohama (25%)	12,962	
Kobe (19%)	8,656	
Nagasaki (33%)	4,224	
Total handling expenses	53,305 [10.9%]	53,305
Depreciation		
Tokyo Maru	5,432	
Nagoya Maru	4,619	
Genkai Maru	7,277	
Takasago Maru (17/24 x 25,240)	17,920	
Hiroshima Maru (7/24 x 5,161)	1,497	
Total depreciation	36,745 [10.3%]	36,745

TABLE 12 (continued)

	Expenses (¥)	
Government Loan	12,960	12,960
Extraordinary Expenses		
Theft from Shanghai Branch Office	12,672	
Major repairs to *Hiroshima Maru*	90,869 [24.8%]	
Subtotal	103,541	103,541
	Estimated total expenses	682,875

Sources: M Sha shi, X, 236, 255-261, 295-296, 344-346; *Wagasha kakukōro,* Chart 1, pp. 129-131.

Notes: [a]Ship expenses represent the total expenses of each ship while operating on the Shanghai line. The figures for the *Takasago Maru* and the *Hiroshima Maru* are highly arbitrary. The former was replaced by the latter on September 12. I have therefore divided the year into 24 periods, assigning 17 to the *Takasago Maru* and 7 (i.e., the 3 1/2 months from mid-September to the end of the year) to the *Hiroshima Maru* and multiplied their recorded expenses for the year by the appropriate fraction. Since the expenses of the ships generally depended more on their type than on the line on which they ran, this seems a justifiable way of estimating expenses. One major problem is that the *Hiroshima Maru* was undergoing repairs between May and September and therefore any fraction for the year is arbitrary. Nevertheless, the total expenses attributed to these two ships correspond closely to the expenses of the other ships and would probably contain only a marginal error. The same method of calculation has been used for depreciation. The full ¥ 90,000 major repair expense to the *Hiroshima Maru* can be charged to the line because (except for the period of repairs) this ship ran on the line from 1876 to 1885. The size of this repair was also not unusual. In 1882 Mitsubishi spent ¥ 77,920 in major repairs for the ships on the line. See *M Sha shi,* IX, 562.

[b]Figures in parenthesis under office and freight handling expenses are rough estimates of the percentage of total expenses of these offices and ports reasonably attributable to Shanghai line business. They reflect the greater dependence of Nagasaki on the line. I have used the 19% figure as a base derived from the Shanghai line's 18.6% share of total income.

[c]Figures in brackets represent the percentage of these expenses incurred through the Shanghai line.

according to the Second Directive's formula and could have used the money as it saw fit. This reasoning supports Shibagaki's contention that the subsidies were actually a form of capital accumulation.

Unlike the Shanghai line, Mitsubishi's domestic lines were lightly subsidized. In these coastal routes, even allowing for the encouragement from Ōkuma regarding the development of a domestic distribution network, Mitsubishi secured its monopolistic position primarily by its own initiative.[58]

Many scholars have focused on Mitsubishi's income from military transport as another source of government funds. Hatade Isao has stated that the bulk of Mitsubishi's business was done in private channels rather than for the government, but he also provides statistics to show that between 1876 and 1885 the percentage of government business in direct operating income in shipping exceeded the profit rate on total shipping income. The significance of these figures (Table 13) is suspect on at least two counts. First, calculations drawn from Hatade's table indicate that 76.3 percent of income from the government between 1883 and 1885 came from normal freight, not from vessels requisitioned for military transport. Second, 93.3 percent of the total income from the government during the period covered by the table came between 1876 and 1882. Using Hatade's figures for those years only, the results, shown in Table 14, reverse the significance of Table 13. Clearly Hatade's results for the full ten years depend on the deficits incurred through competition with the KUK. When military transport was important (1876–1882), the profit rate on total shipping income (17.5 percent) exceeded the percentage of government business in shipping income (14.6 percent). Moreover, there was no general pattern of dependence on military-related income.

The significance of military operations lay not so much in their general contribution to income over a decade as in two other respects. The first was their timeliness. The Taiwan expedition occurred when the YJK was beginning to fall behind Mitsubishi in their competition, and Mitsubishi's service in the expedition deprived the YJK of the government's confidence, which alone could have saved it in its ensuing financial troubles. The Kanghwa Incident provided Mitsubishi with a valuable reserve immediately before its competition with the P. & O. Second, at least in the case of the Satsuma Rebellion, the immediate infusion of profits from military operations was too large to be absorbed in the shipping business alone. If the annual rate of military-related income had been higher but spread more evenly over time, the use of that income might have been different from the actual case in which

TABLE 13 Comparison of Income from Government
with Profit Rate, 1876-1885

	Percentage of Government Business in Shipping Income	*Profit Rate on Total Shipping Income*
1876	9.0	-2.3
1877	72.1	41.1
1878	2.2	2.4
1879	1.4	17.2
1880	0.3	21.3
1881	0.2	14.3
1882	5.5	13.2
1883	2.6	-0.8
1884	3.0	-14.2
1885	5.2	-21.1
Total	11.9	10.9

Sources: Abbreviated from Hatade Isao, "Mitsubishi seiseiki ni okeru shihon chikuseki to tochi shoyū (1)," *Rekishigaku kenkyū* 325:24 (June 1967); and Hatade, *Nihon no zaibatsu to Mitsubishi,* pp. 40-41 (which omits some detail).

Note: This table includes only direct operating income and expenses related to shipping. It omits figures from subsidiary enterprises and expenses for depreciation and insurance.

TABLE 14 Comparison of Income from Government
with Profit Rate, 1876-1882

Total Shipping Income (A)	*Income from Government (B)*	*Percentage (B/A)*	*Profit on Shipping Income*[a] *(C)*	*Profit Rate on Shipping Income (C/A)*
24,247,174	3,534,910	14.6	4,234,689	17.5

Note: [a]According to Hatade's figures, operating expenses in these years were ¥ 20,012,485. These are subtracted from total shipping income (A) to determine the profit.

there was a generally low annual rate but a massive infusion in 1877. Thus, while competitive emergencies, especially that of 1876, provided the motivation, income from military transport, government subsidies, and monopoly profits provided the means for development of new business ventures other than shipping.

INTEGRATED FUNCTIONS AND CHANGING STRATEGY. If we view Mitsubishi as becoming a multifunctional enterprise, it is useful to apply the insights of Alfred Chandler's study of American industry to Mitsubishi's early growth. Chandler discussed two patterns of organizational growth in the emergence of large modern enterprises: the movement into new functions, which he termed "a strategy of *vertical integration*"; and the development of new products, which he called "a strategy of *diversification.*" Chandler's main concern was with multi-unit firms that developed decentralized administrative structures to implement these strategies.[59] Though he did not include transportation enterprises in his study, Chandler's model can be applied to Mitsubishi because it was not simply a shipping firm. Chandler defined the "enterprise unit" as "a regionally or functionally separate enterprise component that could theoretically operate as an independent enterprise. It is managed by a full-time partner or salaried supervisor responsible to headquarters. Its books and accounts, locally kept, can be audited separately from the accounts of the organization as a whole."[60]

Mitsubishi was a highly centralized enterprise, but by the early 1880s it was adding "units" that partially fit Chandler's definition. These units were like embryonic divisions that can be considered harbingers of a later managerial decentralization. In 1882 Mitsubishi's mines were set up with separate administrations under the direct control of the general manager (see Figure 3). Since 1880 they had been under the administration of the Internal Affairs Section. The reorganization of 1882 was not the first time that the mines had been placed under the general manager. Actually, considerable administrative shuffling had occurred since 1875. The mining operations had grown much larger by 1882, however, and

FIGURE 3 Mitsubishi Administrative Structure, 1882

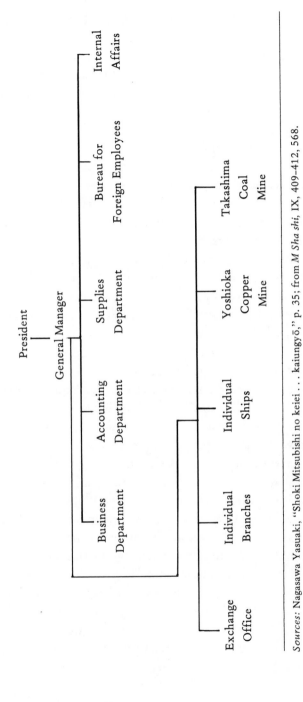

Sources: Nagasawa Yasuaki, "Shoki Mitsubishi no keiei . . . kaiungyō," p. 35; from *M Sha shi,* IX, 409–412, 568.

after that year their managers, as in Chandler's model, reported to the Mitsubishi head office rather than to a section. In 1880, the Exchange Bureau had also become a separate unit, changing its name to the Exchange Office. The old title, "bureau" (*kyoku*), clearly indicated that it was simply a part of Mitsubishi's shipping concern, whereas, "office" (*ten*), implied a separate business entity. The new office had its own internal administrative regulations and, like the mines after 1882, was directly under the Mitsubishi general manager. It also kept separate accounts, one of Chandler's criteria for an "enterprise unit." Finally, its leading managers (*motojime*) met regularly each Friday with the president and general manager to make important decisions and functioned as a Board of Directors.[61]

While the Exchange Office had emerged as a separate administrative unit, to what degree were its business operations still tied to shipping? In 1878 Yatarō had petitioned the government for approval to establish a formal bank, but was refused. This government rejection lay behind Mitsubishi's decision to upgrade the Exchange Bureau to a separate office. By 1880 it had taken on new functions apart from exchange financing to shippers. It began to accept deposits and issue ordinary loans (*tsūjō kashitsuke*) backed by collateral such as public bonds or land certificates. In 1880 the volume of this business exceeded that of the exchange bills issued to shippers. However, the office conducted other loan transactions involving warehousing and exchange financing for freight shipments in areas not served by its individual branches that were clearly part of Mitsubishi's overall shipping business. While the office was possibly capable of operating "as an independent enterprise," in Chandler's use of the term, the interdependence of the parent shipping enterprise and the Exchange Office was still the main characteristic of their relationship.[62]

Mitsubishi's mining ventures were likely more capable of independent operation than the Exchange Office. Like the Exchange Office, the Yoshioka Copper Mine, for example, was managed by a "salaried supervisor responsible to headquarters," but its business was more separate. Nevertheless, Mitsubishi's managerial authority was more centralized than in Chandler's model. Though the Yoshioka Mine's accounts may have officially been separate, a full audit would have disclosed money it was feeding Yatarō for use in shipping competition, as it was designed to do during the struggle with the P. & O. This same pattern of mining profits supporting the parent shipping concern was repeated on a much larger scale beginning in 1881 when Mitsubishi purchased the Takashima Coal Mine from Gotō Shōjirō, whose own investment in the mine had placed him in debt. Located in Kyushu, it was then the largest coal mine in Japan. Mitsubishi used its production for bunker coal and for direct export to Shanghai.[63] Under Mitsubishi's centralized management the head office could shift resources from one field to another as the situation demanded. The growth of the mining enterprise, therefore, presented Mitsubishi with broader strategic options. It could use the profits from the mines as a reserve for its shipping business, or it could concentrate on expanding the mines.

The options which this mining success gave Mitsubishi illustrate the firm's risk-avoidance strategy. Similarly, the pattern of integration that Mitsubishi pursued aggressively in the late 1870s and early 1880s through exclusive contracts with shippers and purchasers was essentially a safe form of expansion, designed at least in its initial stages to provide financial security for the parent enterprise. In this sense Mitsubishi was not unlike other zaibatsu in the early Meiji period, which with unlimited liability preferred to concentrate on familiar businesses like banking, trading, shipping, and mining.[64] In addition to moving into new but closely related functions, Mitsubishi used its profits for secure investments in bonds, stocks, and (to a somewhat lesser extent) land.[65] We may contrast this pattern of expansion with Chandler's model. Although Mitsubishi had pursued a form of integration by adding new functions to expand its shipping operations, its approach to diversification was generally cautious in this period. With the possible exceptions of metal mining and coal mining (the latter itself closely tied to shipping), Mitsubishi's diversification developed primarily from the shipbuilding industry. This did not really begin until the late 1890s even though Mitsubishi had acquired the Nagasaki Shipyard

from the government in 1887. During its first decade under Mitsubishi the yard was used primarily for ship repairs.[66]

As noted in Chapter 2, the stipulations of the First Directive
inhibited diversification based on shipping. There was also a powerful internal inhibition in the tension bewteen zaibatsu ownership
and the general condition of the shipping industry, which has always been one of widely fluctuating profits. In the early 1880s
Mitsubishi was still going through a transition from the period of
exclusive privilege as a "political merchant" to the era of the more
independent zaibatsu. It needed secure profits because it had yet
to acquire the huge financial resources that alone could maximize
its long-term strategic flexibility. But management could not consistently deliver this security despite the monopoly between 1879
and 1882. Yatarō's competitive rhetoric, with its emphasis on
challenging foreigners or crushing domestic competitors, was well
suited to the vicissitudes of shipping but less so to the demands of
the wider group of business "units" that was emerging to provide
the whole firm with a more secure basis. By the early 1880s, Mitsubishi's capital was still overwhelmingly concentrated in shipping,
but even before competition with the KUK began in 1883, Mitsubishi's profits were becoming more broadly based. Table 15 shows
the distribution of profits from the main functional units just before and after the beginning of competition with the KUK. Two
trends are evident: in the early 1880s mining gradually became
Mitsubishi's most profitable enterprise; and in 1883 earnings from
shipping dropped precipitously in the face of competition.

The monopoly which Mitsubishi had built up by the late 1870s
and early 1880s was achieved through a pattern of integrated
functions centered on the shipping industry. As these subfunc-
tions themselves grew, the total enterprise became less dependent
on direct profits from shipping alone. While the subsidiary enterprises had first been established partly to lessen risk and partly to
"feed" the main shipping concern, a more integrated structure was
gradually evolving in which, for example, a significant portion of
the main enterprise's ship expenses would appear as income in the
accounts of the Takashima Mine. Up until 1882 the Takashima

TABLE 15 Index of Profits of Mitsubishi Enterprises, 1879–1883
(Index = 100)[a]

	1879	1880	1881	1882	1883
Shipping	64.2	68.0	40.5	42.9	–
Subunits[b]	23.8	18.5	18.2	5.9	13.3
Takashima Mine			15.0	31.7	54.6
Government subsidies[c]	36.7	24.6	17.3	21.3	40.3

Source: Hatade, *Mitsubishi,* pp. 28–29.

Notes: [a]The total sometimes exceeds and sometimes falls short of 100 because of deficits or profits from miscellaneous categories.

[b]Subunits include warehousing and repair works throughout; bonds until 1879; exchange until the first half of 1881; and stocks until the end of 1881. If the Exchange Office figures were included for the last part of 1881 and subsequently, the percentages for shipping would be even lower.

[c]Subsidies are included as "pure" profit, i.e., income with no expenses.

Mine probably fulfilled the role Yatarō had envisaged for the Yoshioka Mine in 1876. Its profits aided the main shipping concern. But as these profits came to occupy an increasingly large share of Mitsubishi's overall profits and as the shipping operation began to incur deficits, the mine's purpose for Mitsubishi gradually changed. The tactical emphasis on aiding the parent shipping enterprise shifted to the longer-term strategy of broadening the firm as a whole. This strategy was producing a new structure in which mining gave signs of becoming as important as shipping.

This structure had not been part of the government's objective in its shipping policy, even if the ambiguities of the first two directives indirectly contributed to its emergence. On another level, however, one assumption of these directives, articulated by Ōkubo, had been the elimination of competition. The directives tolerated a monopoly rather than providing rules to regulate competition. Domestically, therefore, there was no mechanism to regulate competition in the shipping industry such as there was internationally in the form of the freight conferences that emerged in East Asia in the 1880s and 1890s. Under these circumstances, domestic competition inevitably produced freight rate wars and exclusive contractual agreements. The tension between this competition in the shipping industry and the demands of a group of enterprises for secure profits left an uncertain legacy for the relationship between Mitsubishi and shipping.

Part Two

Formation of the N.Y.K.: 1880–1894

In the late 1870s Mitsubishi enjoyed a favored status. With its monopolistic position in the shipping industry tacitly accepted by the government, it was able to charge high freight rates and watch its profits grow to record amounts. This situation proved to be an aberration. By the early 1880s a growing number of small ship-owners were able to purchase Western-style ships. Large trading firms like Mitsui, suffering under the burden of Mitsubishi's freight rates, willingly supported these smaller shipowners. Challenge to Mitsubishi came from another direction as well. In 1881, its long-time supporters in the government resigned, leaving the adminis-tration of shipping to men anxious to ally with Mitsubishi's enemies. This alliance resulted in a new shipping company, the Kyōdō Un'yu Kaisha, or KUK.

Between 1880 and 1882 Mitsubishi first met its enemies in sev-eral competitive skirmishes and then between 1883 and 1885 it fought them head-on in one cataclysmic life-and-death struggle. Many commentators label the opponents as Mitsubishi and Mitsui, or sometimes the "Mitsui-owned KUK." But to identify Mi-tsubishi's competitor simply as Mitsui is to misrepresent the na-ture of the KUK, which for its time was a broadly based enterprise encompassing a variety of elements, the foremost of which was the government itself.

Most writers have quite appropriately used war imagery to

describe the Mitsubishi-KUK competition. The battle began slowly but reached a crescendo in late 1884. Following a brief pause for negotiations in early 1885, the struggle resumed at a new peak of intensity before the government finally intervened to force an end to the competition. Mitsubishi is usually seen as the victor, if not by unconditional surrender, at least through the negotiations which resulted in the merger of the two and the formation of the N.Y.K. in September 1885. Actually, the commitment of the Mitsui element in the KUK to the competition had waned well before the merger and thus before the new company began shaping an identity in the crucial months after its establishment. Not all the former "enemies" chose to withdraw. Some of the local shipowners who had originally opposed Mitsubishi stayed to participate in the N.Y.K. As an economic organism, however, the KUK crumbled. What remained was a legal structure imposed on the N.Y.K.

Iwasaki Yatarō died on February 7, 1885. Yatarō was the most successful entrepreneur of the early Meiji period, but the shipping enterprise he bequeathed to his brother Yanosuke had incurred nothing but deficits for the two years preceding his death, an ironic end to the career of a man considered a "good capitalist" because of his "cruel heart."[1] Yanosuke was a man of defensive posture, not given to hasty moves and more inclined to long-term planning than his elder brother.[2] This contrast in personalities parallels a change in the popular images of Mitsubishi during the 1880s: the switch from "Mitsubishi of the sea" to "Mitsubishi of the land."[3] Although Mitsubishi continued to exercise an indirect form of control over the new company, it gradually sold most of the N.Y.K. shares it had been allotted at the time of the merger. It then proceeded to reconstruct its business enterprise "on land," concentrating first on mining.

The N.Y.K. was no mere replica of the old Mitsubishi. The most important differences were stricter government supervision and the N.Y.K.'s structure as a joint-stock company rather than a family enterprise. Between 1885 and 1887 the Finance Ministry unilaterally reformed the key aspects of the company's accounting system. In financial and business strategy the government had a stronger influence over the N.Y.K. than did Mitsubishi. By the early 1890s the state had also become the company's largest stockholder. Moreover, between 1885 and 1892 the N.Y.K. was heavily dependent on government subsidies. In these years it was able neither to expand its operations into long-distance overseas lines nor to retain the domestic monopoly inherited at its birth.

FOUR

The Attack on Mitsubishi: 1880–1882

MITSUBISHI'S MONOPOLY

Throughout 1880 and 1881 Mitsubishi's business rivals and their allies in the newspaper world mounted a growing volume of criticism against the company's monopoly. This criticism is not in itself proof that Mitsubishi was increasing its share of the shipping market. In fact, something of the reverse was taking place. Since the Satsuma Rebellion of 1877, Mitsubishi's share of the total number of ships in the country had been declining. The criticism of the early 1880s reflected the frustrations of emerging local shipowners at the extreme tactics used by Mitsubishi to reinforce its monopolistic position attained in 1876–1877. Moreover, during the inflation of the late 1870s Mitsubishi's monopoly had major repercussions on the large companies dependent on shipping transport. In the early 1880s a coalition of small regional shipowners and the major shippers, backed by social critics opposing government subsidies to monopolistic enterprises, united with new political interests to launch a powerful attack on Mitsubishi. The source of the discontent prompting this coalescence of forces was Mitsubishi's business network.

MITSUBISHI'S BUSINESS NETWORK. Mitsubishi's utilization of a system of loans to shippers to overcome the challenge of the

P. & O. in 1876 was greatly expanded during the inflation of the late 1870s. By making loans to merchants conditional upon use of Mitsubishi ships, Mitsubishi deprived small local shipowners of their regular customers. In areas totally dependent on sea transport, Mitsubishi received goods directly from producers and in turn extended loans to them. It then transported the products to the central markets of Tokyo and Osaka; meanwhile, bankruptcies grew steadily among local wholesalers thus cut out of the trade.[1] Two regional examples—Hokkaido and Niigata—illustrate Mitsubishi's network.

Mitsubishi advanced rapidly into Hokkaido following the Satsuma Rebellion. The Mitsubishi Exchange Office took advantage of inadequate local financing to set up branches in the main districts. The size of these branch offices indicates the special importance Mitsubishi attached to its Hokkaido business. The Hakodate Branch was the largest of the Exchange Office's eleven regional branches; the three Hokkaido branches accounted for 30 percent of the capital of these regional offices.[2] The head of the Exchange Office, Hida Shōsaku, described the business as follows:

> We toured Hokkaido to inspect the exchange business and then, after visiting Hakodate, we began to make exchange loans at about 12 percent annual interest. Almost all shippers without exception came to apply for Mitsubishi loans. At the time, interest rates in the Hakodate area were extremely high. They were around 24 percent or even 36 percent. . . Under our Exchange Office's name we made as many loans as possible, and Mitsubishi's influence became truly widespread. We exerted great efforts for the development of local industry by concentrating on the Hokkaido area, and Hokkaido products suddenly underwent a remarkable development and increase. For example, the production [annual?] of goods like *shimekasu* (oil cake) was at a level of no more than 1,000 *koku*. But through the low interest loans from the Exchange Office, we soon saw an increase to 5,000 and then 10,000 *koku*.[3]

Not all loans went to producers. An important exception was an arrangement with the Rakusan Shōkai, an independent trading firm selling Hokkaido products to Honshu. This firm's business had expanded rapidly during the inflation, and in December 1881 it applied to Mitsubishi for a ¥150,000 loan to increase its capital. Mitsubishi granted the loan on condition that all the firm's freight be carried by Mitsubishi vessels.[4]

While certain firms and producers may have benefited from Mitsubishi's services, many local shipowners and wholesalers were forced out of business. Rising freight rates were also of great concern to distributors in Japan's major market centers. For example, in the autumn of 1880 the purchase price of dried herring in Otaru, Hokkaido, was ¥850 per 100 *koku* and salmon, ¥1,250. They sold in Tokyo for ¥1,700 and ¥2,000. The large margin was attributed to Mitsubishi's high freight rates.[5]

Mitsubishi had dealt directly with producers in Hokkaido, but in Niigata it operated indirectly through a trading firm, the Niigata Bussan Kaisha, which it had promoted in 1879. In July of that year it signed a contract with the firm stipulating that all freight covered by Mitsubishi Exchange Bureau loans be carried in Mitsubishi ships and insured by the Tokio Marine Insurance Company. Other clauses of the agreement concerned storage of goods in Mitsubishi warehouses and special loans when Mitsubishi ships were not in port. The Niigata Bussan Kaisha acted essentially as an agent for Mitsubishi, collecting freight from the shippers of the Niigata area. Many of its executives were also officials of the Niigata Rice Exchange, and the company's main shipment was rice destined for Tokyo.[6]

The proliferation of Mitsubishi's exclusive contracts was probably more a reaction to other trends in the shipping industry of the late 1870s than an inevitable by-product of the exchange system the company established in 1876. Large steamships of the type owned by Mitsubishi were still beyond the price range of regional Japanese shipowners,[7] but many of these same shipowners were purchasing Western-style sailing ships to meet the increased demand for shipping. This trend was so pronounced that the late 1870s and the early 1880s have been called the era of the Western-style sailing ship.[8] The rapid increase of ships under 500 net tons at the end of the 1870s would suggest that these new local shipowners were mostly small concerns (see Table 16). Indeed, many

TABLE 16 Ships by Size, 1870–1879: National Totals (NT)

Maximum Size	1870	1871	1872	1873	1874	1875	1876	1877	1878	1879
Steamships										
100	22	41	51	55	68	81	93	105	112	133
500	28	34	37	39	39	42	44	44	40	44
1000	10	11	12	12	21	22	22	23	20	20
over 1000	3	3	4	4	6	10	12	16	13	13
Total	63	89	104	110	134	155	171	188	185	210
Sailing ships										
100	1	2	5	7	8	14	24	36	67	141
500	18	28	32	32	34	32	38	46	71	97
1000	—	—	—	—	—	—	—	2	2	3
over 1000	—	—	—	—	—	1	2	3	1	1
Total	19	30	37	39	42	47	74	89	141	242

Source: Ekitei-kyoku nenpō 9:42 (1880), as reproduced by the Tokyo keizai zasshi, December 2, 1881, in KS, I, 108–109.

Note: The peak year for Western-style sailing ships was 1888 when there were 896 (63,127 NT), compared with 524 steamships (81,066 NT). Steamships regained the lead in tonnage in 1884 and in numbers in 1894. See Wray, p. 219.

apparently possessed only one ship. Mitsubishi's reaction to them indicates a drive for total market hegemony. One popular prewar source describes several one-ship firms driven to bankruptcy. Yatarō's usual tactic was to dispatch one of his ships to the run where the newcomer was operating and destroy him by extreme rate cutting.[9]

Mitsubishi's exclusive contracts were designed to ward off the competition of these smaller owners and, by reinforcing the company's monopoly, to preserve its high freight rates. The most onerous feature of these high rates for shippers was Mitsubishi's imposition of the Mexican dollar as a medium of exchange. With the extensive issue of currency in the late 1870s, Japanese paper currency had depreciated relative to the Mexican dollar, and from 1880 to 1882 the latter increased about 60 percent in relative value. The result was a corresponding increase in shipping charges for many areas of Mitsubishi's operations. Mitsubishi began this policy in 1879, and for the Shanghai line virtually all its freight and more than half its passenger income came in Mexican dollars. It is not clear how much the system was used domestically, but a Mitsubishi order of June 15, 1881, quotes first-class passenger fares in Mexican dollars and second-class fares for the Yokohama-Kobe line in yen. For domestic frieght, it seems that, even when Mitsubishi did not demand payment in Mexican dollars, it set its own rates in dollars and then collected in paper currency at the prevailing rate of exchange. Mitsubishi had its reasons for preferring Mexican dollars—they were used to pay the salaries of foreign crew members and to import ship equipment—but this was little consolation to its customers.[10]

MITSUI AND THE TOKYO SAILING SHIP COMPANY. The principal victim of Mitsubishi's high freight rates was Mitsui Bussan, which relied heavily on maritime transport in handling various domestic products, especially rice, and a small but growing volume of foreign trade. The Mitsui Bank also utilized shipping for transporting currency.[11] Shortly after the Satsuma Rebellion, Mitsui Bussan began exporting coal to Shanghai as the exclusive sales agent for the government-owned Miike Coal Mine in Kyushu, for which it received a government loan of ¥105,000 in 1879 to purchase several ships. As a specialized coal carrier, Mitsui made only a partial entrance into the shipping business. It levied no freight charges; the government simply reimbursed its ship expenses.[12] Overall, Mitsui Bussan's continued dependence on Mitsubishi is said to have cost ¥700,000 annually in freight payments, or about 25 percent of Mitsubishi's income in 1880. This share is large but still credible in the light of roughly comparable figures which show that between 1897 and 1912 Mitsui handled about 15 percent of all Japanese foreign trade.[13]

Saddled with these enormous payments, Masuda Takashi, Mitsui Bussan's president, tried to negotiate a rate reduction with Mitsubishi. When he failed, he rallied together some wealthy regional merchants, traders, and shipowners, and founded the Tokyo Fūhansen Kaisha (Sailing Ship Company).[14] Capitalized at ¥300,000, it was organized in August 1880 and began business early the next year. A Mitsui family member (Takenosuke), Masuda, and Kimura Masami, Mitsui Bussan's vice-president, together held 32 percent of the shares pledged by twenty promoters. The remaining seventeen promoters came from a diverse geographic background—Ishikawa, Niigata, Mie, and Akita prefectures—and four officials were from the Hokkaido Colonization Office.[15] The company, then, was more of an alliance than a Mitsui-run enterprise. Its stated purpose was to carry freight between domestic ports and to China and Korea. More significantly, the new firm's operations place it squarely within the trends of ship accumulation already noted for the late 1870s (see Table 16). It planned to use exclusively Western-style sailing ships in the range of 200–300 tons. Since the Fūhansen Kaisha had few ships to begin with, its founding principles were designed to attract the participation of independent shipowners. It invited them to sell their ships to the company in exchange for shares, and it also chartered ships which did not meet its specifications for purchase (at least 200 tons).[16] Finally, the company's articles of association contained important provisions for the maintenance of reserve funds for insurance, repairs, and ship depreciation. Later shipping companies followed this precedent.

In addition to Mitsui's Masuda, Shibusawa Eiichi played a major role in initiating the Fūhansen Kaisha. Whether it was Masuda who approved Shibusawa's plans, as Shibusawa's biographer suggests,[17] or vice versa, is not clear. But certainly Shibusawa stood ready with loans from the Dai Ichi Bank. Yatarō met this challenge by inviting Shibusawa to a party in August 1880, just at the time of the Fūhansen Kaisha's formation. They engaged in a legendary debate over the principles of one-man rule versus cooperative organization.[18] Failing to win Shibusawa to his side, Yatarō launched a defamatory press campaign against him and the Fūhansen Kaisha—an attack set in motion through payments to newspapers connected with Ōkuma.[19]

The Fūhansen Kaisha's capital, to be sure, was relatively small, but it initially posed a threat to Mitsubishi because it struck at the two sensitive areas examined earlier in this section: Hokkaido and the Japan Sea coast, including Niigata. The company's promoters included several representatives of Hokkaido interests. The ablest, Miyaji Sukesaburō, expressed the hope that the Fūhansen Kaisha would carry all Hokkaido freight.[20] Mitsubishi effectively counterattacked on the Japan Sea coast. First it persuaded Fujii Nōzō, second largest of the Fūhansen Kaisha's stockholders, to establish a separate shipping company, Etchū Fūhansen Kaisha, in a move that split the ranks of Mitsubishi's enemies. Then, it dispatched Kawada Koichirō and Ono Yoshimasa to Niigata, where they dissuaded local merchants from investing in the shipping industry, and united shippers, wholesalers, and wealthy magnates behind the Niigata Bussan Kaisha and against Mitsui.[21]

Though important as the harbinger of a greater challenge, the Fūhansen Kaisha was little more than a temporary scare for Mitsubishi. The growth of Mitsui Bussan's business between 1880 and 1882, especially its shipments of Miike coal, threatened to increase further its dependence on Mitsubishi. The production of the Miike Mine grew from 156,430 tons in 1882 to 574,330 tons in 1891, an average annual increase of 15.5 percent. Exports, about 60 percent

of production, kept pace by growing at 15.2 percent a year.[22]
Mitsui's own ships (or even its charters) could not handle all of this
trade; nor could the Fūhansen Kaisha, with its small fleet of sailing
ships, supply charters. Its major promoters either did not have the
capital, or if they did, as in the case of Mitsui, were not prepared
to take the enormous risk of making a large-scale investment in
shipping. The company's limited capital and reliance on sailing
ships suggest that Mitsui's goals in the venture were likewise quite
limited and its role confined to that of a sponsor. To advance into
the upper ranks of the industry and to build a large organization required a major catalyst. This came in the political changes of 1881.

THE THIRD DIRECTIVE

The inflation of the late 1870s and early 1880s (caused by the
financial strain of the Satsuma Rebellion, the excessive issue of
inconvertible notes by the banks, and the commutation of samurai
payments through a bond issue of ¥173 million) forced the government to revise its economic policy. The urgency of this step
was made apparent by the rapid depreciation of paper currency: in
January 1879 one silver yen was equal to 1.22 yen in paper currency; in 1880 to 1.37; and in 1881 to 1.70.[23] The government de-
vised two programs to cope with inflation. The first was the sale to
private owners of enterprises begun by the government in the
1870s under the Ministry of Industry and the Home Ministry. The
government announced this policy in November 1880, though
most of the sales took place between 1884 and 1889. The second
consisted of a series of deflationary measures to stabilize the government's budget, restore the currency, and establish a central
bank. This program began in earnest when Matsukata Masayoshi
became finance minister in October 1881.[24]

*ESTABLISHMENT OF THE MINISTRY OF AGRICULTURE AND COM-
MERCE.* Fundamental as they were to the economy as a whole,
these financial measures touched only indirectly on shipping. Of the
various reform memoranda of late 1880, however, a joint Ōkuma-

Itō Hirobumi proposal for the establishment of an Agriculture and Commerce Ministry (Nōshōmushō) outlined administrative changes that later affected the government's handling of shipping.[25] Financial reform, it said, depended not merely on curtailing expenses but on creating new institutions, specifically, a single ministry to oversee agriculture, commerce, engineering, and communications. Second, it shifted the emphasis of policy from protective aid (*hogo shōrei*) to guidance (*yūdō*). Third, it implicitly criticized the type of aid program that had enabled Mitsubishi to achieve its monopoly at the expense of others. Government aid, it said, "was being given to only a few people. Before it took the results of these efforts as models for further enterprises, the government should see to it that the recipients of this aid were not competing for [and thereby reducing] the profits of the broad populace engaged in agriculture and commerce." This sentiment marked a departure from Ōkubo's earlier opposition to competition in his May 18, 1875, memorandum on shipping. Finally, and most significantly, the memorandum did not repudiate the shipping subsidies of the 1870s but instead referred to the great increase in international commerce, even holding up transportation as the type of industry to be aided under the new single ministry. In short, from the state's viewpoint, the strategic importance of shipping made the industry more analogous to the navy than to the pilot factories and mines of the 1870s, which the government was willing to sell.

In accordance with the Ōkuma-Itō proposal, a Ministry of Agriculture and Commerce was formed in April 1881. Of direct importance to shipping was the shifting of the Home Ministry's Bureau of Posts and Communications and the Finance Ministry's Commerce Bureau to the new ministry. The Shipping Department was switched from the Posts and Communications Bureau to the jurisdiction of the Commerce Bureau, and a year later was upgraded to a separate Shipping Bureau (Kansen-kyoku) in the Ministry of Agriculture and Commerce.[26] Consequently, shipping policy was greatly affected when this ministry became a hotbed of anti-Mitsubishi sentiment later in 1881. Before the impact of these changes, however, a second skirmish occurred between Mitsubishi and its enemies. This was connected with the government program to sell state-run enterprises.

THE HOKKAIDO COLONIZATION OFFICE AND THE KANSAI BŌEKISHA. Though many of the government-run factories and mines were not sold until the last half of the 1880s, one institution quickly became a prime candidate for sale. This was the Hokkaido Colonization Office (Kaitakushi), set up in July 1869 to develop Hokkaido. Until its abolition in February 1882, this agency consumed ¥20,659,542 in government funds. As evidence of its drain on the treasury, administrative expenses alone accounted for 44.6 percent of this total, whereas expenses directly related to developmental projects came to only 36.6 percent.[27]

In October 1880 Mitsubishi had applied for the government sale of the ships belonging to the Colonization Office and for a government loan.[28] Such favors, however, were harder to come by than they had been in the 1870s. Ōkubo had been assassinated in 1878, and in an administrative change separating the Council of State from the executive (that is, the ministries) Ōkuma had relinquished his post as finance minister in February 1880, though he remained as a councillor.[29] Mitsubishi's support within the government had weakened, and its petition was rejected through opposition from Kuroda Kiyotaka, governor of the Colonization Office. In July 1881 Kuroda made his own recommendation on behalf of four secretaries in the Colonization Office. These secretaries, led by Yasuda Sadanori, planned to leave office and set up a new company, the Hokkaisha, which would then receive the Colonization Office's properties for ¥387,000 to be repaid in thirty years at no interest. The vast range of assets to be sold included factories, farm and grazing land, ships, and offices in Tokyo. The secretaries also petitioned for the right to sell goods used in Hokkaido for payment of tax in kind, for example, salmon, herring, rice cake, and other marine products—just the goods that Mitsubishi was transporting from Hokkaido.[30]

Earlier in this chapter, emphasis was placed on Mitsubishi's role in private commercial shipping from Hokkaido, but up to 1881

Mitsubishi's largest client on its Hokkaido run had been the Colonization Office itself. In turn, Mitsubishi carried more than half of the office's shipments. The sale to the Hokkaisha would be a great blow to Mitsubishi, for the new company seemed intent on using its own ships.[31]

The Hokkaisha was only the tip of the iceberg. Its secretaries had little of their own capital. In the middle of 1881, however, a major new company entered the bargaining, the Kansai Trading Company (Kansai Bōekisha) led by Godai Tomoatsu, president of the Osaka Chamber of Commerce and Industry. Godai played a role in the Kansai analogous to Shibusawa's promotional activities in the Kantō.[32] He was joined in the Kansai Bōekisha by many other prominent businessmen. The most powerful was Hirose Saihei, head manager of the Sumitomo interests. Two others were originally from Choshu. Nakano Goichi was Godai's vice-president in the Osaka Chamber; and Fujita Densaburō headed his own concern, the Fujitagumi, which specialized in forestry and mining. Another participant, Tanaka Ichibē, had a strong interest in shipping. The company's purpose was to promote commerce in the Kansai and engage in foreign trade, especially the exporting of Hokkaido products to China.[33] Though the Kansai Bōekisha was mainly a trading company, it also intended to purchase steamships; indeed, it constituted a greater threat to Mitsubishi than the Fūhansen Kaisha. The former was a much more unified firm—all of its key promoters operated out of the Kansai; furthermore, it was capitalized at ¥1 million. In July Godai sent a petition to Kuroda, which he forwarded to the Council of State along with that of the secretaries: it requested the government sale of Hokkaido's Iwanouchi Coal Mines and Akkeshi forests, properties which the company hoped to utilize to export coal and timber to China.[34]

Assessing the strength of this new opposition to Mitsubishi is complicated by uncertainty whether the Hokkaisha and the Kansai Bōekisha were separate companies or whether "the Hokkaisha not only had the blessing of Kuroda but also was merely a cover for Godai's Kansai Trade Company." In this view Kuroda petitioned the government with Godai's company "masterminding the plan and providing the financial backing."[35] Scholars who stress this "cover" interpretation point to extensive discussion Hirose had with Colonization Office officials during a visit to Hokkaido in May 1881[36] and to similar discussions held by Godai during a June-July trip to Hokkaido in search of investments.[37] Another point is that Godai, Kuroda, Yasuda, and another of the secretaries all came from the same village in Satsuma.[38]

In the end, neither the Hokkaisha nor the Kansai Bōekisha succeeded in obtaining the Hokkaido properties, and the latter was dissolved December 1881. The failure of this apparent alliance seems to have had a long-range negative effect on the opposition to Mitsubishi; but in the short run, the fallout from the issues surrounding the proposed sale proved to be a devastating political blow to Mitsubishi.

Scholars claiming that there were two separate companies base their argument on a Hirose letter to Godai of August 31, 1881, in which he comments on there being no relation between the Hokkaisha's purchase of government factories and the Kansai Bōekisha's plans. The letter, however, was written at the height of opposition to the government sale, and this comment was made in the context of Hirose's advice on how the company should portray itself to the public. In the letter Hirose had asked what the public response would be if in the future the two companies, which now had no formal ties, "should contact one another and come to aid mutually their respective industries." Hirose's questioning seems consistent with the thesis that the two companies planned to merge after the Hokkaisha received the government properties.[39] A similar view is that, after the government sale, Yasuda and the other secretaries intended to enter the Kansai Bōekisha. The effect would have been to create a "private Kaitakushi."[40]

But that was just the problem. The Colonization Office was not a popular institution. As a contemporary newspaper put it, "The abolition of the Kaitakushi will be an extraordinary relief to the poor people of Yezo [Hokkaido], around whose necks the taxes and imposts levied by this institution have hung like huge mill stones, destroying every spark of energy and driving the industrious to desperation."[41] In the midst of the government debate in July over the sale, the newspapers obtained the content of the petitions. Angered by the scandalously low price to be paid for the properties and by apparent favoritism among government cronies, Ōkuma-connected newspapers, the *Mainichi shinbun* and the *Yūbin hōchi shinbun*, attacked the sale in lengthy editorials from July 26 to 29.[42] Even the semiofficial newspaper, the *Tokyo nichinichi*, joined in with the warning that the "sale would give Godai's company power analogous to the British East India Company."[43] Though the government officially approved the sale on August 1, the opposition grew in intensity, and, when the issue became embroiled with other political debates, the government rescinded its decision.

The vocal opposition was not limited to the larger newspapers in the centers of national power. In fact, for this study the local resistance within Hokkaido seems more significant. Traveling separately from Godai, Hirose visited Hakodate in early July and at first received a welcoming reception from the city's principal merchants. But when the problem of the sale of the Colonization Office's properties became known, the Hakodate newspapers voiced disapproval. The townspeople started an opposition movement, claiming that the government properties should be sold to the local inhabitants. Some of the participants entered the Liberal Party (Jiyūtō), founded by Itagaki Taisuke, at about this time.[44]

There are several reasons why all of the various interests and factions opposed to Mitsubishi were unable to coalesce. Godai and his associates were primarily interested in the economic development of the Kansai. Hirose's motives in promoting the Kansai Bōekisha were not unrelated to Sumitomo's then lagging fortunes.[45] Crucial to the outcome was Hirose's failure to forge an alliance with local Hokkaido merchants who were becoming active in shipping. Next, the popular opposition to the secretaries of the Colonization Office was most likely a response to the makeup of Kuroda's executive staff, an exclusive preserve of Satsuma men.[46] Conspicuously absent from this list of factions is Mitsui and its allies in the Tokyo Fūhansen Kaisha, although Mitsui was engaged in financing Hokkaido trade, and one of the Mitsui family heads, Gennosuke, was a large stockholder in the Kansai Bōekisha,[47] but he did not otherwise have a major role in the company. There may also have been a political stumbling block to Mitsui's participation. At the time, Itō Hirobumi and Inoue, Mitsui's adviser, were at odds with Kuroda over the problem of a constitution as well as the issue of Colonization Office properties.[48] With the risk of failure high, Inoue may have advised Mitsui to lay low.

The failure of these interests to coalesce was not just a temporary setback. Several of them went their separate ways to form new shipping firms. While some prospered, their independence meant that future attempts to form nationwide anti-Mitsubishi shipping alliances would be less than complete in their representation. The Colonization Office incident, with its numerous factions searching for alliances, was a rich moment of opportunity for anti-Mitsubishi forces that, once lost, would not come again.[49]

ŌKUMA'S OUSTER, BUREAUCRATIC CHANGE, AND THE THIRD DIRECTIVE. On October 11, 1881, the government announced the cancellation of the sale of the Colonization Office's assets. In the same announcement Ōkuma was ousted from the government, ostensibly because he advocated the rapid establishment of a constitution in which political party cabinets would be responsible to an elected assembly. This contrasted with the gradualist view of Itō, who favored a German model that gave the executive branch more power. Ōkuma's ouster was also a convenient sop to Kuroda's anger. On August 21 Kuroda had written to Terajima Munenori accusing Ōkuma of aiding a conspiracy of Mitsubishi, Fukuzawa, and advocates of popular rights to oppose the Colonization Office sale through payments to newspapers and speaking tours in Hokkaido. Kuroda then had all these charges confirmed in a special investigative report by the Satsuma-dominated Tokyo Metropolitan Police Board.[50]

Kuroda's attack on Mitsubishi was less damaging than the ramifications of Ōkuma's ouster from the government. Fifteen officials followed Ōkuma in resignation; two had special significance for Mitsubishi. Kōno Togama had been Minister of Agriculture and Commerce. His resignation left the ministry in charge of shipping to the machinations of Shinagawa Yajirō. Second, Maejima Hisoka, Mitsubishi's original sponsor, was replaced by Nomura Yasushi as head of the Bureau of Posts and Communications, which still had jurisdiction over the earlier directives to Mitsubishi. Both Shinagawa and Nomura were from Choshu; both were anti-Mitsubishi.[51]

Most accounts, including Yatarō's biography, see in the attacks on Mitsubishi an organized strategy aimed at overthrowing the company. First there were the maneuvers by anti-Mitsubishi businessmen; then the new unfriendly stance of the government; and, after the Colonization Office matter had been dealt with, the Liberal Party turned to challenge Mitsubishi. In short, Mitsubishi was engaged in a "defensive war," and on October 18 Yatarō, beating a hasty retreat, laid down an ironclad company rule of nonparticipation in politics which he commanded future generations to observe.[52]

Like the Liberal Party, many of the newspapers and magazines that had attacked the Colonization Office sale turned their newly charged critical faculties toward Mitsubishi in the autumn of 1881. The most prestigious journal was the *Tokyo keizai zasshi*, founded by Taguchi Ukichi, a proponent of classical liberal economic thought, through the assistance of Shibusawa and Iwasaki Koichirō (no relation of Yatarō!), head of the Banking Section in the Finance Ministry.[53] Beginning on November 19, Taguchi launched a five-part serialized attack on the subsidies to Mitsubishi.[54] Claiming that Mitsubishi's subsidies amounted to more than half the budget of the Ministry of Agriculture and Commerce, Taguchi urged the government to revoke the subsidy clauses in earlier directives to Mitsubishi. In subsequent issues Taguchi focused his critique on Mitsubishi's use of the Mexican dollar and Yatarō's investments in enterprises other than shipping. Calling Yatarō a "daimyo among stockholders," he exhorted Mitsubishi to change its name to the "Mitsubishi Tankō Kawase Kabunushi

Kaisha" (Mitsubishi Mining, Banking and Stockholding Company).[55]

The October upheaval in government personnel soon transformed these attacks into reality. On October 21, Saigō Tsugumichi succeeded Kōno as Minister of Agriculture and Commerce, but the real power inside the ministry gravitated to Shinagawa Yajirō.[56] With the leading government ministers engrossed in other issues—Matsukata in financial retrenchment and Itō in political stabilization—a second-level bureaucrat like Shinagawa had a certain leeway to maneuver.

In its first move against Mitsubishi, the government issued a Third Directive at the end of February 1882. Notwithstanding the criticism of Mitsubishi during the last few months of 1881, the new directive was no mere unilateral order. Before its issuance, extensive discussion took place between Mitsubishi and the government, and Mitsubishi made its weight felt in the final version of the directive.

In late December 1881 Yatarō had been called to a meeting with Saigō, Shinagawa, and Nomura Yasushi at which the government conveyed its intention of revising the earlier directives of 1875 and 1876. The officials began on a conciliatory note, forswearing any intention of interfering in Mitsubishi's business. The purpose of the revision, they stated, was to put aid to Mitsubishi on a long-term footing. Thus the revised clauses would simply clarify ambiguities in the earlier directives and thereby lessen public criticism of government subsidies to Mitsubishi. Suspicious of the officials' tactics, Yatarō replied with a noticeable degree of defiance: "The First and Second Directives have not yet reached their statutory limit. Your revising them now will certainly have repercussions on our enterprises, but I will respect the government's intention of aiding Mitsubishi on a permanent basis and request that you make the revisions as indicated. However, in the event that they do interfere with our enterprises, it will become impossible for me to follow the directive." The subsequent discussion had a similar mixture of accommodation and bargaining. The government produced a first draft on January 30. After

Mitsubishi executives considered it for two weeks, three meetings with Nomura followed. In the first in mid-February, Nomura told Yanosuke and company adviser Ono Yoshimasa "to choose only those parts which Mitsubishi is able to implement" and cautioned them not to let it be known that Mitsubishi itself was making revisions. In two subsequent meetings Nomura and Yanosuke ironed out their differences, and on February 28 a fourteen-article directive was formally issued to Yatarō.[57]

The Third Directive circumscribed Mitsubishi's freedom in buying and selling ships, set a minimum tonnage of 22,000 net tons, regulated ship speed, and set fixed rates for wartime government chartering. The most important article defined Mitsubishi's business activity. The government draft, which Yanosuke and Ono disputed in the first meeting, stated: "The principal business of this company is limited to maritime steamship transport. The company will definitely not engage, either directly or indirectly, in other business. However, the opening of coal mines does not fall under this restriction." After Mitsubishi's revision, this was reduced to: "The principal business of this company is limited to maritime transport. It must definitely not engage in enterprises involving the buying and selling of commodities." Instead of an all-inclusive prohibition, the government accepted a restriction against a specific activity—the buying and selling of commodities—which, one could argue, Mitsubishi was not engaged in anyway. In short, the Third Directive did not force Mitsubishi to suspend any of its operations that had been attacked by Taguchi and other critics in late 1881. Accordingly, the directive is often seen as a compromise, the result of government weakness before Mitsubishi's dominant position as Japan's only powerful shipping company. Others may see in it more guile than weakness, believing that the government was already quietly making plans from which Mitsubishi was excluded.[58] These plans would link the preliminaries with the main bout that followed. Mitsubishi had withstood the competition from the Fūhansen Kaisha; Godai's Kansai Bōekisha had proved only a threat; and one could not foresee from the Third Directive alone the full extent of the fallout from the political changes in October 1881. That only became clear as government planning proceeded through the spring of 1882.

FORMATION OF THE KUK

LOCAL COMPANIES AND GOVERNMENT PROMOTIONAL ACTIVITY. In early 1882 one of the Colonization Office's former directors, Hori Motoi, succeeded where Sumitomo's Hirose had failed. He won the cooperation of wealthy Hakodate merchants intent on establishing a new shipping company. Together they joined to form the Hokkaido Transport Company (Hokkaido Un'yu Kaisha). At about the same time the newly named Tokyo Fūhansen Kaisha was planning a capital stock increase. Indicative of the limited commitment of Mitsui resources, the company's stock subscription drive met with a meager response, and the company petitioned the government for a low-interest loan. The Hokkaido Un'yu Kaisha and the Etchū Fūhansen Kaisha followed suit with similar petitions. Instead of giving separate replies, the government began planning the merger of the three companies into one large concern to challenge Mitsubishi.[59]

Two trends previously discussed finally come together: the gradual amalgamation of local shipowners and merchants into companies and the change in government personnel amid growing criticism of Mitsubishi. Both trends were interdependent insofar as the development of new shipping institutions was concerned. The new companies formed an essential base for a new government policy, and, without government capital and encouragement, it is doubtful that the companies could have reached even the small-steamship stage. But it is essential to see the political dimension that brought the government to this new posture. As one scholar puts it, "The government's real aim was clear: reforming the mismanagement of the previous administration, which had lined Iwasaki's pockets, and recovering maritime power from Mitsubishi. It was not simply the emergence of competing companies."[60] Saigō eloquently expressed this intent while in an inebriated state aboard ship early in 1883. Slandering Mitsubishi's Shōda Heigorō and Yamamoto Tatsuo, he declared that the government had set up the KUK to break Mitsubishi's power and denounced Ōkuma and Maejima for laxity toward Mitsubishi.[61]

Identifying the prime mover behind the government's planning for the new company is not easy. Shibusawa, however, has written that "other promoters and I stood in the public view, but the real power lay in the hands of Shinagawa Yajirō . . . and orchestrating the cast behind the scenes was Inoue Kaoru."[62] Most scholars agree that Inoue was acting in concert with Mitsui; thus Shibusawa's comment is not inconsistent with Masuda's emphasis on Mitsui's role in his autobiography: "Since Shinagawa was himself anti-Mitsubishi, he complied with our request and founded the KUK."[63] Certainly Shinagawa was the major organizer of the new company. Sources differ on the original promoters who cooperated with Shinagawa, but the most commonly mentioned are Shibusawa, Masuda, Hori Motoi, Shibusawa Kisaku, a promoter of the Tokyo Fūhansen Kaisha, Hara Rokurō, an important banker, and Komuro Shinobu, a descendant from a merchant family. Komuro was later involved in promoting railway, mining, and other companies. He had close ties with Choshu leaders and was recommended as a promoter by Inoue Kaoru.[64]

The formal planning for the new company seems to have begun no later than May. On orders from Saigō, Tsukahara Shūzō, head of the Shipping Bureau, produced a draft for presentation to the Council of State. Its essential points were: the company's name would be the Kyōdō Un'yu Kaisha; its authorized capital stock of ¥3 million would be increased to ¥5 million after two months, with the government and public each contributing one-half; and ships would be purchased for both military and commercial use.[65] A Ministry of Agriculture and Commerce plan, eventually presented to the Council of State on May 30, pointed to several disturbing trends—rapidly rising freight rates and the increased chartering of foreign ships by both Mitsui Bussan and Mitsubishi. It stated that a lack of capital was hampering growth of local shipping companies, and it urged the council to aid these smaller concerns by creating one large company, the Kyōdō Un'yu Kaisha, and to launch a nationwide drive for private funds. Finally on July 12 the Finance Ministry approved a government commitment of ¥1.3 million to be paid over four years. Tōtake Hideyuki, president of the Tokyo Fūhansen Kaisha, and Fujii Sankichi, director of the Etchū Fūhansen Kaisha, became promoters of the new company.[66]

On July 14 Shinagawa gave a speech to the promoters illustrating how the volume of freight had eclipsed the increase in the number of ships during the previous few years. He also argued that in promoting one large company the government was not acting unilaterally but was cooperating with other companies without intervening in private industry. Shinagawa intended to rebut the Mitsubishi-connected newspapers that were criticizing the establishment of the new company. The directive issued to the KUK on July 26, however, undercut the force of Shinagawa's arguments by reserving strong supervisory authority for the government. Article 11, for example, stated that for the first three years the president and vice-president would be chosen by the government. Also, article 14 required government consent for matters decided upon at stockholders meetings.[67]

The July 26 directive set the KUK's overall capitalization at ¥3 million, with the government's share the previously approved ¥1.3 million (43.3 percent). The first stock promotion drive to attract private investment was led by Tsukahara Shūzō.[68] During the summer and early fall he traveled throughout western Japan. In Osaka, Hirose Saihei helped him recruit the Nine and Thirteen Shop Union, Mitsubishi's old nemesis in the competition with the P. & O. Tsukahara also visited Godai and Fujita Densaburō, both promoters of the former Kansai Bōekisha. There is, however, no concrete information on subscriptions pledged by these major figures of the Kansai business world. Some sources suggest that Godai did not participate financially but had mediated between the government and company promoters.[69] Tsukahara's success in Osaka and Kyoto was limited to sake brewers and numerous small-scale businessmen. Also of major assistance was Nakai

Hiroshi, governor of Shiga Prefecture, who assembled several local shipping concerns. These concerns elected a group representative, Harada Kinnosuke, who was active in shipping on the Japan Sea coast.

Another major investor, Moroto Seiroku, had been a promoter of the Tokyo Fūhansen Kaisha. A wealthy merchant who was also investing heavily in land, Moroto joined the opposition to Mitsubishi because of his dependence on rice transport. He later retained his interest in shipping and became one of the largest individual stockholders in the N.Y.K.[70]

Inoue, conscious of the Tokyo Fūhansen Kaisha's earlier difficulties in attracting investment, had worried about the KUK's prospects, but Tsukahara's subscription drive satisfied him. A month or so later he wrote to Itō that "even more people than we expected want to become stockholders."[71] The success of Tsukahara's drive enabled the company to petition for an increase in authorized capital stock late in October. Despite visions of a ¥10 million company, it settled for ¥6 million, with the government's share also doubling to ¥2.6 million. Saigō approved its petition on November 27.[72] In the meantime, Shinagawa had set out in mid-October for a second stock subscription drive, which took place amid a volley of Mitsubishi-inspired criticism. For three months he wound his way through the major centers of western Japan, meeting with the local powerbrokers.[73]

THE NEWSPAPER WAR. The newspaper war following the KUK's establishment involved a confrontation both between the supporters of Mitsubishi and the KUK and between Japan's new political parties. It also reveals ties between the two companies and the parties. The Mitsubishi-supported papers argued that by establishing the KUK the government was interfering with private industry and would hinder the sound development of transportation. In an article published before the KUK's formal establishment, the *Yūbin hōchi* gave a favorable review of Mitsubishi's history and expressed the fear that the government would suspend Mitsubishi's subsidies. Now, it said, "through intervention from the political world," another shipping company would be formed. "Is the government not planning a course under which there will be no benefit for the state?"[74] One Mitsubishi-financed paper, the *Tōkai keizai shinpō,* managed by Inukai Tsuyoshi and Toyokawa Ryōhei, a Mitsubishi employee, had to cease publication at the height of the controversy. Since it defended protectionism (*hogoshugi*), simultaneously attacking the KUK and defending Mitsubishi left it in a theoretically untenable position.[75]

What began as a debate over the KUK escalated into a full-scale political controversy. The government had persuaded Itagaki Taisuke and Gotō Shōjirō to travel abroad, thereby removing them from the political arena. This move split the Liberal Party, and leaders like Baba Tatsui and Ōishi Masami left the party. The government had first asked Yatarō to pay for Itagaki's travel expenses. Initially he agreed, but then backed off when Sasaki Takayuki, the conservative former Tosa councillor, argued that "financing political parties is not the business of merchants." Mitsui then had to foot the bill, though the money was nominally given in the name of Hachisuka Mochiaki, a former daimyo of Awa domain for whom Komuro Shinobu was acting as an agent. Komuro, now a KUK promoter, had participated in the political opposition movement in the 1870s. The Liberal Party schism of 1882 brought about a change in the management of the party newspaper, and a Tosa man, Furusawa Shigeru, became editor. According to Masuda Takashi, a group of men under Furusawa had earlier tried to assassinate Yatarō and had put pressure on Shinagawa to act against Mitsubishi. Furthermore, Komuro and Furusawa had studied together in England in the early 1870s. Now that Furusawa had taken charge of the party newspaper, Komuro approached him about instigating an attack on Mitsubishi. Thus began another stage of escalation, despite Yatarō's attempt to intercede with Furusawa through the offices of Gotō. The campaign that followed featured Mitsubishi as the "sea monster" and the Progressive Party (Kaishintō), another political party founded by Ōkuma in March 1882, as a "bogus party."[76]

It is generally assumed that the Progressive Party drew its

financial support from Mitsubishi and other new urban-based businesses. There also seems to have been a financial connection between the Liberal Party and the KUK. Since the KUK had attracted many small investors, it may be that the local men of wealth, the landowners and rural merchants who constituted the Liberal Party, shared a common base of support with, and in some cases were identical to, the stockholders of the KUK. Certainly, several leaders were involved in both the party and the company. For example, Hoshi Tōru, later one of the Liberal Party's most powerful figures, was a KUK stockholder. Komuro was another link, for though he was not active in the party in the 1880s, he had close contacts with it. As one source puts it, the newspaper campaign and its accompanying political movement were probably advantageous for the KUK stock subscription drive.[77]

GOVERNMENT MOTIVATION AND THE KUK

The KUK was an anomaly. While the government embarked upon a drastic deflationary program, it was preparing to invest the enormous sum of ¥2.6 million in a new, untested shipping company. In view of this apparent contradiction in government economic policy, most scholars have located the government's primary motivation for creating the KUK in the political upheavals of 1881–1882. In contrast, this chapter will suggest that the more significant reason for the government's action—related to the longer-term trends in the development of Japanese shipping—was the increasing divergence of Mitsubishi's profit-oriented business from government economic policy and national security concerns. The government's reaction to Mitsubishi's business activity was not primarily a political move. Nor was it simply a response to the pressures of the emerging local shipping companies, even if, as one scholar has pointed out, some of the constituent companies of the KUK antedated Matsukata's deflationary policy and, in that sense, the KUK was not a new venture but an amalgam of older firms suffering from the depressed market.[78] These considerations alone cannot explain the scale of the ¥2.6 million investment, which becomes more apparent when viewed in the light of railway policy. Total government investment in railways between 1877 and 1882 amounted to only ¥3,502,243, and this was offset by ¥4,469,377 in revenue.[79] Furthermore, by the mid-1880s investment in railways was coming increasingly from the private sector. In short, the shipping industry, not the KUK, was the anomaly. The Ōkuma-Itō memorandum on the establishment of the Ministry of Agriculture and Commerce singled out transportation for aid in a period of retrenchment. Also, one of the fundamental policy documents for the program to sell government enterprises, a financial memorandum of August 16, 1880, by Inoue Kaoru, recommended that the government sponsor insurance and export companies to eliminate payments to foreign companies.[80] The same motivation applied to shipping.

THE 1882 DEBATE AND NATIONAL SECURITY. Two secret documents, leaked to the press in October and November of 1882, provide evidence regarding the government's motives. The first was an "opinion paper" (*ikensho*) bearing Yanosuke's name; the second a "defense" (*benmōsho*), a reply to Yanosuke written apparently by someone connected with the Metropolitan Police Board.[81] Yanosuke's *ikensho* claimed that the government had broken its commitment, given at the time of the Third Directive, not to interfere with Mitsubishi's business. More fundamentally, it attacked the concept of competition. The competition between the YJK and Mitsubishi in the early 1870s, he said, had brought only damage to Japan and, to correct this, the government had decided to aid Mitsubishi. By changing its policy to create a new company, however, the government would now inevitably force the shipping industry, with its still insecure foundations, to retreat to the conditions existing before 1875. To the argument that Mitsubishi possessed a monopoly of coastal navigation and was imposing exorbitant rates, Yanosuke countered that other steamship lines were being opened in all regions of the country. The *benmōsho* criticized Mitsubishi for its delusion that the government had promised it the status of a sole agency for coastal transportation, and it argued that Mitsubishi was trying to root out other domestic shipping companies. On the contrary, the *benmōsho* claimed, even if the government should establish "one or two more companies like Mitsubishi," it would not produce losses for Mitsubishi's business. The government, it said, had provided special protection for Mitsubishi's expansion of shipping, not for it to take sole possession of coastal navigation.

In fact, the government's support for competition and opposition to exclusive privileges were contrary to both recent policy and tradition. Yanosuke was quite consistent in rejecting competition, for he was, in effect, appealing to Ōkubo's 1875 policy. While the government of 1882 called for more competition, the legal mechanisms did not favor it. The special directives issued to companies like Mitsubishi still had the aura of exclusive privileges granted to Tokugawa merchants.

Yanosuke devoted most of his *ikensho* to a defense against specific criticisms, centering on two issues: Mitsubishi's freight rates, said to be higher than coastal rates in other countries, and the slowdown in commodity distribution resulting from a shortage of ships. Foreign shipping companies, replied Yanosuke, could afford lower freight rates because of well developed harbor and port facilities. Japan, in contrast, had few conveniences for unloading freight. Numerous port charges as well as the responsibility of shipping companies for damages incurred through inadequate packing and storage all had to be considered in setting freight rates. Yanosuke concluded: "if a reduction in freight rates were carried out because of competition, the huge losses incurred by shipowners would invite disaster for the entire shipping industry." To the charge that there was a shortage of ships, Yanosuke replied that the government should provide Mitsubishi with the wherewithal to increase its fleet rather than investing enormous sums in a new company. The *benmōsho* countered that between 1878 and 1882 Mitsubishi had tried to monopolize profits without building a single new ship; and that it had contravened the First Directive by neglecting repairs so that many of its ships were now unfit for use.

In addition to these specific charges, the *benmōsho* focused on the profits from the Satsuma Rebellion and Mitsubishi's many-sided business activities. Mitsubishi, it said, "had taken advantage of the national difficulty" during the Satsuma Rebellion to demand astonishingly high rates, and then, after garnering enormous profits, had proceeded to ignore the accounting provisions of the First Directive, presenting inaccurate reports the government could not verify. Article 12 of the First Directive had prohibited Mitsubishi from engaging in other businesses under the name of Mitsubishi. But Yatarō, under other names, possessed stock in numerous companies. "There can be no doubt that Iwasaki Yatarō and the Mitsubishi Company are one and the same, but directly or indirectly Iwasaki Yatarō is operating several other kinds of enterprises."[82]

At the heart of many of the *benmōsho*'s conclusions was the issue of trust. The government felt that Mitsubishi's proliferating interests would make the company suspect when called upon to provide government service. The government could well ask, in view of Mitsubishi's "exploitation" of the Satsuma Rebellion, how the company would respond in a broader international emergency. Indeed, could the government really trust Mitsubishi in wartime?

Considerations of national defense were an important motivation for the government's sponsorship of the KUK. Inoue wrote to Itō, "The establishment of this company will be useful for the navy in the event of an emergency." Masuda Takashi observed that "the navy joined hands with the KUK because transport was indispensable. If it had not done so, it would have had to follow a different path, such as building its own ships."[83] The fullest indication of this strategic concern appears in the directive to the KUK. The First Directive to Mitsubishi contained remarkably little about military matters. By contrast, the first 6 of the 17 articles in the KUK directive dealt with the navy. Articles 1, 3, and 5 obligated the company to provide ships in wartime and promised appropriate freight rates. Article 3 stated explicitly that "ships granted to the company will belong to the navy." Under article 4 the Navy Ministry would pay for changes in the structure of ships provided for navy use. Article 6 ordered the company to employ as crew members students of merchant marine and naval schools so that they could undergo practical training as seamen. In contrast to these specifically military clauses, article 2 was mainly financial, but it too had an indirect bearing on the navy: "The government will limit the dividend due it to 2 percent of its stock. Profits exceeding that will be set aside as a reserve fund for insurance." In his July 14 speech to the promoters, Shinagawa tied this article in with defense preparations. "The government," he said, "has decided to use its 2 percent share of the profits for the promotion of the navy."[84]

The government's emphasis on naval preparations was part of a broader defense program that, in the early 1880s, had begun to aim at a continental strategy in contrast to the emphasis on internal security during the 1870s. In fact, on July 15, 1882, Yamagata Aritomo submitted a proposal which combined warnings of "potential continental enemies" and a call "to make a veritable floating fortress of our Imperial nation" through "the expansion of the army and navy." Yamagata's assessment of this expansion as "the most urgent task at hand" is a good measure of how the military context had changed between the time of Mitsubishi's first government subsidies and the establishment of the KUK. From a comparison of the directives to Mitsubishi and the KUK, Yatarō's biographer concludes that "instead of calling the KUK a joint government-private concern, we should regard it as a naval agency under direct government control."[85]

The KUK owed its military character to the broad strategic considerations of the early 1880s, not simply to the reaction to events in Korea in 1882. For six years the Japanese had been trying with only limited success to implement the provisions of the Treaty of Kanghwa, signed in 1876. Finally, on July 23, 1882, a Korean mob attacked the Japanese legation in Seoul, killing a number of Japanese. The Japanese ambassador's report on the incident, however, did not reach Tokyo until July 30, and it did not change the content of the directive issued to the KUK on July 26. But the subsequent requisitioning of commercial ships to support another naval force dispatched to Korea unquestionably speeded up the implementation of the directive. In the meantime Mitsubishi received the lion's share of the military business, earning ¥167,693 over the next two months.[86]

Related to these security issues was a changed attitude toward foreigners. In article 3 of the First Directive the government had encouraged Mitsubishi to select "experienced and skillful foreigners." Article 13 of the KUK directive changed this emphasis, declaring that "ship captains, officers, and engineers should all be Japanese, though for the time being you need not avoid employing foreigners." The *benmōsho* had also criticized Mitsubishi for excessive reliance on foreign technicians for navigation.[87]

Maritime security, moreover, was not limited to the navy. It required as well a strong commercial fleet capable of operating overseas. Government criticism of Mitsubishi's attitude toward this latter role reveals the most significant divergence between government security concerns and the direction of Mitsubishi's business expansion. Shinagawa claimed that Mitsubishi had tried to close down its Hong Kong line shortly after it was opened and that it wanted to discontinue lines to Korea. The reason, he said, was that Mitsubishi "can obtain far and away higher freight rates on coastal than on overseas transport." Mitsubishi's response to these market conditions, Shinagawa suggested, reflected an insufficiency of ships even for coastal shipping and thus the need for a new company.[88] Since the Takashima Mine was providing an increasing percentage of Mitsubishi's overall profits, one of the *benmōsho*'s criticisms is especially telling. "Mitsubishi says that there is no shortage of ships, but why then does it charter foreign ships to transport the coal produced from its own Takashima Mine to Shanghai and Hong Kong?" Because, said the *benmōsho*, "freight rates are so high on coastal routes there is positively no incentive to embark on foreign lines." As a result every year Japan had to pay foreign shipping companies ¥600,000 to ship its coal to China. Increasing exports of coal in the 1880s would soon raise the problem to crisis proportions. As early as 1880 the governor of Nagasaki Prefecture, Utsumi Tadakatsu, had sent a memorandum to the government giving detailed statistics on the relation between freight rates and the exports of the Kyushu coal mines. Despite increased production in the Miike and Takashima mines, profits were unsatisfactory because of high rates charged by foreign ships. In 1879 payments amounted to about ¥570,000. To avoid these charges Utsumi suggested the establishment of a new shipping company through special government aid.[89] Apparently, no action was taken on this petition. However, it was presented before Mitsubishi acquired the Takashima Mine and probably the government expected Mitsubishi to alleviate the foreign payments problem by transporting a sizeable share of its own coal exports. But, according to the *benmōsho,* the change in the mine's ownership had brought no improvement.

This criticism of Mitsubishi was not confined to government pronouncements. Even newspapers friendly to Mitsubishi noted its preoccupation with coastal transport. As Sasaki Seiji has written, "the newspapers of the time show that once Mitsubishi had secured its monopolistic position, it became engrossed in expanding and perfecting its influence in domestic routes and no longer seemed concerned about overseas expansion."[90] But how could this be? After all, had not Yatarō vowed to "cross the earth" with new shipping lines? Certainly other companies were eager to try. The Tokyo Fūhansen Kaisha had spoken of exporting goods to China and Korea. Godai's Kansai Bōekisha had emphasized the export of Hokkaido products to China. The KUK went even further in its petition for an authorized capital stock increase in October 1882. It noted that coal shipped from Kyushu and Hokkaido was still heavily dependent on foreign ships and that Hokkaido marine products were usually transshipped at Yokohama on their way to overseas ports like Shanghai and Hong Kong. The company therefore petitioned for the opening of a direct Hakodate-Shanghai line (though this was not implemented).[91] These professions of intent have one thing in common. They were all made by firms not yet in operation. Even Godai's early idealism about Hokkaido exports quickly faded. Before the Colonization Office sale was canceled his vision had already narrowed from exporting coal and timber to developing machinery for processing fish oil.[92] In the area of overseas expansion there still existed an enormous gap between perception and reality.

It is my contention, however, that this gap no longer existed for Mitsubishi. Yatarō had already abandoned the visionary expansionist aspirations he held in the 1870s. He sought comfort in the immediately realizable profits closer to home, that is, "on land." While he may not have retreated all that way by 1882, he was keeping close to shore. To demonstrate this requires more evidence than just government and newspaper criticism. It is Yatarō's own words which give authority to this impression.

The expansion of Japanese security concerns in the early 1880s occurred mainly in the area of the Korean peninsula. On February 28, 1881, the Council of State ordered the Home Ministry to open a regular monthly line from Kobe to Vladivostok via the Korean ports of Pusan, immediately opposite Japan, and Wŏnsan, on the northeast coast. To buy ships for this line Mitsubishi received a grant of ¥80,000 silver to be repaid over ten years at no interest. In May the line was extended to include stops once every three months at Inch'ŏn (Chemul-p'o), the port on the western side of the peninsula near Seoul. Far from seeking the business of this line, Yatarō wrote to Maejima on March 13 and complained that the port of Vladivostok was located in an undeveloped area that would produce little freight. Even with the ¥80,000 loan the line would not bring a profit; and a monthly passage would be impossible during the winter. While seeing no chance of profits, in another letter on April 22 Yatarō finally gave his consent. "We have decided," he said, "to ignore temporarily the losses to our company's accounts. We will defer to your opinion and operate on a trial basis." He concluded by asking the government to reconsider the merits of the line.

The northern location may explain Yatarō's opposition to the Vladivostok line, but Mitsubishi did not show much enthusiasm for the Korean services either. Since March 1880 Mitsubishi had been receiving a yearly subsidy of ¥10,000 for a line to Wŏnsan that operated every other month, but Yatarō suspended this service in September 1881 shortly after its subsidy was transferred to the new Vladivostok line. Also, in July, Maejima had authorized a reduction to two stops a year at Inch'ŏn. Inch'ŏn was still not an officially "open" port, and whether this reduction was the result of Korean opposition, insufficient cargo, or Yatarō's own wishes is not certain. According to Conroy's account, though, 1881 saw a change in Korea "in the direction of a larger emphasis on foreign relations."[93] And if we are to believe Shinagawa, Mitsubishi wanted to cut back on its Korean lines.

Trends in Japanese-Korean trade help to explain Mitsubishi's reluctance. Until 1882 Korea was still closed to Western countries; therefore, Western exports to Korea were sent via Japan. This gave Korea a small but slowly increasing role in Japanese trade between 1877 and 1881. By 1881 exports to Korea had reached ¥1.9 million, or 6.3 percent of Japan's total exports, up from 1.3 percent in 1877; while imports amounted to ¥1.4 million, or 4.4 percent of Japan's total, compared to 0.5 percent in 1877. These figures, however, are misleading, for almost 90 percent of the goods being shipped to Korea from Japan in this period were re-exports. With the opening of Korea to Western trade in 1882 and the establishment of the Korean treaty-port system, Western countries were expected to export directly to Korea and commercial shipping between Japan and Korea promised to show a corresponding decrease.[94] The Korean lines held little prospect for profitable business.

Yatarō's lukewarm response to the demands of overseas lines in the early 1880s and the widespread criticism of Mitsubishi for its excessive attention to coastal shipping tend to confirm the uncertainties about the direction of the company's investment policy. The preference for coastal over foreign shipping is especially significant because Mitsubishi's other enterprises were more tightly integrated with its coastal lines than its overseas ones. In the ensuing competition with the KUK, the fortunes of Mitsubishi's other enterprises in the business network came to exercise a crucial influence on the decisions Mitsubishi eventually made about shipping.

POLITICAL IDEOLOGY AND CONSPIRACY. Concern for national security was not the government's only reason for establishing the KUK. Political motives and ideology were also important. Scholars who have stressed the political motivation usually refer to an anti-Mitsubishi conspiracy of Choshu interests, Mitsui, and the smaller promoters of the KUK. This perspective overlooks an ideological component in the anti-Mitsubishi campaign, evident especially in the case of Shinagawa Yajirō. Shinagawa's main claim to notoriety was an attempt to rig the 1892 election when he was home minister. He has the image of a political hack doing the dirty work for his fellow Choshu ministers, first Inoue Kaoru and then Yamagata Aritomo, builder of Japan's army. But Shinagawa was a complex figure. Before the 1892 election he was known mainly for his interest in agriculture. His views on farming give a much more positive ideological dimension to his anti-Mitsubishi stance than his negative political image projects. Shinagawa opposed the Meiji government's heavy emphasis on industry, and he tried to formulate programs to protect smaller landowners and farmers against both industrialism and commercialized farming. His best known proposal was for a national system of credit associations designed to aid smaller producers, organized in self-ruling village units and imbued with the "communalism (*kyōdōtai*) of premodern times." He regarded these units as the foundation of the state, but Mitsubishi's exclusive contract system, while contributing to rapid commercialization, threatened to emasculate local credit associations and destroy the organization of small producers' units.[95]

There was an ideological resonance between the communalism of these agricultural units and Shinagawa's own perception of the KUK. In an October 13, 1882, speech to the company promoters he spoke about the first word in the company name, *kyōdō*, meaning "cooperative" or "union." He saw the KUK as a union of investors from each district of the country acting together in one cooperative body. He adamantly rejected the judgment that the KUK was either a joint private-government or government-established concern. Shinagawa maintained that the cooperative body of promoters themselves decided the character of the company.[96]

The clearest link between Shinagawa's activities on behalf of both agriculture and shipping was his promotion of the KUK while he was serving as chief secretary of the Agricultural Society of Japan (Dai Nihon Nōkai), a semigovernmental organization that initiated local farm discussion groups throughout the country. Shinagawa's activity with this organization overlapped at least once with the KUK when he spoke to the Kyoto chapter of Nōkai on January 6, 1883, during his stock subscription campaign. The day before he had delivered a speech to the Kyoto Chamber of Commerce and Industry, summarizing his views on the need for the KUK and including references to agriculture:

> Trade and commerce depend upon shipping for their prosperity; agriculture depends upon shipping for its vigor; and industry depends upon shipping for its development. But the country now has an extreme scarcity of ships and freight rates have risen sharply. Is it proper for the government to entrust to one individual this shipping enterprise which affects so greatly the interests of the general public? No, not at all! And for that very reason the creation of the Kyōdō Un'yu Kaisha is unavoidable. By joining hands with the resources of the public the KUK will develop shipping services, accelerate the prosperity of agriculture, industry, and commerce, and, in turn, strive for the expansion of the sovereign rights of the nation and the flourishing of state power.[97]

Whatever the consistency of Shinagawa's ideological perspective, there is still no denying that he and others in the government acted partly from political motives. Shinagawa's biography claims that he "planned the KUK not simply to destroy Mitsubishi's transport monopoly, but to curb the influence of the Progressive Party." Western historiography on Japan, dominated as it once was by political historians, has usually seen this political dimension as the primary one. Roger Hackett, for example, writes that the "government also helped to establish a transport company to compete with the Mitsubishi Company with the object of weakening a major source of Ōkuma's financial support." The Iwasaki biographies also frequently speak of the political animosity of the "Sat-Chō bureaucracy, which wanted to overthrow Mitsubishi's monopolistic shipping structure without paying any heed to the enormous expenditures of the government." Many sources agree that government leaders feared an opposition movement led by Ōkuma's Progressive Party and supported by Mitsubishi aimed to overthrow the Choshu- and Satsuma-dominated administration. All sides in these political disputes seem to have had their share of anxiety, fueled by their uncertainty over the ultimate motivation of the opposing sides. Inoue Kaoru expressed this in a December 9, 1882, letter to Itō. He wrote that Mitsubishi may have tried to interfere with the establishment of the KUK and stirred up the newspapers against the new company because it feared the government was trying to destroy Mitsubishi. This kind of rampant suspicion makes interpretation difficult, and it may also account for the strong historiographical emphasis on political motivations, for analysis based on conventional primary sources—letters, newspapers, and the like—may reflect simply the pervading atmosphere of fear and fail to detect real underlying motives. [98]

Certainly, however, the political pressure at the height of the newspaper war is evident in Mitsubishi's internal correspondence. In early November Mitsubishi's head office dispatched a message to all branches about certain "false opinions" that Mitsubishi was instigating Progressive Party members to criticize the establishment of the KUK. It further warned employees to concentrate exclusively on the company's principal business and to avoid contact with people active in politics. Similar messages from Yanosuke enjoined employees against slandering the KUK and branded as unfounded the gossip about the alleged alliance between Mitsubishi and the Progressives. [99]

Other sources see not just a reaction against Mitsubishi but a drive by the forces supporting the KUK to utilize the attack on Mitsubishi in order to grasp a more dominant position for themselves. Inoue Kaoru, for example, is pictured as trying to expand Mitsui's influence while Mitsubishi was lying low. That is understandable from a business standpoint, for as one careful source has calculated, by 1882 Mitsubishi's total annual profits had reached the level of Mitsui's, at around ¥600,000. But Yanosuke's biographer goes beyond this to claim that the government "under the pretext of controlling Mitsubishi, was nurturing a new monopolistic enterprise."[100] Is this interpretation not going too far?

A COMPARISON OF DIRECTIVES: GOVERNMENT EXPECTATIONS OF THE KUK. An examination of the directives to the two companies and other KUK documents provides a clearer perspective of just what expectations the government had of the KUK. In comparing the Mitsubishi and KUK directives, government favoritism toward the KUK is most evident in the articles on ships.[101] For example, the KUK had to obtain government permission to purchase ships, and purchases were limited to vessels less than two years old. The government, however, promised to buy ships for the company and to grant other ships presently under the jurisdiction of the Ministry of Agriculture and Commerce (articles 1, 12, and 17). In contrast, Mitsubishi received no promises of aid for ship purchases; it was ordered to deposit annually ¥180,000 with the Bureau of Posts and Communications as a preparatory fund for new ships and major repairs. To improve its fleet Mitsubishi had to sell older ships to raise the required capital for new ones. But the freedom to do so was restricted by other articles prohibiting sale of ships without government permission unless it returned previous loans and payments (articles 2, 3, and 7). The KUK directive said nothing about selling ships. According to the company's articles of association (*teikan,* articles 16 and 17), this was left to the directors.[102]

Mitsubishi had two kinds of repayment obligations: government loans for operating expenses in 1875 and for ships purchased in 1876; and the *myōgakin,* which Mitsubishi had promised for the ships obtained from the government in 1875. When these financial arrangements were made in the 1870s, the government had allowed Mitsubishi to make its repayments over the long term—fifty years in the case of the *myōgakin.* According to this 1882 Third Directive, however, Mitsubishi had to meet these obligations before it could sell ships without government permission. To meet the terms of the directive, Mitsubishi petitioned in January 1883 for the right to repay all government loans quickly instead of over a long term. Most of these loans had been agreed to with little or no interest. In that sense they consisted almost entirely of principal. Mitsubishi petitioned to have the total amount due changed from being viewed as principal to principal *and* interest. The effect was to reduce the principal, for with the loans due over the long term, most of the total debt would become interest. By repaying the loans quickly Mitsubishi was able to eliminate this interest (*ribiki*), which the government had set at 6 percent in response to Mitsubishi's petition. At the time of this petition Mitsubishi still had ¥1,056,000 of the *myōgakin* to repay. By using the formula to eliminate the interest, calculated at 6 percent, Mitsubishi met this obligation entirely in July 1883 by repaying just ¥360,000.[103] Then, in 1885 it returned the other loans, using a similar formula.

Yatarō's biographer has suggested that Mitsubishi negotiated these repayments in order to retain the freedom to dispose of its ships in the event that competition with the KUK threatened its financial stability.[104] This is a significant explanation of Mitsubishi's motives, for if Mitsubishi sold many ships, it would contravene article 4 of its directive requiring it to maintain a minimum of 22,000 net tons. We have noted earlier Yatarō's statement in his negotiations over the Third Directive that he would not be able to follow the directive if the government interfered with Mitsubishi's business. If we assume that he implied that he would sell his ships, such an assumption is consistent with another proposition advanced here—that the increasing percentage of profits from its side enterprises and its reluctance to advance into foreign lines at the expense of its coastal network, where it had a stronger hold on profits, left Mitsubishi's commitment to shipping uncertain.

The government encouraged the KUK to buy new ships. Mitsubishi's ships, however, were all old vessels built some fifteen to twenty years before in Britain or the United States. Article 8 of Mitsubishi's directive required it to "limit ships on the Shanghai line to those which have a speed of more than 11 knots." According to an 1882 naval report, Mitsubishi could not meet the terms of this article. The average speed of Mitsubishi's ships was 8.7 knots; only ten could attain 10 knots; and only one could go 12 knots. Next, article 10 of the Third Directive ordered Mitsubishi to reduce exorbitant freight rates, but added a qualification: "You must not reduce them to such an extent that you lose all the profits you would normally derive from your lines." While this may have been a normal injunction against excessive rate cutting, it could also limit Mitsubishi's freedom in competition with the KUK. By contrast, the KUK directive said nothing about freight rates. Once again, this matter was left to the directors (*teikan,* article 20).

Sasaki Seiji, an early specialist in Japanese shipping history, mentions most of these points. He tries to demonstrate the government's favoritism toward the KUK. On balance, the two directives show favoritism to the KUK, but several qualifications are in order. First, the Third Directive to Mitsubishi concerned the company's implementation of the First and Second Directives. The directive to the KUK was an initial directive and is not strictly parallel to Mitsubishi's Third Directive. More significantly, other aspects to the KUK directive, not mentioned by Sasaki, tend to refute the argument that the government intended to overthrow Mitsubishi and put the KUK in its place as a new shipping monopoly. While the article on outside enterprises in the directives to Mitsubishi had been ambiguous, the comparable article in the KUK directive (article 10) was shorter and more explicit, stating simply: "This company exists for the purpose of carrying passengers and freight with steamships and sailing ships. It must not engage in other business" (*teikan,* articles 5 and 6). Article 7 of the KUK directive ordered the company to transport mail and official freight and stated: "at an opportune time the government will grant a regular subsidy." This promise was never really fulfilled, except for extremely small grants in 1884 and 1885. In fact when the KUK's business began to slump in late 1884, the absence of an operating subsidy became a major source of conflict between the government and the KUK.

In general, the number of regulations imposed on the KUK and the lack of autonomy offered its management point more to a government desire for control over the new company than to an outright wish to crush Mitsubishi or to aid Mitsui by creating a new private shipping monopoly allied with it. If the latter had been the primary motivation, more lenient terms for the KUK would have been a better way of achieving that objective. Instead, the government was responding more to the real needs of the shipping industry: to correct the deteriorating service provided by Mitsubishi and to increase the number of ships.

The government wanted to create a shipping company both profitable and responsive to its policies. Shipping was too vital to the nation's security to be merely part of a private group of enterprises whose criteria for investment might vary dangerously from state security concerns. Yet, while the KUK offered the prospect of more secure support, at the same time the government must have recognized the continued need for Mitsubishi's services. Moreover, the government's failure to provide a regular operating subsidy to the KUK suggests that there was an upper limit to support for the new company. The government's reasoning on the subsidy issue was probably based on two assumptions. First, the KUK could use its capital stock for major ship purchases, leaving internal funds available for operating expenses. Second, aware that Mitsubishi had averaged more than ¥680,000 in profits between 1880 and 1882 and that there was a shortage of ships relative to national requirements, the government may well have believed a KUK pamphlet issued in mid-1883, which predicted that its annual profit would be ¥600,000.[105] Though this figure was probably inflated for stockholder consumption, the government expected the KUK to achieve a good business record. It further assumed that there was room for two competing firms, and it did not anticipate replacing Mitsubishi with a new monopoly.

THE TOKYO FŪHANSEN KAISHA AND THE KUK. One of the three constituent companies of the KUK, the Tokyo Fūhansen Kaisha, was a joint-stock company. As such, the decision to merge with the other two companies had to be approved by its stockholders. This proved unsettling. In an Extraordinary General Meeting of stockholders on August 15, 1882, the merger met with noisy opposition, ostensibly because of concern over future profits. Though it had not effectively challenged Mitsubishi, the Tokyo Fūhansen Kaisha had paid a 20 percent dividend in its two years of existence. One stockholder opposing the merger was Numa Morikazu, a prominent leader of Ōkuma's Progressive Party, an editor of the *Mainichi shinbun,* and a Tokyo assembly official. Numa was cited frequently in the September 1881 Police Board report on Mitsubishi as receiving money from Mitsubishi for speaking tours against the sale of Colonization Office assets. It is generally assumed that he was acting as a proxy for Mitsubishi at the Tokyo Fūhansen Kaisha's General Meeting to issue one last-ditch protest against the formation of the KUK.[106] Whatever the case, this incident provides a foretaste of what would happen at a similar KUK stockholders meeting exactly three years later.

There were three main components that affected KUK management. The first was the government, which gave the company's top leadership a naval cast by appointing as president Itō Shunkichi, a rear admiral. Also, Tōtake Hideyuki, former president of the Tokyo Fūhansen Kaisha and a navy captain on leave, became vice-president.[107] The second was the promoters, who gathered in October to elect a board of directors and to draw up articles of association and a petition to increase the company's authorized capital stock. The third was the stockholders, to whom the articles of association gave certain "rights," such as submitting opinions to directors' meetings and removing officers guilty of inappropriate conduct through a two-thirds vote. Also, voting regulations favored the smaller stockholder (articles 49–51). These three components became a volatile mix, for the stockholders' rights, combined with their demands for high dividends, created strong pressure on both the government and KUK top management during the competition with Mitsubishi.

FIVE

Competition and Merger: 1883–1885

THE MITSUBISHI–KUK COMPETITION

KUK STOCKHOLDING. A complete picture of the N.Y.K. cannot be achieved without a clear understanding of the composition of the KUK and its three-year competition with Mitsubishi which led to the formation of the N.Y.K. in September 1885. To begin, a commonly accepted scholarly view by Edwin O. Reischauer states:

> The mid-eighties, which saw the transfer of most government enterprises to private hands and the first industrial boom, also saw the emergence of a pattern of cooperation and cartel-like organization among big business concerns, in place of sharp competition. . . There was also pressure from government authorities, particularly Inoue, for joint business enterprises that would create strong companies.
>
> The first clear sign of the new tendency was the merger in 1885 of competing steamship lines owned by the two emerging business giants, the Mitsubishi and Mitsui interests.[1]

The KUK is identified as "owned by the . . . Mitsui interests." The previous chapter indicates, however, that the government held a 43 percent share in the KUK. Clearly, then, qualification is needed, but if private stockholding in the company is viewed as central, then Reischauer's generalization regarding Mitsui is widely accepted. Noda Kazuo has written that the N.Y.K. "had the shape of a joint investment of the government, Mitsubishi, and Mitsui."

Many Japanese scholars obscure the issue through a common linguistic device. Ōe Shinobu, for example, says the private shares belonged to "Mitsui and others" (Mitsui *hoka*). However, Shibagaki Kazuo, even without a detailed analysis of the KUK's make-up, has correctly pointed out that much of the KUK's private capital was "scattered among a flock of small shareholders."[2]

Chapter 4 identifies many of these smaller interests. The Hokkaido and Etchū shipping companies were primarily local concerns, and Mitsui possessed less than half the shares held by promoters of the Tokyo Fūhansen Kaisha.[3] The stock subscription drives widened the base of the KUK far beyond these three constituent companies. The following analysis does not deny that Mitsui had the largest private interest in the KUK, but suggests that the extent of that interest has been exaggerated. In fact, the presence of so many other elements behooves us not to label the KUK simply as a "Mitsui interest," because to do so would obscure the vastly different *levels* of motivation. Mitsui wanted to cut back on its enormous freight payments to Mitsubishi and probably also to check Mitsubishi's rising power which threatened Mitsui's standing as the leading Japanese merchant house. Even so, these were limited motivations compared to Mitsubishi's. Because only a small percentage of its interests were in shipping, Mitsui was not, like Mitsubishi, engaged in a virtual "death struggle." True, Mitsubishi may have diversified its profit earnings by 1882, and its commitment to the shipping business may have been less than rocklike, but its assets were still mostly in shipping.

Since no stockholders list is extant, a variety of indirect evidence must be used to analyze who owned the private KUK shares. The three core companies and the stock promotion drives mentioned earlier indicate a widely dispersed pattern of stockholding. This is evident even in the KUK board elected in the General Meeting of April 30, 1883. The leading vote getters were:

Komuro Shinobu	3,741	Shibusawa Kisaku	2,818
Masuda Takashi	3,232	Fujii Sankichi	2,410
Hori Motoi	3,226	Ōkura Kihachirō	2,018

| Sonoda Saneatsu | 1,431 | Shibusawa Eiichi | 1,076 |
| Harada Kinnosuke | 1,360 | Kawasaki Shōzō | 1,025 |

Komuro, because of his close connections with Inoue Kaoru, probably represented Mitsui's interest. Mitsui, through Komuro and Masuda, collected 31 percent of the vote received by the ten leading candidates. The other eight, however, are not so closely linked to Mitsui. Hori and Fujii represented the Hokkaido and Etchū companies; Shibusawsa Kisaku, though Eiichi's brother, was a Tokyo merchant active in the Yokohama silk trade who had invested in the Tokyo Fūhansen Kaisha; Ōkura and Kawasaki were major capitalists. Though originally from Satsuma, Sonoda appears to have represented Hokkaido interests, and Harada Kinnosuke, from Fushiki, represented shipowners from the Japan Sea coast. Shibusawa Eiichi is best regarded as a general sponsor of the company despite his close ties to Mitsui.[4]

Mitsui seems to have achieved dominance over the board by limiting it to five members. The company's articles of association allowed anywhere from four to ten members (article 22), and Hoshi Tōru of the Liberal Party led a heated opposition which favored ten.

Mitsui probably owed its dominance less to an aggregate total of stock than to the fact that it was the largest single bloc amid a flock of individual businessmen. Of the forty-two promoters attending the October 1882 organizational meeting, probably no more than five could be called Mitsui personnel. Mitsui Takenosuke was the Mitsui family member responsible for Mitsui Bussan; then came Masuda, Kimura Masami, Bussan vice-president, and Magoshi Kyōhei, who was in charge of Mitsui Bussan's internal affairs. To these four we could add Komuro. Among the thirty-seven remaining names, four had been independent promoters of the Tokyo Fūhansen Kaisha. Others of major importance were: Asano Sōichirō, an industrialist, Matsumoto Jūtarō and Toyama Shūzō, leading Osaka bankers, and Amamiya Keijirō, a rising capitalist based in Yokohama.[5]

Statistics on the stock subscription campaign further suggest the broad representation in the KUK. By April 27, 1883, the KUK had secured pledges for 62 percent of its private stock (see Table 17). By May 17 this total had reached ¥ 2,161,900. Of this, 41.4 percent came from Tokyo, Osaka, and Kyoto. The other 58.6 percent came from the prefectures.[6] Also, of the forty-two promoters, only twenty lived in these three cities. Finally, the amount pledged by May, presumably representing in large part commitments from the promoters, still accounted for less than two-thirds of the authorized private capital.[7]

TABLE 17 KUK Stock Subscriptions,
        as of April 27, 1883
                (¥)

	Amount Pledged	Amount Paid Up
Tokyo Fūhansen Kaisha	371,100	249,980
Hokkaido Un'yu Kaisha	218,400	72,355
Etchū Fūhansen Kaisha	150,000	150,000
Total from 3 companies	739,500	472,335
Total from stock drives	1,367,550	201,150
Total	2,107,050	673,485

Source: KUK Report of April 30, 1883, *SEDS,* pp. 62–63.

A brief explanation of the Japanese method of stock subscription is necessary to elucidate the meaning of the KUK's stockholding. Most Japanese stocks had a par value of ¥ 50. This par value was relatively high, and commercial organizations frequently sought to reduce it. The government, however, wanted stable stockholders who possessed substantial amounts of property. To reduce the financial burden of this high par value, companies used a system of payment by installments. In the early 1880s an investor could subscribe to a stock issue but would not have to purchase it outright. Under the system, which came into common use in the late 1880s and 1890s, the stockholder paid a certain percentage of the par value of each share when he subscribed. The remainder was paid in installments at times determined by the company.[8]

It is not known whether the KUK used a pledge system, allowing the stockholder to pay for the rest of his subscription whenever he was able to, or an installment system, requiring all stockholders to make payments at specific times. The data in Table 17, however, show that whereas 62 percent of the company's private stock had been subscribed to by April 1883, only 20 percent had actually been paid up. Because of this slow payment, in determining who owned the KUK, its stockholding cannot be regarded as a fixed, stationary matter. Especially after the business began to decline in 1884, major changes occurred in the pattern of holding. According to the company's revised articles of association, the capital was to be fully paid up by the end of 1885 (article 11), but the merger with Mitsubishi speeded up this process. Table 18 gives a chronology of the paying up of the stock and shows that the 1884 changes in holding began when about one-third of the private stock remained to be paid up.

The major protagonist in these stock changes seems to have been Mitsui. According to the *Mainichi shinbun* report of September 12, 1885, the Mitsui Bank had sold all its KUK shares when the stock price had fallen to ¥30 in late 1884.[9] The Mitsui Bank originally had close ties with the KUK, for it had been designated to receive deposits from stock purchases.[10]

To confuse things further, the *Mainichi* report claimed that Mitsui Bussan bought a great portion of the shares sold by the Mitsui Bank. One scholar offers a different view. Without referring to either the bank or Bussan he states that Mitsui quickly sold its stocks when it saw the KUK's prospects worsening.[11] No dates are specified for these sales, but the view that Mitsui sold most of its stock has some corroborating evidence in the events of August 1885. Katō Masayoshi, who became KUK vice-president in June 1885, remarked that at the KUK's Extraordinary General Meeting in August 1885 the government and company officers (*jūyaku*) together possessed less than 50 percent of the company's stock. Since the government portion of KUK stock was more than 40

TABLE 18 Paying up of KUK Stock, 1883–1885

	Total (¥)	Government	Private (A)	No. of Private Holders (B)	Amount per Private Holder (¥) (A/B)
April 27, 1883	673,485	—	673,485	—	—
End of 1883	1,479,325	170,000	1,309,325	—	—
End of 1884	3,904,382	1,470,000	2,434,382	5,509	441.9
Sept. 30, 1885	6,000,000	2,600,000	3,400,000	4,614	736.9

Source: Compiled from KUK Business Reports, *SEDS*, pp. 62, 92–93, 117.

percent, Katō implied that Mitsui, whose votes would be cast by officers representing it, held less than 10 percent of the KUK shares.[12]

Other evidence, however, demonstrates that Mitsui did have substantial control over the KUK in the sense that creditors as well as stockholders can exercise power in a company. This is a list of individuals, institutions, or both with claims against the KUK at the time of the merger. Before the N.Y.K. was legally established, Mitsubishi and the KUK agreed to have the new company take responsibility for debts of ¥1,069,758. The claimants to this debt held a total of 1,069 certificates, each worth ¥1,000. Iwasaki Hisaya (Yatarō's son), with 543 certificates (50.8 percent of the total), held all of Mitsubishi's claim. The remaining 526 claims were all against the debt of the former KUK.

The largest KUK certificate holder, with 165 claims, was Ikeda Shigemasa of the Tokio Marine Insurance Company. Next came Shibusawa Eiichi with 95 and Nishimura Torashirō, a Mitsui Bank official, with 40. All other Mitsui officials on the list were connected with Mitsui Bussan. They held 65 claims, giving Mitsui 105, or 20 percent of the KUK total. If these are added to Shibusawa's claims (in view of his close association with Mitsui), there would be 200 certificates, or 38 percent, a substantial proportion. This list, however, seems to represent bank loans (Shibusawa and Nishimura) and unpaid bills. While it shows that Mitsui and Shibusawa were financing KUK business, it does not provide evidence on stockholding percentages.[13]

This variety of sources, then, leads to two conclusions: (1) it is misleading to say unequivocally that Mitsui "owned" the original KUK; (2) it is inaccurate to claim that "the Mitsui interests" merged with Mitsubishi to form the N.Y.K. This second conclusion will be examined in more detail in Chapter 6.

One more interpretive problem regarding KUK stockholding involves Kansai representation. The discussion of the sale of Colonization Office assets in Chapter 4 suggested that the failure of all interested concerns to coalesce meant that future anti-Mitsubishi shipping alliances would be less than national in composition.

The Iwasaki biographies, though, have argued that "the private capital of the KUK was centered on Mitsui-related interests and the Kansai business world (*zaikai*)."[14] I have argued that the Kansai *zaikai*, which founded the Kansai Bōekisha, did not participate financially in the KUK. The only major financial magnates from the Kansai among the 42 KUK promoters were Toyama Shūzō and Matsumoto Jūtarō. They were exceptions. The most representative figures in the Kansai *zaikai* were the promoters of the Kansai Bōekisha. None of these men, who number 21, appears on the list of the 42 KUK promoters.[15] The Mitsui-Kansai alliance theory cannot stand as a generalization.

In summary, then, the KUK's largest stockholder was the government, but private interests held a majority of its shares. Especially in its early stages its largest private investor was probably Mitsui. However, there were a significant number of other powerful capitalists among the company's promoters. They represented a variety of industries like shipbuilding, mining, and trading, and also included landowners and rice merchants. Finally and perhaps most significantly for day-to-day management, many representatives of local shipowners entered the company. They included some former officials of the Hokkaido Colonization Office, executives of the three constituent companies, and several smaller shipowners who were entering a large shipping company for the first time. In short, the KUK was a patchwork of diverse interests. It was pitted against a gigantic, unified concern, managed, in legend, by one man, Iwasaki Yatarō, and, in fact, by a tightly knit group of his disciples.

THE BATTLE OF THE SEA LANES. The struggle between Mitsubishi and the KUK was the fiercest business competition in the Meiji period. Commentators have described it as a veritable Armageddon. Shibusawa's biographer wrote that "in a way, all Japan was involved in this struggle. Whether Japan would become an industrial nation under the collective system as the Viscount [Shibusawa] would have it so, or under the monopolistic scheme as was advocated by Iwasaki, was forever to be decided by the outcome of this fight." The heart of the competition was in the Yokohama-Kobe and Yokohama-Yokkaichi lines. A former N.Y.K. president has called these lines the two companies' Sekigahara, an allusion to the decisive battle of 1600 won by the forces of Toku-gawa Ieyasu.[16]

The KUK officially commenced its business on January 1, 1883, but the competition emerged gradually. The KUK still lacked the ships to challenge Mitsubishi. At first it operated only small steamers and sailing ships transferred from the Ministry of Agriculture and Commerce and the three constituent companies. Early in 1883, an overseas trip by KUK President Itō Shunkichi, who was assisted by the peripatetic Captain Brown, brought the company sixteen new ships totaling 23,209 tons. All met the government's directive that they be less than two years old. During 1884 the KUK added several more ships, so that the quality of its fleet far surpassed Mitsubishi's. In response Mitsubishi ordered two new ships in 1884, the only large ones it purchased between the Satsuma Rebellion and the formation of the N.Y.K.[17]

The new KUK ships purchased by Itō, however, took a long time to reach Japan. At most only four arrived in 1883; nine came between July and December 1884; and three more in January 1885. As a result Mitsubishi held the advantage in 1883, for the KUK still relied mainly on sailing ships. According to a KUK estimate of sailing time between ports, even with a good wind its ships required 8 days for the Tokyo-Osaka run; 18 days for Niigata-Tokyo; 20 days for Fushiki-Tokyo; 15 days for Niigata-Osaka; and 13 days for Fushiki-Osaka. Mitsubishi ships, even at nine knots, held a much stronger competitive position, covering the Tokyo-Osaka route in 2 days.[18]

During its first year and a half, the KUK ran mostly irregular lines. They extended to each region of the country and overseas to Inch'ŏn in Korea and to Shanghai. By mid-1884 the company was operating thirty irregular lines, about twenty-five of which used Yokohama as their embarkation port. As the new ships began arriving, the KUK assigned them to the key routes between Yokohama and Kobe, lines for which Mitsubishi was already receiving

government subsidies. Both companies stationed their most qualified personnel in the ports of call. As the competition intensified,
the most popular slogan became "the KUK has ships but no men;
Mitsubishi has men but no ships." "Ships" have already been discussed; Figure 4 shows the positions of the "men." Some, especially
the branch managers, became prominent during the competition,
as Mitsubishi gave its branches expanded authority to enable a
quicker response to KUK tactics.[19]

In addition to the KUK's long wait for new ships, it took a
year or more before the competitive rate cutting of the two companies became severe. Mitsubishi began the 1883 competition with
a 10 percent rate reduction. The height of the competition, however, was not reached till 1884. By then second-class passenger
fares were down 20 percent from early 1883 levels (from ¥7 to
¥5.5, for example, on the Kobe-Yokohama run). Also, by late
1884 freight rates for rice on most routes were 35 percent lower
than they had been in 1882. During those two years, rates for rice
shipments of 100 *koku* from Niigata to Tokyo had fallen from
¥100 to ¥65.[20]

There is some question whether these rate reductions were
solely the result of the competition or whether they were also
caused by the Matsukata deflation. Sasaki Seiji has argued the latter
case. He has given figures to show a slight drop in rates between
early 1881 and 1882, though no reduction exceeded 8 percent and
most were much less. The size of the continued decline after early
1882 was certainly due more to the competition than to the deflation.[21]

Mitsubishi also carried out a retrenchment of its overseas lines
in 1884. In April it discontinued its Hong Kong line (begun in
1879) and then its Ryukyu line. Mitsubishi's passenger fares to
the various Korean ports had also fallen by 20–30 percent between
mid-1882 and mid-1884.[22] The impact of the competition, however, fell most heavily on domestic shipping (see Table 19). There
is no marked dissimilarity in the percentage breakdown of Mitsubishi's income by lines between 1884 and 1885; indeed the distribution pattern of 1883 continues. Nevertheless, the 1885 figures

FIGURE 4 KUK and Mitsubishi Management,
        1883–1884

KUK

Executive Directors (*riji*)	Komuro Shinobu, Hori Motoi
—Managers (*shihainin*), Head Office	Akai Zenpei, Ōtawara Noritaka
—Kobe Branch	Sasaki Otoya
—Yokohama Branch	Miyaji Sukesaburō
—Hakodate Branch	Sonoda Saneatsu

Mitsubishi

General Director (*jimu sōkan*)	Kawada Koichirō
General Manager (*kanji*)	Shōda Heigorō
—Accounting Department	Asada Masabumi (Shōda Heigorō)
—General Affairs Department	Nihashi Motonaga
—Business Department	Uchida Kōsaku
—Kobe Branch	Yoshikawa Taijirō
—Yokohama Branch	Kondō Renpei
—Hakodate Branch	Funamoto Ryūnosuke

Source: KD, p. 133; *NYK 50 nenshi*, p. 47; *SEDS*, p. 83.

Note: I am not certain in the case of the KUK whether the *riji* managed directly or through the Head Office's *shihainin*. Similarly, in Mitsubishi's case it is not clear whether the *jimu sōkan* managed directly or through the *kanji*. (Shōda seems to have taken charge of the Accounting Department again in 1884.) As for the personnel stationed on the main lines, the KUK's Miyaji was considered an expert on shipping matters; Sasaki, from Shimonoseki, was one of the company's 42 promoters, and he later continued on in the N.Y.K. For Mitsubishi, Yoshikawa and Kondō were both future N.Y.K. presidents.

are only for the first nine months of the year (that is, up to the time of the merger). To compare the totals of each year we must project the figures on an annual basis. The Shanghai line, for example, would have an income of about ¥400,000, a relatively small dip, considering that Mitsubishi had reduced service from four to three ships in September 1884. Ships taken from the Hong Kong and Shanghai lines were used to strengthen Mitsubishi's coastal services, but projections for 1885 domestic income

TABLE 19 Mitsubishi Income by Lines
(¥)

Line	Freight	Passenger	Total	%
1884				
Domestic	1,377,805	413,829	1,791,634	(74.9)
Shanghai	266,939	201,095	468,034	(19.6)
Hong Kong	49,715	5,124	54,839	(2.3)
Vladivostok	46,681	13,103	59,784	(2.5)
Others	7,566	11,052	18,618	(0.8)
Total	1,748,706	644,203	2,392,909	
1885				
Domestic	866,659	387,124	1,253,783	(77.5)
Shanghai	186,278	112,935	299,213	(18.5)
Vladivostok	43,384	7,293	50,677	(3.1)
Others	7,686	5,731	13,417	(0.8)
Total	1,104,007	513,083	1,617,090	

Source: M Sha shi, XI, 452–453; XII, 703–704.

Note: Silver yen values used in computation: 1884, ¥1.097; 1885, ¥1.0696 (Cf. Table 11). The respective percentages for 1883 were: domestic, 73.5; Shanghai, 18.6; Hong Kong, 5.3; Vladivostok, 1.7; others, 0.9.

still fall short of 1884 totals, despite the increase in the number of ships on domestic routes, showing that income per ship on these routes fell in response to the competition.

Cutbacks and rate reductions were not the most spectacular aspect of the struggle. The competition's notoriety arose from the reckless utilization of the ships, mainly through excessive speed and duplication in departure schedules. These practices became so common that the competition was dubbed the "Sumida River Boat Race." A climax was reached on October 21, 1884, when a Mitsubishi sailing ship of 715 tons bound for Nagasaki from Yokohama collided with the *Yamashiro Maru,* the largest ship in the KUK fleet, just off the eastern coast of the Miura Peninsula, south of Tokyo. The Mitsubishi ship sank. A legal battle ensued that was settled several months later only when Navy Minister Kawamura Sumiyoshi ordered the KUK to pay Mitsubishi an indemnity of ¥20,000.

In the meantime the increasing danger to passengers, freight, and mail finally prompted government intervention in December 1884 when the Ministry of Agriculture and Commerce ordered the companies to abandon the duplications in their schedules.[23] In general, by the end of 1884, government leaders were having second thoughts about the competition because of the deteriorating business results of both companies.

Mitsubishi may still have had an advantage over the KUK in ships during 1883, but the KUK's competitive strength certainly exceeded Mitsubishi's expectations, at least if we can judge from the latter's accounts. Mitsubishi's income had fallen by 16.9 percent between 1881 and 1882 (see Table 9), a decline attributable mainly to the Matsukata deflation and perhaps also to competition from the KUK's constituent shipping companies. But Mitsubishi did not view this decline as the beginning of a trend. Instead, it budgeted for moderate increases of 9.5 percent in freight and 1.2 percent in passenger income for 1883. Thus the actual results for 1883 must have been a shock, especially in freight, where income was 33.4 percent off the projected amount. Passenger income was 10.9 percent below that projected, and, overall, the company suffered a deficit of ¥45,324.[24] On the other hand, the KUK showed a gross profit of ¥145,152, a figure still low enough that the government had to forego its 2 percent dividend. Little was left over for dividends because payments into the KUK's reserve funds were taken from the gross profit. The modest profits in 1883 allowed the company to pay into only two of its three reserve funds (Table 20). This left the KUK with a net profit of ¥77,582. Compared with Mitsubishi's deficit, this was not bad, but in view of the ¥600,000 profit estimated in the company's stockholders pamphlet, 1883 must have been as great a disappointment to the KUK as it was to Mitsubishi, even though it was the KUK's first year of operation. When the modest profit

TABLE 20 KUK Profit Distribution,
        August 1882–1883

(¥)

Gross profit		145,152
Less: 1st reserve fund (insurance)	40,135	
2nd reserve fund (repairs)	27,435	
	67,570	67,570
Net profit		77,582
Stockholders dividend		76,351
Earnings retained		1,231

Source: Compiled from the KUK's First Business Report, *SEDS*, pp. 92–93.

turned to a deficit in 1884, the company was already frightened and on the run. By 1885 Mitsubishi was able to edge out the KUK in profitability (see Table 21). Nevertheless, these profit figures by themselves are misleading. Analysis of the income and depreciation policies of the two companies is needed to evaluate business performance more accurately.

Table 21 gives the impression of an uninterrupted decline in the KUK's business during its three years of operation. The income figures in Table 22 provide more data for comparing the 1884 deficits of the two companies and significantly qualify the KUK's 1883 results. First, the figures for income per ton owned (item a) are an accurate measurement of Mitsubishi's decline because the number of Mitsubishi's ships was relatively constant over the two years. The same averages for the KUK are less meaningful. They are calculated with fixed figures for both income and ships, but the number of KUK ships (item 1) was steadily increasing. The more significant statistics are the average incomes per unit transported. The average income per passenger (item 2) suggests that passenger fares were relatively stable in 1884. Clearly, however, the freight statistics tell the story of the competition. Mitsubishi managed to carry virtually the same amount of freight in

TABLE 21 KUK and Mitsubishi Profits
as Percentages of Assets and Income,
1883–1885

(¥)

	Assets	Income	Gross Profits	Percentage	
	(A)	*(B)*	*(C)*	*(C/A)*	*(C/B)*
KUK					
Aug. 1882–1883	2,210,644	475,331	145,152	6.6	30.5
1884	4,409,634	1,054,015	–25,402	–0.6	–2.4
1885 (to Sept.)	6,482,239	1,291,366	–332,982	–5.1	–25.8
Mitsubishi					
1883	7,426,659	3,735,966	–45,324	–0.6	–1.2
1884	7,405,483[a]	3,026,308	–216,949	–2.9	–7.1
1885 (to Sept.)	6,521,668[b]	2,296,998	–5,569[c]	–0.1	–0.2

Source: KUK Business Reports, *SEDS*, pp. 86–100, 116–122; and "Saimatsu zassai," in *M Sha shi*, X–XII.

Notes: [a]Calculated by deducting accounts payable and receivable from both sides of the ledger. This, of course, is a violation of sound accounting, but these accounts appear only in the 1884 assets table, and I am concerned with trends, not with precise measurement for one given year. Deducting these figures is the only way to compare meaningfully the results of 1884 with earlier years. Second, the assets for 1884 are divided in the account books into paper currency (*tsūka*) and silver yen (*ginka*). The silver yen is calculated at ¥1.097 (see Ibid., XI, 399) and a unified figure is used in this table.

[b]From the report submitted at the time of the merger and thus is somewhat arbitrary. There are no asset tables comparable to earlier years in Mitsubishi's regular business reports for 1885.

[c]This low deficit figure (Ibid., XII, 644–645) has been overlooked by many scholars who list instead a deficit of approximately ¥207,000. This large figure is drawn from a table in Shukuri, p. 435 (also in *SEDS*, p. 101) which is grossly inaccurate, for it lists freight and passenger income in paper currency only. When the silver yen income is included, the deficit figure is reconciled with these official accounts. Cf. *M Sha shi*, XII, 642–643.

1884 as it had in 1883, but its freight income dropped by 24.9 percent. But Mitsubishi's rate of income decline was nothing compared to the KUK's. The KUK had to carry 9 times as much freight just to increase its income by 2.4 times. In fact the ¥9.46 received

TABLE 22 KUK and Mitsubishi Shipping Income, 1883–1884

Item	1883 Mitsubishi Steam	1883 KUK Steam	1883 KUK Sail	1884 Mitsubishi Steam	1884 KUK Steam	1884 KUK Sail
Ships						
Number (1)	32	13	12	33	24	15
Tonnage (NT)	21,597	5,266	3,173	23,026	13,804	4,419
Average	674	405	264	697	575	295
Passengers						
Number	195,267	14,377		157,498	67,499	
Income (¥)	817,979	41,087		634,462	196,113	
Average (2)	4.18	2.85		4.02	2.90	
Freight						
Tonnage	555,207	35,535		551,670	286,539	
Income (¥)	2,216,001	336,200		1,663,214	807,953	
Yen per ton shipped (3)	3.99	9.46		3.01	2.81	

TABLE 22 (continued)

Item	1883		1884	
	Mitsubishi	*KUK*	*Mitsubishi*	*KUK*
Total	3,033,980	337,287	2,297,676	1,004,066
Income (¥)				
Yen per ship ton owned[a]	140.5	44.7	99.8	55.1

Source: NYK 50 nenshi, pp. 48–49. This table contains only direct shipping income, thus the totals differ from income figures in Table 21. Also, figures on Mitsubishi's small number of sailing ships do not appear. The Mitsubishi NT listed here falls below the government's minimum standard. I have computed all averages except for [a], which appears in *Yokohama-shi shi*, p. 554. Numbered references (1, 2, 3) are discussed in the text.

per ton shipped (item 3) in 1883 is so high that one suspects the company was carrying government freight at extra high rates in the form of indirect subsidies. Obviously this ¥9.46 figure explains the "modest profit" of 1883. If it was the result of some temporary subsidy, then we could conclude that even in 1883 the KUK never really got afloat financially. Instead of an "uninterrupted decline," then, the company might well have given its best performance in 1884.

The profit picture given in Table 21 is also obscured by a discrepancy in the two companies' accounting policy regarding ship depreciation. During 1883 and 1884 Mitsubishi had averaged an annual ¥297,860 in depreciation. But in 1885 it did not depreciate at all. From the standpoint of profit, the crucial thing about depreciation is that it appears in the profit and loss statement as an expense. Therefore, by not depreciating in 1885, Mitsubishi avoided a substantial "expense" and ended up with an artificially small deficit. If it had depreciated in 1885, Mitsubishi's deficit would have been as large as in 1884. We cannot conclude, then, that its business performance "improved." On the other hand, the KUK did not depreciate its ships in any of these years. As with Mitsubishi in 1885, the KUK's deficits for both 1884 and 1885 were artificially small.

One more financial difference between the two companies must be noted. Mitsubishi received ¥748,400 in government subsidies during these three years. During the same period operating subsidies to the KUK were exactly ¥26,000. Can we still argue that the government established the KUK in order to overthrow Mitsubishi?[25]

EMERGING BUSINESS PATTERNS. While Mitsubishi and the KUK were busy tearing each other apart, a new challenger arrived, the Osaka Commercial Shipping Company (Osaka Shōsen Kaisha, or O.S.K.), an association of fifty-five shipowners possessing ninety-three ships, established on May 1, 1884, with a capital of ¥1.2 million. It took several decades for this company to reach the general level of the N.Y.K., but it made a profit in its first two years of operation. In fact its income of ¥532,000 in 1884 and ¥938,000 in 1885 compares favorably with the KUK's.[26] Although the O.S.K.'s business in its first years was concentrated primarily in the Inland Sea, formation of this firm made it less likely that either the KUK or Mitsubishi would escape the flow of red ink so long as they continued their competition.

The O.S.K. was probably the most typical case of small local shipowners amalgamating to form a larger company. Indeed, at the time of its formation the O.S.K. owned only one ship over 500 tons. We can trace the origins of the O.S.K. to the Satsuma Rebellion, when small shipowners sprang up "like mushrooms after a rain" to meet the demand for shipping around the government supply base in Osaka. The subsequent business slump and renewed competition prompted the Osaka governor to try to regulate the business. When his efforts failed, the shipowners banded together and in late 1882 approached Sumitomo's Hirose Saihei for help in promoting a new company. Hirose's original planning proved abortive, but participants later reached agreement and on April 29, 1884, received a permit from the Osaka governor to commence operations.

The composition of the O.S.K. also buttresses my argument that the Kansai *zaikai* did not invest heavily in the KUK. The Kansai *zaikai* decided to support its own local firm instead of the KUK. In fact, when Shinagawa Yajirō toured the Kansai on his stock promotion drive for the KUK in late 1882, initial planning for the O.S.K. was already underway. According to Hirose, Shinagawa gave his support to the idea of a separate company in the Kansai.[27] Many of the O.S.K.'s initial stockholders were the local shipowners who had led the movement for amalgamation. Also, several of the large stockholders, including Hirose Saihei and Tanaka Ichibē, had been promoters of the Kansai Bōekisha. Hirose became the O.S.K.'s first president, Tanaka its third. In short, the forces that had opposed Mitsubishi in 1881 failed to build a united alliance, and now, in the form of the O.S.K. and the KUK they were competing with one another.[28]

So far this discussion of the Mitsubishi-KUK competition has emphasized the two companies' deficits. But the resolution of the conflict owed much to the black ink in Mitsubishi's non-shipping enterprises. These outside interests received a hefty injection in June 1884 when Mitsubishi secured the lease of the government-owned Nagasaki Shipyard. The government had been unable to make the shipyard profitable. Between 1871 and 1881 the average annual profit from the shipyard had been a mere ¥1,817.[29] On this basis, Yatarō's biographer has claimed that the government's motivation in leasing the yard to Mitsubishi was to pass on its debts to Mitsubishi, thereby indirectly helping the KUK. As in so many other instances, Yatarō's biographer has probably exaggerated the government's anti-Mitsubishi policy. Once Mitsubishi took over the shipyard it became profitable, clearing ¥50,000 in 1885.[30]

The Nagasaki Shipyard, then, contributed to the further diversification of Mitsubishi's profits. Table 15 showed that this trend toward a varied source of profits had become noticeable in 1881–1883. By 1884 and 1885 Mitsubishi's profit profile had been totally transformed. Profits were now concentrated in outside enterprises, especially the Takashima Mine, while shipping lagged behind with constant deficits. Table 23, a continuation of Table 15, indicates that the Takashima Mine had become the only reliable moneymaker among Mitsubishi's enterprises. By 1885 its performance had matched the level of shipping during the 1879–1882 period. The mine's constantly rising percentages of total Mitsubishi profits was achieved despite this relatively slack period for the output of the mine, a decline which Kobayashi Masaaki has attributed to a reduction in sales caused by the Matsukata deflation and a falloff in demand from Mitsubishi ships in 1883–1885.[31] Nevertheless, except for 1883, the mine's profits rose steadily in absolute terms as well as in the percentage of Mitsubishi's overall profits. Mitsubishi's management became profitable even though the output of the mine in 1885 was only marginally better than the performance achieved by Gotō Shōjirō in 1880 (see Table 24). Kobayashi attributes this to improved organization and skillful utilization of labor and technology that led to a productivity increase of 3.5 between April 1881 and December 1887. During that

TABLE 23 Index of Profits of Mitsubishi Enterprises,
1883–1885

(Index = 100)[a]

	1883	*1884*	*1885*
Shipping	—	—	—
Subunits	13.3	23.5	12.1
Takashima Mine	54.6	87.0	91.6
Yoshioka Copper Mine	0.3	0.1	8.1
Nagasaki Shipyard	—	8.3	9.3
Government subsidies	40.3	55.3	36.7

Source: Hatade, *Mitsubishi,* pp. 28–29.

Note: [a]The index stands for total Mitsubishi profit. The total greatly exceeds 100 in 1884 and 1885 because of the large deficits in shipping. The income figures in Table 21 include subsidies, but in this table (and Table 15) subsidies are listed separately from the shipping account.

TABLE 24 Takashima Mine: Profits and Production,
1880–1888

	Mitsubishi profits *(¥)*	*Production* *(tons)*
1880[a]	—	230,895
1881[a]	244,495 (April to Dec.)	237,666
1882	416,699	254,687
1883	377,164	236,881
1884	422,665	226,912
1885	503,542	258,188
1886	—	270,397
1887	—	302,086
1888	—	306,548

Sources: Combined from Hatade, *Mitsubishi,* p. 29; and Kobayashi Masaaki, *Nihon no kōgyōka to kangyō haraisage,* p. 173.

Note: [a]The mine was under the management of Gotō Shōjirō through March 1881. Profit figures are not entered until April 1881.

period the cost of producing one ton of coal fell from ¥4.64 to ¥1.32.[32] The productivity increase demonstrates that Mitsubishi was focusing more and more attention on the mine.

This shifting attention toward the more profitable outside enterprises contrasts sharply with the shipping deficits of 1884–1885. By then, allocating more resources to mining as a long-term strategy had begun to take precedence over the tactical use of mine profits as a support for shipping. This shift, alongside the deficits in shipping, forced Mitsubishi to reconsider its commitment to the industry. What Mitsubishi had done by late 1884 was to build up a network of outside enterprises that ensured the continuance of its business stability in the event of a withdrawal from shipping.

The Nagasaki Shipyard and the Takashima Mine, both profitable enterprises, were relatively independent of Mitsubishi's main shipping business in that they could sell their products or services to anyone. In contrast, Mitsubishi's Exchange Office had originally been set up to support Mitsubishi's shipping. Although it had diversified its services between 1878 and 1881, it was still closely tied to the main shipping enterprise. The decline in Mitsubishi's shipping income from ¥5.9 million in 1881 to ¥3 million in 1884 constituted a devastating blow to the Exchange Office. The office could no longer conduct its normal financing of shippers and had begun to accumulate a deficit. Finally, in November 1884 Mitsubishi decided to close it.[33] The history of the Exchange Office suggests that Mitsubishi could not operate shipping profitably independently of the office's financing of shippers. It had played an indispensable backup role in Mitsubishi's 1876 competition with the P. & O. and in the building of its monopolistic position in 1880–1881. Abandoning the exchange business signified a foreshadowing of Mitsubishi's later decision to withdraw from the direct management of shipping.[34]

The growing diversity of Mitsubishi's profits and the closing of operations dependent on shipping were part of a pattern, in effect, a strategy of withdrawal from shipping. The central significance of the KUK-Mitsubishi competition, then, was not so much who won, but how the battle changed the business structure of both Japanese shipping and Mitsubishi.

EARLY NEGOTIATIONS. The possibility of a merger between Mitsubishi and the KUK had become a topic of discussion by 1884, albeit in hushed tones. In fact, as early as April 1884 Godai Tomoatsu had urged Yatarō to seek an amalgamation of the two. It was only by late 1884, though, that the effects of the competition began to reverberate inside the KUK. Rumors circulated that the firm's top executives had already submitted written resignations.[35] Finally, in December the prospect of a merger was raised inside the government.

Because of its deficit the KUK was unable to pay its dividend at the end of 1884, and it petitioned the Ministry of Agriculture and Commerce for a ¥250,000 loan. A meeting of state ministers, councillors, and ministers was called to discuss the petition. Secretary to the Council of State, Hijikata Hisamoto, kept a record of the discussion:

> On about the 22nd or 23rd of December 1884 there was a request from Saigō and Shinagawa for a ¥250,000 loan. The reason was that . . . the government would lose prestige if the KUK was unable to pay any dividends even though it was a government-protected company. . . But I opposed the request and said it was not good for the government to intervene. When there are profits, it is natural for a private company to provide a dividend. However, it would not be proper for the government to cover up the fact that there was no profit by giving special aid in times of deficit. Do not Mitsubishi and the KUK both belong to the same Japan? If the government helps only one of them, it will prompt a fratricidal quarrel, and if both should go bankrupt, the ones who would take their place would be the English and American companies. For that reason, in the present situation the government should naturally work to merge the two companies and thus reassure the stockholders. I argued, however, that if a merger were impossible, the government should dissolve both companies and create a new shipping company. Because he was impartial, Saigō said, "Really, what you say is true." Navy Minister Kawamura also commented, "That is a very reasonable opinion," Both state ministers, Arisugawa and Sanjō, just laughed. Itō

and Yamagata said "We cannot decide this matter on the spot today," and the discussion ended on that note. Shinagawa was very angry, but after that this problem [that is, the loan] was not debated.[36]

Hijikata's memory either failed him or he did not reckon with the likes of Shibusawa Eiichi. Early in 1885 Shibusawa intervened with the government to secure the dividend for the KUK. On February 2, 1885, he wrote to Inoue:

> Yesterday I visited Prince Itō regarding the subsidy for the KUK and explained the situation. I asked whether the government could grant ¥160,000 for us to pay the dividend (at 9 percent) to our stockholders this term. He said that the government cannot give us a subsidy simply in response to a petition to the Ministry of Agriculture and Commerce. However, if there is an order from the Finance Minister [Matsukata Masayoshi] to the Bank of Japan, the bank can advance the money. To make arrangements for these proceedings I visited the Finance Minister's residence today together with Itō Shunkichi. The Finance Minister introduced us to the Bank of Japan and the Yokohama Specie Bank. There we found that the term of a general loan could not be long, and moreover, the company would have to pay interest. I explained that under the present financial circumstances of the company, we could not pay our dividend by means of a loan. I made another request of the Finance Minister, but he said the government could not simply grant the money. . . Given the financial situation which I have pointed out, if the government aided us by means of a loan, *we would not be able to announce anything about it to the stockholders* [emphasis added].
>
> I request that your Excellency discuss this matter with Prince Itō and reexamine the issue so that we may receive a grant directly from the Finance Ministry. . . Since Itō Shunkichi and I intend to visit your residence tomorrow, we have postponed our stockholders meeting until the tenth of this month, but we will not be able to delay it any longer than that. We are really at the point where we can neither advance nor retreat.[37]

Shibusawa apparently failed to secure the direct grant from the government, but the company did obtain a loan. The details were recorded in the KUK's second business report submitted to the government on March 3, 1885:

> Although there were no profits to implement reserve funds 1 and 2 or, of course, to distribute to our stockholders, the company devised a plan

to provide a dividend. We petitioned the government to lend us an appropriate sum under an arrangement to repay it when we are able to build up our No. 3 reserve fund, as recorded in article 58 of our articles of association. Through a special favor the government acceded to our request and lent us ¥160,000. Consequently, we will make up our present ¥25,402 deficit in 1885, and we will provide the stockholders dividend through the money from the loan.[38]

For the first two years of the competition the government had by and large let the two companies fight the battle by themselves. With the KUK's deteriorating finances, the issue had been tossed back into the government's lap. Nonintervention was no longer a viable policy.

TOWARD MERGER: NAVIGATING IN MUDDY WATERS

ABORTIVE AGREEMENTS OF EARLY 1885. The government had established the KUK in 1882 because it believed a new company would improve the nation's shipping services. It had taken this action while Mitsubishi was caught in a three-way struggle among the government and the two new political parties. Finally, because of its increasing attention to Korean affairs, the government hoped to make the KUK a supporting agency for the navy. By early 1885, however, it had become apparent that the KUK experiment had not worked as intended. The escalating intensity of the KUK-Mitsubishi competition had brought not improvement but increasing danger and vulnerability to the nation's shipping services. Furthermore, the political context in which the KUK had been launched had now largely been by-passed. In November 1884 the Liberal Party was dissolved and in December, Ōkuma, Kōno Togama, and Maejima Hisoka had withdrawn from the Progressive Party. Finally, in early December an uprising of the pro-Japanese Korean Independence Party in Seoul led to a clash between Japanese and Chinese troops, just the kind of crisis for which the KUK had been established, but for which the competition with Mitsubishi had left it badly unprepared. In the face of another military transport emergency, unbridled competition between steamship companies had become a luxury the state could no longer afford. Clearly, the wheel had turned full circle since 1882.[39]

On January 13, 1885, Saigō summoned the leading officials of both companies to a meeting attended also by Inoue and ordered them to conclude an agreement limiting their competition. They responded with a four-point interim accord dated February 5, which is important mainly for the way it was later violated. Different interpretation arose primarily over point one, which allowed low rates only to shippers already under contract and rebates to shippers with a large amount of freight on a temporary basis. In point two the companies agreed to submit to the Shipping Bureau's arbitration in setting speed limits, because the regulation of departure schedules had proved difficult to implement.[40]

Iwasaki Yatarō died on February 7, just two days after this agreement. The six months following his death witnessed the final battles of the three-year struggle. These months were characterized by a series of deft strategic moves, highly secret negotiations, and a no-holds-barred resumption of the competition. Whether Yatarō set all this activity in motion before he died or whether Yanosuke initiated a shift in policy is a somewhat problematical issue, and it greatly complicates our efforts to discover Mitsubishi's real intentions behind its strategy. Nonetheless, the newly found surface calm between the two companies remained comparatively unruffled for the first six weeks after Yatarō's death. A working group continued negotiations over the articles of the February 5 agreement and by March 6 had extended them into a thirty-article contract. Then on March 16 Yanosuke sent a message to all branches ordering a halt to the competition with the KUK.[41]

Beneath this surface calm a last-minute scramble for advantage was taking place. It was foreshadowed in the January negotiations when Miyaji Sukesaburō, a KUK member of the working group, pressed for a March 15 date for the implementation of the agreement. Mitsubishi argued for March 1. Eventually they compromised on March 10, but behind this squabble over dates lay an explosive issue. Early in February Miyaji, as the KUK's Yokohama

branch manager, signed a contract with Ōkura Kihachirō, one of
the original KUK promoters and now general manager of the Central Tea Industry Union. The contract called for the union to ship
all its tea in KUK ships and to receive in return a 25 percent discount from the company's regular rates. Mitsubishi protested, but
the KUK insisted the contract was valid because it had been signed
before the companies had formally exchanged their thirty-point
accord on March 8.[42]

The Miyaji-Ōkura contract was typical of the deals that led to
the breaking of the KUK-Mitsubishi agreement less than a month
after it was concluded. During their negotiations the two companies had exchanged lists of shippers registered as doing business
with them. These were part of the enforcement procedures related
to point one of the February 5 agreement. On April 4 Yanosuke
wrote to Itō Shunkichi accusing the KUK of lowering its freight
rates and adding to the number of shippers registered in the lists
exchanged. This meant, argued Yanosuke, that the KUK was
giving discounts to shippers not under contract at the time of the
agreement.[43] The KUK's reply, dispatched on April 7, claimed
validity for verbal agreements reached before the March accord
and also contended that contracts with individual shippers who
were members of unions were valid even if the union's name alone
appeared in the registered lists.[44]

In the meantime, on April 6 Yanosuke had written to Matsukata, then acting minister of Agriculture and Commerce, to argue
that agreements reached in late January and signed in early February had become effective immediately. He repeated the same
accusations about the KUK made in his April 4 letter to Itō and
claimed that Mitsubishi could not protect its own business if it
continued to preserve the accord in the face of the KUK viola-
tions. Placing all the blame on the KUK, Yanosuke apologized to
Matsukata that Mitsubishi would have to take "appropriate
measures."[45] On the same day, without waiting for the KUK's
April 7 formal reply to his first letter, Yanosuke notified Itō that
Mitsubishi would be taking "interim measures."[46] Mitsubishi feared
that its freight was decreasing daily, because the KUK was adding

shippers to its lists, and on April 8 Yanosuke sent a telegram to all branch managers urging them to take appropriate action to avoid deficits.[47]

The two companies' views of the renewed competition bears heavily on their comparative strength and their later attitudes toward merger. First, the apparent unilateral timing of Mitsubishi's letters suggests a premeditated plan to resume the competition. The arguments of both companies, however, seem highly contrived. The KUK's insistence on the validity of verbal agreements and its utilization of unlisted members of contracted unions seem to be calculated attempts to evade the agreement, lending substance to Mitsubishi's accusations. On the other hand, Mitsubishi's attempt to make the agreements retroactive to January and February is contrary to the implementation date decided on in the March accord. Indeed, the correspondence implies that neither company felt comfortable with the agreement and both in their own way, one through reinterpretation, the other through repudiation, sought to resume the competition.

This is not a standard interpretation. A different approach, offered by Sasaki Seiji, has received much wider acceptance, but without sufficient scrutiny. Sasaki argues that Mitsubishi had a longer-term strategy that antedated Yatarō's death. By late 1884, he claims, Mitsubishi had realized it could not achieve victory through business competition alone. Therefore, it began buying up KUK stock while selling off some of its own securities to accumulate a preparatory fund for future competition.[48] In this view Mitsubishi used the February and March agreements simply as a tactical compromise designed to cloak its careful preparations for a final drive toward decisive victory. Sasaki sees a further pattern of deliberate deception in Yanosuke's motives behind a salary reduction campaign he launched in late February.[49] The real purpose of this campaign, he claims, was to build up reserves for the struggle with the KUK, just as Mitsubishi had done in competition with foreign firms in 1875 and 1876. The repayment of government loans, also arranged in late February, is judged to be only a surface reason for the salary reductions.[50]

Mitsubishi's strategy, however, was oriented more to its overall business operations than Sasaki suggests. Sasaki's focus, which is primarily on Mitsubishi's tactics for victory in the shipping competition, does not take into account that: (1) Mitsubishi regarded the early 1885 agreements as a means to control competition and as an initial move toward some reorganization of the industry, not simply as a tactic designed to achieve victory. (2) Mitsubishi's repudiation of the agreement in early April was prompted by a change in KUK personnel, a point Sasaki ignores. (3) Mitsubishi used its salary reductions not simply for the competition but for investments outside shipping that became important in Mitsubishi's later post-merger business.

SECRET MANEUVERS, THE KUK SHAKEUP, AND MITSUBISHI TACTICS. Four issues provide evidence regarding Mitsubishi's intentions during the competition in 1885: the formal agreements already mentioned; Mitsubishi's handling of its investments and financial obligations such as loan repayments; the change in KUK leadership; and Mitsubishi's secret maneuvers within the government.

Discussions with the government started before Yatarō's death when Mitsubishi's Kawada Koichirō began meeting secretly with Inoue Kaoru.[51] At the same time Yatarō reportedly gave his trusted follower, Okamoto Kensaburō, a slush fund of ¥400,000 to influence government officials.[52] The recipient of this bribe is often assumed to be Saigō, who came to support the merger in 1885, after having earlier called Mitsubishi an "enemy of the state."[53] Still, Saigō was among the less powerful ministers in the government. Some sources hint that Inoue received money from Mitsubishi; others attribute Inoue's new advocacy of a compromise to his sensitivity to the economic implications of the competition.[54]

Yatarō's biographer takes a different view of these attempts to influence the government. He omits any reference to bribes or to secret negotiations before Yatarō's death. Instead, he claims that Mitsubishi's policy underwent a complete change following Yatarō's death when the new leadership of Yanosuke, Kawada, and

Shōda Heigorō adopted a more flexible attitude. Only then did Mitsubishi launch secret negotiations with the government. As evidence of this flexibility, this new search for accommodation, the biographer cites a March 18 memorial from Yanosuke to Matsukata calling for far more comprehensive countermeasures than the March accord to achieve a permanent peace in the shipping business.[55] While thus absolving Mitsubishi of responsibility for the renewed competition, this official biography blames not so much the KUK but the agreement itself and the government for its willingness to accept a limited compromise.

Yatarō's biographer regards Mitsubishi's posture as defensive. It entered the secret negotiations simply to get the competition under control, to contain it so as to reach an accommodation through "other means."[56] In this view Mitsubishi did not at first anticipate a merger, the argument in favor of which came up only in the process of the secret discussions. As opposed to this Sasaki sees Mitsubishi's strategy as "offensive." He views Mitsubishi's maneuvers as surface tactics designed to camouflage the fundamental commitment to a more aggressive competition, the goal of which was victory.

New personalities entered into the competition just as the struggle resumed in early April. This involved a shakeup of KUK leadership. KUK President Itō, who was not a businessman, had never enjoyed any power in the company. In fact the first year and a half of his presidency was spent abroad purchasing ships. Shibusawa Eiichi once wrote that Itō was "nothing more than a puppet."[57] The government's decision to inject new blood in the form of a new president was probably its most decisive move throughout all of 1885.

The new president was Morioka Masazumi, a samurai from Satsuma, whose pre-Restoration exploits as an executioner amply attest to his sanguine nature. After the Restoration he turned in his sword for a more mundane career as a government official. After several promotions he became governor of Hyogo Prefecture in September 1876.[58] In March 1885 when the government asked him to assume the presidency of the KUK, he at first refused, fully recognizing the difficulties he would face. But Morioka was an appropriate choice among government officials to take the helm of a shipping company, for one of his duties as governor had been administration of the port of Kobe, and he had been instrumental in the construction of a new pier there.[59] The government eagerly sought to obtain his services. Shinagawa led a campaign of persuasion involving government ministers such as Yamagata and Matsukata as well as Tsukahara Shūzō, head of the Shipping Bureau. Eventually this succeeded and on April 7 Morioka was named junior vice-minister in the Ministry of Agriculture and Commerce as a formal prerequisite for his appointment as KUK president, which was finalized on April 9.[60]

The timing of Morioka's appointment clearly seems to be linked with Mitsubishi's renewal of the competition in early April. This linkage suggests an interpretation differing from those of both Sasaki and Yatarō's biographer. The government appointed Morioka not simply to stabilize the KUK's tottering business but to work for an accommodation and perhaps merger with Mitsubishi. Mitsubishi, with its contacts inside the government, must have known of the impending appointment of Morioka. If, as the Yatarō biographer claims, Mitsubishi's primary objective was to contain the competition, why did it choose to repudiate the March accord on April 6, one day before Morioka was appointed to the Ministry of Agriculture and Commerce in order to become KUK president? A likely explanation, in accord with the chronology of the early April KUK-Mitsubishi correspondence, is that Mitsubishi, aware of Morioka's mission to implement the March accord and work for a merger, decided to break the agreement before he became president in the hopes of getting better terms for a merger at a later date.[61]

Morioka's appointment opens up a hornet's nest of questions related to Mitsubishi's secret maneuvers. The appointment was not just a change in presidential chairs; it had wider implications for government personnel. If the "puppet" Itō was being removed, the officials who had earlier controlled the strings would now find their roles changed. Foremost among these was Shinagawa

Yajirō. Shinagawa had participated in the negotiations over the presidential appointment, but his star had clearly passed its zenith. He had already been shunted off the center stage by Mitsubishi's secret discussions with Inoue. As Shinagawa's biographer says, the "KUK governed his fate," and as the company's fortune declined, his influence within the government steadily waned.[62]

Though Morioka's appointment eventually led to a decline in Shinagawa's influence, it was not likely connected with Mitsubishi's alleged bribery. Morioka received widespread support within the government. Both Matsukata and Inoue were committed to a compromise solution, and they did not need bribes to favor Morioka's appointment, which seems to have been a decision by consensus.[63]

On the whole, the popular secondary accounts have exaggerated the significance of the maneuvering behind the scenes during the early part of 1885. The main battles were still taking place on the sea lanes. Whatever Morioka's secret mission, his first task was to investigate the broken accord with Mitsubishi. It was Morioka who compiled an April 15 report to Tsukahara containing the KUK-Mitsubishi correspondence earlier in April.[64] Also, even though Morioka had the support of the government, he could not unilaterally impose his will on the KUK. The company had not been dependent upon Itō Shunkichi for its management. That responsibility was carried by its executive directors and managers in the head and branch offices. These men guarded their independence. Furthermore, at least until late July the KUK directors gave no support to a merger with Mitsubishi. With the limited authority he enjoyed, Morioka was not able to control the course of the competition, and during the first three months of his tenure the independence of the branch managers was more conspicuous than central presidential power.

RENEWED COMPETITION, MITSUBISHI STRATEGY, AND KUK MANAGEMENT. Besides the continuing dispute over the KUK's contract with the tea union, which had a three-year term, traditional ties between shipping agents and the two companies precipitated the renewed competition. Point 3 of the February 5 accord had prohibited exclusive affiliation of passage brokers with the respective shipping companies. It ordered them instead to operate freely with both companies under regulated fees. These provisions collapsed under the pressure for renewed competition for passengers. On May 31 agents managed to obtain a 10 percent discount from the KUK for their passengers on a KUK ship bound for Kōchi. The next day passage brokers connected with Mitsubishi negotiated a similar fare reduction on a ship leaving Kobe.[65] In the next two months, the competition far surpassed in intensity even the recklessness of late 1884. The rate cutting became so severe that Mitsubishi reportedly lost ¥202,500 from May to July alone.[66] The contrast between this operating loss and Mitsubishi's investment behavior, along with the internal dynamics of KUK management, provides the key to understanding the motives of the two companies. Yet, these two issues have generally been overlooked by historians.

To Sasaki Seiji, the more intense competition in mid-1885 is evidence of Mitsubishi's careful preparation for the final struggle.[67] The key assumption in Sasaki's argument is that from late 1884 Mitsubishi had been building a preparatory fund for this ultimate battle. This view, however, overlooks the significance of how Mitsubishi was using its money in 1885.

Some essential background on Mitsubishi's activity in Hokkaido early in the decade is required to explain the company's investment policy in 1885. Earlier we noted that Mitsubishi had extended a ¥150,000 loan to the Hokkaido trading firm, Rakusan Shōkai.[68] In late 1884 this firm went bankrupt, putting its two creditor banks, the One Hundred and Nineteenth Bank of Tokyo and the One Hundred and Forty-Ninth Bank of Hakodate, into a deep financial hole. Both had invested ¥15,000 in the Rakusan Shōkai and had guaranteed the repayment of its loan to Mitsubishi, and both approached Mitsubishi about taking over their management. Since their capital and business operations had many tie-ups, Mitsubishi accepted their proposal and then had them merge. The new bank, the One Hundred and Nineteenth Bank, was capitalized at

¥430,000 (8,600 shares), and the merger contract was approved by the government on April 18, less than two weeks after the suspension of the KUK-Mitsubishi accord and Morioka's appointment. By May 28 Mitsubishi officials had acquired the 6,000 shares formally belonging to the old One Hundred and Nineteenth Bank, and then later in the summer they bought the 2,600 shares of the former One Hundred and Forty-Ninth Bank, making Mitsubishi sole owner of the new bank, the origin of the future Mitsubishi Bank.[69] All this purchasing took place in the midst of the fiercest period in the competition with the KUK, at a time when Mitsubishi was piling up over ¥200,000 in losses. In fact, the total amount of money going out of the Mitsubishi coffers in mid-1885 must have reached colossal proportions: over ¥400,000 for the bank and over ¥600,000 in repayments to the government. These figures dwarf the ¥200,000 lost in shipping competition.

Mitsubishi's enormous outlays demonstrate that conspiratorial theories, emphasizing the build-up of "competition funds," are mere speculation. There is more reason to assume that Mitsubishi's attempts to accumulate cash—the selling of securities and salary reductions—were prompted by these large expenditures, not just by the competition. If Mitsubishi was building a fund for a final victory struggle, why did it expend ¥430,000 on a bank with no relation to the competition? Mitsubishi did not intend to use the new bank to finance shipping, and it later contracted with other banks for some of the functions peformed by its former Exchange Office. Even if there is no direct evidence for the tactical conspiracy thesis that Sasaki develops, many scholars have accepted it uncritically because they view Mitsubishi simply as a shipping company intent on final victory. On the other hand, if one views Mitsubishi as a group of enterprises shifting increasingly away from shipping, then our interpretation of management's goals must change accordingly. Mitsubishi probably sought good enough terms in a future merger to retain a high degree of control in the new company that would be formed, or at least a settlement that would protect it against financial losses and assure it continued income. Certainly by mid-1885 it explicitly sought a merger, and that necessarily meant contemplating a withdrawal from direct management of shipping. The purchase of the bank, which conformed to these managerial goals, suggests that what planning Mitsubishi did for renewed competition was not geared to the narrow tactical goals exclusive to the shipping industry described by Sasaki.[70]

The KUK-Mitsubishi correspondence of early April, which Sasaki did not use, leads to a second consideration. Sasaki says little about the KUK's motivation. Popular Japanese accounts and the Western scholars who have borrowed heavily from them do likewise. They do, of course, emphasize the KUK's heavy losses, but most do not pinpoint the time when the KUK became aware of the extent of its own deficits, an awareness central to any analysis of motivation. The full extent of the loss did not become clear until July 1885. Then too, the local branch managers, more knowledgeable in shipping matters than the company directors, retained considerable independence. These facts, together with the anti-Mitsubishi attitudes of the directors demonstrate how the internal dynamics of the KUK could propel it toward renewed competition. This point is consistent with the evidence of the early April correspondence. In conclusion, both companies sought to renew the competition and both jockeyed for position, with Mitsubishi expecting to take advantage of the Morioka appointment in the hope that its rival's competitive drive would be squelched from within. A theory of long-range Mitsubishi conspiratorial planning is not necessary to explain the intensity of the competition.

There is no denying the severity of the struggle, however. When the passenger competition resumed in late May the second-class fares on the Kobe-Yokohama line stood at ¥5.5. But after the discounting in Kobe in late May and a large-scale transfer of second-class passengers to first-class cabins, the fares for passengers boarding at Kobe plummeted to ¥1.5 by June 14 and continued downward to 75 *sen* and then 55 *sen* by June 27. But by late June the severe rate cutting had spread to Yokohama, and for the westward run to Kobe fares dropped to ¥2.5 and the ¥2. Freight rates fell as well, though perhaps not quite so drastically. The rate for 100 *koku* of rice between Yokkaichi and Yokohama was reported at ¥9 on July 7, a 50 percent drop from late 1884. [71]

Just as in late 1884, some of the worst excesses occurred in the handling of ships. For the sake of speed, boilers were being worked at full capacity, often bringing funnels to a dangerous heat. Many had to put into port to cool off; with the increasing incidence of explosions, some obviously never made it. [72] The timing of this damage to the country's principal fleets could not have been worse from the government's viewpoint. Following regulations passed earlier, in April 1885 it was setting up ship inspection stations. The increasing wear on the ships was clearly one factor that inclined the government toward intervention. Before it did so, however, Mitsubishi had gained an edge over the KUK. By comparing the two companies on the Yokohama-Kobe line (Table 25), we can see that Mitsubishi increased its share from May to June in the two most important categories, freight bound for Yokohama and passengers. The KUK improved in only one category, freight outbound from Yokohama, and in this Mitsubishi still held a large lead. These results, of course, are only for the Yokohama-Kobe line, but this was the most important line in the competition.

At the height of the competition Morioka's position inside the KUK was bolstered when Katō Masayoshi became the company's new vice-president. Katō, a subordinate of Morioka during his tenure as governor of Hyogo Prefecture, had also assisted Saigō in developing distribution programs for tea, silk, and other products. He was appointed assistant junior secretary in the Ministry of Agriculture and Commerce when Morioka entered that ministry in April; in June he moved to the KUK. Katō immediately compiled a report on the company's finances and discovered that the deficit for 1885 was likely to exceed ¥1 million. [73]

On the basis of Katō's report, Morioka sent a secret proposal to Saigō on July 12. [74] He used Katō's report to include projections of the company's deficits (see Table 26) and then added his recommendations. He urged the government to merge promptly

TABLE 25 Mitsubishi-KUK Competition:
Yokohama-Kobe Line, May-June 1885

	May	*June*
Mitsubishi		
Passengers		
Total	2,055	3,208
Average—one voyage[a]	64 (36%)[b]	107 (57%)
Freight		
Yokohama—inbound	(16)75,623[c,d]	(15)64,242
average	4,726 (52%)	4,282 (56%)
Yokohama—outbound	(16) 7,495	(17)14,836
average	468 (72%)	872 (66%)
KUK		
Passengers		
Total	2,869	2,411
Average—one voyage	114 (64%)	80 (43%)
Freight		
Yokohama—inbound	(13)56,558	(11)17,162
average	4,327 (48%)	3,378 (44%)
Yokohama—outbound	(13) 2,150	(13) 5,359
average	179 (28%)	446 (34%)

Source: Sasaki Seiji, *Nihon kaiun kyōsōshi,* pp. 235–236; taken from *KS,* III, 151.

Notes: [a]One voyage is in round-trip units.

[b]Percentage figures in parenthesis represent the share of the business done by the two companies.

[c]Plain figures in parenthesis represent the number of sailings.

[d]The unit of freight is simply "articles" (*ko*) and therefore its value as a statistic is rather limited, but it may show trends over a 2-month period.

the two companies and to regulate shipping charges. The government, he said, should adopt a "policy of full protective intervention" so it could arbitrate disputes. Aside from Hijikata Hisamoto's vague suggestions in December 1884 regarding a merger, Morioka's

TABLE 26　Projected KUK Deficit for 1885
(¥)

Operating deficits:
　Actual monthly deficit: Jan. to May　¥25,000 (x5)　　　125,000
　Additional estimate for all of 1885:　¥50,000 (x12)　　　600,000

Obligations that could not be met with normal income:
　Promissory notes, payments for ship purchases,
　　ship repairs, miscellaneous expenses　　　　　　　　230,000
　Dividend　　　　　　　　　　　　　　　　　　　230,000
　Reserve funds　　　　　　　　　　　　　　　　　200,000

　　Estimated total deficit . . . . . . about ¥1.3 to ¥1.4 million

---

Source: Morioka's secret proposal to Saigō, July 12, 1885, *SEDS*, p. 107.

petition is the earliest documentary evidence of an explicit merger proposal. Its references to government intervention also provided a policy framework for the state's eventual role in the establishment of the N.Y.K.

FINAL NEGOTIATIONS. After Morioka's proposal the pace of negotiations quickened, following two tracks: Mitsubishi's discussions with the government and direct talks between Mitsubishi and Morioka. Although there is a dearth of hard information about Mitsubishi's discussions with the government early in 1885, more is known about the background of one crucial meeting in July. As noted earlier, Kawada Koichirō seems to have had close contact with Inoue Kaoru since the beginning of the year. In July Inoue advised him to meet with Itō Hirobumi and Matsukata, who at the time were in Osaka. As Kawada prepared to embark for the Kansai he took great care in choosing an assistant to accompany him, for his activities were extremely secret, known, even within the company, to no more than a few executives besides Yanosuke. Kawada chose Yamamoto Tatsuo, an able, young, but inconspicuous worker in the Yokohama branch. Yamamoto had just entered the company in 1883, but he was a future bank president, cabinet minister, and political party executive. When told by Kawada that, since his health was failing, he intended to recuperate with some sightseeing in the Kansai and then go on to inspect the shipyard in Nagasaki, the news came as a great blow to the ambitious young Yamamoto, who felt chagrined at being removed from the front lines of the battle. The two first stopped at Yokkaichi to hear reports from the region's branches and then proceeded with a leisurely visit to the Ise Shrine and some sightseeing in the area. Then suddenly, without any explanation, Kawada changed directions and headed toward Kyoto, first by rickshaw—sometimes with three pullers for extra speed—then by train. Upon reaching Kyoto the next day, Kawada finally informed Yamamoto of the purpose of the "vacation." They then left for Osaka, where they met Itō and Matsukata in a restaurant. There Kawada obtained the consent of Matsukata and Itō to a merger between Mitsubishi and the KUK. [75]

This Kansai meeting highlights the influence of Itō and Matsukata. Itō, then Imperial Household minister, [76] was preparing the Meiji Constitution, and was about to become the prime minister in the cabinet system established in December 1885. Matsukata's influence carried weight, for his deflationary program was now nearing completion. [77] Both Matsukata and Itō had played limited roles in the establishment of the KUK in 1882, and they remained more neutral throughout the shipping war than the active promoters like Inoue and Shinagawa. But by 1885 they were prepared to intervene. Their approval put the government's weight overwhelmingly behind a merger. [78]

With the government-Mitsubishi track now smooth, the next step was to open contact between Mitsubishi and Morioka. Shortly after writing his July 12 proposal, Morioka sent a secret messenger to invite Yanosuke to his residence for a meeting with himself and Katō Masayoshi. Over sake the three talked about everything except the competition until Morioka broke in:

Morioka: How long will Mitsubishi be able to continue the competition?

Yanosuke: We can go on for one more year, but after that we'll be left without even a single *mon*.

Morioka: The KUK can compete for only a hundred more days. At that point we'll be bankrupt and will fall under the control of Mitsubishi, I guess.

Yanosuke: If what you say is true, Mitsubishi will be able to win. However, even if we win, the wounds of the competition will leave us in terrible shape. When the foreign ships come, we'll be left with no competitive power and will be defeated. In the end, then, we will probably go bankrupt too.

Morioka: That's certainly true, isn't it. In that case we have no choice other than amalgamation.

Yanosuke (breaking in suddenly): You're right. That's just the point— there's no way except amalgamation. I can endure sacrifice, and for the sake of the country I want your cooperation.

Following more drinks the time came for Yanosuke to depart. As he was leaving he made one final comment to Morioka, "For Mitsubishi I have decided alone, but in your case, it will not be so easy for you to persuade your company. You'll probably need a lot of cooperation, won't you?"[79]

That he did. Immediately after he had won Yanosuke's agreement, Morioka called a KUK directors meeting, attended also by Shibusawa Eiichi. But when he brought up the question of a merger, everyone opposed him.[80] The KUK directors, cognizant of the age and generally poor condition of Mitsubishi's ships, believed that these would have to be scrapped in the not-too-distant future and that then the KUK, with its new ships, could force Mitsubishi into submission. Thus intent on preserving the independence of their company, the directors tried to isolate Morioka. They rejected the content of his July 12 proposal and prepared an antimerger proposal of their own, dispatching it to the government in late July. This proposal began with three basic requests. First, it petitioned the government to buy back the *Yamashiro Maru*, the company's largest ship. The KUK would use the funds acquired to eliminate its debts and then apply what remained to its operating capital. Second, it asked for a special charter for its Shanghai line like the one Mitsubishi had, a permit for a new line to Hong Kong, and an appropriate subsidy for both. Third, it called on the Ministry of Agriculture and Commerce to issue a special ordinance to regulate the competition. The petition also urged the hiring of (1) skilled foreigners who would handle all major ship operations (in contrast to the original directive which favored Japanese seamen) and (2) capable accountants whose reforms would generate about ¥365,000 from additional income and reduced expenses.[81]

This proposal came too late, for the directors had already struck out. On July 27 they were summoned to Inoue's office and one by one were brought before Saigō, who in effect cross-examined them. Saigō asked: "Since you advocate nonacceptance [of the merger], Morioka says that he will resign. Are you prepared to step in and shoulder the responsibility?" Each one in turn replied negatively and then agreed to the union with Mitsubishi.[82]

The next day Saigō issued an official order to the KUK to convene an Extraordinary General Meeting and at the same time informed Mitsubishi of the government's intention to see the companies merge.[83] The exasperated tone of an accompanying secret order to the two companies demonstrated that the government would no longer tolerate the shipping war:

> The competition between the two companies shows no signs of coming to an end, but the government should not be obliged to meet the unlimited demands of both companies. Can both companies permanently sustain losses exceeding the limits of their capital? Will the government remain a spectator, watching these events from the side? If Japan's shipping is destroyed, what will happen? By appropriate means both companies must combine their assets and form one large new company, avoiding the abuses of competition and planning for the expansion of shipping. Both companies should understand this point and give a prompt reply.[84]

Mitsubishi replied with a letter of acceptance dated August 1.[85]

KUK RESISTANCE TO THE MERGER. The opposition to the merger was still not dead, for the KUK had plenty of allies in the Tokyo Chamber of Commerce and Industry. On August 3 the chamber assembled to debate a petition calling on the government to supervise the competition. The petition that emerged in the next meeting on August 14 was essentially an abstract version of the KUK antimerger proposal already rejected by the government.[86] It was too late to be effective, for the KUK Extraordinary General Meeting had been scheduled for August 15.

The petition, then, was little more than a final public gesture; either that or some members were speaking with forked tongues. In the August 14 debate Shibusawa stated that government restraints on competition would not constitute unwarranted intervention. Rather, he argued, government aid and supervision would enable the two companies to maintain their separate existence. But the very next day Shibusawa attended the KUK General Meeting and spoke *in favor of* the merger: "an unavoidable thing," he said.[87] On August 17 Shibusawa's bank, the Dai Ichi Bank, *and* the Mitsui Bank concluded a contract with Mitsubishi under which the two banks would share with Mitsubishi the functions previously performed by Mitsubishi's Exchange Office.[88] Mitsubishi would continue to extend credit to shippers for the value of goods shipped, but the banks would now collect payment from purchasers within ten days receipt of notice and then forward the money to Mitsubishi. In cases where the purchaser could not pay, the goods would either be left in Mitsubishi's warehouses or the banks would extend credit to purchasers and pay Mitsubishi. Clearly, this detailed agreement could not have been drawn up overnight. Shibusawa must have known about it before the August 14 debate, even if his subordinates had negotiated it. The KUK must have had similar arrangements with the Dai Ichi and Mitsui banks. The banks' contract with Mitsubishi, therefore, signifies an end to the competition. It can be regarded not just as a contract with Mitsubishi, but as the forerunner of business relations between these two banks and the new shipping company that was about to emerge.

The KUK's stockholders assembled on August 15 to vote on the merger. Morioka outlined the proposed new company's relation to the government.[89] The company would have limited liability like the Bank of Japan, with the government having a supervisory and protective role. It would, he said, guarantee the company's profits so that the stockholders would not sustain losses from the vicissitudes of business.

Morioka's comments on profit guarantee make more concrete his July 12 proposal for "protective intervention" from the government. There were probably several reasons for the profit guarantee (which had a precedent in the case of the Japan Railway Company), but it is worth noting that the KUK directors had held out almost to the bitter end before accepting the merger. Made in the context of a promerger plea, Morioka's promise may be seen as an attempt to lure other opposition stockholders to his side. In this sense, the need to placate the stockholder was an important factor in the later subsidy program that was so much a part of the N.Y.K.'s identity.

In his plea to the stockholders, Morioka was not as forthright about the KUK's finances as he had been in his July 12 proposal. The figure he gave his audience for company losses represented only a small fraction of his earlier estimate.[90] The stockholders, then, may have been unaware of the extent of the company's deficits when they voted on the merger. If so, that would help to explain the subsequent happenings.

The KUK General Meeting was a spectacular event. It contained all those features that make political and big-business gatherings so entertaining: suggestions of vote buying, questionable legal procedures, parliamentary shenanigans, fistfights, even police intervention.[91]

Some of the disruption was initiated by Mitsubishi. Yanosuke had hired Toyokawa Ryōhei and Asabuki Eiji as agents to arrange for a few people to attend the meeting as holders of small amounts of stock and have them counter the arguments of the antimerger forces.[92] The two chosen to carry the banner of the promerger sentiment were Baba Tatsui and Ōishi Masami, former Liberal Party members. Their actions recall the similar opposition of Numa Morikazu to the KUK merger at the Tokyo Fūhansen Kaisha's General Meeting three years earlier. The intentions of

Baba and Ōishi were unknown even to the organizers of the meeting. Katō Masayoshi admitted that he did not understand why these two, who had no apparent relation to shipping affairs, were speaking so enthusiastically in favor of the merger! Only later did Toyokawa explain the scheme to him.

The antimerger voices, however, virtually drowned out those of the promerger group. Morioka, aware that he had to get through the promerger resolution no matter what, adopted a heavy-handed strategy. He resolved to move immediately for a roll call as soon as the opposition forces had finished their speechmaking, read the resolution aloud, and announce a majority in favor of the merger regardless of the actual voting results. While the arguments went back and forth Morioka rested in the chairman's seat, and when he judged the time to be right he had Katō, as the secretary of the meeting, read the resolution aloud. Then, as planned, he announced a majority in favor of the merger. Pretending not to hear the voices of protest, he immediately declared the meeting closed.[93]

Such extreme precautions may have been superfluous, for the majority of the stockholders voted for the merger anyway. Voting figures come mainly from the principal antimerger speaker, Takanashi Tetsushirō. In September he compiled a lengthy report to the KUK stockholders and had it printed in the newspapers as a public notice.[94] According to this source, the shareholders approved the merger by a vote of 3,369 to 1,273.[95] Takanashi called the decision invalid, because the articles of association required an announcement thirty days before the convening of an Extraordinary General Meeting (article 62). The government, however, had recognized the legality of the decision because of the special July 28 order. Second, 50 percent of the company's stock had to be represented at a meeting to pass major resolutions (article 63; cf. article 67). The ¥1.4 million worth of shares, whose holders had voted, represented only about 23 percent of the company's ¥6 million capital (see Table 27). Also, the KUK had a complicated voting system weighted in favor of the small stockholder. The maximum number of votes per holder was 100 (article 51). Takanashi claimed that proxy voters had cast almost twice as many

TABLE 27 KUK Stock Represented at the General Meeting,
August 15, 1885

Type of Holder	Number of Holders	Value Represented (¥)
Voters in attendance	242	509,950
Voters by proxy	411	879,800
Total	653	1,389,750

Source: Takanashi Report, *KS,* III, 182–184.

votes per holder as had voters in attendance, evidence, he felt, that some had cast more than the permitted 100 votes.

After the voting the antimerger faction followed Takanashi's lead, calling the decision invalid and struggling to cancel the verdict by dragging Morioka, who had temporarily withdrawn to an officials' lounge, onto the assembly floor. Blows were exchanged with police officers who were patrolling the hall. By evening the stockholders had gradually dispersed, but, according to secret information gathered by the police, people were waiting in ambush in the streets outside. Accordingly, Morioka and Katō spent the night in the assembly lounge, and about daybreak they returned to their homes, Morioka escorted by twelve police officers, Katō by two.[96]

ESTABLISHMENT OF THE N.Y.K.

FORMALIZING THE MERGER. One final round of parlays had to be held before the N.Y.K. could see the light of day. After the KUK's General Meeting had approved the merger, as a formal procedural matter the government wanted both the KUK and Mitsubishi to present petitions for a merger. Mitsubishi demurred. After its struggle with the KUK, Mitsubishi feared that a petition could be utilized by the company's enemies to accuse it of using government influence to gain dominance over the KUK. It preferred to shift the public burden of the decision onto the government and hoped for a merger based on a government directive.[97] The government had some last minute palpitations, and on August 22 Inoue Kaoru wrote to Tsukahara:

> I hear that Mitsubishi, which received the message from Shinagawa yesterday, does not want to present a petition on the merger, but they are supposed to reply after Kawada discusses the matter with Yanosuke. They absolutely must do this. In the event they refuse, Itō and I will work to persuade them, so please keep me informed of developments.[98]

It was thus clear within a week of the KUK General Meeting that the final negotiations would pose problems. On August 27 Inoue wrote to Itō, acknowledging that differences in public opinion were causing difficulties for the two companies. By this time he was prepared to warn against "pressing for results too soon," because, he said, "unless we debate these issues thoroughly inside the Ministry of Agriculture and Commerce, problems may arise in the future." Specifically Inoue feared that stockholders would sustain losses in the merger settlement.[99]

The question of the stockholders' interest was raised again in a confidential report dated September 2 from Morioka to three councillors, Inoue, Saigō, and Matsukata. The KUK, Morioka argued, could not have been expected to clear a profit because it had received so little government aid despite its formidable mission of overcoming Mitsubishi's monopolistic abuses. This time Morioka asked for a better deal. The government, he wrote, should provide more aid to satisfy the stockholders.[100] After much debate on Morioka's report, the government decided to guarantee an 8 percent annual dividend on all stock in the new company. Following this decision, Saigō confidentially notified company representatives of the guarantee (which was to have a fifteen-year term), and thereby "obtained their consent" for the merger.[101]

The companies then had to petition the government formally for the privileges already confidentially announced. Mitsubishi obliged on September 15. "Abandoning personal opinions and feelings and discarding even the name of Mitsubishi for the sake of the nation," it said, "we will bow to the will of the public and, owing to these unavoidable circumstances, join in the merger." The petition went on to request formally the guaranteed 8 percent dividend and other matters that had already been decided.[102]

ASSESSING THE COMPETITION: MITSUBISHI VICTORY AND KUK LEGACY. The squabble over the petition signaled the government's determination to establish its supreme authority and rid the negotiating process of troublesome disputes before they could be perpetuated in the institutions of the new company. In that sense one purpose of the petition was to obscure the results of the competition. Evidence suggests that the merger was more a victory for Mitsubishi than a compromise. From an accountant's point of view, the most evident reason for Mitsubishi's victory was the difference in outside support. This may seem paradoxical in view of the government's ¥2.6 million investment in the KUK, but this did not represent operating expenses. Certainly the government provided the KUK with a fleet of new ships. In the recklessness of the competitive struggle, however, the quality of the ships proved less decisive than the possession of a regular subsidy. Mitsubishi enjoyed this, but the KUK did not. The difference was crucial, for in accounting terms, the subsidy appears as income in the profit-and-loss statement and, therefore, is part of the earnings from which the stockholder draws his dividend. The lack of a regular subsidy was fatal to the KUK because without it the company could not pay its dividend. Mitsubishi could rebound from a ¥200,000 deficit in 1884, but a mere ¥25,000 deficit for the KUK sent shock waves through the ranks of its stockholders and destabilized its relations with the government.

One reason the KUK crumbled as an economic organism was the isolation of its directors in late July when their antimerger proposal met with such a stern rebuff from the government. But, given the competitive situation, it was virtually inevitable that the directors should become isolated, for they could not use the peculiar structure of the company to their advantage. Sovereignty, after all, did not reside in the stockholders who elected the directors but ultimately in the government. When the government appointed a president like Morioka to represent its interests, it created two distinct loci of power: the presidential level, occupied by newcomers from the government; and the board of directors, still composed of the original promoters. Mitsubishi did not merge with "Mitsui interests," nor did it defeat the "KUK." Rather, a combination of Mitsubishi and the governmental power represented by Morioka demolished the *original* KUK represented by the directors. In the end the directors were stripped of power.

Many of the scholars who have in effect "blamed" Mitsubishi for renewing the competition in 1885 have overlooked the competitive bent of the KUK branch managers and the dogged persistence of the directors in the face of a plummeting stock price and government alarmism about bankruptcy. These men wanted to retain their independence, and even after they became aware of the extent of the company's losses, they were still willing to tolerate deficits. Yet, in contrast to the managerial freedom of Mitsubishi's "one-man rule," the KUK directors lacked sufficient power inside the company to implement an effective challenge to Mitsubishi. The directors were weak because neither the government, which would have to provide credit, nor the stockholders, who might sell their stock, would permit the company to suffer a large deficit. The government and the stockholders should be viewed not as two unrelated sources of pressure but as two jaws of a vise. This was most evident in the outright grant which Shibusawa strove (and failed) to obtain from the government but which he sought in order to hide from the stockholders the company's true financial condition.[103]

The KUK stockholders, then, had some power, but this power resided not just in the small holder demanding dividends but also in the holders of large blocs of stock, the original promoters of the company. These men, many of whom were very wealthy, exercised a negative influence on the KUK both actively and passively: active in the case of Mitsui executives and probably some others because they sold much of their stock thus shattering public confidence in the KUK; passive in that they were all building up their own personal fortunes and business careers. They were not prepared to help the KUK establish a private network of supporting enterprises—though even if they had been, the strict delineation of the KUK's business in the government's directive probably would have inhibited them. By contrast, Mitsubishi could endure shipping deficits not so much because it had no dividend to pay, but because it had diversified its sources of profit.

Mitsubishi's greater strength thus resided in its structure. The popular slogan, "Mitsubishi has men but no ships; the KUK ships but no men," points to a second advantage. Although the KUK's main branch managers were all capable (see Chart 3), Mitsubishi's managers, as a whole, were more experienced and versatile. Mitsubishi's highest managerial echelon was also more effective than the KUK's directors. Andrew Fraser's conclusion about Komuro Shinobu states: "In his lifetime, few of the business enterprises in which he engaged were successful."[104] The word "effective," instead of "capable," is used intentionally, because Masuda Takashi was obviously a man of immense talent—but his primary loyalty was to Mitsui Bussan. The decisive point was not the quality of Mitsubishi's personnel, but its greater unity.

In view of Mitsubishi's victory, many commentators regard the results of the competition as essentially wasteful. The Iwasaki biographer, Nakano Tadaaki, calls the merger "a complete defeat for the government's shipping administration." Yamamura states that the government "realized the consequences of its past ad hoc actions and turned to subdue the 'sea monster' by means of such wasteful and vain attempts as forming the" KUK.[105] Both reach the same juncture, but in different ways. Nakano, heavily emphasizing the political factor, downplays Mitsubishi's diversification and its influence on the government's economic and strategic thinking in promoting the KUK; whereas Yamamura correctly pinpoints Mitsubishi's outside businesses and the deterioration in its services. He does not, however, provide a detailed analysis of the government's motives in establishing the KUK.

In contrast, the business world's viewpoint, expressed by Terai

Hisanobu, N.Y.K. president (1942–1946), was that "the basic factor which laid the foundation for the progress of Japanese shipping was the emergence of the KUK." Only through the build-up in ships associated with the KUK was Japan able to acquire a merchant marine of international caliber. This is a compelling argument, for most of Mitsubishi's fleet was scrapped relatively soon after the formation of the N.Y.K.[106]

When we talk about "waste," we really must assess cost, the true cost, for example, of the KUK's deficits. Book losses, depreciation not accounted for, private debts, dividends, and loans repaid to the government would total more than ¥1.5 million,[107] equivalent to the cost of four or five good ships. But the KUK now had a fleet of good ships! One cannot say that Mitsubishi would have purchased this fleet by itself, nor assume that Mitsubishi would have tolerated the additional controls that would have been imposed had the government bought this fleet for Mitsubishi.

To argue that the KUK effort was a "waste" is to harbor a hidden corollary that shipping in Japan could have followed a linear pattern of development, thereby ignoring the "structural deficiencies" both Mitsubishi and the KUK had in their service to the state. Mitsubishi's structure, that is, its network of enterprises, had through a risk-avoidance strategy shifted its center of gravity toward those businesses that could deliver secure profits. This strategy did not permit it to respond fully to the increasing demands made by the state upon its shipping enterprise. The KUK, if we can speak of it as a corporate entity, had the virtue of being solely a shipping company, but its structure, which left its directors with little power, could not endure the onslaughts of vigorous competition. Out of this dialectical interaction between the two companies emerged the N.Y.K., a company without these structural deficiencies but possessing a singular commitment to shipping. As an amalgamation of Mitsubishi shipping personnel and the KUK legal structure, at least until World War I it served the purposes of Japanese expansion effectively.

FINANCIAL AND LEGAL STRUCTURE OF THE N.Y.K. At its birth the N.Y.K. was a monopoly. It possessed three-quarters of the country's steamship tonnage. To this total Mitsubishi and the KUK had each contributed twenty-nine ships, with KUK vessels being generally newer and Mitsubishi's ships constituting more than half of the tonnage (see Table 28). The book value of these ships played a crucial role in the merger, particularly in the evaluation of each company's total assets and in the determination of the N.Y.K.'s authorized capital stock.

Before the merger the KUK reported ¥6,526,340 and Mitsubishi ¥6,521,668 in assets to be transferred to the N.Y.K. Since Mitsubishi had to repay the government ¥978,250, its share was reduced to ¥5,543,418. The N.Y.K. then assumed as debt ¥526,340 to the KUK and ¥543,418 to Mitsubishi, to be paid off in five to ten years at 7 percent annual interest. Following these arrangements the N.Y.K. was assigned a capital of ¥11 million, divided into 220,000 shares, each with a par value of ¥50. The KUK stock (Table 29) can be broken down as follows: the government held 52,000 shares, or 23.6 percent of N.Y.K. stock; private sources held 68,000 shares, or 30.9 percent.[108] Mitsubishi, with 45.5 percent, was the company's largest stockholder, a position reinforced by the large number of private KUK shareholders and by the government's representatives in the KUK, Morioka and Katō, who had been on more cooperative terms with Mitsubishi since July than with the original KUK promoters and executives.

The decision to set the N.Y.K.'s authorized capital at ¥11 million had been a highly arbitrary one, determined more by the political need to establish an appropriate ratio of power in the new company than by a true evaluation of the company's assets. These twin questions of power and assets are closely linked to the way the two companies handled depreciation. According to its accounting regulations adopted in 1877, Mitsubishi was to depreciate its ships at 10 percent of their book value per year. Actually Mitsubishi frequently exceeded this rate. Because of this overdepreciation and because Mitsubishi did not buy many new ships, by the

TABLE 28 Steamship Totals at the Time of the N.Y.K.'s Formation, September 1885

Company	Number	Gross Tonnage (GT)	Average per GT	Percentage of National Totals	
				No.	GT
Mitsubishi	29	39,013 (36,599)	1,345 (1,262)	12.7	43.9 (41.2)
KUK	29	29,184 (28,010)	1,006 (966)	12.7	32.9 (31.6)
N.Y.K.	58	68,197 (64,609)	1,176 (1,114)	25.4	76.8 (72.8)
National totals	228	88,765	389		100%
Non-N.Y.K.	170	20,568 (24,156)	121 (142)	74.6	23.2 (27.2)
O.S.K.	83	15,075	182	36.4	17.0
N.Y.K. & O.S.K.	141	83,272 (79,684)	591 (565)	61.8	93.8 (89.8)
Non-N.Y.K./O.S.K.	87	5,493 (9,081)	63 (104)	38.2	6.2 (10.2)

Sources: Plain figures are from *NYK 70 nenshi*, pp. 23–24, 676–677; and *OSK 80 nenshi*, pp. 402, 673. Figures in parentheses are from *YD*, p. 584; and *NYK 50 nenshi*, pp. 81–82.

Note: the figures in parentheses are the most accurate. The plain figures probably represent new measurements taken after the merger. For evidence on these points, see Wray, p. 373.

TABLE 29 N.Y.K. Initial Capital, September 1885

	Shares	Par Value (¥)	Percentage	Guaranteed Profit at 8%
KUK	120,000	6,000,000	54.5	480,000
Mitsubishi	100,000	5,000,000	45.5	400,000
Total	220,000	11,000,000	100	880,000

Source: *NYK 70 nenshi*, p. 22.

end of 1884 ships were valued at only ¥2.10 million. The KUK's depreciation policy, the opposite of Mitsubishi's, was closely connected with the dividend. As Takatera Sadao has written, "it was almost impossible for many companies to allow for depreciation because once they had paid dividends sufficient to satisfy the stockholders there remained little or no surplus . . . for depreciation." The KUK, then, did not depreciate its ships at all.[109] Accordingly, when it completed its business in September 1885, its ships were valued at ¥5.19 million (Figure 5).[110]

The implication of these differences in depreciation policy for the power ratio in the N.Y.K. was simply that stocks would be apportioned to the two companies according to the size of their assets. However, with Mitsubishi ships undervalued because of overdepreciation and with the KUK ships overvalued because of no depreciation, these differences threatened to give the KUK a disproportionate share of N.Y.K. stock. In response to this threat Mitsubishi overturned its accounting procedures in 1885. On March 5, 1885, Mitsubishi had valued its ships at as low at ¥1.89 million, but on August 13 (just before the KUK general meeting) it appreciated them so that in the assets report to the government the ships were valued at ¥3.98 million, even though Mitsubishi had purchased only one ship in 1885! In addition to its ships Mitsubishi also appreciated the value of supporting facilities it intended to transfer to the new company.[111]

The 1885 accounting adjustments adequately solved the problem

FIGURE 5 Book Value of KUK and Mitsubishi Ships,
              1884–1885

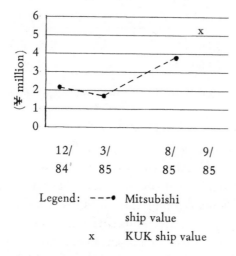

Legend: – – –• Mitsubishi
                   ship value
          x   KUK ship value

of apportioning stock, but the revaluation created more long-term financial difficulties. The capitalization of ¥11 million contained a "vacuum," estimated at more than ¥3.83 million in an internal Finance Ministry planning document of 1886. Thus, the actual value of the assets was closer to ¥7 million.[112] For most of its first decade, this excess of "paper" capital led to greater government financial involvement in the company.[113]

Following the agreement on assets and the dividend, Tsukahara Shūzō and Katō Masayoshi drafted the key merger documents: the government directive to the N.Y.K. and the new company's articles of association (*teikan*), both dated September 29.[114] The N.Y.K. officially began business on October 1, 1885.

The directives and articles of association can be divided into two themes: business operations and legal matters. On operational issues they borrowed heavily from the KUK. The definition of N.Y.K. business removed the ambiguity in the Third Directive to Mitsubishi. It stated: "This company is engaged solely in domestic and overseas shipping and cannot enter other business fields. However, this restriction does not apply to maintaining an ironworks, which is necessary for the repair of the company's ships" (article 5). Regarding the military, the N.Y.K. directive listed both the shipping rates used in the Third Directive to Mitsubishi and the obligations from the KUK directive, though it dropped the statement that the company's ships belonged to the navy (articles 11–15). According to an important new provision, the government would appoint an auditor for all the company's accounts, and he was given broad powers of intervention (article 34). The company also was required to obtain government approval in implementing decisions of the stockholders General Meeting.

Though Mitsubishi accepted the joint-stock form of organization for the N.Y.K., it argued that excessive stockholder rights and restrictions on presidential authority would interfere with company management and urged the government to give the president full authority to wield broad powers.[115] The government did not go as far as Mitsubishi wished, but the N.Y.K. president did have broader powers than his KUK predecessor. The articles of association gave the president the power to make appointments from manager (*shihainin*) on down, and they delineated his responsibilities more clearly. Nonetheless, the more fundamental feature of the N.Y.K. legal structure was the appointive power of the government, retained from the KUK. According to the directive, the N.Y.K. was to have one president, one vice-president, and an unspecified number of directors (*riji*). Throughout the term of the fifteen-year profit guarantee all these officials were to be appointed by the government.

Clearly, at its founding, the N.Y.K., like the KUK before, was a "national policy company" (*kokusaku kaisha*).[116] The national policy companies, established for strategic purposes, became common in the late Meiji period (as with the South Manchurian Railway Company) and especially during the 1930s. The N.Y.K. was one of the first of this kind, and its legal provisions set precedents for later developments. These provisions included the government ownership share, the guaranteed dividend, government powers of appointment, and, in a more general sense, the degree of government intervention in the establishment of the company.

The N.Y.K., however, was institutionally different from later shipping firms set up as national policy companies to increase Japanese influence in China. These firms, established by special legislation, shared many of the N.Y.K.'s legal provisions. But they were jointly owned by other shipping companies (such as the N.Y.K. and the O.S.K.) and, unlike more general purpose national policy companies in China, they did not have large-scale government equity participation.

Its range of attributes made the N.Y.K. a unique company. Within the shipping industry it was the most important firm for national security; for a national policy company it was unusually visible as a *private* firm because of its relation to the Mitsubishi zaibatsu; and it enjoyed more managerial autonomy (after 1893) than did other shipping firms that could be called national policy companies (the O.S.K. being exempt from that definition at least until the 1909 subsidy law). Its origins in the merger between a private company and a partially government-owned enterprise was unique within the shipping industry, and left the company's relationship to the government and to Mitsubishi ambiguous.

Characterizing it as a national policy company serves a useful purpose if it reinforces the legal contrast between the N.Y.K. and the former Mitsubishi Company. The government had earlier placed many restrictions on Mitsubishi, but these were always related to business operations, not to internal management and personnel.

Until the mid-1890s the N.Y.K. presidency was not a powerful office. Government controls set the range of N.Y.K. business activity and limited the president's authority in internal finances. The president was not the representative of the company's major stockholder, but a moderator who would work with the government, the major stockholders, and the executives. There is a popular story that, in view of Mitsubishi's victory in the competition, the government tried to persuade Yanosuke to become the N.Y.K.'s president.[117] But Yanosuke wanted the freedom to rebuild his business empire in industries separate from shipping. Accordingly, the presidency devolved upon former swordsman and now careful negotiator, Morioka Masazumi.[118] When the N.Y.K. began operations it was not yet clear how he would exercise his authority, for the balance of power in the company was still highly unstable. This balance depended mainly on the composition of the executive, and changes there occurred soon after the merger.

SIX

Shaping a Corporate Identity: 1885-1894

PERSONNEL AND THE STRUGGLE FOR CONTROL

There are two dimensions to the problem of control over the N.Y.K. The first, which we may call external, is the general question of government supervision of the N.Y.K.'s finances. The second, which is internal, concerns the influence of private interests on the company. In this second dimension, Mitsubishi was able to secure a dominant influence through its stockholding and its former personnel, but of these two means, personnel was the more visible and important.[1]

EXECUTIVE RESIGNATIONS. At the time of the N.Y.K.'s establishment, its executive officers represented the two founding companies in a rough numerical balance (Figure 6). At the level of branch manager, however, Mitsubishi's influence was stronger both in quality and quantity. First, Mitsubishi's Kondō Renpei and Yoshikawa Taijirō retained the two key posts, Yokohama and Osaka-Kobe. Overall, the N.Y.K. had 18 branch offices with 17 managers. Of these 17 men, 10 were from Mitsubishi; 4 were from the KUK; and 3 cannot be identified. The greater imbalance between the former adversaries at the lower administrative level than at the top left the total structure highly unstable.

Finally, just two months after the establishment of the N.Y.K.,

FIGURE 6 The N.Y.K.'s Initial Administration, October 1885

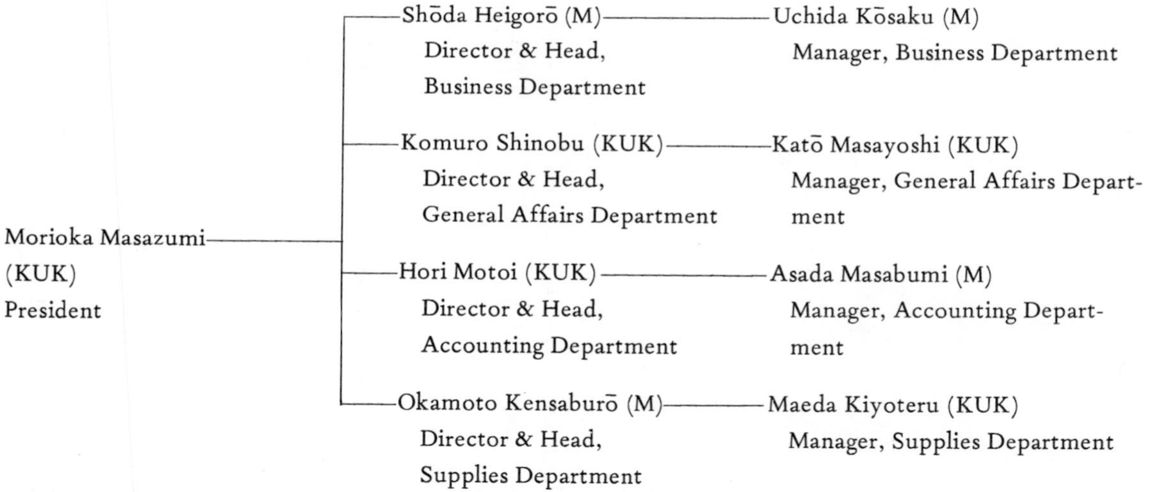

Morioka Masazumi (KUK)
President

— Shōda Heigorō (M) —————— Uchida Kōsaku (M)
    Director & Head,   Manager, Business Department
    Business Department

— Komuro Shinobu (KUK) ————— Katō Masayoshi (KUK)
    Director & Head,   Manager, General Affairs Depart-
    General Affairs Department   ment

— Hori Motoi (KUK) —————— Asada Masabumi (M)
    Director & Head,   Manager, Accounting Depart-
    Accounting Department   ment

— Okamoto Kensaburō (M) ————— Maeda Kiyoteru (KUK)
    Director & Head,   Manager, Supplies Department
    Supplies Department

Sources: *KD*, p. 146; and *NYK 70 nenshi*, pp. 617, 619, 630–631, give the designations shown here with the directors (*riji*) concurrently serving as department heads (*kachō*) and presiding over middle-level managers (*shihainin*). See also Wray, p. 383.

Notes: In large joint stock companies the term *riji* was generally abolished after the Commercial Code in 1893.

The (M)—meaning Mitsubishi—and (KUK) show the former affiliation of these executives.

there occurred what I shall dub the "December 3 massacre." Three directors, Shōda, Komuro, and Hori, as well as several KUK-affiliated branch managers, all resigned from the company, and there was a drastic reshuffling of other branch personnel. When the dust had cleared, 14 branch managers remained: 10 from Mitsubishi; 3 from the KUK; and 1 cannot be identified. Quantitatively this was not much of a change, but qualitatively it was. Two KUK men had resigned from the important offices of Otaru (in Hokkaido) and Niigata. More significantly, the remaining KUK branch managers, Sonoda Saneatsu at Hakodate, Sasaki Otoya at Shimonoseki, and Harada Kinnosuke at Fushiki, were all serving in the local areas where they had worked before the formation of the KUK. They had been recruited in the stock drives of 1882, but they had not been among the early KUK planners.[2]

As a result of the "massacre" the influence of the original KUK members in the N.Y.K. executive completely disappeared. In addition to the resignations of Komuro and Hori, Maeda Kiyoteru was also forced out when the government abolished the Supplies Department on December 4, leaving only one director, Okamoto, and three managers (*shihainin*), Uchida, Katō, and Asada, below Morioka. None of these executives came from the original KUK.

The explanation most frequently given for this upheaval comes from Taguchi Ukichi, who in an article in late December 1885 attributed the resignations to Mitsubishi's gaining control over the former KUK's stock. The resignation of a Mitsubishi executive like Shōda, he wrote, was simply a strategy to facilitate the departure of the former KUK officials.[3] Taguchi's estimates of Mitsubishi's stockholding in the N.Y.K. were highly exaggerated, as will be shown in the next section, but Mitsubishi was the N.Y.K.'s largest stockholder. On that basis alone Taguchi's reasoning does have merit. Nevertheless, the extent of Mitsubishi's stockholding was not the only cause of these resignations. Other explanations point to the relation between the company's financial problems and the unstable alignment of its officers. Kondō Renpei's biographer states that with their deep-seated antagonism, the employees of the two former companies never became reconciled to one another. To make matters worse the four directors and four managers were like "too many cooks spoiling the broth." Morioka, who tried to remain neutral and aloof, warned them that "everyone's energy will soon be dissipated from the endless disputes." The directors, it is said, became so frustrated at their inability to get any work done that they decided to resign before being "cautioned from outside."[4] By this account the very number of executives made resignations inevitable.

Apparently the directors waited one day too long, for on December 2 Finance Minister Matsukata ordered the company to reduce the number of land employees so that their annual salaries would total less than ¥200,000. Following this order the business of the Supplies Department was transferred to the Accounting Department, and on December 7, three branch offices and seven of the company's thirteen representative offices were abolished. The retrenchment must have been just as devastating for the lower-ranking employees as for the executives. Yanosuke's biographer claims that Mitsubishi transferred 515 office employees and 1,200 seamen to the N.Y.K., but by late 1886 the N.Y.K. personnel totaled only 965 (364 on land and 609 seamen).[5]

The resignations and then the untimely death of Okamoto stripped away the top executive level leaving the N.Y.K.'s daily business in the hands of three managers. With the retrenchment program in full force these three were not able to damp the fire under the "seething cauldron" of disputes between the two factions as the strife extended into the lower ranks of the company. Apart from Morioka, however, who did not become an activist administrator, there was no one person with the superior executive authority to deal with this crisis. The company finally took the decisive administrative step in mid-1886 with the promotion of Yoshikawa Taijirō.

EMERGENCE OF STABLE MANAGEMENT. Yoshikawa became the N.Y.K.'s most important executive during the company's first decade. Like many Mitsubishi men he had studied at Fukuzawa's

Keiō School. After serving as an English teacher and administrator in the Ministry of Education, he entered Mitsubishi in October 1878 through the recommendation of former Keiō classmates. Described as a "man of conspicuous ability who could take charge in the midst of a dispute," Yoshikawa became business manager in the head office in the summer of 1886, and then in January 1887 moved up to director and head of the Business Department, posts he held until July of the next year when he rose to the vice-presidency, with Uchida Kōsaku taking over his vacated posts.[6]

Yoshikawa brought quiet to the company's management, but the retrenchment program soon met new and more difficult challenges. In its initial stage the N.Y.K.'s retrenchment had essentially meant getting rid of excess baggage—ships, personnel, and unwieldy financial regulations. By the end of 1887 most of these problems had been solved. But in the late 1880s expenses began to increase rapidly and the thrust of the company's retrenchment policy had to shift from financial and purely administrative measures to cutbacks in supplies throughout its operations. Since the company had departments for only business, general affairs, and accounting, it revived the former Supplies Department and gave its head overall responsibility for the new austerity program. Kondō Renpei's installation as manager of this department in September 1888 was, along with Yoshikawa's 1886 promotion, one of the two most important appointments of the 1885–1893 period.

Although Kondō's appointment filled a gap in the company's administration, the awkward two-tier structure of department heads (*kachō*) and managers (*shihainin*) serving the same function remained. This structure had outlived its purpose of allowing a sufficient number of executives (of the two merging companies to receive important positions in the N.Y.K.) and was done away with in April 1889 when the position of *shihainin* was abolished and the current managers, Katō, Kondō, and Asada, all joined Uchida as both department heads and directors.

With this final rationalization the N.Y.K. now had one president, one vice-president, and four directors. Of these six men, four had been Mitsubishi employees (Yoshikawa, Uchida, Kondō, and

Asada); the other two, Morioka and Katō, had been the government appointees to the KUK. Consequently, the only elements
from the KUK to contribute to the N.Y.K.'s identity were the two
government appointees, who remained with the N.Y.K. for the
balance of their careers, and the former local shipping agents, who
were now serving as branch managers. None of the early planners
of the KUK remained. In sum, then, the N.Y.K.'s personnel was
overwhelmingly dominated by former Mitsubishi men at all levels
of the company's operations.

N.Y.K. STOCKHOLDERS, 1885–1899

MITSUBISHI AND N.Y.K. STOCK. The issue of N.Y.K. stockholders
has been the subject of more scholarly myth-making than any
other problem related to the company. Dispelling these myths is
made difficult by the lack of data on the early N.Y.K. years. There
is a short list of major stockholders for late 1887, but the first full
official list does not appear until 1892. One common view, about
Mitsubishi in the 1890s, expressed by Nakagawa Keiichirō, is that
"the stock dividend from the [N.Y.K.] was the largest item in
[Mitsubishi's] revenue."[7] This generalization assumes that Mitsubishi retained most of its N.Y.K. stock. In fact, it did not.

Mitsubishi began in October 1885 with a guaranteed dividend
of ¥400,000 from the N.Y.K. On March 14, 1886, just as it was
closing down its shipping enterprise and starting a new firm, Mitsubishi gave 12,200 shares of N.Y.K. stock to 160 of its employees. These shares had a par value of ¥610,000 and made up
12.2 percent of Mitsubishi's N.Y.K. holdings. Many scholars have
mentioned this special stock bonus, but there has never been a
satisfactory analysis of the reasons for it. Officially, it was given
out of gratitude for services rendered.[8] Mitsubishi may have also
been looking to the future and using the shares to retain the loyalty
of its employees. The N.Y.K.'s articles of association (article 44)
adopted voting regulations similar to the KUK's favoring the small
shareholder. These appear in Table 30, which indicates that the

TABLE 30 Voting Rights in the N.Y.K. General Meeting

Shares	Votes per Share	Total per Category	Cumulative Total
1–20	1 per 10	1	2
21–100	1 per 20	4	6
101–1000	1 per 50	18	24
1001–5000	1 per 100	40	64
Over 5000	1 per 200	36	100 [max]

Source: Compiled from the N.Y.K.'s articles of association, article 44, *SEDS*, p. 135.

maximum number of votes allowed was 100. Holding the large number of shares originally awarded it would thus not in itself enable Mitsubishi to control the outcome of a General Meeting. Mitsubishi actually enhanced its potential for control by giving away stock to friendly employees, who could now also cast votes "guided" by Mitsubishi.[9] The near debacle of the August 15 KUK meeting must certainly have reinforced the importance of securing strong voting rights in a General Meeting.

The most controversial aspect of Mitsubishi stockholding is whether it had bought up KUK shares before the merger. There are several versions of this theory. One is that by late 1884, when the KUK stock price fell, Mitsubishi bought up a majority of the KUK shares. Another view is that Mitsubishi's purchases took place just prior to the merger.[10] As evidence for this latter interpretation Shibagaki Kazuo used the *Tokyo keizai zasshi* article of December 26, 1885, in which Taguchi Ukichi claimed that "almost all the KUK stock had come into Mitsubishi's possession."[11] There is other contemporary evidence of heavy stock purchasing. On August 17, 1885, the *Chōya shinbun* noted that the KUK stock price, which had fallen to ¥30 in late 1884, rose to nearly ¥50 when news of the proposed merger began to circulate. Then on September 5 the *Tokyo keizai zasshi* reported that the price had rapidly risen above ¥50.[12]

There is also contemporary evidence against the theory that

Mitsubishi controlled the KUK's stock before the merger. For example, on September 12, 1885, the *Mainichi shinbun* claimed that Mitsubishi had bought large quantities of KUK stock when the price had fallen to ¥30 but that it had later sold this stock.[13] Furthermore, Taguchi's frequently cited article is open to question. In it he speaks of the ¥6 million capital stock of the KUK—formerly Mitsubishi's formidable enemy—virtually being presented as a gift with the resignations of the KUK officials in early December. This is an abstract description of power and control, not an analysis of specific stockholding percentages. This article simply does not contain the kind of hard evidence required for the categorical conclusions held by most scholars. In fact, the claim that "almost all the KUK stock had come into Mitsubishi's possession," can be dismissed, for this totally ignores the 43 percent government share in the KUK.

On the other hand, to acquire a majority of the N.Y.K.'s stock at the time of the merger Mitsubishi would only have needed an additional 5 percent to go with its allotted share of 45 percent. In 1932, Nishino Kiyosaku, using the earliest partial list of N.Y.K. stockholders, tried to show that Mitsubishi's holdings did not exceed its assigned share in the N.Y.K. and that therefore it could not possibly have bought up KUK stock. To demonstrate this he added up the shares held by the Iwasaki family and Mitsubishi-related figures (66,940), estimated the number given to employees, and concluded that the total was less than 100,000 (Mitsubishi's allotted portion). Nishino's basic conclusion may be correct, but his argument is flawed, for he misdated the list by a whole year, taking it as October 1886 instead of October 1887.[14]

A more fruitful avenue of analysis is to examine Mitsubishi's transactions in N.Y.K. shares after the merger. Its first major deal was in April 1887 when the stock price had risen to ¥88.8. Mitsubishi then sold one-third of its original stock and thereby obtained a capital fund of about ¥2.5 million. At that price this would have involved the sale of approximately 28,000 shares. Second, in September 1887, Yanosuke, after consultations with Asabuki Eiji on the current high price of N.Y.K. stock, ordered Shōda Heigorō to make preparations for the sale of 10,000 shares no matter what the obstacle.[15]

If Yanosuke did make this sale, the Iwasaki family unloaded close to 40,000 shares in 1887. Although most of these shares were sold *prior* to the date of the stockholders list used by Nishino, the turnover of N.Y.K. stock in the two years following the merger (Table 31) was too immense to provide hard evidence about 1885 holdings based on 1887 lists. The turnover in 1887 alone came to ¥24,850,000.

The 1887 stockholders list contains few holders who were original KUK promoters. They likely sold most of their shares prior to the heavy turnover in 1887. In the 1887 list the only mention of a Mitsui holder among those with more than 500 shares is Kimura Masami of Mitsui Bussan who had 969 shares, or 0.4 percent of the total. Shibusawa Eiichi, whom Hirschmeier has called "one of the chief shareholders of the N.Y.K.," held only 200 shares.[16] In fact only Kimura among the original KUK promoters held more than 500 N.Y.K. shares in 1887. According to 1899 surveys, Toyama Shūzō and Matsumoto Jūtarō, the fourth and fifth largest non-zaibatsu shareholders in Osaka, had no financial holdings in shipping; nor did Amamiya Keijirō, the largest non-zaibatsu shareholder in Tokyo, though all three men had been KUK promoters. The only important KUK promoter among leading N.Y.K. stockholders was Moroto Seiroku, who ranked eleventh in 1892, but he had purchased most of his 1,365 shares after 1887.[17] The stock sales of the original KUK promoters thus left their representation in N.Y.K. stockholding as meager as it was among N.Y.K. personnel.

THE ROLE OF THE IMPERIAL HOUSE. The key point about N.Y.K. stock purchases in the 1880s was that the former shares of the Iwasaki family were not all being dispersed but instead were being concentrated in a different way. The largest single buyer in the two years following the merger was the Finance Ministry, which acquired 13,800 shares apart from the government's original

TABLE 31 N.Y.K. Stock Prices and Turnover,
1886–1893

	High	Low	Average	Turnover	Dividend
	(¥1)			(1,000 shares)	(%)
1886	73.0	56.9	63.7	331	8
1887	89.5	69.1	76.1	497	8
1888	92.6	71.2	77.0	207	12
1889	96.0	78.6	86.5	115	12
1890	81.6	65.5	73.4	15	11
1891	68.0	58.7	61.6	5	9
1892	67.5	60.0	62.7	12	8
1893	82.3	63.8	72.1	137	8

Source: Okaniwa Hiroshi, *Nihon kaiun kin'yū,* p. 70. The "low" for 1887 is contradicted by NYK-KSG, December 15, 1887, Supplement I, p. 11, which gives the December 1887 price as ¥66.5. See also Shimura Kaichi, *Nihon shihon shijō bunseki* (Tokyo Daigaku Shuppankai, 1969), p. 41.

holding in the KUK that had been transferred to the N.Y.K.[18] This new government purchase was related to a planned decrease in the N.Y.K.'s authorized capital stock and to an elaborate program to broaden the financial connections between the state and the N.Y.K. through the Imperial Household Ministry.

Following the government's 1881 promise of a constitution, debate began on the proper role of the Imperial House in the new political era. Iwakura Tomomi feared that the emperor's status could not be guaranteed if debates over people's rights intensified after the opening of the Diet. As a way to "protect the constitution" he proposed in 1882 that army and navy expenses be paid out of income derived from the assets of the Imperial Household so as to free the military from dependence on the Diet. To strengthen these assets he advocated turning over state forest lands, mines, railways, and certain industrial plants to the autonomous control of the Imperial Household, whereby they would become the "material foundation" of the constitution.[19]

Iwakura's fellow oligarchs did not accept all these ideas, and in particular, the proposal for the direct financing of the military by the court was not adopted. In general, however, after Itō Hiro-bumi became Imperial Household minister in March 1884, the government began to turn over lands and capital investments to the Imperial Household with the goal of consolidating the court's financial autonomy. In a November 1884 memorandum Matsukata brought the issue of Imperial Household assets specifically into the realm of business by urging that government stock in banks be given to the Imperial House. In May 1885, ¥1 million worth of Yokohama Specie Bank shares and ¥2.5 million of the government's ¥5 million subscription to Bank of Japan shares were turned over to the Imperial Household Ministry with the promise of more to come once the government had fully paid up its subscription.[20]

Matsukata's next step was to transfer to the Imperial Household the government's ¥2.6 million worth of N.Y.K. shares.[21] This transfer, which took place sometime in the summer of 1887, necessitated revision of the government's directive to the N.Y.K., because the government's design in building up the financial independence of the court had been to increase the legal and administrative separation between the government and the Imperial House. Henceforth Imperial House shares would not be designated as "belonging to the government" as expressed in the original version of article 2 of the directive, which contained an explicit statement that the government owned 52,000 shares. The revision, ordered by the minister of communications, simply dropped all mention of the identity of the stockholders.[22]

Another reason for deleting explicit reference to shareholders was to prepare for a second stage in the government's design to broaden the financial connection between the state and the N.Y.K. In 1884 the government had created a new European-style peerage of 500 members as the nucleus for a conservative upper house in the Diet that was to convene in 1890. To strengthen the peerage and make it the "bulwark of the throne," the government promulgated the Peers Hereditary Property Law on April 29, 1886.[23] Jurisdiction over this hereditary property became the responsibility of the Imperial Household Ministry, and on August 9, 1887, it made an imperial grant of its own N.Y.K. shares to 80 peers. This involved 17,050 shares, which were allotted as follows: 350 shares each to 19 counts, 200 shares each to 43 viscounts; and 100 shares each to 18 barons. In September, 7 princes were also given a total of 3,640 shares, bringing the grand total of peerage-owned stock to 20,690 shares, or 9.4 percent of the N.Y.K.'s paid-up capital.[24]

Under this new law a peer holding 350 shares would be assured an annual income of ¥1,400 from the N.Y.K. dividend. Imperial Household Minister Hijikata Hisamoto liberalized the law on October 4, 1887, by permitting peers to transfer their N.Y.K. stock to other forms of property provided they obtained the ministry's permission. Whichever course the peers chose, a fat purse now awaited them. They could keep the stock and the annual dividend, or if they sold it even at the low ¥66.5 market price of December 1887, the counts at least would each receive ¥23,275. The recipients of all this wealth were virtually all the major figures in the Meiji government: Yamagata, Itō, Matsukata, Inoue, and even the opposition leaders. Both Itagaki and Ōkuma got 350 shares. Also represented were former Tosa officials like Hijikata, Sasaki Takayuki, Tani Kanjō, and Fukuoka Kōtei. All these figures had become members of the "merit" aristocracy.

Among the many changes taking place between the experimental age of the 1870s and the hardening of the institutional structure in the 1880s was the accumulating wealth of government leaders. The contrast with the 1870s is striking. In 1889, for example, a count like Itō could sell his mansions in the Takanawa and Shinagawa sections of Tokyo to Yanosuke for ¥100,000. But a decade earlier Kido Kōin had died without wealth, and Ōkubo Toshimichi's "family needed a special bequest from the emperor to pay for his funeral expenses."[25] Certainly a thorough study of the drafting of this peerage law, the motives for it, and its complex impact on society would seem to be in order. The conventional wisdom suggests that it was an attempt to copy the social structure of Europe in preparation for a constitutional order, the foundation of which was the Imperial House. But one can hardly forget that much of this new wealth was legislated into existence by the beneficiaries themselves. At the top of the new nobility was the Imperial Household Ministry, "the bureaucratic means of fusing the hierarchy of social status with that of wealth." In creating this new social stratum, that is, a peerage that would be the bulwark of the throne, it was necessary that the people who had the power become wealthy as well.[26]

The law illustrates why it is not enough to conclude simply that Mitsubishi was victorious in the competition with the KUK and that it later gained control over the N.Y.K. The transition to the new company was not so simple. Compared to the pre-1885 Mitsubishi, the N.Y.K. was subject to a much stricter government directive, and its legal and financial interests were far more closely intertwined not only with the state but also with the private interests of government leaders. Under a complicated web of ownership the N.Y.K. was a vastly different company from the old Mitsubishi. The latter had received state subsidies, but the government bestowed upon the N.Y.K. the more intangible quality of "legitimacy." The peers law, by designating "shares of banks or companies under special supervision" as suitable for hereditary property, ensured the stability of this marriage between subsidized companies and imperial politics. Wed to the "bulwark of the throne," the N.Y.K. would not be allowed to fail. But by the same token, it would not have the freedom to deviate from state policy the way Mitsubishi had.

Despite the changes of 1887, Mitsubishi was still the largest N.Y.K. stockholder. Between them Hisaya and Yanosuke retained 56,417 shares, or 25.6 percent of the total. Table 32 shows the dominance of the Iwasaki family and the government. Together they held 101,527 shares, or 46.1 percent. But by the mid-1890s, the relative standing of Mitsubishi and the Imperial Household had been reversed as a result of major changes involving first a decrease and later an increase in capital stock.

As noted at the end of Chapter 5, the N.Y.K.'s initial ¥11 million authorized capital stock contained a vacuum of ¥3.83 million. It was assumed at the time that this paper capitalization would have unhealthy inflationay effects on company finances. Accordingly, in March 1886 the company had obtained government approval to decrease its authorized capital stock to ¥ 8.8 million, but to amortize the decrease of ¥ 2.2 million involved buying back 44,000 shares from the company's stockholders at market value. Given the high stock price, this amortization would have cost close to ¥ 3 million. Raising such a huge sum was virtually impossible, especially since it had to be done without disturbing the stockholders, and thus the whole matter had to be delayed. Finally in the fall of 1887 the N.Y.K. requested the Imperial Household Ministry to sell its shares at par value. As shown in Table 32, the ministry had 31,310 shares at the time. The company hoped to purchase the other 12,690 shares at market prices with profits and reserve fund surpluses. The N.Y.K., however, could not raise the money to meet scheduled payments to the ministry or to buy back the other shares. As a solution, in September 1892, the company received government approval to issue bonds totaling ¥ 2.25 million. The bonds were quickly purchased, and in January 1893 the company amortized the remaining shares. [27]

This transaction typifies the intertwining of state and business interests, for the origins of the capital decrease lay in the manner of accounting that revalued assets prior to the merger. Table 33 shows that the Imperial House saved the N.Y.K. almost ¥ 500,000 by selling its shares at par value. This may be regarded, then, as a form of indirect subsidy.

The bonds with which the N.Y.K. amortized its shares had sold quickly because they were issued at 6 percent, considered high for that time. They bore such high interest because Mitsubishi's Kawada Koichirō, president of the Bank of Japan, had intervened to secure a favorable rate for the N.Y.K. ensuring the rapid sale of the bonds. Mitsubishi was the largest purchaser of the bonds with 20.6 percent, but the Imperial House bought 16 percent. This made the transaction a partial exchange of stocks for bonds, with the Imperial House earning back in interest on the bonds part of the indirect subsidy it gave the N.Y.K. This exchange led to further financial ties in December 1895 when the N.Y.K. deposited ¥ 750,000 with the Imperial Household Ministry under a contract

TABLE 32 Leading N.Y.K. Stockholders,
October 31, 1887

Stockholder	No. of Shares	Par Value (¥1)	% of Total
1. Iwasaki Hisaya	36,417	1,820,850	16.6
2. Imperial Household Ministry	31,310	1,565,500	14.2
3. Iwasaki Yanosuke	20,000	1,000,000	9.1
4. Finance Ministry	13,800	690,000	6.3
5. Hiramitsu Mohē	3,146	157,300	1.4
6. Morioka Masazumi	3,052	152,600	1.4
7. Toki Ryūjirō	2,319	115,950	1.1
8. Kawada Koichirō	2,000	100,000	0.9
9. Kameda Sukejirō	1,569	78,450	0.7
10. Watanabe Haruuemon	1,563	78,150	0.7
11. Kuroda Kiyotaka	1,350	67,500	0.6
12. Suenobu Michinari	1,340	67,000	0.6
13. Ōya Tomijirō	1,062	53,100	0.5
14. Naitō Tamesaburō	1,017	50,850	0.5
15. Imamura Seinosuke	1,000	50,000	0.5

Source: SEDS, pp. 148-149.

Note: The only N.Y.K. officers on this list are Morioka and Suenobu (a branch manager). Kuroda was a peer. He was the former head of the Hokkaido Colonization Office and was prime minister, April 1888-October 1889.

that allowed the ministry to retain the money for five years. The Imperial House returned the deposit in early 1899, but in the interim, like any good financial institution it paid the N.Y.K. 6 percent annual interest.[28]

The Finance Ministry's purchase of 13,800 N.Y.K. shares following the merger was also related to the company's overcapitalization problem. By 1892, this Finance Ministry holding had grown to 32,300 shares, almost the same number that the Imperial House had held before selling its shares back to the company at par value. Shortly after the merger, an 1886 internal Finance Ministry policy draft had predicted that the N.Y.K. would have to ask the

TABLE 33   Estimated Savings from Imperial Household
Ministry's Sale of N.Y.K. Shares
(Par Value in 1893 Capital Stock Decrease)

Purchase Date	Shares Purchased	Cost to N.Y.K. (A)	Market Value per Share[a]	Market Value of Purchase (B)	Savings (B–A)
Sept. 1890	5,000	250,000	70.00	350,000	100,000
Jan. 1893	39,000	2,132,172	64.36	2,510,040	377,868
Total	44,000	2,382,172		2,860,040	477,868

Sources: Materials cited in footnote 27.

Notes: [a]The market value per share for the first purchase is my own estimate based on the data in Table 31. That for the second purchase is calculated from the cost to the N.Y.K. of the 39,000 shares which is given in *NYK 50 nenshi,* p. 542. This purchase involved two transactions: (1) 26,310 Imperial House shares at par value (¥1,315,500); and (2) the remaining 12,690 shares at market value (¥816,672). (NYK), Teishutsu shiryō #14, suggests that the Imperial House's 31,310 shares were transferred to the N.Y.K. in 1888. The N.Y.K. then held its own shares, but it did not pay for them until the dates indicated here.

government to lend it shares to reduce the ¥3.83 million in paper capital. This explains why the Finance Ministry had purchased the 32,300 shares. By doing so it retained an amount equivalent to that which the Imperial Household Ministry had in effect "lent" to the N.Y.K. for the decrease in capital stock. In October 1895 the Imperial House secured the return of this "loan" when the Finance Ministry transferred to it the 32,300 shares, giving it 18.4 percent of the N.Y.K.'s stock and making it the company's largest stockholder.[29]

Between 1887 and 1892 Yanosuke had sold all his N.Y.K. shares to finance Mitsubishi's new enterprises. Hisaya, meanwhile, remained the N.Y.K.'s largest stockholder until mid-1892 when he sold 6,430 shares, leaving him with 30,814, or 14.3 percent, and below the Finance Ministry in the rankings. With improved business opportunities following the Sino-Japanese War, in 1896 the N.Y.K. decided to increase its authorized capital stock to ¥22 million. After this subscription was fully paid up in July 1898, the Imperial Household Ministry remained the N.Y.K.'s largest stockholder with 80,550 shares, or 18.3 percent of the total.[30] By contrast, the share of Hisaya, the second largest stockholder in 1899, came to only 6 percent. Perhaps the name originally proposed for the KUK, Teikoku (Imperial) Yūsen, would have been more appropriate for the N.Y.K.!

The Imperial House, then, held three times as much N.Y.K. stock as did Mitsubishi. Unfortunately, there is not enough documentation on liaison with the ministry to determine how much influence it exerted on the company. In 1895, however, a representative from the Imperial House, the director of the Bureau of Imperial Property, nominated the company auditors, and in 1900 was himself named auditor. Through him the Imperial House appears to have been consulted on major company decisions. In one example, from mid-1896, the N.Y.K. was negotiating with the Ministry of Communications over subsidies for government-designated lines to India and Australia. Certain provisions of the subsidies struck the company as disadvantageous. The N.Y.K. directors debated whether to accept the government's terms but put off any immediate response. Instead, the following decision was recorded in the minutes of the directors meeting:

> [The terms of the subsidy] will exert great influence on the company in the future. Therefore, it was decided that, in accordance with our agreement with the Imperial Household Ministry to hold prior discussions on important matters, before taking any action we will first consult with the Imperial Household Ministry and the Iwasaki family, [the company's] large stockholders whose interests will be affected.

This is only a single piece of evidence, but it is explicit enough to conclude that the Imperial House's holdings in the N.Y.K. were not just an indirect form of government financing, given without strings attached. At the very least, the company had to take cognizance of the Imperial House's interests.[31]

Another way to assess the Imperial House's influence is to ask what was the general purpose of its stockholding. According to a

survey of large holdings (5,000 or more shares) by the newspaper
Jiji shinpō in the spring of 1899, the Imperial House's major investments, expressed in percentages of shares, were: banking, 43.5
percent; shipping, 34.9 percent; and railways, 21.6 percent (Table
34).[32] In his memorandum of March 24, 1887, on N.Y.K. stock,
Matsukata compared the role of the Imperial House to that of
banks. Loans made by the Bank of Japan and the Yokohama Specie
Bank to companies would come from the banks' reserves, not
from government revenue. The main purpose of bank loans, he
said, was to promote the nation's economy, not to increase government revenue. Similarly, when the Imperial House invested in
companies like the N.Y.K., the dividends received would be separate from the government's budget and could be used independently for financial aid.[33] In this comparison, Matsukata seems to
be describing the role of an institution like a major investment
bank that could be closely coordinated with state economic policy
yet legally separate enough to prevent Diet interference.

OTHER HOLDERS. Besides Mitsubishi and the Imperial House, a
third component in N.Y.K. ownership, albeit a smaller one, was the
Mitsui Bank (Table 35). The bank bought 3,292 shares in 1891–
1892 just after Nakamigawa Hikojirō became its head and before he
became an N.Y.K. director in 1893.[34] By the mid-1890s a new element, namely stockbrokers, began entering the top ranks of N.Y.K.
stockholders. By 1899, two of the wealthiest, Nomoto Teijirō and
Fukushima Namizō, brokers on the Tokyo Stock Exchange, were
the third and fifth largest holders in the company (see Table 36).[35]
Brokers may have purchased many of the shares given away in the
1880s first to Mitsubishi employees and then to peers. Few of the
"merit" peers who received stock gifts in 1887 appear as large
N.Y.K. holders in the 1890s. On the other hand, peers from the
old nobility increased their shares. Inaba, Maeda, and Nabeshima
in Table 36 represented families of former domain lords.
    Only Iwasaki Hisaya and the Imperial House were among the top
15 stockholders in both 1887 and 1899. Large purchasing by other
holders, such as Mitsui, stockbrokers, and the old nobility, had

TABLE 34 Major Imperial Household Ministry Stockholdings,
Spring 1899

Institution	No. of Imperial House Shares	Par Value per Share	Total Par Value (¥)
N.Y.K.	80,550	50	4,027,500
Bank of Japan	69,660	200	13,932,000
Yokohama Specie Bank	30,200	100	3,020,000
Japan Railway Company	24,422	50	1,221,100
Hokkaido Colliery & Railway Co.	18,460	50	923,000
Total	223,292		23,123,600

Sources: A stockholding survey by *Jiji shinpō,* spring, 1899. For the list of shares, see Murakami Katsuhiko, "Shokuminchi," in Ōishi, ed., *Nihon sangyō kakumei,* II, 302. *Nihon Ginkō 80 nenshi,* ed. Nihon Ginkō shiryō chōsa shitsu (1962), pp. 197–212; *Yokohama Shōkin Ginkōshi* (secret internal publication, 1920), pp. 16, 95, 165, 187, 211, 217, 273, 301. *Hokkaido Tankō Kisen 50 nenshi,* pp. 144–154.

TABLE 35 Mitsui Bank's Stockholding in the N.Y.K.,
1891–1916

	Shares	% of Total	Ranking
October 31, 1891	0	0	—
April 30, 1892	3,292	1.5	?
October 31, 1897	8,212	1.9	4th
October 31, 1900	8,312	1.9	3rd
October 31, 1902	7,912	1.8	3rd
November 8, 1915	5,212	1.2	3rd
April 30, 1916	0	0	—

Source: NYK–KNS; (NYK), Ketsugi yōkenroku, 1891–1892.

by and large prevented any rapid dispersal of company stock to smaller owners. Mitsubishi's sales had, however, led to some deconcentration of holding, especially among the higher ranks. In

TABLE 36　Leading N.Y.K. Stockholders,
　　　　　　October 31, 1899

Stockholder	No. of Shares	Par Value (¥1)	% of Total
1. Imperial Household Ministry	80,550	4,027,550	18.3
2. Iwasaki Hisaya	26,447	1,322,350	6.0
3. Nomoto Teijirō	23,558	1,177,900	5.4
4. Mitsui Bank	8,212	410,600	1.9
5. Fukushima Namizō	6,850	342,500	1.6
6. Tokuda Kōhei	4,230	211,500	1.0
7. Kaizuka Uhē	3,000	150,000	0.7
8. Baba Kinsuke	2,530	126,500	0.6
9. Yamane Yasuo	2,500	125,000	0.6
10. Inaba Kenkichi	2,310	115,500	0.5
11. Yokoyama Hisatarō	2,200	110,000	0.5
12. Maeda Toshitsugu	2,075	103,750	0.5
13. Wada Tetsutarō	2,000	100,000	0.5
14. Nabeshima Naoki	2,000	100,000	0.5
15. Shimomura Chūbē	2,000	100,000	0.5

Source: NYK–KNS.

1887, 7 stockholders possessed more than half the total shares; in 1899, 60 did, a considerable change even allowing for the doubling of the authorized capital stock from ¥11 to ¥22 million. By other perspectives the change appears less radical. In 1887, the number of holders with 1,000 or more shares was 15; in 1899 the same number held 2,000 or more (the parallel figure, since the capital had doubled). However, the overall share of the top 15 had fallen from 55.0 percent to 38.7 percent.[36]

Dispersal proceeded more quickly in executive stockholding. Table 37 shows that company officials held a mere 0.38 percent of total shares in 1899, compared to 2.97 percent in 1887. Though N.Y.K. directors did maintain medium-sized holdings, by the turn of the century an official's stockholding had no relation to the power he exercised in the company. Of course, even in 1887 the

TABLE 37 Leading Stockholders among N.Y.K. Officials,
1887 and 1899

	1887			1899	
Name	*Ranking*	*No. of Shares*	*Name*	*Ranking*	*No. of Shares*
Morioka Masazumi	6th	3,052	Nakamigawa Hikojirō	115th	500
Suenobu Michinari	12th	1,340	Kondō Renpei	176th	350
Yoshikawa Taijirō	19th	842	Hama Masahiro	195th	300
Kondō Renpei	25th	700	[a]5-way tie	266th	250
Yoshitake Seiichirō	31st	600			
Total		6,534			1,650[a]
Percentage of paid-up capital		(2.97%)			(0.38%)

Source: SEDS, p. 148; *NYK–KNS.*

Notes: [a]250 counted only twice. Those in the 5-way tie in 1899 were Yoshitake Seiichirō, Asada Masabumi, Sonoda Kōkichi, Shibusawa Eiichi, and Shōda Heigorō. Suenobu, Yoshitake, and Hama were branch managers at the time of these lists; Sonoda, Nakamigawa, Asada, Shibusawa, and Shōda were directors.

number of shares a manager held was not necessarily decisive for the position he occupied in the company, but at least it was a badge of closeness to Mitsubishi, from whom the manager probably received the stock in the first place (with the exception of Morioka). Thus Table 37 also reflects the gradual dispersal of Mitsubishi stock. Having this stock in the hands of Mitsubishi-related personnel may have been important for strategic reasons in the early years of the N.Y.K., but once the company's management became stable, especially in the mid-1890s, such tactics were superfluous. The best evidence for this is that the officials listed under 1899 in

Table 37 did not purchase (or receive) new shares in the capital stock increase of 1896–1898. Nor did other leading Mitsubishi officials unrelated to the N.Y.K. have substantial holdings in the company.

MITSUBISHI'S WITHDRAWAL FROM SHIPPING

HISTORICAL CONTEXT OF MITSUBISHI STRATEGY. The N.Y.K.'s increasingly stable management enabled Mitsubishi to conduct, in effect, a "phased withdrawal" from the company, best typified by Hisaya's relatively small 6 percent share in 1899. The formation of the N.Y.K. resulted, in the long run, in triumph for Mitsubishi *because* it withdrew from the shipping industry. By World War I, Mitsubishi grew into one of Japan's two largest zaibatsu, an institutional growth based primarily on mining, banking, and shipbuilding. The primary needs of institutional growth leading to zaibatsu formation were: first, the capital to make massive investments in primary industry, most commonly mining; second, the managerial freedom to start new forms of industry or trade, for example, the development of the electrical engineering industry as a spin-off from shipbuilding. The restrictiveness of the shipping industry – at least as a subsidized common carrier – would have made these kinds of managerial decisions impossible.

Thus far, we have emphasized both Mitsubishi's indifference to ship purchasing and overseas line expansion and its concentration on profits from domestic lines and other enterprises. Such a managerial disposition reveals less about Yatarō and Yanosuke as "economic men" than about the objective conditions surrounding the development of Japanese trade in the early 1880s. In 1880, when Japan conducted only 22.0 percent of its foreign trade with Asia, as much as 54.5 percent was with Europe, and 22.8 percent with North America. But in the 1880s the outer limit of Japanese shipping capacity was still within Asia. Japanese ships could not go where most of Japan's trade went. This was the main reason why the country's foreign trade, the basis for any overseas shipping, was still mainly in the hands of foreign merchant houses and why the transport of commodities remained in the control of powerful foreign shipping companies with close connections to the trading houses. The development of Japanese overseas shipping, however, coincided with a radical reversal in the pattern of foreign trade. By 1910 44.7 percent of Japan's trade was with Asia and only 29.5 percent with Europe (the American share remained about the same at 22.1 percent).[37] The growing proximity of its major trading partners enabled Japan to take a larger role in the transport of its imports and exports. Thus, the shifting pattern of foreign trade, not just government subsidies, aided the development of Japan's overseas shipping, and trade ultimately depended upon industrial development.

In addition to the adverse foreign trade conditions in 1880, high costs in the shipping industry were a continuing burden to Mitsubishi. Though the government had covered most of the purchase cost of Mitsubishi's steamships, these were still expensive to operate. That is one reason why most of the country's newly acquired tonnage in the late 1870s and early 1880s consisted of Western-style sailing vessels. Some of Mitsubishi's steamships had been emergency purchases and required expensive repairs; continued reliance on foreigners as skilled seamen sustained high labor costs; and the undeveloped state of Japanese ports prevented potential savings. This last issue was especially acute in northern Japan, where Mitsubishi was expanding its services around 1880. Government vacillation and cancellation of some northern port projects in the 1880s did not augur well for the immediate future. Even on the international ports of Yokohama and Kobe major construction did not begin until the 1880s.[38]

These prevailing high costs help to explain the motive behind Yatarō's rhetoric and tactics. In the mid-1870s he had attacked low freight rates as expedient, and he consistently strove for a monopoly, for total market hegemony, because he saw it as essential to profitability in the shipping industry. The high freight rates that Mitsubishi could charge because of its monopoly in steamships offset the high operating costs and enabled it to earn large profits from 1879 to 1881. But when it lost its monopoly through the competition from the KUK it could no longer offset these costs. An attempt to recover its market share in the face of high costs and lower freight rates induced by competition offered little hope of profit maximization.

In the long run the cost of repairs, labor, and ports would decline. Indeed, this prospect of declining costs helped to justify government subsidies to a monopolistic firm like Mitsubishi. These were not subsidies aimed simply at helping an inefficient firm. Nevertheless, it would take time (at least until the late 1880s) for this decline to be felt. Mitsubishi could not afford this patience. By allowing its assets to remain in shipping it would miss out on emerging new opportunities in the 1880s. It therefore shifted its assets into mining, where costs were falling sharply during this decade and which offered better prospects for profit.[39] In summary, in the years when Mitsubishi came to the forefront of Japanese shipping, government intervention, high costs, and eventually competition prevailed.

This situation was not conducive to the sustained profitability necessary for the expansion and diversification of assets. Consequently, it was only by detaching itself from the direct management of shipping that Mitsubishi acquired the resources and the freedom to grow into a fully diversified group of enterprises. This long-term result does not necessarily mean that as early as 1885 Yanosuke envisaged a full-fledged zaibatsu. But we do know that following the merger Mitsubishi rapidly increased its investments in those industries that had enabled it to diversify its profit structure before 1885, and to do so it utilized income from the sale of N.Y.K. stock. In that sense the withdrawal from shipping was strategic and not simply a victory or a forced compromise.

MITSUBISHI'S NEW STRUCTURE. Institutionally Mitsubishi began a new course in March 1886 when Yanosuke established the Mitsubishi Company (Mitsubishi Sha).[40] The transition from the old to the new Mitsubishi and the separation of the N.Y.K. can be summarized by referring to three groups of employees. The first group were those who continued on in the new Mitsubishi. The most important were the top-ranking executives who had served the Iwasaki family for a decade or more, such as Kawada Koichirō and Shōda Heigorō (whom we can include despite his two months in the N.Y.K.). Also in this group were leading executives who had not had major roles in shipping. Yamawaki Masakatsu remained head of the Takashima Mine, while Hida Shōsaku and Toyokawa Ryōhei successively led the One Hundred and Nineteenth Bank.[41] A second group included young, capable employees who had joined Mitsubishi in the early 1880s. For this group, interest in their own careers took precedence over any long-term loyalty to Mitsubishi, for after leaving the N.Y.K., instead of returning to Mitsubishi they set out on altogether new paths in the political and business worlds. Two examples were Katō Kōmei and Yamamoto Tatsuo. Katō, a future foreign minister and prime minister, joined Mitsubishi in July 1881, went immediately to the Hakodate Branch, and became involved in opposition to the sale of Hokkaido Colonization Office properties. He left the N.Y.K. in January 1887 to enter the Foreign Ministry. According to his biography he wanted to be successful on his own, and since he had married Yatarō's daughter in 1886, he felt he would never be recognized for his own talent if he stayed in Mitsubishi. Yamamoto had joined Mitsubishi in January 1883. He left the N.Y.K. in January 1890 to follow his mentor Kawada Koichirō into the Bank of Japan.[42] Kawada had left Mitsubishi to become president of the bank in September 1889. A third group consisted of employees who had long experience in Mitsubishi, who had worked in shipping during the competition with the KUK, but who did not enjoy the same high status or rank within Mitsubishi as Kawada or Shōda. These were people like Yoshikawa Taijirō, Uchida Kōsaku, and Kondō Renpei who transferred to the N.Y.K. and became its leaders.

Mitsubishi's investments during this period quickly turned the new firm into a "land" company. In coal mining Mitsubishi relied at first on the rich Takashima Coal Mine, but its main purchases between 1886 and 1888 were metal mines. In 1888 two occurrences changed the pattern of Mitsubishi's coal business. First, the production of the Takashima Mine reached its peak and began to decline after 1888. Second, Mitsubishi tried to buy the Miike Coal Mine from the government but was outbid by Mitsui by a mere ¥2,000. The mine was sold for ¥4,590,439.[43] To compensate for this setback, in 1889 Mitsubishi began purchasing additional coal mines, most of them in Kyushu. By the mid-1890s it had acquired approximately 15 coal and 30 metal mines. By 1894 the output of the company's leading four coal mines was back up to 360,000 tons; and by 1901 the leading five mines produced 760,000 tons. Mitsubishi's first major sales of N.Y.K. stock, in 1887, had financed much of its mining expansion in the late 1880s. Similarly, in the mid-1890s additional sales, which left Hisaya with only 6 percent of N.Y.K. stock, helped Mitsubishi to purchase the rich gold and silver mines in Sado and Ikuno. Mitsubishi bought these two mines in 1896 for ¥1.73 million from the Imperial Household Ministry.[44]

Real estate was a second major area of investment for Mitsubishi in the late 1880s and early 1890s. Of the ¥2.4 million the company spent, almost ¥2 million went for land in Tokyo, but there were other substantial investments as well: a rice cultivation project in Niigata, the Koiwai dairy farm in Iwate Prefecture, and a land reclamation project in Kojima Bay in Okayama Prefecture.[45] The most famous purchase of all was the Marunouchi district of Tokyo, a vast area opposite the Imperial Palace, which, in the late 1880s, was part grass plain and part military drill field. It also contained many barracks and some government offices. In the late 1880s the army decided to vacate these barracks, which were mostly renovated homes of former domain lords, and build new Western-style barracks in a different section of the city. To do so the army needed ¥1.5 million, and it decided to sell the land. Since it was directly opposite the palace, the government wished to sell the land to one buyer, fearing many separate buyers might cause problems in the future. This policy eliminated all but a few prospective purchasers, and in March 1890 Mitsubishi bought the land for ¥1.28 million.

With the land purchase, the background images for Mitsubishi's development came to the fore. Mitsubishi's exchange of the risky ways of the "sea" for the haven of "land" was not a traditional, safe investment but an innovative, forward-looking move.[46] Yanosuke had been strongly urged to buy the land by Shōda Heigorō and Suenobu Michinari, who were in London at the time on business. The modern office center in London led them to dream of creating a similar one in Japan. Yanosuke concurred, and construction planning began soon after the purchase. Mitsubishi's Building No. 1, completed in 1894 in the English style, was Japan's first office rental building. Building No. 3, finished in 1896, housed the N.Y.K.'s head office.[47]

The significance of this land purchase becomes apparent when Mitsubishi's other options for use of its N.Y.K. stock are examined. The "sea" image is used as a symbol for risk because of the shipping industry's unpredictable profits and need for huge capital investment. But N.Y.K. stock, with its government subsidies, was not "risky"; that was why it had been given to the peers. Mitsubishi's safest option would have been to treat the stock as a financial cushion, content with its annual ¥400,000 dividend. Instead, it took the more progressive step of selling it and using it for productive purposes.

Mitsubishi's positive investment strategy of the late 1880s, spearheaded by managers like Shōda, led also to tentative planning for industrial manufacturing. In 1888–1889, several Mitsubishi managers persuaded Yanosuke to begin a steel enterprise. Yanosuke's commitment, however, was conditional upon receipt of government subsidies, which, after negotiations, were not forthcoming, and the project proved abortive.[48] In one sense, then, Mitsubishi maintained a conservative approach to industrial manufacturing until its shipbuilding investments of the mid-1890s. From another perspective, though, the key variable was less Mitsubishi conservatism than government financing, which became available in 1896.

Until the early 1890s more than two-thirds of all Mitsubishi's profits came from mining and stock dividends (see Table 38). Though these dividends at first represented N.Y.K. stock, they

TABLE 38 Mitsubishi Profit Structure, 1886–1892
(Index = 100)

	Public Bond Interest	Stock Divi- dends	Deposit & Loan Interest	Real Estate	Coal Mining	Other Mining	Ship- build- ing
1886	13.0	25.8	10.2	0.4	41.5	3.9	5.2
1887	16.4	20.4	1.9	1.1	51.9	5.6	2.7
1888	18.6	19.9	0.8	1.4	40.5	15.1	3.7
1889[a]	19.3	24.6	0.8	2.4	45.1	0.9	4.1
1890[a]	15.4	22.5	0.3	1.9	52.6	–	3.6
1891	18.1	27.4	–	2.9	39.9	7.2	4.5
1892	17.8	27.1	–	3.0	37.5	10.5	4.1

Source: Hatade, *Mitsubishi,* pp. 32–33.

Note: [a]The totals for 1889 and 1890 fall short of 100 because of losses in copper mining.

increasingly came from railway investments. The Nagasaki ship-yard, for which Mitsubishi paid ¥527,000 in 1887, brought in only a small percentage of the profits, but then in this period its functions were mainly construction of small vessels and repair work. By 1894 shipbuilding constituted only 12.1 percent of company assets, compared to 37.6 percent for mining and 38.8 percent for real estate. This asset structure changed radically after 1896. Whereas real estate investments came to a temporary halt, subsidies spurred the growth of shipbuilding and Mitsubishi's purchases of expensive metal mines made mining the dominant area of company business (48.5 percent of assets in 1898).[49]

Profits from banking are not included in the percentages in Table 38 because the One Hundred and Nineteenth Bank remained legally independent of Mitsubishi during this period. The bank's profit tripled after its capital was increased to ¥1 million in 1890, but this would never have amounted to even 1 percent in the percentages shown in this table. Following the establishment of the Commercial Code in 1893, Mitsubishi became a Limited Partnership (Mitsubishi Gōshi Kaisha). Hisaya and Yanosuke divided ¥5 million in capital between them. Business officially began on January 1, 1894, and in October 1895 the company established a banking department to exercise more formal supervision over the One Hundred and Nineteenth Bank. The bank itself disappeared as a legal entity in 1898 when its charter expired, and the banking business legally became what it had always been in practice— another Mitsubishi department.[50]

FINANCIAL RETRENCHMENT AND BUSINESS, 1885–1893

RATIONALIZATION OF COMPANY FINANCES. Apart from the personnel upheaval in late 1885, the N.Y.K.'s greatest problem in its early years was clarifying the legal ramifications of the financial clauses in the government directive. This issue focused on the status of the government subsidy and the related questions of profit guarantee, reserve system, and debt.

According to the N.Y.K.'s interpretation of the subsidy, the government was legally obliged not only to guarantee the 8 percent dividend but also to subsidize the company's payments into its reserves if it had a deficit.[51] There were, however, no explicit guidelines in the directive on how to handle these financial contingencies. In a November 4 memorandum Matsukata rejected the N.Y.K.'s interpretation of the directive, arguing that there was a limit to the government's obligation. He emphasized that the Minister of Agriculture and Commerce had the power to issue revisions in the directive if the N.Y.K., in conforming to it, would produce losses for the government. He also laid down several guidelines that the company had to follow in the event of a deficit. First, if operating profits were insufficient to cover the stated percentages for reserve funds and depreciation, the company could reduce these percentages proportionately. That way the company would simply break even, and the government would then pay the full 8 percent dividend. Second, if there were no operating profits at all, the company would have to forego reserve payments and depreciation. On December 5, in another memorandum Matsukata set limitations on the company's expenditures and established accounting regulations.[52] This came right after the retrenchment order on land employees and the mass resignations of December 3.

The genesis of these financial problems seems to have been poor judgment in setting rates for reserve funds and not just the legal loopholes in the directive. Every year the company was obligated to pay 22 percent of the value of its ships for two reserve funds and depreciation. Broken down, this involved 7 percent for an insurance reserve; 10 percent for a repair reserve; and 5 percent for depreciation (article 28). In its first year of operation these regulations brought the N.Y.K. over ¥3 million in obligations to the three funds. It ended the year ¥974,822 short of the stated percentages.[53] Apparently in March 1886 the government decided to reduce the 22 percent requirement to 17 percent. This lower figure was then jettisoned in late 1887 when a government study using the 17 percent requirement estimated an annual average overall shortage of ¥647,038 for 1888–1900 (calculated with the dividend obligation but without the subsidy).[54]

Finally, in the revised directive issued to the N.Y.K. General Meeting in December 1887 the insurance reserve fund was lowered to 5 percent and the repair fund to 3 percent. With depreciation remaining at 5 percent, the total requirement was now 13 percent. Any shortages in these funds were to be made up in subsequent years.[55]

The second step in overcoming financial chaos was to give the subsidy a new legal status. The government decided to eliminate the 8 percent profit guarantee and to borrow a French formula for subsidizing ships on the basis of distance traveled while carrying mail. The government estimated that the company's ships would travel 786,760 nautical miles with the mails. They decided to maintain the subsidy at ¥880,000 (that is, the equivalent of the 8 percent profit guarantee), but to express it in fixed terms as ¥1.1 per mile.[56]

The government's rationale for such a huge subsidy (when Mitsubishi's subsidy had been considered large at ¥250,000) was that, apart from the Shanghai line and a few important coastal services, Mitsubishi had had a relatively small number of regular lines. On the other hand, under government order the N.Y.K. had taken responsibility for many such lines, some of which were expensive to operate. Since ships had to leave port on schedule, they could not wait until they were assured of a full cargo. The corresponding loss of income from freight thus justified the large subsidy.[57]

The new formula for the subsidy imposed a risk on the company that had not previously been explicit. Liability for deficits would now fall entirely on the company. But an improved business outlook in 1887 made the new system seem less risky. Yoshikawa reported to the 1887 General Meeting that income for October and November 1887 was up 10 percent over the same period a year earlier. Also, in October the government ordered the company to begin transporting coal overseas from the Miike Mine. This contract enabled the N.Y.K. to order a large specialized vessel, the *Miike Maru*, which at 3,308 tons was the largest ship in the company's fleet.[58] A refurbishing of the fleet had begun in 1887. Article 19 of the directive prohibited the N.Y.K. from purchasing ships more than two years old without government permission. In 1885, however, only half of its ships were less than ten years old. Between 1887 and 1892 the company purchased eleven new ships, totaling 24,676 tons for ¥2.89 million. In the meantime it sold off many of its older vessels, so that by 1892 ships less than ten years old constituted 71 percent of the company's tonnage.[59]

After settling the subsidy problem and enhancing its earning capacity with new ships, the company decided to pay off its debt without waiting for the full ten-year term. There were two reasons for this decision. First, the interest rate of 7 percent was considered higher than what the company could earn through utilizing the unpaid portion. Second, the directive limited the dividend to 8 percent while the debt remained outstanding. Repayment was made in two lump sums, in December 1887 and in 1888.[60]

There is some ambiguity about the extent of government control over the N.Y.K. reflected in these financial reforms between 1885 and 1887. In one sense they simply eliminated the vagueness that the government had inserted in the 1885 directive and once the ambiguities had been cleared up the N.Y.K. enjoyed considerable freedom within the new financial standards. This is a strong argument. But the fact remains that the government set the standards. All of the reforms are mentioned in the Finance Ministry policy draft found in the Matsuo papers. This draft and Matsukata's memoranda show that the government forced the company to agree with its interpretation of the subsidy and its relation to reserves and profits. Nor could the company change the fixed percentages for the reserves. In this sense we cannot call the N.Y.K. a fully independent private company. The road to independence only began in 1888 when the company paid off its debt and acquired the right to set its dividend rate. But the continuing official supervision through the directive suggests it is best to call the N.Y.K. a joint private-government concern, at least until the commercial reforms of 1893.

DECLINING PROFITABILITY OF COASTAL SHIPPING.   After a stormy first two years the N.Y.K.'s business improved markedly in the late 1880s. In 1888 the dividend went up to 12 percent (Table 39), and profits were well in excess of the government subsidy. Unfortunately we do not have a percentage breakdown of business for the line categories to show the source of this improvement. Probably it came in domestic lines as a consequence of the industrial boom in the late 1880s. In the meantime overseas lines increased only very slowly. In 1885 the N.Y.K. had continued the three basic East Asian lines that were in operation before the merger, those to Shanghai, Vladivostok, and Inch'ŏn. In the next few years it added additional services to Tientsin and Manila. The N.Y.K. domestic lines ordered by the government were either connected with Hokkaido or concentrated in the main Yokohama-Kobe route. The first signs of trouble arose on this main route at the end of the decade. Before the recovery of 1888 could become sustained, the N.Y.K. was hit by a series of shocks over the next five years in all phases of its business: in 1889, a fall-off in passenger business; in 1889–1890, a rapid increase in expenses; and

TABLE 39 N.Y.K. Business Results, 1886–1893

(¥1,000)

	Assets	Income	Expendi-tures	Profit	Profit as % of Assets	Profit as % of Income	Dividend	
	(A)	(B)		(C)	(C/A)	(C/B)		(%)
1886	13,168	4,546	3,666	880	6.9	19.4	880	8
1887	13,647	5,160	4,280	880	6.5	17.1	880	8
1888	12,907	5,617	4,136	1,481	11.5	26.4	1,320	12
1889	13,254	5,904	4,515	1,389	10.5	23.5	1,320	12
1890	12,784	5,937	4,685	1,251	9.8	21.1	1,182	11
1891	12,486	5,346	4,294	1,052	8.4	19.7	967	9
1892	12,249	4,975	4,104	871	7.1	17.5	860	8
1893	12,507	5,145	4,218	927	7.4	18.0	704	8

Sources: NYK–H 1–8, 1887–1893; NYK 70 nenshi, pp. 39, 701–707.

after 1890, a decrease in freight revenue. Few of these shocks were temporary. All were related to changes in the country's industrial structure which were having a profound impact on the profitability of the shipping industry.

The first major shock to N.Y.K. business was the decline of almost 50,000 passengers in 1889 (see Table 40), caused primarily by the opening of the government-owned Tokaido Railway line in July 1889 between Tokyo and Kobe. This paralleled the N.Y.K.'s most important business line. At ¥ 3.76, one-way tourist fares by train were lower than steamship charges. Travel by rail took twenty hours; by sea, two days. As a result of this competition, between 1888 and 1891, N.Y.K. passenger business fell off by about 40 percent in both income and numbers. The growth rate of the railway business was also much more rapid than shipping in the early 1890s. Between 1891 and 1896 railway passengers increased by 93 percent, from 11.8 million to 22.7 million. The corresponding figure for the N.Y.K. was 41 percent, but this merely represented a climb from the 1891 low of 170,000 to 240,000, the same level as 1889. Changes in freight income were not as dramatic but were still substantial. Railway freight increased 58 percent between 1891 and 1896, from 820,000 to 1.3 million tons; N.Y.K. freight incrased 32 percent from 1.3 to 1.7 million tons, but this latter figure included a growing amount of overseas business.[61]

Despite the fall-off in passenger business, overall income rose in 1888–1890, but during the same years profits fell steadily, by 6 percent in 1889 and 10 percent in 1890. Expenditures were rising much more quickly than income, and the company set up a special committee headed by Yoshikawa to curtail expenses. Between 1888 and 1892 the number of foreign employees was reduced by 39 percent. Japanese employees were cut by 16 percent between 1889 and 1892. Analysis of the percentage of each major expense item in the company's budget during this period leads to the conclusion that the rising price of coal was the main cause of the crisis. Between 1886 and 1892 most items in the budget maintained a fairly constant percentage of overall expenses. Coal,

TABLE 40 N.Y.K. Freight and Passenger Transport,
1886–1893

	Freight (tons)	Income (¥)	Number of Passengers	Income (¥)
1886	?	2,703,076	?	787,431
1887	1,044,579	3,138,454	262,702	886,085
1888	1,212,650	3,285,479	290,874	1,024,469
1889	1,279,599	3,484,452	242,303	1,008,644
1890	1,356,939	3,749,268	220,491	755,146
1891	1,290,180	3,561,952	173,669	625,926
1892	1,239,698	3,197,437	191,609	664,861
1893	1,352,858	3,362,471	208,128	626,839

Sources: NYK–H 1–8, 1887–1893; NYK 70 nenshi, pp. 39, 701–707.

however, increased from 11.6 percent of the budget in 1887 to 18.1 percent in 1889 and 17.7 percent in 1890. Calculated in terms of the distance traveled by steamships, the cost of bunker coal rose 45.1 percent between 1887 and 1889. Concretely this meant that coal expenses per mile rose from ¥0.43 in 1887 to ¥0.62 in 1889. To combat this "energy crisis" the N.Y.K. purchased the Katsuno Coal Mine in Kyushu in November 1889. The company did not expect a profit but felt it would gain simply by using its own coal.[62]

The fuel crisis eased in 1891 when the price of a ton of coal fell from ¥4.50 to ¥4.15.[63] The cost per mile fell to ¥0.56 in 1891 and ¥0.48 in 1892, and by 1892 coal's share of the company's budget had declined to 15 percent. But no sooner had the company pulled out of this fuel crisis than it was hit by a decline in freight shipments. This resulted from competition with railways and other shipowners, and the accounts suggest a decline in freight rates. For example, the amount of freight carried fell by 8.6 percent between the peak year of 1890 and 1892, but in the same period freight income was off by 14.7 percent (see Table 40).

In 1892 these numerous problems culminated in what was

probably the worst business performance since the company's founding. Also, for the first time since 1887 the company's profit was less than the government subsidy. The N.Y.K. business report gave the following reasons for the decline in income in 1892: (1) There had been a recession in which (a) a crop failure in northern Japan reduced rice shipments (income from rice shipments from Niigata and other northern prefectures to Tokyo still constituted most of the company's freight revenue); and (b) fishing in Hokkaido had only brought half the catch of the previous year. (2) Income from coal shipments fell by nearly 50 percent from 1891 because of a rapid decline in freight rates following a drop in the price of coal. (3) Fewer people emigrated. (4) An unusually large number of ships had been wrecked or were undergoing repairs. (5) As a result of new shipbuilding laws recently passed in Western countries, many Western steamship companies had begun to purchase new fleets. At the same time, they were selling off their older ships. Year by year more and more smaller Japanese shipowners had begun to buy these ships. By penetrating the domestic monopoly of the large companies these smaller owners brought more competition to coastal routes and a rapid decline in freight rates. [64]

All these business problems came at an especially inauspicious time. In 1890 Japan's Diet had convened following the country's first general election. This had been successfully contested by revived versions of the political parties that had emerged in the early 1880s. In the intensified political debate of the time, journalists had stepped up their opposition to the large N.Y.K. subsidy. And in 1891 there had even been talk in the Diet of slashing it to ¥500,000.

This opposition greatly frightened the N.Y.K.'s stockholders, especially since the case against the N.Y.K.'s subsidy had been buttressed by the performance of the independent shipowners, many of whom were apparently making profits even without subsidies. All these problems came out in the open in the N.Y.K.'s 1892 General Meeting. Stockholders sought assurance from management that the government subsidy would be retained and demanded that the company allow the establishment of two committees of stockholders to deal with problems of accounting and business expansion. Morioka reaffirmed the government's fifteen-year term for the subsidy but refused debate on the stockholders' demand for greater participation.[65]

The 1892 slowdown raised doubts about the profitable limits of traditional shipments like rice, fish, and coal that still constituted the bulk of the N.Y.K.'s freight. A related question was the long-term viability of concentrating business on domestic lines. The late 1880s and early 1890s, a hiatus for the shipping industry, was a period during which the large companies had begun to suffer from the competition of railways and smaller shipowners, but had not yet developed long-distance overseas lines. This relative lull, coming only a few years after the N.Y.K.'s founding, stands in contrast to the business climate temporarily enjoyed by Mitsubishi during the late 1870s and early 1880s. Through its monopoly Mitsubishi had profited from domestic lines and had concentrated its energies there. But the N.Y.K. had to look overseas because by 1890 coastal routes no longer offered the prospect of sustained profitability.

During this period, however, lines to Tientsin and Manila had merely been local extensions of East Asian traffic. The only N.Y.K. innovation in its overseas services was transport of emigrants.

By the late 1880s overseas emigration had become a popular subject for discussion and publication. Many writers emphasized the need for emigration and focused on Hawaii as the primary target, seeing it as a way station toward further expansion into Mexico, South America, and Australia. One of these writers, Ōishi Masami, had been a Mitsubishi agent in the 1885 KUK General Meeting. In a book published in 1891 he discussed the relation between shipping, emigration, and the expansion of Japanese trade, calling on the government to encourage the peaceful emigration of Japanese overseas. Much of the proemigration activity of the time was semiofficial. To take one case, in 1893 a number of prominent government officials and journalists, including Taguchi Ukichi, established the Colonization Society.[66]

Emigration of Japanese to Hawaii had first been approved in 1884, and over the next decade the N.Y.K. carried the great majority of emigrants under government sponsorship. Between 1885 and 1894 N.Y.K. vessels made twenty-four voyages to Hawaii, transporting more than 27,000 emigrants. This business was actually the first regular long-distance ocean shipping by Japanese steamships, but it was an exceptional case, and from the standpoint of developing overseas shipping, it did not set a precedent for additional lines.[67] That could only come through the mainstay of freight transport.

Prior to the 1890s most Japanese planning for transoceanic lines concentrated on the Pacific. Mitsubishi cooperated with the government in this planning, at least until the rise of its domestic competitors. Yatarō had approved the January 1875 report from Ōkuma's Steamship Office on a trial run to San Francisco.[68] The government could not afford to subsidize that, and the first seriously considered proposal was for a line to Canada. In 1879 Mitsubishi had written to Canadian Prime Minister John A. Macdonald, offering to establish a trans-Pacific service if the *Canadian* government would subsidize it! The next year Tsukahara Shūzō was appointed to go to Canada for formal negotiations over opening a line that would connect with the Canadian Pacific Railway. On the eve of his departure, however, the matter was suspended. Macdonald regarded the proposal as premature because the C.P.R. was not even nearing completion. Later, in 1884, Macdonald revived the idea, advocating a line under the "joint control" of Mitsubishi and the C.P.R. By this time the Mitsubishi-KUK competition diverted planning away from such international ventures, though in any case the C.P.R. (with its railway completed in 1885) would probably have insisted on a monopoly of Canadian subsidies.[69]

The best opportunity for a Pacific line during the early N.Y.K. years came in the late 1880s. In May 1886 the N.Y.K. had concluded a through-freight transport agreement with the American Pacific Mail Company and the O. & O. Company that was based on an earlier contract between these two firms and Mitsubishi. The

N.Y.K.'s portion of the agreement covered the Shanghai-Yokohama route, whereas the American companies ran between Yokohama and San Francisco.[70] This contract acted as a deterrent to the N.Y.K. moving into the Pacific. As a result of a decline in the fortunes of the Pacific Mail, by the mid-1880s the O. & O. had taken over the major share of Pacific shipping. Nevertheless, despite the O. & O.'s highly profitable record during the 1880s, managerial changes in its parent firm, the Central Pacific Railway Company, presaged a more exclusive attention to the railway business. Consequently, the O. & O. appeared willing to relinquish its San Francisco-Hong Kong line, which made stops at Hawaii and Yokohama.

The N.Y.K. began secret negotiations with the O. & O. and soon reached informal agreement on taking over its line. The N.Y.K. then sent two petitions to the minister of communications, on November 13, 1888, and on March 4, 1889, requesting a mail subsidy.[71] In its attempts to persuade the government, the N.Y.K. wrote of visionary prospects in a propagandistic manner. The main points of the petition were: (1) The governments of all enlightened countries provided subsidies without which steamship companies could not operate overseas lines. (2) Emigration was the best way to expand a country's trade. Opening lines throughout the world would enable many Japanese to emigrate overseas without the anxiety of being cut off from Japan. (The N.Y.K. hoped to use the emigration issue to duplicate the profitable experience of European steamship companies.) (3) Unlike the O. & O., the N.Y.K. would not have to be concerned about the dictates of a parent railway company. On the positive side, the N.Y.K. could conclude a contract for services with the Central Pacific Railway. A chance for such an arrangement with an American railroad might not come again. (4) The N.Y.K. believed it could absorb the remaining East Asian business of the Pacific Mail, which was oriented toward the New York trade via the Panama rail link. Entry into this trade would give the N.Y.K. a headstart on a round-the-world service once the Panama Canal opened. (5) The government was urged to respond quickly and secretly because other companies contemplating a Pacific service, such as the P. & O., might also bid for the O. & O. business. Presenting a detailed budget, the N.Y.K. requested an annual subsidy of ¥500,000 for twelve years. Despite extensive lobbying of cabinet ministers (and Itō Hirobumi, head of the Privy Council), the government refused, saying that the "time was not yet right."[72]

While the subsidies required may have been beyond the government's means during the 1880s, the failure of Mitsubishi and then the N.Y.K. to exploit these opportunities on the Pacific left the N.Y.K. in a comparatively disadvantageous position in later years. Timing was an important factor in the success of overseas lines begun by the N.Y.K. in the 1890s. In contrast to the strategic lines to India and Europe, where for almost two decades the N.Y.K. was the only Japanese participant, on the Pacific the N.Y.K. had Japanese competition soon after the beginning of its service in 1896. An earlier start might have given the company more bargaining power over the long-run.

THE 1893 COMMERCIAL CODE
AND COMPANY REORGANIZATION

NEW LEGAL STATUS. Before the N.Y.K. began its expansion in the mid-1890s, it underwent a major internal administrative reform. This reform was the result of the Commercial Code of July 1893 which defined new regulations for Japanese companies.

Although the government had instituted bank regulations in the 1870s, little was done in establishing regulations defining the legal status of companies until around 1890. This ten- to twenty-year hiatus was less the result of delays in government planning than the lack of a pressing need for a company law. The large firms dominating the economy in the 1870s, like Mitsui and Mitsubishi, found that a company law was not necessarily compatible with a family-centered enterprise structure. For Mitsui a new law would entail certain disadvantageous disclosure requirements; for Mitsubishi it was somewhat superfluous in that the company was already being regulated through special legislation.

By the late 1880s there were both external and internal pressures leading the government away from its previous nonintervention. The increasing number of foreign transactions carried out by smaller firms dictated a clearer legal regulation of their responsibilities. The significance of this problem was heightened by the government's negotiations regarding the revision of the unequal treaties with the Western powers. The need to implement a commercial code, along with the civil and criminal codes, became another strategy aimed at regaining full sovereignty. Domestic pressures for legal reform were probably even more compelling. Following the completion of the Matsukata deflation program in the mid-1880s there had been a great "company boom." This boom occurred mainly in railways and cotton spinning companies, but the number of banks, electric light, and even smaller shipping companies increased rapidly. By 1889 enterprises with the joint-stock pattern of organization constituted more than half of all the companies in Japan.

The proliferation of new companies helped bring on Japan's first modern financial panic in 1890, and many of the less sound firms, especially in the cotton spinning industry, went bankrupt. Against this background Japan's first commercial code, promulgated in April 1890, was slated to go into effect the next year, but through problems in the Diet was delayed until July 1893. Only part of it, however, was implemented: a company law, a law governing bills and promissory notes, and a bankruptcy law. The company law had several inadequacies: a licensing system for establishing companies and issuing company bonds and no regulations concerning mergers.[73] For the first time, however, it clearly defined the forms of companies, recognizing three types: the joint-stock company (*kabushiki kaisha*); the limited partnership (*gōshi*—form taken by Mitsubishi); and the unlimited partnership (*gōmei*—form chosen by Mitsui).[74]

In general, the new law brought most companies under closer governmental scrutiny. The basic requirement was the submission of regular business reports to the Finance Ministry. The N.Y.K. was less affected by the new rules than were other companies, for the N.Y.K. and its predecessors had been subject to financial disclosure ever since the first directive to Mitsubishi in 1875. In fact, for the N.Y.K. the new law meant less, not more, government control. The government withdrew its special supervision, revised the company's articles of association (hereafter called articles of incorporation), and gave more legal rights to directors and stockholders. For the first time the N.Y.K. could be called an independent private company.

The new freedom did not mean that the company would revise its articles of incorporation by itself. On the contrary, Itō Hirobumi, the prime minister in 1893, wanted to make the N.Y.K.'s new articles an example for other companies. Katō Masayoshi was placed in charge of drafting the articles, but Itō, through the assistance of Kawada Koichirō, invited all concerned to his private residence on October 14, 1893. Attending the meeting were the N.Y.K.'s president and vice-president (Morioka and Yoshikawa), the company's four directors (Uchida, Asada, Kondō, and Katō), Vice Minister of Communications Suzuki Tairyō, Shibusawa Eiichi, Yanosuke, and Chief Cabinet Secretary Itō Miyoji, who attended because he had participated in drafting the 1885 N.Y.K. articles. Prime Minister Itō served as chairman of the group, which deliberated over the draft line-by-line from 9:00 A.M. to 5:00 P.M.[75]

The incorporation procedure of the new Commercial Law gave the company a new name, Nippon Yūsen Kabushiki Kaisha, but the official foreign name remained Nippon Yusen Kaisha (without the macron!).[76] The new articles of incorporation stated the company's purpose as "managing the shipping business" (article 3), but the definition omitted the negatively phrased restrictions present in directives to earlier shipping companies.[77] Administratively, the N.Y.K. was to have between five and eleven directors (*torishimariyaku*) and at least two auditors. These officials were to be chosen at the General Meeting from among stockholders with more than 100 shares, though it was not explicitly stated that there had to be a vote. Appointments could be made merely by designation.[78] The new Board of Directors was empowered to elect from among its members one president, one vice-president, and an unspecified number of managing directors (*senmu torishimariyaku*). This article replaced the government's earlier power of appointment (article 11). Similarly, the new auditors gave the company the right to audit its accounts, a function performed by the Finance Ministry since 1885. Auditors were required to submit to the General Meeting: a business report; a statement of accounts which included a profit and loss statement and a reserve funds statement, a catalog of assets; a balance sheet; and a statement on profit distribution.

On December 1, 1893, the government also released the N.Y.K. from most of the restraints of the earlier directive (though not those relating to military obligations). The only major control provision remaining was the need for government approval in revising the articles of incorporation (article 7).

The revised directive of 1887 had fixed executive bonuses at between 5 and 10 percent of operating profits (article 28). This provision was eliminated in 1893. The new articles authorized the General Meeting to set salaries, while official bonuses were left to the discretion of the executives (article 16). The scale approved in December 1893 was: president, ¥400; vice-president, ¥300, executive directors, ¥200 (all monthly), and directors and auditors, ¥800 a year. Bonuses were dependent on profits and were always approved as a whole. Judging from the number of executives and the accounts of the mid-1890s, each individual executive could expect around ¥5,000 a year in bonuses.[79]

ADMINISTRATIVE CHANGES AND THE NEW BOARD. The N.Y.K. appointed a maximum of eleven directors. Six were already company officials continuing in their previous positions: the president, vice-president, and four directors (*riji*)—now renamed managing directors. The remaining five directors constituted a major innovation for the N.Y.K. Yoshikawa had proposed that powerful outside people be appointed who could use their influence on behalf of the N.Y.K. These new board members were chosen in consultations among Morioka, Yanosuke, and Kawada Koichirō before the October 14 meeting with Itō Hirobumi. The new directors were

Shōda Heigorō, representing Mitsubishi; Nakamigawa Hikojirō of Mitsui; Shibusawa Eiichi, a general representative of the business world who was particularly useful in dealing with the Japan Cotton Spinners Association; Sonoda Kōkichi, president of the Yokohama Specie Bank; and Isobe Kaneyoshi, a reserve rear admiral proposed by Itō Hirobumi. The two auditors were Abe Taizō of the Mitsubishi-affiliated Meiji Life Insurance Company and Yamamoto Sugunari of the Fifteenth Bank (the stock of which was held mostly by peers).[80] In general, these new members represented the company's major stockholders and to some extent its business clients, at least in the case of Shibusawa and the cotton spinners.

Shibusawa is certainly the most surprising member of the board, in view of his earlier clash with the Iwasaki brothers on matters of principle. Shortly after the mass resignations of December 1885, however, Mitsubishi had sought to pacify the departed members of the former KUK. At a New Year's banquet on January 2, 1886, Kawada had met with Shibusawa and reported Yanosuke's desire for a mutual understanding. Following several meetings between Yanosuke and Shibusawa, some of the planners of the KUK met with Mitsubishi executive and achieved a reconciliation, agreeing to let bygones be bygones.

This 1886 reconciliation between Shibusawa and Mitsubishi did not result in any immediate role for Shibusawa in the N.Y.K. It was only in 1893 that Mitsubishi itself felt the need for Shibusawa's services on behalf of the N.Y.K.'s business expansion. Mitsubishi also desired to change the N.Y.K.'s image. In the public mind of the early 1890s the company was completely dominated by Mitsubishi. The N.Y.K. felt this image was unfair, and by employing Shibusawa, one of the founders of the KUK, it hoped to "correct this misunderstanding." Employing him, however, was no simple matter. Shibusawa claimed that he agreed to become a director only after Yanosuke's assurance that "Mitsubishi" [meaning the N.Y.K.] was no longer "controlled by one family" but had become a "public enterprise" (*kōkyō no jigyō*).[81]

Between late 1885 and 1893 most of the leading N.Y.K. officials had been former Mitsubishi personnel. The 1893 reform did not lessen Mitsubishi's dominance at the N.Y.K.'s executive level. But the new system of outside representative directors greatly broadened the character of the company. These directors participated in fundamental decisions; for the next decade or two they provided the board with a remarkable stability; and through their outside influence they helped to give the N.Y.K. an immense clout in the business world. Shōda and Shibusawa in particular proved invaluable to the N.Y.K. in negotiating contracts of international scope and in pressing for favorable legislation for the shipping industry.

The other component on the board, the executive directors, initially proved to be less stable than these outside directors. One of the legacies of the Mitsubishi-KUK merger had been a lack of clarity regarding the locus of executive authority. The need to satisfy both parties to the merger had proved nearly disastrous for the company's management in its first few years of operation. Those disputes had since passed, but two problems remained in the new structure. The first was the nature of the presidency. From at least the beginning of 1887 Yoshikawa had been the N.Y.K.'s main executive officer. Morioka had been of crucial importance in consummating the merger in 1885 and had shepherded the company through the reforms of 1893. With these reforms in effect his role was now superfluous. His election as president by the company in December 1893 was an expression of gratitude, for he resigned in March 1894. The presidency and the locus of executive authority were then united in Yoshikawa's hands.

The second problem had been the presence of too many executives to manage the daily business of the company, but this too was solved in 1894. Simultaneously with Morioka's resignation, Uchida and Asada both resigned as managing directors (though for the time being they remained directors as did Morioka). Their resignations can only be attributed to the company's desire to rationalize the shape of its exectuive.

The next problem confronting the directors was who would fill the position of vice-president. In terms of the length of executive service in the shipping industry and the N.Y.K., both Uchida and Asada had seniority over Kondō Renpei, and Uchida had already been passed over once before in favor of Yoshikawa. During the past six or seven years, however, Kondō had earned a reputation for talented management through his handling of the N.Y.K.'s retrenchment. In fact, several years earlier Kondō was about to be appointed a director of the Bank of Japan, but Yanosuke intervened to block the appointment specifically to keep Kondō's talents in the N.Y.K. When the question of the N.Y.K. vice-president arose in early 1894, Yanosuke pressed vigorously for Kondō's promotion to the post, and the recommendation was quickly accepted. Kondō's biographer states that the executive changes of 1894 were made by the "large stockholders, Yanosuke and Kawada, together with the new directors," and that the number of executive directors had been reduced so that the remaining executives "could make more efficient use of their abilities."[82]

The resignations of 1894 left the N.Y.K. with three executive officers: Yoshikawa, the president; Kondō, the vice-president; and Katō, the managing director. Kondō and Katō, the two executives under the president, now enjoyed greatly expanded powers. Kondō managed both the business and supplies departments; Katō, both accounting and general affairs (See Figure 6 for 1885). This concentration of power solved the excessive dispersal of authority, but it also left something of an administrative vacuum in that there were no middle-level managers. Accordingly, in April 1894 the company carried out the first administrative reform of its head office, which retained the distinction between senior executives and middle-level managers (Figure 7). Thus the responsibilities of Kondō and Katō were consolidated into a Business Division and a Legal Division. Under these divisions, managers (*shihainin*) headed sections (*kakari*) which had the same functions as the old departments.

The April 1894 reform marks the emergence of the N.Y.K.'s first real middle-level managers. The two new managers, shown in Chart 5, were both ex-Mitsubishi men who had been strategically situated during the competition with the KUK. Before the merger Haruta Gennojō was Mitsubishi's branch manager in Yokkaichi.[83]

FIGURE 7 N.Y.K. Executive Structure, April 11, 1894

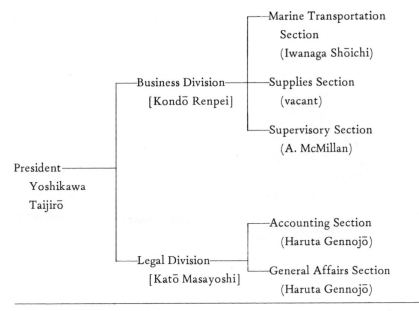

Sources: NYK-TG#18, March 21, 1894; and #21, April 11, 1894; *NYK 70 nenshi,* pp. 630-631.

Note: The N.Y.K. histories do not list Kondō and Katō as division heads, but the directors' minutes clearly indicate that their responsibilities were divided as shown here.

Iwanaga Shōichi served under Yoshikawa in the Kobe branch in the 1880s, and after the merger succeeded Kondō Renpei as Yokohama Branch Manager. Iwanaga played a leading role in the N.Y.K.'s later expansion, and from 1899 to 1911 he was managing director.

This new structure still did not make clear how much authority would be delegated to the executive directors. ("Executive directors" is used as a collective term to refer to the managing director as well as to the president and vice-president, both of whom were also formally designated "managing directors" [*senmu torishimariyaku*]). According to administrative regulations adopted in April, the executive directors were to carry out the decisions made by the Board of Directors. However, the board had been unable to draw a clear distinction between what had to be decided by the

FIGURE 8 Kondō Renpei
N.Y.K. president, 1895–1921

FIGURE 9 Katō Masayoshi
N.Y.K. vice-president, 1895–1915

FIGURE 10 Iwanaga Shōichi
N.Y.K. managing director, 1899–1911

Photographs: courtesy of the Internal & Public Relations Chamber, NYK LINE.

board and less important matters which could be left to the discretion of the executive directors. The company decided to postpone further reform until this distinction had worked itself out in practice. In the meantime executive directors were required to seek approval at the directors meeting "as the occasion demanded" (*zuiji*).[84]

Yoshikawa Taijirō lived a full life as an educator and a businessman. He was a gregarious man who drank heavily, but that was not necessarily the cause of the illness that began to overtake him shortly after the outbreak of the Sino-Japanese War in the summer of 1894. During the war he conducted company affairs from his bed, but by spring 1895 he developed lung complications and died on November 11, 1895. Yanosuke then held discussions with each director and without delay secured the appointments of Kondō as president and Katō as vice-president.[85]

Following Yoshikawa's death the N.Y.K. had eight directors (Isobe and Uchida had resigned in August 1895). Of these only Kondō and Katō were executive directors. They were joined by Iwanaga in 1899 when he became managing director. As a team these three stayed together for more than a decade, giving the company sustained managerial calm and stability.[86] Together they presided over the N.Y.K.'s overseas expansion during which the company increased the size of its fleet sixfold through wars and new subsidy laws, extended its lines around the world, and sailed proudly into new waters as the flagship of Japanese imperialism. This burgeoning new power was preceded by fundamental changes in Japan's industrial structure that forced a change in the business strategy of the shipping industry.

THE N.Y.K. IN THE BUSINESS WORLD

Though the N.Y.K. had been a monopoly at its birth, during its first decade many smaller shipping companies emerged and rather quickly increased their share of the country's tonnage. These new firms benefited from the increasing business opportunities afforded by the growth of mining, railways, and manufacturing industries like cotton spinning. For large firms like the N.Y.K. and to a lesser extent the O.S.K. there were causal links between this changing industrial structure and expansion into overseas shipping lines. These links consisted of "pull" factors, namely, developments in foreign trade which created new opportunities for overseas shipping, and "push" factors, that is, competitive forces within Japan which cut into profits from domestic business.

STRUCTURE OF THE DOMESTIC SHIPPING INDUSTRY. In domestic shipping the geographic distribution of the N.Y.K.'s lines in the early 1890s remained virtually identical to that of its predecessors, Mitsubishi and the KUK. The N.Y.K. was strong in northern Japan and in shipping between the Japan Sea coast north of Niigata and Tokyo. It was also still dominant in the country's main coastal artery, the Yokohama-Kobe route. But its operations in western Japan were limited to tramps.[87] This area was serviced primarily by the O.S.K., though it had encountered severe competition from small shipowners there following its establishment in 1884. By 1890 these small owners had joined with the O.S.K. to form the Kansai Steamship Union (Kansai Dōmei Kisen), which agreed to a sharing of income and common services for passengers.[88]

It is sometimes said that the N.Y.K. devoted its attention to consolidation and retrenchment in its early years, whereas the O.S.K. concentrated on growth.[89] This generalization is not borne out by O.S.K. ship statistics or by the company's income over its first seven or eight years. Like the N.Y.K., the O.S.K. followed a ship consolidation program during these years. In 1893 its fleet of 17,875 tons was barely above its 1885 level. But in the meantime it had scrapped many vessels, reducing the number from 99 to 51; implemented a ship acquisition program in which 26 of the 35 vessels it purchased were newly constructed; and doubled its average ship size to 350 tons. This last figure contrasts with the N.Y.K.'s average of 1,426 tons in 1893 and strengthens the impression of the O.S.K. as a regional company confined mostly to western Japan.

Financially, the O.S.K.'s 1892 income of ¥893,000 was lower

than that of 1885, but then the N.Y.K.'s own income had increased by only 9.4 percent between 1886 and 1892. The O.S.K.'s initial ¥1.2 million authorized capital stock, however, had been increased to ¥1.8 million in May 1893, and between 1885 and 1892 its assets had grown by 38 percent to ¥2.1 million. In the same period the N.Y.K.'s assets had declined by 7 percent.[90] Rather than demonstrating a faster O.S.K. growth rate, these figures reflect the elimination of the N.Y.K.'s excess paper capital and not a real decline of its assets in terms of market value. The O.S.K. began to grow into a large company only after the stimuli of more rapid industrial growth, war, and increased government aid in the mid-1890s.

A different, more common view of the O.S.K. is that, in contrast to Mitsubishi and the N.Y.K., the Osaka company "developed through its own efforts without governmental support."[91] On the contrary, government aid was an important factor in enabling the O.S.K. to achieve its dominant position in western Japan. In August 1887, the O.S.K. petitioned the government for an annual ¥50,000 subsidy for ship improvement to last for eight years. This subsidy, which began the following year, was extremely small compared to the N.Y.K.'s. But the O.S.K.'s fleet was also small in comparison, and in view of the limited geographic scale of the company's services, the subsidy was substantial enough to give the O.S.K. a decisive edge over its competitors. Later, beginning in 1890 the O.S.K. received an additional ¥20,000 annual mail subsidy for lines which the company had been operating under government designation as a condition for its earlier subsidy.[92]

The third major Japanese shipping company of the late nineteenth century was the Tōyō Kisen Kaisha (Oriental Steamship Company), established in 1896 by Asano Sōichirō. Asano's shipping interests originated in the early 1880s when he was selling coal from Hokkaido mines and expanding the Fukagawa Cement Works, leased from the government in 1881 and purchased in 1883. Asano had become a KUK promoter in 1882 in the hope that the new company would lower freight rates for his shipments.

When the KUK merged with Mitsubishi in 1885, however, he severed connections with the N.Y.K. Freight rates soon increased, and Asano found himself in the same situation he had been in before the formation of the KUK. After consulting with Shibusawa Eiichi, he decided to establish his own shipping company. In November 1886 he set up the Asano Marine Transportation Office (Asano Kaisōbu) with a capitalization of ¥200,000. This firm did not have a strong regional economic base similar to that enjoyed by the O.S.K. in the Kansai. Instead Asano followed a strategy of specializing in large shipments, as indicated by the four ships he purchased averaging 1,279 tons. Unlike the N.Y.K. and the O.S.K. he did not open regular lines. He preferred to operate in areas not serviced by the two large companies. Asano soon became a powerful figure in the shipping world because he brought together many of the country's independent shipowners into the Association of Shipping Enterprises (Kaiungyō Dōmeikai), formed to avoid fruitless competition. By 1895 it had grown to thirty-five members.[93]

The number of independent shipowners grew steadily. In 1885 shipowners outside the two main companies held less than 10 percent of the country's tonnage, whereas the N.Y.K. alone possessed about 75 percent. But by 1893, as shown in Table 41, for the first time the combined fleets of the N.Y.K. and O.S.K. constituted less than half the country's tonnage. The N.Y.K. retained its monopoly of large ships, but had lost its overwhelming dominance in total tonnage by the eve of the mid-1890s expansion. Though these new shipowners hurt the N.Y.K.'s domestic business by offering lower freight rates, they also had an integral function in the financial consolidation of both the N.Y.K. and the O.S.K. By the early 1890s, these small owners had begun to purchase older ships from Western countries, but they were also the only market for the older ships being sold by the N.Y.K. and the O.S.K.

INDUSTRIAL INTERDEPENDENCE AND OVERSEAS EXPANSION. By any standard the N.Y.K. remained a large company. In the late 1880s, by its own reckoning, it was the third largest steamship

TABLE 41 National Steamship Totals, 1885–1893
(Number of Ships, Tonnages, and Percentages of National Tonnage)

	N.Y.K.			O.S.K.			Rest of the Country			Totals	
	No.	GT	%	No.	GT	%	No.	GT	%	No.	GT
1885	58–	68,198	(76.8)	83–	15,075	(17.0)	87–	5,496	(6.2)	228–	88,765
1886	51–	61,990	(67.1)	74–	14,137	(15.3)	102–	16,288	(17.6)	227–	92,415
1887	50–	64,905	(60.2)	63–	13,177	(12.2)	139–	29,726	(27.6)	252–	107,808
1888	50–	67,516	(55.5)	55–	12,933	(10.6)	176–	41,178	(33.9)	281–	121,627
1889	47–	68,305	(50.8)	54–	13,717	(10.2)	210–	52,526	(39.0)	311–	134,548
1890	46–	66,638	(46.6)	56–	16,067	(11.2)	223–	60,292	(42.2)	325–	142,997
1891	47–	65,671	(44.5)	52–	15,973	(10.8)	236–	65,930	(44.9)	335–	147,574
1892	47–	66,780	(42.5)	50–	15,881	(10.1)	278–	74,486	(47.4)	375–	157,147
1893	45–	64,157	(38.3)	51–	17,875	(10.7)	304–	85,458	(51.0)	400–	167,490

Sources: OSK 80 nenshi, pp. 405, 762–763; NYK 70 nenshi, p. 675.

Note: The "Rest of the Country" category is calculated by subtracting the N.Y.K. and O.S.K. figures from the national totals. I have computed all percentages.

company in the world. Several European shipping companies had faster growth rates in the 1890s, and in 1900 the N.Y.K. ranked fifth in the world in capital and seventh in tonnage.[94] In 1894, before its capital stock increase in the mid-1890s, the N.Y.K. was more than twice the size of the new Mitsubishi Gōshi Kaisha in assets (¥14,366,000 to ¥6,356,000).[95] Finally, as shown in Table 42, in 1896 it was still almost five times larger than its nearest competitor, the O.S.K., and overall it was the second largest joint-stock company in Japan.

Railways had achieved the leading position among the country's joint-stock companies through a combination of government support and private investment. The government had constructed all routes in the 1870s, but by the end of the decade there were two opposing pressures on railway policy. The first, in the wake of the Satsuma Rebellion, was the military's recognition of the strategic importance of railways. The second was the inflationary crisis of the late 1870s and the retrenchment policy adopted in 1880. The second proved the strongest, and the government cut back on its railway construction in the 1880s. As a substitute, the government encouraged railway construction through private capital. In many respects this was an ad hoc policy. It was never affirmed or delineated fully as government shipping policy had been in the 1870s. Though private groups raised the capital and operated new railways which lacked direct government financial backing, the government retained its own options through numerous supervisory controls and rights to military expropriation. This policy left the future ownership of railway lines more open to question than that of shipping companies.[96]

The first concrete expression of the new railway policy was the Japan Railway Company, formed in November 1881 to build a line from Tokyo to Aomori Prefecture. This was no more a "private company" than the N.Y.K. of the late 1880s, for the government exempted its land from national taxation, guaranteed an 8 percent dividend on paid-up capital, and had the Railway Bureau build part of the line. Peers and institutions they owned purchased most of the company's stock during its first year. Mitsubishi itself

TABLE 42 Japan's Largest Joint-Stock Companies
by Assets, March 1896
(¥1,000)

Company	Assets
Communications	
1. Japan Railway Company	32,867
2, N.Y.K.	18,330
3. Hokkaido Colliery & Railway Co.	12,896
4. Sanyō Railway Co.,	10,698
5. Kyushu Railway Co.	10,481
6. Kansai Railway Co.,	7,053
7. Chikuhō Railway Co.	4,175
8. O.S.K.	3,865
9. Osaka Railway Co.	3,236
10. Toyosu Railway Co.	2,559
Manufacturing	
1. Kanegafuchi Cotton Spinning Co.	3,284
2. Osaka Cotton Spinning Co.	2,413
3. Mie Cotton Spinning Co.	2,245
4. Hokkaido Flax Spinning Co.	1,506
5. Settsu Cotton Spinning Co.	1,436
6. Okayama Cotton Spinning Co.	1,397
7. Tokyo Cotton Spinning Co.	1,358
8. Kanekin Cotton Weaving Co.	1,333
9. Osaka Alkali Manufacturing Co.	1,309
10. Amagasaki Cotton Spinning Co.	1,264

Source: Nakamura Seishi, "Wagakuni ni okeru jōi kigyō no hensen," Nakagawa Kei-ichirō et al., *Kindai Nihon keieishi no kiso chishiki*, pp. 450–451.

held 8 percent. After 1883 the company was able to raise more capital from the public, for early business results following initial construction pushed profits beyond the government's 8 percent dividend guarantee. This success helped to stimulate Japan's first railway boom that produced the private companies listed in Table 42.

The stockholding in these railway companies sheds light on the relationship between shipping and Japanese industrial development in general. The railways became a major target of Mitsubishi investment activities in the 1890s. Mitsubishi held a substantial, and in some cases dominant, share of six of the seven largest joint-stock companies in Japan: the Japan Railway Company, the N.Y.K., the fourth ranking Sanyō Railway (the company's largest stockholder and a 9.8 percent share in September 1891), the Kyushu Railway (34,659 shares), the Kansai Railway (11,700 shares in 1895), and the Chikuhō Railway (35,726 shares).[97]

Earlier in this chapter, it was shown that the rise of the railways had cut sharply into the N.Y.K.'s shipping income. The dual pattern of Mitsubishi's holdings in both the N.Y.K. and railway companies was not simply a risk-avoidance tactic to offset these losses; it was also part of a more positive strategy. Yoshikawa Taijirō gave the clearest explanation of this in the N.Y.K.'s 1887 General Meeting:

> Some people worry that the shipping industry may decline because of the development of railways and the consequent competition from overland transport. This is nothing but a shortsighted view. Land transport and shipping are like the two wheels of the same vehicle. They are interdependent, and together will help each other's development. We can say for sure that if overland rail traffic becomes heavy, it will give rise to prosperous trade in regions which until now have had no means of transport, and these regions will quickly be able to transport their products overland to the ports. As a result, railways will lead to more and more traffic on sea routes and bring increasing vigor to maritime enterprises. In fact, this trend is inevitable. All European and American countries have followed the same pattern in the development of their sea and land transport systems.[98]

Yoshikawa's comments were made in a climate of anticipation encouraged by new construction on the Japan Railway that began in 1886 and by a government proclamation on private railway regulations in May 1887. The content of his explanation, however, was not new to Mitsubishi or N.Y.K. personnel. Yatarō's motives for originally investing in the Japan Railway had been to open up a transport network to remote areas like the Tōhoku region and to bring inland products to coastal ports. He expected this to increase the volume of Mitsubishi's freight. In later years this railway became integrated with Mitsubishi enterprises in the north, especially mining and products from the Koiwai dairy farming enterprise. In addition to his capital investment Yatarō had strengthened his hand by placing several Mitsubishi executives in the company as directors. Yatarō's own adviser, Ono Yoshimasa, became vice-president of the company in 1887 and president in 1892.[99]

The reasoning of Yatarō and Yoshikawa was equally applicable in Kyushu where the railways ran through the rich coal basins to the ports, thereby integrating mining, railway, and shipping enterprises. The desire to integrate business functions, however, was not Mitsubishi's sole motive for investing in Kyushu railways. There was an added element of competition. Mitsui had purchased the Miike Coal Mine in 1888, but even earlier it had been the government's sole agent for the sales of the mine. Furthermore, after 1888 Mitsui bought more coal mines in Kyushu, and through its sales network, Mitsui Bussan managed to control the distribution of much of the coal in Kyushu. Mitsui's movement into Kyushu was a setback for Mitsubishi, for its reliance on Kyushu coal was almost as great as its reliance on shipping had been in the early 1880s. Accordingly, its investment in Kyushu railways, in addition to providing transport for its own coal, was a means of compensating for Mitsui's advantages in distribution.[100]

The same symbiotic relationship between railways and shipping existed in the case of the Hokkaido Colliery & Railway Company. This is the only one of the top seven joint-stock companies in Japan where I have been unable to document Mitsubishi investment. However, the N.Y.K.'s Morioka and Yoshikawa were both members of its promotion committee, and even more significantly, Yoshikawa served from 1889 to 1891 as a company standing committeeman, a position filled through a stockholders election.[101] Again, this interest was consistent with the N.Y.K.'s transport of coal and its traditionally strong position in Hokkaido trade.

Yoshikawa's confidence in railways may not have anticipated the dual impact of their development. Some lines benefited the shipping industry, as he described, but others hurt. The greatest exception to his positive outlook was the Tokaido line, though this opened two years after his speech to the N.Y.K. stockholders. The Japan Railway Company's line to Aomori, completed in 1891, also led to a rapid decline in steamship passenger traffic.[102] What does seem true is that, whether railways were good or bad for short-term shipping profits, they all influenced the N.Y.K. to expand its operations overseas. The Tokaido line exerted this influence indirectly. By capturing the majority of the passenger business and a substantial portion of the freight in the country's main traffic artery, it brought to an end the profitability of shipping based mainly on coastal trunk lines. The long-term income projections dictated by railways made overseas expansion a necessity for the shipping industry. On the other hand, the integrated functions of the Kyushu railways had a more direct impact on expansion. By facilitating the distribution of coal they made possible its rise as a major export item to East Asia in the mid-Meiji years.

Railways constituted an immense industry in the late 1890s. In 1896 they had one-quarter of all the paid-up capital stock of the country's joint-stock companies (¥89 out of ¥357.5 million), and by 1894 there was about three times as much private as government track (1,537 to 581 miles).[103] There had, however, long been sentiment in the Railway Bureau favoring nationalization of railways. When the business crisis of 1890 exposed the shaky finances of many private railways, the government passed the Railway Construction Law in 1892, which included the principle of nationalization for those lines unable to fulfill state construction goals. This act saw increased state railway building, but the second investment boom, which followed the Sino-Japanese War, led to new private construction both of local railways and extensions of trunk lines.[104] A ten-year debate over nationalization then ensued, with

Mitsubishi one of the leading opponents.[105] In the end, however, the compensation Mitsubishi received following the railway nationalization in 1906 was a major stimulus to its diversification into other industries.

While railways and shipping constituted the largest industries in the communications field, cotton spinning companies, as shown in Table 42, were the largest manufacturing enterprises. In contrast to railways and shipping, cotton spinning companies had emerged in the 1880s almost exclusively through the investment of private entrepreneurs and their success in importing foreign technology.[106] Zaibatsu families and the government had been major investors in railways and shipping. Cotton spinners, on the other hand, generally remained independent of zaibatsu investment, and especially in the late 1880s and 1890s they raised their capital internally.[107] The main stockholders in the cotton spinning industry were people who either worked in the firms or had close business connections with them. One survey of occupations has shown that 55 percent of the major stockholders in the industry in 1898 were either directors of cotton spinning companies or dealers in dry goods, cotton cloth, and cotton yarn. Other clearly non-zaibatsu occupations represented were rice fertilizer merchants and brewers.[108] This pattern of stockholding had important implications for the relations cotton spinning companies had with one another. In contrast to the diverse enterprises in the zaibatsu that were oriented vertically toward their head offices, the individual cotton spinning companies developed strong horizontal ties within their own industry. As early as 1882 the Japan Cotton Spinners Association (Nihon Bōseki Rengōkai) had been set up under the leadership of Shibusawa Eiichi, who had invested heavily in the Osaka Cotton Spinning Company, the first successful large-scale firm in the industry. This superior industry-wide organization gave the cotton spinners a stronger influence in negotiating import and export contracts than that of the producers of Japan's largest export items like tea and raw silk. The distribution of these latter products was still controlled by wholesalers and their exports were handled mostly by foreign merchants.[109]

The year 1890 was a major transition point for the cotton spinners. Too many companies had been established in the boom of the late 1880s. The resulting overproduction helped spark the financial crisis of 1890 when many firms went bankrupt as banks turned off the supply of short-term credit upon which the industry depended. The overproduction problem strengthened the horizontal ties among the big cotton spinning companies and encouraged them to enlarge their export markets. A related point of transition was the industry's shift from the use of Japanese raw cotton, which made up half of all consumption in 1888, to imported supplies. By 1896 Indian and Chinese raw cotton accounted for 75 percent of total consumption, with the superior Indian variety occupying 58 percent of the total.[110]

These changes in Japanese cotton spinning meant more import and export business for the shipping industry. In short, the key industries which emerged in the 1880s—mining, shipping, railways, and cotton spinning—became interdependent and helped make the country's industrial growth self-propelling. Acting on the basis of their mutual economic needs, leaders of these industries developed business alliances which encompassed their key firms as well as trading companies, industrial associations, and, in some cases, governmental institutions. This coordinated strategy led to effective cross-industrial organization that overcame the lack of resources possessed by any one firm or industry and presented a common front against foreign competitors. This pattern of growth had for the first time laid the basis for the potential profitability of long-distance overseas shipping and the period of rapid expansion to come.

Part Three
The Era of Expansion: 1893–1914

In 1892 N.Y.K. shipping lines were limited to a few relatively short routes within East Asia. By late 1896 N.Y.K. services extended to India and Australia, across the Pacific to the United States, and through the Suez Canal to Europe, all but "encircling the globe." What had wrought this revolution in transport? One factor was the emergence of organized alliances among Japanese business institutions. Designed primarily to support the textile industry in its struggle with foreign competition, these trading networks enabled the N.Y.K. to begin a service to India in 1893, the company's first transoceanic line. The major impetus for this expansion, however, was the Sino-Japanese War. The war provided the government with increased financial strength (as a result of the indemnity received from China), and it furnished the military with a heightened sense of urgency regarding wartime transport support. Enhanced financial capacity and national security concerns led the government to pass greatly expanded subsidy programs for shipping in the late 1890s.

Subsidies played a decisive role in the early years of the N.Y.K.'s transoceanic lines. The company was dependent on government aid because of the barriers to entry into these lines. A system of shipping conferences, the principal obstacle, maintained various exclusionary policies to prevent the entry of newcomers. The conference system, whose leading members were British, was especially strong on the European line, which also became the most important area of N.Y.K. business. Between 1896 and 1902, then, the N.Y.K. waged a well-planned tactical campaign that enabled it first to enter this European conference and then to achieve parity with its other members. As early as 1899, however, N.Y.K. leaders recognized that the lack of Japanese freight on the westbound voyage to Europe could undermine their drive for parity. In order to buttress this main line the N.Y.K. took steps to load more Europe-bound China freight. This policy of establishing branch lines in China that would connect with the European line I have called the "feeder strategy."

Even with the N.Y.K.'s successful entry into its overseas lines, until the Russo-Japanese War the company remained a multi-service firm, active in all areas of Japanese shipping, namely, coastal, near-seas, international feeder, and transoceanic services. Between 1904 and 1909, however, the N.Y.K. withdrew from the feeder lines and some coastal services. Prompting these withdrawals were: (1) competition in international feeder lines from foreign companies; (2) competition in coastal routes from domestic tramps, which had grown rapidly during the Russo-Japanese War; and (3) government intervention, first, through control over feeder lines in China and second, through stricter subsidy legislation that gave the government more regulatory power and reduced aid to all but near-seas and designated transoceanic services. In adjusting to these forces the N.Y.K. adopted a strategy of specialization for its transoceanic lines that can be called conservative because it exhibited a reluctance to open new long-distance lines prior to subsidization and a disinclination to develop tramp services.

Between 1900 and 1914 government subsidies and management's decision to limit the dividend enabled the N.Y.K. to accumulate enormous reserves. Since the company had virtually no debt, its reserves gave it the capacity to develop new services independent of government programs. With a few exceptions, notably in India, it did not utilize its reserves for this purpose. The fact that it did not leads to the ironic conclusion that in the very period when the company was becoming wealthy it was adopting a conservative strategy of specialization. Besides competition and government intervention, the N.Y.K.'s internal situation helps to account for this seeming anomaly. Kondō Renpei, the N.Y.K. president, was less innovative than his counterpart in the O.S.K., and the Imperial House's large ownership share in the N.Y.K. tended to make him even more cautious. The N.Y.K., too, was more than just a shipping firm. A large portion of its reserves were unavailable for new shipping services, for they were tied up in long-term investments in port construction, industrial firms, and banks, thereby fulfilling national developmental functions. Finally, management wished to retain control over reserves in case they were needed for a future Panama Canal line. Many stockholders, however, objected to N.Y.K. financial policy, for though reserves increased, the capital stock from which the stockholders drew their dividend remained frozen at the level established in 1896.

The subsidies which stabilized the N.Y.K.'s overseas lines and enriched the company also profoundly affected Mitsubishi. As described in Part Two, the establishment of the N.Y.K. led to a major transformation in Mitsubishi from a company of the sea to a company of the land. Government subsidies, especially those for the N.Y.K., led to a second, more far-reaching transformation of Mitsubishi. The subsidies and their accompanying protective legislation prompted the N.Y.K., after 1900, to buy most of its large ocean-going ships from Mitsubishi instead of from British firms. These N.Y.K. purchases established the base for Mitsubishi's diversification into heavy industry. The N.Y.K. was thus in the forefront of two major economic legacies of the pre-World War I period: the emerging international competitiveness of textiles, achieved through cooperation with trading companies, and the successful beginnings of heavy industry.

SEVEN

International Lines: Commercial Diplomacy, 1893–1902

THE BEGINNINGS OF OVERSEAS LINES

The N.Y.K.'s initial service outside of East Asia was the Bombay line, started in 1893 (Map 2). New trading companies and the growth of the textile industry provided the commerce that made this line successful. The growing financial strength of the government after the Sino-Japanese War led to larger subsidies, making possible the establishment in 1896 of the European line, the most important of several new overseas lines. These developments bridge the events of the early 1890s, described in Chapter 6, and the rapid expansion that occurred in the late 1890s.

BOMBAY LINE AND THE COTTON SPINNERS, 1893–1896. Individual firms in the cotton spinning industry that sustained the N.Y.K.'s first transoceanic line were not vertically integrated; that is, the firms did not have the sales and purchasing organization either to market their product abroad or secure the raw materials necessary for production. The industry did not have the time or resources to add these functions to its management, given the sudden switch to imported raw cotton in the late 1880s and the rapid emergence of exporting early in the 1890s. Instead, these functions were performed by trading companies. Naigaimen and Nihon Menka were the two most important trading companies specializing in the

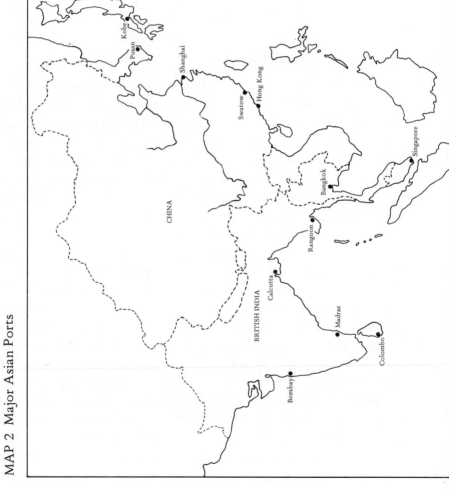

MAP 2 Major Asian Ports

import of raw cotton. Mitsui Bussan, in contrast, performed a wider range of functions for the cotton spinners. Like the specialized importers, Mitsui obtained raw cotton abroad; in addition it monopolized the import of machinery through its exclusive dealership with Platt Brothers, a British firm, and utilized its own trading network to market Japanese cotton yarn abroad, especially in China. These trading firms also had exclusive sales contracts with the largest spinning companies. Naigaimen, the leader in the import of Indian cotton, was, for example, the sole agent for Osaka Spinning Company and the Mie Spinning Company. Mitsui Bussan, which was stronger in China and which handled more than half of all raw cotton imports, had an exclusive contract with the Kanegafuchi Spinning Company. This institutional apparatus served the principal international needs of the cotton spinners: to import raw cotton from China and India and to export the manufactured yarn, principally to China.[1]

Despite this impressive institutional growth, in the early 1890s two obstacles remained to thwart the competitiveness of the Japanese cotton spinners in East Asian markets: government tax policy in the form of duties on exported yarn and imported raw cotton and the high freight rate on Indian raw cotton between Bombay and Kobe. According to an 1889 study by the Spinners Association the import duty and the freight rate respectively accounted for 3 percent and 4.5 percent of the production cost of yarn. In 1893 the total expense for production and exportation of one bale of Japanese cotton yarn to Shanghai was ¥93.4, compared to ¥90.3 for the competing yarn from India. This expense included ¥2.7 for freight charges on raw cotton from Bombay to Kobe, ¥1.4 for the import duty, and ¥3.2 for the tax on the yarn exported from Japan. During the 1890s intensive lobbying by the Cotton Spinners Association and the Chambers of Commerce led to government abolition of the export tax on yarn in 1894 and the import duty on raw cotton in 1896. The next obstacle, the high freight rate, was created by the monopoly on the Bombay-Kobe line held by a shipping conference of three companies: the P. & O. (the dominant member), the Austrian Lloyd, and the Navigazione

Generale Italiana. To meet this challenge an alliance emerged between cotton spinners and the N.Y.K. against the conference rate
of 17 rupees (Rs.) per ton for raw cotton. Opposition, however,
could not be effective as long as the shipping conference controlled
the Indian shippers.[2]

The action which led to an effective alliance was taken by the
large diversified Indian firm of Tata & Sons. Tata exported raw
cotton to Japan and Indian cotton yarn to China. In 1891 the firm
had set up a branch in Kobe and from this vantage point became
aware of how the P. & O.-controlled freight rates obstructed the
growth of trade between India and Japan. In May 1893 one of
the firm's senior partners, J.G.N. Tata, came to Japan for discussions with the N.Y.K. and the Spinners Association. The commitments he received from them enabled him to persuade Indian
shippers to bind together to fight the P. & O. by providing cargo
guarantees for a competing shipping service between Bombay and
Kobe. This would be jointly run by Tata and the N.Y.K., each
contributing two ships. With the Indian link secure, the chain was
completed by agreements between the N.Y.K. and the Cotton
Spinners Association in the autumn of 1893. Early in September
the largest firms in the association, the Kanegafuchi, Osaka, and
Mie spinning companies and the Naigaimen and Nihon Menka importers, took the lead in signing a formal contract with the N.Y.K.
They then persuaded smaller firms to join, and a new contract
was drawn up on October 28, summarized as follows: (1) The
N.Y.K. promised one sailing every three weeks (or at the very
least, four weeks) with a ship of more than 3,000 tons. (2) The
formal freight rate would be 17 Rs. per ton, but the N.Y.K. would
pay loyal members of the association a rebate of 4 Rs. (3) Companies using non-N.Y.K. ships would be penalized 50 *sen* per bale.
(4) The N.Y.K. promised to transport at least 30,000 bales of raw
cotton each year. (5) The association guaranteed annual shipments
of at least 50,000 bales.[3]

Though the N.Y.K.'s first ship sailed on November 7, the competition with the conference had begun in earnest several weeks
before. On October 16 the P. & O.'s East Asian branch managers

visited Japan and delivered their first blow to the N.Y.K. in the form of a scare tactic. If the N.Y.K. did not withdraw from its planned Bombay line, they warned, the P. & O. would reopen the Yokohama-Shanghai line from which it had retired after the competition with Mitsubishi in 1876.[4]

The underlying economics of the competition gave the P. & O. cause for alarm. Essentially three shipment trades were involved: raw cotton from India to Japan; cotton yarn from India to China and, to a lesser extent, Japan; and cotton yarn from Japan to China. The P. & O. fought hard to maintain its dominance over the raw cotton shipments to Japan; but, because its own trade between India and China was more important than its shipping to Japan, the P. & O. fundamentally depended on continuing strong exports of Indian cotton yarn to China. The principal threat to this export trade was the potential strength of the Japanese cotton manufacturers in the China market. The growing strength of the Japanese industry during the 1890s thus constituted the dynamic behind the changing structure of this shipping competition.

When the N.Y.K. did not submit to heavy threats, the P. & O. adopted the more conventional tactic of severe rate-cutting. By early 1894 its rate had fallen to 2 Rs., with a rebate to contract shippers making the effective rate only 1.5 Rs. In response, the N.Y.K. agreed to cut its rate from 13 to 12 Rs. (that is, the rebate was increased to 5 Rs.), while the association guaranteed additional shipments. The association also imposed heavier penalties on shippers who deserted the Japanese-Indian alliance to import raw cotton in non-N.Y.K. vessels. By spring these "disloyal" shippers had to pay penalties of ¥3 a bale (equivalent to ¥12 a ton) on shipments they had made with the P. & O. if they wished to resume business with the N.Y.K. The penalty, equivalent to 22.8 Rs. a ton, was more than the former freight rate of 17 Rs.[5]

The competition greatly stimulated demand for raw cotton. The association estimated that Japanese cotton manufacturers would require 230,000 bales a year. These needs led the N.Y.K. to place two extra ships on the line during the peak growing season between March and June. The association then increased its guarantee to an annual 150,000 bales, and the N.Y.K. transported shipments that exceeded the guarantee for 7 Rs. a ton.[6]

Toward the end of the peak period for raw cotton the focus of the competition shifted toward the second trade, the shipment of cotton yarn from India. By June discounts on exports to China had reached 85 percent. The P. & O. also adopted more aggressive tactics in the Japanese market. What alarmed the Japanese most were the low rates at which the P. & O. was shipping cotton yarn to Japan (also at 2 Rs.). These rates made Indian yarn cheaper in the Japanese domestic market than Japan's own yarn. It was thus a threat not only to the cotton spinners' export market but also to their domestic sales.

The P. & O. received a temporary boost from the outbreak of the Sino-Japanese War in July 1894, for the government quickly requisitioned all N.Y.K. ships over 1,000 tons, including those on the Bombay line. A burst of hopeful telegrams soon flowed into the P. & O.'s head office in London. On August 7 the company's Bombay agent cabled that "the stoppage of the N.Y.K. steamers coming to this port has of course greatly weakened the opposition in the eyes of the Native shippers here and they consider it doubtful if the Japanese line will, even when the present war is over, resume running to Bombay." This prediction was capped by a "rumor" that the spinners' agreement with the N.Y.K. would not be renewed because they had not benefited from it and that "but for a feeling of sentiment & patriotism the Union would break up at once."[7]

Such false optimism was the hallmark of British firms operating in East Asia during the 1890s. In fact, after a temporary suspension of the service at the beginning of the war, the N.Y.K. was soon able to resume operations on the Bombay line by using charters. Moreover, the N.Y.K. had as an essential bulwark the organized business alliance of many Japanese institutions. Rather than signaling retreat, this alliance portended a steady advance of Japan into the Indian trade. First, as early as February 1893, Mitsui Bussan had set up a branch in Bombay to extend the range of its raw cotton imports. Then, in late 1894, through the urging of the Cotton Spinners Association the Japanese government established a consulate in Bombay. The Yokohama Specie Bank quickly followed with its own branch there in November 1894. By mid-1895 it had made available an exchange fund of 500,000 Rs. to the members of the Japanese-Indian alliance.[8]

In late 1894 and early 1895 two other adjustments helped to bring about a structural shift in the competition in the N.Y.K.'s favor. In September 1894 the N.Y.K. signed an additional contract with the Cotton Spinners Association for the export of yarn to Shanghai. Specially packaged units of four bales (equivalent to 1 ton) bearing the certificate of the association would be charged only ¥2 from Kobe (compared to the normal rate of ¥3, a reduction of 33 percent). The second change was the withdrawal of Tata in February 1895 from the shipping arrangement with the N.Y.K. In the first eleven months of the competition Tata had lost ¥72,338 (compared with the N.Y.K.'s ¥20,901), and its fortunes had worsened with the intensified competition in cotton yarn transport in the summer of 1894.[9]

These changes favored the N.Y.K. because a specialized strategy catering to the cotton spinners' needs (imports of raw cotton and exports of cotton cloth) offered the best hope for long-term profitability. As opposed to this, the transport arrangement with Tata, though useful at first in mobilizing Indian shippers, had imposed a certain inflexibility on N.Y.K. tactics, for it obligated the company to participate in the direct export of Indian cotton yarn to China, which had been one of Tata's two main concerns. With Tata's withdrawal the N.Y.K. placed two more ships on the line, thus taking over full responsibility for the transport. Then, by eliminating the stop at Shanghai it shortened the return voyage to Japan by several days and gained an advantage over the P. & O. in the speed of raw cotton deliveries.[10] This adjustment in its lines highlights the N.Y.K.'s priority—shipments of raw cotton to Japan—in contrast to the P. & O.'s own specialized strategy of concentrating on the transport of cotton yarn to China.

The P. & O. did not confine its tactics simply to business operations within Asia. Company Chairman Thomas Sutherland and other stockholders influential in the British Parliament and the Conservative Party issued frequent demands for government intervention against the Japanese coalition. Nevertheless, the P. & O. had incurred heavy losses in the struggle, and in late 1895 it asked the British government to mediate. British officials then held discussions with Katō Kōmei, a former Mitsubishi employee who was now serving as a special ambassador to England. Rather than working through government channels, the N.Y.K. entrusted the negotiations to Shōda Heigorō, the Mitsubishi member on its board, who had left for Europe in late 1895 to plan for the establishment of the N.Y.K.'s European line.[11]

Shōda's negotiations with the P. & O. in the early months of 1896 likely were helped by the impending passage of legislation which would give the N.Y.K. a special subsidy for the Bombay line. N.Y.K. discussions with the government concerning this subsidy had received support as early as May 1894 from a report of the Tokyo Chamber of Commerce recommending subsidies for overseas lines. Plans for such legislation, however, had been derailed temporarily by the Sino-Japanese War.[12] The passage of new subsidies in 1896 put the N.Y.K. in a much stronger position. The N.Y.K.'s final bargaining point was its European line, begun in March 1896, which Shōda skillfully utilized to extract from the P. & O. an agreement on the Bombay line. The settlement, reached on May 6 and implemented on July 1, provided for a yearly quota of sailings between Japan and Bombay with the P. & O. to have 48, the N.Y.K. 16, and the Austrian and Italian firms 12 each. The freight rate was set at 17 Rs., with a rebate of 5 Rs. per ton to contract shippers, the same rate that the N.Y.K. had been using since the revised agreements of early 1894. Finally, all earnings from the service were to be pooled with each company drawing a fixed quota of units, or "points." The P. & O. received 30 points, the N.Y.K. 14, and the other two firms 8 each.[13]

While this settlement was the outcome of a vigorous tactical struggle and skillful diplomacy, the resolution of the battle was foreshadowed by the increasing specialization in the trades that created a kind of division of labor conducive to a lessening of competition. For example, N.Y.K. ships leaving Bombay during February 1896 carried twenty-two times more raw cotton than the P. & O., while P. & O. boats exported five times more yarn from Bombay than the N.Y.K. during the same month. The overall growth of trade made it more profitable in the short run for the P. & O. to continue its dependence on Indian yarn. Cotton yarn shipments from Bombay to China increased from 120,614 bales in 1888 to 220,372 in the first six months of 1896. In these same years, shipments of yarn from Bombay to Japan fell from 26,071 bales to a mere 1,694.[14] Japanese demand fell especially after 1890, the year when domestic production of yarn surpassed total imports for the first time.

The late 1890s saw an especially rapid increase in exports of Japanese cotton yarn. Between 1896 and 1899 exports of yarn grew from just over 10 to more than 40 percent of production, and 90 percent of these exports went to China (including Hong Kong). Furthermore, by 1897 Japanese exports had surpassed imports of cotton yarn.[15] Insofar as this performance depended upon easy and reasonably priced access to the superior Indian raw cotton, the N.Y.K.'s strategy of specializing in direct shipments from India to Japan helped the cotton spinners not only to dominate the home market but also to decrease their dependence on it through the rapid growth of exports. In turn, this growth ensured future N.Y.K. profits on its Bombay line and also strengthened the company's lines to China.

The early Bombay line marks a specific stage in Japan's industrial revolution when Japan attained a degree of equality in full-scale international economic competition. The key feature of this line was the coalition that emerged to struggle against the freight rates imposed by foreign competitors. In this sense, the line had a greater impact in shaping an organized business strategy than in contributing to either the cotton spinning industry or the N.Y.K. in particular. As Yasuba Yasukichi has shown in his study of ocean freight rates, the abolition of the import duty on raw cotton and the export duty on cotton yarn achieved greater savings for the cotton textile industry than did the reduction in the freight rate.

Yasuba, however, then proceeded to downplay the importance of the shipping battle for the cotton spinners and to agree with contemporaries, who viewed the three-year struggle primarily as an event in maritime history.[16] Yet, in retrospect, describing the struggle as an event in maritime history seems too narrow an assessment. Other lines later became more important to the N.Y.K. Also, the institutional contribution to the cotton spinners of the business coalition (as distinct from the actual savings achieved through lower rates) cannot be overlooked. The cotton spinners needed institutional allies because they themselves performed only the function of production. Even in narrower financial terms the struggle was of considerable benefit to the cotton spinners. For example, between 1894 and 1897, some 5 to 10 percent of the Osaka Spinning Company's profits came from the rebate paid by the N.Y.K.[17] The Bombay line, then, was a major development in the emergence of Japanese business institutions and strategy and not simply an event in the history of the shipping industry.

Despite the rapid growth in India-Japan trade, the *relative* importance of the Bombay line to the N.Y.K. inevitably declined after 1896 with the opening of more distant overseas lines. Furthermore, the connection between the N.Y.K. and the cotton spinners was by no means confined to the Bombay line. The bulk of the machinery which Mitsui imported for the industry from England was carried by N.Y.K. ships. This freight gave the N.Y.K. a strong competitive position in the eastbound trade of its European line. The financial strength for the establishment of this line came from the Sino-Japanese War.

THE SINO-JAPANESE WAR AND SUBSIDY LEGISLATION, 1894–1899. A long-standing conflict between China and Japan over which country would control the Korean peninsula lay behind the outbreak of war in 1894, though the war itself was precipitated by local unrest in Korea. The N.Y.K. had suffered business setbacks there partly of its own making and partly because of the increase of Chinese influence in Korea since the Sino-Japanese accord of 1885.[18] A distinction must be drawn, though, between the conflict over Korea which led to the war and its broader effects. Korea was of minor significance to the N.Y.K., but the outcome of the war was to have worldwide implications for the company's business operations. The one-sided treaties imposed upon China after the war opened up new areas for Japanese shipping. Relevant to the diplomatic concerns of this chapter was Japan's enhanced reputation for military and commercial strength. While British official circles had sufficient respect for Japan's military prowess to anticipate her victory in the war, the same cannot be said for British businessmen who were involved with East Asia and with whom the N.Y.K. had to deal on a daily basis. Early in the war John Swire, the leading British business figure in Chinese shipping, commented that "[Japan is] bound to be beat in the end and the War may tend to open up China."[19] Perhaps even more astonishing was a remark made during the war by P. & O. Chairman Sutherland that many of the company's stockholders might live to see the day when the P. & O.'s ships were built on the Yangtze instead of in Britain.[20] No mention here of Nagasaki! Despite the Triple Intervention of Germany, Russia, and France in April 1895, which forced Japan to return to China the Liaotung Peninsula, the war helped to change these attitudes and made the N.Y.K.'s diplomatic march toward equality with Western companies much easier.

Despite a decade of strategic planning, Japan's military was shaken at the beginning of the war by the inadequacy of the country's merchant fleet. Similar to earlier military engagements, the government had to rely upon emergency purchases of foreign vessels.[21] As a result, the total tonnage in the country grew from 167,000 to 331,000 tons during 1894 and 1895, while the size of the N.Y.K.'s fleet doubled from 64,000 to 128,000 tons. This led to a postwar excess of ships, and many were designated to service new possessions such as Taiwan or to open up new lines in East Asia.[22] Most of these ships were old, in need of repairs, or of only medium size. The military need for larger vessels that could be converted to cruisers, however, provided a strong motive for the development of transoceanic lines. As Shōda Heigorō explained in a February 1895 speech, the American route, where speed was essential, would be an appropriate line on which to place new ships that could be interchangeable as merchant vessels or navy warships.[23]

The military motive for acquiring a larger fleet was matched by Japan's greater capacity for purchasing it. At ¥360 million, the indemnity from China was approximately four and a half times the size of the government's 1893 regular expenditures of ¥84.6 million. Despite civilian planning for the use of the indemnity, 85 percent of it was soon swallowed up by the military. An additional 14 percent was spent on imperial property, Taiwan, education, and a fund for natural disasters, leaving 1 percent, ¥579,762 of which was used to establish the Yawata Iron and Steel Works in Kyushu. Another ¥3.2 million was designated for the 1897 regular budget under the categories of emergency military expenses, transport, and communications. The small amount left for transport was a negligible portion of that needed for shipping subsidies. This was good news to competing foreigners. When Butterfield & Swire, the East Asian subsidiary of John Swire & Sons, heard from Masuda Takashi that "the Chinese indemnity is already fully dissipated," they asked, "where is the money [for subsidies] to come from?"[24] The indemnity did not contribute directly to postwar subsidies but rather covered emergency military and further priorities that otherwise would have been charged to the regular budget. In this sense it helped to consolidate national finance and increase Japan's international credit. This gave more flexibility to the regular budget in creating new funds for subsidies.

The movement for subsidy legislation began in the years 1892 to 1894, when several bills were presented to the Diet. Most of these favored general aid to shipping for anyone meeting certain criteria, whereas the N.Y.K. at that time was more concerned with receiving subsidies for specific lines.[25] By May 1894 N.Y.K. planning had become coordinated with that of the Tokyo Chamber of Commerce, which issued a report on May 29 recommending a subsidy for the Bombay line. On June 5, just as Japan was preparing to launch its expedition to Korea, the chamber appointed a nine-man committee to undertake a more detailed investigation of methods of shipping promotion. The most important members of this committee were Mitsubishi's Shōda Heigorō and Mitsui Bussan's Masuda Takashi. A speech delivered by Shōda to the committee on February 6, 1895, contained the key points which later appeared in the committee's final report. Shōda outlined three target areas for funding: training of seamen, shipbuilding, and aid to shipping. The principal point about shipping was the clear differentiation between two kinds of aid: (1) general promotion based on government standards and (2) subsidies for designated lines.[26] This distinction appears in the N.Y.K. records as early as May 1894, and study of the drafting process that led eventually to the maritime legislation suggests that the N.Y.K. and the Tokyo Chamber of Commerce were the main architects of the navigation law passed in 1896.

Partly because of the war the committee took over a year to complete its findings. In August 1895, its report was circulated to Diet members and formally presented to the cabinet as a memorial. Then, early in September the Shipping Bureau consulted with the N.Y.K. to see whether the company wanted to make any final amendments before it was presented to the Diet as a bill. The legislation sailed through the Diet with little opposition and was promulgated on March 24, 1896, going into effect on October 1.[27]

The principal legislation passed was the Navigation Encouragement Law. Briefly, this gave aid to vessels over 1,000 tons with a speed of more than 10 knots and less than 15 years old; ships built abroad were eligible if they were less than 5 years old. Ships meeting these criteria were to be given 25 *sen* per ton for every 1,000 miles traveled to, from, or between foreign ports, with the amount of subsidy increasing 10 percent for every additional 500 tons and 20 percent for each extra knot of speed up to a maximum of 6,000 tons and 17 knots. Together with this general aid the law also provided for Specified Line Subsidies. This gave the N.Y.K. annual payments of ¥192,108 and ¥348,960 for its Bombay and Australian lines. These lines, according to Shōda's explanation in his February 1895 speech, were subsidized at this time because the Bombay line needed help in its battle with the P. & O. and could lead to expanded services, whereas the Australian line, though less important than the other lines, such as the European and American, was presently without a major competitor; the Japanese felt that if they seized the opportunity they could monopolize the service. The promise of emigration also seemed to hold good prospects for the Australian line. On the other hand, government and industry decided to wait before subsidizing other major lines, because the European line needed additional planning before a specific budget could be presented and the N.Y.K. had to have a connection with an American railway before plans for the U.S. line could be finalized.[28]

Certain clauses in the Navigation Law encouraged speculative business. Because the payment formula was based on distance traveled, some shipping companies planned to increase the length of their lines to receive a larger subsidy.[29] Another problem was that the law indirectly subsidized foreign shipyards, for Japan's yards were not yet sufficiently advanced to provide the many large ships needed for the longer overseas lines. In response to these problems the government revised the law in 1899 to reduce the subsidy for ships built abroad to one-half that for ships constructed in Japan. Finally, in 1899 the N.Y.K. received special annual subsidies for its European and American lines in the amounts of ¥2,673,894 and ¥654,030, respectively.

The precise meaning of this subsidy legislation in the late 1890s has been the subject of considerable misinterpretation. Arthur Tiedemann has claimed that the Navigation Encouragement Law illustrated the "shift from *ad hoc* aid for specific favored companies to aid extended to any company meeting general qualifications set forth by law."[30] This assessment applies only to the general portion of the law, whereas the Specified Line program was more important. For example, between 1896 and 1914 the line subsidy program provided 75.7 percent of N.Y.K. subsidies. In comparison the general bounties under the Navigation Encouragement Law contributed only 18.8 percent. (The remaining 5.5

percent came from the direct annual ¥880,000 subsidy which lasted until 1900).[31] Also, since the line subsidies were given primarily to the large companies operating overseas, after 1900 the program as a whole temporarily retarded the trend toward deconcentration in the industry evident during the 1890s.

Teratani Takeaki, a specialist in shipbuilding history, has provided a more detailed interpretive framework which basically agrees with Tiedemann's assertion. Teratani argues that the 1896 program marked a change from the earlier policy of designating specific companies to a policy of general promotion based on specific standards. He thus sees the large line subsidies of 1899 as "a big step backward" which foreshadowed the 1909 law with its even greater emphasis on liner service.[32] This is an inaccurate picture in that it ignores the principle of "designation" as a major part of the 1896 program. Teratani does not mention the line subsidies given that year for the Bombay and Australian lines. Furthermore, it was certainly government policy in 1896 to "designate" the European and American lines for eventual special aid. It was simply assumed that subsidies would be provided for them when their planning was complete. The line subsidies of 1899 therefore should not be regarded as a "step backward" but rather as the logical development of discussions between the N.Y.K. and the Ministry of Communications between 1894 and 1896. In that period the dual principle of general bounties *together* with designated line subsidies originated.

One final point on the subsidies of the 1890s relates to business strategy. In his February 1895 speech to the Chamber of Commerce Shōda argued that the government should not impose burdensome obligations on companies receiving aid. The final result did, of course, include the usual requirement that subsidized firms had to make their ships available to the government in times of war. But in general the laws reflect Shōda's advice. They might even be called "liberal" in that they allowed companies a considerable degree of managerial autonomy in their operations. This point is not inconsistent with the principle of "designation" as applied to the overseas lines, for the requirements set there, such

as minimum ship size and speed, were no more than what the
N.Y.K. had intended to follow. Subsidies of the 1890s, then, provided massive funds for overseas lines, but unlike later laws, which
limited the range of business strategy, they left room for the autonomous planning of the firms themselves, a tendency that lasted
until the Russo-Japanese War.

THE EUROPEAN LINE AND THE FREIGHT CONFERENCE

WAR PROFITS AND ESTABLISHMENT OF THE LINE, 1894–1896.
Although the European line became the most important of the
N.Y.K. services, planning for it originated as an offshoot of the
Bombay line. In February 1894 the board decided that "as a first
step towards checking the competition on the Bombay line, the
company should extend this line to Europe and request the government to grant a subsidy for it."[33] They followed this up by
presenting a preliminary budget based on twelve sailings a year
(Table 43). The company had to lower its projected income by
¥234,138 because of the need to reduce rates in competing with
the freight conference that controlled most of the shipping between Europe and East Asia. The board then petitioned the
Ministry of Communications for a subsidy equal to the projected
annual deficit of ¥882,934, but they added a separate request
that the government provide a supplementary grant to cover
deficits in excess of the projected figure. That, of course, would
have amounted to a guarantee, and it forms an interesting parallel to the debate between the company and Matsukata in late
1885 over the meaning of the 8 percent guarantee in the original
subsidy.

The Ministry of Communications replied with an offer of ¥1.3
million, provided that the N.Y.K. utilize new ships, all of which
would have to be constructed in Britain. Since the aforementioned
budget covered only normal operating expenses, the ministry's
offer was considered insufficient, for the cost of the ships would
run to several million yen. The company, therefore, decided to

TABLE 43 Preliminary N.Y.K. Budget for the European Line,
         April 4, 1894

(¥)

Income normally expected	1,013,792	Expenditures	1,662,588
Reduced income on account of competition	234,138	(Based on 12 sailings at 138,549 each)	
Actual income	779,654		
Deficit	882,934		
	1,662,588		1,662,588

Source: NYK-TG#20, April 4, 1894.

defer planning for the European line and to concentrate instead on two other goals: obtaining a subsidy for the Bombay line and working towards a general navigation law.[34] At this point the differentiation between general aid and subsidies for designated lines becomes clear, and the N.Y.K. enters into the subsidy planning described in the last section.

The impact of the Sino-Japanese War on company finances reversed this pessimistic forecast regarding the European line.[35] Betwen 1894 and early 1896 profits from the N.Y.K. ships requisitioned for the war came to roughly ¥5 million.[36] By no means all of this massive sum was available for business expansion. Expensive repairs cut deeply into the war profits. The company, however, was able to set aside an emergency reserve of ¥2.55 million. Of this total, ¥2.25 million had been placed in the reserve in the business term ending in September 1895. Just days later, on October 9, the company formally decided to open the European line by using the war profits to compensate for deficits on the line. From a financial point of view, the next two years did not go according to plan. First, in early 1896 ¥1.2 million was removed from the reserve in a mysterious accounting procedure, which involved writing down the value of ships used during the war. This left a reserve of ¥1.35 million. In late 1896, ¥924,000 of this reserve was used for a special stockholders dividend (33 percent for the term). The remaining ¥428,000 was placed in a dividend reserve, and rapidly worsening business conditions forced the company to use all of it to pay its dividend in March 1897.[37] It is important to keep this financial situation in mind, for while the company was awash in yen when it decided to open the European line, two years later it suffered the worst internal revolt of stockholders since the KUK meeting of August 1885.

To implement its decision, on December 4, 1895, the board appointed Shōda to go to Europe to prepare for opening the line and entrusted him with full authority to negotiate on behalf of the company. In touring the various ports of England and the continent, Shōda was to establish branch offices, select agents, designate the ports of call, and order new ships. Six ships, placed on the line in 1896, had an average size of approximately 4,600 tons, substantially below the 6,000-ton standard aimed at.[38] To pay for new ships the company increased its authorized capital stock in June 1896 from ¥8.8 million to ¥22 million. The increase of ¥13.2 million was paid up through four installments over the next two years, and all of it was used to purchase ships (Table 44).

TABLE 44 Ships Purchased in the
1896 Capital Stock Increase

Line	Date of Opening	No. of Ships	Cost (¥1,000)
European	March 1896	12	9,480
American	August 1896	3	2,850
Australian	October 1896	3	1,690
Coastal	Various	7	1,520
Total		25	15,540

Source: NYK 70 nenshi, p. 57.

Overall, it is hard to overestimate the importance of the war for the opening of the line. True, the major ships employed on the line after 1897 were financed by the N.Y.K. itself through the capital stock increase, and planning for subsidies had already begun before the war in 1894. Without the war, then, subsidies might have been enacted sooner—but only by a few months and on a smaller scale. It is highly unlikely that the line subsidies of 1899 would have swollen as they did without the extra military motivation resulting from the war. If in late 1895 there had been smaller subsidies and no war profits, the N.Y.K. would have been hard put to start the line. The extra profits, then, probably gave the line a good two-year head start. Even the financing of the capital stock increase can be tied to the war, for the Imperial House subscribed to 18.3 percent of the new stock issue (equivalent to ¥2.4 million) after receiving ¥20 million from the indemnity.

INITIAL AGREEMENT WITH THE CONFERENCE, 1896-1897.   War profits enabled the N.Y.K. to initiate its European line, but they alone could not sustain it in the face of major institutional and economic barriers to entry into this European-dominated business. One barrier was the conference system, the cartel-like organization of European shipping companies. Another related obstacle was the steadily increasing ratio of ship capacity to cargo during the last two decades of the nineteenth century. The resulting excess capacity created a downward pressure on freight rates, one of the main reasons for the strengthening of the conference system during these years.[39]

The European-Far East Conference, which the N.Y.K. confronted when it began its line, had been formed in 1879. "In reading over this strange document," editorialized the *China Mail* about the original combination of shipowners, "one is apt to get confused as to whom the ocean belongs, or whether 'the sea, the open sea' appears as an asset on the books of the various companies here named."[40] Shipping companies viewed their institution in more defensive terms, arguing that they offered shippers a regular, dependable, and safe service at all times of the year. They combined to protect themselves against the predatory tramp, which came only at peak seasons to take the cream of the trade when freight rates were high.

The effectiveness of conferences depended on a number of exclusionary devices to prevent the entry of outsiders and control measures to regulate the business of member companies. The most important exclusionary device was the "deferred rebate." The rebate, usually 5 to 10 percent of the freight, was deferred to ensure that the shipper avoid using nonconference vessels during a fixed period of six months or a year. The "loyal" shipper would receive his rebate at the end of this period. A second device was the allocation of access to ports. Most members of the European-Far East Conference had, over the years, built up their own trades around home ports, the most important being Liverpool and London. Generally members of the conference were allowed to load or discharge cargo at only one of these two ports. In other circumstances, an outsider seeking access to berthing facilities without the sanction of the conference might be subject to a rate war, or shippers aligned with the conference could boycott his ships. Because of the British dominance of the conference, control of port access was the most restrictive measure from the viewpoint of the N.Y.K.

Regulation of freight rates was part of the internal control mechanism of the conference. The European conference regulated rates by quoting a maximum, rather than a common, figure in order to allow firms whose ships were slower to charge, by agreement, slightly lower rates. It was also a tactic, as John Swire explained: "We do not agree in the policy of fixing a *minimum,* it gives outsiders a knowledge what to quote in order to secure business. To name a *maximum* is often politic, so as to prevent merchants fearing 'a corner.'"[41] Full members of the conference also had an agreement to pool their cargo tonnage, which they were to carry in stipulated proportions. At the end of the year each member firm would either pay into or receive from the pool shares reflecting how much its ships had either overcarried or undercarried its allotment. Finally, the European conference, unlike the Bombay conference, had no quota on the number of sailings a member could make.

Shipping conferences were by no means monolithic, unchanging organizations. Although there was a core body of fully participating members which held voting rights, there were also a large number of companies which cooperated with only one or two of the measures just described. For example, the conference might accept cooperation from an outsider on one issue, such as rates, on the condition that it stay out of another conference area, such as a particular port. Or, an outsider's access to a port might be contingent on that firm agreeing to join the conference pool. "Associate members" frequently changed, and there were occasions when a core member would temporarily withdraw. Furthermore, the conference control devices and agreements were constantly being revised.

The two most important members of the conference were the P. & O. and the Ocean Steam Ship Company, two highly different firms. The P. & O. was London based, government-subsidized for its mail service to most parts of Asia, bureaucratic, and hesitant about expanding the conference system. Ocean Steam Ship, usually known as the Blue Funnel Line, was basically a family-owned firm led by Alfred Holt and built up through its own reserves with a strong regional base in Liverpool and powerful agents in East Asia. Several other smaller British firms such as the Ben, Shire, and Glen lines and the China Mutuals made up the other core members. Leading European firms like the French Messageries Maritimes, the other lines from the Bombay conference, and the German firms which entered in the 1890s participated as associate members. [42]

The key individual in the conference system, however, was John Swire. His ties to the conference were twofold. First, his firm of John Swire & Sons and its subsidiary, Butterfield & Swire, acted as agents for Holt's Blue Funnel. Second, in the early 1870s Swire began his own shipping company, the China Navigation Company, which operated on the Yangtze River and served as a feeder line for Holt's service to the East. During the 1870s Swire pioneered pool agreements on the Yangtze which later became models for the European-Far East Conference. He helped to found the latter organization in 1879 and nurtured it until his death in 1898. In his obituary he was called the "Father of Shipping Conferences."[43]

An idiosyncrasy of the conference was its Eurocentric nomenclature. The conference was two separate entities: the "Outward" (that is, Europe to East Asia) and "Homeward" (East Asia to Europe) conferences. For clarity, hereafter these will be called the eastbound and westbound conferences.

For the N.Y.K. the conference system represented a major institutional barrier to entry into a full-scale European service. Unlike the Bombay line, the European line was not dominated by a single cargo in which a shippers union such as the Cotton Spinners Association could stand behind the N.Y.K. Even for raw silk, Japan's most important export, the N.Y.K. felt the effects of the deferred rebate which "tied" shippers to the conference lines. These lines generally had exclusive contracts with the foreign houses in Yokohama which still controlled the export of raw silk.[44] To attract shippers the N.Y.K. had to lower its rates below conference levels, thereby accumulating large deficits. Whereas the rebate system limited the N.Y.K.'s carriage of a particular trade like raw silk, conference influence over ports through its allied shippers deprived the company of a whole range of general cargo. In particular, the conference system impeded full N.Y.K. access to the major ports on the line, London and Shanghai.

Conferences sought to govern cargo shipment as a self-protective measure in the face of the growing ratio of shipping capacity to cargo, probably the most important phenomenon in world shipping in the late nineteenth century. One scholar has estimated that between 1873 and 1897 the annual increase in the effective capacity of British ships, 5.3 percent, was more than twice the annual increase in the growth of British overseas trade, which in volume grew at 2.6 percent a year.[45] The resulting competition for cargo constituted an economic barrier for the N.Y.K. This was especially formidable on the westbound voyage because Japan ran a large trade deficit with Europe and plentiful cargo was hard to come by.

Since the conference utilized numerous interdependent control devices, a full-fledged attempt at entry by the N.Y.K. would probably have been met with a multipronged and simultaneous reaction on all fronts. During the first few years on the European line, then, the N.Y.K. was primarily concerned with tactical maneuvering. It avoided frontal challenges in its vulnerable areas and pursued a selective thrust against certain weak points of the conference. Only after the company had secured an initial and limited position within the conference did it begin to develop a broader business strategy to integrate the European line with other aspects of its business. In the meantime it followed a careful tactical approach toward its goal of parity with other conference members.

Fortnightly reports on westbound business make it possible to trace initial N.Y.K. forays into rate competition. These were generally successful. Since early 1895 the rate per ton on ordinary cargo from Yokohama to London had remained steady at 40s. In canvassing for freight in preparation for its first sailing, the N.Y.K. offered to take cargo at 25s. This shook the conference rate structure. A March 14 report stated, "shippers are holding back cargo for lower rates and those who will ship do so on the understanding that they are afterwards put on the same footing as actual shippers by the [N.Y.K.]." By late March the conference had cut rates to 27s. 6d. to counter the N.Y.K.[46]

The departure on March 15 of the *Tosa Maru* (Figure 11) had even more impact on the N.Y.K.'s policy. The company had long assumed that the European line would have a close link with the Bombay line. The *Tosa Maru*, however, found that there was insufficient London-bound freight at Bombay to justify calling there. Shippers in Singapore and in Japanese ports raised more serious objections to the long delay caused by the stop at Bombay. The *Tosa Maru* had taken 68 days to reach London, 10 of which had been spent in Bombay. Cables were sent to the second ship, which left Yokohama on April 18, instructing it not to call at Bombay. Henceforth the European line became independent of the Bombay line.[47]

The *Tosa Maru* enjoyed greater success than anticipated, especially on its return voyage. In England Katō Kōmei provided

FIGURE 11 *The Tosa Maru*

The sendoff of the *Tosa Maru* from Kobe in March 1896 inaugurating the N.Y.K.'s European line. Courtesy of the Internal & Public Relations Chamber, NYK LINE.

extensive support in publicizing the N.Y.K. and in securing freight, which helped to cut the projected deficit on the first sailing. The N.Y.K. was also able to tap discontent with the conference among Manchester shippers. In response the conference began a campaign to get the N.Y.K. to cooperate with it. Shōda's advice to the board before the *Tosa Maru* sailed had been to defer the N.Y.K.'s participation for as long as it operated inferior ships but at the same time to check out the possibility of a freight rate agreement. The N.Y.K.'s price for cooperation with the conference was a special discount on its rates to offset the disadvantages of its poorer quality ships. On May 22 a provisional agreement was reached that led to a 5 percent discount for the N.Y.K., which was allowed to quote 30s.5d. as opposed to 32s. for conference lines.[48]

The agreement on freight rates brought the N.Y.K. into the deferred rebate system and put the company's name on the westbound conference's Rebate Circular, which listed the shipping companies cooperating with the conference and the terms of payment to shippers. Exporters who confined their support to the conference for a period of six months were given a rebate of 5 percent. If they continued for a full year, they would receive an additional 5 percent on freights contributed during the first six months and a straight 10 percent for the last six months. The rebate payments were made through agents in London. They applied only to tea and general cargo; they were not payable for rice and oils from Japan or for silk and treasure. A second part of the agreement allowed the N.Y.K. to retain its own earnings rather than having them placed in the conference pool, because the company did not call at Shanghai or other China ports north of Hong Kong. This left them in a disadvantageous position on the westbound voyage.

The terminus of the line became Antwerp, the only major "open" European port—principally because the Belgians did not have an oceangoing fleet, the interests of which would otherwise have placed restrictions on entry, as in Liverpool and Hamburg. The other aspect of the agreement's port policy allowed the N.Y.K. to stop at London on its outbound voyage but not on the return from Antwerp. Instead, ships called on the east coast at

Middlesbrough (Map 3). They could not ship East Asia-bound cargo from any other British port without special application. Generally Southampton was the only other port for which such application was approved.[49]

This agreement, which obviously placed the N.Y.K. in an inferior position to the other companies on the European line, was part of the company's tactic not to antagonize the conference. Two years later, when the N.Y.K. was much stronger, its London manager admitted that the company's management had accepted this "humble position" in 1896 even "though it was irksome to them."[50] From the beginning, then, the N.Y.K. sought equality while recognizing that it could be achieved only through a step-by-step approach. Curiously, the British, unaware that the Japanese company had deliberately chosen this "low posture," greatly feared the N.Y.K. during negotiations in 1896. But by late 1898, when it appeared the conference was working more harmoniously, the British had become somewhat complacent—just when the N.Y.K. was preparing its major move toward equality, a move that in general terms had been planned from the time the company entered the line in 1896.

Two other related agreements were concluded in 1896. First, the Bombay settlement had been confirmed on May 22, the same day as the agreement on the westbound conference. The port of Middlesbrough played an important function in these agreements, which were settled by a trade-off. In the negotiations Shōda discussed only the Bombay line, saying nothing about the European conference even though he was aware that the P. & O. anticipated an N.Y.K. application both for conference membership and London berthing privileges. Shōda did nothing to disabuse the P. & O. of this notion. His acceptance of Middlesbrough instead of London appeared to the P. & O. to be a compromise by the N.Y.K. for which the British were willing to pay in the form of the Bombay agreement. Had the N.Y.K. requested immediate entry into the European conference, the P. & O. would have demanded stiffer terms for a Bombay settlement.[51] The second major agreement was the reestablishment of the Homeward Straits Conference,

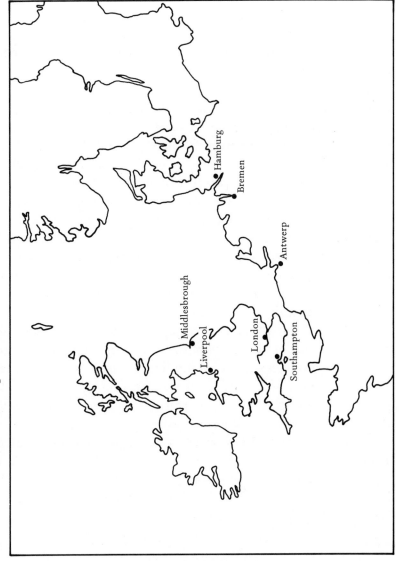

MAP 3 British and European Ports

which involved shipping from the Singapore area to Europe. Straits shipping was less susceptible to the conference system, for Singapore cargo was usually loaded on steamers returning to Europe from China. Singapore merchants, rather than gambling upon China steamers having sufficient space for their freight, often chartered their own vessels. In 1896, however, a slump occurred in westbound freight from China, resulting in an excess of ships diverted to Singapore to compete for cargoes there. A precipitous fall in rates ensued, which in turn led to the negotiations for a new conference. The N.Y.K. entered this conference as a full member, agreeing to pool its earnings.[52]

N.Y.K. negotiating success in 1896 had other tangible results. The entry into the European-Far East Conference had facilitated arrangements with more powerful shippers, and the company was able to load metal goods and heavy products such as iron rails, as well as cotton cloth and other Manchester exports at Middlesbrough. Also, the lack of a stop at either Bombay or Shanghai was advantageous to the eastbound voyage, for it gave the N.Y.K. a more direct service than most of the European companies, which frequently relied on transshipment. Consignees were able to obtain their goods more quickly, thus saving interest. Despite these gains, the early success of the *Tosa Maru* was not matched by later ships, and deficits quickly accumulated. Indeed, apart from the success in obtaining cargo on the eastbound run, 1897 was a disaster—the worst year thus far in the company's history. It produced four interrelated problems: political instability; unanticipated obstructions to business operations; a stockholders revolt; and new competition which threatened the gains from the N.Y.K.'s initial agreements with the conference.

In late December 1896, after a thorough audit and financial assessment of its new transoceanic lines, the N.Y.K. petitioned the Ministry of Communications for special line subsidies of ¥2.6 million for the European service and ¥770,000 for the American line. Early in 1897 the government of Prime Minister Matsukata Masayoshi approved the N.Y.K. request, and in March the Specified Line Subsidy bill went before the Diet. Here misfortune beset the N.Y.K., for several days later the Diet was dissolved. N.Y.K. officials, anxious over the mounting losses on the European line and unwilling to wait for the next Diet session, approached Matsukata and other cabinet ministers to seek out "other means" to obtain the subsidies.[53]

Unfortunately, the Meiji Constitution was not so easily circumvented! The N.Y.K. petition had fallen into a political maelstrom. A battle was being waged among government leaders vying with one another for ascendancy while trying to work out arrangements with the opposition parties to create a more stable government. The upshot was a series of short-lived cabinets and frequent Diet dissolutions. Between March 24, 1897, and December 3, 1898, the Lower House was in session for only 23 days and did not meet at all during the four-month Ōkuma cabinet of 1898. As a result, when Yamagata Aritomo became prime minister in November 1898 he was faced with a backlog of urgent economic legislation.

As the political logjam built up in 1897, N.Y.K. officials became increasingly worried. Company president Kondō Renpei had warned stockholders in May that it might become impossible to maintain the overseas lines if means could not be found to make up for the losses. The public, too, was by no means on the company's side. The *Tokyo keizai zasshi,* which was leading a campaign against the special line subsidies, strongly supported the navigation law because it encouraged the purchase of good ships and thus strengthened the country's fleet. But the magazine opposed the special subsidies, for it felt they served no important strategic purpose, such as linking Japan with overseas possessions.[54]

Business problems of 1897 exacerbated the growing sense of crisis among N.Y.K. executives. The rate war in the Straits trade to Europe had cut income drastically in the first term of the business year. Expenses on the line were greater than anticipated, especially the Suez Canal tolls. A strike of lighters in Yokohama tied up N.Y.K. ships for five days; and an engineers' strike in England delayed delivery of three of the new ships ordered there. By the end of the business year in September, six of the twelve ships ordered for the line had arrived, but only two had completed the certification process making them eligible for navigation aid.[55] A profit of ¥56,084 during the second term was not enough to wipe out the effects of a first term deficit of ¥163,327. In September, for the only time prior to 1929, the company decided not to provide a dividend.

The stockholders responded in a near-riot. They began the November General Meeting by issuing two demands: (1) revision of the articles of incorporation to ensure that there would always be a dividend and (2) disclosure of the company budget for overseas lines. The stockholders clearly saw that the Navigation Encouragement Law subsidies were wholly inadequate for overseas lines. Kondō tried to mollify them by predicting that the government would submit a new bill in the coming year. He urged the stockholders to exercise patience until "next March," when he hoped aid would be forthcoming. Such tepid reassurance did little to quiet the gathering. Stockholders argued that there was virtually no chance of a bill passing the Diet in the coming year. All the talk about "waiting until next March," they complained, was too "vague." They then called an Emergency General Meeting to be convened the following month, December 1897.

The attitudes revealed in these meetings showed the essential conservatism of the stockholders toward overseas lines. As a P. & O. report of early 1896 put it, the N.Y.K. had opened the European line "without waiting for support from the State, although that is confidently expected to follow."[56] Stockholders, critical of this decision, saw that the line was an enterprise started for the good of the country, but they now denounced the executives for opening it before receiving subsidies, because the company was "wearing itself out for the sake of the state." Postwar management had been irresponsible, they claimed, for the company should have conserved some of the profits from the Sino-Japanese War as a hedge against future emergencies rather than using them all on overseas lines.[57]

Most of the resentment was coming from the smaller stock-holder. One colorfully expressed the rift in the company by point-ing to the large stockholders like the Iwasaki and Mitsui families, who could endure without dividends for five or ten years, whereas the small stockholder depended upon the dividend to provide the wherewithal for his daily living costs. Without it, he would "even face the prospect of death by starvation." During the Emergency General Meeting in December these sentiments crystallized in a remarkable demand. The protesters argued that as long as the com-pany could not provide a dividend, the value of its shares would diminish. Their statement suggested that, if company officials could find no solution to the problem, the N.Y.K. should be dis-solved as a profit-making company, thereby enabling the stock-holders to retain whatever value might be left in their shares.[58]

With such internal upheaval, late 1897 was the worst possible moment for external danger. But, indeed, two new disasters loomed on the horizon in the form of additional competition. One was the expansion of German service in East Asia. Until 1897 the principal German shipping firm in Asia was the subsidized North German Lloyd. But in January 1898 the Hamburg America Line, which that year surpassed the P. & O. in tonnage to become the largest shipping company in the world, also began a freight service to East Asia. In February the two German firms initiated a joint service. Kondō worried that the German challenge would prompt all the other European companies to try to improve their posi-tions, an action that could lead to the breakup of the conference and plunge the N.Y.K. into even greater competition.[59]

The second potential disaster was an announcement by the Blue Funnel that it intended to withdraw from the westbound conference at the end of January. The Blue Funnel was dissatis-fied with the amount of cargo it was loading in China and Japan and wanted a differential rate similar to the N.Y.K.'s. The an-nouncement sent conference rates on general cargo down from 32s. to 22s.6d. by early December 1897. The N.Y.K. feared that it would have to suspend its own 5 percent discount so as not to offend the conference, but when it learned that the Blue Funnel was primarily in a dispute with the P. & O. and not with the conference as a whole, the company decided to retain it.[60]

THE PORT OF LONDON AND STEPS TOWARD PARITY, 1897–1899.
The end of 1897 marked in a sense the nadir of the N.Y.K.'s fortunes, but it also offered the promise of a new beginning. The first two years of the European line had been a preliminary exercise, undertaken at considerable risk and resulting in near catastrophe. Problems had arisen primarily because of the unexpected delay in two kinds of subsidies: the special line grants (yet to be approved by the Diet) and the general navigation encouragement program. The immediate problem in 1897 was that, of the original six ships on the line, only the *Tosa Maru* qualified for this navigation aid. By the spring of 1898, however, nine of the twelve ships ordered for the line had reached Japan. The addition of these new vessels changed the fortunes of the line in two ways. First, it drastically increased the amount of navigation aid from the ¥111,692 of 1897—which had not even been enough to cover Suez Canal tolls—to ¥2 million in 1898 and to ¥2.9 million in 1899. The second effect was to increase scheduled departures from once to twice a month as the new ships arrived.

While Kondō was worrying about the Germans breaking up the conference, it was the rapid deployment of new ships by the N.Y.K. that most alarmed the British members. In January 1898 the P. & O.'s Yokohama manager, a man named Woolley,[61] was appointed to convey a consensus reached by the other conference members regarding the N.Y.K. and its 5 percent discount. Woolley pointed out that the discount had always been considered a temporary concession based on the small size of the original N.Y.K. ships. But there had also been, he said, "a tacit understanding that if the N.Y.K. should begin to use new ships on the regular line, the concession should naturally be withdrawn." Nevertheless, the N.Y.K. was reluctant to give up the discount until it had received enough ships to start its fortnightly service. On January 25, then, it replied to the conference that it would retain the discount until the end of June 1898.[62] The conference's acceptance of this commitment may have given the N.Y.K. increased clout, for the company was able to assist Swire in mediation between the P. & O. and the Blue Funnel, which led to the signing of a new westbound agreement on February 24. For the full members of the conference this restored the previous rate of 32s. for general cargo from Yokohama to London. On May 1 a general increase went into effect, which restored westbound rates to the 40s. level maintained before the opening of the N.Y.K.'s line in March 1896.[63]

Through a combination of humility in weakness and tenacity in strength the N.Y.K. had waged a well-planned diplomatic campaign.[64] The acquisition of new ships, the new role as mediator, the restoration of the 40s. rate, the doubling of service which was implemented on May 14, and the subsequent abolition of the special discount together constituted the first major step toward parity with the other conference members. Port policy was now the sole remaining obstacle to full-scale equality.

Business conditions in 1898 forced the N.Y.K. to accelerate its drive toward equality. Doubling service had made the company more competitive, but the business recession of 1898 caused expenses to rise more rapidly than income. The new ships created an additional need for cargo, which was simply not available, especially as East Asia-bound freight from Antwerp had fallen off markedly. There was thus a need to diversify the sources of cargo by calling at additional ports. A second problem for the immediate future was the increase in Japanese import tariffs scheduled to go into effect in 1899. This caused a sudden rush of extra shipments in the last two months of 1898, as importers made purchases before the tariff went into effect. It clearly forecast, however, more depressed conditions for 1899. As one response to this predicament, in late 1898 the N.Y.K. sought concessions from the conference that would give the company a virtual monopoly on shipments of Japanese government cargo from Britain. Swire realized that "the alternative to our conceding means that the [N.Y.K.] would retire from the Conference, and a break up of rates on both East and West coasts [of England] would follow."

But the conference did insist that the N.Y.K. "make special application for each lot not shipped at Middlesborough," and that shipments from other ports not include general cargo but be restricted to government freight. Some of this was military cargo, which in 1899–1900 contributed roughly 4 percent of total eastbound freight receipts.[65]

Despite these concessions, the British did not feel as threatened by the N.Y.K. as they had in 1896 or earlier in 1898. One reason for this, Swire stated, was that "outwards and homewards the N.Y.K. are not doing near as well as their competitors." He concluded his letter of November 22 with: "Rest and be thankful."[66]

Within days the Swire firm had reason to revise this opinion, for on November 24 the N.Y.K. board met to consider a proposal from the company's London branch manager, T. H. James, a former navigation supervisor for the N.Y.K. in England. James, now the principal company negotiator with the conference, suggested that the N.Y.K. abandon Southampton and make London its port of call on the eastbound voyage. The board approved the recommendation with the qualification: "Since there will be fierce competition because of this move, to prevent the negative effects from spreading beyond London, implement the decision only after first negotiating with the P. & O."[67] James rejected this tactic as overcautious. In a November 29 cable he argued that "it is better not to negotiate with the P. & O. before implementing the move." He suggested that the company simply give notice. The directors then recorded the following decision:

> In the beginning, despite the fact that our original plans called for a stop at London, the world's largest center of commerce, we made Southampton our last port of call in England. We adopted this policy simply to avoid competition with the advanced companies. When we established the line we thought this would be a convenient stop. But now, with the decline in our freight shipments and the poor business condition of the line, we can no longer follow a policy of patience and endurance. Certainly the standing of the company in the European area has greatly advanced and it can no longer be compared to what it was two years ago. For these reasons at this time we will adopt an enter-

prising policy. We accept the opinion of the London manager and, while fully expecting competition, as planned before we will make London our port of call on the homeward [eastbound] voyage and then entrust the bargaining with the P. & O. to the London manager.[68]

Several days later, as planned, James sent a withdrawal notice to the eastbound conference. He then discussed the matter with an official of John Swire & Sons, who described their meeting:

I have seen James, he was most frank. Their present action was determined when they began the line; they then accepted a humble position in deference to James' counsel, though it was irksome to them. Now their service they consider on a par with the best of the other lines, and are determined to obtain an equality with them. *They do not seek to touch the West ports.* London is their objective. With Antwerp, Middlesborough and London they would be content . . . The position desired by N.Y.K. will be a great blow to P. & O., still I will put it to them and endeavour to reconcile Barnes [the P. & O. manager] to the inevitable, for the N.Y.K. are determined to fight. The only sop the N.Y.K. would yield is not to call at Shanghai, which is something.[69]

Further comment on the N.Y.K.'s motives was given in a letter from the Swire firm to the Ben Line:

Their explanation of the secession is that they are dissatisfied with their being barred from the London berth. They wish equality in this respect with the P. & O. To rule their name out of the "Rebate" Circular would mean active competition, to let it remain, would perhaps indicate our weakness, and not prevent the N.Y.K.'s competition. In these circumstances smashing of outward rates may be expected, and the strong probabilities are the war would extend to the homeward [westbound] agreements also.[70]

Consistent with the anxious tone of this letter, the Swire firm desperately tried to bring about a negotiated settlement between the conference members and the N.Y.K. It failed to do so before January 10, 1899, when James informed Swire & Sons that the N.Y.K. considered the matter closed and that it would now "take steps to retire from all agreements subsisting between them and others in the Far East Trade."[71] At the same time, however, a letter containing a more detailed explanation of the N.Y.K.'s future policy was shown to the P. & O. According to the Swire firm, this "worked wonders," with the P. & O. manager, Barnes, verbally giving John Swire & Sons "carte blanche to come to terms. The P. & O.," continued this account, "fully recognize the magnitude of the issues now raised. James is willing to negotiate afresh."[72] The precise content of the letter that jolted the P. & O. management and caused its change of position is not known, but since the Swire firm had been conciliatory from the beginning it is appropriate to ask why it took another month for negotiations to achieve any success. Since the reasons had less to do with N.Y.K. demands than with disagreements among British firms, the content of these negotiations will be summarized briefly.

The principle of the N.Y.K. loading at London was accepted and agreement on standard clauses was attained fairly quickly, including the stipulations that the N.Y.K. would adhere to the rebate circulars and that its departures from London would be fortnightly and on the same day as those of the P. & O. mail steamers. The N.Y.K. was not to call at or carry goods for transshipment to Shanghai. The main obstacle to a negotiated settlement, however, was how to parcel out among British firms the decreased share that the N.Y.K. entry was expected to bring.

British companies were organized in two structural groupings around their respective ports. Based at London were the P. & O. and the "Three London Lines"—the Glen Line, the Shire Line, and the Ben Line, smaller firms which stood to suffer the most from the N.Y.K. entry onto the London berth.[73] John Swire & Sons thus tried to leave the negotiations among the London-based lines to the leadership of the P. & O. These talks constituted the first reason for the month's delay in negotiations. The second grouping, based at Liverpool, consisted of the Ocean Steam Ship Company (Blue Funnel) and the smaller China Mutuals. During its original planning for the line, the N.Y.K. had hoped to make Liverpool a port of call—only to discover that the Ocean Steam Ship Company had an iron grip on the port.[74]

Although it was the London berth to which the N.Y.K. aspired, this did not mean that the London-based firms were the only ones threatened. No legal reason prohibited London firms from stopping at Liverpool. Port policy was regulated by conference agreement, and the N.Y.K. entry not only modified this agreement but called into question the relations between the London- and Liverpool-based groupings and their system of exclusive port privileges. Thus, to force the Liverpool lines to share the burden of the N.Y.K.'s entry, the P. & O. could demand concessions from the Ocean Steam Ship Company in exchange for the "non-invasion" of the port of Liverpool.[75] One privilege which the Blue Funnel enjoyed was the right to three annual "loadings" at London for the eastbound voyage. It took two months of persuasion, but Swire & Sons and the P. & O. eventually induced the Blue Funnel to relinquish this privilege.[76] This was the second reason for the delay in the negotiations.

Delaying negotiations the longest was the Swire firm's attempt to work out an overall indemnification formula to compensate all lines for cargo lost to the N.Y.K. This extremely complex formula eventually failed, partly because its basis was a pooling arrangement for earnings from London general cargo. The N.Y.K. preferred a pool, as did the Liverpool firms, which felt that would be the only fair way to ensure adequate compensation for the loss of their own privileges. The three smaller London lines, however, strongly opposed a pool on the grounds that it would be inequitable to them. In the end the scheme was abandoned and replaced by an arrangement involving simply an agreed upon freight rate for London cargo, which would then be applied to all other British ports. An agreement on this basis was signed on February 10, 1899, that finally made the N.Y.K. a full voting member of the eastbound conference.

Two categories of freight covered by conference regulations were: general cargo, the subject of Swire's attempt at indemnification; and "Fine Goods," otherwise known as "Lancashire and Yorkshire Goods," or "L. & Y. Goods." This cargo consisted of "yarn and all fabrics of wool, cotton, silk, or mixtures thereof manufactured and packed in Lancashire and Yorkshire."[77] Prior

to 1899 the N.Y.K. had the right to take 600 tons of Fine Goods
per departure. Permanent members operated a pool for their earnings from Fine Goods. The problem of how to fit the N.Y.K. into
this pool was another reason for the delay in negotiations, though
a solution here was more easily reached than that involving general
cargo from London. The Swire firm suggested that putting the
N.Y.K. on an equal footing with the P. & O. would lead to a stable
agreement. [78] The P. & O., which had held an 18.5 percent share in
1897, objected to this equality, and in the end the pool's percentage system was changed to a point system, similar to that used
by the Bombay conference, in which the total "points" were increased from 100 to 116 for cargo to China and Japan. The N.Y.K.
received a 16-point share in the pool, which replaced its previous
right to take 600 tons per departure. The British felt that the
N.Y.K. would probably take less under the new formula but
that their prestige would be enhanced, for they would now "be
parties to the Pool instead of outsiders." [79]

The agreements on the London berth and on the Fine Goods
pool were another major step for the N.Y.K. towards equality
within the conference, leaving only the matter of Shanghai to be
resolved. The N.Y.K.'s withdrawal notice and the subsequent
negotiations are of special interest because they highlight the
seeming reluctance of the British firms to fight the N.Y.K. The
Swire firm expressed this hesitancy in a letter to the Ben Line:
"It is certain a general fight would mean serious loss to all concerned, with any arrangement, after a period of exhaustion, on
perhaps less favorable conditions than could be made before the
rupture, and the money wasted in the fight would never be recovered." [80] The P. & O.'s view was that "we did our best to combat this invasion of our trade, but found that the only alternative
would be a free fight which might involve us in considerable loss
of money without producing any satisfactory result." [81] One reason for this sudden acquiescence to the N.Y.K. was that it competed as a single Japanese firm against many British firms whose
squabbles among themselves were almost as much of a threat as
the N.Y.K. itself. The second reason was the explicit British

concern about Japanese subsidies. As the Swire firm explained, "The recent confirmation by the Japanese Government to the N.Y.K. of their subsidy as *special steamers* has induced that Company to take the earliest advantage of their position."[82]

The subsidies not only made the British realize the futility of resistance but also bolstered the N.Y.K.'s confidence. These subsidies seem to be the long-awaited special line subsidies. The Yamagata cabinet had come into office in November 1898 and was preparing a program of economic legislation of which the subsidies were a part. Throughout January 1899 frequent meetings occurred between government officials and representatives of the N.Y.K., primarily Shibusawa, Kondō Renpei, and Iwasaki Yanosuke. One meeting with Yamagata took place on January 9,[83] which coincided with the N.Y.K.'s "withdrawal" from the conference announced by James on January 10.

Although the N.Y.K. now had the solid support of the cabinet as well as the confidence in a stable government as a result of an agreement between Yamagata and the Liberal Party, substantial public opposition to the special line subsidies continued. The final Diet vote on the bill, March 7, 1899, was preceded by the fiercest debate of the year among the supplementary budget proposals, the category under which the bill had been presented. The principal opposition speaker, Shimada Saburō, president of the *Mainichi* newspaper, argued that owing to the scarcity of Japanese in England, the amount of mail did not justify a subsidy. Government use of foreign ships would be preferable, especially since, in his opinion, the European line, unlike the Bombay line, did not carry freight of special value to Japan's economic or strategic interests. If huge sums were to be spent, he suggested they be used instead for lines within Asia. The progovernment arguments stressing the value of the transoceanic lines for Japanese foreign trade and diplomacy enlivened the debate, but because of the prior commitment of the Liberal Party to support the bill, they were not decisive in changing anyone's mind. The final vote in favor of the subsidies was 165 to 78.[84]

The line subsidies, which went into effect on January 1, 1900, were given for a ten-year period. The law provided ¥2.7 million annually and required the N.Y.K. to place on the European line twelve ships of at least 6,000 tons with a minimum speed of fourteen knots—standards already met by the company.[85] Since this law did not go into effect until 1900, the N.Y.K. operated the European service for almost four years without the special line subsidies and for a year and a half with virtually no subsidy at all from the Navigation Encouragement Law. Despite the confident expectation of subsidies in 1896, this record suggests that the opening of the line was a major example of entrepreneurial risk-taking, certainly commensurate with the achievements of the Bombay line in light of the fact that the European line had no shippers union like the Cotton Spinners Association to support it. Still, it was the special subsidy that brought the N.Y.K. into the conference as an equal in 1899—evidence that subsidies cannot be evaluated in narrow economic terms. Calculations which simply compare the subsidy to the amount of a company's annual profit to determine the degree of dependence on the government over-look a major function of subsidies. Toward the British in 1899 they were clearly an effective diplomatic weapon even before they passed the Diet.[86]

THE PORT OF SHANGHAI AND THE FREIGHT CONFERENCE, 1899–1902. In the aftermath of the N.Y.K. entry into the eastbound conference the company began longer-range strategic planning. This was carried out primarily by Kondō Renpei in two overseas investigation tours—to East Asia in 1899 and to the West in 1900 and 1901. Planning focused on integrating European line business with Chinese freight. China was more important in the company's westbound service to Europe than in the eastbound line because of the dearth of Europe-bound Japanese cargo and China's ability to supply additional freight. After evaluating Kondō's reports in 1901 and 1902, the N.Y.K. took measures to make Shanghai a stop on its westbound European line. The eastbound line, by contrast, was less dependent on China because of the large shipments of indus-trial cargo from Europe.

In the year following its admission to the conference, the N.Y.K. concentrated on modifying agreements to expand its carriage rights to these industrial goods, which were, contrary to Shimada Saburō's opinion in his Diet speech, strategic freight. The company tried, for example, to increase its shipments of spinning machinery. This was covered by conference agreements, though exports from Britain had fallen off in 1899, probably because of the new Japanese import tariff. The N.Y.K. also made significant gains in "open" cargo, a third freight category in addition to London general cargo and Lancashire and Yorkshire goods. Open cargo was freight not covered by conference agreements. That is, the conference did not have a specific freight rate for open cargo; no rebate was paid on it; nor were shippers penalized for transporting it in nonconference vessels.[87] Key freights in this category were locomotive machinery, wheels, and axles, and the principal carrier was the Ocean Steam Ship Company, with its base at Liverpool. Because of Liverpool's proximity to England's industrial heartland, it was more economical to ship these heavy products from the west coast than from east coast ports like Middlesbrough, where the N.Y.K. had loading rights. Despite these disadvantages, the N.Y.K. worked out agreements with Ocean Steam Ship to carry a certain share of this "open" machinery.[88]

Another version of a Japanese business alliance, akin to that practiced on the Bombay line, seems to have been responsible for the N.Y.K.'s success in obtaining heavy industrial cargo. At the time, Mitsui Bussan was importing large volumes of iron products from England. In the late 1890s its annual shipments came to around 30,000 tons, and this volume helped to compensate the N.Y.K. for the disadvantages of shipping via British east coast ports.

The business relationship between these two Japanese behemoths is suggested by a fascinating proposal put to the N.Y.K. by Mitsui Bussan early in 1897. As a condition for entering into an exclusive transport contract with the N.Y.K., Mitsui proposed that the N.Y.K. provide a rebate of 5 percent to be paid in London, as was done by the conference. In addition, when Mitsui's freight exceeded 10,000 tons, the N.Y.K. was to deliver a rebate of 1s. per ton to be paid secretly in Tokyo. Although Mitsui was an excellent business partner, the N.Y.K. worried that the public bidding on what was mostly open cargo would cause problems. No matter how much the company tried to keep the contract secret, public offers better than Mitsui's but habitually refused by the N.Y.K. would invite suspicion and expose the arrangement, thereby damaging the company's reputation in Britain. Even without an exclusive contract, however, the N.Y.K. was prepared, on a provisional basis, to pay rebates to Mitsui on high-quality freight such as machinery. Whether to pay rebates on lower-quality iron products, the N.Y.K. board decided, was best determined on a space-available basis. The board did admit that in view of the irregularities in the kinds, volume, and origin of freight, the Mitsui offer was tempting, and they decided to study the matter further. It is not known precisely what decision was later adopted, but since Mitsui remained the principal importer of locomotive machinery, iron rails, and spinning machinery, it is likely that some arrangement was worked out with the N.Y.K. Mitsui's proposal is also typical of the methods of general trading companies—handling large volumes for small commissions.[89]

In 1899 the conference had been amenable to giving the N.Y.K. concessions on open cargo partly because it did not call at Shanghai. However, in the two years between the supplementary agreements of 1899 and the time the N.Y.K. prepared to demand Shanghai port-of-call privileges, the company's influence had grown to the point where the British Consul at Yokohama claimed that the N.Y.K. could virtually control conference freight rates. This testimony, given before a British parliamentary committee, was contradicted by Samuel Samuel of M. Samuel & Company who argued that it was the P. & O. which dictated to the conference. Samuel's anti-P. & O. bias as an agent for the Shire line, one of the three small London lines, may have colored his opinion.[90] Thomas Sutherland of the P. & O. stated: "We never dictate to anybody; we persuade."[91] Perhaps the strongest evidence in this debate was that the P. & O. cut back on some of its services to

Japan in 1900. All testimony pointed to the increased influence of the N.Y.K., the main reason for which seems to have been its direct eastbound service which, unlike that of many of the British lines, avoided frequent transshipment.

In 1900 shipments of Fine Goods to China increased rapidly. Since the N.Y.K. did not stop at China ports, it did not participate in the transport of these shipments. This situation on the eastbound voyage, however, was not necessarily to the N.Y.K.'s disadvantage. Not stopping at China ports on the one hand made the company's direct service to Japan more competitive and on the other hand virtually assured, in times of brisk trade to China, that the N.Y.K. would transport less than its full allotment as a pool member (16 out of 116 points). In this case, it could still share in the increased earnings, because it received from the pool an amount equivalent to its "undercarriage."[92]

Unlike the good financial condition of its eastbound service, the N.Y.K.'s westbound service was deficit ridden during the early years of the line, in part due to the different content of the trades. Most eastbound freight from Europe to East Asia consisted of manufactured goods, high-value general cargo, and heavy industrial products. These goods could be shipped without seasonal variation and could be more easily integrated into a rebate system than westbound freight. The raw materials, foodstuffs, and bulky items in the westbound trade attracted more tramp shipping in competition with the liner service. A second reason, directly relevant to the N.Y.K.'s lack of privileges in China ports, concerned Japan's own unbalanced trade relations with Europe. While 44.0 percent of Japan's imports in 1900 still came from Europe, only 21.6 percent of its exports went there. Not surprisingly, then, N.Y.K. ships bound for Europe in early 1901 were loaded only to one-fifth of capacity. Quite clearly, Japan's export trade to Europe was insufficient to sustain the N.Y.K.'s westbound service. Loading freight at China ports en route to Europe was thus the only hope for profit. Basically, the company intended to ship Chinese agricultural exports like soybeans, vegetable oil, grains and cereals, and tea as well as hides and skins. This N.Y.K. strategy of dependence on China was unwelcome to British firms, for China's export trade to Europe was not increasing rapidly during these years. N.Y.K. entry to China ports would therefore result in a redistribution of carriage to the detriment of the British.[93]

British companies were fully aware that the N.Y.K. was carrying less than other lines. Although the N.Y.K. was not a full member of the westbound conference, it did, of course, quote the same freight rates and there were general stipulations in conference agreements about how much cargo the N.Y.K. should be allowed to transport. Not being a member of the westbound pool, the N.Y.K. was able to retain its own earnings, and British companies consistently allowed it to "overcarry" its stipulated cargo. This concession, like those on eastbound cargo, served as an "inducement" to dissuade the N.Y.K. from stopping at Shanghai, for in that case, the N.Y.K. would enter the westbound pool and "their allotment would be considered more than what they are securing in Japan."[94]

In 1901–1902 the most contentious issue between the westbound conference and the N.Y.K. was the freight rate on raw silk. Ultimately this became linked with N.Y.K. negotiations for entry to the Shanghai berth. The government order for the N.Y.K.'s European line, issued on July 1, 1899, recognized the centrality of the raw silk trade on the westbound voyage by regulating the maximum sailing time, not between Kobe and Britain, but from Kobe to Marseilles, the main destination for the cargo. The voyage had to be completed in 46 days. (The eastbound voyage, to be completed in 48 days, was regulated from British ports to Kobe.) Freight rates as such were not subject to official approval, but there seems to have been a considerable amount of governmental "guidance," motivated by the desire to protect Japan's strategic dependence on raw silk exports.[95]

Ties between foreign trading houses and shipping firms seem to have exerted a more sustained influence over raw silk shipments than over other cargo. In January 1901, however, the N.Y.K. slashed its rates on raw silk, waste silk, and silk goods to 30 percent below conference levels. Following complaints from conference firms, in June the N.Y.K. reduced its discount on silk goods and waste silk to 10 percent, but kept its 30 percent discount on raw silk. It then sought to become a full member of the westbound conference while retaining these lower rates. Kondō, in the meantime, warned James (the London branch head and principal negotiator) about the strategic nature of raw silk, for he feared there might be complaints in the Diet about the N.Y.K. colluding with foreign shipping firms to raise freight rates.[96]

The N.Y.K.'s weaker position in the westbound trade left the company exposed to rougher confrontation tactics than it had faced with London. In particular, an unattractive pool formula offered by the conference thwarted the N.Y.K.'s goal of stopping at Shanghai with conference approval. As negotiations bogged down in late 1901, the N.Y.K. acquired Ministry of Communications approval to include Shanghai as a port of call and decided to act unilaterally and institute its stop there before an agreement with the conference had been reached.[97] Then came the classic response of the shipping conference—the N.Y.K.'s name was removed from the westbound Rebate Circular and a warning to shippers not to provide cargo for the N.Y.K. was substituted. Unable to obtain adequate freight at Shanghai, the company was forced to compromise in January 1902. It agreed to a three-month trial of the pool formula in exchange for the retention of its existing discounts on raw silk, waste silk, and silk goods.[98]

The outcome of this settlement proved more advantageous than the N.Y.K. had anticipated. At first, the N.Y.K. assumed its share of pool cargo would be limited to 500 tons per vessel. Within weeks this was increased to 900 tons because of larger than expected demand. Also, British companies sometimes accused the N.Y.K. of giving disguised rebates by allowing shippers to load cargo in excess of its stated measurement. Though these complaints continued, the British abolished the practice of remeasuring Japanese cargo in May 1902. Also in May, the N.Y.K. was able to retain its rate discounts when it renewed the conference pool agreement. There was, however, one dissenter to this renewal. The North German Lloyd announced that it would cut its rates on

waste silk to match the N.Y.K.'s 10 percent discount. Nevertheless, the German firm's bargaining position seems to have been
rather weak, for the P. & O. and Messageries Maritimes apparently
feared that they would have to follow suit with cuts against their
wishes. This potential conflict within the conference may explain
how James successfully dissuaded the North German Lloyd from
implementing its cut the day before it was to go into effect, thereby winning recognition for the N.Y.K.'s special discount.[99]

These favorable developments following its entry into the pool
contributed to the rapid growth of N.Y.K. influence on the line
between 1902 and 1904. In September 1905, in a discussion of
westbound cargo, a Butterfield & Swire official wrote that the
Russo-Japanese War had given the P. & O. a chance to *recapture*
"the carrying supremacy" on the European run, which before the
war had been held by the N.Y.K.![100] In short, the dominance the
N.Y.K. achieved in the eastbound conference between 1899 and
1901, attested to by many witnesses before the 1901 British parliamentary committee on foreign subsidies, seems to have been
paralleled between 1902 and 1904 on the westbound service.

The N.Y.K. achieved this success in a period of increasing competition for freight resulting from the growing capacity to cargo
ratio. Several factors accounted for the high growth rate of shipping capacity. To some extent it was a response to market trends,
namely, the rapid increase during the three decades prior to World
War I in the international trade of countries distant from Europe.
Also, France, Germany, and Japan were building national fleets to
increase their political influence and to enhance their prestige.
Finally, in the era of the "new imperialism," countries built larger
fleets to connect home territories with overseas colonies and
spheres of influence. The growing capacity created downward
pressure on freight rates. In the late 1890s the precise timing of
freight rate changes suggests that immediate competition—the
N.Y.K. entry and the Ocean Steam Ship's temporary withdrawal—
was the most important cause in the downward movement of
rates on the European line from 1896 to 1898. After 1898 the
recovery of rates may have been influenced by temporary shortages

of tonnages brought on by the Spanish-American War, the Boer War, and then the Boxer Rebellion. In August 1899 rates on the European line had risen from 40s. to 45s., but by 1903 the long-term secular changes seem to have taken over again, for these rates had fallen to 20s.[101] The dual challenge of the secular decline in rates and the expanded efforts of Western fleets made the formulation of new strategies an urgent priority.

During the N.Y.K.'s entry into the conference system the development of the company's strategy can be divided into two periods. During the first, 1896–1899, the N.Y.K. was primarily concerned with gaining equality with Western companies, and to attain this it concentrated on establishing its trunk lines, especially the European line. During the second, 1899–1902, strategy shifts toward feeder lines, because of the lack of cargo on the N.Y.K.'s European westbound line and the encroachment of Western imperialist powers in East Asia. Kondō's principal fears were that the Trans-Siberian Railway would make a land passenger route to Europe more economical than the sea route and that the railway would enable Russia to set up an agency for coastal shipping in East Asia. His second great bogeyman was the Hamburg America Line. Large companies like this, he said, threatened to dominate China's shipping. They were "starting main lines and then setting up strategically placed branch services or buying up lines already in existence."[102] By 1901, then, parity with the European firms on the trunk lines was no longer enough, for these lines were threatened by the shipping companies of the new imperialists, particularly the Germans. The trunk lines, the mainstay of the company's operations, could not be secure without reinforcement by branch lines that could act as feeders. The stop at Shanghai was not simply the final step in the march toward equality with the West, an equality that could make the westbound voyage profitable; it was also the first step in a new strategy. This new feeder strategy, evolved between 1901 and 1904, had three designs: (1) a strategic, "defensive" goal of preventing Western takeover of Chinese trade; (2) creation of new commercial institutions to penetrate China; and (3) the building of a business structure to buttress the main

lines to the West. In a July 1901 board meeting, Kondō expressed
the great concern with China that motivated the new strategy:

> This meeting is not the time to discuss this, but I expect our profits will
> increase when we make Shanghai a stop on the European line. We are
> already in contact with relevant branch offices with regard to expenses,
> and in the near future, when it comes time for the board to consider
> this, we will have to examine the degree of preparation at Shanghai.
> Making Shanghai a stop on the European line will lead to yearly in-
> creases in the trade to and from the Yangtze region, and we will need to
> cultivate the main line by establishing a branch line. Our first task then
> will be to undertake detailed inspection tours and investigate the num-
> ber of passengers and the amount of freight. We have heard that the
> China Merchants Steam Navigation Company, which presently occupies
> a leading position in the shipping of the Yangtze region and other parts
> of the Chinese coast, has received a request to be bought out by the
> Hamburg America Line. Following the decisions on problems relating
> to the indemnity at the ambassadors conference in Peking, the [Chinese]
> government asked the China Merchants for funds, and there is some
> doubt that the company can maintain its shipping prerogatives under
> Chinese leadership. In other words, we will secretly keep a check on the
> future movements of the China Merchants and determine whether or
> not it may be necessary to buy it out. An investigation of the situation
> of the Western powers with regard to China shows that this is no time
> for Japan to be a silent bystander when so much is at stake for our
> trade. If our countrymen do not advance *now,* with a positive policy
> towards China, we will very soon regret that we have been left behind
> by the other countries. As the leading Japanese shipping company we
> must do all in our power. We must resolve to acquire navigation leader-
> ship on the Chinese coast. But no matter how great our resolution, if
> the proper opportunity does not come, it will be difficult to implement
> this goal. [103]

EIGHT

China and the Issue of Imperialism, 1896–1904

JAPANESE SHIPPING IN CHINA

China, especially Shanghai, became the key to the feeder strategy developed by the N.Y.K. after 1900. The goal was to link China ports with the company's new transoceanic lines, creating thereby an international integration of business operations. The N.Y.K. moved first into North China and then, beginning in 1902, into the Yangtze valley. This strategy illustrates how business participated in Japanese imperialism more for its own needs than for the purposes of the state.

N.Y.K.–O.S.K. COMPETITION IN NORTH CHINA, 1899–1901. Kondō's grand vision of the role of China originated in a tour of East Asia during the autumn of 1899. In December he submitted a memorial to the cabinet on the threat to Japan's strategic interest. His first warning was that once Russia had connected Europe and East Asia by rail, it would expand its shipping operations in East Asia, and, in the near future, might even gain control of Korea's coastal navigation. Second, he predicted that the building of railways in China by the Western powers would inevitably lead to the development of the country's natural resources. Japan, however, had no agency to exploit those resources, and would have to expand East Asian shipping services to avoid being deprived of influence in the area.[1]

Kondō's memorandum carefully delineated the strategic objectives now common to both government and the shipping industry. During his tour Kondō had cabled the board regarding the company's lines to North China. This provides a useful contrast with the formal memorandum to the government because it more explicitly recognized competition within the shipping industry as a motivation for expanding the company's lines. "Looked at from the viewpoint of profits," the telegram stated, "it would be safer to wait until the state comes to subsidize lines for this area before beginning our operations. However, if we wait until then, other Japanese companies will seize the opportunity and we will lose our advantageous position here."[2]

Kondō had good reason to worry. While the N.Y.K. had been building up its transoceanic lines, the O.S.K. had concentrated its expansion on new services to China, especially the Yangtze region, South China, and Taiwan. Also, in July 1898 the immensely able Nakahashi Tokugorō, future cabinet minister and party politician, became president of the O.S.K. By mid-1899, with several ships in receipt of aid under the navigation law, the O.S.K. was exporting railroad ties and coal to North China while importing soybeans and bean cake. Believing that they could operate a regular service if they had a subsidy, the O.S.K. petitioned the government in July 1899 to aid two lines: a direct service from Japan to North China ports and a Shanghai-Tientsin line, which would act as a feeder to the company's already subsidized Yangtze operation. In September, following a report by company director Sugiyama Kōhei, who had also visited North China, the O.S.K. instituted a regular line to North China without waiting for government subsidies. This line ran parallel to the N.Y.K.'s.[3]

Prior to the O.S.K. entry into the North China trade, the N.Y.K. had only an unscheduled line to Tientsin and its vessels were still transporting important cargo such as cotton yarn via Shanghai. In response to the O.S.K. competition, the N.Y.K. upgraded this service and began shipping yarn direct to North China in 1898. Then, in September and October 1899 the company began regular Kobe-Tientsin and Shanghai-Tientsin services.[4]

Before this late 1899 offensive by the N.Y.K., things seemed to be going the O.S.K.'s way. The cabinet had accepted its subsidy proposal and was preparing to submit it to the Diet session which opened on November 22. Successful discussions were also underway to have the Imperial House make its first purchase of O.S.K. stock, thereby placing the government's imprimatur on the company. Following the N.Y.K. moves, however, newspapers began reporting rumors of changes in the government's commitment. A worried Nakahashi quickly began a lobbying campaign. In mid-December he wrote to Itō Hirobumi, who at the time was developing close relations with the Liberal Party as it prepared to transform itself into the Seiyūkai, an alliance between one faction of the oligarchy and the leading opposition party. Another letter was dispatched to Matsukata, the finance minister in Yamagata's cabinet. In his letters Nakahashi presented plans for the extension of O.S.K. services in North China, the Yangtze, South China, Taiwan, and Korea. The company intended to expend large sums for new ships and additional land facilities. He then presented his own grand vision of a Pacific Rim strategy, in which O.S.K. services to China and Southeast Asia could link up with the major ports of both North and South America. He did, however, add that the O.S.K. would not persist if the N.Y.K. continued to challenge it on the North China run, but it was determined to maintain its Yangtze and South China services.[5]

The N.Y.K. was not prepared to take any chances. To prevent a loss of influence to the O.S.K., it sought help from its superior political contacts. Before departing on his East Asian tour, Kondō had called on Prime Minister Yamagata and acceded to his request to take along several army spies to China, which may partly account for the national security rhetoric of Kondō's December memorandum to the cabinet. Not satisfied simply with its government ties, the N.Y.K. undertook to bribe Hoshi Tōru, leader of the Liberal Party, who then, according to O.S.K. sources, proceeded to block the O.S.K. subsidy measure.[6] These events arose just as the N.Y.K.'s original fifteen-year ¥880,000 subsidy expired. In 1900 the government replaced this with a series of individual line subsidies for services to coastal and East Asian ports. Included in the new subsidies were ¥250,000 for the Shanghai line and ¥100,000 for a Kobe-North China line—the very line over which the N.Y.K. had thwarted the O.S.K.'s attempt to obtain a subsidy.

The remarkable contrast between the urgent nationalistic tone of Kondō's December memorial and the N.Y.K.'s successful maneuvering to monopolize the government's favor should be viewed as the normal pattern of Japanese company-government relations in the rapid expansion after the mid-1890s. The public posture of acting on behalf of the state disguised the private struggle for advantage among competitors in the shipping industry.

The N.Y.K. went to such lengths because the North China business was considered essential to the development of the new feeder strategy. As part of this strategy, freight from the North China region would be shipped from Tientsin to Shanghai and from there to Europe and America. Shanghai thus played a major role for the American as well as European line. Prior to the opening of the American line in 1896, the N.Y.K. had a through-freight agreement with the Pacific Mail and O. & O. firms which linked its Shanghai line with the Yokohama-San Francisco services of the American companies. This contract was canceled in 1896 when the N.Y.K. began to carry through freight itself. During Kondō's tour, however, it was decided that neither Yokohama nor Kobe could provide sufficient freight for the U.S. line to justify the extra cost of transshipment from the Shanghai line. In December 1899, then, Shanghai was made the departure port for the U.S. line. Upon returning to Japan, Kondō explained to the stockholders that the hub of the "Big Three" lines (Europe, America, and Australia) was moving from Yokohama to Shanghai. By connecting with China coastal lines and other East Asian routes, the business flowing through Shanghai would complete the integration of the three major lines.[7]

EARLY JAPANESE FIRMS ON THE YANGTZE & BRITISH OPPOSI-TION, 1896-1902. Maximizing the use of Shanghai required a business network along the Yangtze, but the N.Y.K. had come late to Yangtze shipping. By the time it entered the competition on the river, the British had almost a thirty-year head start. The first important British firm on the Yangtze had been Swire's China Navigation Company, which had developed a pooling arrangement with the American firm of Russell & Company in 1874. In 1877 the China Merchants Steam Navigation Company purchased the Russell firm and then took its place in the pool. Joining in 1881 was the Indo-China Steam Navigation Company, a subsidiary of Jardine, Matheson & Company, the leading British trading firm in East Asia. In the 1882 agreement which pooled the earnings of these firms, the China Merchants had a 42 percent share, Swire 38 percent, and Indo-China 20 percent. By 1897, the year of the last renewal of the agreement before the Japanese entry, the China Merchants share had fallen several percentage points and that of Jardine, Matheson's subsidiary had risen accordingly.[8] Two other firms cooperated with the pool as associate members: the Chinese firm of Hoong On and, most importantly for the present discussion, a small British outfit called McBain & Company.

The basis for British business on the Yangtze was the 1858 Treaty of Tientsin, which gave Britain and subsequently other major Western powers the right to navigate on the Yangtze. By 1862 major inland ports such as Hankow had been opened. Japan's relations with China had been governed by the 1871 Sino-Japanese Treaty of Peace and Commerce. Unlike treaties which China signed with major Western powers, this 1871 treaty did not have a most-favored-nation clause. Under this clause, major Western powers automatically acquired the same rights as Britain, which acted as the vanguard in opening new ports and extending its privileges. Because the 1871 treaty lacked this clause, Japan did not share in the right to navigate on China's inland waters and Japanese goods were taxed more heavily than those of Western countries. For Japan, the Treaty of Shimonoseki following the

Sino-Japanese War brought about several legal changes: it opened additional ports and gave Japan the right to manufacture goods in China and to navigate on her inland waters; but most importantly it also contained the most-favored-nation clause. Thus Japan could benefit from new ports that were opened when Britain negotiated regulations for Yangtze navigation in 1898 as part of an effort to expand its sphere of interest in the Yangtze valley.[9] (See Map 4.) The first major Japanese shipping company on the Yangtze was the O.S.K.[10] Operating with a government subsidy, it opened a Shanghai-Hankow line in January 1898 and a Hankow-Ichang line in May 1899.

Because the O.S.K. had no wharves or other facilities along the river, before it began the Yangtze line it explained to the China Navigation Company that it had no intention of starting an opposition to the pool. It only wanted a 10 percent discount on freight rates. The pool firms, known to themselves as the "Three Friendly Companies," were not inclined to be charitable. According to an O.S.K. report, the pool increased rebates to its shippers to dissuade them from using O.S.K. services and tried to prevent the Japanese firm from leasing land and buildings in Hankow. The O.S.K.'s isolation in the trade made it more vulnerable to these tactics. When it began the line it had no services which connected with the Yangtze line. Very little of the early freight which it carried to the Yangtze delta was bound for Japan; most went to ports in North and South China. The problem was that the coastal China routes were dominated by the pool companies, which refused to carry O.S.K. freight. With the proper land and sea facilities the O.S.K. might have been able to compete with the pool, but without them it had to pay bribe money to get the Three Friendly Companies to accept connecting shipments.[11]

By 1900 the situation had begun to improve. In January of that year the company decided to increase its capital stock from ¥5.5 million to ¥11 million, and ¥2.5 million of this increase was allotted for the Yangtze line. Also, in October 1901 the government boosted the Shanghai-Hankow subsidy from ¥70,000 to ¥160,000 and set the Hankow-Ichang subsidy at ¥60,000. Several newly

MAP 4 Chinese and Korean Ports

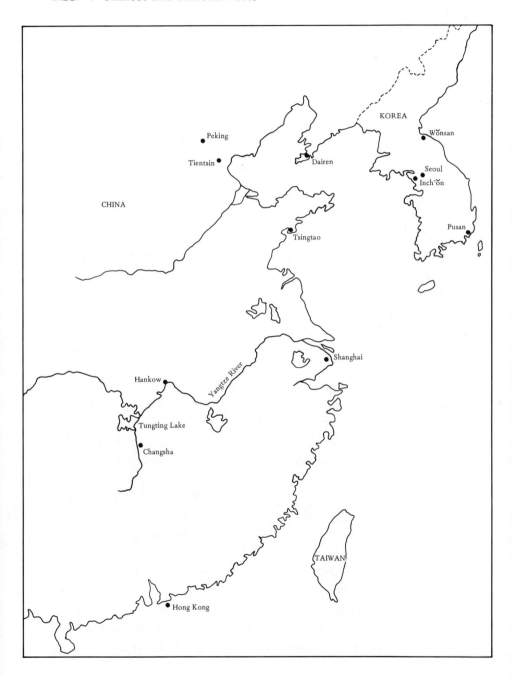

built ships were placed on the line, and the Shanghai representative office was expanded into a full-scale branch office manned by the company's most skilled young officials.[12]

The expansion of the O.S.K. service and the entry of the Germans into the Yangtze trade complicated the negotiations of the British firms for the renewal of their pool agreement due to expire in 1902. By 1901 the two main German firms, the Hamburg America Line and the North German Lloyd, had developed a joint shipping service on the Yangtze between Shanghai and Hankow, and the latter firm operated as far as Ichang. There were reports that the Germans planned to extend their lines farther inland and then integrate this extensive Yangtze service with connecting routes to achieve a dominant position on both the North and South China coasts. These reports, plus rumors of the Hamburg America Line takeover of the China Merchants, inclined the British to negotiate when the two German firms jointly applied in October 1901 to enter the pool. These talks failed because of major disagreements over the standard by which pool shares would be allocated and because of British objection to the direct Hankow-Swatow line of the North German Lloyd, which the German firm refused to relinquish.

This latter point was also a major reason why the O.S.K. refused to join the pool, for by 1901 they had established connecting services between their Yangtze line and South China ports. In addition, they felt that the pool would encroach upon the independence of their management, for its stipulations would have prohibited an increase in new steamers planned for the line. This would have been unacceptable to the company and to the government, which was providing aid expressly to increase Japanese influence in China.[13] When the pool was renewed by the British and the China Merchants, July 1, 1902, the Germans and the Japanese remained on the outside, with the O.S.K. being the "worst competitor"[14] (see Table 45).

The N.Y.K.'s first direct connection with Yangtze business was an investment in the Hunan Steamship Company, formed in 1902 to operate between Hankow and Tungting Lake in the northern

TABLE 45 Shipping Companies on the Yangtze,
ca. 1901–1902

Company	Lower Yangtze (Shanghai-Hankow)		Upper Yangtze (Hankow-Ichang)	
	No. of Ships	Tonnage	No. of Ships	Tonnage
O.S.K.	3	7,200	2	3,900
China Merchants	4	5,800	2	1,200
China Navigation[a]	3	5,500	2	1,000
Indo-China S.N.[b]	3	5,500	2	1,500
Hoong On	4	2,700		
McBain & Co.	2	1,600		
Melchers & Co.[c]	4	?		
Arnhold Karberg & Co.[d]	2	?		

Sources: Nisshin Kisen, pp. 14, 25–26; *Nakahashi Tokugorō*, II, 106–107.

Notes: [a]Butterfield & Swire.   [c]agent for the North German Lloyd.
[b]Jardine, Matheson.   [d]agent for the Hamburg America Line.

part of Hunan Province. The N.Y.K. became involved in the planning in October 1901 when the company's vice-president, Katō Masayoshi, toured Hunan. His report, emphasizing the need for larger facilities and a government subsidy, brought the government into the planning process, which soon involved consular officials in China and naval personnel. Promoters of the firm, who met in February 1902, represented a cross section of all the major Japanese firms dealing with China, including four representatives from the N.Y.K. (five if Shibusawa is included), two from Mitsui Bussan, and others from the Yokohama Specie Bank, the Yasuda Bank, and the Ōkura Trading Company.

Following this meeting, the Diet quickly approved a subsidy for the new Hunan firm, and the Imperial House became one of its stockholders. The N.Y.K. invested ¥300,000, equal to 20 percent of ¥1.5 million authorized capital stock, on which the government guaranteed a 6 percent dividend. Katō became chairman of the company.[15]

The Hunan Steamship Company played an important role in opening more of China's interior for Japanese trade. As it began planning its operations, the company realized more ports were needed in Hunan, which spurred a strong lobbying effort by the shipping and trading community. In October 1903 the government signed a supplementary treaty with China which opened Chang-sha, the major city in Hunan, located some distance south of Tungting Lake.[16] Kondō spoke to the stockholders of the Chang-sha area as a potential market for Japanese goods, but he put greater emphasis on the impact Hunan's exports would have on the N.Y.K.'s feeder strategy:

> The most urgent need is to establish branch lines which shall serve as feeders to our main lines. Goods will not come to us if we merely wait for their advent. We have to go in search of them into the very gardens of their owners. Thus in the case of goods for shipment at Yokohama, we have to go into the interior to seek them, and in the case of Kobe cargo we must go to look for it as far as Nagoya and surrounding districts. If that is necessary in our own country, how much more essential must it be in China and Korea. Sitting placidly in Hong Kong and Shanghai will not bring cargoes for our steamers. We must establish feeding lines into the interior of China and a network of communication with shippers.

As Kondō ventured into his announcement of the new firm, he emphasized that the Hunan firm would be "a feeder of the [N.Y.K.'s] main services." The goods that the new company would bring to Hankow "will come to Shanghai to be loaded in the Yusen Kaisha's steamers for the latter's main lines to Japan, America, and Europe, and the reverse operations will be similarly performed for cargo going into the interior of China."[17]

By the time the Hunan company actually began operations in March 1904, the N.Y.K. had taken even farther-reaching steps to expand its feeder network in China. Its entry into the Yangtze trade, however, was with a quality of innocence, like a stranger entering a garden unaware that a lion awaited him.

N.Y.K.'S MCBAIN PURCHASE & BRITISH OPPOSITION AT HANKOW,
1903–1904. In mid-1903 Hayashi Tamio, N.Y.K. Shanghai branch
manager and a rising star within the company, detected rumors
that the small British firm of McBain & Company might be willing
to sell its Yangtze shipping business. Kondō, sensing that this was
the "proper opportunity" he had spoken of to the board in 1901,
gave Hayashi the go-ahead to proceed with negotiations. Hayashi
conducted affairs in absolute secrecy until word began circulating
in June that the N.Y.K. had purchased all of McBain's property
at a price of ¥1.53 million.[18] Interestingly, an earlier O.S.K. report had dismissed McBain as a one-family firm which sold kero-
sene on the side, and all foreign observers agreed that the N.Y.K.
price exceeded the value of McBain's property. Yet, there was
plenty of foreign interest in McBain. In March 1901 McBain had
refused a Hamburg America Line offer of at least one million
taels; and in 1903, before Hayashi stepped in, a "Hankow syndicate" was negotiating for the purchase.[19] What made the McBain
property so desirable?

As the British had developed settlements, or concession areas,
along the Yangtze since the 1860s, they had secured the best
sites in the open ports for berthing facilities. Though McBain
owned only two steamers, he was the oldest British shipowner
operating in China, and had secured the most convenient lots in
Chinkiang, Wuhu, Kiukiang, and Hankow. The most important
facilities were in Hankow, where he occupied the best berth in the
British settlement. His long experience had also reportedly given
him the full confidence of Chinese shippers. His two ships, then,
valued at a mere 30,000 taels, were of minor signficance. The key
was the wharfage facility and the goodwill.

The McBain purchase fit perfectly into N.Y.K. strategy, enabling
direct participation in the rich trade of the Tungting Lake region
and Hunan, the "rice-granary of China," and establishing ties with
the railways which would connect with the shipping routes at
Hankow. Company reports pointed primarily to the value of the
new Yangtze service for the main overseas lines which had come to

intersect at Shanghai, the new hub of the N.Y.K.'s global transport network. Between 1899 and mid-1903, N.Y.K. storage facilities in Shanghai had grown from 15,000 to 50,000 tons and new wharves were also being constructed to accommodate its European liners. During these years of growth at Shanghai, however, the N.Y.K. had lagged behind in inland organization and feeder lines. For several years management had been looking for the "proper opportunity" to expand the inland network.[20] The Hunan Steamship Company, the first initiative in this respect, was expected to transship Shanghai-bound freight to O.S.K. ships at Hankow. But now, with the McBain purchase, the N.Y.K. not only had a new Yangtze service but it also had virtual control over the Hunan firm and its routes, which would connect with the new line at Hankow, thereby giving the N.Y.K. a direct link between Shanghai and Changsha. The company had thus achieved a full integration of services back into the interior of China and outward toward the major international lines. This marked the culmination of the feeder strategy— or so it seemed.

Not unexpectedly the main British companies refused to let the N.Y.K. have the best berthing facilities on the Yangtze without a fight. The effect of this dispute over McBain's wharves left a long-standing bitterness in N.Y.K. executives toward the British companies. Since the dispute occurred shortly after the Anglo-Japanese Alliance of 1902, it also raises questions about the alliance's applicability. In the preamble of the treaty, Britain and Japan had pledged to "secure equal opportunities in [China and Korea] for the commerce and industry of all nations." For Britain, the intent of this promise was to secure its interests in the Yangtze valley. However, Britain's principal worry regarding the Yangtze, as Nish suggests, "was the economic encroachment of other trading powers there," including Japan. The preamble, then, was a general statement of principle without the same degree of applicability as the diplomatic and military clauses of the treaty. In fact, the dispute over McBain's wharves, which seemed to contravene the spirit of the preamble, shows that the undercurrent of Anglo-Japanese commercial competition flowed directly against the stream of the better-known diplomatic relations.[21]

McBain's berth at Hankow was held under a lease arrangement. The N.Y.K. assumed it could take over the lease when it purchased the McBain firm. As opposed to this, the major British shipping firms, the China Navigation Company and the Indo-China S. N. Company, argued that McBain did not have the right to transfer the lease, and they sought to obtain the use of the berth for themselves.[22] In the British concession area of Hankow, where the berth was located, customarily a Landrenters Council consisting of both British and "Alien" (that is, non-British) members had the authority to approve and renew leases. Some members of this council, who opposed the Yangtze pool, favored more competition by letting the N.Y.K. use the berth under the principle of free trade.[23] When the lease for McBain's wharf came up for renewal in February 1904, the Landrenters Council supported the N.Y.K. application by a vote of 78 (60 "Aliens" and 18 British) to 43 (all British).[24]

After several more months of legal maneuvering, the British Foreign Office aided the British firms by changing the rules of the Landrenters Council. Reacting against the decisive role of the "Alien" Landrenters, the Foreign Office declared that in future "the Bund Frontages will be allotted in accordance with the majority of British votes." The British companies then obtained the berth themselves.[25] So much for "equal opportunities" under the Anglo-Japanese Alliance.

One argument that the British frequently used was that since Japan had its own concession in Hankow, the N.Y.K. should find accommodation there. The Japanese settlement, however, lacked good berthing facilities. Accordingly, it took several years before the N.Y.K. obtained land for a wharf, this time in the French settlement. What exacerbated the N.Y.K.'s antagonism toward the British, however, was the action of the Russian Consul in Hankow, who, during the Russo-Japanese War (!) offered the N.Y.K. accommodation in the Russian settlement. This area, which adjoined the British concession, also contained good facilities, and the offer was tempting enough that the N.Y.K. certainly would have accepted had the two countries not been at war![26]

The immediate business impact of the wharfage controversy is difficult to measure, for the Russo-Japanese War naturally was the major impediment to N.Y.K. operations during most of this period. But the McBain purchase had been made eight months before the war, and company records indicate that the dispute at least delayed business expansion during that interval and in that sense frustrated the implementation of the feeder strategy. The dispute also had considerable impact on the Hunan firm, whose stockholders had expressed anxiety as early as 1903 over their inability to obtain a landing place in Hankow. The N.Y.K.'s acquisition of McBain's property seemed to solve this problem by promising the Hunan company landing facilities at the McBain wharf. British opposition thus frustrated the N.Y.K. in its interior branch lines as well as along the Yangtze.[27]

Ironically, the wharfage dispute arose when Japan was supposedly enjoying her maximum benefits from the Anglo-Japanese Alliance. But these were diplomatic benefits, and Kondō viewed the matter differently: "As England is our ally . . . I imagined that even in matters of trade we should not have experienced such unsympathetic treatment. But that was a mistake on my part. I find that in national commerce there is no distinction between ally and national enemy." Opinion in Japan generally echoed this sentiment, for Britain was seen as having abandoned the principles of liberty and free trade. Many worried that a bad precedent had been set and, in the aftermath of the Russo-Japanese War, with Japan having gained new territorial possessions in South Manchuria, some asked what the foreign reaction would be if the Japanese declared Dairen off-limits to all ships not flying the Japanese flag. Later, when Japan seized the German possession of Kiaochow during World War I, it did indeed block British ships from the port of Tsingtao, and British complaints then resembled the N.Y.K.'s in 1903.[28] All of this forms an interesting precedent for the "exclusive spheres" doctrine of the 1930s. Even if it be admitted in retrospect that the N.Y.K. entered into the McBain purchase with a degree of legal naiveté, one can also conclude that the British were good teachers.

IMPERIALISM AND WAR

BUSINESS IMPERIALISM. Through its business activity in East Asia, especially its dependence on China in the development of its feeder strategy, the N.Y.K. became a participant in economic imperialism. To justify this assertion requires some definition of, and some distinction among, the types of imperialism. Since this study is of a particular firm, however, Japanese imperialism will be discussed only to comment on issues pertinent to the N.Y.K.[29]

Historians usually make a distinction between formal empire, involving occupation and colonial rule, and informal empire, implying a degree of commerical and financial penetration, backed perhaps by informal political methods and resulting in extensive control by one country over another.[30] The N.Y.K. acted within the formal empire, for it carried on business with Taiwan, the territories in South Manchuria, and Korea (acquired by Japan respectively in 1895, 1905, and 1910). With the exception of South Manchuria, however, the company conducted only a small percentage of its business with these territories and they exerted little influence on the development of its strategy. The informal empire, that is, China, is more germane to an examination of the N.Y.K. as a business imperialist.

China became the essential support for the European line and a major trading area for the N.Y.K.'s key partners in its business alliances, namely, the cotton spinners and Mitsui Bussan. Japanese goods, produced and marketed by these firms, meant increased N.Y.K. export freight. Between 1890 and World War I, N.Y.K. officials were as enthusiastic as any businessman about the potential of the China market. For example, when the N.Y.K. began planning for government subsidies in early 1895, its first drafts would have limited even general navigation aid to ships engaged in transoceanic transport. Nakamigawa Hikojirō, the N.Y.K. board member from the Mitsui Bank, objected to this. "China," he said, "will absorb Japanese manufactured goods, and to the extent that it develops itself, it will become our largest market. Consequently, we must plan today for the growth of Sino-Japanese trade by giving increasing aid for shipping lines to China. To exclude this excellent market from the areas designated for subsidies would be to oppose the objectives of the state."[31] Following the Russo-Japanese War, Kondō wrote that China is "now ready to develop her resources, while her five hundred millions of inhabitants are in a position to purchase manufactures and products from abroad. China ought to be a great market for the world's trade."[32]

Though the China market was, in general, a myth, N.Y.K. business partners did develop a high degree of dependence on China trade.[33] As shown earlier, in certain industries like cotton spinning, exports to China accounted for a large proportion of total production. Mitsui Bussan, of course, marketed these goods through its excellent sales network.[34] Some Japanese scholars have related Mitsui's dependence on China to domestic business structure. Since trading surpassed mining as the most profitable of Mitsui's enterprises after 1900, and since Mitsui did roughly 15 percent of its business in China, its trading there is seen as indispensable to the rapid accumulation of the Mitsui zaibatsu's capital resources.[35] Dependence on China by enterprises crucial to Japan's changing industrial structure tended to legitimate opinion makers who stressed China's economic value to Japan. China was not only a market for manufactured goods in which Japan increasingly enjoyed a comparative advantage but also an exporter of resources. Attempts to guarantee a secure supply of these resources led to a more forceful Japanese diplomacy culminating in the Twenty-One Demands of 1915. The prominent economic issues in these demands concerned the control of iron ore supplies, a matter in which both Mitsui and Mitsubishi, and to a lesser extent, the N.Y.K., became involved.[36]

The most important N.Y.K. interests in the shipping industry in China were the navigation rights on the Yangtze and other inland waters acquired after the Sino-Japanese War. Also, it had made extensive direct and indirect investment in China to create a shipping infrastructure. Some of these investments, such as the interest in the Hunan Steamship Company, the property owned in Shanghai, and the leases of wharves on the Yangtze have already been mentioned. Others will be discussed in the next two chapters.

At least two criteria should be present to regard "economic expansion" as "imperialist."[37] First, an economic privilege must be acquired by force, and second, its impact must contribute to an erosion of the subject country's autonomy.[38] In general, N.Y.K. business in China fits these criteria. The company originally acquired its right to navigate on the Yangtze through military force, that is, by the treaty imposed on China after the Sino-Japanese War. Then, in 1898, under British pressure, China removed existing restrictions on inland steam navigation by foreigners. Under the most-favored-nation clause, this provided new opportunities for Japan. China agreed to Britain's demands, however, partly out of the hope that more foreign shipping would promote trade without simultaneously damaging Chinese shipping.[39] While these navigation rights perhaps were not given entirely under duress in 1898, China's hope seems to have been in vain, at least with respect to Yangtze traffic and the four major groups operating there (the two British firms, the Japanese, and the China Merchants). Between 1903 and 1911, Japan's share of the steamship tonnage held by these four groups almost doubled from 24 to 47 percent, while that of the China Merchants fell from 27 to 16 percent.[40]

This growing Japanese strength was one factor (though not the most important) that prevented the China Merchants firm from developing an effective ocean-going fleet. Foreign shipping did, of course, bring many benefits to China, improving domestic distribution and stimulating the traditional economy. In response, Chinese junk shipping also increased its activity.[41] Still, foreign domination of China's modern economy is justifiably labeled imperialist because it eroded China's autonomy by reducing its capacity to exploit its comparative advantage as a means to future strategic development.[42] One manifestation of this impact within the shipping industry was the increased risk it imposed on Chinese businessmen when investing in their own companies. As a result, Chinese capital tended to be diverted into foreign enterprises. For example, in 1900 several small Chinese firms had been set up to run between Hankow and Changsha, but in the face of foreign competition only one of these firms survived, and Chinese capital flowed into the N.Y.K.-controlled Hunan Steamship Company. This was made possible by the Hunan Company's own directive from the Japanese government, which exempted Chinese from a prohibition against foreign stockholding. Chinese were allowed to hold up to 20 percent of the company's shares.[43]

The N.Y.K.'s activity in China can be thought of as a kind of auxiliary imperialism. From the beginning the N.Y.K. regarded its Yangtze line as a feeder necessary for the profitability of the European service, the company's major concern.[44] In this sense its European business "pushed" the N.Y.K. into becoming an economic imperialist in China. In short, imperialism in China became an integral unit in the internationalization of the company's business operations.

The relation between imperialism and the N.Y.K. must therefore be seen within the context of the world economy. If we apply to the European line the common distinction in the historiography of imperialism between the metropolis and the periphery, then the N.Y.K.'s "metropolis" consisted of both Japan and Europe, while China, because it was not industrialized and because it had only a supporting role, acted as the "periphery." This distinction, however, should not obscure the fact that, for the N.Y.K., there was no bifurcation between policies oriented to the West and those oriented to China. Both areas were part of an integrated operation.

N.Y.K. RESISTANCE TO WAR SERVICE. Besides the function of China as a feeder and the attractions of its market, Kondō and other N.Y.K. officials urged Japanese expansion into East Asia because of their strategic concern about the increase of European influence there. This raises questions about the connection between

N.Y.K. strategy and government military policy. Did being an economic imperialist inevitably entail promotion of imperialist wars? There have been very few well documented studies of the response of Japanese companies to war. One study by Hilary Conroy almost seems to have discouraged such research. He argued that there was no business pressure for war with China in 1894 and as a corollary tended to dismiss economic imperialism as a factor in Japanese expansion, though his focus was on Korea.[45] More recently, however, Akira Iriye and Peter Duus have provided considerable detail about the vast amount of rhetoric on economic expansion coming from popular writers, businessmen, and government leaders. Duus in particular has pointed to the perception by businessmen of the economic benefits to be gained from military expansion. More specifically he has argued that "big business leadership fell into line behind the government's foreign policy" before both the Sino-Japanese War in 1894 and the Russo-Japanese War in 1904.[46]

The basic problem with the work done by Western scholars on economic expansion, including that which focuses on imperialism, lies with the limitations of its evidence. Most scholars have relied primarily on writings, public statements, or on published records of meetings between businessmen and government officials. Since they have not used company records in their research on Japanese imperialism before World War I, not surprisingly they have overlooked the issue of normal business strategy.[47] It is interesting that scholarship on Britain's "informal imperialism" in Latin America has had a more precise focus on business strategy. D.C.M. Platt suggests that generalizations about economic imperialism must "be founded on some expertise with respect to the day-to-day operations of business." Robert Greenhill argues that though the nature of their business operations sometimes dragged British shipping companies into colonial disputes, these companies "preferred peace and the *status quo* which permitted normal business."[48]

Greenhill's conclusion anticipates my argument about the N.Y.K.'s response to military ventures—that the N.Y.K.'s principal concern was always with normal business. A slightly different approach has been offered by Duus with his characterization of business leaders "falling into line" behind government policy. Such a posture implies a willingness to tolerate the disruption of normal business, though it is, of course, less aggressive than various forms of pressure for war. Put briefly, the view which Duus seems to share with Iriye is that, whereas business leaders may have anticipated benefits from war, they did not lobby for military expansion nor did they engage in economic imperialism. They only favored "economic expansion" and adopted a posture of "falling into line" on military policy. There is, in this view, an assumed negative link between economic imperialism and war, namely, that because business did not actively support the latter, it did not support the former either. The principal purpose of this section is to break the analytical link between economic imperialism and war by showing that the N.Y.K.'s business strategy led the company both to engage in economic imperialism and, at least in certain cases, to resist participation in wars. Some evidence has already been given on economic imperialism. The second part of the question confronts a common perception that shipping was an adjunct of the navy and thus of all industries had the most to gain from wars. Certainly the N.Y.K. derived enormous benefits from the Sino-Japanese War.[49] But generally the N.Y.K. considered military ventures too disruptive. The outbreak of a war inevitably led to a threefold response: sudden military requests for transports, secret negotiations with government leaders, and the interruption of normal business. The N.Y.K.'s response to specific wars deserves detailed attention, for the priority the company placed on normal business operations led it into a number of embarrassing contradictions, dilemmas, and at least once into a position of potential total resistance.

The N.Y.K. does not seem to have resisted government requests prior to the Sino-Japanese War. In fact it profited from negotiations on the eve of the war. On June 4, 1894, two days after the cabinet's decision to send troups to Korea, Kawakami Sōroku, the vice-chief of the Army General Staff, urgently demanded ten transports from Kondō. This was granted only after a debate over the possibility of a news leak regarding the government's secretly planned expedition to Korea if the N.Y.K. followed normal procedure in seeking approval of the request for transports from its directors. Kondō complained to Kawakami that it was always the government that leaked secrets and furthermore, if this secret should be disclosed, no one would know which of them, Kondō or Kawakami, was responsible. If such a situation should arise, said Kondō, the issue could only be settled by the two of them dueling to the death with swords.

Impressed by Kondō's decisiveness, Kawakami ordered the army to give the wartime contract for coal transport to the N.Y.K. After the end of hostilities in 1895 he told Kondō and Katō that "we could not have fought the war without the N.Y.K."[50]

That much is clear from the statistics. The N.Y.K. accounted for 59 percent of the requisitioned tonnage and carried 83 percent of military personnel and 75 percent of the horses during the war.[51] The company apparently responded according to government expectations. Some doubt, however, must remain about what was actually happening behind the scenes. Some shipping firms were less than zealous in their patriotism. The following comments by John Swire seem to pertain to the ships of Mitsui Bussan:

> We are in receipt of your telegram of this date [23 July] respecting the transfer of the M[itsui] B[ussan] fleet to the English flag and our agency. We are opposed to this business—it would injure us greatly in China, would probably rupture our arrangement with the C[hina] M[erchants] Co., and we might be boycotted by the China guilds.
>
> Besides, the transfer would not have legal effect in event of capture, our Government would not support any claim for redress, for no one could contend that *ownership* had been conferred upon us.[52]

The Butterfield & Swire agency subsequently refused to accept a request to take charge of the China Merchants fleet, which instead was fictitiously "purchased" by Jardine, Matheson for the duration of the war. Having rejected the Japanese request, Swire felt he could hardly accept responsibility for the Chinese fleet.[53] It is unclear, though, whether Japanese firms were trying to avoid government requisition or whether they were fearful of physical damage and capture. Actually Mitsui seems to have made substantial gains from requisitioning. During 1895, 94.5 percent of Mitsui shipping income came from requisitioned ships. The corresponding figure for the N.Y.K. was 54.3 percent.[54]

The next major military service performed by the N.Y.K. occurred during the rescue operation on behalf of foreign legations in Peking during the Boxer Rebellion of 1900. In contrast to the domestic orientation of its business in 1894, the N.Y.K. now had an established network of regular overseas services. Not surprisingly, then, its response to government demands in 1900 was considerably more equivocal than Kondō's decisiveness with Kawakami Sōroku in 1894. Kondō was traveling in the West when the Boxer Rebellion broke out, and Katō took charge of negotiations with the government. In mid-June 1900 he met with General Terauchi Masatake and offered some resistance to government requests. Terauchi suggested that, if supplying the government with ships produced a shortage in the N.Y.K.'s regular domestic routes, the company could charter ships from independent shipowners. The N.Y.K., however, could not accept charters at rates charged by independents without incurring a substantial loss, a loss which it could recoup only by raising its own freight rates, thereby contradicting the government directive concerning stable freight rates for regular lines. Katō was especially worried about foreign lines. The army should be aware, he told Terauchi, that these services were not just the property of the N.Y.K. but that they were a public service. Marshaling his arguments, Katō claimed that, during the Boer War, Britain had utilized 1.5 million tons of shipping for military purposes without making cutbacks in either its domestic or overseas services. He saw no reason why Japan could not perform in the same manner. Under the government directive, Katō explained, the N.Y.K. had a dual obligation—to regular lines, on the one hand, and military transport, on the other. Which of these should take precedence in the present situation, he said, only the government could decide. Terauchi then hastily asked for 80,000 tons of shipping and the N.Y.K. directors called an emergency meeting to consider how to meet the request.

The ensuing discussion provides an interesting commentary on the N.Y.K.'s changing business commitments. In particular it marks the transition from the company's almost total dependence on coastal shipping in its early years to the now dominant concern for overseas business. The directors set priorities for providing ships to the government. The first would be pulled off domestic lines, and in fact, if the company could have followed its own preference, it would have supplied only coastal ships. It could not do this for fear of incurring public criticism. When the new ships for the European line had been delivered, there had been considerable public discussion about how useful they would be in times of war! Regretfully, then, the directors felt they would have to offer several ships from transoceanic lines as well, even though they feared this would result in a loss of confidence in the N.Y.K. abroad.[55]

Another reason for Katō's reservations was the ambiguity over government rates. There was a contradiction between the rate of ¥4.5 per ton per month mentioned in the 1885 directive and the orders for the special lines of the late 1890s, which had promised higher rates for ships requisitioned from these services. Negotiations with the government were unsuccessful, and the company had to be content with the original ¥4.5 rate, while it paid ¥5 for the ships it had to charter.[56]

Promising business conditions just prior to the Boxer Rebellion also influenced N.Y.K. reservations about military transport. The year 1900 had seen a recovery from the 1897–1899 recession, and the N.Y.K. had placed several temporary steamers on domestic lines to cover the increased shipments. More importantly, British ships requisitioned for the Boer War had been pulled off East Asian routes (an interesting contradiction to Katō's statements to Terauchi), creating an extra demand for Japanese vessels. This occurred just when the N.Y.K. was expanding lines to North China as part of the early development of the feeder strategy. The Boxer

Rebellion was thus ill-timed from the perspective of strategic business growth, for the company had to suspend the Shanghai-Tientsin lines with the exception of stops at Chefoo.[57]

No matter how ill-timed, the Boxer Rebellion was a minor interruption compared with the Russo-Japanese War. Negotiations in the fall of 1903, before the government's decision for war was made, provide the greatest contrast between what the N.Y.K. said to government officials and what it did behind the scenes. In the second week of October 1903 Kodama Gentarō, vice-chief of the Army General Staff, presented Kondō with extreme demands, namely, that to show the united spirit of the Japanese people and thus induce the Russians into a more conciliatory attitude, the N.Y.K. and the O.S.K. should jointly declare that they would offer their ships to the government free of charge upon the outbreak of war. To this Kondō replied, "it would be necessary to have a General Meeting of our stockholders agree to this for us to make the kind of announcement you desire, but since we are a profit-making corporation, it is extremely unlikely that our stockholders would decide to make such an offer." Fujita Densaburō of the O.S.K. also appears to have given Kodama the same advice. In another meeting with Kondō several days later, Kodama claimed that railway and coal companies had agreed to provide their services without charge, but again Kondō put him off by advising him to discuss the matter with Shibusawa, Masuda Takashi, and Yanosuke. To Kodama's frustration their opinion was the same as Kondō's. In a third meeting with Kodama, Kondō became more aggressive, calling the proposed announcement an unnatural demonstration that would have no effect on the Russians. He then asked Kodama point-blank whether the government was planning to initiate the war. Kodama replied that, if matters could not be settled through negotiations, there would be no alternative to war, but such a war would entail enormous costs, somewhere in the neighborhood of ¥1.5 billion, and chance of victory was slim. For that reason he wanted the companies to cooperate in a demonstration of support. Kondō took a different tack. He suggested that, rather than worrying about costs, the government should make a definite decision to begin the war and then assemble important business leaders who could offer opinions about war expenses.[58]

It is possible that Kondō's more aggressive, questioning tone in his meeting was an attempt both to acquire information and to stall for time. The N.Y.K. needed both information and time, for it was engaged in momentous decisions of its own. While Kodama was trying to get the N.Y.K. to offer its fleet free of charge, the company conspired behind his back to attempt a transfer of its ships to the British flag. The N.Y.K. carried on simultaneous, secret negotiations with both the P. & O. and Jardine, Matheson, though the talks with the latter eventually reached into the British government itself. The first well-documented evidence of these negotiations appears in a telegram of October 16, 1903, from the P. & O. agent in Kobe, Woolley, to his head office in London:

> For your private information only—Nippon Yusen Kaisha have communicated confidentially with me that, from the unsettled state of political affairs, it has been decided that, *if necessary, most* of the N.Y.K. fleet must be transferred at once to British flag, in which case N.Y.K. will request put name P. & O. Company. [emphasis added].

The next day the head office replied that "unless privately requested by British Government to act as suggested, with ample guarantees with regard to consequences, it is impossible to regard transaction suitable to P. & O. Company's position." On the nineteenth Woolley again urged secrecy, for the "position of affairs is critical still," and then on October 21 he sent another telegram, virtually identical to the one quoted above, except that the words "if necessary" were omitted and "N.Y.K." in the last sentence was replaced by "Their Directors." Woolley, the agent, then concluded: "On what terms can you undertake the business?" On the same day the P. & O. directors replied, confirming that they could not "make any proposal."[59]

Similar N.Y.K. negotiations with Jardine, Matheson became known to the British minister in Japan as early as October 16. The evidence suggests that Jardine, Matheson was more willing than the P. & O. to accept N.Y.K. ships, for in late October the British government discussed the feasibility of such a transfer to the British trading firm.[60] In a telegram of October 28, the British minister in Japan had asked the Foreign Office whether, in the event of a transfer, provisional certificates of British registration could be issued as long as "purchase money actually" passed. British officials at least considered helping the N.Y.K., and they even sought legal opinion. Of course, even without such advice they realized that a transfer of the N.Y.K. fleet would be neither genuine nor permanent and that payment would only be a "loan transaction," a "serious irregularity" that would violate a British policy established in 1898 against such bogus sales.

It is not known how many N.Y.K. directors, mentioned in the P. & O. telegram of October 21, were aware of these approaches to the British. We do know, however, that on October 21, probably *before* the dispatch of the P. & O. telegram, an N.Y.K. directors meeting was held, and Kondō revealed some of the content of his talks with Kodama the day before. The directors decided to promise the government company support in a special letter sent on October 24 to the minister of communications.[61] On October 28 in a meeting of leading businessmen convened to discuss the crisis with Russia, Kondō urged support for an early beginning to the war.[62] Everyone present was surprised at Kondō's statement, an indication perhaps that, with the exception of his talks with Kodama, he had not previously revealed his opinions. Though N.Y.K. negotiations with the P. & O. agent probably broke off after October 21, Kondō was still talking with two voices, for the company's Jardine, Matheson card seems to have been kept alive at least until October 31. The end of the war scare in November then temporarily freed the N.Y.K. from the horns of its dilemma.

Taken together, the demands made by Kodama (the implications of which would have been obvious to Kondō), the government directives on the military obligations of subsidized shipping firms, and the internal evidence of the British documents imply that the N.Y.K. was trying to evade war service. The crucial word in the P. & O. telegram of October 16 is "most" (that is, most of the N.Y.K. fleet), for it creates a context within which we can judge the meaning of the N.Y.K.'s approach to the P. & O. from the perspective of government policy. During the Russo-Japanese War the N.Y.K. provided all of its large and medium-sized ships to the government. In short, the vast majority of its tonnage was requisitioned, and surely Kondō, from his conversations with Kodama earlier in October, must have expected this. Placing "most" of its fleet under the British flag would have constituted nothing less than a massive evasion of war service. The consequence of such action would have been far-reaching indeed. At the very least, it would have transformed the N.Y.K. from a heavily subsidized company into a nonsubsidized independent concern.[63]

The British government's discussion of the Jardine, Matheson connection confirms the meaning of the P. & O. telegram, for officials estimated the worth of the ships to be transferred at several million pounds sterling, roughly equivalent to the book value of the *whole* N.Y.K. fleet. They also clearly assumed that the N.Y.K. wanted temporary protection for the duration of the war, after which their ships would be returned. Most important, a comment by British Foreign Secretary Lord Lansdowne supports the view that the N.Y.K. carried on these talks without the knowledge of the Japanese government. Lansdowne wrote, "It is I understand not the Japanese Gov. but a Japanese Company which asks us to connive at this conspiracy."[64]

To my knowledge there is no evidence in Japanese of these approaches to the British. N.Y.K. records, however, provide a plausible explanation of the company's October panic. Between mid-October and early November there was heavy telegraph traffic between the head office and ports on the European line concerning cargo insurance. The war scare had made insurance on N.Y.K. cargo prohibitively expensive, prompting shippers to desert the N.Y.K. for other lines. In response the head office accepted the advice of the branches that the N.Y.K. itself incur the extra insurance charges to retain its shippers. At one point the N.Y.K. contemplated paying foreign insurance firms because rates of Japanese companies had risen more steeply. Despite these countermeasures, by early November receiving agents in London were instructing their shippers in Japan not to load with the N.Y.K. Whatever action the N.Y.K. took, then, it feared that freight would inevitably go to the British and German flags.[65] In this context, a transfer of N.Y.K. ships to the British flag would have solved the insurance crisis and enabled the company to maintain its service.

In early 1904, Japanese military planning reached a more decisive stage, and by mid-January the N.Y.K. had received secret notice from government sources that it might be necessary to suspend the European line. The board then decided on January 13 to try to monopolize as much as possible the market for requisitioned ships by encouraging the government to lease N.Y.K. ships before those of other companies.[66] This apparent reversion to patriotism superficially appears to contradict the meaning of the October approach to the British, but it was still a *business* decision. Because of the insurance problem and the likely damage to its ships, commercial operation of company vessels in wartime would be uneconomical and potentially disasterous. If no transfer to the British flag could be effected, the only way the company could earn income with its own ships was to have the government requisition them.

Japan opened the Russo-Japanese War on February 8, 1904, by attacking Port Arthur. Despite its seeming resolve of January 13, however, the N.Y.K., in a continuing series of contradictory moves, appears to have kept its options open through inquiries to James, the London manager. On February 17 the N.Y.K. directors met to decide the future of the European line. When the war began several ships on the homeward voyage were in or west of the Mediterranean Sea. It seemed that all of these would have to return via the relative safety of the Cape of Good Hope route. Another possibility, however, was to have them return to London and operate under one of two options that James had presented. Option one entailed cooperating with British businessmen to establish a new company under British law which would then be the legal owner of the ships. Option two involved setting up a dummy firm, placing the ships under its name without transferring ownership.[67]

Along with the P. & O. telegrams and the British government response to the possible transfer of N.Y.K. ships, this N.Y.K. meeting raises a host of questions about N.Y.K. contingency planning. Though somewhat ambiguous, the evidence of this meeting suggests the N.Y.K. was still contemplating some form of evasion, for the meeting focused on the use of a dummy firm for commercial purposes. A possible counterargument to this is that the company considered using the British flag to secure safe passage home. On February 10, for example, it had consulted with the navy about the safest course for a ship docked at Colombo.[68] Yet, company decisions do not portray the military danger of a return voyage as sufficiently serious in itself to justify a transfer to the British flag. The February meeting viewed the Cape route as an acceptable alternative. In early January, despite brisk business, the London branch could not attract cargo to N.Y.K. vessels and James recommended loading ships with coal and routing them via the Cape. But the board rejected this, arguing that it was premature (as of January 13) to abandon Suez for the escape route round the Cape.

A more plausible tactical explanation is that the new options were considered in February as a means to maintain the European line while operating emergency purchases for the government. The N.Y.K. planned to purchase more ships for government use and in March even prepared special accounting categories for them.[69] Nevertheless, besides the fact that such purchases never materialized on the scale envisaged, the internal evidence of the February 17 meeting undermines this tactical explanation. The minutes do not provide a precise count of the ships still in Europe, but judging from the size of those mentioned they totaled at least 30,000 tons. Though equivalent to approximately one-eighth of the company's fleet, this would represent a much higher percentage of ships most appropriate for war service. Purchasing replacements for these ships at war-inflated prices would have required two-thirds of the company's reserves (a decision likely to meet stockholder resistance) or a government loan (an action contradicting the purpose of the directive on military obligations). Whatever the company's *intent* (which was probably both to maintain the line and to operate separate ships in war service), the *effect* of setting up a British company with some 30,000 tons of its best ships would have been evasion, representing on a smaller scale the kind of resistance evident in the approach to the P. & O. and Jardine, Matheson. The directors, however, decided that the procedures for setting up a new company in Britain would be too burdensome, and, worst of all, there would be no prospect of receiving a subsidy![70] In the end they had no choice but to suspend the European line—with great regret that the foundation of everything they had built up over the years was so suddenly collapsing.

There can be no greater testimony to the primacy of "economic man" over the "patriotic samurai businessman" than the N.Y.K.'s contingency planning in the face of military obligations. The transfer of the China Merchants' ships to foreign ownership during both the Sino-French War in 1884 and the Sino-Japanese War in 1894 is typical of the popular contrast between the nationalistic Japanese businessman and the more purely money-oriented Chinese entrepreneur.[71] As the above evidence shows, however, this contrast was not so marked as the popular image would have us believe. The N.Y.K. tried to act much as the China Merchants had done in earlier wars. The distinctive point about Japan was not any special "samurai spirit" but its governmental and institutional context which eventually led the N.Y.K. to fulfill its national obligations. Part of this context included the precisely worded directives on requisitioning. Actual evasion, if it had come to that, would surely have had to cope with overwhelming legal difficulties. In China, on the other hand, it was a relatively simple matter.[72]

The N.Y.K.'s reluctant response to the military in the Boxer Rebellion and the Russo-Japanese War somehow seems out of touch with the company's common image of close military cooperation, but it should not be surprising in view of the relations between the leading shipping firms and the military since the Restoration. A rather consistent pattern of resistance begins in the

1870s with the YJK and the Taiwan expedition, followed in the 1880s by Mitsubishi's reluctance to become involved in Korea. The N.Y.K.'s response in 1903 and 1904 is a continuation of this pattern. Certainly there were notable exceptions, such as Mitsubishi's transport for the Taiwan expedition, but this was unusual because the company was newly formed and had to maneuver to win the government's favor. Two other major exceptions were the Satsuma Rebellion and the Sino-Japanese War. In the case of the former, Mitsubishi had recently defeated all challengers to its dominance and did not have to worry about competitors threatening its domestic lines. In 1894, apart from the Bombay line, the N.Y.K. had few important overseas services that were vulnerable to disruption. Its coastal lines, however, were challenged during the war by domestic tramps and foreign shipping firms. Also, as noted, there seems to have been some initial resistance from Mitsui Bussan to war service in 1894. Generally, once companies became established and their services institutionalized they became committed primarily to their normal business operations. For the N.Y.K. the Russo-Japanese War in its initial prospects spelled utter disaster for these operations.

This account of the three-stage transition from the Sino-Japanese War to the Boxer Rebellion and the Russo-Japanese War suggests that, as the N.Y.K.'s principal overseas lines became more and more institutionalized, the company became less and less inclined to support the government's military ventures. By contrast, throughout the decade from 1894 to 1904, the N.Y.K. was becoming more deeply involved in business imperialism (or "informal empire") in China through its growing investments and lines there. These operations were made possible by the Sino-Japanese War, but the Russo-Japanese War did not promise the same rewards. A principal characteristic of Japanese management in the modern era has been its emphasis on the stability and expansion of the market. But when shipping executives were forced to put their vessels at the disposal of the military, they feared the loss of their markets.

While the N.Y.K. management did not view the prospect of war service with enthusiasm, the effects of war and the resulting changes in government policy were principal factors in the evolution of company operations. Money flowing from the Sino-Japanese War at least indirectly made possible the subsidies for the major lines, and the postwar treaty forced China to open the Yangtze valley to Japanese penetration. The war thus provided a basis for the N.Y.K. feeder strategy, which depended primarily on Yangtze transport. The effects of the Russo-Japanese War also brought a significant shift in N.Y.K. strategy. Before the war the company had expanded through the accumulation of new routes and their integration into an international network. While the company made several attempts to further this strategy after 1905, the aftermath of the war brought new pressures which gradually forced the N.Y.K. toward more specialization in its operations and away from the grander visions of the feeder strategy.

NINE

Nationalism and Regional Strategies: 1904–1914

THE RUSSO-JAPANESE WAR AND ITS AFTERMATH

In the Russo-Japanese War of 1904–1905 the N.Y.K. on balance lost more than it gained. All of the company's main lines were interrupted—without the same compensating degree of profits that occurred during the Sino-Japanese War. In contrasting the effects of the two wars it is best to highlight the business situation before the wars began. In 1894 the N.Y.K. had just initiated its overseas lines; it needed government support in the form of both strategic commitment and money. This it received, for the Sino-Japanese War acted as an enormous booster, propelling the company into its rapid expansion. In 1903 the company was reaching the fulfillment of its institutional growth, linking its main and feeder lines, for which it had planned since at least 1899. The Russo-Japanese War was like an earthquake, shaking the structure of a nearly finished building.

The quantitative contrast is as great as the institutional. Prior to 1900 the record year for profits had been 1895, the peak of the Sino-Japanese War, when the company cleared ¥4.77 million. As the overseas lines matured, however, for four consecutive years from 1900 to 1903 profits were at or above the record level of 1895. Following the Russo-Japanese War they did not reach this level again until 1912. A comparison of the aftermath of the two wars shows that company income grew at an annual rate of 11.2 percent between 1896 and 1903 but at only 3.0 percent a year between 1906 and 1911.

Another loss from the war was a redirection in government policy away from the tolerance of company autonomy toward greater state intervention, which affected both the main lines and the feeder strategy. Some of these losses were offset by the war's principal gain, the freer access to South Manchuria. This area became a major feeder for the European line, helping to solve many of the earlier problems of cargo shortage on the westbound voyage. This gain, however, typifies another new direction of government policy which was to transform the feeder strategy, namely, the more explicit orientation toward colonialism and control of East Asian resources.

EFFECT OF THE WAR ON COMPANY LINES AND FINANCES. When the Russo-Japanese War began, the N.Y.K. possessed seventy-five ships with a total capacity of 244,000 tons. Virtually all of these were requisitioned, leaving the company with only nine ships of 13,594 tons for its own services. By the end of 1904 the government had requisitioned well over half a million tons of shipping from Japanese owners. This included 48,000 tons from the O.S.K. and approximately 25,000 tons each from Mitsui Bussan and Asano's Tōyō Kisen. The war temporarily suspended all of the company's overseas lines. The Bombay line, in fact, was not resumed until after the war. Later in 1904 several ships were made available for a reduced service on the less hazardous American line, but foreign vessels had to be chartered for a monthly service on the European line. East Asian and coastal lines also relied mostly on charters.[1]

In sum, the company's financial situation was: all of its ships were earning income from the government and for all of its services it had to pay charter fees on foreign ships. The effort to balance this and come out with a profit was hampered by the loss of most of the government subsidy. Since foreign charters were ineligible for navigation subsidies, the company received no aid under that category for the duration of the war. Line subsidies were given for "services performed," but the charters could conduct only a greatly reduced service. Subsidies for this amounted to less than 25 percent of aid in normal years. The bottom line, then, was what rate the government would pay for requisitioned ships and how much the N.Y.K. would have to pay in charter fees.

Rates for requisitioned ships had long been a source of disagreement between the N.Y.K. and the government. In private conversations following the Sino-Japanese War, General Terauchi Masatake had tried to persuade the N.Y.K. to lower the previously promised rate of ¥4.5 per ton per month to ¥3.5. Since Terauchi had managed to get other companies to accept this lower figure, the N.Y.K. worried that if it refused it could damage its relations with the army. Though the ¥4.5 rate held good for the Boxer Rebellion, before the Russo-Japanese War a compromise was reached at two classes of ¥4.5 and ¥3 according to ship size.[2]

The issue of rates was not confined to confidential negotiations but became a matter of public debate. Kondō argued that government rates were equivalent to no more than 8s.6d., whereas the British government had paid anywhere from 15 to 25s. during the Boer War, and they had even offered the N.Y.K. 20s. for the ships on its European line (just under ¥10). Critics, however, circulated rumors that the N.Y.K. had demanded ¥7 for its ships before the war, and in early 1905 a movement arose to reduce the company's subsidies. Usual opponents such as Taguchi Ukichi and Shimada Saburō were joined by the hard-line liberal Ozaki Yukio in introducing a Diet resolution against subsidies.[3]

Kondō's complaints had some validity at the beginning of the war when the market rate for charter fees was still extremely high. But as the war progressed and Japan's credit improved, charter rates dropped in tandem with the falling interest rates on government war loans raised abroad. To maintain the confidence of its shippers, the N.Y.K. continued the European line, though with fewer sailings, by chartering from the Blue Funnel and medium-sized British firms. As early as May 1904 these agreements set fees considerably below the requisitioned rate for large ships. The

N.Y.K. guaranteed the British firms 4s.6d., but promised to pay up to 6s. (about ¥3) if it cleared a profit.[4]

The favorable differential between the charter fees and the rate for requisitioned ships helps explain the company's profits of ¥3 million in both 1904 and 1905 despite the cutback in subsidies. In any case, the company had learned from the stockholders revolt of 1897 to prepare for hard times. Between 1900 and 1902, the years of plenty, ¥3.3 million had been placed in a special reserve for the "equalization of dividend payments" to protect against a potential deficit like that of 1897. This special reserve, the institutional outcome of the earlier revolt, never had to be drawn on, and indeed the company paid a 15 percent dividend following the war, the highest since the Sino-Japanese War. Even during the ensuing depression it kept its dividend at 12 percent until 1909.

Financially the N.Y.K. adequately survived the war, but its wartime profits, 40 percent lower than those of the previous four years of peace, belie a common assumption that shipping companies greatly benefited from the war.[5] Liner companies like the N.Y.K. had mediocre results, but tramp shipping earned huge profits. The war proved especially timely for Yamashita Kamesaburō, the most famous Japanese tramp shipper, for he had just turned his coal distributorship into a shipping business. To the tramps also went most of the emergency purchases of ships made during the war. The N.Y.K. fleet size before and after the war starkly indicates the rise of the tramps and the relative decline of the N.Y.K. In 1903 N.Y.K. ships were measured at 242,000 tons, or 36.8 percent of the country's tonnage. While the fleet had grown to 253,000 tons by 1906, this represented only 24.4 percent of Japan's total capacity.[6]

The war's hindrance of the N.Y.K.'s feeder strategy, despite company efforts to develop additional branch lines, substantially effected company finances. In 1902 the N.Y.K. established a special reserve for line expansion and improvement of the fleet. In the first term of that year ¥500,000 was placed in the reserve, which grew rapidly to ¥3.5 million by the outbreak of the war. No more funds were added until 1912, testifying to the war's disruption of company planning. A second financial impact, which all Japanese firms likely suffered, was the obligatory purchase of government bonds and securities to finance the war. In early 1906 the company held approximately ¥5 million in government securities issued expressly for the war. This represented more than half of all N.Y.K. investments in stocks and bonds and constituted 10 percent of the firm's total assets. Although the N.Y.K. held these securities for only three years and naturally drew interest, this forced "investment in war" made fewer funds available for expansion of normal business during the 1904 to 1907 period when the company was trying to transform the feeder strategy into an institutionalized structure.

POSTWAR COMPETITION AND STRATEGY. Though the Treaty of Portsmouth formally ending the war was signed on September 5, 1905, it was not until April 17, 1906, that the N.Y.K. was able to resume the European line with its full assignment of twelve ships. The next month Katō was dispatched overseas to investigate company lines. One of his missions in Europe was to extend N.Y.K. port privileges to make the company more competitive on the European line. In late 1906 he met with Albert Ballin, the powerful head of the Hamburg America Line, to request berthing rights in Hamburg. Since Katō could make no headway himself, he called upon the diplomatic skills of Takahashi Korekiyo, president of the Bank of Japan, who happened to be in Hamburg. Takahashi, the principal negotiator for the loans from the United States and Europe that had enabled Japan to fight the war, was a personal acquaintance of Ballin. Takahashi took up the cause of the N.Y.K. with Ballin and at least opened the door to a compromise. Hamburg was a closed port because Germany wanted to direct as much of its overseas export trade as possible through its own ports. If foreign shipping companies called at Hamburg, they would reduce the share carried by German firms. Competition from the port of Antwerp, through which a considerable portion of Germany's exports were shipped, made Hamburg less inclined to grant privileges to foreign shipping companies. The Hamburg America Line, however, had a contract with the French Messageries Maritimes to regulate their share of Antwerp cargo, just as the N.Y.K. had a working arrangement with the P. & O. regarding Antwerp that was tied to conference agreements. Ballin suggested that the N.Y.K. might be admitted to the Hamburg berth in exchange for a similar deal that would give the Hamburg America Line rights to a certain portion of N.Y.K. Antwerp cargo.[7]

It is not known how long these talks continued into 1907 or whether the N.Y.K. was amenable to Ballin's suggestions. What is clear is that 1907 was a bad time to bargain with the Hamburg America Line, for by mid-year the world's shipping industry had fallen into its worst recession in decades and by 1908 Ballin's firm, which was heavily dependent on the depressed North Atlantic passenger traffic, had 136,000 tons laid up. A combination of excess tonnage and a business recession had produced a severe worldwide impact on the shipping industry. In Britain freight rates were lower than they had been for fifty years. In Japan, 1907 had begun with the N.Y.K. stock at a pre-World War I record high of ¥154.6, but by December it had dropped precipitously to ¥77. Generally, in Japan the recession hit hardest those services already suffering from postwar competition with tramp shipping, principally domestic and near-seas operations. On the other hand, liner services withstood the recession better, for the conference system suppressed competition and was able to maintain profitable rates. In fact, freight rates on westbound general cargo jumped during the war years from the low of 20s. in 1903 to a high of 45s. in 1907. Accordingly, the European line became the mainstay of the N.Y.K.'s operations during the lean years.[8]

While the European line remained a money-earner, the recession brought a major structural shift in its trade. The standard pattern of heavy shipments of eastbound European merchandise and uncertain cargoes from Asia prevailed through mid-1907, and several charters were placed on the eastbound line in addition to the twelve regular ships. But in the following two years of recession, the westbound became the more profitable of the two services. In 1908 European-bound freight from China became so plentiful that most westbound ships could not accommodate cargo from the Straits. Conversely, with the decline in demand for European manufactured goods brought on by the business recession in Japan, eastbound ships loading at London were only half full. Somewhat offsetting this decline were two charters employed to carry increased freight direct to colonial ports such as Inch'ŏn in Korea and Dairen in South Manchuria as well as to Hokkaido.[9]

Of the four main areas of N.Y.K. services—overseas, feeder, near-seas, and coastal lines—the overseas lines, especially the European, pulled through the recession in the best shape. Coastal services were hurt by competition from tramps. Feeder lines, still in the development stage in the aftermath of the war, suffered from resistance of Western competitors to N.Y.K. penetration of their markets. Near-seas services, where the N.Y.K. had traditional strength, were invaded by the British who seized the opportunity of war to try to recapture what their countrymen had long since lost. These last two crises can be illustrated by the most vigorous competitive struggles in the postwar years, one in Southeast Asia, another on the Yokohama-Shanghai line.

Consideration of a Southeast Asian line goes back to 1901 following Kondō's tour of the West. In his report Kondō suggested that operations in Southeast Asia could act either as a branch line to the European service or as a basis for a Japan-New York line via Suez. Under this visionary proposal, goods from both Southeast Asia and Europe would be exported to America. Imports from the United States would include oil, general cargo, and manufactured goods such as iron products and railway equipment, which were considered cheaper than their English equivalents.[10]

Planning for this line was derailed by the Russo-Japanese War. In the meantime, the North German Lloyd strengthened its hand in the Southeast Asian trade. As early as 1899 it had purchased a Blue Funnel subsidiary, the East Indian Ocean Steamship Company, which had been a feeder for the British company's European line. Based at Singapore, the German firm built up a commanding position in the trades to Penang, Bangkok, and Borneo and linked this business with its China shipping. In May 1906 the N.Y.K.

launched a challenge by running charters from Hong Kong and Swatow to Bangkok. By mid-1907, after it reportedly began carrying passengers without charge, N.Y.K. losses on the line had mounted to an annual ¥300,000, though various testimony suggests that the German firm was doing even worse. At this point Mitsui Bussan, on behalf of the N.Y.K., tried to mediate the dispute with Butterfield & Swire, which was acting as the North German Lloyd's agent. The German firm refused to accept any settlement except on its own terms, while the N.Y.K.'s freedom of action was circumscribed by contracts with Chinese shippers which stipulated that it would maintain the line for three years. Nevertheless, in late 1907 the company reevaluated the line and found that it had failed to achieve its original goals, which were to promote trade between Japan and Siam and to serve as a feeder for the European line. Instead, the line had become increasingly preoccupied simply with regional shipping. The N.Y.K. board therefore decided that the best solution was to hand over the line to the North German Lloyd for a price, provided that accepting money in such a fashion did not damage the company's reputation overseas. In the end an N.Y.K. delegation led by Iwanaga Shōichi, the company's managing director, met with North German Lloyd representatives in a Hong Kong hotel in December 1907. The N.Y.K. accepted £15,000 in exchange for a commitment to relinquish the line for ten years.[11]

The withdrawal from the Hong Kong-Bangkok line did not mean a loss of N.Y.K. interest in Southeast Asia. One member of Iwanaga's delegation, Ōtani Noboru, N.Y.K. president from 1935 to 1942, became one of the company's leading experts on the area, and, while serving in Hong Kong prior to World War I, he helped to plan the New York line via Suez.[12] In the short run, however, the failure to establish an effective feeder line, analogous to the initial frustration after the McBain purchase, was a significant setback for company strategy. The more problems it encountered in developing feeder services, the more likely it was to retreat to the posture of a strictly main-line company.

The second major competition of these years grew out of the

excess capacity problem following the war. Here the N.Y.K. was the victim, not the attacker. The method of resolution was the same as that employed in the competition with the North German Lloyd, but the results were different. During the Russo-Japanese War the N.Y.K. had maintained its Yokohama-Shanghai service by chartering ships from Butterfield & Swire. Since these ships were not in demand elsewhere after the war, Butterfield & Swire decided to leave them on the line even after they had been released from charter and the N.Y.K. had resumed running its own ships. Since the N.Y.K. had decided to double the Shanghai service by running lines from Yokohama and Kobe, the Butterfield & Swire action led to a fierce three-year struggle. As was its wont, the British firm soon proposed a freight rate agreement and a pooling of traffic. This struck the N.Y.K.'s pride because of the special tradition of the Shanghai line as Yataro's first successful overseas effort. Relations with the British deteriorated, and when Mitsui intimated to them in mid-1907 that the N.Y.K. wanted a settlement, Butterfield & Swire commented that this "would be greatly to the N.Y.K.'s interests, as well [?] as of other Japanese who thought the whole world out here should belong to them."[13]

It was the British who finally gave in, however. In the spring of 1909, Butterfield & Swire offered to withdraw if the N.Y.K. bought two of the firm's three ships on the line for a total of £30,000 (about ¥300,000). The N.Y.K. could see no use for the ships, but since the Butterfield & Swire withdrawal would generate an additional ¥50,000 in annual earnings, the company agreed to pay the British £10,000. This "withdrawal fee" was paid in annual installments of £2,000 over the next five years.[14] However one regards this method of resolution, it was certainly used frequently enough to become an institutionalized practice, albeit one conducted in hushed tones.

The most significant aspect of this competition with Butterfield & Swire was the diplomatic flap which accompanied its intensification in mid-1906. On June 15, 1906, the pro-British *Japan Gazette* published a translation of remarks made by the N.Y.K.'s Iwanaga Shōichi. In resolute tones he was reported to have commented on "several measures for dealing the rival a deadly blow," and on "the duty and object of the N.Y.K. to check the arrogance of foreign steamers to the East of Suez." The pro-N.Y.K. *Japan Weekly Mail* roared its disapproval at what it saw as an inaccurate translation. In fact the *Gazette*'s wording hardly seems misleading; it was more like an attempt to render succinct a typical Japanese circumlocution.[15] In any case the protests could not stop the damage. Rumors soon circulated that the Finance Ministry was providing secret subsidies to Japanese shipping firms to oust foreigners from East Asian waters. Picking up on Iwanaga's statements, a German newspaper in New York predicted that the Anglo-Japanese Alliance would receive its "death-blow" in the field of trade and further suggested that the British were building a military port at Singapore to thwart Japan's designs on India. The N.Y.K. tried to treat the matter as if nothing unusual had happened. Free competition, said Kondō, naturally invited a clash of interests. In July Iwanaga sent a long letter of explanation to James, the N.Y.K.'s London manager, which James then passed on to the Swire firm.[16] In reassuring words he expressed confidence in Japan's support for "the open door and equal opportunities for all." The competition with Butterfield & Swire on the Shanghai line was no more unusual than competition among British firms; and the cause, said Iwanaga, was simply excess capacity and the need to find "employment for the additional steamers." But while Iwanaga spoke of the English as "our best friends," his translated statement hardly lends itself to that sentiment. He had not confined his remarks to the Shanghai line but had complained in detail about the McBain purchase. News of the McBain affair of 1903–1904 seems to have been kept under wraps until Iwanaga's statement, possibly because the N.Y.K. did not acquire its berth in the French concession area until April 1906. Also in the latter half of 1906, following Iwanaga's statement, Kondō made his own extremely critical remarks about the British attitude toward the McBain purchase.

The competition with Butterfield & Swire and the McBain wharf dispute signaled a change in the N.Y.K. attitude toward the British. While the company's European and East Asian lines remained integrated in a business sense, with each feeding the other, in diplomatic terms a bifurcation had developed between a cooperative posture in European business and a more nationalistic stance toward the British within East Asia.

From 1896 to 1904 the N.Y.K. had moved in measured but steady fashion from a concentration on trunk lines in its quest for equality to their integration with feeder services. After 1904 company strategy did not follow the same measured steps or undergo a linear evolution as before. Increasingly complex pressures make it more difficult to characterize policy in such straightforward ways as "the quest for equality" or "feeder strategy." These pressures can be summed up in two limiting forces which impinged on company management. One was the growth of government intervention and the restrictions it placed on managerial autonomy, partly through control over strategic business in China and more sweepingly via the 1909 subsidy law. This law abolished navigation aid except for the most important designated lines and gave the government broader authority even over operational matters. The second was the increased competition in coastal and feeder lines which limited the services that could still operate profitably.

As a result of these forces, the innovative and internationalist strategy of the 1896 to 1904 years becomes a mix of conservatism and nationalism after 1904. Conservatism here is defined primarily as specialization. Retrenchment in coastal services, cutbacks in feeder lines, and a more exclusive reliance on subsidized routes (both near-seas and transoceanic) add up to what can be called liner strategy. This is a conservative strategy not simply because of specialization but because of its reluctance to risk starting new and more distant transoceanic lines, such as the Panama-New York line in 1914, without prior subsidies.

The nationalist dimension of this strategy expresses itself within Asia, where the company tries to expand its influence by dominating a conference at the expense of the Europeans (the Bombay line) or by achieving an independent position of strength outside the conference (on the Yangtze). And since expense is less of an inhibiting factor for Asian than for trunk lines, unilateral response to new opportunities (British India) tends to displace the diplomacy of the earlier period. China business illustrates a number of these themes: the N.Y.K. Yangtze service suffers from government intervention; the company adopts a more nationalistic, uncompromising stance toward the British; and it continues to build an infrastructure of imperialism.

SUBSIDIARY COMPANIES AND INVESTMENTS IN EAST ASIA

ESTABLISHMENT OF THE NISSHIN KISEN KAISHA, 1905-1914. One of the principal themes of post-1904 management was the decline of consensus and the growth of conflict in government-company relations. Tension between the N.Y.K. and the government over Yangtze shipping began before the end of the Russo-Japanese War. In July 1905 the minister of communications, Ōura Kanetake, met privately with Kondō and Katō to express the government's displeasure at the competition between four Japanese companies on the Yangtze. Ōura presented several options for an amalgamation of Japanese operations. Either one company might buy up the ships of the other three, or the N.Y.K. and the O.S.K. should merge the assets of their Yangtze services with the Hunan and Daitō firms to create a new company. The N.Y.K., however, felt it would be difficult to implement either scheme because of the different circumstances of the four companies. Some were subsidized, whereas others were not. Their purposes differed, with the Hunan and Daitō servicing single areas, the O.S.K. integrating its Yangtze line with other China business, and the N.Y.K. connecting with transoceanic lines. And it would be difficult to evaluate fairly each company's assets.

Ōura further asked the N.Y.K. to take the role of "representative" in explaining the plan to the other three companies and then to report back to the government. The N.Y.K. was reluctant on both substantive and tactical grounds to assume such a role. First, the board concluded that "from the standpoint of our company we do not want this merger to be carried out." The reason was simple: "Since we believe our company has the strength to expand the business of the Yangtze line by itself, there is no need at present to be active in bringing about an amalgamation." Second, the N.Y.K. felt that if it gave details about the other companies' assets in its reply to the government, it would weaken its own bargaining position. It therefore chose a tactical response. Katō was appointed to communicate verbally an N.Y.K. request that the government take the initiative in drafting more concrete proposals before inquiries were made to the other companies.[17]

The N.Y.K. was clearly reluctant to cooperate with the government if it felt it could further its own interests independently. Its first step in trying to ward off a government-imposed merger was an attempt to transform the Hunan Steamship Company into a virtual subdivision of the N.Y.K. The Hunan firm itself wanted to "entrust" the operational phase of its business to the N.Y.K. It had failed so far to become profitable, and operating in only one area (between Changsha and Hankow) necessitated transshipment at Hankow to either O.S.K. or N.Y.K. vessels. This placed the Hunan firm at a competitive disadvantage vis-à-vis the British companies which could run direct from Changsha to either Shanghai or Ichang on the Upper Yangtze. Since the N.Y.K. still hoped to monopolize the Yangtze business, it had the Hunan company formally request the government to let the N.Y.K. handle its business operations. This would have allowed the N.Y.K. to run direct from Shanghai to Changsha and to establish a more fully integrated service.[18]

On March 7, 1906, as a first stage in the collapse of the N.Y.K.'s takeover plans, Uchida Kakichi, head of the Shipping Bureau, refused to sanction this Hunan request. This left the N.Y.K. in a tenuous position on the Yangtze. The earlier denial of McBain's berthing rights in Hankow had delayed extension of its Yangtze service, and the two ships it had purchased from McBain were rapidly deteriorating. Meanwhile, the O.S.K., with its subsidy, had expanded its facilities, and the assets of its Yangtze business had grown to ¥3.1 million. Clearly the N.Y.K. was no longer the prime candidate to purchase the other lines. The three unattractive

options remaining reveal the company's dilemma. First, with three
ships of the 3,500 ton class ordered from the Kawasaki Shipyard
earlier in 1906, the N.Y.K. could launch a major competition
against the O.S.K. This course, however, would go directly contrary
to government policy, which had stiffened since Ōura raised the
issue of a merger in July 1905. Second, the N.Y.K. could accept a
minority position in a new company that would result from a
merger. Third, it could sell its Yangtze property and work out a
business agreement with the purchasing firm. [19]

The first option (outright competition) would have been the
most consistent with goals pursued by the N.Y.K. since 1903.
The McBain fiasco, however, had prevented the N.Y.K. from effectively challenging the O.S.K., and a competitive struggle in
1906 held out little promise, for by that time thirty-three steamers
were operating on the Shanghai-Hankow run. First-class passenger
fares, normally at ¥10, were ¥7 and occasionally as low as ¥4.
Freight rates, too, had declined by more than 40 percent. Furthermore, the N.Y.K. had traditionally enjoyed good relations with
the O.S.K. on the Yangtze. When the Osaka firm began its operations in 1898, the N.Y.K. became its agent and let it use its
wharves and warehouses in Shanghai until the O.S.K. established
its own branch there in 1902. Even the promotion of the Hunan
firm in 1902 initially was not meant as a challenge to the O.S.K.,
for Kondō accepted the fact that the O.S.K. would carry N.Y.K.-
bound freight from Hankow to Shanghai. [20]

This raises the larger question of why the N.Y.K. had not relied
more on the O.S.K. in the development of its feeder strategy.
Instead of starting its own Yangtze line, at considerable expense, it
could have contracted with the O.S.K. to feed its European line.
The large scale of the N.Y.K.'s initial plans for a Yangtze operation, indicated by the price paid for the McBain firm, seems to
have militated against a more active cooperation with the O.S.K.
In 1903 the O.S.K. did not have the financial resources to risk additional commitments of the size undertaken by the N.Y.K. Also,
the O.S.K. had inferior berthing facilities at Hankow. Thus, to
act as a feeder to the N.Y.K.'s European line, the O.S.K. would

have had to make financial commitments to obtain better berths as well as new ships to carry European-bound freight to N.Y.K. vessels at Shanghai. To make these commitments the O.S.K. would have needed guarantees from the N.Y.K. But the two firms were strong rivals elsewhere—they had yet to work out agreements on pooling or rates on lines they jointly served. To the N.Y.K., allowing the O.S.K. to become the dominant Japanese firm on the Yangtze would be giving its rival too much of an advantage. The N.Y.K. further assumed that after the McBain purchase it would no longer need to rely on the O.S.K. for transshipment of Hunan freight at Hankow. By 1906, however, the delays in its own Yangtze service, its failure to win government approval to take over the Hunan operations, the excess capacity problem after the war, and the increased government pressure against competition among Japanese firms swayed the N.Y.K. away from the first option (continued competition) and inclined it instead to choose option three (selling out). To implement this it asked the Ministry of Communications in March 1906 to mediate the sale of its Yangtze business.[21]

Shortly after this approach to the government the N.Y.K. was finally able to acquire a berth in the French settlement in Hankow. This wharf, as well as several small steamships presently under construction and, of course, the property in Shanghai, were excluded from the sale offer. The company assessed its remaining ships and other Yangtze property at ¥1.5 million (not including the three large ships, worth ¥1.8 million, which would not be delivered until later that year). In order to preserve the feeder function of the Yangtze service the N.Y.K. set precise conditions for the sale of its property. The purchasing company, presumably the O.S.K., would have to give the N.Y.K. first rights to Yangtze freight transshipped at Shanghai enroute to Japan and priority to incoming N.Y.K. freight bound for Yangtze ports. Second, a through-rate agreement would have to be concluded for all freight transshipped at Shanghai that connected with N.Y.K. routes. In the end, however, the N.Y.K.'s asking price of ¥1.5 million was considered excessive by the O.S.K., which offered only ¥550,000. At that price the N.Y.K. was unwilling to sell and the deal fell through, though not before rumors circulated that the O.S.K. would surrender its foreign lines to the N.Y.K. and would receive in return a monopoly of the latter's coastal services. Such broader prospects may have been discussed, but they never reached the stage of concrete decision-making.[22]

With neither the O.S.K. nor the N.Y.K. able to achieve a take-over of the other's Yangtze business, the Shipping Bureau in September 1906 "informally ordered" the four Japanese companies to set up a committee to measure their asets with a view to merger. After the committee evaluated total assets at ¥8 million and investments by individual promoters added ¥100,000, a newly promoted company, Nisshin Kisen Kaisha (Japan-China Steamship Company), was established with a total authorized capital stock of ¥8.1 million.[23] This settlement left the N.Y.K. in a minority position which did not significantly change later in 1907 when it added its share of the Hunan stock after the dissolution of that firm (see Table 46). The N.Y.K. then held 43.3 percent of the new company, but the O.S.K.'s share was 46.6 percent.[24]

The establishment of the Nisshin Kisen Kaisha has obvious parallels to the N.Y.K.'s own formation. Both companies were the result of a government-imposed merger which restricted managerial autonomy. Like Mitsubishi in the original N.Y.K. of 1885, the N.Y.K. also entered Nisshin Kisen with less than half of its capital stock. And again, just as Mitsubishi had appreciated its assets in the months prior to the 1885 merger, so too the N.Y.K. ordered sufficient tonnage in 1906 to increase its stake to the point where it could claim joint control over the Nisshin Kisen with the O.S.K. There the parallel stops, for unlike the KUK, the stock of which was widely scattered in the early N.Y.K., the O.S.K. stock was held as a bloc. There was no chance for the N.Y.K. to take virtual control of the Nisshin Kisen as Mitsubishi had done with the N.Y.K.

Insofar as it was a joint venture, the new company initially seemed a setback for the N.Y.K.'s feeder strategy. Unable to cater exclusively to N.Y.K. routes, the Nisshin Kisen had to connect

TABLE 46   Nisshin Kisen Kaisha: Original Assets,
March 25, 1907

	Tonnage	Value of Assets (¥)	No. of Shares	% of Shares
O.S.K.	13,423	3,700,000	74,000	45.7
N.Y.K.	12,798[a]	3,290,000	65,800	40.6
Hunan S.S.	3,329	810,000[b]	16,200	10.0
Daitō S.S.	1,556	200,000	4,000	2.5
Other promoters		100,000	2,000	1.2
Total	31,106	8,100,000	162,000	100.0

Source: Nisshin Kisen, pp. 38–46, 302–303.

Notes: [a]Represents new ships ordered in 1906.

[b]The Hunan's authorized capital stock of ¥1.5 million had not been fully paid up.

with O.S.K. lines to South China which were outside the N.Y.K.'s business network. Also, there were extensive government controls over the new firm. The directive issued on April 1, 1907, made freight rates, departure times, and scheduling all subject to approval by the Ministry of Communications, and it specified in minute detail the operations of company lines. Although the firm's executives could be elected by its stockholders, the first president was the head of the Inspection Department in the Shipping Bureau, Ishiwata Kuninojō. Most controversially, the directive set up a government supervisory office within the company. Lobbying by Shibusawa and Katō succeeded in eliminating this office, but it failed to remove the clauses relating to "guidance" of normal business operations.[25]

The transformation of an N.Y.K. feeder line into a jointly controlled subsidiary had begun with the British denial of berthing rights at McBain's wharf. Of course, even if the McBain purchase had gone smoothly, it is unlikely that the N.Y.K. could have bought out the O.S.K. A faster development of its Yangtze service, however, might have enabled it to achieve a more controlling interest in an eventual amalgamated firm like the Nisshin Kisen.

Though the Nisshin Kisen marked a switch in N.Y.K. strategy away from development of its own feeder lines, it was not necessarily detrimental to the company's overall business. For one thing the N.Y.K. did retain a strong influence in the new firm. Iwanaga became one of its principal negotiators with its British competitors, and after Ishiwata's retirement in 1914 Kondō himself served as Nisshin president until his death in 1921. One can further argue that the Nisshin Kisen was more useful to the N.Y.K. under government control than any independent N.Y.K. line, locked in battle with other Japanese firms, could have been. As a strong united company with an ¥800,000 annual subsidy, the Nisshin Kisen quickly became the dominant force on the Yangtze. Following the merger it continued to operate from an independent position of strength outside the Yangtze pool and actually improved feeder services for the European line. In 1908 it signed a contract with the N.Y.K. providing for through rates to overseas lines. By 1911, according to the Swire firm, the Nisshin Kisen had a "practical monopoly of the carriage of European cargo from Hankow," and there "can be no doubt," it stated, "that the Japanese success with this transhipment cargo has prevented a [Yangtze] Pool being formed."[26]

There was in fact an interdependent relation between the dominance achieved by the Nisshin Kisen on the Yangtze, as shown by the tonnage figures in Table 47, and the success of the N.Y.K.'s European line during the 1907 to 1911 depression. The Nisshin Kisen grew primarily because it integrated international operations with its improved feeder network, which adroitly capitalized on the increase in Chinese exports during these years. For example, between mid-October and mid-November 1910, 90 percent of the freight carried by the Nisshin Kisen from Hankow was destined for transshipment at Shanghai for Japan, Europe, and the United States. The total amount carried was 321,091 piculs, with 288,768 piculs bound for overseas and only 32,325 piculs for other Chinese ports. During the same period the Indo-China S.N.

TABLE 47 Relative Market Share of Main Companies on the Yangtze
(Number of Ships, Tonnages, and Percentages)[a]

	China Navigation	Indo-China S.N.	Nisshin Kisen	China Merchants	Totals
1903	4–6,757 (23.8)	5–7,236 (25.5)	5–6,727 (23.7)	6–7,688 (27.1)	20–28,408 (100)
1911	9–9,863 (17.9)	6–10,648 (19.3)	12–25,678 (46.6)	7–8,864 (16.1)	34–55,053 (100)

Source: Nakamura Tadashi, "Chōsha kaikō zengo," p. 7.

Notes: I have corrected a typographical error in Nakamura's table. The 1903 figure for Nisshin Kisen represents the totals for Japanese firms at that time.

[a] Figures before the dash represent number of ships; those after the dash, tonnage; and those in parentheses, percentages of tonnage.

carried 67,050 piculs from Hankow, 72 percent of which was for transshipment at Shanghai, though the bulk of this was bound for Vladivostok, not western Europe. The China Navigation Company carried only 54,405 piculs, but their transshipment percentage is not known. In contrast to the British firms, the Nisshin Kisen was committed primarily to the foreign transshipment trade which was growing much faster than the domestic Chinese trade.

The Japanese success in this trade from Hankow stemmed partly from a coordinated strategy and partly from the dictates of government policy. The amalgamation of the four Japanese firms into the Nisshin Kisen left the new firm with an excess of tonnage for the trade that existed in 1907. Nisshin Kisen used this excess to provide guarantees to shippers who, in return, promised it exclusive support. The Japanese firm also took advantage of the nature of the river trade to extend this system of guarantees. In seasons when the river was low it was difficult for the steamship companies to forward enough cargo to Shanghai to meet the demand of the ocean steamers. With its "excess" tonnage the Nisshin Kisen was able to guarantee cargo to exporters even when the river fell. Again, these guarantees were conditional on shippers' use of the Nisshin Kisen during the high-water season. The Japanese also made a concerted effort to attract business from Western firms in China, employing a foreigner whose sole function was to secure freight from these firms. They even paid for the towing of cargo from the British, French, and German concessions to their own berth, now in the Russian concession. Another reason for this success was the decline of the Germans in the Yangtze trade since their failure to secure entry into the pool in 1902. By 1911 Arnhold Karberg & Company, an agent for the Hamburg America line, was one of the shippers accepting guarantees from Nisshin Kisen.[27] Whether the Japanese government foresaw this success is open to question, but its policies certainly contributed to it. The directive of 1907 had ordered the company to maintain at least 28,000 tons on its lines. Without this order, the company, in the interests of more prudent, profitable management, might well have reduced the number of its ships before realizing that excess tonnage was the key to dominating the foreign transshipment trade. The excess tonnage meant that the Nisshin Kisen at first barely broke even, but as a subsidiary serving the wider operations of the N.Y.K. and to a lesser extent the O.S.K., the small profit was more than compensated for by the extra freight it brought its parent companies. Also, by accepting this initially low profit it rapidly expanded its market share. With the larger share, its performance so improved that by 1910 its profits exceeded the amount of the government subsidy.

By contrast the Yangtze pool companies were beset by the disadvantages of managerial conservatism. First, they were still primarily oriented to the domestic Chinese trade. Second, their own pool prohibited them from employing extra tonnage. As Butterfield & Swire complained, "we are bound hand and foot by the Pool Agreement from attempting to recapture the trade [the Japanese] have so quickly and successfully built up."[28] Third, the presence of the China Merchants in the pool reinforced the orientation toward the domestic business, for this firm took little interest in the transshipment cargo. After considerable negotiation the two British firms finally persuaded the China Merchants in December 1910 to let them place several additional steamers on the Yangtze that would operate outside the pool simply to compete with the Nisshin Kisen in the transshipment trade.[29]

The British firms had not been fully aware of the extent of Nisshin Kisen dominance until a report was prepared for them in November 1910. Prior to that they had maintained a tough negotiating posture with regard to Nisshin Kisen entry into the pool despite the fact that the formation of the Japanese firm seems to have greatly reduced their profits, which were already heading downward as a result of the depression. Between 1907 and 1910 the China Navigation Company did not earn enough to cover depreciation charges on its fleet and could not pay a dividend. This set off a radical movement among the stockholders, who demanded a consultative committee with management and a lowering of the depreciation rate to allow for high dividends (shades of the KUK of 1883 to 1885 and the N.Y.K. of 1897!). The

Indo-China S.N. had averaged £110,000 in annual profits between 1898 and 1905, but from 1906 to 1908 its profits fell to only £12,405 a year.[30]

After 1910 the British became more conciliatory to the Nisshin Kisen, but several problems remained before a pool agreement could be concluded. The Japanese wanted a four-party pool, whereas the British and Chinese insisted on a two-party pool which would consist of the Nisshin Kisen as one party and the three pool companies as the other. This latter formula would require less financial disclosure to the Nisshin Kisen. The principal obstacle, however, was the Nisshin Kisen's excess tonnage, which the company could not reduce because of the government directive. The existing pool arrangement was based on a combination of the total measurement capacity of each company's steamers and the number of "trips," or sailings, each year. Because the Nisshin Kisen had the greater number of ships, the British proposed that one trip by its steamers should, for the purposes of pooling, count only as three-quarters of a trip. Negotiations over these issues finally began to make headway in 1912, and an agreement was reached early in 1913. This increased freight rates by 50 percent, thus setting off a Chinese boycott against the Nisshin Kisen.[31]

INVESTMENTS IN CHINA AND COLONIAL BUSINESS. In the three to four years prior to the Chinese Revolution of 1911 the N.Y.K. substantially increased its property in China. First, between 1908 and 1911 it made frequent additions both to its port facilities and office space in Shanghai. It purchased more than an acre of land in the foreign settlement area, two warehouses, and a two-story brick building; it had another three-story brick building constructed as a new branch office; and in 1911 it paid ¥800,000 to take over the permanent lease of excellent wharves and pontoons. Also, in September 1907 it bought two acres of land in Newchwang in South Manchuria.[32] In the field of investment, it purchased ¥800,000 worth of Chinese railway bonds in 1911. It is difficult to measure its interest in the Nisshin Kisen Kaisha. The par value of its holdings was ¥3.5 million, but it had written this down in its books to a level much below its real value. [33]

Taken together, these property holdings and investments as well as its interest in Korean shipping would account for slightly less than 10 percent of overall company assets. This is about twice the percentage represented by property involving China and Korea before the purchase of new ships for the Yangtze in 1906.

Indirect investments gave the N.Y.K. a larger stake in China than either its accounts or visible property would suggest. The most famous case of Japanese investment in China prior to World War I was the Hanyehping Company, a complex located just south of Hankow which included an arsenal, iron ore mines, and a colliery. These constituent units were incorporated into the company in 1908. Japan depended upon this firm for the development of its steel industry. Between 1900 and 1914, 61 percent of all the iron ore used by the state-run Yawata Iron and Steel Works in Kyushu came from the Tayeh mines, one of the units of the Hanyehping complex. Japan's first major direct financial involvement with this complex came in 1903, a year in which *all* of Yawata's iron ore came from these mines. In November of that year the Industrial Bank of Japan signed a contract with the Chinese to provide a ¥3 million loan to the Tayeh mines to be repaid over thirty years at 6 percent. In the business term ending in March 1903 the N.Y.K. had purchased ¥1 million worth of Industrial Bank debentures. This investment in the Industrial Bank was actually earmarked for the Tayeh mines. [34]

As the Chinese Revolution of 1911 approached, the N.Y.K. became increasingly involved in political activities on behalf of the revolutionary party. Many felt that a new revolutionary government would tend to develop China more quickly, perhaps (it was hoped) after the model of Meiji Japan; also the revolutionaries were strong in the Yangtze area where the Japanese had their main commercial interests. Unfortunately, these activities are not documented in internal company sources. It will suffice, then, to say that both the N.Y.K. and the Nisshin Kisen were carrying arms shipments to China. Some of the N.Y.K. shipments were seized, but the Nisshin Kisen seems to have enjoyed a protected status. Like the Hunan Steamship Company before it, the Nisshin Kisen allowed the Chinese to hold up to 20 percent of its stock. This policy apparently spared it, for example, during the 1910 Changsha riots against foreign economic influence in which the facilities of the two major British shipping firms were destroyed.[35]

During the emergence of the revolutionary government in late 1911 and early 1912 there were sudden and opportunistic attempts by large Japanese firms such as Mitsui, the Yokohama Specie Bank, the Ōkura Trading Company, and the N.Y.K. to take over the Hanyehping Company and the China Merchants. Here we will deal only with the China Merchants. In early 1912 the revolutionaries pressured the Chinese shipping firm either to sell the company or to accept huge loans. According to the plan the proceeds would then be given to the new revolutionary government, which promised to repay the company at a later date with certain unspecified privileges. The N.Y.K. and the Nisshin Kisen came forward as the willing lenders, promising 10 million taels, with the Chinese firm's fleet as security. This loan was approved virtually without discussion at a China Merchants stockholders meeting on February 1 that was under the control of the revolutionaries. A majority of the 200 stockholders present apparently opposed the loan but were afraid to speak out, while telegrams received from other stockholders were ignored by the leaders of the meeting. In the end, however, the loan was scuttled partly by Yuan Shih-k'ai, the northern-oriented, more conservative, and anti-Japanese military figure who became provisional president of the new republic in March, and partly by the intervention of the Hong Kong and Shanghai Banking Corporation. It provided the China Merchants with a loan of 1.5 million taels, one-third of which went to the revolutionaries.[36]

The Hong Kong and Shanghai Bank had intervened in this affair at the instigation of Butterfield & Swire. In a manner reminiscent of the McBain fiasco, following the abortive takeover Butterfield & Swire seems to have been rewarded with some of the China

Merchants Hankow property for saving the Chinese firm from the Japanese. Butterfield & Swire then began to act as agents for the China Merchants on a commission basis, and by 1914 they had assumed an extensive managerial role in the Chinese company. Once again, the N.Y.K. was left holding the bag. This time it controlled its resentment and tried a more diplomatic tact, apparently in response to Butterfield & Swire's increased influence. In Tokyo in December 1913, Koike Chōzō, head of the Political Division in the Foreign Ministry, held informal discussions with E. F. Crowe of the British Embassy. He suggested that the Anglo-Japanese Alliance should be broadened beyond the political realm to include commercial and industrial fields. One area where British and Japanese interests could combine, he said, was in aiding the financially troubled China Merchants. Specifically he recommended that a combination of Japanese interests represented by the N.Y.K. and Nisshin Kisen and British interests represented by Jardine, Matheson and Butterfield & Swire should take over the Chinese shipping company. The British, however, saw that they had much to lose and little to gain by cooperating with the Japanese, and, as one official put it, the Chinese had no particular desire to have their firm taken over.[37]

Before World War I, then, the O.S.K., N.Y.K., and Nisshin Kisen had failed to translate their successful business advances in China trade into effective political leverage. They had also exacerbated an already bitter relationship with the British, who had capitalized on the Japanese failure. On the other hand, relations with the Japanese government over Chinese matters, which had basically been in conflict in 1905, especially over N.Y.K. plans on the Yangtze, had become more cooperative. The large subsidies to the Nisshin Kisen and its business expansion supplemented the resources of the N.Y.K. to give the two Japanese firms the financial wherewithal to attempt the takeover of the China Merchants. That attempt failed, and it had not, of course, received official endorsement. But the Foreign Ministry's initiative in late 1913 shows that the government and companies were beginning to cooperate more for common goals. This development probably encouraged the growing Japanese tendency toward interventionism in China just prior to the Twenty-One Demands.

Since the Russo-Japanese War the N.Y.K. had taken on new roles in South Manchuria and Korea. South Manchuria, especially, helped to reinvigorate the N.Y.K.'s near-seas business after 1910. Also, like the Yangtze area, it played a major role as a feeder to the main European line. Efficient transport of the area's agricultural goods was made possible by the opening of the South Manchurian Railway in 1907. As early as 1908 freight from Dairen was sufficient to take up the slack caused by the depression at Shanghai and prop up the fortunes of the European line. Further institutionalization occurred in 1910 when the N.Y.K. and the South Manchurian Railway signed an agreement on through rates and bills of lading.[38] By 1913 the bean trade from Manchuria was supplementing the China trade to make East Asian continental exports a principal area of N.Y.K. business. The expansion that they brought to the European business is described in a board meeting of that year:

> Trade between East Asia and Europe has been developing remarkably each year, and since the capacity of our ships is small, it has become difficult to provide satisfaction to shippers. Quite obviously if this state of affairs continues, in the future—and for that matter today as well—as China develops we will not be able to provide sufficient cargo space to handle such exports as soybean oil from Dairen, wheat straw, braid, and peanuts from Tsingtao, and soybeans from the Shanghai area. Even on the return voyage from Europe there is enough freight to justify calling at regional ports like Dairen, Nagasaki, Kure, and Yokkaichi in addition to those ports where we must call by government order. We will therefore employ extra ships to run once a month or every four weeks.[39]

Japan had begun a major economic penetration of Korea in the late 1890s, but it was not until after its victory in the Russo-Japanese War that it attained a free hand to establish its own institutions. In August 1905 a navigation treaty signed with Korea gave Japanese vessels the right to ply between all ports and in inland waters.[40] Following the Japanese annexation of Korea in 1910 the government amalgamated the operations of the major shipping firms to create a colonial company, Chōsen Yūsen Kaisha (Korean Mail Steamship Company), formed in 1912. It operated under the supervision of the Korean Governor-General with a head office in Seoul, in contrast to the Nisshin Kisen, which retained its head office in Tokyo. The capital of the firm was set at ¥3 million, divided into 60,000 shares. Of these, 32,500 were to be subscribed to in Korea. The N.Y.K. and the O.S.K., however, each held one-sixth of the shares. It was thus a joint venture, though not to the same degree as the Nisshin Kisen. The N.Y.K. influence in the Chōsen Yūsen was strong from the beginning, for its first president was Harada Kinnosuke, the Fushiki shipowner who had entered the KUK and then transferred to the N.Y.K. Harada's principal labors for the N.Y.K. had been performed in the Kansai, where he served as head of the Osaka branch from 1894 to 1906, after which he became head of the Supplies Department. In 1911 he was appointed a company director, a position he continued to occupy while serving as president of the Korean firm.

The Chōsen Yūsen, not simply a shipping company, was authorized to participate in diverse activities that gave it a broad impact on the Korean economy. In addition to acting as an agent and performing port-related functions such as lighterage and warehousing, it also engaged in commercial trading and financing to shippers.[41]

Prior to World War I the large Japanese shipping firms in China and the Japanese colonial areas of East Asia were brought under government control, taking two forms: a colonial institution (Chōsen Yūsen) and a national policy company (Nisshin Kisen). For the government these companies were part of the apparatus of imperial control; for companies like the N.Y.K. they served as feeders for wider international business. Some, like the Nisshin Kisen, fulfilled these functions more effectively than the N.Y.K. had originally foreseen. But insofar as the government controlled the scope of the new firms' operations it limited the N.Y.K.'s flexibility. The company could no longer autonomously diversify its business within East Asia. Nevertheless, government intervention, together with the ownership structure of the Nisshin Kisen, created an institutional stability between the parent companies and their new subsidiary. This made possible a rapid increase in Japanese influence within China.

STRATEGIES FOR INDIAN AND AMERICAN LINES

In contrast to N.Y.K. business in East Asia, shipping to India and America was relatively free from government controls. The Indian Raj, then still securely part of the British Empire, was far enough away that Japanese shipping there was beyond the bounds of its government's imperial policies; it was also near enough that the N.Y.K. could afford to begin new lines without subsidies. Shipping to America essentially involved transport between two terminal ports, Shanghai and Seattle. The American line operated without the diplomatic disputes over ports characteristic of European business. The N.Y.K. responded differently to the new opportunities in these two areas. In India it was an aggressively expansionist response; in America, a rather cautious conservatism. The obvious variable was the greater distance and dependence on subsidies in America, especially as the potential for a New York line via the Panama Canal emerged in the 1912 to 1914 years. Also, in contrast to the strong Bombay freight conference, where the N.Y.K. exercised an increasingly dominant influence, the American line had a more open and less stable conference. Its rules were less restrictive, members changed frequently, and raw silk and tea, the most important U.S.-bound freights, were outside the rebate system.

THE BOMBAY AND CALCUTTA LINES, 1896-1914. Shipping between Japan and India in the two decades prior to World War I is the story of Japanese expansion and the relative decline of the British. N.Y.K. success prior to the 1896 Bombay-line pool agreement had been achieved partly by specializing in the shipment of raw cotton directly to Japan in contrast to the P. & O.'s main activity, carrying Indian cotton yarn to China. The favorable trends behind this success continued after 1896. Between 1895 and 1900 exports to Japan from Bombay grew at an annual rate of 30.1 percent, while Bombay exports to China treaty ports grew at only 6.6 percent a year. The great increase in trade between Japan and India followed Japan's abolition of its import duty on raw cotton in 1896. Between 1895 and 1897 the value of Indian raw cotton imports grew from ¥ 8.2 million to ¥ 26.4 million.[42]

Favorable trade patterns plus a five-year renewal of the Bombay line subsidy in 1901 (cut from ¥ 192,108 to ¥ 178,785) enabled the N.Y.K. to increase its share in the pool, renegotiated in 1902. The 1896 agreement had allotted the N.Y.K. 16/60 points, or 23 percent, while the P. & O. had 30/60 points, or 50 percent. Under the 1902 agreement the N.Y.K.'s share rose to 30 percent; the P. & O.'s fell to 35 percent.[43]

The N.Y.K.'s close ties with the Cotton Spinners Association, the weight behind the company's growing influence within the Bombay Conference, served the N.Y.K. well in the face of numerous shocks to the Bombay line in the mid-1900s. When the N.Y.K.'s ships were requisitioned during the Russo-Japanese War, the company's principal motivation for employing charters on its trunk lines was to retain the confidence of its regular shippers. Because of the stable alliance between the N.Y.K. and the Spinners Association, "trust" was not an issue on the Bombay line. This freed the company from the need to run expensive charters, and instead, together with the cotton spinners, the N.Y.K. persuaded the European companies to take up the N.Y.K. share, retain the same net freight rate of 12 Rs., and thus assure the Japanese industry of adequate supplies during the war. Following the war, then, the N.Y.K. did not have to rebuild a shippers network, and it was thus able to accept a government decision in 1906 not to renew the Bombay line subsidy without untoward worry about the future.

The principal problem of the line between 1906 and World War I was how to keep the peace with the P. & O. in the face of increasing Japanese influence. A new pool agreement in 1906 had for the first time given the N.Y.K. an equal share with the P. & O. at 32.5 percent. Also, despite the postwar recession, Japanese demand for raw cotton continued to grow, and in 1908 N.Y.K.

income from the Bombay line was 2.7 times what it had been in 1901. To meet this demand conference firms employed charters in addition to their regular sailings. These charters, which operated outside the pool, were usually unprofitable. In 1912, the P. & O. demanded that the Cotton Spinners Association bear its losses from these charter operations, a request it quickly withdrew when the N.Y.K., in response, threatened to leave the conference. The Spinners Association did agree, however, to incur one third of the deficit from conference charters. Another contentious issue was the N.Y.K. subsidy, which P. & O. Chairman Thomas Sutherland had attacked in a well-publicized speech in December 1907. His remarks, coming shortly after the termination of the Bombay line subsidy, had the quality of a self-fulfilling prophecy, for the N.Y.K. soon began to assign to the line ships still eligible for navigation aid. In 1910–1912 this aid averaged ¥ 268,000 annually, contrary to the common assumption that the line was unsubsidized after 1906.[44]

It is ironic that the N.Y.K., a Tokyo-based firm, had been the principal beneficiary of the Spinners Association's support when the bulk of the Japanese market for raw cotton was in the Osaka area. If the 1896 distribution patterns were typical, 83.7 percent of Indian raw cotton imports went to Kobe and only 12.5 percent to Yokohama. The N.Y.K. had begun to diversify this pattern in May 1912 when it instituted a stop at Yokkaichi on behalf of the Mie Cotton Spinning Company, which paid an extra 1 R. per ton for the service. Nevertheless, the N.Y.K. had earlier lost its exclusive position when the O.S.K. began an experimental line to Bombay in 1907. By late 1912, the O.S.K. had asked the N.Y.K. to sponsor its entry into the Bombay conference, a request the N.Y.K. deemed impolitic to refuse. The next year, then, saw several changes in the conference: the O.S.K. entry (without a stop at Shanghai) and a switch from a percentage to a point system for the pool following the withdrawal of the Italian firm (which had had a 16 percent share). Out of a total of 84 points, the N.Y.K. and P. & O. each had 28, the Austrian firm, 16, and the O.S.K., 12. Overall, then, from 1896 to 1913 the Japanese share in the conference pool had grown from 23 percent to 47 percent, while the P. & O.'s share had declined from 50 to 33 percent. These pool shares, however, were for the business of the line as a whole. A clearer picture of Japanese growth can be seen in the conference schedule for raw cotton shipments (expressed in bales) to be carried on regular sailings in 1914: N.Y.K. – 403,000; O.S.K. – 304,200; P. & O. – 139,140; and the Austrian Lloyd – 10,558.[45]

While the P. & O. was suffering from Japanese dominance on the Bombay line, the principal victim of N.Y.K. expansion to other Indian ports was the British India Steam Navigation Company (known also as the British India Line). In September 1911, following unsuccessful negotiations with the British India Line and two other firms active along the east coast of India, the N.Y.K. opened a line to Calcutta to compete with the British-led Calcutta Conference in both the Japan-India trade and British Indian coastal shipping. The government refused to provide a special subsidy for this line and reportedly cautioned the N.Y.K. against even starting it in view of the expected competition. As with most of its business in India, the N.Y.K. received its basic support for the line from private sources. Mitsui Bussan, delighted at the prospect of new business, gave assurances that its own shipments could fill three ships, the same number that the N.Y.K. had expected to begin with. Mitsui's backing enabled the company to start the line with five ships and fortnightly sailings.[46] A contract was also signed with the Cotton Spinners Association, and raw cotton became the largest item in the trade, with raw cotton imports from Calcutta alone growing from ¥1.3 million in 1911 to ¥4.3 million in 1913. Other major imports were pig iron, rape seed cake, and timber. In addition, substantial quantities of rice were imported from Rangoon because of a sharp rise in the price of rice within Japan, and tea was carried to Hankow. The leading exports from Japan were matches and glassware. The threat to the British India Line, however, came not just from this direct Japan-India trade but primarily from the N.Y.K.'s penetration of the British India Line's sphere of influence—British Indian coastal shipping. By the British firm's definition this included the route between Calcutta and the Burmese port of Rangoon by which more than 300,000 Indian emigrant laborers annually traveled. By slashing passage rates from 10 Rs. to 1 R. the N.Y.K. soon captured more than half of this traffic.[47]

With the average freight rate per ton between India and Japan also down from ¥9 to ¥2, N.Y.K. losses on the line soon mounted to an annual ¥300,000, though this was more than matched by the British India Line's ¥600,000 deficit. The N.Y.K.'s use of ships in receipt of navigation aid, which brought in ¥50,000 a year in 1912–1913, provided only a small financial cushion, but to the company the rapid growth of the India-Japan trade and the favorable response from Indian merchants justified the line's heavy losses.[48]

The British Indian Line's chairman, Lord Inchcape (formerly J. L. Mackay) followed a carrot and stick approach to the N.Y.K., promising negotiations but planning for countermeasures. After several unsuccessful meetings with N.Y.K. officials (in Bombay and London) in the spring of 1912, Inchcape tried to use the P. & O. as a mediator. The gist of his message to the P. & O. (somehow obtained by the N.Y.K.'s London branch) was: "By reason of the British India Line's competition with the N.Y.K. on the Calcutta-Rangoon-Straits route, we wish to take retaliatory action against the N.Y.K.'s Bombay line. Since this will result in losses to the P. & O., we would be most grateful if you, as a friend of the N.Y.K., could hold discussions on this matter with the Japanese firm." The British India's Line's threat was to withdraw its services as a feeder for the N.Y.K.'s Bombay line in which it carried raw cotton from Tuticorin (south of Madras) to N.Y.K. vessels at Colombo. The N.Y.K. correctly regarded the British India Line's tactics, which it labeled extortionist, as a bluff, and instead planned its own stop at Tuticorin should the British India Line sever these business ties. Inchcape then offered a pool conditional upon N.Y.K. withdrawal from the Calcutta-Rangoon-Straits line, but this was unacceptable to the N.Y.K. because of the high priority it placed on the trade along this route. Additional meetings the next year in Tokyo and London failed to break this impasse.[49]

With no light at the end of the negotiating tunnel, Inchcape sought government intervention. Because of its potential political repercussions within India, the N.Y.K. competition was sufficiently important to be considered by the British cabinet in early 1914. The British believed that the N.Y.K.'s "astonishingly large" subsidy indicated "a definite political intention," and the government of India feared that the N.Y.K.'s share of the Indian coastal trade would give the Japanese a growing "influence over the general population" that would not be "in the interest of British rule in India."[50] Inchcape exploited these concerns. Writing to the Foreign Office, he invoked the fear of Pan-Asianism by claiming that the N.Y.K. was "advertising that the Captains and officers are Japanese and therefore more likely to be friendly to native passengers than Englishmen!"[51]

The British government's tactics in responding to Inchcape's request were shaped by its underlying assumption that the Japanese government controlled the N.Y.K. through its subsidy. The British saw no hope for a compromise with the N.Y.K., but since in their view the N.Y.K. was the "foster child" of the Japanese government they felt that a direct approach to Japanese officials might bring about the desired result.[52] Specifically they hoped to persuade the government to reduce the N.Y.K. subsidy. The British dismissed the point that the N.Y.K. received no special line subsidies for its Indian services, for they argued that the size of the overall subsidy enabled the N.Y.K. to incur the large deficits in its Calcutta and neighboring lines. The British employed two threats to induce cooperation from the Japanese. The first, to exclude foreign or subsidized shipping firms from the Indian coastal trade, was never carried out. Opposition of Indian shippers to exclusion legislation was too strong; and Japanese Foreign Ministry officials hinted that, should an exclusion law single out subsidized firms, a new Japanese company would be started to run separately from the N.Y.K. The second threat was to pressure Japan into opening its own coastal trade. But since the British India Line would not benefit much from such a change in Japanese law, this was considered ineffective retaliation; the British dropped this threat as well.

Japanese negotiators encouraged the British to renew direct discussions with the N.Y.K., but World War I prevented any resolution by these means. Several desperate telegrams from Inchcape to Kondō in early August failed to bear fruit. The British government informed Inchcape that, in the wartime crisis, its relations with Japan took precedence over the British India Line's plight and thus it could no longer pressure the Japanese government. By staving off an agreement prior to the outbreak of war, the N.Y.K. now was in an excellent position to expand its influence in India even further.

In their many competitive struggles with the N.Y.K. prior to World War I, British shipping firms always pictured themselves as victims of Japanese subsidies. Despite the long-standing dominance of British commercial power in Asia, there was some justice in their complaints. Certainly the Japanese government was playing a more supportive role in the shipping industry than was the British government (with the important exception of the McBain incident on the Yangtze). Nevertheless, British perceptions, which shaped their negotiating tactics in the Calcutta trade dispute, overlooked certain crucial aspects of Japan's industrial development. The major assumption was that because of its subsidies, N.Y.K. profits on its other trunk lines left a surplus that could be "transferred" to the Indian services. Reducing the subsidy would eliminate this surplus, thereby forcing the N.Y.K. to withdraw from the Calcutta line. In all likelihood, this would not have been the result if the subsidy had been reduced through diplomatic pressure. The British assumed this result because they misread Japan's industrial situation. In 1913, 97.6 percent of N.Y.K. subsidies went for designated lines. If these subsidies had been reduced, the N.Y.K. would most likely have cut services on the same expensive lines for which they were given. Reducing the Calcutta service was an improbable response for, as they had proved on the

Bombay line, shipping to India was a market they could potentially handle without subsidization. The N.Y.K. received no navigation aid for ships on the Bombay line in the 1913/2 term, but it still cleared a profit, just as it had in 1909/1. By exaggerating the impact of subsidies in general and the Indian line deficits in particular, the British failed to perceive fully the N.Y.K. strategy of accepting short-term losses as a way to acquire the market, which in the long run would enable it to maximize profits.

The priority placed on market acquisition relates to a second British misconception. N.Y.K. success in India was attributed to its subsidies rather than to its network of private shippers, namely, the trading companies, the cotton spinners, and the match exporters (on whose behalf Mitsui Bussan had instituted standardized marketing techniques). India was strategic for these enterprises as a supplier of raw materials and as a market for light industrial products, whose growth was spearheading a gradual change in Japan's industrial structure. The N.Y.K. could acquire and operate in new markets even at low freight rates because of guaranteed support from this shippers network.

Though they misunderstood the role of the N.Y.K. subsidy, the British were aware of the N.Y.K.'s shippers network. The British India Line had taken steps to attack it when the competition heated up in 1912, somewhat as the P. & O. had done to Mitsubishi in 1876 and to the N.Y.K. between 1893 and 1896. Lord Inchcape had tried to establish contracts with Japanese enterprises exporting to Southeast Asia and to attack the N.Y.K. "citadel" through direct dealings with Mitsui and Mitsubishi. These approaches failed to penetrate the N.Y.K. network, and they are of interest instead because of how they were perceived by other British shipping executives. Many felt that whatever success Inchcape might have would hurt the P. & O.'s East Asian business more than it would that of the N.Y.K. In the end, the setbacks the P. & O. and the British Indian Line suffered at the hands of the N.Y.K. constituted one among several factors which prompted these two British firms to amalgamate in 1914. This merger can be seen as an indication of stagnation within Britain's Asian shipping. By contrast, the appearance of the O.S.K. in South Asian waters alongside the N.Y.K. points to the increasing dynamism of the Japanese.[53]

PACIFIC SHIPPING: SEATTLE AND PANAMA. About the time the N.Y.K. began its Calcutta line in 1911, the impending completion of the Panama Canal was bringing fresh choices for the company's American line. This line originated with a July 1896 contract between the N.Y.K. and James Hill's Great Northern Railway. Using Hill's rail network, with which it connected at Seattle, the N.Y.K. could quote through-freight rates for trade between Asia and the Midwest as well as the east coast of the United States. Japan's principal export, raw silk, could reach east coast ports one day faster via the Seattle route than it could through San Francisco. This gave the N.Y.K. an advantage over the Tōyō Kisen Kaisha, which had opened a line to San Francisco in 1898. The N.Y.K.'s principal competitors on its northern Pacific line were the China Mutuals, purchased by Holt's Ocean Steamship Company in 1902, and the Canadian Pacific Railway, which specialized in raw silk transport with a fleet of fast ships and an efficient transcontinental railway.

The American service generally utilized less than half the tonnage employed on the European line and was seldom as successful prior to World War I. Furthermore, shortly before the war the line was beset by two new obstacles. One was a 1908 ruling by the U.S. Interstate Commerce Commission affecting through rates. Previously the through rate was publicly quoted only for the whole route, say, between Yokohama and Chicago. The new ruling, which required that both the land and sea portions of the total rate be made public, resulted in an increase for the rail portion and a 20 percent decrease in the sea rate. The immediate consequence for the N.Y.K. was a decline in the line's income of 34 percent between the first and second terms of 1908 and of 50 percent from 1908 to 1910. The ruling also had a long-term negative effect, for the company substantially reduced tonnage on the American line, which until the war never regained the profit level of 1907–

early 1908. A second problem was increased competition, first from the O.S.K., which started a line to Tacoma in 1909 and entered the Pacific conference the next year through N.Y.K. mediation, and then from large British firms like the Royal Mail Steam Packet Company and the Blue Funnel. The N.Y.K. might have thwarted some of this competition had it accepted a late 1912 offer of a three-year, $75,000 annual subsidy from the city of Portland, Oregon, to operate a line from Hong Kong. Judging the offer insufficient, but enticed by future prospects, the N.Y.K. avoided a direct refusal, telling Portland officials that the matter would be placed under consideration. This ambivalent response failed to prevent the Hamburg America Line from opening a Pacific service to Portland in 1913 as part of its round-the-world network. [54]

The geography of Japanese-American trade posed another disadvantage for the Seattle line. Except for flour, the principal American exports to Japan, machinery and raw cotton, were produced in the eastern and southern states. Most of these goods were shipped to Japan eastward via Suez rather than by the westward route via the Pacific ports from which the railways received the major part of the freight income. The Panama Canal promised to transform this trade. Instead of moving eastward, it could now be carried westward by Japanese lines via the more direct and less expensive Panama route. [55]

The opening of the Panama Canal, August 15, 1914, is beyond the chronological scope of this study. The planning for the N.Y.K.'s Panama line between 1912 and 1914, however, reveals much about the company's business strategy. Essentially the N.Y.K. had two choices. One was to increase capital stock to finance ship purchases necessary to begin the line as soon as the canal opened, gaining an advantage over potential competitors, on a gamble that the government would then provide a subsidy to cover operating deficits. A second choice was to wait for the Diet to approve an operating subsidy and then to increase the capital stock to buy ships. While some public speculation occurred about the N.Y.K. using its own funds for the projected line, company executives unequivocally chose the second option. Though a conservative decision, it was not simply a reflection of a "bureaucratic," no-risk managerial mentality.[56] Rather, the decision was made within a complex set of political and economic pressures.

The N.Y.K.'s caution arose partly from apprehension over stockholder dissension if a subsidy were not granted once the line was started. The company feared a repeat of what had happened with the European line, which it had initiated on its own in 1896 only to suffer a deficit because of an unexpected delay in the subsidy. Indeed, the company lacked a sufficient guarantee that an adequate subsidy bill would in fact pass the Diet. As late as January 1914, company demands (¥1.97 million) and the Shipping Bureau's estimates (¥1.26 million) were still wide apart. The disparity resulted partly from lower bids presented by the O.S.K. and the Tōyō Kisen Kaisha. This Panama Canal subsidy debate arose coincidentally just as the 1909 subsidy program was to expire. In the new subsidy program beginning in 1915, the government wanted to reduce overall payments, including that for the Panama line, below the total 1909 level. The more money that went into the Panama line, the less would be available for other subsidies. While few seriously expected the O.S.K. or Tōyō Kisen to defeat the N.Y.K. for the Panama subsidy, these companies likely presented low bids to help justify a smaller government estimate in its negotiations with the N.Y.K. By thus lowering the amount for the N.Y.K.'s Panama line, they left more money for other line subsidies from which they would benefit.[57]

Eventually the N.Y.K. persuaded the government to increase its offer to ¥1.5 million, but this may have been a tactical mistake. On March 23, 1914, the Diet refused to pass the subsidy bill, helping to defeat the government budget and precipitate the downfall of the cabinet headed by Admiral Yamamoto Gombei.[58] Yamamoto's cabinet had been supported by the Seiyūkai, which during these years had occasionally assisted the N.Y.K. The new prime minister, Ōkuma Shigenobu, was backed by the recently formed political party, the Dōshikai. Among its leaders were well-known opponents of subsidies such as Shimada Saburō. Committed

to economic retrenchment, the Dōshikai slashed the overall subsidy by twice the Seiyūkai's planned reductions and postponed the
Panama bill. Some accounts suggest that Tōyō Kisen had lobbied
the Dōshikai because it feared that an N.Y.K. Panama line via San
Francisco would destroy its own line to San Francisco. In the end,
the Dōshikai came to support another Tōyō Kisen proposal, a
syndicate amalgamating the Pacific services of the N.Y.K., the
O.S.K., and Tōyō Kisen to operate the Panama service, but this
idea died after several months of N.Y.K. resistance. Certainly the
political change in 1914 delayed the beginning of the N.Y.K.'s
Panama line.[59]

Another reason for the N.Y.K. reluctance to initiate the line
without official aid was the uncertainty of the trade. The company
did expect to pick up some import business from the eastern and
southern regions of the United States. But the outward voyage
was much less economically viable. By value, two-thirds of Japan's
exports to the United States in 1913 consisted of raw silk. The
freight rate on the Panama-New York line was expected to be 50
percent less than that for the northern rail route to the east coast.
The largest expense incurred in shipping raw silk, however, was the
interest charges in transit. Because the Panama route took twice as
long to reach New York, raw silk continued to go by overland
rail.[60]

In a 1912 General Meeting, Kondō had replied to a question
about the company's Panama strategy by asking that if such a
large deficit was incurred on the relatively short Calcutta run,
how much more would the company lose on a major world route
like Panama.[61] His question pointed to the greater distance involved
in the American service, but it also draws attention to other fundamental differences. The more important variables were, first, the
political situation, that is, the competition and intrigue among
Japanese firms over the Panama issue (absent from the Calcutta
line), and second, N.Y.K. control over freight. This control it was
not assured of on the Panama service; it lacked the shippers network available on the Calcutta line. Had these two factors differed,
with the political climate more amenable and the trade prospects

more predictable, starting the line prior to subsidization would have been a risky but financially responsible decision. In view of the company's healthy financial state in 1914, the ¥1.3 million operating deficit projected for the Panama line would have had less of an adverse impact than the ¥800,000 loss predicted for the European line in 1897.[62] In short, then, although the company's responses to opportunities in India and America were very different, they both point from their own perspective to the key ingredient in Japan's shipping success, namely, "organized entrepreneurship," the ability to integrate networks of shippers to control a trade.

Nevertheless, the Panama matter cannot be viewed as one particular subsidy problem. The broader issue, which shaped N.Y.K. responses during these years, was the uncertainty regarding future subsidization following the expiration of the 1909 program. Concern over this influenced decisions on company lines, forced innovations in accounting, and rekindled stockholder restlessness. A full account of business strategy between 1909 and 1914 requires an examination of the 1909 program and a more internal analysis of finances and decision-making.

TEN

Expansion: A Financial and Institutional Analysis,
1893-1914

COMPETITION, REGULATION, AND LINER STRATEGY

Between the mid-1890s and 1912 the European line together
with the domestic and near-seas services almost always generated
more than three-quarters of N.Y.K. operating income. Within
these principal services, major changes occurred following the
Russo-Japanese War in the distribution of tonnage and the sources
of company profits. Before 1904 the N.Y.K. tried to integrate all
phases of its operations—coastal, near-seas, feeder, and overseas
lines. Between 1905 and 1909, factors such as increased competition and government intervention forced the company to adopt a
new strategy of specializing on overseas lines and subsidized near-
seas services, in short, a liner strategy. This new strategy led to retrenchment in many local services and feeder lines.

CHANGING PROFIT STRUCTURE AND COASTAL RETRENCHMENT.
Prior to the formation of the N.Y.K., three-quarters of Mitsubishi's
shipping income came from its domestic lines, and the remaining
quarter from near-seas services. Generally this percentage continued for the N.Y.K.'s business until its overseas expansion in the
mid-1890s. By 1903 domestic and near-seas business used a third
of the company's tonnage (see Table 48) while generating roughly

TABLE 48 N.Y.K. Line Categories by Tonnage,
              December 1903

Line Category	No. of Ships	Tonnage	(%)
European	12	74,210	
American	6	36,078	
Australian	3	12,711	
Bombay	5	19,392	
Overseas lines (Total)	26	142,391	57.9
International feeder lines (Yangtze)	2	1,999	0.8
Near-seas	10	24,815	10.1
Coastal	31	56,990	23.2
Others	8	19,333	8.1
Total	77	246,128	100.0

Source: Adapted from *NYK 70 nenshi,* pp. 93–94.

40 percent of operating income and 6 percent of operating profit. In the same year, the European line accounted for 30 percent of tonnage, roughly 35 percent of income, and 57 percent of operating profit (reflecting the impact of subsidies). As high as this profit share was in 1903, in no other period in the N.Y.K.'s history was the European line as important as in the five years after the Russo-Japanese War. Between 1907 and 1910/1, as the company purchased six new ships of the 8,500 ton class to replace the older 6,000 ton vessels, the line's profits, which came to about ¥7 million, were equivalent to 120 percent of total operating profit. In contrast, between 1906 and 1910/1, domestic and near-seas lines ran up deficits of at least ¥4 million.[1]

A combination of the postwar business recession and excess capacity resulting from wartime emergency purchases was the main factor behind these huge deficits. Competition among tramps during the recession drove rates for key freights like rice and coal down by 50 percent between the end of the war and 1909. Also, both Mitsubishi and then the N.Y.K. did much of their coastal business in northern Japan and along the Japan Sea coast. During the 1894 to 1904 decade, the opening of railways in these areas cut deeply into revenue from the shipping lines serving them. Rather than eliminating these lines the N.Y.K., prior to 1907, "transferred" the surplus from overseas profits to cover their deficits. Finally, the major factor in the near-seas deficit was the competition on the Shanghai and Southeast Asian lines. Nevertheless, in general, the near-seas lines were becoming increasingly strategic. Most were retained, and some, like services involving South Manchuria, were strengthened after 1910.

The government had long subsidized the N.Y.K.'s coastal lines to ensure a regular and efficient national service. But after the Russo-Japanese War, the emergence of competing Japanese shipping firms able to operate profitably on these domestic services reduced the need for special aid to the N.Y.K. in this area. Between 1906 and 1908 the government either eliminated many coastal and some near-seas subsidies or replaced them with reduced mail subsidies. At first the N.Y.K. tried to continue some of these lines independently, but losses (¥100,000 a year on the westward Kobe-Otaru run) eventually forced the company to devise a new strategy to cope with the crisis in domestic shipping.[2] A special Business Investigative Committee (Gyōmu Chōsa Iinkai) was formed in May 1907 with Katō as chairman and Iwanaga as vice-chairman. The committee recommended the abolition of many lines and presided over a broad retrenchment program, including the downgrading of local and some near-seas branches to representative offices, the selling of older ships, and the dismissal of several hundred seamen.[3]

For company organization the most important aspect of this program was the downgrading of branch offices. For two decades these branches had continued to perform many of the functions inherited from Mitsubishi and the KUK, but by 1907 new developments had superseded their usefulness. Kondō described these changes as one reason for the N.Y.K.'s cutbacks in coastal services:

In the period when shipping companies monopolized the transportation system, ships departed for all regions of the country and it was necessary to maintain shore-based agencies with appropriate facilities. We can characterize that time as a period when enterprises like exchange financing, insurance, and warehousing were all operated by shipping companies as side-businesses. However, as society has advanced and progressed, we find that today the exchange business has been taken over by banks and the insurance business by insurance companies. Even the warehousing business has so grown that it is operating in certain districts with hardly any difficulty as an independent enterprise. These commercial agencies have all developed to the point where shipping companies no longer have to operate shore facilities by themselves.[4]

Katō's committee recommended retrenchment not only in coastal but also in feeder lines. "The major transoceanic lines are important from the standpoint of the nation's economy... As a company we have to preserve our own profits by entrusting to other shipping companies the relatively unimportant feeder lines and concentrating instead solely on the principal trunk lines."[5] This conclusion led to a new and specialized liner strategy. The company had freely chosen this strategy in 1908, but its implementation after 1909 was shaped primarily by government intervention.

THE 1909 OCEAN LINES SUBSIDY LAW. The Ocean Lines Subsidy Law of 1909 reversed the basic feature of the 1890s shipping legislation—the distinction between aid to ships based on standard criteria and aid to designated lines. The new law amalgamated these two forms of aid, providing subsidies only to specified companies operating on designated lines. Whereas the old law had given fixed payments to these lines the new one funded them according to criteria similar to those used under the old Navigation Encouragement Law. Deficiencies in this navigation law and broader strategic concerns prompted the government to adopt the more unified approach to subsidization. First, several companies had extended their lines simply to increase their navigation bounty. Since some of these firms operated tramps on unscheduled routes, the government often found its treasury being drained by ships in ballast. Second, the minister of communications, Gotō Shinpei, an official with long experience in colonial and emigration matters, wished to strengthen government control over the principal trunk lines and to open up new commercial opportunities by a line to South America. Sentiment for emigration was another motive for this new line.[6]

Under the basic standards of the 1909 law, ships of over 3,000 tons with a speed of at least 12 knots were eligible for up to 50 *sen* per ton every 1,000 miles. To the N.Y.K. these standards contained two major objectionable features: the payment formula and the greatly extended authority given the minister of communications. Earlier restrictions, such as a maximum eligibility of fifteen years and a 5 percent annual reduction for ships beyond the age of five years, had applied only to grants under the navigation law and had not affected the fixed subsidies for designated lines. Without the fixed amount guaranteed by these subsidies, the restrictions would result in a steady reduction in aid unless the lines were outfitted with new ships after five years.

Also, while the new law gave a progressive increase of 10 percent for each additional knot of speed, it provided no extra allowance for size. Thus, although the basic unit grant had increased from 25 to 50 *sen,* the subsidy for a ship of 6,000 tons and 15 knots actually fell from 75 to 65 *sen* per ton per 1,000 miles. Even the basic grant was not guaranteed, for vague phrases in the law, which promised payments of "up to" 50 *sen* "depending on the conditions of the line," accorded the minister discretionary power to reduce the grant. Government authority had its greatest impact at the actual operating level, for the minister was empowered to approve freight rates and to designate the terminal ports of the line as well as the number and type of ships.[7] Despite extensive debate, the only major amendment to the government bill was a requirement that the Diet, in accordance with its constitutional duties, set the annual subsidy budget. This reduced slightly the minister's discretionary financial power.

Initial N.Y.K. studies anticipated that the new law would cut subsidies by 30 percent and necessitate an expensive building program to avoid the reduction in aid to ships older than five years.

The company prepared various amendments, but its efforts to persuade the Seiyūkai to adopt these and to limit further the minister's authority proved unavailing and the bill became law on March 24, 1909.[8]

At least superficially the government gave companies a choice between adhering to the new law, in which case subsidies could be renewed at a reduced rate after five years, or opting to remain under the provisions of the old law with its larger subsidies. The latter would render a company ineligible for renewal after the five-year term of the 1909 law and force it to proceed entirely without aid. In late 1909 the government pressured the N.Y.K. to accept the new law, but prior to that N.Y.K. discussions revealed a high degree of disenchantment and a desire for a more autonomous strategy.

Mitsubishi's Shōda began an April N.Y.K. board meeting by questioning how much the new law would do for the company. "Based on its results to date," he said, "I don't think the American line has sufficient value to be worth maintaining at this point. Nor do I think we can expect the European line to progress beyond its present state." Acceptance of the new law, he suggested, would leave only a slim hope for improvement on the two lines. Nor could better prospects be expected under a renewal of the contract at the end of the five-year term. He concluded that "it would be more suitable to continue the business under the [old navigation] encouragement law and to defer a decision on these lines to a later date." Katō supported Shōda's preference for the old law with a strong financial argument. A projected fifteen-year budget, he said, showed that profits under the new law would be "less than the interest obtainable from the equivalent investment in government securities. Placing ourselves under the new law with such meager returns," Katō insisted, "would be a ruinous decision for future business. In the present situation there is no way other than to stay with the Navigation Encouragement Law."[9]

Because of the five-year limit for subsidies attached to the navigation law option, the arguments of Shōda and Katō implied a potential withdrawal from the government's overseas subsidy program, a radical departure in N.Y.K. thinking. Though this withdrawal did not occur, the fact that it was even considered is important. It suggests that the company was reluctant to operate the trunk lines which were in the national interest unless it had a guarantee of constant financial return. These lines would be even more expensive to operate with the increased government regulation under the new law. By reducing the subsidy and imposing additional costs through upgraded standards for new ships, the 1909 law threatened the guarantee of financial return and undermined the company's rationale for operating subsidized lines. Certainly, Shōda and Katō could not have anticipated World War I or probably even the extent of the shipping recovery after 1912. But if their recommendations had prevailed and the company had opted for the old law, thereby freeing itself from the government controls accompanying the subsidies just as the war was beginning, it might have been able to exploit its opportunities more effectively than it did.

The views of Shōda and Katō did remain N.Y.K. policy until October 1909. Until then, the company had planned to operate the U.S. line under the old law, for it did not believe the line's prospects warranted the expense of upgrading it to the standards of the new law. It also considered several options for the European line, such as operating a combined fleet of new and older ships or making the contractual term only three years. These and other last-minute alternative plans were all objectionable to the government, which strongly "advised" (*kankoku*) the company in mid-October to adhere to the new law. The government insisted the European and U.S. lines be placed under the law for the full five years. As a final trump card against the government, N.Y.K. executives schemed to utilize the company's stockholders. Accepting a five-year contract under the Ocean Lines Subsidy Law, the board argued, was tantamount to committing the company to a nonprofit-making endeavor. Directors alone, they rationalized, could not decide a matter of such import, which affected the very purpose of the company as a profit-making enterprise. The N.Y.K. executives informed the Ministry of Communcations they would accept the new law only if the stockholders expressed their agreement. The government sidestepped this scheme (really a bluff designed to achieve a compromise) by calling it "awkward" (*kurushii*). That evasive maneuver was enough to make the N.Y.K. desist, and it finally submitted to the new law in November.[10]

With its emphasis on new ships, the 1909 law accelerated the retrenchment already under way within the company. The elimination of navigation subsidies for ships from 1,000 to 3,000 tons led to the sale of many of the company's smaller and older ships and encouraged more withdrawal from coastal operations and specialization in overseas liner services. This growing specialization was not an autonomous strategy. The extensive government controls over liner operations suggested to many that conditions had returned to the pre-1893 days when the government had supervised the early N.Y.K.

In sum: in two stages following the Russo-Japanese War the government first intervened to take control over the N.Y.K.'s main feeder operations in China and then extended its authority over transoceanic lines. In neither case were the results quite what the company expected. The Nisshin Kisen actually improved feeder services, while the shipping recovery after 1912 dissolved company anxiety over the viability of its overseas lines. The new controls, however, prevented the company from profiting from that recovery as much as it might have done.

PROBLEMS OF LINER STRATEGY. The transformation of the N.Y.K. into a specialized liner company was an outgrowth of government intervention, conservative management, and the company's experience as a relatively new member of international conferences. These developments can be examined by comparing the N.Y.K.'s performance with that of other companies, both Japanese and foreign, and by analyzing certain problems it confronted peculiar to liner strategy.

To begin with several elementary measures of performance, in 1910 N.Y.K. profits rose above ¥4 million for the first time since the boom of 1900–1903, results attributable primarily to the retrenchment campaign. Not until 1912, the first year of the pre-war boom, did income exceed ¥ 30 million. Between 1911 and 1913 income increased by 21 percent, and in the latter year a pre-war profit high of ¥ 5.9 million was recorded. Also, by 1914 the N.Y.K., more than any other Japanese firm, had been responsible for fulfilling an aim of the subsidy program—balancing Japan's international shipping payments. Prior to the Sino-Japanese War only 10 percent of Japanese trade was carried in Japanese ships. This figure rose to 30 percent in 1899, after the opening of the major overseas lines, to 40 percent in 1908, and to 50 percent in 1914.[11] Since the N.Y.K. garnered virtually all of the freight carried by Japanese ships on transoceanic lines prior to the Russo-Japanese War, it is little wonder that by 1903 it had grown into the seventh largest shipping company in the world, behind the Hamburg America Line, the North German Lloyd, the French Messageries Maritimes, the British India Line, the P. & O., and the Union Castle. By 1913 it ranked eleventh, a slide caused by its retrenchment between 1907 and 1910, a shipbuilding boom in Europe, and the merger of several British firms.[12]

Within Japan the N.Y.K.'s share of the nation's tonnage fell steadily after the Russo-Japanese War, while the share held by tramps, the O.S.K., and to a lesser extent, Tōyō Kisen, increased proportionately (Table 49).[13] There has been a common assumption that during these years the N.Y.K. followed a conservative, bureaucratic policy, while the O.S.K. was vigorous and innovative.[14] At first glance growth rates, calculated from Table 49, support this assumption, for between 1904 and 1913 O.S.K. tonnage increased at an annual rate of 11 percent, the N.Y.K.'s at only 4 percent. These growth rates, however, are less indicative of managerial performance than of different stages of development. First, during this period the O.S.K. undertook two principal innovations, lines to Tacoma, Washington, and Bombay. These necessitated, for the first time, the purchase of large, ocean-going vessels. In short, the O.S.K. was undergoing the same process that the N.Y.K. experienced earlier when its annual growth rate in tonnage was 14 percent between 1892 and 1901. By the Russo-Japanese

TABLE 49   Share of National Tonnage
           Held by Three Main Companies
           (Unit: 1,000 tons)

	O.S.K.	N.Y.K.	Tōyō Kisen	Total of 3 Firms	All-Japan	National Share of 3 Firms (%)
1894	19(7)[b]	86(33)	–	105	264	40
1899	43(9)	196(39)	18(4)	257	498	52
1904	69(9)	236(30)	26(3)[a]	331	790	42
1909	122(10)	307(26)	61(5)	490	1,190	41
1913	177(12)	346(23)	88(6)	611	1,514	39

Source: OSK 80 nenshi, p. 27.

Notes: The three firms' share in 1913 would be close to 36% if 170,000 tons of mostly tramp steamers registered in Dairen (to avoid ship taxes) were included. Yoneda, pp. 256–257.
[a]Figures from 1903.   [b]Figures in parentheses are percentages of national totals.

War the N.Y.K. had all but reached the geographic limits of its expansion (until the opening of the Panama Canal), and its growth from then until 1914 generally involved replacing ships rather than starting new lines. Second, the N.Y.K.'s rate of new ship purchasing was much higher than the growth figures imply. They reflect, after all, the retrenchment program with its selling of old ships, a structural transformation the O.S.K. had yet to undergo—in part because overseas expansion was less urgent for the O.S.K., since the more intense freight traffic in western Japan sustained the profitability of its coastal services longer than those of the N.Y.K. in the north. By 1913 the Bombay and Tacoma lines still seem to have accounted for little more than 10 percent of the O.S.K.'s income.[15]

A second misconception about N.Y.K. strategy prior to World War I is that it was excessively dependent on passenger business. Nakagawa Keiichirō, for example, has stated that after 1900 O.S.K. President Nakahashi "gave priority to freight over passengers in contrast to the N.Y.K.'s policy of placing emphasis on passengers before freight."[16] This assumption stems from the company's image during the 1920s and 1930s, when it built several very large passenger vessels, and does not accord with the facts. Table 50 shows that, while the share of freight income was increasing for both companies, even in 1913 in relative terms the O.S.K. was still almost twice as dependent as the N.Y.K. on passenger business.

TABLE 50   Freight-Passenger Ratios: N.Y.K. and O.S.K.
(Based on Income)

	N.Y.K.	*O.S.K.*
1903	4.35	1.82
1908	4.75	2.04
1913	5.31	3.07

Sources: Calculated from *NYK 70 nenshi,* p. 701; and *OSK 80 nenshi,* p. 798.

Although the N.Y.K. did occasionally boast about its European passenger business, in its early years the company charged about ¥100 less per round trip than its European competitors. By 1903 it was confident enough to begin quoting equal fares and increased its London-Japan one-way trip from £50 to £55.[17] During these years the North German Lloyd had by far the best passenger service between Europe and East Asia. Thomas Sutherland of the P. & O. called this assertion "jolly humbug," but in fact British officials often traveled home on North German Lloyd boats.[18] On the Pacific just prior to World War I, larger and specialized passenger vessels began to appear, some of them operated by Tōyō Kisen to San Francisco. The N.Y.K., in contrast, still used ships equipped for both freight and passengers. These were less popular than the new specialized vessels, and the company found itself losing much of its Pacific passenger business.[19]

In the two decades prior to World War I, Japanese shipping grew more quickly and gave a better business performance than did foreign, especially British, shipping. Between 1890 and 1909 the average annual growth rate for Japanese tonnage was 11.2 percent, for Germany 5.1 percent, and for Britain 2.7 percent. Thus, between 1895 and 1914 Japan's share of world tonnage grew from 1.7 to 3.8 percent, while Britain's declined from 60.6 to 41.6 percent (compared to increases by Germany from 8.0 to 11.3 and the U.S.A. from 5.5 to 9.4 percent).[20] Table 51 shows that the N.Y.K.'s earning power per ton was much steadier than that of the P. & O. The rise in O.S.K. earning capacity stems partly from a lower base in the late 1890s, after which it derived increased income from expanded services, and partly from the greater profitability of its coastal business.

Several comparisons between British and Japanese strategies help to explain, in part, the different levels of business performance. Nakagawa has argued that the specialization of British firms in markets and routes deprived them of the flexibility to integrate their operations on a worldwide basis. Although the N.Y.K.'s liner strategy generally led to excessive specialization in main routes, one example, albeit a rather late one, suggests that the company was prepared to take more of a "systems approach" of integrating different sectors of its operations when the opportunity merited it. In June 1907 the company had begun running three tramp ships on its European line. The later use of these ships illustrates the risk-sharing strategy employed to open new, unsubsidized operations. In 1912, the N.Y.K. signed a contract with the Oriental Emigration Company (Tōyō Imin Kaisha) to carry emigrants to Brazil. The emigration firm guaranteed a minimum of ¥120,000 in passage fees, while the N.Y.K. promised to pay a rebate of one-third on fares above the guarantee. The operation appears to have become profitable, though, only when the N.Y.K. carried lumber to Europe on its return via Suez. These sailings to Brazil, which as early as 1896 had been planned with a stop at New York on the return to Europe, provided a precedent for the westward round-the-world route via Panama that the company began during World War I.[21]

One aspect of British specialization that contrasts with Japanese

TABLE 51 Index of Major Companies' Earnings per Ton,
1898–1914

(1900 = 100)

	P. & O.	N.Y.K.	O.S.K.	Cunard
1898	64.07	75.81	101.71	89.76
1899	76.34	78.06	95.58	83.46
1900	100.00	100.00	100.00	100.00
1901	62.87	104.58	103.54	95.28
1902	100.29	96.86	115.69	92.91
1903	87.29	93.10	125.44	81.10
1904	82.63	96.82	178.20	71.65
1905	78.44	104.82	155.10	76.38
1906	69.91	96.11	123.03	97.64
1907	70.80	104.84	134.78	79.53
1908	64.22	102.70	139.63	79.53
1909	60.32	80.38	126.69	101.57
1910	65.12	92.36	134.40	106.30
1911	67.21	94.38	128.11	90.55
1912	64.07	97.00	134.08	108.66
1913	80.09	101.75	145.92	100.79
1914	57.03	92.07	129.96	100.79

Sources: Derek H. Aldcroft, "The Depression in British Shipping, 1901–1911," p. 18;
NYK 70 nenshi, pp. 675, 701; *OSK 80 nenshi,* pp. 763–765, 798–802; Francis E. Hyde,
Cunard and the North Atlantic, 1840–1973 (Macmillan, 1975), p. 132.

Note: Indexes calculated for Cunard and the Japanese companies. Subsidies are not
included. The N.Y.K. and O.S.K. figures include income from charters operated but not
tonnage for such vessels. This creates some distortion, in particular a slight bias favoring
the O.S.K., which was relatively more active as a charter operator than the N.Y.K. (see
n. 45 of this chapter). For trend purposes, however, the distortion is minimal, for the
degree of O.S.K. chartering in 1900, the base year, was about the same level as in later
years.

practice was a reluctance to develop feeder lines. Holt's Ocean
Steam Ship Company had begun a feeder in Southeast Asia but
then sold it in 1899 to the North German Lloyd. According to
Holt's biographer, John Swire "had never had much patience with
what he called 'wayside earnings' and largely condemned deviation
from the main line trades." Similarly, with regard to tramps

Richard Holt remarked in 1908 that "we have never been interested in tramps, and we have never had any."[22] Of course the N.Y.K. had had to give up its feeder lines as it grew into a more specialized liner firm. The difference in the Japanese case, at least in China, was that the government took control of the feeder line and left its ownership as a joint subsidiary of the N.Y.K. and O.S.K. In this sense the Japanese government played a much stronger role in buttressing private firms than did the British government. Also, the leaders of the N.Y.K. and Nisshin Kisen were often the same executives. Especially after their 1908 contract on through rates, they shared strategic goals. Their degree of common purpose seems to have been stronger than that which existed between Holt's Europe-East Asia line and Swire's Yangtze feeder, the China Navigation Company.

As a response to their competitive decline, British firms adopted a strategy of merger. From 1900, and especially between 1912 and 1914, "a well-defined process existed whereby a small and declining number of companies absorbed their rivals and acquired an increasing volume of British tonnage."[23] By contrast there were no mergers among main line companies in Japan during this period, only the transformation of subsidiary operations into national policy companies. In addition, the number of large independents was rapidly growing.

Liner strategy itself became a restrictive mode of operation which limited the N.Y.K.'s managerial flexibility primarily because it necessitated a large percentage of the company's business being tied up in conference agreements. In this sense Nakagawa's comment about British specialization can also apply to the N.Y.K. The most famous illustration of this arose over a freight rate dispute in 1912. In the spring of that year the European-Far East Conference decided to increase its westbound rates by 10 percent. Since the Japanese government, under the 1909 subsidy law, had the authority to limit the freight rates of subsidized companies, the conference decision provoked a classic confrontation between a private multinational economic organization and the nation state. The N.Y.K. was caught between the two.

The conference justified its rate hike on the grounds of increased costs for shipbuilding, labor, and coal. Of the thirteen conference members only the N.Y.K. dissented, because it could not obtain government permission for the increase. The Japanese government resisted because of the impact the new rates would have on the growing number of cheap exports like porcelain, toys, and straw braid. For many of these items freight rates were over 50 percent of cost price, and in some cases above it. An increase in the rate, it was felt, would destroy the competitive edge in Europe which these exports had just won. A strong lobbying campaign by exporters quickly arose, and within days the Yokohama Chamber of Commerce had presented a formal petition. The Ministry of Communications, meanwhile, assigned the matter for study to the Ministry of Agriculture and Commerce.[24]

The Japanese government also refused to sanction the increase because it would contravene the purposes of the subsidy, which was given to keep freight rates low. Many observers argued, in fact, that should the N.Y.K. succeed in increasing its rates it would be morally bound to give up its subsidy for the European line.[25]

Early in May the Ministry of Communications took tentative steps to break the impasse by approving an increase, provided that rates "remain intact on goods of a special nature, which have rivals in . . . foreign markets, those which show favourable prospects, low-priced exports, and imported foreign-made machinery and staple materials."[26] This list of exemptions was so broad that it heightened conference opposition to the Japanese stand, but it did at least defer the deadline for N.Y.K. compliance from June 1 to July 1, 1912. In the ensuing negotiations with the conference, the N.Y.K., it should be noted, was acting primarily under government instructions and not as an autonomous firm. For its own part, the Ministry of Communications was sensitive to N.Y.K. needs. If the company refused to enforce conference decisions, it faced possible expulsion. Since it handled only 20 percent of conference business with Japan, even if it were forced to compete outside the conference with lower rates it could hope to carry only a portion of the cheap exports. Discord, therefore, could not help Japanese trade, and the adverse effects of expulsion would create additional financial demands on the government from the N.Y.K. The government recognized the needs of the shipping industry for an increase but felt it "necessary to place a limit" on the rates "in the spirit which gave birth to the policy of shipping subsidies as well as trade protection."[27]

Eventually on June 18 the conference capitulated and accepted the Ministry of Communications's May formula which limited the increase to 5 percent while exempting 52 items. These items, which retained the existing rate, included bamboo ware, ginger, pepper, porcelain, canned goods, bamboo blinds, screens, straw braid, tea, vegetable wax, toys, and beans.[28]

The exporters of the goods were the principal winners in this dispute. The N.Y.K. claimed that by hard bargaining with the conference it had secured the market for them. On the contrary, it was the government that had taken the hard line. But it must be emphasized that the government stand was efficacious only because of N.Y.K. strength within the conference. The European members of the conference compromised because the cost of competing with an independent N.Y.K. exceeded the loss of anticipated freight revenue under the exemptions and 5 percent increase. On the other hand, the N.Y.K. was a victim of the dispute, for the compromise placed a lid on its profits during a boom period when expenses were rising.

Ironically, China was a victim of the conference rate hike, though only temporarily. The Ministry of Communications regulated N.Y.K. rates not simply from Japan but also from intermediate ports on the European line. Whereas it resisted increases for Japanese exports, it accepted the conference request for intermediate ports and then in December 1912 permitted a second 10 percent hike on Chinese exports.[29] These measures, however, were soon superseded by a countervailing influence on liner strategy, namely, the pressure to lower freight rates to confront outside challengers. In 1913 a German firm, the Rickmers Line, began undercutting conference rates. By 1914 rates from Antwerp on iron materials had fallen from 25s. to 16s. a ton and on glass products from 28s. to 19s. The westbound trade was also affected, with many Japanese goods bound for Europe falling from the 40–50s. range to 25–30s. and agricultural products from China's interior from 61s. to 25s. This rate war also affected Manchuria. Beginning in May 1914 its agricultural products were brought into the rebate system, tying shippers in Dairen to the conference as a means of fighting the Rickmers Line.[30]

Liner strategy and the conference system to which it adhered seem to have been most effective in times of depression, such as 1907–1910. In more prosperous times, like 1912–1914, the restrictions of the system and government intervention limited the profit-making capacity of liner companies. Business trends in these latter years reversed those which followed the Russo-Japanese War. The deficit-ridden, domestic-near-seas services, which since 1900 had usually placed second in total business income, surpassed the European line in 1912/2 to become the company's largest earner. This recovery probably resulted from lessening of competition on the Shanghai line, increased business with South Manchuria, and perhaps domestic inflation. On the other hand, European line tonnage reached its peak in 1910. Because of the greater capacity of its new ships, in that year the N.Y.K. reduced the number of regular vessels on the line from 12 to 11. This freed the old ships for use as tramps, as in the Brazil operation. But by 1913, despite a marked increase in cargo all the major conference lines had to cut back on their extra ships because of competition from outsiders. N.Y.K. extra ships were, in some cases, 30 percent empty, while several regular vessels carried coal below deck in place of normal cargo (Figure 12). Also, despite management's continuing pessimism about its future, the N.Y.K.'s Seattle line improved relative to the European line. From 1910 to 1913 the ratio of European to U.S. line income fell from 6.39 to 2.94 and that for profits from 6.29 to 4.50.

These trends on the European line suggest that the failure to build integrated tramp services and the company's dependence on liner operations were narrowing its strategic options. In a comment on Gabriel Kolko's *Railroads and Regulation,* Alfred Chandler

FIGURE 12 The *Katori Maru*

The *Katori Maru*, a combined freight and passenger vessel of 10,513 tons, was built in 1913 for the European line. It carried coal below deck in 1914 because of a loss of cargo to nonconference operators. HG, June 3, 1914. (This photograph was taken some years later, for the N.Y.K. only began using its distinctive funnel mark in 1929.)

Courtesy of the Internal & Public Relations Chamber, NYK LINE.

criticized Kolko for failing "to recognize the importance of system-building as an alternative to pooling in railroad competition."[31] The observation is relevant to N.Y.K. strategy. In the early years of expansion the company promised to develop a "systems" approach, meaning the integration of different sectors of its overall operations, through the feeder strategy. As the company became more specialized, it lost full control over the feeders and did not extend the concept to its liner network. Instead it relied on a pooling strategy, that is, cooperation with the conferences. "System-building," then, was left primarily to the tramps and independents. Clearly, though, it was difficult for the N.Y.K. to avoid the conference system in the established trades. For the European line, operating on a regular basis was a strategic national priority. Such a line could not be continued on a long-term basis outside the conference. In short, the "conservatism" of the N.Y.K. was a reflection of the "national" functions which it performed and which made it an essentially different company from the still primarily locally oriented O.S.K. or the tramps which thrived in times of opportunity.

CAPITAL AND SHIPPING COSTS

THE ECONOMICS OF SHIP PURCHASING. During the Sino-Japanese War the N.Y.K. received approximately half of all the tonnage purchased on an emergency basis by the government. Following the war most of these ships (roughly 65,000 tons) were handed to the N.Y.K. on easy terms at ¥3.6 million to be repaid at no interest over twenty years.[32] Though a few of these were large enough (4,500 tons) for use on the European line, generally they were of poor quality. In fact, John Swire regarded them as useless for the European and East Asian lines, and he further predicted that "having the steamers on hand, will probably deter them from contracting for further boats."[33]

Swire correctly assessed the ships as uncompetitive, but he misjudged long-range Japanese policy. Other than as a ragtag initial entry into the European line, these ships did not play a major role in the N.Y.K.'s era of expansion. They were the last of a kind—an emergency purchase in time of military crisis, following the precedents of the Taiwan expedition and the Satsuma Rebellion. Instead, beginning in 1896 the structure of N.Y.K. ship purchasing was revolutionized. No longer relying on long-term government loans, down to World War I the N.Y.K. bought all of its ships through self-financing.[34]

Generally the N.Y.K.'s upgrading of its fleet won the praise of foreign observers. One commented in 1902 that "the Company is not showing any laggard disposition in the matter of adding to its fleet. That was the mistake made by the old Mitsu Bishi; a mistake which led to the establishment of its rival, the Kyōdō Unyu Kaisha."[35] Specifically, the N.Y.K. did most of its purchasing in three periods. First, in 1897 and 1898 the capital stock increase of ¥13.2 million was used to buy new ships for the main overseas lines. Second, as noted in Chapter 9, the N.Y.K. had about ¥5 million tied up in government securities between 1904 and 1906 to finance the Russo-Japanese War. Revenue from the sale of these and other securities as well as older ships financed six new 8,500 ton ships, worth about ¥1.61 million each, that were assigned to the European line as replacements upon their completion in 1908 and 1909.[36] The 1909 Ocean Lines Subsidy Law, with its emphasis on new ships, ushered in the third period of purchasing. By 1911 about half the ships still on the European line were nearing the limit of their fifteen-year eligibility for subsidies. Cash assets, grown from ¥3.1 million in 1907 to ¥12.5 million in 1911, helped to finance six new 10,000 ton ships for the European line at a budgeted cost of ¥2.13 million each.[37]

Within the framework of the N.Y.K.'s financial procedure, between 1897 and 1914, the net purchase price of ships amounted to ¥54.4 million. Of this total, 24.3 percent came from the capital stock increase, 48.3 percent from income equal to depreciation cost, which the company used to upgrade the fleet on a regular basis, 1.8 percent from a short-term loan in 1909, and 25.6 percent from other internal funds.[38]

The key question is what were these "other internal funds"? A fairly precise analysis of these funds can be attempted from the data in Figure 13. This figure and Table 52 attempt to show—by balancing off current assets against current liabilities for four sample years—how much money the company could expect to have available to work with in twelve-month periods following the selected years. Basically I will argue that government subsidies enabled the N.Y.K. to maintain large current assets, to minimize current liabilities, and to utilize the balance to buy ships.

It is important to note, however, that the N.Y.K. accounts do not distinguish between fixed and current assets or between long-term and current liabilities. This distinction can be determined by the nature of the categories listed in the balance sheet and from their use in the two decades before 1914. First, *assets* were of three types: (1) Fixed assets are ships, land, and buildings. (2) Investments are company holdings of government securities, industrial bonds, and bank debentures, as well as its share in subsidiary firms. (Strictly speaking, investments could be regarded as current assets, but since the company generally held them for a fairly long period, I have placed them in a separate category.) (3) Current assets are primarily cash (84 percent in 1914). Next, *liabilities* were of two types: (1) In 1914 long-term liabilities and retained earnings consist of reserves (88 percent), a pension fund (7 percent), the amount of bonds or loans not due within one year (1 percent), and that portion of retained earnings that is appropriated for reserves or otherwise kept within the firm (4 percent). (2) Current liabilities are accounts payable, installments and interest on loans and bonds due within the next year, plus that portion of retained earnings to be paid out in dividends or bonuses.[39]

Figure 13 depicts three increasingly significant relationships: The first, the decreasing percentage of capital stock (stockholders' equity) on the liabilities side of the balance sheet, is more relevant to the internal politics of the company than to ship purchasing. Second, there is the rapid increase in long-term liabilities—reserves. "Reserves" are not money; rather they are simply the expression of an obligation. For example, when a figure in the company's

FIGURE 13 N.Y.K. Financial Structure, Selected Years
(%)

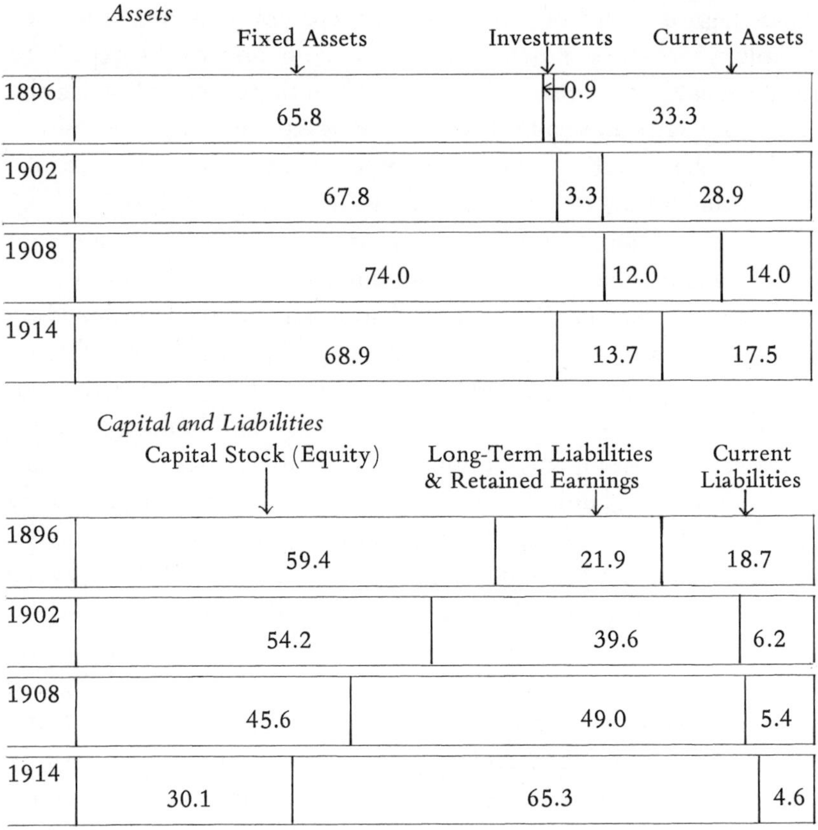

Assets	Fixed Assets	Investments	Current Assets
1896	65.8	←0.9	33.3
1902	67.8	3.3	28.9
1908	74.0	12.0	14.0
1914	68.9	13.7	17.5

Capital and Liabilities	Capital Stock (Equity)	Long-Term Liabilities & Retained Earnings	Current Liabilities
1896	59.4	21.9	18.7
1902	54.2	39.6	6.2
1908	45.6	49.0	5.4
1914	30.1	65.3	4.6

(¥1,000)

	1 – Fixed Assets 2 – Investments 3 – Current Assets (CA)			1 – Capital Stock 2 – Long-Term Liabilities & Retained Earnings 3 – Current Liabilities (CL)		
Year & Total	1	2	3	1	2	3
1896 (20,254)	13,333	185	6,737	12,022	4,445	3,789
1902 (40,574)	27,518	1,335	11,723	22,000	16,079	2,495
1908 (48,224)	35,683	5,799	6,745	22,000	23,643	2,583
1914 (72,189)	50,387	10,020	12,781	22,000	47,795	3,391

Source: Adjusted and calculated from *NYK–EH*.

expense or profit distribution statement was earmarked for a particular reserve, the amount in question represented actual cash which became part of current assets or was used for investments. All N.Y.K. reserves were long-term obligations; therefore, the company did not have to keep large sums on hand to cover these reserve funds. Instead, it could use the cash that was technically obligated to a particular reserve in order to buy ships. This was true even of the insurance and repair reserves, which together totaled ¥22.2 million in 1914, for especially after 1907 the company spent well under 1 percent of these funds each year, while putting in 10 to 15 percent of their total; hence their rapid growth. (For total accuracy, a small amount should be added to current liabilities to represent the yearly withdrawals from the pension fund. However, this amount, which unlike insurance and repair payments is not recorded, was negligible.)

TABLE 52 N.Y.K. Working Capital, Selected Years

Year	Current Ratio (CA/CL)	Working Capital (CA–CL) [¥1,000]
1896	1.78	2,950
1902	4.70	9,264
1908	2.61	4,162
1914	3.77	9,390

Source: Calculated from Figure 13.

Having substantial reserves did not in itself enable the company to freely use current assets to buy ships. That depended on the third major relationship in Figure 13 (see also Table 52), that between current assets and current liabilities. This is expressed as the "current ratio," which is a measure of debt-paying ability (the ratio of current assets to current liabilities). If the N.Y.K. had had large current liabilities (for example, loans requiring high interest payments or short-term loans), the current ratio would have been lower and more current assets would have been directed to financing debt. As it was, the N.Y.K. had no loans (except for two small interest-free ones from the government and the Red Cross, which essentially made them long-term liabilities). As current assets grew between 1909 and 1914, the company built up a large excess of current assets over current liabilities, in short, an enormous pool of *working capital* (a term meaning the amount of current assets against which there is no current claim, that is, money the company could use as it pleased). For example, in the first half of 1914, cash accounted for 87 percent of current assets, but with large ship purchases in 1914 cash assets fell from ¥13.5 million to ¥10.7 million. Nevertheless, working capital continued to grow, for whatever the company spent on ships (¥15 million between 1912 and 1914) was soon matched by the amounts designated for reserves, which in real terms became cash expressed as current assets.

One final point about Table 52 that requires explanation is how superior the 1914 financial situation was to earlier years. The working capital for 1902 was almost as large as that for 1914 because 1902 had been a slack year for ship purchasing, allowing a large cash surplus to accumulate. In contrast, 1912–1914 had been the peak period for purchasing. Despite that, the company still had more working capital than in 1902.

Overall, Table 52 represents a healthy financial picture and demonstrates how the N.Y.K. could purchase its ships through self-financing. Nevertheless, the financial meaning of "self" must be defined by subsidies. Table 53 demonstrates that even in the boom period before World War I profits exceeded subsidies only in 1913. Though subsidies were given for operating expenses, to cover deficits on the major overseas lines, from the viewpoint of working capital their relevance to ship purchasing is that they created the reserve system. Subsidies were listed as income in company accounts. That made possible an increase in expenses. In other words, the subsidies covered those expenses like depreciation and reserves which created the financial means to buy ships. For example, depreciation and funds earmarked for certain reserves were listed as expenses *before* the determination of profit.

In addition, other reserves (as well as dividends, executive bonuses, and retained earnings) were taken out of profits. Since most of these categories (depreciation, reserves, retained earnings) all became actual cash, the subsidies, while technically given for operating expenses, also financed N.Y.K. ship purchases and thus were responsible for capital accumulation.

Although the N.Y.K. did not actually draw on its reserves, except for small amounts from the insurance and repair funds, their development provides a useful index of company planning and strategy. First, to identify them by accounting categories, the insurance and repair reserves were recorded as expenses prior to profit; the preparatory fund (shown in Table 54) was a legal reserve required of all companies by the Commercial Code and it was taken out of profits.[40] The remaining funds were all optional and came out of profits. One can divide the build-up of reserves into four periods. First, between 1899 and 1901, during the first years of large profits following the stockholders' riot of 1897, the company set up its dividend equalization fund, reflecting the need to preserve internal stability. Second, between 1901 and 1903, as the feeder strategy took shape, ¥3.5 million was placed in the line extension fund. Then, during the long recession from 1904 to 1910 no new funds were started, and additions were made only to the insurance, repair, and preparatory funds as required by the company's articles of incorporation. Finally, the 1909 subsidy law prompted and the business recovery of 1912 made possible a new build-up between 1911 and 1914. Over ¥4 million was added to the line extension and fleet improvement fund, and a reserve to prepare for the anticipated subsidy reduction after 1914 was started in 1911.

Generally, the N.Y.K.'s financial structure differed from other shipping companies. Its dependence on subsidies, as measured by percentage of gross income, was greater than the O.S.K.'s, though only by 18 percent to 13 percent for the whole period from 1894 to 1913. This was nowhere near the 33 percent figure for Tōyō Kisen, a company in dire financial shape prior to World War I. The O.S.K. also relied more on capital stock and loans than the

TABLE 53 N.Y.K. Business Results, 1894–1914

(Unit: ¥1,000)

	Assets (A)	Income (B)	Expenditures	Profit (C)	Profit as % of Assets (C/A)	Profit as % of Income (C/B)	Dividend (¥1,000)	Dividend (%)	Subsidy (D)	Subsidy as % of Profit (D/C)
1894	14,365	6,514	4,945	1,568	10.9	24.1	880	10	899	57.3
1895	18,002	15,494	10,723	4,770	26.5	30.8	1,760	10 30	899	18.9
1896	20,254	11,243	9,581	1,661	8.2	14.8	2,244	18 33	889	53.5
1897	28,088	10,600	10,727	-127	-	-	605	10 0	1,490	loss
1898	32,752	14,846	12,545	2,300	7.0	15.5	1,584	8	3,480	151.3
1899	34,669	16,675	13,958	2,717	7.8	16.3	2,090	9 10	4,425	162.9
1900	38,213	21,116	16,360	4,755	12.4	22.5	2,420	10 12	4,664	98.1
1901	38,783	23,281	17,837	5,444	14.0	23.4	2,640	12	4,649	85.4
1902	40,574	22,615	18,044	4,570	11.3	20.2	2,640	12	5,143	112.5
1903	43,096	23,642	18,820	4,822	11.2	20.4	2,640	12	5,355	111.1
1904	44,406	21,301	18,401	2,900	6.5	13.6	2,640	12	2,646	91.2
1905	47,374	22,535	19,524	3,010	6.4	13.4	2,640	12	1,100	36.5
1906	47,001	24,202	20,733	3,468	7.4	14.3	2,970	15 12	2,782	80.2
1907	46,796	28,370	25,932	2,438	5.2	8.6	2,640	12	5,220	214.1
1908	48,224	27,610	24,762	2,848	5.9	10.3	2,640	12	5,369	188.5

TABLE 53 N.Y.K. Business Results, 1894–1914

(Unit: ¥1,000)

	Assets	Income	Expenditures	Profit	Profit as % of Assets	Profit as % of Income	Dividend		Subsidy	Subsidy as % of Profit
	(A)	(B)		(C)	(C/A)	(C/B)	(¥1,000)	(%)	(D)	(D/C)
1909	51,303	26,666	24,046	2,619	5.1	9.8	2,200	10	6,516	248.8
1910	53,718	27,485	23,435	4,050	7.5	14.7	2,200	10	6,130	151.4
1911	57,884	28,120	23,724	4,396	7.6	15.6	2,200	10	5,825	132.5
1912	62,707	31,077	26,114	4,963	7.9	16.0	2,200	10	5,088	102.5
1913	68,401	34,032	28,158	5,874	8.6	17.3	2,200	10	4,836	82.3
1914	73,189	34,185	29,348	4,837	6.6	14.2	2,200	10	5,043	104.3

Sources: NYK 70 nenshi, pp. 701–707; NYK-EH.

Note: Where two figures appear under the dividend percentage, different amounts were given in the two halves of the business year.

TABLE 54 Growth of N.Y.K. Reserves, Selected Years
(Unit: ¥1,000)

	1896	1904	1910	1914
Insurance	2,153	2,532	6,202	10,478
Repair	591	2,886	7,617	11,719
Preparatory fund	624	1,987	2,863	3,871
Dividend equalization		3,300	3,300	3,300
Line expansion & fleet improvement		3,500	3,500	8,100
Preparation for subsidy reduction				2,643
Construction of head office				1,500
Special reserve				900
Total	3,368	14,205	23,482	42,509

Source: NYK-EH.

N.Y.K. In 1913 the O.S.K.'s total assets were ¥32.2 million:[41] 51 percent stockholders' equity (32 percent for the N.Y.K. in 1913), 23 percent reserves, 22 percent bonds and loans, and 4 percent other liabilities. Although the O.S.K.'s three legal reserves (preparatory, insurance, and repairs) made up less of its total reserves than the N.Y.K.'s (54.9 percent compared to 62.9 percent for the N.Y.K. in 1913), the O.S.K. had only two other categories of reserves, dividend equalization and retained earnings, and nothing specifically put aside for business improvement.

While the N.Y.K.'s reserve funds were unusually large, one feature the N.Y.K. had in common with the O.S.K. as well as many industrial manufacturing firms was a relative lack of reliance on bank loans. Yamamura reached this conclusion by studying representative firms like Oji Papers, Tokyo Electric Light, the O.S.K., Japan Flour Milling, and Kurashiki Cotton Spinning. He found they relied on capital stock increases, bonds, or internal reserves much more than bank loans. Unfortunately, there is a gap in Yamamura's data between 1905 and World War I, the period when most established firms were rapidly increasing their reserves.[42]

Though subsidies were clearly the foundation for the N.Y.K.'s reserve system, or internal financing, by 1914 the company was no longer dependent on subsidies. Following the 1909 subsidy law, when management had cut the dividend rate from 12 to 10 percent to leave more cash under its own control, there occurred an increasingly heavy flow of funds into the reserve system. By 1914 its new ships, massive investments, and huge working capital had given the N.Y.K. a measure of autonomy to act independently of subsidies. Business results, even under the company's specialized strategy, show a lessening of dependence on subsidies. Operating income grew at an annual rate of 1.9 percent from 1901 to 1910 but at 11.7 percent a year from 1910 to 1913. In these latter years subsidies as a percentage of operating income fell from 32 to 18 percent overall and from 45 to 35 percent on the European line. Most revealingly, both the European and U.S. lines had one term in 1913 when their operating profit exceeded their subsidies for the first time since 1900 when the full subsidy program was implemented.

This interpretation conflicts with official statements and scholarly assessments, which have placed more emphasis on the high subsidy-profit ratio. For example, an American report of 1916 concluded that the Japanese shipping industry had "not got beyond the need for financial assistance from the State. In other words, the 'infant industry' has never grown up." Teratani expresses a similar view that both the N.Y.K. and the O.S.K. "would have gone bankrupt if they had not received government subsidies."[43] Such ahistorical speculation goes contrary to the financial trends of the early 1910s. Without subsidies the N.Y.K. would have reduced or eliminated its most expensive overseas lines and concentrated on those it could still handle, especially the Indian and probably European lines. The American line would likely have led to an amalgamation with the O.S.K. and Tōyō Kisen. But most importantly, giving up subsidies would have freed the company from many extra expenses in meeting onerous government standards and allowed it more managerial flexibility. That is why some company members favored dispensing with subsidies under the 1909 law.[44] By consensus, to finance future expansion such as the Panama line, the executives preferred to stick with the subsidies rather than rely on capital stock increases or loans. This was a managerial choice. It was a conservative one, but hardly one forced upon the company through "infant dependency" or "imminent bankruptcy."

COSTS. The N.Y.K.'s international competitiveness in the two decades prior to World War I stemmed in part from moderate, and in some cases declining, operating costs. For example, N.Y.K. ship expenses per ton were 7.7 percent lower in 1913 than they had been in 1898. Only in 1907–1908 did inflation threaten to reach runaway proportions as it had in the late 1880s for the shipping industry. Although data are unavailable for a precise comparison, O.S.K. costs appear to have been similar to the N.Y.K.'s (see Table 55) at the beginning of the expansionary period. Only in the latter part of the 1898 business year, for example, was the full complement of ships assigned to the European line. In later years,

TABLE 55 N.Y.K. Ship Costs
(Unit: ¥/owned ton)

1898	1903	1908	1913
52	51	60	48

Source: NYK-EH. These figures include expenses shown in Table 56 plus depreciation and payments made from reserves for insurance and repairs. Until 1899 the N.Y.K. did not insure its ships. Instead, when necessary it drew upon its reserves. This policy changed after extremely heavy payments (over ¥1.4 million) from the repair reserve in 1898. It then began insuring its ships, the fee for which appears for the first time as an expense in the profit-and-loss statement for 1899/1. Incurring insurance as a regular expense removed a potential obstacle to the growth of the insurance and repair reserves. See also notes 45 and 55 of this chapter. (If calculations included only the operating expenses in Table 56, the results for these selected years would be: ¥39, ¥43, ¥52, and ¥41, respectively.)

when N.Y.K. overseas lines were in full operation, O.S.K. costs per ton were 10 to 20 percent less than the N.Y.K.'s.[45] The principal difference was that overseas operations involved numerous extra expenses. Port dues were heavier overseas, and the Suez Canal tolls were, of course, unique to the European line. Also, the cost of coal in Southeast Asia or Europe was 30 to 50 percent higher than in Japan. Finally, N.Y.K. wages were higher not only because it relied on foreigners for its overseas lines but also because it paid its Japanese crews more than did other Japanese shipping companies.

Ship operating costs are broken down in Table 56, and Table 57 shows their increase up to 1914 by using an index of 100 for 1900. This measures actual expenses, not prices or wages. Labor costs showed only a moderate rise until 1912. Despite the rising number of officers and crew to meet expanded operations, costs were kept down by the gradual dismissal of foreigners. Actually a 30 percent reduction in foreign officers had occurred between 1886 and 1893, but in the early years of expansion the number of foreigners almost doubled. This development seems to have been resisted by Japanese seamen. At the time, crews consisted of a volatile mix of "coolies" and native Japanese seamen presided over mainly by foreign officers. In 1896 several mutinous incidents occurred on N.Y.K. ships. According to one report, "as soon as officers exercise authority the crew rebel and leave the ship at the next port."[46] By

TABLE 56 N.Y.K. Ship Operating Expenses by Percentage,
          1900 and 1913

	Salaries	Victuals	Coal	Repairs	Port Dues	Suez Canal Tolls	Charter Fees	Others
1900	16.2	12.6	30.6	6.7	7.8	7.8	3.8	14.5
1913	18.2	11.7	29.4	10.1	10.2	5.2	6.5	8.7

Source: NYK-EH. Ship expenses constituted 67.4% of operating expenses in 1900 and
    60.3% in 1913.

1901, however, the number of foreign officers had fallen to 119,
about the level of 1893. It then decreased gradually until the 1909
subsidy law, which made approval of their employment much more
restrictive. By 1913 only 16 remained, 12 of them ship captains.[47]

While the foreigners were being dismissed, the wages of Japanese
seamen were being kept down. This pattern began to change in
1912, however, when Japanese seamen made their first effective
gains through a strike in Yokohama. On April 22 about 60 seamen
and firemen with a month's strike fund walked off an N.Y.K. ship
in Yokohama harbor, thereby delaying the departure of this and
several other ships. Monthly wages of N.Y.K. crew ranged from ¥10
to ¥20, on average about 20 percent higher than wages of other
Japanese shipping firms. On April 27 the O.S.K. and Tōyō Kisen
forced the N.Y.K.'s hand by increasing their wages by ¥3; early in
May the N.Y.K. followed suit with its own ¥3 increase, rationalized
as a "temporary allowance" (*rinji teate*). This wage settlement sent
the index for company salaries up from 120 in 1911 to 166 in
1913.[48]

These seamen's wages may seem abnormally low because in 1912
the Home Ministry was using ¥20 a month in household income
as the poverty line. At the time, however, even the typical worker's
household income was only ¥21 a month, and most unskilled
workers, including the lower ranking seamen, were below the poverty line. It is possible, of course, that while on a transoceanic
voyage, a seamen might have received free of charge from his com-

TABLE 57 Index of N.Y.K. Operating Expenses, 1898–1914
(1900 = 100)

	Ship Expenses						Other Expenses	
	Salaries	Victuals	Coal	Repairs	Port Dues	Suez Canal Tolls	Branches	Business
1898	73	77	89	82	23	56	80	71
1899	89	79	98	109	79	98	83	75
1900	100	100	100	100	100	100	100	100
1901	104	101	114	177	115	108	108	102
1902	109	106	115	158	124	99	116	106
1903	112	108	105	149	126	97	126	122
1904	121	149	56	121	113	50	124	92
1905	133	134	31	130	64	–	141	78
1906	118	134	94	154	104	4	189	96
1907	131	156	164	179	185	95	171	155
1908	134	146	152	196	175	106	168	147
1909	134	127	131	170	181	135	159	143
1910	128	108	123	172	187	139	158	149
1911	120	108	118	164	180	127	182	162
1912	144	125	124	213	194	108	209	183
1913	166	139	143	223	195	98	157	214
1914	166	150	153	240	227	105	166	206

Source: NYK-EH.

pany a higher percentage of his daily living expenses than would the shore-based factory worker.

Upper-class seamen, whose special training in maritime institutes made them skilled employees, naturally received much higher pay. For deck officers the average monthly wage among all Japanese seamen serving on steamships in 1914 ranged from ¥30 for a third-officer to ¥70 for a first-officer. Overall, the chief engineer received the highest wage among seamen, ¥110 a month. The upper-class seamen were also much better organized than the crew. As early as

1896 they had formed their own nationwide organization, which in 1907 was incorporated as the Maritime Officers' Association (Kaiun Kyōkai). Although this was not a trade union, its labor activities following World War I provided a model for the formation in 1921 of the Japan Seamen's Union, which acted on behalf of crew members.[49]

Like executives in many industries prior to World War I, N.Y.K. leaders were trying to establish more permanent employment among their officers and crew. During the retrenchment of 1907, when the company had laid off many seamen and shore employees, it provided special allowances to those who remained to ensure their loyalty. After the 1912 strike, it also revised its wage system to provide greater increases according to length of service.[50] Such incentives were in some cases important in the shipping industry, for seamen were considered employees only while they were aboard ship. Nevertheless, along with the increasing disharmony between managers and stockholders, the discrimination felt by seamen at the hands of shore employees was one of the principal destabilizing factors within the company during and after World War I.

According to the index of expenses, repairs were the most rapidly increasing category down to 1914. The 1914 figure, however, is misleading, for the base year of 1900 was very low for repairs, only 3.1 percent of ship value compared to 5.1 percent in 1901.

The category showing the steadiest upward trend is port dues. A major cause of this was the frequent strikes in Britain which increased docking expenses, especially in London. Also, according to Thomas Sutherland, Calcutta was "one of the most expensive ports in the world."[51]

The cost of coal had risen rapidly in the late 1880s and mid-1890s, but during its era of expansion, with the exception of 1907, the N.Y.K. was generally successful in keeping down coal expenses, evident from virtually every measure available. As shown in Table 57 the index for coal expenses for 1911 (118) was barely higher than for 1902 (115), whereas the cost of coal per mile in 1913 (¥1.13) was lower than in 1901 (¥1.24). Certainly the newer, more efficient ships contributed to this saving. Between 1909 and 1914 the cost of coal per ship ton fluctuated between ¥11.2 and ¥12.8, but from 1898 to 1902 it had risen from ¥14.2 to ¥15.3. Another reason for the moderate coal price was improvement in Japanese ports and in rail networks connecting them with mines.[52]

Although many decisions on coal contracts are recorded in the minutes of N.Y.K. board meetings, it is difficult to perceive any trend in coal prices because the price varied greatly depending on the type of coal (unsifted, lump, or powdered) and the place of purchase. Obviously it cost less to buy coal near Yokohama than to have it hauled from Hokkaido or Kyushu. During the recession in 1908, when there was insufficient freight to fill coastal vessels, the N.Y.K. actually began buying direct from the coal ports to provide cargo rather than buying coal on order to Yokohama. Domestic prices generally ranged between ¥4 and ¥8 a ton. Overseas purchases, such as at Singapore to which Mitsui exported, usually cost at least 30 to 50 percent more. In 1898 the N.Y.K. switched from purchasing through an agent in Singapore at ¥12.5 a ton to a direct deal with Mitsui at ¥10 a ton.[53] The N.Y.K. appears to have followed a flexible purchasing policy. After 1900, the O.S.K. temporarily bought coal only from the big four coal producers: Mitsui, Mitsubishi, Yasukawa, and Furukawa. By contrast, in late 1905 the N.Y.K. was unable to agree on a satisfactory price with these companies and signed an agreement with several independents for 220,000 tons, more than half of its needs for the next year.[54]

In the first decade of the twentieth century, British firms made discernible savings in operating costs through more technically efficient ships. For example, on the Cunard Line, ship costs per ton in 1898 were roughly ¥93. In comparison with the N.Y.K., Cunard figures for the years in Table 55 show that its costs fell to ¥85 in 1903 and ¥71 in 1908 before rising to ¥89 in 1913. Primarily, the use of the turbine engine brought costs down between 1898 and 1908. On the other hand, overall British expenses were much greater than those in Japan because of higher wages and victualing costs as well as stricter safety standards and manning regulations. One measure of the lower Japanese wages is that in 1912 Japanese freighters of 8,000 tons carried 45 crewmen compared to 38 for 7,500 ton British ships. The cost curve for the two countries also was different. In 1908 Cunard's costs were at their lowest during this period, whereas the N.Y.K.'s were at their highest. The different curve can probably be explained as follows: N.Y.K. costs were high in 1908 because the company was still using relatively old ships. By 1913, however, despite the wage increases of 1912 (very moderate by British standards), the company had begun to benefit from technologically superior ships, which had cut costs in Britain when they were introduced there a decade or so earlier. For Cunard, however, rising labor costs between 1908 and 1913 had begun to eat into the savings previously generated through ship improvements.[55]

One nonoperating cost, taxation, involved the N.Y.K. and other Japanese shipping companies in considerable controversy following 1900. The chief of the Tokyo Tax Administration Bureau had ruled that the N.Y.K. had to declare depreciation and reserve funds as part of profit rather than claiming them as expenses beforehand. In 1903 the N.Y.K. appealed the ruling and won a court verdict upholding its interpretation of the 1900 revised tax law. This allowed it to continue claiming depreciation and reserve contributions as expenses prior to profit. Had the N.Y.K. lost the legal battle, it would have paid about 50 percent more in taxes, the difference between ¥1.4 million and ¥925,000 in 1913, for example. As it was, the percentage of profit paid as taxes (both national and local, as they are combined in the accounts) rose from 3.4 percent in 1898 to 7.0 percent in 1903. The high figure of 20.5 percent in 1908 reflected continuing burdens from the Russo-Japanese War, but by 1913 it had fallen to 13.6 percent. These payments were quite steep relative to those of British companies. In 1913, for example, Cunard's taxes were roughly 3.7 percent of profit. In the same year, the P. & O. paid no taxes, and in the five years prior to the war they never exceeded 0.3 percent of profit.[56]

BUSINESS RELATIONS AND INDUSTRIAL STRUCTURE

FREIGHT AND INVESTMENTS. Japan's present industrial structure, which imports raw materials and exports manufactured products, began to take shape in the 1930s. Its foundations, however, were laid between the late 1880s and the start of World War I. The development of industrial manufacturing prior to 1914 proceeded through three stages. The first, which began in the 1880s, was led by the cotton spinning industry which grew primarily through private investment. Government financing became important during the second stage, which began in the mid-1890s. Especially after the Sino-Japanese War and the indemnity, subsidies and government banks helped spur the development of heavy industry in fields like shipbuilding and steel. A third stage, which emerged between the Russo-Japanese War and World War I, was marked by somewhat more sophisticated technological change, especially in the electrical and chemical industries. Enterprises in these fields sometimes began as diversifications of earlier zaibatsu heavy industry. Others were initiated by younger entrepreneurs, who were early products of Japan's technical education. Among these new industries started just prior to World War I, bank loans became important. Zaibatsu funds and foreign technical licenses provided the basis for these industries.

The industries that developed during these stages all required imports of machinery and raw materials, and except for cotton spinning, which had a growing export trade, their products were generally sold in the home market. To balance these import needs Japan relied on exports of primary goods like raw silk, tea, and coal, though coal was declining as an export because of the high domestic demand for bunker coal. An early hint of how Meiji industrial development would affect the export structure came in the 1890s with the growth of the market in China for Japanese cotton yarn. However, the first wedge in the flow of manufactured exports beyond East Asia, a wedge that became an open floodgate in the 1930s, came with the advance of inexpensive exports, such as matches to India, or toys and ceramics to Europe. Many of these inexpensive items were traditional goods that cannot be called products of the industrial revolution described above. But they were the forerunners of a changing trade structure, for they provided trading companies with essential experience in developing marketing organizations overseas. Matches were especially noteworthy as one of Japan's first competitive manufactured products abroad. Between 1895 and 1914 they displaced Scandinavian and German competitors in East and South Asia, a success partly attributable to Mitsui Bussan, which established common trademarks and made large volume purchases from domestic producers to facilitate export sales.[57]

The N.Y.K. contributed to this changing industrial structure by reducing freight rates and by providing better access to markets and sources of raw materials. In his study of ocean freight rates, Yasuba concluded that "reductions may have occurred without the Japanese entries, but such reductions were certainly made earlier and most probably by larger margins because of these entries."[58] The most famous illustration of this trend was the rate on Indian raw cotton imports. The N.Y.K. provided the cotton spinners with a 5 Rs. rebate when it began competing with the P. & O. in 1893. After it entered the Bombay Conference in 1896 it not only kept the rebate but, except for 1901 and 1902, it gradually increased it so that by 1911 the rebate (8.7 Rs.) was higher than the net freight rate (8.3 Rs.), as the official rate was still 17 Rs.[59]

The verdict is more ambiguous on the European line. From 1896 to 1907 rates on general cargo fluctuated between 20s. and 45s. and from 1907 to 1912 between 40–50s. Rates probably would have gone higher without the N.Y.K.'s participation in the conference. More clearly, government intervention in certain strategic cases kept rates down. The government's "administrative guidance" over raw silk rates, for example, was permitted by the conference after the N.Y.K. began calling at Shanghai in 1902. And in 1912 the freight conference had to bow to the Japanese government and put a 5 percent limit on increases. In more general terms, the N.Y.K. saw the advantage to its European line in promoting the restructuring of Japan's industry. In a 1911 New Year's message, Kondō criticized banks for not investing enough in manufacturing enterprises. Behind his comment was the fact that 64 percent of the freight on the eastbound voyage from Europe in 1910 consisted of machinery and iron products used in Japanese manufacturing establishments. By 1913, supplies for chemical manufacturers had become plentiful enough on the eastbound run to warrant mention in the company business report, a reflection of the company's interest in one of the "new" industries of the 1910s.[60]

The N.Y.K.'s role in securing markets for cheaper exports was possibly decisive. In November 1903 Kondō claimed that the N.Y.K.'s competitive entry into the conference had driven down freight rates and led to greater export capacity for Japan's manufacturers.[61] Earlier in the year he had provided a more precise measure of the N.Y.K.'s contribution. The increasing number of vessels on the European line, he argued, had "naturally caused a competition of freight rates, bringing them down to such a point that this cheap carriage enables inferior grades of commodities to be transported. It is a fact that owing to the low rate between Japan and Europe, cheap articles can be sent from this side . . . If commodities can be carried to a distance of over ten thousand miles for something like ten *yen* [about 20s.] a ton, cheap grades of goods will be transported . . . [If] this carrying business were limited to British vessels alone, there can be no doubt that rates of freight would go up."[62] Rates were at their lowest point prior to World War I when Kondō made these remarks; but since the cheap exports were competitive even in 1911 when general cargo was at 50s., the brief period of extremely low rates just before the Russo-Japanese War must have led to a major boom for these items. As it was, even in 1911 inexpensive toys still went to London for only 35s. (about ¥17). Again, government intervention in 1912 on behalf of these exports backed up the rationale Kondō had given in his 1903 speech. In nearer locales the N.Y.K. could provide the same advantage to the small goods without government backing. The strength behind the 1911 entry into the Calcutta line was the company's large cash assests. By enabling it to incur annual deficits of more than ¥300,000 between 1912 and 1914, they helped win markets for inexpensive Japanese exports.

Yasuba agrees that the international competitiveness of Japanese shipping firms reduced freight rates, but he questions the "net welfare effect to the Japanese economy as a whole," because the firms were subsidized. Yasuba's skepticism about the value of subsidies stems from his assumption that shipping was not a terribly important industry "in this period from an economic viewpoint."[63] As opposed to this view, the foregoing argument that the N.Y.K. contributed to the changes in Japan's industrial structure is based on evidence from a variety of specific cases involving freights essential to that emerging structure rather than on extensive quantitative data. This evidence is more representative of the "tip of the iceberg" than of exceptional cases. If this is accepted, then the economic argument for subsidies gains weight (at least prior to 1912 and especially when the government controls which accompanied subsidies are included). This would apply even to India for the years 1896 to 1906, when the Bombay line received special subsidies. Yasuba rejects this view, arguing instead that only military considerations could justify subsidies.

Yasuba's view overlooks two essential features of Japanese business and industrial strategy: (1) the role played by organized business alliances in acquiring markets for Japanese goods; and (2) the government policy of designating strategic industries for special promotion, in order to produce a long-term net social benefit. Certainly there were more reasons for providing subsidies than simply lowering freight rates and supporting the military. Further analysis of this second point will be covered in the following section on Mitsubishi. The key point about freight is that the support subsidies provided business alliances helped to change the country's industrial structure. That in itself was an important social benefit.

In questioning the economic importance of shipping, Yasuba argued that textile machinery would have been a more logical candidate for subsidies because of the relative importance of the textile industry. Logic, on the contrary, would suggest that subsidies be given to enterprises that would otherwise have difficulty operating (the N.Y.K.'s regular transoceanic lines beyond Asia would qualify prior to 1912) rather than to industries already profitable. The textile industry did not require domestic machinery to be profitable. By 1900 it was doing quite well with imported machinery thanks in part to the close business relationship between Mitsui Bussan and the N.Y.K. (involving British exports) made possible by subsidies for the European line.

But shipping cannot be judged by the same standards as the textile industry. Shipping was part of the infrastructure, an essential link in the chain of organized business alliances. If we take, for example, the 1893 Bombay line alliance of the cotton spinners, the Japanese government, the Yokohama Specie Bank, Tata's Indian raw cotton exporting firm, Japanese importers like Mitsui Bussan, and the N.Y.K., it is hard to imagine this organized entrepreneurial system working for several decades with a foreign shipping company in place of the N.Y.K. Without the N.Y.K. there would have been a missing link in the chain. Yasuba rightly concludes that government tariff policy had a greater financial impact on the textile industry than did the freight rate. However, the point is not that shipping did a lot for one industry (textiles) but rather that it did a little for a lot of industries, especially those which integrated their business with Japanese overseas trading networks. Ranking industries by quantitative measures (percentage of labor force employed, for example) overlooks the interdependence of business firms, an interdependence essential to Japan's industrial strategy in gaining access to markets and securing raw materials.

The N.Y.K. probably performed more of a developmental function before World War I than since. For example, it is common to view the shipowner, with his membership in a collusive organization, the conference, as having a partially antagonistic relation to the shipper, who searches for the cheapest rates and the most reliable service. Indeed, N.Y.K. records contain extensive evidence on quarrels between the company and the cotton spinners over rates. Still, the presence of shippers in organized alliances suggests a view which differs from the emphasis on shipowner-shipper conflict. The alliances were effective when the N.Y.K., on behalf of the shipper (and needless to say, its own market share), undercut a conference or forced a conference of which it was a member either to lower rates or to moderate increases. At the same time, the alliances were not necessarily indicative of business strategies that Japanese firms have followed to the present. Today, for example, Japanese exporters of electrical goods often avoid exclusive ties with Japanese shipping companies in favor of the most competitive service available, no matter what the nationality. Prior to World War I, however, there were two distinctive features of business alliances that relate to the developmental function of shipping: (1) They were formed in times of crisis, as when the development of a crucial industry like textiles was hampered by foreign-controlled freight rates. (2) They were initiated on behalf of industries that required low rates to achieve competitive breakthroughs in overseas markets.

N.Y.K. investments began to increase rapidly around 1902 as the company started to build up its reserves. Between 1901 and 1903 they grew from 1.3 percent to 7.2 percent of assets. The pattern of company investments, the largest of which are shown in Table 58, can be divided into four periods. Prior to 1902, when company reserves were still quite small, the only investments were in various public bonds and a Hakodate waterworks project. Between 1902 and 1907, besides the forced investment in government securities to finance the war with Russia, three new trends emerged. One was the financing of a domestic infrastructure for shipping, primarily through port improvement projects in Nagasaki and Osaka, and on a smaller scale through railways in Hokkaido. Some of these investments, as in Kyushu railways and Nagasaki Port, were undertaken as integrated projects. Second, an initial investment was made in the Kanegafuchi Cotton Spinning Company, a firm related to company freight. Third, there was the large ¥1 million purchase of Industrial Bank debentures earmarked for the bank's loan to the Tayeh iron ore mines in China. In general the Industrial Bank was a principal promoter of the shipping industry in Japan. It provided large loans for the purchase of ships. Its connection with the N.Y.K., however, was quite atypical of this

TABLE 58 Principal N.Y.K. Investments in Bonds and Securities
(Unit: ¥1,000)

1902		1905	
Osaka Port Construction	500	Finance Ministry Securities	3,500
Finance Ministry Securities	300	Japan Industrial Bank	990
Hereditary Pension Bonds	285	National Treasury Bonds	856
Military Bonds	149	Osaka Port Construction	500
Consolidated Bonds	79	Hokkaido Railway	300
Total Investments	1,335	Total Investments	7,894
1908		**1913**	
Japan Industrial Bank	961	Class A Imperial Bonds	3,258
National Treasury Bonds	619	Japan Industrial Bank	1,475
Special 5% Interest Bonds	374	Otaru City	1,147
Imperial Bonds	283	Japan Hypothec Bank	1,022
Nagasaki Port Improvement	249	Korean Enterprise Bonds	1,000
Military Bonds	168	Chinese Railway Bonds	800
Naval Bonds	117	Fuji Gas Cotton Spinning	700
Korean Treasury Bonds	100	Kanegafuchi Cotton Spinning	469
Tōbu Railway	100	Hokkaido Development Bank	100
Kanegafuchi Cotton Spinning	61	Tōbu Railway	100
Total Investments	5,799	Total Investments	11,076

Source: NYK-EH.

Note: The holdings are bonds unless otherwise specified.

general pattern. As a large purchaser of the bank's debentures, the N.Y.K. was acting as the primary financial institution. The bank did not aid the N.Y.K. directly, but contributed to building an infrastructure that improved the business climate for the shipping industry.

Between 1907 and 1909, following the sale of government securities, few major new purchases were made and investments fell from ¥10.3 million to ¥5.8 million (16.8 to 11.6 percent of assets). Between 1909 and 1914 some new trends supplemented the patterns established prior to 1904. By 1914 investments had increased again to about 15 percent of assets. In one respect, the N.Y.K. was financing its own interests such as the infrastructure of ports or business partners in the cotton spinning industry. It is also clear that the company was buying bank debentures and public bonds simply because they were a good investment. Finally, the interest in Chinese railways, which began in 1913, seems unexpectedly late in view of the company's business and political activity in China up to 1912.

In addition to the entries listed in Table 58, important direct investments, such as Nisshin Kisen and Chōsen Yūsen, appear in the totals for each year. In several stages between 1907 and 1913 the N.Y.K. wrote down the book value of its Nisshin Kisen shares from the ¥50 par value to about ¥12 in 1913. This reduced the book value of the stock in the company's assets from the ¥3.5 million settled on in late 1907 to about ¥800,000. Why this was done is not clear, but in implementing it the N.Y.K. wrote it off as depreciation by claiming it as an expense.[64]

The N.Y.K. did not invest in the stock market but preferred the greater security of bonds. Based on the rate of interest of most of these bonds, around 5 percent, it probably earned between ¥300,000 and ¥500,000 annually. In the best traditions of "economic man" the company took particular care in making its investments. For example, in June 1910 the Hypothec Bank was offering subscriptions at ¥96 to 5 percent debentures with a par value of ¥100. The discount made the effective rate of interest 5.39 percent, and the N.Y.K. decided to buy ¥500,000 worth provided the subscription price did not go above ¥96. Apparently it did, for after recording its decision, the company did not buy Hypothec Bank debentures until 1911 and then only ¥200,000 worth.[65]

While the N.Y.K. continued to hold large amounts of public bonds, by 1914 over 60 percent of its investments were in industrial enterprises, public construction projects, or government development banks. Like its one-fifth owner, the Imperial House, the N.Y.K. was large enough to act like a long-term investment bank. In this sense it was fulfilling a national policy that made it more than just a shipping company. This multifunctional dimension can be related to the conservatism of its business strategy. All these investments were made with funds obligated to the company's reserves. Since there was a strong disinclination among N.Y.K. executives against increasing the capital stock, the only other means of furthering business expansion were the reserves, some of which were earmarked for line extensions. The company had over ¥10 million in cash assets to cover some of these reserves, but (assuming the continuance of the no-debt strategy) especially risky or large-scale ventures would also have entailed a cutback in the investments to finance the new business. Such cutbacks would have been hard to reconcile with the "national policy" functions of the company's investments.

THE N.Y.K. AND MITSUBISHI'S SECOND TRANSFORMATION. Performing national policy functions meant more than investing in an industrial infrastructure for the benefit of the nation in general and the shipping business in particular. It also involved coordinating investments with Mitsubishi. Although Mitsubishi had withdrawn from shipping in the 1880s and concentrated instead on mining, the N.Y.K.'s overseas expansion became the principal agent in transforming Mitsubishi into a full-fledged zaibatsu based primarily on heavy industry. On the whole, this process created a closer association between Mitsubishi and the N.Y.K. than had existed in the decade following the 1885 merger. Technology became the basis for this new relationship, but the two companies also coordinated some of their investment decisions, and personnel ties remained strong, though not as extensive as during the N.Y.K.'s first decade.

Prior to the mid-1890s Mitsubishi followed a generally conservative investment strategy in industrial manufacturing. This policy changed after the Sino-Japanese War, as shipbuilding became the new technological link between Mitsubishi and the N.Y.K. During his inspections of European shipyards in early 1896, Shōda became convinced that Mitsubishi's Nagasaki Shipyard could build 6,000 ton steamships for the N.Y.K.'s European line. At first, Shōda's initiative met with opposition from the former conservative policies. One faction within Mitsubishi, led by Yamawaki Masakatsu, the ex-manager of the Takashima Mine and the Nagasaki Shipyard, feared that the heavy capital requirements of shipbuilding would act as a drain on Mitsubishi's Kyushu enterprises, which were primarily in coal. The promise of the N.Y.K. as a market won the argument for Shōda in an epoch-making decision strongly supported by Iwasaki Yanosuke and Hisaya.[66] Also helpful for Mitsubishi's prospects was the Shipbuilding Encouragement Law of 1896, which gave subsidies for vessels over 700 tons, though this law was less decisive in promoting shipbuilding in Japan than the revised 1899 navigation law, which halved subsidies for foreign-built vessels.[67]

From the time the N.Y.K. purchased its first new ships for the European line in 1896 to World War I, the company's total orders for new ships came to 316,343 tons. Of this, 43.1 percent came from Mitsubishi's Nagasaki Shipyard, 35.6 percent from Britain, and 20.5 percent from the Kawasaki Dockyard in Kobe. Virtually all of this British tonnage, however, was purchased prior to the revision of the navigation law. After 1900 all large N.Y.K. ships assigned to overseas lines were built in Japan. The N.Y.K. also bought 41.8 percent of the 313,376 tons of ships constructed under the shipbuilding subsidies. Mitsubishi built 64.1 percent of that total, or 200,897 tons, and N.Y.K. purchases from Mitsubishi under the program came to 96,493 tons.[68]

The N.Y.K. was by far the largest customer for the Nagasaki Shipyard. The company's purchases enabled Mitsubishi to diversify its business structure after the Sino-Japanese War. Between 1896 and 1904 Mitsubishi's assets in mining grew from ¥6.6 million to ¥7.9 million, a modest 19 percent increase. During the same period shipbuilding assets jumped from ¥2.1 million to ¥7.5 million, or a 262 percent growth. Though shipbuilding had thus reached the level of mining by the Russo-Japanese War, its profit performance was uneven, especially between 1903 and 1910. Partly for that reason Mitsubishi made extensive new investments in mining. That

TABLE 59 Mitsubishi's Operating Profits, 1894–1913

Category	%
Shipbuilding	10.0
Coal mining	17.0
Metal mining	38.2
Business (trading)	11.5
Real estate	7.9
Banking	15.4
Total	100.0

Source: Hatade, *Mitsubishi,* pp. 70–71, 109–111. Unlike Table 38, these figures do not include income from stocks and bonds.

explains why, as Table 59 shows, Mitsubishi's mining operations brought in five and a half times as much profit as did shipbuilding in the two decades prior to World War I. By 1914 the main industrial assets and their percentage of total company assets were: (1) shipbuilding, ¥11.3 million (22.8); (2) metal mining, ¥9.9 million (19.9); and (3) coal mining, ¥9.3 million (18.7).[69] Mining, especially metal mining, also played a major role in Mitsubishi's diversification. In fact, the continuing profitability of mining suggests that the strategy of risk avoidance which Mitsubishi had followed at least since the early 1880s still lay behind the company's diversification. Furthermore, the contributions of shipbuilding and mining to new ventures were closely intertwined and often interdependent. Fundamentally, though, despite its uneven profit record prior to 1912, shipbuilding soon became the core of Mitsubishi's operations because it was the industry most closely related to the market demand that stimulated new business ventures in the acquisition of raw materials and diversification into more specialized manufacturing. Perhaps the most important development in this latter category was Mitsubishi's establishment of a second shipyard in Kobe in 1905. The Kobe yard concentrated on building engines and later became the basis for a separate electrical engineering division within the company.[70]

Since World War II Mitsubishi has emerged as Japan's largest zaibatsu (or "industrial group" in the postwar parlance), known especially for its development of heavy industry. Clearly, the foundation for its diversification into heavy industry was laid by the ship purchases of the N.Y.K. and other Japanese shipping companies prior to World War I. This strategic development provides another economic rationale for the government subsidies to shipping firms. Yasuba's argument that shipping was not important from an economic viewpoint but that shipbuilding subsidies may have been justified because of the "spread effects" of the shipbuilding industry is contradictory.[71] Without the shipping subsidies, which enabled the N.Y.K. to buy ships, it is unlikely that a large enough domestic market for ships would have emerged to prompt Mitsubishi to shift its earlier conservative investment strategy and commit as much as it did to shipbuilding.

Mitsubishi's diversification illustrates the function of shipping as a *trigger* industry. Increasing sales of bunker coal to shipping firms between 1885 and 1895 fueled the profits of the major zaibatsu. After 1896, as a market for the shipbuilding industry, shipping produced extensive mutual ties among industries, which, in a two-stage process, triggered a feedback mechanism leading to increased demand for shipping. The steel industry (and the shipbuilding industry which it supplied) depended on machinery imports from Europe, carried by the N.Y.K., and on iron ore from China. More ships then had to be built to handle this freight. Through this interdependence shipping generated major changes in Japan's industrial structure while enlarging its own business.[72]

The N.Y.K.'s purchasing of ships resulted less from an autonomous managerial decision in favor of Mitsubishi than from the protectionist nature of the 1899 shipping legislation. It did not mean that there would be a special Mitsubishi-N.Y.K. business relationship involving price preference in interfirm transactions. There were certainly rumors of such favoritism when Mitsubishi built its first ship for the N.Y.K., the 6,000 ton *Hitachi Maru*, in 1898 (Figure 14). Prior to 1900, buying from Mitsubishi instead of the British offered the N.Y.K. no direct economic advantage.

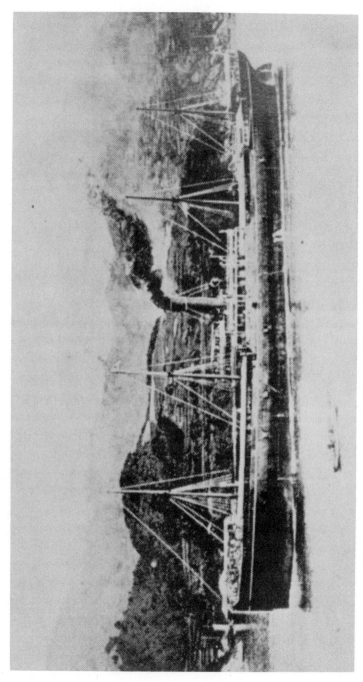

FIGURE 14 The *Hitachi Maru*

The *Hitachi Maru*, at 6,172 tons, was the first large ocean-going vessel constructed in Japan. Courtesy of the Internal & Public Relations Chamber, NYK LINE.

Since the cost of building in Japan was about 15 percent greater than in Britain, rumors circulated that Mitsubishi would bear the extra cost itself.[73] If this did transpire, it was less indicative of a special Mitsubishi–N.Y.K. connection than of a simple incentive to get the N.Y.K. to buy. Other evidence concerning the first ships built by Mitsubishi demonstrates that, while the N.Y.K. was willing to make some sacrifices to get Mitsubishi started, this did not constitute an institutional preference.

The *Hitachi Maru* has received great fame as Japan's first large ocean-going vessel. Less well known is the fact that the N.Y.K. actually ordered two new ships from Mitsubishi. Even though the materials for construction of the second ship had already been purchased, production delays on the *Hitachi Maru* forced the N.Y.K. to cancel the order for the other ship. Pressed by the urgency to upgrade its European line, in March 1898 the N.Y.K. board decided it was willing to go only so far for Mitsubishi:

> Transferring our order from Mitsubishi to Britain will be a damaging blow to Mitsubishi's reputation. Even more than that, it will be an extremely regrettable blow to Japan's manufacturing. Nevertheless, the delay in construction time for the second ship will have a great bearing on company interests. From the standpoint of company profits, in response to Mitsubishi's inquiry, at this time we must cancel the agreement for the second ship.[74]

In the end the N.Y.K. received the *Hitachi Maru* and the British ship, which replaced the second Mitsubishi ship, seven months behind its schedule for the original two ships. This delay entitled the N.Y.K. to claim ¥169,600 in compensation, but in view of Mitsubishi's lack of experience the N.Y.K. agreed to its request for a reduction and settled instead for half of the indemnity, or ¥84,800.[75]

In later years the N.Y.K. was less inclined to be tolerant, especially as Kawasaki developed into a competitor for Mitsubishi. In a similar construction delay in 1909 involving both shipbuilders, contracts entitled the N.Y.K. to ¥370,000 in compensation. In the course of the delays, however, improvements in ship speed and carrying capacity had been achieved. In response, the N.Y.K. cut

Mitsubishi's indemnity by 75 percent and Kawasaki's by 66 percent. The difference in the reductions was determined by a formula for the increased earning power built into the ships and not by any business preference for Mitsubishi.[76] Of course, the N.Y.K. board had to act in a legal, impartial manner. The evidence from its meetings does not preclude matters being adjusted behind the scenes. But the minutes do show that if preference for Mitsubishi existed, it was not conducted through normal channels.

Officials who entered the N.Y.K. around the time of World War I have also denied that any preference was given to Mitsubishi.[77] In the contracts for bunker coal, discussed earlier, there is no evidence of N.Y.K. favoritism to Mitsubishi or vice versa, and of course, in 1905 the N.Y.K. had rejected bids from Mitsubishi and other large companies in favor of independents. Also, though Mitsubishi became a major domestic supplier and exporter of coal, it transported the coal itself rather than by N.Y.K. ships. Primarily because of its coal business, it had changed its articles of incorporation in 1899 to allow for "ship transport" and in 1912 it set up a shipping section within its Business Department. Mitsui Bussan was an even larger carrier of coal than Mitsubishi, especially in the export field. In fact the shipping activity of these two firms expanded enough that Mitsui Bussan and Mitsubishi, respectively, had 15.6 and 6.2 percent of the tonnage constructed under the Navigation Encouragement Law. And between 1894 and 1904 Mitsubishi purchased 16.2 percent of the tonnage built by its own Nagasaki yard (compared to 69.6 percent for the N.Y.K.).[78]

Generally speaking Mitsubishi transported most of its own products bound for East Asian ports, while entrusting its European cargo to the N.Y.K. The European-bound cargo was less important, but it illustrates the supporting role performed by Mitsubishi. In 1902 it had established a representative office in Hankow, partly to sell bunker coal, but by 1908 it had begun dealing in Chinese commodities unrelated to its industrial enterprises. It soon turned its sales of sesame seeds, soybeans, and paulownia oil into exports to Europe, thereby expediting the feeder function along the Yangtze that the Nisshin Kisen performed for the N.Y.K.

The most important aspect of Mitsubishi's shipping centered around the development of the Yawata Iron and Steel Works. The N.Y.K. became involved in this more as a financial investor than as a business partner. In 1900 Mitsubishi secured a ten-year contract (subsequently renewed) to transport iron ore from the Tayeh mines near Hankow to Yawata (in Kyushu). The N.Y.K.'s ¥1 million purchase of Industrial Bank debentures in 1903, earmarked for the bank's loan to the Tayeh mines, was coordinated with Mitsubishi's development of this closely integrated business project. On the one hand, Mitsubishi used Yawata's steel in its ships; in 1896 Japan had had to import 95 percent of its steel, but by 1914 Yawata could meet 25 percent of domestic demand. On the other hand, Mitsubishi was supplying Yawata with both coke and iron ore, financed in part by the largest N.Y.K. investment outside of government securities. These investments in Yawata's development were strategic for Mitsubishi's broader diversification. The coke sales to Yawata served as a base for tar and glass production (and supplied the Mitsubishi subsidiary, Asahi Glass) and later chemical enterprises; by providing an entry into China for Mitsubishi, this integrated business network facilitated export sales of the Kirin Beer Brewery Company, a Mitsubishi subsidiary also financed by the N.Y.K. and of which Kondō Renpei became chairman in 1907.[79]

Surprisingly, despite the forward-looking quality of Mitsubishi's diversification, its shipping and trading activity probably helped to make the N.Y.K.'s strategy conservative prior to World War I. For example, if the N.Y.K. had tried to continue tramp operations within East Asia, it most probably would have ended up competing with some of Mitsubishi's services. Also, the essential differences between Mitsui and Mitsubishi structure help to explain why the N.Y.K. did not develop as extensive an overseas tramp service as Mitsui Bussan. Mitsui Bussan was a general trading company, handling all sorts of products and integrating its transactions across several continents. In contrast, Mitsubishi's trading was still limited primarily to mining products and the goods involved in the integrated Yawata project. Virtually all of this trade was conducted within East Asia. Any N.Y.K. development of overseas tramp services was not likely to provide direct benefit to Mitsubishi, whereas Mitsui's overseas tramps were essential to its functions as a general trading firm. From Mitsubishi's viewpoint, the N.Y.K.'s first priority was to remain financially healthy so that it could buy ships. At least prior to World War I, chartering ships in the manner of a tramp operator would not increase the sales of the Nagasaki Shipyard. Buying was essential.

The N.Y.K.'s relationship to Mitsubishi, then, was primarily as a purchaser of its ships and as an investor in its strategic projects. There were other ties, such as the Tokio Marine Insurance Company, but unlike Mitsui Bussan, Mitsubishi did not become a major shipper for the N.Y.K. As Nakagawa has pointed out, even in the Inter-War Years the N.Y.K. and the O.S.K. did not develop close ties with the shippers within the Mitsubishi and Sumitomo zaibatsu to which they were connected.[80] The N.Y.K., as we have noted, did not carry much of Mitsubishi's coal. And in other respects, Mitsubishi was still not a large export shipper. At least prior to World War I, however, the dependence of Mitsubishi's shipbuilding on imported machinery helped to increase N.Y.K. cargo on its eastbound European line.

It is difficult to say how much control Mitsubishi exerted over the N.Y.K. On the one hand, Mitsubishi, even with its machinery imports, was responsible for only a small portion of N.Y.K. freight. On the other hand, the business relationship had become closer between 1896 and 1914. N.Y.K. deposits in Mitsubishi's banking department had grown from about ¥1 million to over ¥2 million. These deposits illustrate the way some of the N.Y.K. subsidy flowed to Mitsubishi. Since subsidies became cash assets, in effect a portion of them went directly from the government to Mitsubishi's bank in the form of an N.Y.K. deposit, and from there to the Mitsubishi shipyard as payment for ships in what was essentially an interdepartmental transaction within the Mitsubishi zaibatsu. Yet, the most telling feature of these deposits for the Mitsubishi-N.Y.K. relationship was the fact that, though Mitsubishi usually received the largest share (on average, roughly 18 percent), it was not substantially favored over other banks. The Third Bank (that is, Yasuda) was often less than 2 percentage points behind, and in at least four business terms between 1900 and 1913 it held as much as or more than Mitsubishi. The Mitsui and Dai Ichi banks followed closely with around 12 percent each, while both the Fifteenth and Yokohama Specie banks often had 9 percent or more. If Mitsubishi had controlled the N.Y.K. the way most scholars assume, it would likely have received a larger share of N.Y.K. deposits. On the contrary, wide dispersal of its funds (partly to take advantage of higher interest rates) rather than exclusive ties to Mitsubishi was the dominant feature of N.Y.K. banking.

Other aspects of the Mitsubishi connection had weakened somewhat. In 1899 Mitsubishi, through Hisaya, owned 6.0 percent of the N.Y.K., or 26,447 shares. In 1900 Hisaya transferred 2,000 of these shares to Yanosuke, but the Iwasaki share remained constant until 1907 when they sold about one-third of their holdings. By 1910 Hisaya held 16,072 shares, or 3.7 percent, a figure he retained to World War I. Some of these shares may have been sold to Mitsubishi personnel, but non-Mitsubishi stockholders still had enough to prevent Mitsubishi from controlling the N.Y.K. simply through stock. Shōda, of course, had represented Mitsubishi on the N.Y.K. board until 1911, but when he left there was no longer a high-level Mitsubishi executive in the N.Y.K. However, the most important day-to-day executive in the N.Y.K. after 1911 was probably Hayashi Tamio (of McBain fame). He had succeeded Iwanaga as managing director in that year, and he just happened to be Iwasaki Hisaya's intimate friend.[81]

COMPANY ORGANIZATION AND DISSENT

LEADERSHIP, ADMINISTRATION, AND POLITICAL CONNECTIONS. N.Y.K. leadership between the mid-1890s and World War I remained remarkably stable, too stable some would say, for the company may have been somewhat slow in allowing fresh blood to rise to the top. Throughout the era of expansion the two major executives were Kondō Renpei, the president, and Katō Masayoshi, the vice-president, while Iwanaga Shōichi served as managing director from 1899 to 1911. Of these leaders, Kondō is usually singled out for criticism as being too conservative. While there is no positive evidence to upgrade Kondō's reputation, the criticism needs more accurate perspective. Though the company suffered leadership problems even before World War I (especially after 1911), the negative view of Kondō's presidency has been shaped too much by the problems of World War I and its aftermath. Had Kondō resigned in 1915, he might have left a hero with his successor being blamed for the problems of the 1920s. Moreover, while he did preside over an increasingly conservative business strategy between 1907 and 1914, that strategy seems to have been determined less by N.Y.K. management decisions than by government intervention, intensified competition, and the East Asian orientation of Mitsubishi's business.[82]

In the early years of his presidency, 1896–1904, Kondō instituted a vigorous and innovative policy that saw the company achieve equality with European competitors and develop the feeder strategy in East Asia. This strategy took shape during Kondō's trips to East Asia, Europe, and North America between 1899 and 1901. There is some doubt, however, whether Kondō himself was its principal architect. A younger N.Y.K. official, Masaki Shōzō, accompanied Kondō on his Western tour. According to a contemporary in the O.S.K., Masaki was the hardest working, most brilliant of N.Y.K. leaders. Masaki, in fact, had drawn up the plans for the three new overseas lines of 1896. Quite likely, then, his ideas contributed to Kondō's presentation of the feeder strategy when he returned to Japan. As Masaki's own career progressed, he remained a specialist in foreign lines, becoming head of the department so named in the 1911 administrative reform. Masaki never became a director, but if his influence as a second-echelon idea man remained strong, it may help explain the receptivity within the company to a concentration on liner strategy. It certainly matched his speciality.[83]

Recruitment is one aspect of Kondō's leadership often contrasted unfavorably with that of the more innovative Nakahashi of the

O.S.K. Nakahashi became famous for bringing many graduates of Tokyo Imperial University (Tōdai) into his firm. During its retrenchment campaign, however, the N.Y.K. had laid off many shore employees, and when business began to expand rapidly between 1912 and 1914 the company found itself short of personnel. The problem was rectified somewhat in 1913 when an effort was launched to recruit Tōdai graduates. One of the Tōdai graduates entering the company in 1913 was Terai Hisanobu, a future president and one of the most intellectually brilliant executives in N.Y.K. history.[84]

Finally, a few additional generalizations can be made about Kondō. First, between 1898 and 1902 he was out of the country about half the time, leaving actual management to Katō and, increasingly, Iwanaga. Second, following the Russo-Japanese War he became more and more of an elder statesman of the business world and a sort of company ambassador to the political world. Both of these points are related to a third attribute—his distance from the stockholders and the lower ranks of the company, namely, the seamen. On this last point, especially with regard to stockholders, he provoked dissent even before World War I through his insistence that management maintain exclusive control over the company's burgeoning reserves.[85]

Vice-President Katō seems to have performed three principal functions for the N.Y.K. (1) He took charge of long-range planning after the Russo-Japanese War, heading the committee that planned the postwar retrenchment and the orientation toward liner strategy. Though this committee was formed to deal with a specific crisis and was only temporary in nature, it was a precedent for the kind of planning staff that began to play a major role in later Japanese corporate history. In 1915 the N.Y.K. institutionalized it by creating a separate Business Research Chamber (Gyōmu Chōsa) whose first head was Masaki Shōzō. (2) Katō served as a liaison with early subsidiaries like the Hunan Steamship Company. (3) Most importantly, he was the company's main contact with the government and political parties.

Of all N.Y.K. officials it is easiest to find favorable comments about Managing Director Iwanaga. From 1899 to 1911 he ran the daily management of the company, which meant frequent contact with business partners and competitors. Many of these were foreigners, and his fluent English eased his relations with them. He is credited with a great many achievements: visiting Southeast Asia and planning the Bombay line in the early 1890s, overseeing troop transport during the Sino-Japanese War, examining prospects for a New York line in 1901, and generally acting as the company's principal international negotiator. It was Iwanaga who signed the contract with James Hill's Great Northern Railway in 1896; and he later settled disputes with the North German Lloyd in 1907 and Butterfield & Swire in 1909. The latter company complimented him on being "keen and well posted." His active role in the early Nisshin Kisen may be related to a report that he became "a wealthy man" and did "well for himself in engineering the combination" (that is, Nisshin Kisen).[86]

Overseas, N.Y.K. management was affected by the 1909 subsidy law, which prohibited employment of non-Japanese managers and clerks in overseas branches without government consent. The company had long relied on the services of T. H. James, who was London branch head from 1897 to April 1910. He was replaced by Negishi Renjirō, who stayed in the post until December 1911, when he returned to Japan to become a company director.

The company's major administrative change prior to the war came in 1911 and had three features: (1) a shift in the composition of the board from a mix of external and internal directors to a purely internal cast; (2) divided responsibility among an increased number of managing directors; and (3) a restructuring of second-echelon management. This change is important because of the adverse effect which departures from both the board and management had on subsequent administration.

In the board, there had been a gradual attrition of some of the outside directors prior to 1911. Nakamigawa, Mitsui's representative, had died in 1901, and Shibusawa resigned in 1909. In 1911 all nonexecutive members of the board resigned in a perhaps well-intentioned but overdue attempt to allow younger officers to run the company. Shōda Heigorō was certainly the most important board member who left in 1911. His opinions are quoted frequently in the minutes of the board meetings, and he seems to have acted as a counterweight to Kondō in helping to shape a consensus on policy. The failure to replace him with a top-level Mitsubishi official seems to have lessened coördination after 1911, though there is no evidence of a serious conflict in policy with Mitsubishi before the war, for the N.Y.K. undertook its heaviest ship purchasing between 1912 and 1914.

Shōda's departure would have been less of a blow if it had not been for the simultaneous resignation of Iwanaga for health reasons. In one sweep the N.Y.K. had lost its leading outside director and its most important internal manager. Iwanaga was considered the "central pillar" (*daibokubashira*) of the N.Y.K. and the brains behind Kondō (*bakuryōchō*). As managing director he had concurrently served as head of the company's Freight Department, the key post for overseas lines. For a long time following his resignation, it is said, there was a stagnant atmosphere within the company.[87] Without Shōda to balance him and without Iwanaga to run the company, Kondō seems to have become a more authoritarian president. He had already, of course, become remote from day-to-day administration. Since Iwanaga's replacements lacked his long experience, Kondō's decisions seemed to weigh more ponderously upon the company, tending to make Kondō himself unpopular.

In the long run this situation might have corrected itself, for Hayashi Tamio, who became head of the Business Division, and replaced Iwanaga as managing director, was by all accounts a good executive, and it is said he soon surpassed Kondō in popularity among company staff. However, even though Hayashi had served as head of the strategic Shanghai branch from 1900 to 1906, he had had a rather short tenure in the head office as Passenger Department head prior to 1911. Furthermore, in 1911 he was one of three new managing directors, and, although he had the most important function, he was ranked third in seniority. The other two were Suda Toshinobu, a technical specialist who took charge of the Ship Administration division, and Hori Tōru, a former secretary to the board who became head of the General Affairs Division.[88]

During its early expansion the N.Y.K. had replaced the two-division- five-section structure shown in Figure 7 with six departments. This change of 1897, shown in Figure 15, allowed Kondō and Katō, who had earlier been responsible for the two divisions, more time for planning. Following Iwanaga's resignation in 1911, management authority was dispersed among the three new managing directors, who each supervised his own division, under which there were eight departments.[89]

Partly because of their longevity in office, N.Y.K. leaders developed considerable clout in the political world. Kondō, Katō, and Iwanaga all participated in the Yūrakukai, an organization of businessmen designed to coordinate policy and influence government legislation. Earlier, in 1895, Kondō, Shibusawa, Mitsubishi's Toyokawa Ryōhei, and others had established the *Tōyō keizai shinpō* (The Oriental Economist), a business journal that competed with the *Tokyo keizai zasshi*. The N.Y.K. subsidized the new journal with a ¥35 a month advertisement.[90] Also, when conflict with the government arose, Kondō was able to see the minister of communications, or in some cases to go over his head. However, it was always Katō who was first dispatched to lobby with the government. Katō had ties with Katsura Tarō, prime minister for approximately seven of the years from 1901 to 1913. Following his retirement as N.Y.K. vice-president in 1915, Katō was also a frequent visitor to the retreat of Yamagata Aritomo, the most influential elder statesman of the time.[91] Never were Katō's contacts in greater demand than during the 1909 subsidy law controversy.

Briefly, the political situation in 1909 was as follows. The government of Prime Minister Katsura had brought in the Ocean Lines Subsidy Bill, described in the beginning of this chapter, which would cut aid to the N.Y.K. The Seiyūkai, which opposed the government, held half the seats in the Diet and could influence government legislation. The Seiyūkai executive was inclined to help the N.Y.K. Unfortunately for the company, a strong minority faction

FIGURE 15 N.Y.K. Executive Structure, 1897 and 1911

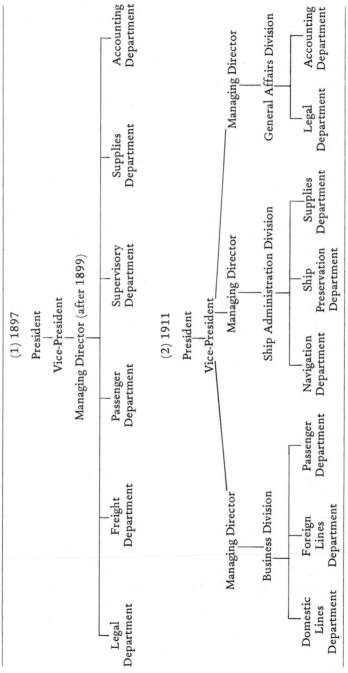

Source: NYK 70 nenshi, pp. 631–632.

within the Seiyūkai favored an even more stringent law than the government's bill and tended to align on this issue with antisubsidy parties in the Diet.[92] Nevertheless, the N.Y.K. decided the Seiyūkai executive was movable, provided it had some lubrication.

In mid-February 1909, after having publicly stated that the new law would force the N.Y.K. to abandon its European line, Katō met with Gotō Shinpei, minister of communications, and Terauchi Masatake, army minister. He reported on the meeting to the N.Y.K. board:

> Gotō and Terauchi stated that it would be difficult for the government to present a revised bill to the Diet, but if company action prompted the Diet to adopt amendments, the government would then disclose that its opinion was the same [as that of the Diet]. Based on these comments, once we open negotiations with the Seiyūkai's executive . . . we can anticipate some expense. We must urgently put into motion some procedure to add amendments to the draft bill.[93]

Several days later Katō met with Motoda Hajime, a leading Seiyūkai executive, who informed him that the N.Y.K.'s only option was to appease the opponents of the subsidy within the Seiyūkai. Katō's subsequent advice to the board was recorded as follows:

> Katō stated that "Motoda did not say how much money would be necessary to handle this matter, but inferring from points made in the conversation I assume that the Seiyūkai executive is hoping for twice the amount of cash that the company has been planning to give." It goes without saying that as a company we do not want to create a bad example of political corruption or engage in secret manipulations that would arouse public criticism . . . [However, calculations show that] if our amendments pass, we can achieve an increase of about ¥500,000 a year over the original bill. When we consider the fact that the outcome of these amendments will not only have an enormous impact on the interests of our stockholders but will also greatly shape the destiny of the country's shipping industry, there is no way that we can sit passively looking on. There will be no hope for the continued development of shipping under the new law. To prevent that situation from occurring, no matter how much public criticism is aroused, the company must decisively resolve to execute a procedure for passing our amendments. Our

decision is to prepare a successful outcome by arranging for the necessary expense, or twice the amount of cash we anticipated in our previous meeting.[94]

Such iron resolution, however, did not move the unbending opposition of the Seiyūkai's minority faction. There was, moreover, increasing criticism of the N.Y.K. for trying to "buy up" this faction. In the end, the most the Seiyūkai's Business Committee could offer were the two amendments limiting the term of the law to five years and reducing slightly the minister's powers.[95] It is unclear whether N.Y.K. funds had failed to influence the Seiyūkai executive or whether they succeeded in preventing the minority opponents from forcing a tougher law on the executive.

Perhaps it was frustration with this "informal" means of influence that prompted the N.Y.K. to establish a more personal connection with the Seiyūkai in 1914 as the Panama line and renewal of the 1909 law came up for debate. Early in 1914 newspapers circulated reports that the N.Y.K. had decided to appoint Okazaki Kunisuke, a Seiyūkai leader, as its vice-president. Okazaki was a close friend of Hara Kei, the powerful head of the Seiyūkai, which in 1914 held 55 percent of the seats in the Diet. Opposed to the Seiyūkai was the newly formed Dōshikai, which wanted to slash the subsidy budget. The potential benefits from the Okazaki appointment were obvious, but its partisan nature invited risk also and appalled many of the company's stockholders. In the May 1914 General Meeting, opposition to Okazaki's appointment focused on several points. First, it was unseemly for the N.Y.K. to imitate the South Manchurian Railway and Tōyō Kisen, which had Seiyūkai men as vice-presidents. Second, the company's future would be in jeopardy if a party opposed to the Seiyūkai should come to power and react accordingly against the N.Y.K. Third, subsidies were given by the state. They should not be used to reward political parties. There was concern that management bonuses, already over ¥70,000 a term, would be increased for Okazaki and that the company would thereby be indirectly funding the Seiyūkai.

When Kondō finally had a chance to respond to the criticism, he simply denied that Okazaki was going to enter the company, though contemporary reports suggest that the denial was forced by the opposition and that previously the company had at least made an informal decision to appoint Okazaki.[96]

This political imbroglio provides a fitting contrast with the O.S.K. While the N.Y.K.'s internal leadership was withering and casting about to bring a politician *into* the company, Nakahashi Tokugorō *left* the O.S.K. presidency in 1914 to enter the Seiyūkai. He did so with the comfort of a completed mission, having groomed capable successors *within* the O.S.K.

STOCKHOLDERS, RESERVES, AND BUSINESS DECISIONS. A final reason why the N.Y.K. did not pursue a more flexible policy of expansion between 1907 and 1914 lies with a problem that had been with the company from its inception—the restlessness of its stockholders. Management's inability to handle its internal finances in a way compatible with both its own business plans and the wishes of the stockholders led to a paralysis in decision-making by 1914. By hoarding the company's wealth in reserves, management was inciting the stockholders to revolt.

Table 60 shows the leading stockholders in 1906 and 1913. Four of the top five holders in 1899 (see Table 36) were still in the top six in 1906. Between 1899 and 1913 the principal change in stockholding was less the composition of the main holders than the increasing dispersal of stock. Mitsubishi's sale of one-third of its shares in 1907 was the main impetus for this. The number of holders jumped from 3,530 in October 1906 to 4,618 in March 1908. Also, in 1913 the number of holders possessing 2,000 or more shares (15) was the same as in 1899. But in 1913 these 15 held only 139,126 shares, or 31.6 percent, compared to 38.7 percent in 1899.

The main effect of this dispersal was to make the medium-to-large holder, principally the stockbrokers, more influential. These brokers, though not a coordinated group, had similar interests. Their main concerns were the share price and the dividend. For them the N.Y.K. was an attractive investment, for its share price was consistently high(Table 61), which, between 1912 and 1914,

TABLE 60 Leading N.Y.K. Stockholders, 1906 and 1913
          (October)

1906			1913		
	No. of Shares	%		No. of Shares	%
1. Imperial Household Ministry	80,550	18.3	1. Imperial Household Ministry	80,550	18.3
2. Iwasaki Hisaya	24,947	5.7	2. Iwasaki Hisaya	16,072	3.7
3. Murai Kichibei	10,000	2.3	3. Mitsui Bank	5,112	1.2
4. Fukushima Namizō	6,680	1.5	4. Murai Kichibei	5,000	1.1
5. Maeda Toshitame	5,215	1.2	5. Tsukamoto Sadauemon	4,000	0.9
6. Mitsui Bank	5,112	1.2	6. Chiba Kamenosuke	3,500	0.8

Source: NYK-KNS.

never fell below double the par value of ¥50. By contrast, the
O.S.K. stock was only marginally above par, and Tōyō Kisen's
rarely even reached par.

The N.Y.K. had a special place in the stock market beyond being the most attractive investment among shipping firms. Prior to
World War I the Japanese stock market was still underdeveloped,
partly because many of the largest enterprises were zaibatsu owned.
They were not joint-stock companies and therefore had no shares
that could be traded on the exchange. Also, the nationalization of
the railways in 1906 removed from the stock market a large number of big firms that had previously attracted money. In short,
there were few firms listed on the stock exchange which combined the attributes of large size, growth, secure assets, and high
share prices. Firms that possessed these attributes—the N.Y.K. and
Kanegafuchi Spinning were perhaps the most famous—attracted an
enormous amount of speculative investment.[97]

The clearest example among N.Y.K. stockholders of a speculator
was Fukushima Namizō. This Tokyo broker held shares throughout the period shown in Table 61, but the quantity he held fluctuated in almost exact proportion to the stock price. In 1902 he had
6,830 shares; but by late 1905, during a postwar slump, he had cut

TABLE 61 N.Y.K. Stock Prices, 1894–1914

Year	High	Low
1894	80.7	51.3
1895	117.0	73.6
1896	124.5	70.3
1897	81.3	50.0
1898	58.8	45.1
1899	76.4	57.3
1900	71.2	55.5
1901	76.1	60.3
1902	84.1	76.1
1903	86.1	77.7
1904	83.2	58.7
1905	102.7	76.2
1906	133.9	94.2
1907	154.6	77.0
1908	86.4	75.5
1909	85.9	72.7
1910	106.9	84.3
1911	111.9	92.1
1912	125.2	104.1
1913	121.8	102.5
1914	121.9	102.9

Source: Okaniwa, p. 96.

his holdings to 880. He had 6,680 in late 1906, 330 in 1909, and 4,380 in 1912.

The N.Y.K.'s role as a leading magnet for speculative funds ensured that important decisions concerning its internal finances would be given full public attention. In fact, between 1912 and 1919, few issues in the financial world excited such controversy— another reason why the success of N.Y.K. management often hinged on how well it could handle the company's stockholders and why stockholders caused more disruption in the N.Y.K. than in other companies. Furthermore, other stockholders of lesser means but greater commitment caused management as much trouble as the speculators and stockbrokers. Some of these people could be called the idle rich, for they were permanent investors who lived off the N.Y.K. dividend.[98] They allied with other groups, dependent mainly on the N.Y.K. dividend, and they were the most vocal opponents of management, sometimes rationalizing their stand in idealistic tones.

Stockholder protest went through various stages. In the late 1890s it was a matter of avoiding "poverty." In 1897, when there had been no dividend, they haggled over procedural questions, trying to get management to promise a guaranteed dividend. This led to the Dividend Equalization Reserve. In 1898, when profits had improved somewhat, stockholders became too impatient to wait for a government decision on subsidies. Their demand for more than a mere 8 percent dividend was rejected by Mitsubishi's Toyokawa Ryōhei, who warned that while the government was considering the matter of the specified line subsidy it was dangerous for the stockholders of the company to appear too overly concerned with profits and dividends. It would be expedient, he said, if they appeared more concerned with the national interest. If the company seemed already to enjoy a healthy profitable situation, the government might be less inclined to provide a large subsidy.[99]

When the first stage of plenty arrived in 1900, more organized agitation arose to protect the interest of the small holder. This movement crystallized in 1900 and 1901 over the issue of choosing company auditors. A "reform faction" wanted to appoint an auditor as representative of "smaller" holders. The faction was led by Ozaki Saburō, a prominent member of the House of Peers, whose 1,030 shares made him the thirty-third largest holder, and Kishimoto Tatsuo, an ex-judge with 320 shares. Kishimoto was the faction's candidate for auditor. In putting forward his name the faction attacked the large holders like Mitsubishi, Mitsui, and especially the Imperial Household Ministry. In 1895 the Imperial Household Ministry had nominated the two auditors, Abe Taizō of Mitsubishi's Meiji Life Insurance Company and Arishima Takeo, a former director of customs in Yokohama. The representative of the ministry to the N.Y.K. in 1895 had been Iida Son, director of the Bureau of Imperial Property. In 1900 management's candidate for auditor was Iida himself, who was expected to watch over the interests of the Imperial House within the company. The reformists attacked the voting system, which, with the large stockholdings of Mitsubishi and the Imperial House, made every outcome inevitable. In more idealistic tones they called for a decision on the auditor to be reached by consensus (*manjō no dōi*).

The reformists saw themselves as idealists opposed to incompetent bureaucrats. One of their members, Tsunaga Kiyoshi, launched a strident personal attack on Watanabe Senshū, the Imperial House official who was the nominal holder of the N.Y.K. stock and who had been asked to nominate the auditor. "What business should our company have with an objectionable blockhead like Watanabe?" Tsunaga asked. "If we have to accept some official appointed from the Imperial Household Ministry, he won't be able to do anything for us. I say this with no disrespect for the Emperor. I am merely giving my opinion of superannuated officials."[100] Needless to say, the reformists lost.

The other issue, arising around 1900 and more directly related to the increasing plenty, was the use of N.Y.K. reserves. Although reserves in 1901 stood at only ¥6.2 million, presenting a still modest reserve-capital stock ratio of 0.34, they had doubled since mid-1899. Critics began calling on management to provide larger dividends instead of hoarding its money. The *Mainichi shinbun* complained that "the big shipping company, while clutching at large subsidies from the State and sucking the blood of the people, shows its indifference to the constricted state of the money-market by keeping a reserve of ten millions of *yen* distributed among various banks, and . . . if socialism ever becomes a power in Japan, the Nippon Yusen Kaisha will be the first victim of its fury."[101]

The N.Y.K. had three choices in the matter of reserves. It could increase dividends as demanded. It could use the funds for immediate business expansion. Some large stockholders (unnamed) who preferred this option specifically advocated using the reserves to buy the China Merchants S.N. Company.[102] The third option, which the company chose, was to retain the reserves for future use as a bulwark against recessions.

Although the stockholders were quiet throughout the remainder of the decade, the terms of the 1909 subsidy law did not augur well for peaceful General Meetings in the future. The law limited the period of eligibility during which a ship could receive subsidies to fifteen years. This presented the N.Y.K. with a potential problem for ship financing. Because no such limitation had existed for the designated line subsidies, since 1901 the N.Y.K. had used a system of depreciating, or redeeming the cost of, its ships over a period of twenty-five years. In fifteen years, however, they could only write off 60 percent of ship value, and the law would not allow ships to be sold to foreigners until three years after their subsidies had expired. Normally the N.Y.K. would sell ships no longer eligible for subsidies, thereby maintaining a fleet that would earn the benefits of both subsidies and depreciation.[103] After 1909, to avoid having old ships ineligible for subsidies, the N.Y.K. would have to upgrade its fleet more quickly. This required putting additional funds into reserves to prepare for more frequent ship purchases. Since these new reserves were taken out of profit, less was available for the dividend. This was the main reason the company cut its dividend from the 12 percent it had maintained through the post-Russo-Japanese War recession to 10 percent in 1910. To the stockholders' chagrin, the dividend was kept at 10 percent even through the years of plenty from 1912 to 1914.

The decision to limit the dividend, plus several trends that began in 1912, namely, renewed profits, large ship purchasing, and the prospects for the Panama Canal line, heightened debate about how the company would use its reserves. All these new trends came into the limelight just after Iwanaga's resignation. They portended a period of drift, as Kondō seemed to be losing some control over the company's destiny. Beginning in 1912, promanagement stockholders proved incapable of rushing through voice votes and preventing long rambling questions about company finances. In 1912 and 1913 most of these questions focused on how the company would finance its new ships or whether it would call for a capital stock increase to open the Panama line. Kondō insisted that new ships would all be paid for from company earnings and that the Panama line would not start until subsidies had been approved.

In the meantime, reserves were escalating rapidly. Between 1906 and 1910 they grew by 37.2 percent, between 1910 and 1914 by 81 percent. The ratio of reserves to capital stock, 0.34 in 1901, grew to 0.78 in 1906, 1.07 in 1910, and 1.93 by 1914! For company politics this increasing ratio was like the ticking of a time bomb. The stockholders wanted to see the ratio reversed by increasing the company's capital stock. After all, they could only receive dividends from the capital stock. But this sole portion of company funds from which they drew was rapidly decreasing relative to the burgeoning reserves. Management favored increasing reserves, on the other hand, because (1) no dividends were paid from them, (2) it had exclusive control over them, and (3) it feared more expensive times ahead.

Since reserves are not money but "expressions of obligation," the company could *renege* on these obligations and use the reserves for something other than their stated purpose. This is precisely what the stockholders wanted. As early as 1912 there had been demands that the company increase its capital stock not simply by inviting new funds but by converting its reserves into new shares, in short, by issuing *free* shares (that is, stock dividends) to its existing stockholders. A precedent for this had already been set by several banks, including the Bank of Japan.[104] Anticipation of these stock dividends also helped to keep the N.Y.K. stock price above ¥100 after 1912.

These soaring expectations can be blamed in part on Kondō. Had he been less hesitant in the use of the reserves by providing, over the course of the years, a little extra for both dividends and business expansion, he might have lessened the confrontation that existed by 1914. Business decisions would also have been subject to less of a dilemma. The major point here is that stockholder expectations created obstacles for business decisions and thwarted potential expansion between 1912 and 1914.

Every company option was beset by dilemmas. If it decided to finance expansion, such as the Panama line, simply out of reserves (which it could have done financially), stockholders who wanted the reserves transferred to stock dividends would be alienated. For internal political reasons it could not finance expansion through a capital stock increase without simultaneously converting a large portion of the reserves into stock dividends. But management was opposed both to increasing the capital stock and to losing its exclusive control over the reserves. One reason for this was that the company's thirty-year business term was due to expire in 1915. Its renewal would require negotiation with the government; and, because it was unsure of government intentions, management wanted to maintain control until the renewal.[105] Finally, if the company gambled on a capital stock increase, with its accompanying stock dividends drawn from reserves, and then found in 1915 that its subsidy was to be reduced, it would have lost its financial edge, an edge which management in the person of Kondō regarded as essential for expanding its present services.

To the stockholders, such hesitancy seemed unjustifiable in the face of continuing large profits. Two additional events in 1914 exacerbated this stockholder discontent. In March the O.S.K. increased its authorized capital stock to ¥24.75 million (compared to the N.Y.K.'s ¥22 million). Then, while the N.Y.K. dividend was kept at 10 percent, executive bonuses, which for the previous few years had been in the range of ¥60,000 to ¥70,000 a term, were suddenly increased to ¥110,000.[106]

On the eve of World War I the N.Y.K. had become a tinderbox ready to be lit by the fires of plenty. Kondō, with large expectations of his own, still seemed to be above the fray. In a 1914 New Year's article he wrote "In any event . . . it is absolutely certain that not only in the shipping world but in all departments of human activity this year will be a memorable one, adverse or favourable."[107]

Conclusion

PRINCIPAL THEMES

This study has been concerned with three principal themes: expansion, strategy, and finance. With the exception of the 1880 to 1885 period, when Mitsubishi undertook to withdraw from shipping, expansion—in the sense of development of overseas lines and services—was the constant goal of management throughout the years from 1870 to 1914. Even after 1907, when the N.Y.K.'s expansionist thrust slowed, its conservatism was rationalized as financial preparation for greater expansion (new lines and bigger ships) in the future.

Strategy had two dimensions. One was innovative. The business alliances centered around the early Bombay line, the integrated goals based on shipbuilding which inspired Shōda Heigorō to plan the European line, and the skillful negotiating with which the N.Y.K. entered the freight conferences were all innovations that led to changes in Japan's industrial structure and a strengthening of its overseas trade. A second dimension of strategy, however, was passive in that management often allowed outside forces to shape its direction. Shipping firms were frequently at the mercy of government policy changes or dependent on the undeveloped state of the economy. The strategic response to these forces, as illustrated by Mitsubishi in the 1880s, was sometimes a departure from the goal of overseas expansion.

Finance was in one sense the means of implementing the goal of expansion; hence the emphasis on government subsidies. In a broader institutional context, however, finance encompassed a variety of different issues. Stockholder interests worked to shape the company's internal structure. Policy toward reserves was a measure of managerial goals, as company leaders sought to consolidate funds to lessen future risk. And investment policies were a gauge of company interests outside shipping, as illustrated by Mitsubishi's shift toward land and the N.Y.K.'s assumption of national policy functions through its investments.

The interrelationship of these themes makes it apparent that only the innovative business strategies and the subsidies contributed directly to expansion. Strategies forced on the company and institutional trends relating to internal finance often militated against it. Management, therefore, could not easily maintain consistent strategies in pursuit of expansion. For this reason this study has focused on how conflict among these institutional and economic forces shaped company strategy.

When the N.Y.K. did expand into overseas lines and, in certain cases, supplant foreign competition, there were many reasons for its success, the most important of which were: (1) Business alliances, in which the N.Y.K. participated and which emerged from Japan's growing trading strength and changing industrial structure, provided the company with competitive advantages on crucial lines. (2) Subsidies, the result of both government industrial policy and the efficacy of a war machine that could demand heavy indemnities, furnished both financial strength and a diplomatic weapon. (3) The timing of entry into overseas lines meant that the N.Y.K. was the exclusive Japanese participant with a monopoly of government favor, which gave the company extra bargaining clout with foreigners. (4) Lower costs, which enabled the N.Y.K. to charge competitive freight rates, reflected both the lower wages in Japan and other factors like subsidies and business alliances that made it possible for customers to tolerate the company's older and slower ships in its early years.

This study has also examined several institutional issues both for their own sake and for their connection with the themes of expansion, strategy, and finance. The most important of these have been zaibatsu evolution, as seen in the relations between Mitsubishi and the N.Y.K.; the role of the government, particularly with regard to subsidies; and the internal dynamics of the N.Y.K. The remainder of this conclusion, where possible, will use a comparative perspective to treat these institutional issues and the reasons for N.Y.K. success.

THE MITSUBISHI ZAIBATSU, THE GOVERNMENT, AND THE N.Y.K.

Until the mid-1960s, Western scholarship on Japanese business of the Meiji period was heavily influenced by interpretations that Japanese scholars had formulated before World War II. These views attributed the dynamism of Japanese business to the initiatives of a government manned by samurai and the leadership qualities of patriotic entrepreneurs. In the 1960s Kozo Yamamura set out to overhaul these interpretations. He argued that the entrepreneurs themselves, not government policy, provided the impetus for industrial growth and that Meiji business leaders were motivated more by profit incentives than by a nationalism derived in part from Japan's late development.

Japanese scholarship has greatly changed, however, since Yamamura conducted his research. Emphasis has shifted away from Japan as a late developer and from the *origins* of the zaibatsu to their internal institutional growth, resulting in more studies of the transition from early to late Meiji and less attention to the Restoration period. For example, Kobayashi Masaaki has described how Mitsubishi originally integrated the business of the Takashima Mine into the functions of its main shipping enterprise but then moved toward mining as its principal activity. In studies of zaibatsu finance, Yasuoka Shigeaki has attributed the hesitancy of the zaibatsu to diversify into industrial manufacturing to the concern of their leaders with secure profits. More so than Yasuoka, Morikawa Hidemasa has stressed the initiative of salaried managers in

the diversification of the zaibatsu. Like Yamamura's emphasis, this
downplays the role of the government in zaibatsu formation. These
scholars have confirmed many of Yamamura's revisions, but in
their discussion of business growth they have focused more on
institutional change and strategy than on general questions of
motivation or social origins.

In addition, there is reason for skepticism about Yamamura's
primary emphasis on the initiatives of private entrepreneurs, at
least in the shipping industry. Since this study has concentrated on
internal company finance, the most important feature to be noted
is the greater use of subsidies for shipping than for other industries.
Clearly, subsidies—a type of government initiative—were crucial to
the formation of a strong shipping company in Japan.

Though Mitsubishi could have operated profitably without subsidies between 1879 and 1882, its experience shows that subsidies
had to be closely supervised by government with a consistent policy
to have their desired effect. During these profitable years Mitsubishi concentrated on preserving its monopoly of long-distance
transport among Japanese shipowners rather than improving its
shipping services. The fact that costs in the shipping industry during this period had not yet begun to decline encouraged Mitsubishi
to maximize its profits on a short-term basis. By accumulating
funds rapidly it diversified its business options, one of which was
to withdraw from shipping, taking a considerable fortune with it.
Finally, subsidies received in these years in effect financed not just
shipping but also Mitsubishi's purchase of mines.

Government policy toward shipping differed from that towards
most other industries. In the 1870s the government tried to promote new industries through its own investment and management
but, finding this too costly, decided to sell these enterprises. On
the other hand, though it heavily subsidized Mitsubishi in the
1870s, it did not exercise strict control. Closer supervision over
shipping began in the 1880s. This coincided with the major turning point in the evolution of the zaibatsu, namely, the government's
sale of mines and factories to private concerns in the mid-1880s—
the very time that Mitsubishi was withdrawing from shipping. In

this sense the government's supervision of shipping was the reverse of its attitude toward the emerging business combines which came to be known as zaibatsu. The 1880s saw a significant bifurcation in the strategic and financial purposes of the government's control over industry. It sought to control what was strategic (especially in the military sense) even if it was expensive; but it was willing to sell nonstrategic industries.

Whereas Yamamura underestimated the government's role in shipping, others have overemphasized it in the zaibatsu's case. Western historiography on the sale of government enterprises has focused more on the 1880 decision to sell than on the precise government-zaibatsu relationship in its aftermath. Characterizations of this relationship tend to be too general. Chalmers Johnson argues that "Meiji Japan began to shift away from state entrepreneurship to collaboration with privately owned enterprises, favoring those enterprises that were capable of rapidly adopting new technologies and that were committed to the national goals of economic development and military strength. From this shift developed the collaborative relationship between the government and big business in Japan."[1]

To be fair, Johnson's comment encompasses the twentieth century, and I can support it after 1896. Yet, since it is prefaced by reference to "Meiji Japan," it needs qualification for 1885–1895, the second stage of zaibatsu capital formation, achieved mainly through mining profits. Government-zaibatsu relations were looser and less important in this decade than in any other period in modern history. Certainly there were "collaborative relationships." The monopoly of the Bank of Japan presidency from 1889–1903 by the Iwasaki family and former Mitsubishi personnel (Kawada Koichirō, Iwasaki Yanosuke, and Yamamoto Tatsuo) testifies to that. But, in the early 1880s Mitsubishi's shirking its "commitment to national goals" gave it the autonomy to grow into a zaibatsu. Before the mid-1890s, the government generally did not succeed in inducing the zaibatsu into "strategic industries" as we know that term today, in the sense of pioneering "new technologies;" or, if a zaibatsu was inclined to enter such fields (for example, steel, as illustrated by Mitsubishi's 1889 plans), the government failed to provide the requested financing.[2] Furthermore, at the institutional level of zaibatsu firms, the accumulation of wealth through mining, development of commercial trading networks, and gradual diversification into manufacturing after the mid-1890s were all aided by the government in one way or another, but the combining of these processes in giant business concerns was primarily the result of private business strategy.

The N.Y.K.'s relationship with this new Mitsubishi zaibatsu remained ambiguous for some time after 1885. Though partially owned by Mitsubishi and managed by its former personnel, the N.Y.K. for several decades was the much larger firm. By all accounts the N.Y.K. was a unique company, for, if one were to compare Mitsubishi and the N.Y.K. to a parent-child relationship, viewing it historically one could not say precisely which was the parent and which the child. This ambiguity is ultimately rooted in Mitsubishi's withdrawal from shipping in the 1880s before the economic preconditions of overseas expansion had been met.

Mitsubishi's withdrawal, however, helped bring these preconditions to fruition. Its investments in railways, mines, and other productive enterprises, together with the concomitant growth of industrial manufacturing, and the new overseas trading opportunities spearheaded by Mitsui Bussan opened the way for overseas shipping in the early 1890s.

The N.Y.K.'s image as a Mitsubishi firm stems from its origins in 1885, from the situation today when Mitsubishi-related companies hold 30 percent of N.Y.K. stock (compared to 3.7 percent in 1914), and from the Inter-War Years when Mitsubishi frequently intervened to appoint N.Y.K. presidents. The ambiguous era in the relationship was between 1885 and World War I. True, in the decade after the N.Y.K.'s establishment, Mitsubishi's Iwasaki Yanosuke usually had the decisive voice in N.Y.K. executive promotions, but, with the major exception of bunker coal, business activity was quite separate. After Mitsubishi began building N.Y.K. ships in the late 1890s, the two firms developed more mutual interests. During this period Shōda Heigorō acted as Mitsubishi's principal manager, and as an N.Y.K. board member till 1911 and a contemporary of Kondō he seems to have coordinated policy by consensus without requiring any extraordinary measures of intervention.

If there had been more conflict in the relationship, there might well have been more evidence of Mitsubishi attempts to control the N.Y.K. As it was, such conflict began after 1914 when Iwasaki Koyata, the soon-to-be Mitsubishi president, and Kondō clashed over fleet expansion. Kondō, expecting a short war and an ensuing recession, was at first reluctant to undertake large ship purchases.[3] In response Iwasaki Hisaya sold half his N.Y.K. shares in 1915. This seems to indicate a loss of confidence in Kondō that set the stage for later Mitsubishi intervention. That began after World War I and before Kondō's death in 1921 when other companies in the Mitsubishi zaibatsu objected to N.Y.K. ship-purchasing plans on the eve of the recession. In 1924 intervention spread to the most important personnel decisions when, after prolonged dissension among N.Y.K. executives, Iwasaki Koyata imposed an outsider on the company as its new president. Normally a 3 percent stock-holder would not possess such automatic veto power. But despite the selling of stock, the traditional ties between Mitsubishi and N.Y.K. had not died out. Furthermore, the recession of the 1920s, with its severe impact on Mitsubishi's shipbuilding, made a healthy N.Y.K. an urgent priority.

We have tried here to qualify the Mitsubishi–N.Y.K. relationship by suggesting that the degree of intervention varied with the period. However, if our principal focus were the zaibatsu rather than the individual firm, we would have to examine this relationship in a broader framework. Virtually all historical studies of the zaibatsu have had a top-down orientation. From the perspective of the family and the zaibatsu's top management councils, the main subjects of analysis have been the methods of control over member companies and the kinds of internal preference arrangements among these individual firms. On the other hand, examining individual subsidiaries or affiliates clearly shifts the focus toward normal every-day business activity and the firm's business partners outside the zaibatsu. In contrast to the top-down perspective, this more "horizontal" focus on the firm acting within its industry brings forth a wealth of detailed records, suggesting perhaps a lesser amount of encumbrance from "vertical" zaibatsu controls and a greater degree of autonomy than is commonly assumed. A study of an individual zaibatsu firm down to World War II would probably reveal frequent shifts between the two poles of control and autonomy. In good times the pendulum would shift toward autonomy; in a crisis or when a crucial decision was pending, intervention would prevail. How frequently such decisions arose would depend partly on the closeness of the business relation between the firm and the zaibatsu as a whole.

For the N.Y.K., business connections with Mitsubishi increased in importance after World War I. Prior to the war the relationship remained basically harmonious. This was first because times were generally good and second because the N.Y.K.'s principal business concerns focused less on Mitsubishi than on relations with trading firms like Mitsui or shippers like the cotton spinners, on the competitive state of the shipping market, and on the vagaries of government policy. In this context the top-down perspective has seemed inappropriate, for Mitsubishi was more dependent on the N.Y.K. (as a market for its ships) than the N.Y.K. was on it. The steady growth of N.Y.K. ship purchases until 1914 was a third reason for the harmonious relationship.

One final point about Mitsubishi apparent from this study concerns political parties. It is usually assumed that Mitsui supported the Seiyūkai while Mitsubishi backed the various groups descended from Ōkuma's Progressive Party that helped form the Dōshikai just before World War I. During the period under study, the N.Y.K. departed about as far as possible from this common perception of Mitsubishi's political orientation. But the N.Y.K. was a business rather than a political entity. It had to come to terms with the Seiyūkai, which was the only powerful party between 1900 and 1913. The N.Y.K. tried to nurture its ties to the Seiyūkai by planting seeds of a financial and personal nature. They did not always

yield the desired fruit, but by comparison the Dōshikai, with subsidy opponents among its leaders, was downright poisonous.

THE N.Y.K., THE GOVERNMENT,
AND COMPARATIVE PERSPECTIVES

Though government supervision over subsidies became stricter in
the 1880s, in looking over the whole period from 1875 to 1914, a
linear evolution from the supportive to regulatory functions of
subsidy policy is not discernible. Rather these two aspects of policy
varied according to legislative timing. Specifically, new policies
initiated in the aftermath of a military venture, were primarily
supportive. If some time had elapsed since the conclusion of a war
(say, four or five years), the policy was likely to stress regulation.
Supportive legislation received prior approval of companies and indeed was virtually drafted by them. Regulatory laws tended to be
handed down from the government ministry to a shocked company,
which would then resort to various schemes to try to change them.

There were four major cases of subsidy legislation before World
War I. The first was the initial commitment to Mitsubishi in 1875,
with its accompanying directives. The second began in 1882 with
the Third Directive to Mitsubishi, which was part of the process
leading to the formation of the N.Y.K. and the larger, more supervised, subsidy given to it. The third was the vastly increased aid in
the 1896 laws and their 1899 revisions. The fouth was the 1909 law.

Of these various measures, those of 1875 and the late 1890s were
the most supportive. The first was drafted by Maejima and Ōkubo
(in consultation with Yatarō) after the Taiwan Expedition. The
1896 laws were the most liberal measures. That fact reflects both
the political context and the drafting process. They were passed in
a mixed atmosphere of new wealth from the Chinese indemnity
and military preparedness following the Triple Intervention. The
N.Y.K., the Tokyo Chamber of Commerce, and the Ministry of
Communications all had an input into the drafting of these laws.
Though not hastily written (they had been under consideration
since 1894), they contained loopholes which were partially filled

by revisions in 1899. One might place these revisions in a separate
category, for they imposed tougher regulations with regard to ship
age, but they were important primarily for the boost they gave to
domestic shipbuilding and for the extension of the designated line
program, the most supportive measure of all.

In contrast to these laws, the new programs of the 1880s and
1909 stressed regulation. Though the Third Directive to Mitsubishi
in February 1882 and the new subsidy for the N.Y.K. in 1885 allowed for some input from Yatarō and Morioka, they greatly increased government intervention, especially in the early N.Y.K.,
the legal framework of which was patterned after the closely
regulated KUK. In 1909 the government's bill was fully prepared
before Kondō was even informed of the details. In both cases, in
the 1880s and 1909, there seemed less need for emergency legislation than in 1875 and 1896. Though Japan became involved in
several military skirmishes in Korea in the early 1880s, these were
less indicative of a perceived emergency than of a gradual shift in
military planning toward a continental strategy calling for a more
reliable government hold over its merchant marine as a necessary
complement to the navy. In 1909, some four years beyond the
Russo-Japanese War, although military expansion was still a priority, the country already had a large fleet thanks to the purchases
of 1904–1905. The military had first call on the armaments budget
in a tight fiscal period, and there was less sense that war was inevitable than, say, in 1896 after the Triple Intervention.

While the legislation during these four periods was clearly influenced by the immediate political context, there is also no question
that the regulatory functions accompanying subsidies were much
broader in 1914 than in 1875. The controls extended over freight
rates, types of ships, personnel, ports of call, and other line operations. At the same time, companies enjoyed more legal protection
under the Constitution and Commerical Code than they had in the
1880s. The greater clarity of law obviated the need for the subject
status imposed on a company like the KUK. And indeed, the
N.Y.K. had successfully used its rights to defend itself against
government interpretation of tax laws in 1903.

One way to assess the significance of Japanese subsidy laws and government controls over shipping is to provide a comparative examination of subsidies and other government aid. China presents one possible comparison, for Mitsubishi began operations at about the same time as the China Merchants Steam Navigation Company. This firm's tonnage registered virtually no growth between the late 1870s and 1914, and one reason for that was certainly the lack of government aid. The China Merchants received no operating subsidies but only various forms of exclusive transport privileges which, in terms of aid per gross ton, never amounted to more than a third of the support given to Mitsubishi after 1875. Neither capital stock, which was insufficient, nor borrowed funds, which were actually loans placed on deposit with the company at guaranteed interest rates, could be used to upgrade the fleet without solid prospects for business expansion.[4]

In entrepreneurial terms, management's custom of using the firm's reserves to invest in real estate presents another contrast with the more development-oriented N.Y.K. Overall, though, this contrast with China should qualify the emphasis some scholars have placed on the initiative of private entrepreneurs in Japan. The dynamic, risk-taking Japanese entrepreneur is often seen as the great variable in any contrast between the economic development of China and Japan. In the early shipping industry, however, governmental stability and its capacity to provide aid were as important.

A second instance of a weak or inconsistent government aid program undermining one of Mitsubishi's competitors occurred in 1877 when the subsidies of the American Pacific Mail Company were suspended. This firm suffered from numerous takeover bids in the 1870s, eventually becoming a subsidiary of the Southern Pacific Railway. Its decline as a Pacific shipping power demonstrates the importance of both subsidies and consistent long-term planning.[5] Both the China Merchants and the Pacific Mail lacked either the capacity or the managerial autonomy to pursue an expansionist policy like the N.Y.K. This clearly limits their value for comparative analysis. More appropriate comparisons can be made with the large European firms whose services, financial structure,

and relations with their governments bore greater similarity to the
N.Y.K. Some of these firms, such as the P. & O. and the North
German Lloyd, were N.Y.K. competitors. Another, the Cunard
Line, operated in a different business environment because of its
location (the Atlantic) and emphasis (passengers), but in certain
respects it offers the closest resemblance to the N.Y.K. In discussing government aid, subsidies provide the most easily measurable
statistical evidence, but rough approximations of how government
policy affected matters like depreciation and reserve structure can
also be attempted.

The P. & O., the company with the longest tradition of subsidized mail service between Europe and East Asia, was receiving an
annual mail subvention of £305,000 in 1913. The terms of this
subsidy differed from that received by the N.Y.K. for it carried
mail free of charge while the P. & O. obtained revenue from this
service. After subtracting these mail receipts, we find that the
P. & O.'s net subsidy came to about ¥4.12 per ton in 1913, about
the same scale as the principal German program. Under that the
North German Lloyd had begun its East Asian service after the
Reichstag passed a subsidy bill in 1886. In 1913 the German firm's
subsidy of DM 6.1 million was equivalent to roughly ¥2.9 million,
or ¥3.34 per ton. Both these figures were less than a third of the
N.Y.K.'s ¥13.98 per ton in the same year.

These rates are useful for comparing whole fleets, but they need
qualification to be applied to the competition of individual lines.
N.Y.K. subsidies were spread over three services (European, Australian, and Pacific) compared to two for the North German Lloyd
(Europe to East Asia and Australia). More important, the German
firm's fleet was 2.3 times the size of the N.Y.K.'s in 1914, and it
operated a far higher percentage of nonsubsidized services. Figures
for 1914 show that the German company allotted nine ships totaling 82,453 tons to its European-East Asia line and received ¥1.7
million for it. This was equivalent to ¥20.74 per ton, considerably
higher than the N.Y.K.'s overall subsidization rate. By comparison,
during the 1910 to 1912 period, when the N.Y.K. had 91,502 tons
allotted to its European service but before it introduced its new

ships of the 10,000-ton class, its European line was subsidized at about ¥35 per ton. Such a high rate reflects this line's utilization of about a third of the company's tonnage while receiving 60 percent of its subsidies. The N.Y.K.'s rate of ¥35 for 1910–1912, however, had certainly declined by 1914, for the interim saw a decrease in subsidies. In conclusion, though, it seems that the N.Y.K. received substantially larger government aid for its European line than did the North German Lloyd for its East Asian service, but the difference in the subsidization rates for the two lines was nowhere near as great as that for the two companies' whole fleets.[6]

Most scholars have argued that subsidies were not crucial in giving any one European country an edge over another in shipping competition between 1890 and 1914, that the subsidies were relatively small (as illustrated by the British and German examples above), and that they were given for uneconomical services such as mail and passenger transport or for national prestige.[7] As a corollary, some of these services would not have been started without subsidies. The experience of the North German Lloyd supports these propositions. Even with its subsidy, at least until the late 1890s this firm ran a constant deficit on its East Asian service. In 1898 the government gave it a new contract, increasing the subsidy from DM 4.1 million to DM 5.6 million (¥1.9 million to ¥2.6 million). The boost provided by this contract enabled the company to purchase its Southeast Asian branch line from the Blue Funnel in 1899 and to begin planning for new services in China. Nevertheless, these China initiatives, conducted jointly with the Hamburg America Line, fell short of expectations. Not only was the new contract insufficient to cover large-scale expansion in China but it also failed to give the North German Lloyd an edge (except in passenger operations) on the European line in the intensified competitive environment following the late 1890s. In fact, after 1900 some of the firm's services were actually constricted, as it was forced into cooperative arrangements with the Hamburg America Line, to which it paid part of its subsidy. In effect, then, the 1898 contract merely kept the North German Lloyd competitive; it did not ensure any particular advantage over other firms. Beyond that, it authorized extensive government intervention in matters like freight rates, ship size, and port-of-call decisions, offering something of a model for Japan's 1909 subsidy law.[8]

The North German Lloyd's East Asian service, then, failed to grow beyond a national service role into a primarily money-making operation. By contrast, the company derived its largest profits from its nonsubsidized North Atlantic service, where, in addition to the Hamburg America Line, it became one of Britain's principal competitors. In short, rather than being crucial to the growth of European shipping companies, subsidies functioned to offset expenses for services performed on behalf of the state. A full perspective, however, requires us to distinguish between the types of services before we can assess the impact of subsidies on N.Y.K. success.

The cooperative arrangements between the North German Lloyd and the Hamburg America Line in East Asia involved primarily mail. The latter firm apparently found these agreements unprofitable, for by 1904 it had withdrawn from them, concentrating instead on freight.[9] Clearly, cargo services were less dependent on subsidies, as Holt's Ocean Steam Ship Company illustrates. It began operating to East Asia in the late 1860s without government aid and initially felt the pinch of competition from the subsidized P. & O. In 1874 Holt's firm unsuccessfully tried to block the renewal of the P. & O.'s mail contract in a debate which, in its arguments against subsidies, resembled the attack on Mitsubishi in the 1880s. Thereafter, Holt, secure in his Liverpool base, became the dominant carrier of industrial exports, and down to World War I his firm built up its fleet from accumulated earnings and a carefully planned reserve fund.[10]

The P. & O. and Holt's Ocean Steam Ship represent extremes in types of service (the former emphasizing mail and passengers, the latter, freight); the N.Y.K. falls in between, though somewhat closer to Holt's model. Like the P. & O. and the North German Lloyd, the N.Y.K carried mail and passengers, but the scale of these services was much smaller for a Japanese firm operating to Europe than for a British firm like the P. & O. servicing colonial possessions in Asia. The North German Lloyd, with the relatively small German possession in Shantung, had much less of a burden in this respect than the P. & O. The German firm was also a large cargo carrier, but it had invested heavily in passenger business, the most expensive service to operate. The N.Y.K.'s European line bore more resemblance to Holt's in that its principal function was to carry industrial cargo. Since the Ocean Steam Ship Company did not require subsidies, this suggests that the N.Y.K., with its concentration on freight, may have benefited more from its subsidies than did the P. & O. and North German Lloyd from theirs. Its subsidization was an advantage over Ocean Steam Ship; and its less-expensive services were an advantage over the P. & O. and North German Lloyd.

N.Y.K. subsidies covered more areas than did those of the North German Lloyd (which did not operate in the Pacific) and the N.Y.K. lacked a large independent moneymaker like the North Atlantic route (the Bombay line being small by comparison). But at ¥13.98 per ton, the N.Y.K.'s higher rate of subsidization gave it a competitive edge. Why, for example, did the North German Lloyd not become a strong competitor in China shipping, as it had hoped in 1902? Was it lack of funding or simply the distance from Europe? Both were important, but one wonders what the company might have done in East Asia had its whole fleet been subsidized at ¥14 a ton.

The N.Y.K.'s subsidization rate, however, was not excessively high by Japanese or other European standards. As stressed earlier, the O.S.K. was *not* much less dependent on subsidies than the N.Y.K. In fact, in 1913 the O.S.K.'s subsidization rate was ¥14.56 per ton, compared to the N.Y.K.'s ¥13.98. Tōyō Kisen, at ¥37.51 per ton, more than doubled these figures. Even this high rate was average by French standards. The failure of France's program, however, illustrates that no amount of subsidization could overcome a weak trading position. Comparative gross figures for 1901 show that France had the largest national subsidy program at ¥19 million, equivalent to ¥36 a ton. Second was Britain with ¥9.3 million. This represents ¥1.22 per ton for the approximately twenty-five leading steamship firms and probably less than half of that for the national fleet. Japan was third with ¥8.3 million, or ¥15.28 per ton. The German rate cannot be calculated for 1901, but for 1914 it was reported to be 82 *sen* per ton.[11] Japan, then, like the N.Y.K., falls between the two extremes of the low British-German rate and the massive French aid.

The most common reasons given for the failure of the French program to free its shipping firms from such massive dependence are the absence of a strong trading network, excessive regulation, and the lack of a major port like Hamburg or Antwerp through which to channel European goods. By contrast, Japan's vigorous trade made the subsidy program effective. Also, unlike Britain and Germany, Japan's subsidy rates were high enough to contribute effectively to the capital structure of firms, at least those like the N.Y.K. and the O.S.K. which skillfully utilized trading networks.

Among major international firms operating to East Asia, the French Messageries Maritimes had the highest subsidization rate at ¥17.73 per ton. Another example of a firm subsidized in the same "moderate" range as the N.Y.K. was the Cunard Line. Its rate in 1913 was about ¥9.45 a ton, though this figure includes a government loan.[12] Cunard's situation had three other similarities to the N.Y.K.: (1) Its subsidy was given not simply for mail and other routine services but also for the express purpose of combating its competition. (2) Among British shipping companies it was probably the most crucial for national security. (3) During the years 1903 to 1908 Cunard was under extreme competitive pressure from firms in an unstable North Atlantic conference system. The N.Y.K. shared these features during the early years of its European line. Hyde's conclusion that Cunard could not have survived the difficult times after 1900 without government aid[13] seems applicable by analogy to the larger N.Y.K. services like the European and the Pacific between 1898 and 1902. Unlike the P. & O. subsidy, which was mainly for "routine" services, the comparison with Cunard shifts the emphasis away from the size of the N.Y.K.'s subsidy toward its goal—the intertwining of national defense and competitive trading advantage. Complemented by advantages like lower costs and effective trading networks, the N.Y.K.'s subsidy was effectively utilized in pursuit of this goal. It is not surprising, then, to see a British scholar often critical of European aid programs conclude that "probably the only country which achieved any degree of success with subsidies in the pre-1914 period was Japan."[14]

From the viewpoint of costs alone, Japanese government subsidies to the N.Y.K. were effective in two ways. Between 1896 and about 1910 subsidies offset high operating costs, caused in part by high salaries for foreign personnel and inefficient fuel consumption of the relatively old ships of that era. As shown in Table 55 (Chapter 10) N.Y.K. costs per ton had declined substantially between 1908 and 1913 as a result of the reduction in foreign seamen and the introduction of more fuel-efficient ships. In this latter era, then, the function of subsidies seems to have changed from offsetting high costs to providing funds for new technology, namely, the expensive new ships with their lower operating costs.

Most countries adopting subsidy programs did so in part to support their navies. Japan was perhaps the most conspicuous example of this military emphasis. But in addition, Japan seems to have had more of an economic motive behind its subsidies than the other countries mentioned here. The British government generally refused to sanction subsidies for primarily economic reasons, providing them instead to facilitate communication among different parts of a far-flung empire and to buttress the navy. Germany, with much less an empire, was more concerned with prestige, though the North German Lloyd subsidy was passed following the adoption of a colonial policy. Also, the desire for trade and close communication with German possessions in China probably motivated the 1898 increase in that subsidy. Japan, of course, also subsidized shipping services to its colonies, but these territories were too nearby to constitute a major rationale for the size of its subsidy program. Prestige was important to France. Like Germany it too had colonial interests in Asia, but these were minor compared to Britain's, and they had little impact on the size of the French program. France's mammoth subsidies can be better explained by two points: (1) French shipping policy never experienced the kind of transformation that occurred in Britain with the switch from the Navigation Acts to a free trade posture. Flag preference remained a stronger force in France than in other European countries. (2) This form of shipping nationalism was designed less to achieve positive economic goals or even to buttress the navy than to compensate for high shipbuilding costs and for geographic disadvantages such as the lack of major ports near industrial centers and the expense of maintaining many small ports.

Besides subsidies the Japanese government provided other forms of aid to the N.Y.K. The Imperial House shares were a kind of government investment in the company. Also, there were vigorous trade promotion efforts, especially through institutions like the Yokohama Specie Bank. Subsidization of shipping, however, was unique in scale among direct government grant programs. Between 1896 and 1913, 66 percent of all industrial subsidies from the regular budget went to shipping.[15] Not without reason, then, did Japanese companies assume they could always count on government support. The N.Y.K. even requested a subsidy for its Calcutta line when it began to pile up deficits in 1912 despite the government's original advice not to start the line.[16]

Though Japan's subsidy policy had both supportive and regulatory functions for business operations, in comparative terms emphasis on its supportive component has seemed more appropriate. Comparing internal finance similarly highlights the supportive role. First, however, we must ask how taxation affected the firms under consideration. In the discussion of costs in Chapter 10, we showed that in the years just prior to World War I the N.Y.K.'s relative tax payments were roughly three and a half times those of Cunard and that the P. & O. frequently paid no taxes at all. However, because of the relatively small amounts involved (N.Y.K. taxes being less than one-fifth of subsidies), these differing rates do not constitute a significant variable and do little to cancel out the advantage to the N.Y.K. of its larger subsidies.

Because of their connection with the reserve system, pretax deductions were certainly more important than taxes themselves.

Depreciation, insurance, and sometimes repair funds designated for reserves formed the principal deductions. A comparison of the N.Y.K., the P. & O., and Cunard shows that their deductions were not based on the book value of their fleets. If 1.00 represents N.Y.K. totals, the relative values in 1914 were: Cunard, 1.57; N.Y.K., 1.00; P. & O., 0.75.[17] All three companies, however, had annual pretax deductions of some ¥5 million just prior to World War I. The principal difference among the three appears in the way they built their reserves. The N.Y.K. and Cunard funded their reserves from both retained earnings (that is, after-tax profits) and pretax deductions; the P. & O.'s reserves came exclusively from pretax deductions, which represented a higher percentage of ship value than those of the N.Y.K. and Cunard. Why it could do this is not clear, but this method seems to be how the P. & O. avoided paying taxes.

This favorable write-off and taxation treatment probably did not give the P. & O. a major advantage over the N.Y.K. Rather, it seems to reflect different methods of financing. The N.Y.K. depended less on depreciation. Its subsidies gave it such large current assets that it could continue to designate greater amounts for reserves than could the British firms while still buying new ships. As as result N.Y.K. reserves grew much faster. In 1900 its reserves stood at ¥6.2 million compared to ¥5.5 million for Cunard; by 1914 these reserves had increased, respectively, to ¥42.5 million and ¥11.8 million.[18] As a percentage of income, N.Y.K. reserves in 1914 were among the largest of all international shipping firms. By this measurement Table 62 also shows the firms with the highest subsidization rates, the N.Y.K. and Messageries Maritimes, possessed respectively the largest and smallest reserves among the six firms listed. Building up reserves for the autonomous use of management was a low priority for French firms, whose subsidy contracts were so overburdened with regulation that they became virtual state agents.[19] Compared to the British and German examples, the size of the N.Y.K. reserves shows the effectiveness of subsidies in stabilizing company finances. On the other hand, the reserves had grown especially quickly after 1910 because management

TABLE 62 Reserves of Leading Shipping Firms as a Percentage
of Income, 1914

Firm	Reserves/Income (%)
N.Y.K.	124
Hamburg America Line[a]	96
North German Lloyd[a]	68
P. & O.	35
Cunard	31
Messageries Maritimes[b]	9

Source: Calculated from U.S. Department of Commerce, *Government Aid to Merchant Shipping,* pp. 60–61, 85–86, 165.

Notes: [a]1912 [b]1913

had placed a higher priority on retaining earnings than on business expansion. The N.Y.K.'s position at the top of the list in Table 62 reflects, in part, the increasing conservatism of its business strategy between 1910 and 1914.[20]

The large size of the N.Y.K. subsidy, which made possible the rapid growth of these reserves, should not obscure the fact that especially after 1899 the government was increasingly selective in its grants. The government provided subsidies for six main reasons. In rough order of importance they were:

(1) The military needed a reliable body of transports. The expense of maintaining these ships between wars necessitated an operating subsidy. When subsidies came under attack after 1900 their supporters almost always resorted to this military consideration as their first defense, arguing in particular, that Japan could not have fought the Russo-Japanese War without the subsidy laws of the 1890s.

(2) Shipping subsidies, with their preferential clauses favoring Japanese ships, provided an indirect stimulus to key heavy industries like shipbuilding and steel. This trigger function provides perhaps the easiest measurement of the efficacy of the shipping subsidies,

for the shipbuilding subsidy alone was too small to have encouraged rapid growth in the industry.

(3) The government wanted Japanese firms to operate trans-oceanic lines for economic security. First, they would help balance international payments, a goal achieved by 1914, at least with regard to shipping payments. Second, by operating overseas, Japanese shipping firms would facilitate the formation of trading networks among shippers, importers, trading companies, and banks—in short, the entrepreneurial alliances the government itself supported.

(4) Subsidies enabled the government to have some control over freight rates. Its reasoning varied over time. In the 1870s Ōkubo supported subsidies to sustain higher freight rates. He reasoned that excessive competition was driving rates down and preventing the emergence of a strong, internationally competitive shipping firm. In other times the opposite goal of restraining freight rates seemed to have been so overtaken by events that many questioned whether the government was committed to it. In the 1909 subsidy debate Shimada Saburō had complained in the Diet that "the N.Y.K.'s ships on its European line cannot compete with those of Britain, Germany, and France. They cannot survive except by entering into agreements and setting rates. Since they have this accord with all the other companies to set rates, there's no way anyone can travel cheaply."[21] However, the large Japanese presence in overseas lines and participation in conferences probably kept rates from going higher. This particular motivation for subsidies became more important as more Japanese exports became competitive. The government's successful resistance to the rate increase requested by the European-Far East Conference in 1912 was the best illustration of this reason.

(5) As part of its program of political consolidation, especially in the early and mid-Meiji years, the government wanted to establish protected companies to serve as channels for investments by the Imperial House and the peers that were to be the bulwark of the throne. Even in the late Meiji period, when more private firms expanded and became attractive investments, the high reliability of

the N.Y.K. dividend ensured a continuing relationship with the Imperial Household Ministry.

(6) For diplomatic reasons, especially before 1902, the government wanted to have a strong merchant marine that could be seen as a support for the military. It was felt that this would make Japan a more attractive partner in a potential alliance with a Western power.[22] This objective, while designed to appeal to British officialdom, conflicted with the interests of private British shipping firms, perhaps illustrating in its achievement a disjunction between British diplomacy and economic interests.

The subsidy program also can be related to a more general tendency of Japanese government economic policy—designating certain industries as strategic and singling them out for special promotion. Variations of this policy have been in effect since the early eighteenth century, when the Tokugawa shogun, Yoshimune, designated raw silk for special promotion, to the 1980s, when the government aided the development of silicon chips. The period of this study was one of building an economic structure. It can be compared to the immediate post-World War II era when the rebuilding of the economy led the government to designate steel, coal, electric power, and shipping for special aid on the grounds that these industries would provide an infrastructure and a base for development in other sectors of the economy. I am not suggesting that the Meiji government had a master plan that gradually evolved between 1870 and 1914. The emphasis of subsidy laws shifted greatly depending on immediate circumstances, and companies played a major role in having themselves designated. But at least since the Ōkubo memoranda of the mid-1870s shipping had been designated a strategic industry, and by 1909 government policy toward shipping had become increasingly oriented to specific goals.

THE N.Y.K. AS AN AUTONOMOUS FIRM

Strategic industrial policy in Japan has had three major features: the jettisoning of industries that have become uncompetitive; the maximization of profit from areas of comparative advantage; and the promotion of industries considered important for the future. From 1906 to 1914 the N.Y.K. experienced these three courses: it jettisoned many of its deficit-ridden local services; it recovered its competitive edge on important near-seas services; and it upgraded its transoceanic fleet under the encouragement of the 1909 subsidy law, which designated only strategic lines for aid. In the process the N.Y.K. became a more specialized liner company.

Increased specialization was more the result of strong external pressures than internal, autonomous managerial decisions. Neither the 1909 law, with its exclusive attention to regular overseas lines, nor Mitsubishi's trading system, limited as it was to East Asia, provided the N.Y.K. with incentives to develop overseas tramp services. Adhering to the 1909 law meant offering regular transoceanic liner services, which could not be operated profitably outside of conference systems. Conferences tended to dictate the kind of shippers the N.Y.K. did business with. Shippers who needed guaranteed supplies or industrial products on a regular or predictable basis generally did not depend on tramp services. Certain internal dynamics, however, also inclined the company toward specialization.

It was not simply dependence on subsidies that led to N.Y.K. conservatism between 1909 and 1914. The company owed its rich financial position to the long-term build-up of reserves via the subsidies, but these reserves were substantial enough that the company could have used them to break away from its specialized orientation. In general, the company's internal structure discouraged this because:

(1) Though the role of the Imperial Household Ministry in the N.Y.K. is not well documented, there were consultations with the ministry on some crucial decisions and a company auditor was an Imperial House official. The Imperial House's one-fifth ownership of the N.Y.K. seems to have given the company a particular posture as the national flag carrier. The principal interest of the Imperial House was in a secure long-term dividend. This was virtually guaranteed as long as the company chose to remain protected by government subsidies. Perhaps the first alternative business option

for the company was to develop more extensive tramp services. Tramps operated best in times of peak business activity, when they took the cream of the trade. They succeeded between 1912 and 1919, but in the postwar recession many had to be absorbed by larger firms. In short, tramp services were not the best way to provide long-term dividend guarantees.

(2) Between 1912 and 1914 stockholder demands for converting reserves into free shares inhibited potential expansion. By 1914 the N.Y.K.'s internal structure had evolved in a manner analogous to the KUK of 1885. The management of both companies was caught in a vise between the government and the stockholders. There were differences, of course. In the KUK's case, the government refused to provide a subsidy. Management still wanted to expand its business, but the stockholders would not tolerate the inevitable deficits. As for the N.Y.K., government policy had forced it into a particular specialization, and stockholder demands discouraged management from expanding beyond that.

The emphasis placed on stockholders in this study may seem unusual in view of the mere formality of most General Meetings today. However, the situation was different before World War I and it contrasted with experience in Western countries. The joint-stock system originated in the West, whereas Japan deliberately imported it. The Meiji government actually courted potential stockholders as a way to introduce the system and channel money into industrial enterprises. Expectations encouraged by the government led stockholders to take seriously their rights and anticipate just returns, especially if their firm was also subsidized. In order to maximize their returns, large holders, especially stockbrokers, speculated heavily in N.Y.K. shares. In addition, smaller holders had more influence than their percentage of shares because of proportional voting systems which favored them. Finally, the number of N.Y.K. stockholders (around 4,500) was small enough that stockholding did not become wholly impersonal but large enough that alienated holders could organize to oppose management decisions. The N.Y.K. stockholders resembled less the impersonal post-World War II investor than the late Meiji local political power broker lobbying the Diet for pork-barrel legislation.

(3) Comparisons between O.S.K. and N.Y.K. policies often over-look a key variable, namely, the longer association between the N.Y.K. and the Imperial House and peers as well as the higher N.Y.K. share price and the greater expectations that it induced in the stockholders. N.Y.K. stockholders, then, seem to have inhibited management more than was the case in the O.S.K. Despite this qualification, Kondō was without question a more conservative president than the O.S.K.'s Nakahashi. One conclusion of a recent comparative study of Japanese and American management seems relevant to Kondō's long tenure as N.Y.K. president: "Case studies of incumbents whose terms of office spanned the time periods when their organizations were moving from one era to another seem to indicate that they 'failed' more often than they 'succeeded.'"[23]

In retrospect, Kondō's bureaucratic management has been blamed for the post-World War I ills of the N.Y.K. There are two common explanations for these ills: prewar conservative manage-ment and ramifications of wartime controversies. One of these wartime conflicts involved the capital stock, which the company doubled in 1915 and again in 1917. But the process of doing so split company management and led to wholesale resignations. Obviously, the two explanations cannot be separated, for the same man was in charge and there was continuity in policy. The second perspective, however, seems more plausible. The N.Y.K.'s huge reserves gave the company options a more flexible manager might have been able to implement to avoid conflict during the war.[24] Decisive action at the beginning of the war might have defused the subsequent controversies before they sparked the postwar dissen-sion. Kondō, though, can still be seen as a conservative prior to 1914 without reading this wartime situation back into the prewar period. Nakahashi, for example, started the O.S.K.'s Bombay line on a trial basis for several years before upgrading it to a regular service, and he began the Tacoma line prior to subsidization. In contrast, despite the N.Y.K.'s greater resources, Kondō was adamant about retaining large reserves and he refused to consider a Panama line prior to subsidization.

(4) To expand its services prior to 1914 the N.Y.K. would have had to cut back on its extensive investments. Some of these investments served national policy functions, especially in ports and development banks, and were crucial to national progress. Some also were related to the interests of board members or stockholders, for example, the Tōbu Railway (Asada Masabumi, a director till 1911), Kanegafuchi Cotton Spinning (Mitsui), and the Industrial Bank (Mitsubishi via the Tayeh mines). Retention of these investments was another factor inhibiting flexibility in the shipping business.

In short, the N.Y.K.'s internal structure was not simply a group of managers committed to shipping. Rather, it was knit closely into the fabric of Japan's political and business institutions. This pattern tended to create a greater degree of external pressure on the N.Y.K. than in a company with a less complex ownership and a narrower range of investments. Company structure, then, circumscribed the autonomy of management.

THE N.Y.K. AND BUSINESS ALLIANCES

In contrast to the conservatism of N.Y.K. liner strategy, the company showed a flexible response in areas like India, initiating a vigorous competition against British firms. The key variable in the N.Y.K.'s Panama and Calcutta lines was not so much dependence on subsidies as possession of a dependable market network. Cooperation with shippers provided the basis for these networks, or business alliances. By helping to import raw materials for newly emerging industries and to market their products abroad, they played a role in Japan's development similar to the government's strategy of inducing changes in industrial structure by designating key industries for promotion. Examples of goods that became competitive in this period through the actions of organized alliances were cotton yarn in China and matches in India.

These organized alliances contained specialized importing firms, trading companies, shipping firms, industrial producers, and banks. To operate they usually needed freedom from foreign participation. Even the Tata firm's role in the Bombay line illustrates this. Though its participation was advantageous to the Japanese alliance at first, when it proved otherwise it withdrew. Shipping firms were essential to the autonomous direction of these alliances. They provided the Japanese transport without which the alliance's strategy would falter.

The principal strategy was risk sharing, that is, risk was accepted in exchange for certain guarantees. The N.Y.K. could tolerate large rebates to shippers because of the cargo guarantees they offered. This strategy reduced the costs of shipment, enabling the producer to market his goods more cheaply, and it led to the N.Y.K. obtaining a larger market share on the shipping route in question. Such alliances usually emerged in crisis situations. Their first mark of success might occur when a foreign conference accepted the terms of the Japanese alliance, allowing the N.Y.K. to enter the conference and stabilizing the trade. Such an accommodation would end the crisis but would not necessarily mean the end of the Japanese alliance. In cases where a single cargo dominated a route, as raw cotton did on the Bombay line, the Japanese shippers, that is, the cotton spinners, were powerful enough to exert a long-term controlling influence over the freight rate and to enable the N.Y.K. to gain an increasing share of conference revenue. In other cases, where producing firms were numerous, small, and scattered throughout Japan, trading companies would act as the actual shipper providing guarantees to the N.Y.K.

These alliances emerged from the interdependence among cotton spinners, trading companies, and shipping firms. This interdependence arose in the nineteenth century because of the lack of vertical integration in producing firms. Based on studies of the 1930s, however, many scholars and businessmen have long assumed that the vertical ties among importers, financial institutions, producers, shippers, and transporters first developed within single zaibatsu. Yet, the richest firms, like the zaibatsu, generally failed to enter industrial manufacturing before the mid-1890s. Alliance participants, then, came from different zaibatsu (hence the term "alliance," which would be inappropriate for a purely intra-zaibatsu network), and furthermore, those that did take up industrial manufacturing in this period were usually non-zaibatsu firms hard pressed to raise sufficient capital for production. They had none left over to create divisions for acquiring raw materials, which were mostly obtained overseas, or for marketing. These functions were performed by the trading companies, with the shipping companies actually carrying the goods. Trading companies, then, compensated for the lack of vertical integration in Japan. Also, one of the reasons why industrial manufacturing was risky during the Meiji period was Japan's lack of tariff autonomy prior to 1911. This situation prompted the government to participate in entrepreneurial alliances through its consular offices and banks.

The organized business alliance was a nationalistic phenomenon but not a manifestation of patriotism; there are too many examples of unpatriotic behavior or resistance to national policy to warrant such a generalization. Nor was the entrepreneurial alliance simply a reaction to the unequal treaties. In his 1876 denunciation of the P. & O.'s alliance with the Osaka-based Nine Shop Union, directed against Mitsubishi, Yatarō blamed the "customs" of merchant firms for Japan's backwardness more than the unequal treaties. The custom criticized in this instance was that of forming business alliances with foreigners. Yatarō implied that alliances should instead be established among Japanese for the benefit of his own firm. The exclusive Japanese membership in these alliances flowed more from interdependence of needs and common managerial strategies than from patriotism.

A contrasting form of entrepreneurship, discussed by John McKay with regard to pre-revolutionary Russia, defined an entrepreneur as one who not only controlled or had access to capital but as one who possessed organizational skills. But in Russia it was the French investor who became tied in with the Russian entrepreneur in developing business alliances, a situation recalling the practice of the Chinese comprador investing in foreign shipping firms.[25] Thus, while entrepreneurship as conceived by McKay is in some ways like that which evolved in Japan (organization substituting for capital), the more national application of it in Japan seems to have led to a more determined pursuit of goals.

Another foreign example illustrates the way the nationalism of Japanese trading alliances helped the shipping industry. Japan was the fastest growing trading nation in Asia, and participation in that trade was the best assurance of long-term profit. Despite this, British trading firms long active in East Asia retained their traditional orientation to China. For example, in 1901 the London-based John Swire & Sons advised its East Asian trading subsidiary, Butterfield & Swire, against opening a branch in Kyushu. Regarding this proposed new agency, the parent firm wrote that the "prospect for foreigners continuing to trade successfully in Japan is . . . extremely doubtful . . . [and so we] desire to strengthen our borders in the country where our chief interests lie, . . . China not Japan."[26]

Both their established positions in China and the difficulty of participating in the increasingly nationalistic Japanese trade led the British to retain their traditional strategies. Foreign firms still handled an enormous share of Japan's trade in the early twentieth century, but their hold was strongest in the older trades like raw silk and tea. The most farsighted among them saw that foreign trading firms could not accommodate themselves to Japan's changing industrial structure by following traditional strategies. For example, Marcus Samuel, who had been a general merchant in Japan since the Restoration, withdrew almost entirely from his trade in rice, coal, and silk and instead hatched his visionary scheme to transport oil to Japan.[27] Samuel, whose plan was the origin of Shell Oil, was an exceptional entrepreneur. In general, the failure of other British firms to become leading participants in the business alliances based on Japan's new industries was a major reason why Japanese shipping firms began to outperform their British counterparts in Asia.

Despite the nationalism of Japanese business alliances, the trend toward deconcentration in Japan's shipping industry made it difficult for one firm like the N.Y.K. to retain its exclusive or

monopolistic position within an alliance. On the Bombay line, for
example, the O.S.K. had broken the N.Y.K.'s exclusive tie with
the Cotton Spinners Association by 1913. This new development,
which sometimes saw competition among Japanese alliances,
emerged rather late in the period under study, but its timing does
have some bearing on the particular evolution of N.Y.K. strategy.

The N.Y.K.'s major expansion occurred in the late 1890s, when
the company was the exclusive Japanese representative on its new
lines with a monopoly of government favor. This monopoly broke
down earliest on the Pacific and Bombay lines. The N.Y.K. had,
since 1900, always had some competition on the Pacific from
Tōyō Kisen's San Francisco line, but when the O.S.K. began
running to Tacoma in 1909 talk shifted its focus from expansion
to amalgamation of services. In Indian shipping, where trade prospects were better, the N.Y.K. continued an expansionist strategy
after it lost its monopoly of Japanese participation. It might be
argued, however, that one of the company's motives for starting
the Calcutta line in 1911 was to protect its overall position in India
by diversifying its lines there at a time when the O.S.K. was entering the Bombay line.

Besides the main liner firms like the O.S.K., competition also
came from the tramps, with some of them, Yamashita and the
Suzuki Trading Company in particular, developing into large enterprises. Finally, there were the principal trading enterprises, especially those of Mitsui and Mitsubishi, which often used their own
ships rather than entrusting their goods to companies like the
N.Y.K. Though three firms possessed 39 percent of Japan's tonnage
in 1913 (an oligopoly with a high level of concentration), the other
firms mentioned here were primarily charter operators; hence their
shipping activity would not necessarily appear in statistics of owned
tonnage. Data are insufficient to determine whether the shipping
industry, as measured by overall operations, was still an oligopoly
in 1914, but certainly in the decade after 1904 it experienced an
increasingly lower level of concentration.

Comparative data bear out this emphasis on deconcentration
and competition within Japan's shipping industry. In 1905 seven

companies owned 60 percent of German tonnage; a larger number of tramps made the British industry less concentrated. Trends in Germany and Britain, however, were quite the opposite of those in Japan. The dominance of the Hamburg America Line and the North German Lloyd in Germany continued to be greater than that of the N.Y.K. and O.S.K. in Japan. Nakagawa has commented that, in contrast to Britain and Japan, Germany had only one coastline. Much of Germany's foreign trade, therefore, was carried on the Rhine River to Rotterdam and Antwerp and then handled by British shipping companies. Germany's only coastline was dominated by just two major ports, Hamburg and Bremen, which contributed to the high concentration in the German shipping industry.[28] Also, while concentration ratios may have been lower in Britain, the trend there toward massive amalgamation was the reverse of that in Japan, where new companies were sprouting up together with business alliances to serve the country's growing trade.

THE N.Y.K. AND THE WIDER WORLD

The N.Y.K.'s presence on the world stage was first felt in a major way when the company penetrated the European-dominated freight conferences in the late 1890s. It was thus one of the earliest Japanese enterprises to achieve parity with its Western counterparts in an international economic organization. One is tempted to find an analogy between this successful penetration and the efforts of Third World countries today to gain a larger share of their own trade now carried by conference members. In general, the analogy is inapplicable, for the strategy of the Third World has been to gain access through preferential treatment, whereas the N.Y.K. achieved entry through its own strength, with the British backing down in the face of Japanese subsidies. Yet, some Third World countries with oil wealth, such as Indonesia, have unilaterally adopted a rather vigorous national flag policy for carrying their own cargo outside the conference system without showing the same inclination as the pre-World War I Japanese for joining the existing order.

Another analogy with the Third World is China's situation around 1900. Virtually all of its long-distance overseas trade was carried by foreigners. The relevant point for this study, however, has been the critical role the N.Y.K. developed as a carrier of Chinese trade (and its dependence on that freight), which became the key to its success within the conference system on the west-bound voyage to Europe. For this reason it integrated its East Asian and European business by trying to develop the Yangtze as a feeder for the lines to the West. This provided the motive for the N.Y.K. to participate in a form of economic imperialism in China.

By eroding China's autonomy, imperialism made Chinese businessmen less directed toward state goals. Japan-style nationally oriented business alliances were out of the question in China when so many of its most effective businessmen either worked as compradors or continued to invest in foreign firms like the Nisshin Kisen. Chinese steamship enterprise was the first victim of aggressive penetration by the N.Y.K. and other Japanese shipping firms.

British shipping was the second major victim of N.Y.K. expansion. The measures of British decline are numerous: the fall from a majority share by the P. & O. on the Bombay line to only one-third, the decline from a combined 50 percent to a 37 percent British share on the Yangtze between 1903 and 1911, and the various testimony about N.Y.K. influence on the European line. This was not a precipitous decline but the beginning of a long competitive rivalry. Britain, however, was a good commercial competitor to have. Despite the complaints of British firms about the Japanese, the British government, with the important exception of the McBain case on the Yangtze, took little anti-Japanese action.

We have pointed to several strategies, such as mergers and the disinclination to start feeder lines, which may reflect a contracting British industry. What was the British perception of Japanese strategy? Although British businessmen often complained about the networks of shippers behind the N.Y.K., in their correspondence and speeches they usually attributed N.Y.K. success to its subsidies rather than to its business alliances. In contrast, some British scholars have downplayed the impact of subsidies, but stressed the overall stimulus to shipping of Japanese trade. Writing about the pre-World War I period, S. G. Sturmey commented that "the increase in Japanese shipping was . . . justified by the growth in Japanese trade and was clearly not at the expense of foreign shipping: the extension of trade depended on an increase in the shipping services to and from Japan which it is doubtful if non-Japanese shipping would have provided." Sturmey continues: "Had subsidies not been given, the expansion of the Japanese fleet would have been slower, but the eventual size would not necessarily have been smaller."[29] Thomas Sutherland of the P. & O. would not have accepted this judgment without qualification. In 1901 he stated that "I should say in all probability while the British shipping trade has increased with Japan, it will not have increased as fully as we should have liked it to increase."[30] Furthermore, the ability of shipping to function as a trigger industry, helping to change Japan's industrial structure and stimulating more trade, would have been greatly diminished without subsidies.

Sturmey's comment fails to distinguish between the gross revenue of British firms (which was increasing) and the market (which they were losing, at least in Asia). My impression is that without subsidies the N.Y.K. would have been unable to begin some of the more distant overseas lines for perhaps another five years or more and could not have gained full entry to the European conference. Such a major institutional setback would have had more of a delaying effect than Sturmey's evolutionary economic perspective suggests. Government subsidy programs, crucial for the large sums they provided and for their assurance of support, led companies to assume they could count on the government, an assumption that sometimes encouraged them to take risks they would otherwise have avoided. The best example of this was the European line, which the N.Y.K. had initiated on the assumption that it would soon receive special subsidies, even though these subsidies were later unexpectedly delayed. Without that initial assumption the company might well have deferred its commitment.

In the years prior to 1900, when the N.Y.K. was struggling to enter new lines and conferences, its funds were too fully utilized to have allowed for a prolonged nonsubsidized competitive battle. It had already relied on a capital stock increase to finance new ships because its reserve funds were still miniscule. Only in the 1902 to 1903 years when cash assets began to accumulate (because of the subsidies), did the company venture beyond subsidized operations into feeder lines. This leaves us with an incongruous conclusion. Major expansion came in the late 1890s, when the N.Y.K. had no significant investments, had little in the way of reserves, and had waited much longer than expected for subsidies. But from 1904 to 1914, as reserves grew, strategy became more conservative. While not exactly parallel, the N.Y.K.'s use of its reserves to invest in government banks and industrial firms seems reminiscent of Mitsubishi's purchases of mines in the 1880s with its shipping subsidies, an apparent retrogression in financial policy away from the goals of expansion. Of course, there were important contrasts between the environments of the late 1890s and of the post-1904 period. One was the fact that the N.Y.K. had already expanded virtually to its geographic limits prior to 1904 (but without a parallel growth in the types of services, such as tramp shipping). A second was the greater pressure, especially from government intervention, that limited N.Y.K. autonomy in 1909 more than it had in 1896. Still, the following conclusions can be drawn. Subsidies were crucial to the company's early success in encircling the globe; they kept the company competitive on its trunk lines by enabling it to buy new ships through its reserves from 1912 to 1914. But the size of these reserves shows that expansion depended not so much on the degree of wealth as on a strategic commitment by management. The company's major innovation prior to World War I, the opening of the lightly subsidized Calcutta line, demonstrated the key to further expansion to be the business alliances in which the N.Y.K. joined with other Japanese firms in quest of their corporate goals.

Appendixes
Notes
Bibliography
Index

Appendix A
A Note on Ship Tonnages

The following are definitions of the two kinds of tonnage referred to in this book.

Gross tons (GT): The gross tonnage of a ship is the total volume of the ship.

Net tons (NT): Net tonnage refers only to that part of a vessel which carries cargo.

Statistical Usage: Meiji period government statistics on ships were kept in net tons. Consequently, most official yearbooks contain net tonnage figures. Generally speaking these statistics are available only for the total number of ships and total tonnage in the country. They do not include a breakdown by company. Shipping companies kept their own statistics in gross tons. For this reason the government tonnage statistics are of little value in computing concentration ratios. For comparative analysis it is necessary to use company histories to collect data on individual firms.

Unless otherwise indicated all references in the text to "tons" are to gross tonnage.

Appendix B
Company Administrative Terminology

1. *Middle Management*

In recent years there has emerged a series of English terms for contemporary Japanese administrative offices which some scholars have regarded as standard translations. (See Rodney Clark, *The Japanese Company,* Yale, 1979, p. 105; and Johannes Hirschmeier and Yui Tsunehiko, *The Development of Japanese Business, 1600-1980,* 2d. edition, Allen & Unwin, 1981, pp. 379-383). Terms relevant to this book are as follows:

bu	department
ka	section
kakari	subsection

For two reasons I have not used these translations: (1) They are not as standard as these authors suggest. The N.Y.K. does not use them on its business cards. (2) More important, it would be difficult to apply translations of contemporary administrative terminology to the nineteenth century. It would be quite misleading, for example, to call an administrative unit of a company in the 1890s a subsection (just because its Japanese title at that time happened to be *kakari*) when it clearly performed the functions of what Clark would now call a department (*bu*). Another problem is that administrative terminology underwent numerous changes at least until the 1890s (there were further changes after World War I). To have described that evolution in my text would have necessitated changing the translations of Japanese terms several times in the course of the study. I therefore decided to use a standard translation for the same Japanese term whenever it appeared throughout the period covered, from 1870 to 1914. Next, I chose a set of translations that would make sense historically. Finally, the N.Y.K. still uses these translations on its business cards. They are as follows:

bu	division
ka	department
kakari	section

2. *Top Management*

In this case the translations are more standard. Certain administrative offices, however, did not evolve until after World War I. The terms in question are (Clark's translations):

senmu torishimariyaku	senior managing director
jōmu torishimariyaku	managing director

Since the office of *jōmu* arose after World War I, prior to the war the *senmu* was not "senior" to another class of director. I have, therefore, used the following translation:

senmu torishimariyaku	managing director

APPENDIX C-1: Value of Owned Tonnage by Line
(Unit: ¥1,000)

	Europe	USA	Australia	Bombay	Domestic & Near-Seas	Calcutta	Brazil	Requisitioned Ships	Total
1900/2	9,314 (45)	1,121 (5)	2,241 (11)	496 (2)	5,084 (24)			2,694 (13)	20,950
1901/1	9,797 (47)	1,462 (7)	2,052 (10)	763 (4)	5,482 (26)			1,412 (7)	20,968
1901/2	9,721 (48)	2,669 (13)	1,705 (9)	817 (4)	4,147 (21)			1,100 (6)	20,157
1902/2	8,830 (39)	4,460 (20)	2,949 (13)	873 (4)	5,283 (24)				22,395
1903/1	8,619 (38)	4,595 (20)	2,885 (13)	1,195 (5)	5,187 (23)				22,481
1903/2	8,195 (34)	5,109 (21)	2,757 (12)	1,384 (6)	6,408 (27)				23,853
1904/1	6,476 (26)	4,047 (17)	1,904 (8)	868 (4)	4,320 (18)			6,981 (28)	24,596
1905/1	0	1,757 (7)	313 (1)	0	1,319 (5)			21,198 (86)	24,588
1905/2	0	1,676 (7)	0	0	891 (4)			22,028 (90)	24,595
1906/1	571 (2)	1,468 (6)	483 (2)	15 (0)	2,567 (10)			19,509 (79)	24,612
1906/2	5,662 (24)	4,403 (19)	3,042 (13)	2,045 (9)	6,558 (28)			1,895 (8)	23,605
1907/1	7,422 (30)	5,099 (21)	2,968 (12)	1,520 (6)	7,509 (31)				24,518
1908/1	7,884 (32)	5,144 (21)	2,822 (12)	468 (2)	7,979 (33)				24,296
1908/2	8,436 (36)	5,006 (21)	2,749 (12)	123 (1)	7,032 (30)				23,346
1909/1	11,061 (42)	4,869 (18)	2,675 (10)	315 (1)	7,545 (29)				26,465
1909/2	16,085 (52)	4,149 (13)	2,602 (8)	672 (2)	8,000 (25)				31,508
1910/1	16,258 (53)	2,719 (9)	2,529 (8)	1,485 (5)	7,840 (25)				30,832
1910/2	15,011 (51)	2,364 (8)	2,456 (8)	2,127 (7)	7,539 (26)				29,496

APPENDIX C-1 (continued)

	Europe	USA	Australia	Bombay	Domestic & Near-Seas	Calcutta	Brazil	Requisitioned Ships	Total
1911/1	14,812 (52)	2,316 (8)	2,382 (8)	2,001 (7)	7,162 (25)				28,673
1911/2	14,274 (51)	2,225 (8)	2,309 (8)	2,032 (7)	7,046 (25)	12 (0)			27,898
1912/1	13,540 (50)	2,296 (9)	2,236 (8)	1,806 (7)	6,679 (25)	315 (1)	131 (1)		27,004
1912/2	12,712 (45)	3,555 (13)	2,162 (8)	1,801 (6)	7,120 (25)	768 (3)	327 (1)		28,446
1913/1	12,580 (42)	3,883 (13)	2,089 (7)	2,105 (7)	8,275 (27)	1,179 (4)	109 (0)		30,220
1913/2	12,251 (41)	3,729 (12)	2,167 (7)	2,233 (7)	8,244 (27)	1,312 (4)	343 (1)		30,279

Notes: All data in Appendix C are taken from SKS unless otherwise stated. Data are unavailable for omitted terms. Figures in parentheses are percentages of the total.

APPENDIX C-2: Freight Income by Line
(Unit: ¥1,000)

	Europe	USA	Australia	Bombay	Domestic & Near-Seas	Calcutta	Brazil	Total
1900/2	2,788 (43.4)	417 (6.5)	326 (5.1)	302 (4.7)	2,578 (40.2)			6,413
1901/1	3,393 (49.8)	395 (5.8)	308 (4.5)	268 (3.9)	2,453 (36.0)			6,817
1901/2	3,005 (43.4)	578 (8.3)	292 (4.2)	339 (4.9)	2,713 (39.2)			6,927
1902/2	2,779 (42.0)	750 (11.3)	280 (4.2)	376 (5.7)	2,429 (36.7)			6,614
1903/2	2,526 (36.9)	698 (10.2)	235 (3.4)	484 (7.1)	2,893 (42.3)			6,837
1904/1	2,058 (38.9)	591 (11.2)	147 (2.8)	465 (8.8)	2,024 (38.3)			5,285
1906/2	1,078 (17.9)	849 (14.1)	249 (4.1)	775 (12.9)	3,073 (51.0)			6,024
1907/1	3,142 (40.1)	979 (12.5)	261 (3.3)	629 (8.0)	2,831 (36.1)			7,842
1908/1	3,595 (40.2)	1,122 (12.6)	282 (3.2)	888 (9.9)	3,052 (34.1)			8,939
1908/2	3,294 (42.2)	692 (8.9)	293 (3.8)	811 (10.4)	2,710 (34.7)			7,800
1909/1	3,239 (44.6)	703 (9.7)	231 (3.2)	879 (12.1)	2,211 (30.4)			7,264
1910/1	3,974 (48.7)	495 (6.1)	279 (3.4)	827 (10.1)	2,579 (31.6)			8,154
1910/2	3,400 (42.3)	418 (5.2)	320 (4.0)	873 (10.9)	3,016 (37.6)			8,026
1911/1	3,795 (44.9)	637 (7.5)	325 (3.8)	818 (9.7)	2,869 (34.0)	16 (0.2)		8,444
1911/2	3,367 (39.2)	608 (7.1)	408 (4.7)	754 (8.8)	3,446 (40.1)			8,599
1912/1	3,734 (40.2)	849 (9.1)	384 (4.1)	856 (9.2)	3,181 (34.2)	286 (3.1)	3 (0.0)	9,292
1912/2	3,613 (34.0)	950 (8.9)	472 (4.4)	1,018 (9.6)	4,141 (39.0)	421 (4.0)	0	10,615
1913/1	3,650 (32.9)	1,126 (10.2)	379 (3.4)	866 (7.8)	4,305 (38.8)	549 (5.0)	213 (1.9)	11,088
1913/2	3,473 (30.8)	1,041 (9.2)	512 (4.5)	819 (7.9)	4,713 (41.8)	584 (5.2)	61 (0.5)	11,274

APPENDIX C-3: Rebates as a Percentage of Freight Income
(Selected Lines)

	Europe	USA	Bombay	Shanghai	Kobe-Otaru
1901/1	8.0	?	7.2	?	9.8
1901/2	7.0	?	17.4	2.6	7.8
1902/1	7.7	5.6	16.3	5.1	12.4
1902/2	8.1	6.2	25.4	3.6	9.7
1903/1	8.5	6.9	16.3	5.1	9.6
1903/2	8.2	9.5	31.0	2.9	7.8
1904/2[a]	51.8	38.0		?	6.6
1906/2	11.6	3.0	0.4	3.3	9.7
1907/1	2.7	9.6		7.8	
1907/2	6.2	1.3		3.6	
1908/1	8.4	1.0		7.5	
1908/2	10.7	0.2		2.9	
1909/1	8.9	1.4		8.4	
1909/2	9.3	1.3		3.0	
1910/1	8.0	3.7		7.5	

Source: (NYK), Ketsugi roku. These figures come from reports presented to the government several months after the regular business report (*NYK-EH*). They appear to come from separate accounts, for income figures often differ substantially from those in SKS in Appendix C-2.

Notes: The above data are available only for the years when the lines received special subsidies under the laws of the late 1890s.

[a]Despite large rebates, the Bombay line is recorded as having a minus income in this term.

APPENDIX C-4: Passenger Income by Line
(Unit: ¥1,000)

	Europe	USA	Australia	Bombay	Domestic & Near-Seas	Calcutta	Brazil	Total
1900/2	469 (34.7)	106 (7.9)	204 (15.1)	12 (0.9)	558 (41.3)			1,350
1901/1	352 (34.2)	37 (3.6)	173 (16.8)	12 (1.2)	454 (44.1)			1,029
1901/2	486 (35.1)	71 (5.1)	189 (13.7)	12 (0.9)	627 (45.3)			1,383
1902/2	403 (26.4)	250 (16.4)	204 (13.4)	15 (1.0)	655 (42.9)			1,527
1903/2	396 (22.1)	419 (23.4)	191 (10.6)	17 (0.9)	769 (42.9)			1,794
1904/1	351 (28.2)	285 (22.9)	112 (9.0)	10 (0.8)	489 (39.2)			1,246
1906/2	200 (13.2)	242 (15.9)	168 (11.1)	19 (1.3)	891 (58.6)			1,520
1907/1	371 (22.4)	418 (25.2)	131 (7.9)	10 (0.6)	730 (44.0)			1,659
1908/1	421 (23.1)	472 (25.9)	186 (10.2)	9 (0.5)	734 (40.3)			1,821
1908/2	444 (26.1)	365 (21.4)	208 (12.2)	3 (0.2)	684 (40.1)			1,704
1909/1	477 (37.2)	266 (20.8)	142 (11.1)	1 (0.1)	396 (30.9)			1,281
1910/1	606 (45.5)	190 (14.3)	152 (11.4)	1 (0.1)	384 (28.8)			1,333
1910/2	559 (35.5)	234 (14.9)	208 (13.2)	1 (0.1)	571 (36.3)			1,573
1911/1	631 (45.4)	237 (17.1)	139 (10.0)	1 (0.1)	383 (27.6)			1,390
1911/2	607 (34.5)	321 (18.2)	251 (14.3)	1 (0.1)	580 (32.9)			1,761
1912/1	712 (41.4)	262 (15.2)	195 (11.3)	5 (0.3)	455 (26.5)	2 (0.1)	78 (4.5)	1,720
1912/2	637 (30.8)	432 (20.9)	307 (14.9)	1 (0.0)	590 (28.5)	23 (1.1)	77 (3.7)	2,067
1913/1	817 (41.5)	361 (18.3)	193 (9.8)	6 (0.3)	445 (22.6)	65 (3.3)	84 (4.3)	1,971
1913/2	653 (29.2)	396 (17.7)	301 (13.4)	3 (0.1)	710 (31.7)	82 (3.7)	92 (4.1)	2,238

APPENDIX C-5: Total Operating Income by Line
(Unit: ¥1,000)

	Europe	USA	Australia	Bombay	Domestic & Near-Seas	Calcutta	Brazil	Total
1900/2	3,257 (42.0)	523 (6.7)	530 (6.8)	314 (4.0)	3,136 (40.4)			7,763
1901/1	3,745 (47.7)	432 (5.5)	481 (6.1)	280 (3.6)	2,907 (37.1)			7,846
1901/2	3,491 (42.0)	649 (7.8)	481 (5.8)	351 (4.2)	3,340 (40.2)			8,310
1902/2	3,182 (39.1)	1,000 (12.3)	484 (5.9)	391 (4.8)	3,084 (37.9)			8,141
1903/2	2,922 (33.9)	1,117 (12.9)	426 (4.9)	501 (5.8)	3,662 (42.4)			8,631
1904/1	2,409 (36.9)	876 (13.4)	259 (4.0)	475 (7.3)	2,513 (38.5)			6,531
1906/2	1,278 (16.9)	1,091 (14.5)	417 (5.5)	794 (10.5)	3,964 (52.5)			7,544
1907/1	3,513 (37.0)	1,397 (14.7)	392 (4.1)	639 (6.7)	3,561 (37.5)			9,501
1908/1	4,016 (37.3)	1,594 (14.8)	468 (4.3)	897 (8.3)	3,786 (35.2)			10,760
1908/2	3,738 (39.3)	1,057 (11.1)	501 (5.3)	814 (8.6)	3,394 (35.7)			9,504
1909/1	3,716 (43.5)	969 (11.3)	373 (4.4)	880 (10.3)	2,607 (30.5)			8,545
1910/1	4,580 (48.3)	685 (7.2)	431 (4.5)	828 (8.7)	2,963 (31.2)			9,487
1910/2	3,959 (41.2)	652 (6.8)	528 (5.5)	874 (9.1)	3,587 (37.4)			9,599
1911/1	4,426 (45.0)	874 (8.9)	464 (4.7)	819 (8.3)	3,252 (33.1)			9,834
1911/2	3,974 (38.4)	929 (9.0)	659 (6.4)	755 (7.3)	4,026 (38.9)	16 (0.2)		10,360
1912/1	4,446 (40.4)	1,111 (10.1)	579 (5.3)	861 (7.8)	3,636 (33.0)	288 (2.6)	81 (0.7)	11,012
1912/2	4,250 (33.5)	1,382 (10.9)	779 (6.1)	1,019 (8.0)	4,731 (37.3)	444 (3.5)	77 (0.6)	12,682
1913/1	4,467 (34.2)	1,487 (11.4)	572 (4.4)	872 (6.7)	4,750 (36.4)	614 (4.7)	297 (2.3)	13,059
1913/2	4,126 (30.5)	1,437 (10.6)	813 (6.0)	894 (6.6)	5,423 (40.1)	666 (4.9)	153 (1.1)	13,512

Note: Total operating income is the sum of Appendixes C-2 and C-4. I have omitted requisitioned ships, since I do not have figures for their income.

APPENDIX C-6: Total Subsidies by Line
(Unit: ¥1,000)

	Europe	USA	Australia	Bombay	Domestic & Near-Seas	Calcutta	Total
1900/2	1,327	149	258	76	51		1,860
1901/1	1,411	126	262	84	329		2,213
1901/2	1,398	287	253	108	390		2,436
1902/2	1,328	497	264	128	437		2,654
1903/2	1,333	569	281	153	435		2,771
1904/1	977	467	165	90	319		2,018
1906/2	856	491	242	101	466		2,156
1907/1	1,289	577	235	87	411		2,599
1908/1	1,417	551	274	14	388		2,643
1908/2	1,492	561	218		454		2,725
1909/1	1,736	475	212		411		2,834
1910/1	2,077	391	211	100	410		3,189
1910/2	1,744	310	215	174	489		2,941[a]
1911/1	1,768	311	212	196	406		2,893
1911/2	1,730	306	214	189	493		2,932
1912/1	1,622	269	213	131	387		2,622
1912/2	1,507	268	184	15	442	50	2,466
1913/1	1,509	279	211	49	386		2,433
1913/2	1,510	253	158		430	53	2,403

Notes: [a]This total includes ¥9,000 in miscellaneous grants, mostly for service to Hawaii. SKS lists specified line subsidies and navigation aid separately. I have added these together to obtain the total subsidy for each line. Bombay line subsidies after 1906 all came in the form of navigation aid. Likewise, increased navigation aid explains the swelling of the European line's subsidy in 1909–1911.

APPENDIX C-7: Profits by Line
(Unit: ¥1,000)

	Europe	USA	Australia	Bombay	Domestic & Near-Seas	Calcutta	Brazil	Requisitioned Ships	Total Operating Profit	Other Profit	Total Profit
1900/2	1,361 (46)	188 (6)	193 (7)	25 (1)	701 (24)			56 (2)	2,524 (85)	436 (15)	2,960
1901/1	1,406 (50)	74 (3)	111 (4)	110 (4)	181 (7)			387 (14)	2,270 (81)	535 (19)	2,805
1901/2	1,202 (46)	182 (7)	103 (4)	114 (4)	473 (18)			107 (4)	2,182 (83)	458 (17)	2,640
1902/2	1,110 (48)	344 (15)	105 (5)	131 (6)	187 (8)				1,878 (81)	454 (19)	2,332
1903/1	1,154 (52)	496 (22)	66 (3)	154 (7)	-23 (-1)				1,848 (83)	385 (17)	2,233
1903/2	1,076 (42)	465 (18)	104 (4)	170 (7)	249 (10)				2,064 (80)	526 (20)	2,589
1904/1	620 (42)	338 (23)	-54 (-4)	165 (11)	-125 (-9)			50 (3)	995 (68)	475 (32)	1,469
1905/1	-18 (-1)	189 (13)	-14 (-1)	9 (1)	367 (25)			1,270 (86)	1,803 (121)	-318 (-21)	1,486
1905/2	-41 (-3)	252 (17)	-2 (0)	93 (6)	310 (20)			1,307 (86)	1,919 (126)	-394 (-26)	1,525
1906/1	62 (3)	109 (5)	-21 (-1)	113 (5)	-549 (-25)			1,034 (47)	747 (34)	1,477 (66)	2,224
1906/2	530 (43)	316 (25)	-43 (-3)	-215 (-17)	-823 (-66)			243 (20)	8 (1)	1,236 (99)	1,244

APPENDIX C-7 (continued)

	Europe	USA	Australia	Bombay	Domestic & Near-Seas	Calcutta	Brazil	Requisitioned Ships	Total Operating Profit	Other Profit	Total Profit
1907/1	1,028 (80)	413 (32)	-89 (-7)	-169 (-13)	-1,055 (-82)				128 (10)	1,152 (90)	1,281
1908/1	946 (65)	527 (36)	10 (1)	-41 (-3)	-603ª (-41)				840 (57)	627 (43)	1,467
1908/2	787 (57)	263 (19)	-24 (-2)	-8 (-1)	-233 (-17)				785 (57)	596 (43)	1,381
1909/1	847 (72)	140 (12)	-84 (-7)	147 (13)	-502 (-43)				548 (47)	630 (53)	1,178
1909/2	1,083 (75)	239 (17)	47 (3)	60 (4)	121 (8)				1,550 (108)	-108 (-8)	1,442
1910/1	1,321 (78)	292 (17)	-71 (-4)	91 (5)	-214 (-13)				1,420 (83)	282 (17)	1,702
1910/2	989 (42)	74 (3)	83 (4)	238 (11)	604 (26)				1,987 (85)	361 (15)	2,348
1911/1	1,399 (82)	173 (10)	-12 (-1)	201 (12)	-41 (-2)				1,719 (100)	-2 (0)	1,717
1911/2	1,176 (44)	274 (10)	129 (5)	125 (5)	526 (20)	3 (0)			2,235 (83)	444 (17)	2,678
1912/1	1,579 (73)	230 (11)	40 (2)	142 (7)	-211 (-10)	-148 (-7)	-22 (-1)		1,611 (75)	550 (25)	2,160
1912/2	1,395 (50)	249 (9)	132 (5)	156 (6)	461 (16)	-155 (-6)	-10 (0)		2,227 (79)	576 (21)	2,803
1913/1	1,712 (57)	262 (9)	51 (2)	-17 (-1)	386 (13)	-193 (-7)	114 (4)		2,315 (77)	675 (23)	2,990

APPENDIX C-7 (continued)

	Europe	USA	Australia	Bombay	Domestic & Near-Seas	Calcutta	Brazil	Requisitioned Ships	Total Operating Profit	Other Profit	Total Profit
1913/2	1,157	376	113	0	882	-171	-100		2,258	627	2,885
	(40)	(13)	(4)	(0)	(31)	(-6)	(-4)		(78)	(22)	

Notes: (1) Figures in parentheses are percentages of total profit. "Negative percentages" are included to indicate more clearly the scale of the deficit. (2) The "other profit" shown in SKS for 1910–1911/1 does not match total profits. The figures are marginally different for 1910 but add over ¥400,000 in 1911/1. Since both the operating profit and total profit in SKS are consistent with *NYK-EH*, I have "corrected" the other profit figure here simply by subtraction. (3) Operating profits here include results of charter business. (4) The N.Y.K. referred to the Brazil operation not as a "line," but usually as a "sailing west of Europe."

ªThis contains a deficit of ¥86,911 recorded under the Bangkok, or Southeast Asian, line. In earlier years this line had been placed in the domestic and near-seas category.

APPENDIX C-8: Subsidies as a Percentage of Operating Income

	Europe	USA	Australia	Bombay	Domestic & Near-Seas	Calcutta	Total
1900/2	40.7	28.5	48.7	24.2	1.6		24.0
1901/1	37.7	29.2	54.5	30.0	11.3		28.2
1901/2	40.0	44.2	52.6	30.8	11.7		29.3
1902/2	41.7	49.7	54.5	32.7	14.2		32.6
1903/2	45.6	50.9	66.0	30.5	11.9		32.1
1904/1	40.6	53.3	63.7	18.9	12.7		30.9
1906/2	67.0	45.0	58.0	12.7	11.8		28.6
1907/1	36.7	41.3	59.9	13.6	11.5		27.4
1908/1	35.3	34.6	58.5	1.6	10.2		24.6
1908/2	39.9	53.1	43.5		13.4		28.7
1909/1	46.7	49.0	56.8		15.8		33.2
1910/1	45.3	57.1	49.0	12.1	13.8		33.6
1910/2	44.1	47.5	40.7	19.9	13.6		30.6
1911/1	39.9	35.6	45.7	24.1	12.5		29.4
1911/2	43.5	32.9	32.5	25.0	12.2		28.3
1912/1	36.5	24.2	36.8	15.2	10.6		23.8
1912/2	35.5	19.4	23.6	1.5	9.3	11.3	19.4
1913/1	33.8	18.8	36.9	5.6	8.1		18.6
1913/2	36.6	17.6	19.4		7.9	8.0	17.8

Note: Operating income is from Appendix C-5 and includes neither subsidies nor income from requisitioned ships. Thus, the *ratio* of subsidies to operating income in 1900/2 would be 0.24.

APPENDIX C-9: Subsidies as a Percentage of Operating Profit

	Europe	USA	Australia	Bombay	Domestic & Near-Seas	Total
1900/2	97.5	79.3	133.7	304.0	7.3	73.7
1901/1	100.4	170.3	236.0	76.4	181.7	97.5
1901/2	116.3	156.8	245.6	94.7	82.5	111.6
1902/2	119.6	144.4	251.4	97.7	233.7	141.3
1903/2	123.9	122.4	270.2	90.0	174.7	134.3
1904/1	157.6	138.2	—	54.5	—	202.8
1906/2	161.5	155.4	—	—	—	26,950.0
1907/1	125.4	139.7	—	—	—	2,030.5
1908/1	150.0	104.6	2,740.0	—	—	314.6
1908/2	189.6	213.3	—	—	—	347.1
1909/1	205.0	339.3	—		—	517.2
1910/1	157.2	133.4	—	109.9	—	187.4
1910/2	176.3	418.9	259.0	73.1	81.0	125.3
1911/1	126.4	179.8	—	97.5	—	168.5
1911/2	147.1	111.7	165.9	151.2	93.7	131.2
1912/1	102.7	117.0	532.5	92.2	—	162.8
1912/2	108.0	107.6	139.4	9.6	95.9	110.7
1913/1	88.1	106.5	413.7		100.0	105.1
1913/2	130.5	67.3	139.8		48.8	106.4

Note: Operating profit includes both subsidies and profits from requisitioned ships. The dash indicates a deficit despite subsidies.

Appendix D
Banking of N.Y.K. Term Deposits

(Unit: ¥1,000)

	Mitsubishi	Mitsui	Dai Ichi	Third (Yasuda)	Fifteenth	Yokohama Specie	Sumitomo	Others (%)	Total
1900/1	1,250 (21)	550 (9)	950 (16)	950 (16)	800 (13)			(24)	5,950
1901/1	1,300 (15)	1,200 (14)	1,100 (13)	1,100 (13)	950 (11)		100 (1)	(33)	8,600
1901/2	1,100 (15)	950 (13)	950 (13)	950 (13)	800 (11)		150 (2)	(33)	7,350
1903/1	900 (14)	650 (10)	750 (12)	750 (12)	700 (11)		400 (6)	(35)	6,400
1903/2	900 (15)	800 (13)	750 (12)	800 (13)	550 (9)		150 (3)	(31)	6,100
1904/1	550 (15)	450 (12)	450 (12)	450 (12)	400 (11)		100 (3)	(37)	3,800
1905/1	900 (15)	650 (11)	800 (13)	810 (14)	550 (9)		400 (7)	(31)	5,960
1905/2	1,150 (18)	800 (13)	750 (12)	810 (13)	600 (9)		350 (6)	(30)	6,360
1906/1	1,150 (18)	800 (13)	750 (12)	810 (13)	600 (9)		450 (7)	(29)	6,410
1906/2	400 (12)	300 (9)	300 (9)	601 (18)	250 (8)		200 (6)	(37)	3,258
1907/1	350 (12)	300 (10)	300 (12)	648 (22)	150 (5)		120 (4)	(37)	2,948
1908/1	700 (20)	450 (13)	350 (10)	600 (17)	300 (9)	350 (10)	250 (7)	(16)	3,550
1908/2	550 (15)	500 (14)	450 (12)	450 (12)	300 (8)	400 (11)	300 (8)	(19)	3,650
1909/1	1,000 (24)	450 (11)	400 (10)	900 (22)	300 (7)	350 (9)	200 (5)	(12)	4,100
1910/1	1,000 (15)	900 (13)	850 (13)	900 (13)	700 (10)	800 (12)		(23)	6,700
1910/2	1,250 (14)	1,200 (14)	1,100 (12)	1,200 (14)	950 (11)	1,150 (13)	500 (6)	(17)	8,900
1911/2	2,200 (18)	1,650 (13)	1,650 (13)	1,700 (14)	1,150 (9)	1,350 (11)	650 (5)	(18)	12,547

APPENDIX D (continued)

	Mitsubishi	Mitsui	Dai Ichi	Third (Yasuda)	Fifteenth	Yokohama Specie	Sumitomo	Others (%)	Total
1912/1	2,200 (18)	1,700 (14)	1,700 (14)	1,700 (14)	800 (7)	1,150 (9)	650 (5)	(19)	12,250
1912/2	2,150 (17)	1,650 (13)	1,650 (13)	2,150 (17)	900 (7)	1,150 (9)	600 (5)	(18)	12,550
1913/1	2,150 (17)	1,550 (13)	1,550 (13)	2,150 (17)	1,100 (9)	1,000 (8)	500 (4)	(19)	12,400
1913/2	2,350 (19)	1,150 (9)	1,150 (9)	1,950 (16)	1,150 (9)	650 (5)	50 (0)	(31)	12,250

Source: SKS.

Note: These deposits were called term deposits (*teiki*) until 1911 and notice deposits (*tsūchi*) thereafter. Figures in parentheses represent the percentage total held by each bank.

Abbreviations Used in the Notes

FO
: Foreign Office, Records. Great Britain, Public Record Office. My citations use the hand-stamped pagination in the upper outside margin of the page.

GN
: Great Northern Railway Company Records, Minnesota Historical Society.

HG
: (NYK), Hōkoku (Reports), Gaikō-ka no bu (Foreign Lines Department). 1912–1914. A continuation of TH–KG, these reports often give chronological summaries of key issues. For business operations they rival NYK–TG in importance.

HK
: (NYK), Hōkoku (Reports), Kaikei no bu and Kaikei-ka no bu (Accounting Department). 1893–1914. Useful for stocks, bonds, and investments. Before 1907 I have used the date of entry (which precedes the item) rather than the date of the report.

JSS
: John Swire & Sons Ltd., Archive, School of Oriental and African Studies, University of London. See Hook for a guide to these papers which are useful for conferences and the early history of the Nisshin Kisen Kaisha.

JWM
: *Japan Weekly Mail.* This Japanese government-subsidized newspaper frequently went to great lengths to support the N.Y.K., but it is still extremely useful, for it specialized in international issues and catered to the shipping community.

KD
: Suehiro Kazuo, *Danshaku Kondō Renpei den narabi ikō* (The life and posthumous papers of Baron Kondō Renpei). 1932. Based partly on interviews, this official biography is unusually candid and detailed about internal company affairs.

KS

Kaiun shiryō (Historical materials on sea transport), ed., Koshino Kiyone. 3 vols., 1886. This set of newspaper articles is indispensable for following the Mitsubishi-KUK competition. It is useful for information on freight rates, stock prices, KUK personnel, and events at stockholders meetings. Since its facts are sometimes unreliable, it should be used as a supplementary source.

M Sha shi

Mitsubishi Sha shi (1870–1893). (Records of the Mitsubishi Company), ed., Mitsubishi Gōshi Kaisha Sōmu-bu Chōsa-ka. 1910–1919. This indispensable source for the period up to 1886 was partially classified as a secret internal record until the end of World War II, and it has been little utilized by Western scholars. It contains the company's annual accounts, important petitions, internal memoranda, and ship records. I used the original edition in the Mitsubishi Economic Research Institute, since reprinted by Tokyo University Press.

NYK 50 nenshi

Nippon Yūsen Kabushiki Kaisha 50 nenshi (A 50-year history of the N.Y.K.). Dōshahen, 1935.

NYK 70 nenshi

Nippon Yūsen Kabushiki Kaisha 70 nenshi (A 70-year history of the N.Y.K.). Dōshahen, 1956.

NYK–EH

Nippon Yūsen Kabushiki Kaisha eigyō hōkokusho (1899–1914) (N.Y.K. business report). Beginning in 1895, each business year (which lasted from October 1 to September 30) had two *terms,* the first ending in March, the second in September. Thus, the citation *NYK–EH* 16/1, March 1901, p. 37, refers to an item on page 37 of the N.Y.K. business report covering the first term of the company's 16th year of operation, which ended in March 1901. Similarly, a citation to *NYK–EH* 16/2, September 1901, would be to the second term of the same year.

NYK–H

Nippon Yūsen Kaisha hōkoku (1887–1893) (N.Y.K. business report).

NYK–JH

Nippon Yūsen Kabushiki Kaisha jigyō hōkokusho (1894–1899) (N.Y.K. business report).

NYK–KNS

Nippon Yūsen Kaisha kabunushi seimeibo and *Nippon Yūsen Kabushiki Kaisha kabunushi seimeibo* (N.Y.K. stockholders lists).

NYK–KSG

Nippon Yūsen Kaisha and Nippon Yūsen Kabushiki Kaisha kabunushi sōkai gijiroku (Minutes of the N.Y.K. stockholders meetings). Stockholders meetings were focused on the business report and thus their minutes contain useful elaboration. At times of major decisions or controversy the minutes (verbatim) sometimes run to more than 100 pages. These documents have no pagination. The page numbers in the notes are based on my own system of paginating copies. Under this system each copied impression on B4-sized paper contains two pages (like a book), one on the right hand side, a second on the left.

NYK–TG   Nippon Yūsen Kabushiki Kaisha torishimariyakukai gijiroku (Minutes of the N.Y.K. directors meetings). These board minutes, the most useful N.Y.K. materials, are records of decisions, not verbatim minutes, but they frequently quote telegrams or comments made in the meetings. Explanations of particularly important matters are often lengthy.

OM   Ōkuma monjo (Papers of Ōkuma Shigenobu), in Waseda University. These are useful for the 1870s when Ōkuma was finance minister. Few of the documents relating to shipping have appeared in the published collections of Ōkuma papers, though a number have been printed in biographical materials on other Meiji leaders.

OSK 50 nenshi   *Osaka Shōsen Kabushiki Kaisha 50 nenshi* (A 50-year history of the O.S.K.). Osaka, Dōshahen, 1934.

OSK 80 nenshi   *Osaka Shōsen Kabushiki Kaisha 80 nenshi* (An 80-year history of the O.S.K.). Osaka Shōsen Mitsui Senpaku Kabushiki Kaisha, 1966.

P&O   P. & O. Management Report to the Board. P. & O. Archives. National Maritime Museum, Greenwich. These reports end in 1898. Literally patched together, they contain occasional correspondence from agents in Asia and some statistical data, especially on freight rates, from which it is possible to construct a series over several years.

SEDS   *Shibusawa Eiichi denki shiryō* (Biographical materials on Shibusawa Eiichi). 1957–1958. This set of 56 volumes is a vast collection of documents on virtually every company and organization Shibusawa had anything to do with. They are indispensable for the KUK, for the accounts, relevant letters, and memoranda printed here probably constitute the most unified collection on that company.

The volume number is omitted in citations to vol. 8.

SKS   (NYK), Sho kanjō setsumeisho (Explanations of various accounts). 1899–1913. An accounting historian's dream, these reports were the basis for *NYK–EH*. My calculations from them are in Appendix C. Along with other documents listed in my bibliography under "(NYK). Miscellaneous material," they were discovered in a warehouse in March 1983.

TH–KG

(NYK), Torishimariyakukai hōkoku (Report to the board of directors), Kamotsu-ka Gaikō (Freight Department, Foreign Lines). 1898–1911. Prepared primarily for Managing Director Iwanaga Shōichi. See also HG. I have used the date of entry before 1904 and the date of report (inside the board's red seal) after that.

Yanosuke den

Iwasaki Yanosuke den (Biography of Iwasaki Yanosuke). Denki Hensankai. 2 vols., 1971. This has fewer documents than *YD*, but it is the most comprehensive survey of Mitsubishi in the post-1885 era.

YD

Iwasaki Yatarō den (Biography of Iwasaki Yatarō). Denki Hensankai. 2 vols., 1967. This contains many documents, but where possible it is wise to check with the original.

The volume number is omitted in citations to vol. 2.

Two additional items deserve mention because they have been little used by Japanese scholars. Most popular prewar accounts of Japanese business have limited value today. One exception is Nishino Kiyosaku's *Hanseiki zaikai sokumenshi* (Tōyō Keizai Shuppanbu, 1932). Nishino could provide much inside information on the Mitsubishi–KUK merger because he had partial access to the *M Sha shi* and because he interviewed some of the same contemporaries on whom Suehiro relied for his biography of Kondō Renpei. Second, one mine of material I have not used is the 400-odd volumes of N.Y.K. ledger books stored at Hitotsubashi University covering the years 1885 to 1945. Professor Nakamura Masanori introduced them to me in late 1975, and I was only able to check a few details from the company accounts. These ledgers would be useful for a case study of a particular year's accounting or for an attempt to trace a particular issue over a span of years.

Notes

INTRODUCTION

1. *YD*, I, 430–433; Tanaka Sōgorō, *Iwasaki Yatarō den* (Tōyō Shokan, 1955), pp. 69–72, and Marius Jansen, *Sakamoto Ryōma and the Meiji Restoration* (Princeton, 1961), pp. 276–277.

2. *YD*, p. 585.

3. One *koku* equals 5.1 American bushels, 0.278 cubic meters, about one-sixth of a net ton, or one-tenth of a gross ton.

4. Miwa Ryōichi, "Suijō kōtsū," in Toyoda Takeshi and Kodama Kōta, eds., *Kōtsūshi*, vol. 24 of *Taikei Nihonshi sōsho* (Yamakawa Shuppansha, 1970), pp. 477–478. For a more positive interpretation of Bakumatsu shipping as well as shipbuilding, see Thomas C. Smith, *Political Change and Industrial Development in Japan: Government Enterprise, 1868–1880* (Stanford, 1955), pp. 7–11.

5. See Togai Yoshio, "'Zaibatsu' to iu kotoba," (The term "zaibatsu"), in Nakagawa Keiichirō et al., eds., *Kindai Nihon keieishi no kiso chishiki* (Yūhikaku, 1974), p. 126. In popular writing on the early zaibatsu great emphasis has been placed on the relationship between businessmen and politicians from Satsuma and Choshu, the two western domains which led the Restoration movement. The common view is that politicians from Satsuma secured special favors for Mitsubishi, and politicians from Choshu did likewise for Mitsui. Some confirmation of this interpretation is presented here, but in general a more compelling interpretation of government business policy can be found in rational economic considerations.

6. Morikawa Hidemasa, "Nihon zaibatsu no keiei senryaku: ishi kettei katei o chūshin ni," *Keiei shigaku* 13.1:30–36, 44–48 (October 1978).

7. On "trigger" industries, see Sanuki Toshio, *Sangyō kōzō* (Nihon Keizai Shinbunsha, 1981), pp. 23–62, which describes a similar role played by shipping after World War II.

8. Alfred D. Chandler, Jr., *Strategy and Structure: Chapters in the History of the Industrial Enterprise* (Anchor Books, 1966), p. 16.

9. See Chalmers Johnson, *MITI and the Japanese Miracle: The Growth of Industrial Policy, 1925-1975* (Stanford, 1982), p. 99 and p. 88, where the generalization that between the Matsukata reforms and the 1920s "the government's overall policy toward industry and foreign trade had become a more or less orthodox version of laissez faire" is hedged too much by the word "overall."

10. Johannes Hirschmeier and Yui Tsunehiko, *The Development of Japanese Business, 1600-1973* (Harvard, 1975). The revised edition of this work, *The Development of Japanese Business, 1600-1980* (George Allen & Unwin, 2d edition, 1981), contains more information on organization and structure. All citations here, however, are to the first edition.

11. Richard Tanner Pascale and Anthony Athos, *The Art of Japanese Management* (New York, 1982), esp. pp. 120-130.

12. An exception is Yoshihara Kunio, *Sogo Shosha: The Vanguard of the Japanese Economy* (Oxford, 1982), which contains a lengthy, well-researched historical section.

13. I have used the word structure to mean (1) organization in the administrative sense, the hierarchy of managerial authority within a firm and also its network of operations, as discussed by Chandler; and (2) the percentage distribution of different kinds of industrial or business activity within a company or enterprise group, and in certain cases, within Japan as a whole, as in "industrial structure."

14. See Mishima Yasuo, ed., *Mitsubishi zaibatsu,* in *Nihon zaibatsu keieishi* (Nihon Keizai Shinbunsha, 1981).

15. *Nihon kaiun keieishi,* 6 vols., ed., Kaiji Sangyō Kenkyūjo (Nihon Keizai Shinbunsha, 1980-1984).

16. A recent exception to this generalization is Sugiyama Kazuo, *Kaiungyō to kin'yū,* vol. 4 of *Nihon kaiun keieishi,* (Nihon Keizai Shinbunsha, 1981) which makes use of NYK-TG in chapters on the N.Y.K. in the Inter-War Years.

17. See Kozo Yamamura, "Japan, 1868-1930: A Revised View," in Rondo Cameron, ed., *Banking and Economic Development* (Oxford, 1972), pp. 168-198; and Gary Saxonhouse, "A Tale of Japanese Technological Diffusion in the Meiji Period," *Journal of Economic History* 34.1:149-165 (March 1974). Mark Fruin's work on Kikkoman, to be published in the Harvard Business History Series, will deal with strategy and structure. See also Kawabe Nobuo, "Japanese Business in the United States before World War II: The Case of Mitsubishi Shoji Kaisha, The San Francisco and Seattle Branches," PhD dissertation, The Ohio State University, 1980.

18. My impression is that N.Y.K. executives are more conscious of the conflict in cases like this than many scholars who write about Japanese government-business relations.

19. For a discussion of social gain and private benefit, see Douglass North and Robert Paul Thomas, *The Rise of the Western World: A New Economic History* (Cambridge, Cambridge University Press, 1976), pp. 1–8.

20. This is not to deny that industrial developments prior to 1914 laid the foundation which enabled Japan to exploit its opportunities during the war.

21. Information from the Editorial Department of Tōyō Keizai Shinpōsha. The N.Y.K. is not the "world's largest shipping company in bottoms owned," as claimed in *Japan Company Handbook, 1st Half, 1983* (Tōyō Keizai Shinpōsha, 1983), p. 1009.

PART ONE: THE EMERGENCE OF MITSUBISHI: 1870–1880

1. THE FIRST SHIPPING COMPANIES: 1870–1874

1. Yatarō's social origins were typical of many borderline samurai who often sold and bought status for pragmatic reasons. Financial problems prompted an Iwasaki ancestor to sell the family's rural samurai (*gōshi*) status in 1795. Yatarō repurchased the status in 1861 because he thought it would prove useful to his future prospects. See *YD*, I, 58–66, 115, 258–259; and Kozo Yamamura, *A Study of Samurai Income and Entrepreneurship* (Harvard, 1974), pp. 143–144. The section in Yamamura's book on Yatarō appeared earlier as the "The Founding of Mitsubishi: A Case Study in Japanese Business History," *Business History Review* 41.2: 141–160 (Summer 1967).

2. Quoted in Nakagawa Keiichirō and Yui Tsunehiko, eds., *Keiei tetsugaku, keiei rinen: Meiji-Taishō* (Daiyamondosha, 1969), p. 121.

3. For useful lists of Yatarō's "practices," see Yamamura, *Samurai Income and Entrepreneurship*, pp. 145–147, 217–218. See also *YD*, passim and for the problem of domain notes, pp. 612–619.

4. Unless otherwise noted the following summary of Yatarō's role during the years 1870–1873 is taken from *YD*, pp. 1–49.

5. *YD*, I, 644.

6. For the sale of domain enterprises, see *YD*, pp. 22–32, 73. For documents and comments on Yatarō's borrowing and purchases, mostly from foreigners, see *YD*, I, 589–597, 740–741; and *YD*, pp. 678–686. The largest of the domain's debts was to the American firm of Walsh, Hall & Co., from which Yatarō had borrowed 400,000 *ryō*. (The *ryō* was the monetary unit preceding the yen. In 1868 it was officially readjusted at

the rate of 1 *ryō* to ¥1.0832. See Yamamura, *Samurai Income and Entrepreneurship*, p. 217; and Araki Nobuyoshi, *En no rekishi* (Kyōiku-sha, 1979), pp. 23-45.) As security for the loan Yatarō granted the American firm rights to deal in the domain's camphor. The Finance Ministry assumed the outstanding portion of this debt upon the domain's abolition. See also n. 48 of this chapter.

7. *YD*, p. 22.

8. Nagasawa Yasuaki, "Meijiki Mitsubishi no toppu manejimento soshiki," *Keiei shigaku* 14.1:30, 44n5 (September 1979), favors early 1872 and the establishment of the Mitsukawa Shōkai as the time by which Yatarō had turned the enterprise into his own firm. See also the same author's "Iwasaki Yatarō to Mitsubishi no hasshō," in Miyamoto Mataji, ed., *Kamigata no kenkyū* (Osaka, Seibundō, 1976), IV, 223-248. On the meaning and origins of the name "Mitsubishi," see *YD*, pp. 34-35, 46-47; *Yanosuke den*, II, 114-115; and Furuta Ryoichi and Hirai Yoshi-kazu, *A Short History of Japanese Merchant Shipping* (Tokyo News Service, 1967), p. 111. Literally "three water caltrops," Mitsubishi is sometimes translated as "three diamonds" because of the similarity in appearance between diamonds and leaves on the surface of a pond. The Mitsubishi crest is a combination of the crests of the Iwasaki family and the Tosa domain.

9. Quoted in Irimajiri Yoshinaga, *Iwasaki Yatarō* (Yoshikawa Kōbunkan, 1960), pp. 104-105.

10. Quoted in Hirschmeier and Yui, p. 139; from *YD*, p. 75. On early Mitsu-bishi management, see Nagasawa Yasuaki, "Shoki Mitsubishi no keiei soshiki: kaiungyō o chūshin ni shite," *Keiei shigaku* 11.3:26-49 (March 1977), and "Meijiki Mitsubishi no toppu manejimento."

11. Irimajiri, p. 106; Nakagawa and Yui, p. 132.

12. Yoshino Toshihiko, *Nihon Ginkō* (Iwanami Shoten, 1963), pp. 72-76.

13. *YD*, p. 19. The phrase "for the good of the domain" is a translation of "*kuni no tame.*" The word "*kuni*" has the meaning of both "domain" and "country." In this context Yatarō seems to be referring to the local area, Tosa, rather than to Japan as a whole.

14. *YD*, p. 412.

15. Morikawa Hidemasa, "The Organizational Structure of the Mitsubishi and Mitsui Zaibatsu, 1868-1922: A Comparative Study," *Business History Review* 44.1:62-83 (Spring 1970). For comments on the influence of the Keiō school on Mitsubishi personnel, see the same author's *Nihon-gata keiei no genryū* (Tōyō Keizai Shinpōsha, 1973), pp. 51-56. For official biographies, see *KD;* and Shukuri Shigeichi, *Shōda Heigorō* (1932).

16. *Yanosuke den*, I, 166, 167.

17. Quoted in Irimajiri, p. 108.

18. *KD*, pp. 93-108.

19. For a list of shipping regulations in the Meiji period, see Tominaga Yūji, *Kōtsū ni okeru shihonshugi no hatten* (Iwanami Shoten, 1953), pp. 111-115. For the 1/1870 proclamations, see "Ōkurashō enkakushi," vol. 2, in Tsuchiya Takao and Ōuchi Hyōe, eds., *Meiji zenki zaisei keizai shiryō shūsei* (Kaizōsha, 1931-1934), III, 269-272.

20. Saitō Yoshihisa, "Meiji shonen no kaiun seisaku," *Dōshisha shōgaku* 22.5-6:64 (March 1971). See also Shibusawa Yeiichi, "Joint-Stock Enterprise in Japan," in Ōkuma Shigenobu, ed., *Fifty Years of New Japan* (New York, 2d ed., 1970), I, 466.

21. *NYK 70 nenshi*, p. 3. The suffix *"gumi"* indicated a family partnership organized as a purveyor to the government.

22. Miyamoto Mataji, "Kaisō Kaisha no kōhai," in *Uozumi sensei koki kinen ronsō* (Suitashi, Kansai Daigaku, 1959), pp. 666. This same essay is reprinted with minor changes as part of "Kaisō Kaisha to Nihon Koku Yūbin Jōkisen Kaisha," in Miyamoto's *Meiji zenki keizaishi no kenkyū* (Osaka, Seibundō, 1971). See pp. 128-129.

23. Quoted in Saitō, "Meiji shonen," p. 69. This directive is scarcely different in content from Honda Toshiaki's criticism of shipping practices written in 1798. See Donald Keene, *The Japanese Discovery of Europe, 1720-1830* (Stanford, 1969), pp. 95, 177.

24. Saitō, "Meiji shonen," p. 67.

25. *SEDS*, II, 552.

26. U.S. Department of Commerce, *Government Aid to Merchant Shipping* (Washington, 1925), pp. 277-278; Jesse E. Saugstad, *Shipping and Shipbuilding Subsidies*, U.S. Department of Commerce (Washington, 1932), p. 58 (known commonly as the *Saugstad Report*); *OSK 80 nenshi*, p. 2; John G. B. Hutchins, *The American Maritime Industries and Public Policy, 1789-1914* (Harvard, 1941), pp. 529-530.

27. *NYK 70 nenshi*, p. 2. See also Arthur E. Tiedemann, "Japan's Economic Foreign Policies, 1868-1893," in James W. Morley, ed., *Japan's Foreign Policy, 1868-1941, A Research Guide* (Columbia, 1974), p. 120.

28. Miyamoto, "Kaisō Kaisha to Nihon Koku Yūbin Jōkisen Kaisha," pp. 130-132.

29. *Teishin jigyōshi* (1940), VI, 757-759; *Meiji zaiseishi*, ed., Ōkurashōnai Dō Hensankai (Yoshikawa Kōbunkan, 1971), I, 304, 309, 315.

30. On 11/3/1872 the company changed its name to the Japan National Mail Steamship Company (Nihon Koku Yūbin Jōkisen Kaisha), and it is commonly known by this name.

31. Shiroyanagi Shūko, *Zaikai taiheiki* (Nihon Hyōronsha, 1929), p. 93.

32. Miyamoto Mataji, "Nihon Seifu Yūbin Jōkisen Kaisha ni tsuite," *Osaka*

daigaku keizaigaku, 9.1:2–7 (July 1959). This article also appears in revised form as part of "Kaisō Kaisha to Nihon Koku Yūbin Jōkisen Kaisha." See pp. 132–142.

33. Miyamoto Mataji, *Onogumi no kenkyū* (Ōhara Shinseisha, 1970), III, 131.

34. Okaniwa Hiroshi, *Nihon kaiun kin'yū hattatsushi* (privately printed, December 1959), p. 55.

35. See the writings of Johannes Hirschmeier, "Shibusawa Eiichi: Industrial Pioneer," in William W. Lockwood, ed., *The State and Economic Enterprise in Japan* (Princeton, 1965), pp. 209–247; and *The Origins of Entrepreneurship in Meiji Japan* (Harvard, 1964).

36. Shibagaki Kazuo has called the YJK a *kokusaku kaisha* in *Nihon kin'yū shihon bunseki* (Tokyo Daigaku Shuppankai, 1965), p. 57.

37. John R. Black, *Young Japan: Yokohama and Yedo, 1858–1879* (Oxford, 1969, reprint of original 1883 ed.), II, 365, 451–452.

38. For an example of government arrogance, see the Council of State "advertisement" in Irimajiri, p. 114. Yamamura also comments that Yatarō offered "longer and better-connected shipping schedules." See *Samurai Income and Entrepreneurship,* p. 147.

39. Black, II, 451–453.

40. Quoted in Irimajiri, p. 116.

41. Quoted in *YD,* p. 83. For Yatarō's letters to Yanosuke in 1872 and 1873, see *Iwasaki Yatarō nikki* (Denki Hensankai, 1975), pp. 635–651.

42. For brief comments on industrial policy, see Ōe Shinobu, *Nihon no sangyō kakumei* (Iwanami Shoten, 1968), p. 24.

43. Miyamoto, "Kaisō Kaisha to Nihon Koku Yūbin Jōkisen Kaisha," pp. 164–165.

44. For the YJK accounts, see Yamaguchi Kazuo, "Meiji shoki no gaikoku kaiun to Mitsubishi Kaisha," *Sekai keizai bunseki – Wakimura Yoshitarō kyōju kanreki kinen ronbunshū* (Iwanami Shoten, 1962), p. 142 (also in OM, A2957).

45. Proposal from Ōkubo to Chief Minister Sanjō Sanetomi concerning export industries, 1875, in *Meiji Japan Through Contemporary Sources, III, 1869–1894* (The Centre for East Asian Cultural Studies, 1972), pp. 18–23.

46. Some scholars have mistakenly assumed that this repair subsidy was actually given to the company. See for example Ōe, p. 22. For details on the episode, see Miyamoto, *Onogumi no kenkyū,* IV, English summary, p. 11; and "Kaishō Kaisha to Nihon Koku Yūbin Jōkisen Kaisha," pp. 164–165; *KS,* I, 381–382; and *SEDS,* p. 67. The Finance Ministry's accounting reform involved a switch in the fiscal year.

47. Okaniwa, p. 60.

48. Shiroyanagi Shūko, *Nihon kaiun no kensetsusha, Iwasaki Yatarō* (Chō-bunkaku, 1942), pp. 175–179; Jansen, *Sakamoto*, p. 276; *YD*, p. 71. Mishima, ed., *Mitsubishi zaibatsu*, pp. 136–137, notes that, since Yatarō's many foreign loans were short-term, they did not constitute a long-term means of raising funds. This distinction is less important than it seems, for Yatarō's abilities as a speculator enabled him to accumulate capital through the use of short-term loans.

49. *YD*, pp. 71–72; Black, II, 451; Lewis Bush, *The Life and Times of the Illustrious Captain Brown* (Voyageurs Press, 1970), p. 69.

50. *YD*, p. 73; *Yanosuke den*, I, 154–155. The Mexican dollar was an international currency in East Asia. The Meiji government created a silver yen as a special "trade dollar" equivalent to the Mexican dollar. Until the post-Satsuma Rebellion inflation the paper yen was equivalent to this silver yen and approximately equal to the U.S. dollar. For this reason yen and dollars were used interchangeably in foreign trade transactions until the late 1870s. Hiroshi Shinjō, *History of the Yen* (Kinokuniya, 1962), pp. 15–16, 28, 97.

51. Ono, head of the Finance Ministry's Public Works Department and in charge of planning for the construction of Osaka port, later became a key adviser to Mitsubishi. *YD*, I, 639–640; Shiroyanagi, *Zaikai taiheiki*, pp. 92, 98; Hatade Isao, *Nihon no zaibatsu to Mitsubishi* (Rakuyū Sho-bō, 1978), pp. 36–37.

52. Kajinishi Mitsuhaya, *Seishō* (Chikuma Shobō, 1963), p. 78; *YD*, I, 592; *YD*, pp. 72–73.

53. On camphor, see *YD*, p. 680; and n. 6 of this chapter.

54. For comments on this "centripetal" phenomenon in connection with the Restoration, see Albert M. Craig, *Chōshū in the Meiji Restoration* (Harvard, 1961), pp. 369–371.

55. For an account of the incident and subsequent expedition, see Grace Fox, *Britain and Japan, 1858–1883* (Oxford, 1969), pp. 280–310.

56. Kondō Renpei, "Japanese Communications: The Mercantile Marine," in Okuma, ed., *Fifty Years of New Japan*, I, 448.

57. After the expedition Mitsubishi operated 8 steamers over 1,000 tons. The YJK had but 2 of that capacity. See William D. Wray, "Mitsubishi and the N.Y.K. Line, 1870–1894: The Beginnings of the Modern Japanese Shipping Industry," PhD dissertation, Harvard University, 1976, p. 82.

58. Itō Yonejirō, *Nihon no kaiun* (Hōbunkan, 1922), p. 14; letters from LeGendre in OM, C445–C510; Bingham correspondence, OM, C76–C77. For a fuller treatment of the expedition and the foreigners involved, see Wray, pp. 59–85.

59. Iwata Masakazu, *Ōkubo Toshimichi: The Bismarck of Japan* (California,

1964), p. 199. See also *Ōkubo Toshimichi monjo* (Nihon Shiseki Kyōkai, 1927–1929), V, 499–500.

60. Shibusawa, "Joint-Stock Enterprise," p. 468.

61. See John G. Roberts, *Mitsui* (Weatherhill, 1973), p. 119. Roberts states that Yatarō "was on intimate terms" with Ōkubo and Ōkuma and that the "trio used to make nocturnal excursions to the pleasure quarters of Yoshiwara." Yatarō did move his head office from Osaka to Tokyo in April 1874, but his frequent visits to the pleasure quarters were to Shimbashi, not Yoshiwara, and his companions were Tosa men (NHK documentary in April 1983 based on newly discovered photographs of Yatarō's many geisha).

62. Shiroyanagi Shūko, *Iwasaki Yatarō den* (Kaizōsha, 1932), p. 305; and Wray, pp. 66–67. On Brown, see Bush, pp. 1–33, 61, 64; and OM, C131–C143; on Batchelder, see OM, C37–C54.

63. To cope with a financial crisis caused by heavy purchases, Ōkuma proposed allocating an emergency fund for the army and navy and reducing each ministry's budget. Nakamura Naomi, *Ōkuma Shigenobu* (Yoshikawa Kōbunkan, 1961), pp. 89–90. For Ōkuma's financial proposal, see *Ōkuma monjo* (Waseda Daigaku Shakai Kagaku Kenkyūjo, 1958–1962), I, 78–79.

64. Sugii Rokurō, "Meiji seifu no kaiun seisaku," *Geirin* 7.5:8–9 (1956).

65. Saitō, "Meiji shonen," p. 74.

66. For Kido's comments on resigning from the government in April 1874, see Irimajiri, p. 121.

67. See *YD*, pp. 102–105. Actually the YJK did undertake some token transport for the government, but it apparently did "not show any success." Obata Kyugoro, *An Interpretation of the Life of Viscount Shibusawa* (Tokyo, 1939), p. 115.

68. This is the opinion of Miyamoto Mataji, who also believes that the main reason why the YJK refused the government's request was its fear of domestic competition from Mitsubishi (personal communication).

69. Sugii, "Kaiun seisaku," pp. 10–11.

70. Shukuri, p. 369.

71. For a typical view, see Nagata Masaomi, *Meijiki keizai dantai no kenkyū* (Nikkan Rōdō Tsūshinsha, 1967), pp. 181–182.

72. Quoted in Segawa Shizuo, *Kaiun kōkokushi* (Kaiji Ihōsha, 1927), p. 216. Segawa states that Mitsubishi did not petition the government until after the foreigners had withdrawn and the government was searching for someone to continue the transport.

73. This record appears in a bound handwritten but unpublished series of reminiscences about Yatarō entitled "Ko shachō jiseki shiryō." The only copy was formerly in the possession of the Iwasaki Biographical Compil-

ation Committee, which in 1976 was incorporated into the Mitsubishi General Research Institute. Quoted in *YD*, pp. 106-107.

74. Segawa, p. 216.
75. "Ko shachō jiseki shiryō," in *YD*, p. 131; Maejima Hisoka, *Jijoden* (Dō Denki Kankōkai, 1956), p. 102.
76. Katsuta Magoya, *Ōkubo Toshimichi den* (Dōbunkan, 1910), III, 532- 533. Katsuta refers to Ōkubo's meeting with Yatarō in discussing the disposition of the ships purchased in 1874, the manner of aid to Mitsubishi, and the liquidation of the YJK. Decisions on these issues were made in June and July of 1875. For Ōkubo's activity in 1874, see Iwata, pp. 182-203; and Mōri Toshihiko, *Ōkubo Toshimichi* (Chūō Kōronsha, 1969), pp. 189-190, 198.
77. Yamamura, *Samurai Income and Entrepreneurship*, p. 148; Shiroyanagi, *Kaiun no kensetsusha*, p. 216. The section which Yamamura quotes contains no reference to a "contract," but only a general reference to Yatarō getting Ōkuma and Ōkubo "completely under his thumb" (kotogotoku kore o jika yakurōchū no mono to shite shimatta). The confusion arises because Yamamura does not mention the repair subsidy issue.
78. Yamamura, *Samurai Income and Entrepreneurship*, p. 148 (my emphasis).
79. OM, A2922; Sugii, "Kaiun seisaku," pp. 9-10.
80. Arthur E. Tiedemann, "Big Business and Politics in Prewar Japan," in James W. Morley, ed., *Dilemmas of Growth in Prewar Japan* (Princeton, 1971), pp. 267-269.
81. Shibagaki Kazuo, *Mitsui, Mitsubishi no hyakunen* (Chūō Kōronsha, 1968), p. 21.
82. These figures are from *NYK 70 nenshi*, p. 7. This source contains several errors regarding the purchasing of the ships. See Wray, p. 80n38, for comment on discrepancies among primary sources.
83. Shibagaki, *Mitsui, Mitsubishi*, p. 21.
84. For a list of the 9 ships used in the expedition, see *M Sha shi*, I, 202- 204. See also Wray, p. 82, Table 4.
85. OM, C363, C365, C837, and A2923; *M Sha shi*, I, 276; Wray, pp. 81-83.
86. Bush, pp. 26, 59-71; *M Sha shi*, II, 77-82, 85-86.
87. *M Sha shi*, I, 280. Yanosuke had taken charge of Mitsubishi's operations in 1874 because Yatarō was ill.

2. THE YEAR OF DECISION: 1875

1. Sugii, "Kaiun seisaku," p. 11; *Meiji zaiseishi*, I, 303, 318.
2. Memo of conversation recorded in "Ko shachō jiseki shiryō" and quoted in *YD*, pp. 130-131.
3. See Maejima, *Jijoden*, pp. 100-101. Maejima recorded this proposal in

his autobiography 40 years after he wrote the original memorandum, and he admitted not remembering well the language of the document. Despite places where the wording might be slightly different, he believed there were no great discrepancies in the general content. See also Sugii, "Kaiun seisaku," p. 11.

4. For comments on this memorandum, see Sidney D. Brown, "Ōkubo Toshimichi and the First Home Ministry Bureaucracy," in Bernard Silberman and Harry D. Harootunian, eds., *Modern Japanese Leadership: Transition and Change* (University of Arizona, 1966), p. 212.

5. *Ōkuma monjo*, III, 103–116. Also in OM, A7.

6. Averages calculated from Smith, pp. 24–25. For figures on the outflow of specie, see Ōe, p. 12.

7. Nakamura Naomi, *Ōkuma zaisei no kenkyū* (Azekura Shobō, 1968), pp. 64–67. Ōkuma's memorandum was important in shifting the focus of government transportation policy from railways to shipping. Yoneda Fujio, *Gendai Nihon kaiun shikan* (Kaiji Sangyō Kenkyūjo, 1978), p. 6.

8. This was a common sentiment. As Thomas Smith remarks, in the early Meiji period "there was scarcely an official document proposing the establishment of a new government enterprise that did not argue that private capital was too weak for the undertaking." Smith, p. 37.

9. For the general context of Ōkuma's proposals on shipping, see *Ōkuma monjo*, III, 110–111; and Joyce C. Lebra, *Ōkuma Shigenobu: Statesman of Meiji Japan* (Canberra, 1973), pp. 30–31.

10. Memorandum from Ōkuma to Sanjō, January 1875, "Kisen Jimukyoku o mōkuru no gi," OM, A6.

11. Quoted in *YD*, pp. 137–140; also in OM, A2927. No date appears on this petition, but the index to OM, *Ōkuma monjo mokuroku*, ed., Waseda Daigaku Ōkuma Kenkyū Shitsu (1952), p. 99, dates it as 1874, identifying it as a Mitsubishi request to absorb the YJK. The *YD*, p. 141, dates it as 1875. Internal evidence suggests that it was presented sometime between November 1874 and January 1875. For further discussion of the dating of this petition and of discrepancies among sources regarding the Taiwan Bureau, see Wray, pp. 93–94 n 12.

12. Maejima, *Jijoden*, pp. 99–100. See also *Maejima Hisoka: yūbin sōgyōdan* (Dō Denki Kankōkai, 1956), p. 105.

13. Joyce Lebra has claimed that Ōkuma's January memorandum on the economy demonstrates his "significance as an innovator over a broad range of economic activity" and that Ōkubo "pushed" Ōkuma's proposals. This statement is probably true for Ōkuma's memoranda on the economic crisis as a whole, but there is no evidence that Ōkubo supported his ideas on government-managed shipping, and Maejima appears to have denounced them. See Lebra, p. 31.

14. *YD*, pp. 204–207; *Wagasha kakukōro no enkaku*, ed., N.Y.K. Kamotsuka (1932), p. 64.

15. *NYK 70 nenshi*, p. 8. Later in February 2 more of the ships received in 1874 were commissioned for Mitsubishi to open a northern route between Yokohama and Hakodate.

16. Ibid. In 1874 imports from China had been ¥8.7 million; exports, ¥3.7 million. In 1875 Japan did 25.9% of its trade with Asia, 18.4% with North America, and 54.5% with Europe. The trade with Asia was roughly balanced, that with North America was heavily in Japan's favor, and that with Europe ran a large deficit. See Kaji Teruyoshi, "Mitsubishi zaibatsu no seisei to kaiun," *Shōdai ronshū* 25.1–3:153 (September 1974); and Miwa Ryōichi, "Kaijō yusō," in Andō Yoshio and Matsuyoshi Sadao, eds., *Nihon yusōshi* (Nihon Hyōronsha, 1971), p. 392. On the Chinese merchants, see Noriko Kamachi, "The Chinese in Meiji Japan: Their Interaction with the Japanese before the Sino-Japanese War," in Akira Iriye, ed., *The Chinese and the Japanese: Essays in Political and Cultural Interactions* (Princeton, 1980), pp. 60–66.

17. Ōe, pp. 23–24.

18. Maejima, *Jijoden*, p. 100.

19. "Ko shachō jiseki shiryō," in *YD*, pp. 131–132.

20. Maejima, *Jijoden*, p. 99.

21. Ibid.; Black, II, 453.

22. M.Y. Yoshino, *Japan's Managerial System: Tradition and Innovation* (MIT Press, 1968), pp. 254–260; Eugene J. Kaplan, *Japan: The Government-Business Relationship*, U.S. Department of Commerce, Bureau of International Commerce (1972), p. 74. The *ringi* system was especially appropriate for the early Meiji bureaucracy because the nominal leaders of the Council of State were generally neither as powerful nor as capable as the officials who headed the ministries. Leaders like Sanjō, for example, at the most acted as mediators. Nevertheless, their approval was essential to legitimize a decision. Yoshino's comments about modern Japanese corporations, however, may be too much of an idealization of what is only the most apparent phenomenon. He stresses the initiative of lower-echelon officials in drafting *ringisho*. My impression, based on discussion with N.Y.K. employees, is that an executive may order a lower-echelon department to prepare a *ringisho* and have it circulated and then forwarded to superiors for formal approval. Since the *ringisho* is written in the form of a proposal, it implies that the initiative was with the drafter, thereby masking the fact that the drafter is actually following a superior's verbal order of which there is no record—to the frustration of the historian. These observations are confirmed by a number of scholars who have stressed that lower echelon personnel frequently draft *ringisho*

in response to decisions already made by company leaders. See Ezra F. Vogel, ed., *Modern Japanese Organization and Decision-Making* (Berkeley, University of California Press, 1975); and Kozo Yamamura, "Entrepreneurship, Ownership, and Management in Japan," in Peter Mathias and M. M. Postan, eds., *The Cambridge Economic History of Europe* (Cambridge, 1978), vol. vii, pt. 2, pp. 258–260.

23. Maejima, *Jijoden,* p. 99.

24. See Wray, p. 101 n 25.

25. Students of Meiji political history will notice the similarity of Ōkuma's behavior in this shipping debate to his precipitous handling of the constitutional issue in 1881.

26. On the industrial promotion policy, see Ishizuka Hiromichi, *Nihon shihonshugi seiritsushi kenkyū* (Yoshikawa Kōbunkan, 1973); and Kobayashi Masaaki, *Nihon no kōgyōka to haraisage: seifu to kigyō* (Tōyō Keizai Shinpōsha, 1977). For a more specialized list of works, see Wray, p. 102 n 28.

27. *Ōkubo monjo,* V, 561–566. This memorandum is translated in *Meiji Japan through Contemporary Sources,* III, 13–17; and an abbreviated version appears in David John Lu, *Sources of Japanese History* (New York, McGraw-Hill Book Company, 1973), II, 48–49.

28. Kobayashi Masaaki, "Nihon no kōgyōka to kangyō haraisage," *Keiei shigaku* 6.1:72–73 (September 1971); and the same author's "Shokusan kōgyō seisaku," in Nakagawa et al., *Keieishi no kiso chishiki,* p. 24.

29. Memorandum from Ōkubo to Sanjō, May 24, 1875, *Ōkubo monjo,* VI, 363–366. Detailed statements on the four categories were made in separate memoranda. On the Home Ministry's economic program, see Sidney Devere Brown, "Ōkubo Toshimichi: His Political and Economic Policies in Early Meiji Japan," *Journal of Asian Studies* 21.2:194–197 (February 1962).

30. Nakamura, *Ōkuma zaisei,* p. 66; YD, pp. 118, 128; Maejima, *Jijoden,* pp. 101–102.

31. *M Sha shi,* II, 15–17.

32. *Yanosuke den,* I, 164; YD, p. 150. See Chapter 1, n. 73; and Wray, pp. 105–106.

33. Memorandum from Ōkubo to Sanjō, May 18, 1875, "Shōsen jimu kanshō sanyō no kubun," *Ōkubo monjo,* VI, 354–360.

34. Despite Ōkubo's concern about Japanese losses to the American company, in February he had returned from the Osaka political conference on a Pacific Mail ship. See Brown, "Ōkubo Toshimichi: His Political and Economic Policies," p. 196.

35. Nakamura, *Ōkuma zaisei,* p. 74.

36. "Ōkuma Shigenobu tsuikairoku," in Maejima, *Jijoden*, p. 250; quoted also in *YD*, p. 129.
37. Maejima, *Jijoden*, p. 103. There are accounts of initial meetings between Yatarō and government officials like Maejima and Ōkubo. These meetings have in common an extraordinary rapidity with which the participants recognize Yataro's talents.
38. Sugii, "Kaiun seisaku," p. 18; *YD*, p. 133.
39. Memorandum from Ōkuma to Sanjō, September 1875, *Ōkuma monjo*, III, 121. Also in OM, A9. See also Nakamura, *Ōkuma zaisei*, pp. 66–67, 70, 74.
40. Maejima, *Jijoden*, p. 102; *Maejima: yūbin sōgyōdan*, pp. 106–107.
41. There is a suggestive resonance between Ōkubo's policy and reform proposals concerning shipping made by late Tokugawa thinkers like Honda Toshiaki. While seemingly different in that Ōkubo favored a private company whereas Honda argued that shipping should be conducted by the "ruler" and not left to "merchants," both attacked the Tokugawa merchant and both shared what could be called a statist mentality. See Keene, pp. 91–122, 175–226, esp. p. 176; and Wray, pp. 113–114.
42. Smith, pp. 36, 43; Uda Tadashi, "Wagakuni tetsudō jigyō keieishi ni okeru seifu to kigyō: 'tetsudō seiryaku' no tenkai kōzō," *Keiei shigaku* 6.1:124–126 (September 1971). For discussion of railways in the 1880s and 1890s, see Chapter 6.
43. Adapted from Hirschmeier, *Origins of Entrepreneurship*, pp. 225–226; and Shibagaki Kazuo, "The Early History of the Zaibatsu," *Developing Economies* 4:541 (December 1966). The full five-article code appears in *M Sha shi*, II, 37–38. For controversies regarding the exact dating of this code and subsequent revisions by Shōda Heigorō, see Takaura Tadahiko, "Mitsubishi no 'shasoku' ni tsuite," *Keizaikei* 101:114–122 (October 1974); and Wray, p. 117 n51. One matter not in dispute is that Shōda produced Mitsubishi's accounting rules, incorporating double-entry bookkeeping, in 1877.
44. Morikawa, "The Organizational Structure of Mitsubishi and Mitsui," p. 65; *M Sha shi*, II, 38–39; Nagasawa, "Shoki Mitsubishi no . . . kaiungyō," p. 29–32.
45. This information on personnel is taken from a company employee ledger, "Yōin jiseki," formerly in the Iwasaki Biographical Compilation Committee room. The ledger shows that there was still no standardization of names for company offices. There is some doubt about the extent of Ishikawa's and Kawada's supervision over their respective departments, for they had to travel several months at a time, visiting branch offices. See Nagasawa, "Meijiki Mitsubishi no toppu manejimento," p. 31.

46. *M Sha shi,* II, 97–100; Nakagawa and Yui, pp. 133–136.
47. Maejima, *Jijoden,* p. 102; Bush, p. 68; *Ōkubo monjo,* VI, 389–390.
48. Matsukata ke monjo, vol. 61, Kōtsū (Transportation), no. 31, n.d.
49. *YD,* p. 141; Yamamoto Mitsuhiko, *Kawasaki Shōzō* (1918), pp. 85–90. Kawasaki had earlier been in charge of the YJK's Ryukyu line. See Mishima Yasuo, "Kawasaki Shōzō no zaisan chikuseki katei," *Keiei shigaku* 12.3:1–21 (June 1978).
50. *NYK 70 nenshi,* p. 10. For comments on the date these ships were actually given to Mitsubishi, see Wray, p. 127n61.
51. The date of the meeting is inferred from internal evidence in Katsuta, *Ōkubo den,* III, 532–533.
52. The only copy I have seen of this June memorandum is held by the Iwasaki Biographical Compilation Committee.
53. July 10, 1875, *Ōkubo monjo,* VI, 353.
54. Memorandum from Ōkubo to Sanjō, July 29, 1875, "Chakushu hōhō mikomisho," *Ōkubo monjo,* VI, 383–384.
55. *Ōkubo monjo,* VI, 381–382.
56. Ibid., p. 382. The subsidy designated ¥250,000 for operating expenses. For the proposed allocation of the remaining ¥50,000, see ibid., p. 390; and Wray, p. 129n68.
57. *Ōkubo monjo,* VI, 415–423.
58. *YD,* pp. 142–148; *NYK 50 nenshi,* pp. 8–11.
59. Yamamura, *Samurai Income and Entrepreneurship,* p. 162.
60. Irimajiri, p. 126.
61. See Wray, pp. 131–132; and Maejima memos to Ōkuma, October 16 and December 20, 1875. OM, B193-3, B193-10.
62. Figures compiled from *M Sha shi* by Shibagaki in *Nihon kin'yū shihon,* p. 63.
63. *YD,* p. 135; *Ōkubo monjo,* VI, 385.
64. Maejima, *Jijoden,* p. 102.
65. For related comments, see *Yanosuke den,* I, 145–146.
66. Nakamura, *Ōkuma zaisei,* pp. 68–69.
67. Smith, p. 35.
68. As recorded by Maejima in "Ko shachō jiseki shiryō," and quoted in *YD,* p. 132.
69. *Maejima: yūbin sōgyōdan,* p. 106.
70. *Saugstad Report,* p. 321.
71. Saitō, "Meiji shonen," pp. 60–61.
72. Yamamura, *Samurai Income and Entrepreneurship,* p. 162.
73. Kobayashi Masaaki, "Kindai sangyō no keisei to kangyō haraisage," in Kajinishi Mitsuhaya, ed., *Nihon keizaishi taikei,* vol. 5, *Kindai* I (Tokyo Daigaku Shuppankai, 1965), pp. 304–305.

74. Shibagaki, *Nihon kin'yū shihon,* p. 64.
75. In his work on Mitsubishi's early history Yamamura made two major points relevant to this study. Arguing that the early Meiji government did not have a consistent industrial promotion policy in the case of the shipping industry, Yamamura emphasized Mitsubishi's strong bargaining position. I have qualified this by giving more credit to the government in its 1875 policy formulation, but I agree with his emphasis on Yatarō's profit motivation.
76. Also, in October the Department of Ships changed its name to the Shipping Management Department, formalizing the shift from the supervision of ships to general maritime administration. See Wray, p. 141n92, for comments on discrepancies among sources regarding this name change.
77. *Wagasha kakukōro,* p. 116; Wray, p. 122.
78. Saitō, "Meiji shonen," pp. 76–77; Irimajiri, p. 130.
79. Quoted in *YD,* pp. 208–212; also in OM, A2928.
80. Quoted in *YD,* p. 214; also in OM, A2929.
81. *YD,* p. 217; taken from the *Japan Mail,* February 20, 1875.
82. OM, C844.
83. U.S. Department of Commerce, *Government Aid to Merchant Shipping,* p. 278; Hutchins, *The American Maritime Industries,* pp. 530–531; and the *Saugstad Report,* pp. 58–59. For further detail on the switch in U.S. subsidy policy, see Sasaki Seiji, *Nihon kaiun kyōsōshi josetsu* (Kobe, Kaiji Kenkyūkai, 1954), pp. 148–149.
84. Bush, p. 69. As the largest American trading house in Japan, Walsh, Hall & Co. also had close connections with Mitsui. Several years before he set up Mitsui Bussan, Masuda Takashi acquired his knowledge of foreign trade during a one-year stint as an employee of Walsh, Hall & Co. See Togai Yoshio, *Mitsui Bussan Kaisha no keiei shiteki kenkyū* (Tōyō Keizai Shinpōsha, 1974), pp. 52–53; and Masuda Takashi, *Jijo Masuda Takashi ō den* (Uchida Rōkakuho, 1939), pp. 122–124, 130–131, 167–170.
85. *M Sha shi,* II, 308–311, 314–324. For a convenient summary, see Yamaguchi, "Gaikoku kaiun to Mitsubishi," pp. 144–145.
86. *Meiji un'yushi* (Nippōsha, 1913), p. 21; Black, II, 454.
87. Letter from Batchelder to Ōkuma, July 25, 1874. OM, C38.
88. Black, II, 454.

3. COMPETITION AND BUSINESS INNOVATION: 1876–1880

1. *M Sha shi,* III, 619, 663–664(66?); and Wray, pp. 149–150. This operation is known as the Kanghwa Incident.
2. Francis E. Hyde, *Blue Funnel: A History of Alfred Holt and Company of Liverpool from 1865 to 1914* (Liverpool, 1957), pp. 41–43, 59.

3. P. & O. Minute Book #11, February 1, 1876, p. 144, and February 15, 1876, p. 149.

4. Nakagawa Keiichirō, "P. & O. Kisen Kaisha no seiritsu," *Keizaigaku ronshū*, 26.1 & 2:295 (March 1959).

5. Batchelder to Ōkuma, February 24, 1876, OM, C60.

6. In Nakagawa and Yui, pp. 137-139; *YD*, pp. 692-694; and Lu, II, 80-82.

7. Yamaguchi, "Gaikoku kaiun to Mitsubishi," p. 150; *YD*, pp. 220-221; Wray, p. 154n10.

8. *KD*, pp. 101-106.

9. Report from J. M. Batchelder to Ōkuma, May 3, 1876, Matsukata ke monjo, vol. 61, Kōtsū, no. 28.

10. *Tsukahara Mushū ō* (1925), pp. 21-22; Irimajiri, p. 133.

11. Batchelder report to Ōkuma, May 3, 1876 (see n. 9 above); *Tsukahara*, pp. 21-22; *Yamamoto Tatsuo* (Dō Sensei Denki Hensankai, 1951), p. 114. I have no figures for P. & O. fares, but during the competition Mitsubishi's second-class fare for the Yokohama-Kobe run was ¥3. At that rate, the 25 *sen* would have been an 8% surcharge. See *Wagasha kakukōro*, p. 116. The threat of arrest was probably a greater deterrent than the surcharge itself.

12. Yamaguchi, "Gaikoku kaiun to Mitsubishi," p. 150.

13. Miwa, "Kaijō yusō," p. 401.

14. In 1867 a report on commerce prepared by Mutsu Munemitsu, Japan's foreign minister from 1892 to 1896, "contrasted the advantages of the Western shipper, who simply charged freight for the tonnage he carried and insured its safety, with the Japanese system wherein the shipowner paid to the shipper part of the value of the goods loaded, on the premise that he would more than recover his expenditure on delivery." Jansen, *Sakamoto*, p. 310.

15. *Tokyo Kaijō Kasai Hoken Kabushiki Kaisha 100 nenshi*, I, ed., Nihon Keieishi Kenkyūjo (Dōsha, 1979), pp. 52-77, esp. pp. 67-69.

16. Quoted in *Iwasaki Hisaya den* (Dō Hensan Iinkai, 1961), p. 110. For an account of the Nine Shop Union in the Tokugawa period, see Furuta and Hirai, pp. 68-78. This alliance between the Nine Shop Union and the P. & O. against the government-supported Mitsubishi brings to mind one of the paramount issues in the early 1850s debate about opening Japan. One reason for the strong anti-foreign sentiment of both the bakufu and domain leaders had been the fear that the "common people" would be led astray by the advantages of foreign trade and would become less amenable to control. As one memorial to the bakufu remarked: "All merchants are led astray by profits . . . In a crisis, we cannot predict what they might not do in league with the enemy." Quoted in Maruyama

Masao, *Studies in the Intellectual History of Tokugawa Japan,* trans. Mikiso Hane (Tokyo University, 1974), pp. 338–339.

17. *Mitsubishi Ginkōshi* (Dō Hensan Iinkai, 1954, special 2d ed., 1959), p. 10.
18. Yamamura, *Samurai Income and Entrepreneurship,* p. 150. See also Nakamura, *Ōkuma zaisei,* pp. 75–76.
19. Miwa, "Kaijō yusō," pp. 400–401.
20. This discussion of the freight business is taken mainly from *YD,* pp. 221–227; *Iwasaki Hisaya den,* pp. 109–111; Nakamura, *Ōkuma zaisei,* pp. 74–76; and *Mitsubishi Ginkōshi,* pp. 9–14.
21. *M Sha shi,* III, 617; *YD,* 706–708; Wray, pp. 164–167.
22. Nakagawa and Yui, pp. 140–143; *YD,* pp. 695–699.
23. Until 1885, "foreign vessels carried over 90 per cent of Japan's overseas trade and represented about 83 per cent of the steamship tonnage entering and clearing Japanese ports." Francis E. Hyde, *Far Eastern Trade, 1860–1914* (A. & C. Black, 1973), p. 157.
24. Kwang-Ching Liu, *Anglo-American Steamship Rivalry in China: 1862–1874* (Harvard, 1962), pp. 152–153; and Albert Feuerwerker, *China's Early Industrialization: Sheng Hsuan-huai (1844–1916) and Mandarin Enterprise* (Harvard, 1958), p. 183.
25. Yamaguchi Kazuo, "Kaiun," in Arisawa Hiromi, comp., *Nihon sangyō 100 nenshi* (Nihon Keizai Shinbunsha, 1966), p. 84; Miwa, "Suijō kōtsū," p. 481, "Kaijō yusō," pp. 394–396; Wray, pp. 171–176. For a study of the competition between Japanese and Western-style ships, see Sasaki, *Nihon kaiun kyōsōshi,* esp. pp. 32–117; and Sasaki Seiji, *Nihon kaiungyō no kindaika* (Kobe, Kaibundō, 1961). The best work on pre-Restoration shipping is Yunoki Manabu, *Kinsei kaiunshi no kenkyū* (Hōsei Daigaku Shuppankyoku, 1979).
26. Fernand Braudel, *Capitalism and Material Life, 1400–1800,* trans. Miriam Kochan (New York, Harper & Row, 1975, Colophon Books), pp. 265–266.
27. Furuta and Hirai, pp. 58–107. I have studied the *wasen* in a separate project on the Tokugawa-Meiji transition sponsored by the Social Science Research Council and led by Marius Jansen and Gilbert Rozman.
28. Furuta Ryōichi, "Kaijō kōtsūshi," in *Miyagi kenshi* (Zaidan Hōjin Kankōkai, 1960), V, 624–625.
29. For interpretive comments and a partial though useful list of freight goods compiled from *M Sha shi,* see Shibagaki, *Nihon kin'yū shihon,* pp. 65–68. I am also indebted to Professor Miwa Ryōichi for discussion of this point.
30. *NYK 50 nenshi,* pp. 11–12; *YD,* pp. 229–230.

31. This article set an important precedent in the evolution of government-subsidized regular lines (*meirei kōro,* literally, "ordered lines").
32. Irimajiri, p. 139.
33. *YD,* pp. 242-247. Marius B. Jansen, "Mutsu Munemitsu," in Albert M. Craig and Donald Shively, eds., *Personality in Japanese History* (California, 1970), p. 322. Yatarō paid his debt of gratitude by showering gifts on Hayashi while he was in prison.
34. Iwata, pp. 247-250.
35. *Zaikai bukko ketsubutsu den* (Jitsugyō no Sekaisha, 1936), I, 112. The Hagi Rebellion was led by discontented samurai from Choshu. Mitsubishi earned ¥40,000 in its suppression. See n. 1 of this chapter.
36. The most reliable sources list from 42 to 46 ships employed in military transport. See *M Sha shi,* IV, Appendix, *Seinan sen'eki un'yushi; YD,* pp. 249-253.
37. *M Sha shi,* IV, 187-188. At the time Yatarō was negotiating with the Finance Ministry for a loan, the Tosa radicals were plotting the exchange of government bonds for Yatarō's cash. For the ships, see *Yanosuke den,* I, 158-161.
38. OM, C692.
39. Yamaguchi, "Kaiun," p. 84; Wray, p. 183 n 54.
40. Quoted in Irimajiri, pp. 143-144. The *myōgakin* applied to 29 ships, the 13 received during and after the Taiwan expedition and 16 still remaining from the YJK. A *myōgakin* was originally a donation which merchants presented to the bakufu or domain upon receiving permission or a charter to engage in business. It gradually came to be set at an annual rate and became a form of tax which merchants paid to the bakufu.
41. *Iwasaki Hisaya den,* p. 116.
42. Okaniwa, pp. 56-57. The *myōgakin* demonstrates that scholars are incorrect in assuming without qualification that the government "gave" Mitsubishi these ships in 1875. See Yamamura, *Samurai Income and Entrepreneurship,* p. 148; John K. Fairbank, Edwin O. Reischauer and Albert M. Craig, *East Asia: The Modern Transformation* (Houghton Mifflin, 1965), p. 254.
43. Takaura, p. 114; Takatera Sadao, *Meiji genka shōkyakushi no kenkyū* (Miraisha, 1974), pp. 91-124.
44. The data for this account are in *M Sha shi,* IV, 629-633, and V, 751-760; and *Yanosuke den,* I, 154-159. For an analysis, see Wray, pp. 185-188. Professor Takatera Sadao kindly reviewed my calculations and supported my explanation of this matter.
45. Many prewar accounts which greatly exaggerated Mitsubishi's profits ignored the basic fact that government ship transport expenditure during the rebellion came to about ¥3.5 million. The official figures are in

M Sha shi, IV, 582–583. See also Wray, p. 189; and Tanaka, *Iwasaki*, p. 182. The government's total expenditures for the rebellion are often listed at ¥42 million. See Tominaga, p. 118.

46. This deficit included a depreciation expense of ¥782,835 (compared to an average depreciation of ¥243,579 for 1879–1882).

47. *YD*, pp. 699–702.

48. Computed from *Yanosuke den*, I, 160–161.

49. Besides mining, the main enterprises which Mitsubishi had entered by 1880 were exchange financing, warehousing, and ship-repair work. This last was begun in 1875, when Mitsubishi purchased the Yokohama Engine Works (Yokohama Seitetsujo) through a joint investment with the English firm of Boyd & Co. In 1879 the foreign firm withdrew from the venture and Mitsubishi began operating it by itself. See Kobayashi Masaaki, "Nagasaki Zōsenjo no haraisage," *Keizaikei* 73:16–17 (June 1967); and the same author's *Nihon no kōgyōka*, pp. 223–224. The Yokohama Engine Works was the forerunner of the Yokohama Dock Company, which later became a subsidiary of the N.Y.K. until merging with Mitsubishi Heavy Industries in 1935. Also, by 1880 Mitsubishi had an indirect interest in insurance and a small beginning in real estate. In general, most of Mitsubishi's subsidiary enterprises were intertwined with its main shipping business. It had given up its silk reeling and camphor works in 1875. See ibid., p. 220; and Hatade, *Mitsubishi*, p. 26.

50. Compare *Mitsubishi Ginkōshi*, p. 34; and *M Sha shi*, VIII, 462–464. The profit in the first half of 1881 was ¥83,661.

51. I am indebted to Professor Uekusa Masu for discussion of this point.

52. Shibagaki, "Early History of the Zaibatsu," p. 545.

53. Hatade, *Mitsubishi*, p. 31.

54. Shibagaki, *Nihon kin'yū shihon*, p. 75.

55. *M Sha shi*, IX, 552–553.

56. See Wray, p. 198, for comments on line budgets.

57. In 1881 the 5 ships listed in Table 12 had insurance expenses of ¥15,722. *M Sha shi*, VIII, 470. In 1882 regular insurance charges were removed as a separate entry in the accounts and transferred to depreciation. See Wray, pp. 199, 312–313n26.

58. Shibagaki, *Nihon kin'yū shihon*, p. 65.

59. Chandler, *Strategy and Structure*, pp. 17, 19.

60. Alfred D. Chandler, Jr., "Institutional Integration: An Approach to Comparative Studies of the History of Large-Scale Business Enterprise," in Nakagawa Keiichirō, ed., *Strategy and Structure of Big Business* (Tokyo University, 1976), p. 122.

61. Nagasawa, "Meijiki Mitsubishi no toppu manejimento," pp. 33–34.

62. For a different emphasis, see Nagasawa, "Shoki Mitsubishi no . . .

kaiungyō," pp. 43–45, who argues that the office's loans, which accounted for almost three times as much business as exchange financing to shippers in the second term of 1880, indicate that the office's own business, rather than its role as a supporting division for the shipping enterprise, was now its principal sphere of activity. Nagasawa's view overlooks two points: (1) In 1881 ordinary loans totaled about half what they had been in 1880. (2) Loans in other categories were related to shipping, and these increased in 1881. In this case the evidence is strong enough only to modify but not to contradict the assertion of the official Iwasaki biographer that "because the Exchange Office was a supporting enterprise of Mitsubishi Steamship, it could not develop its own activity as a bank, and its fortune and destiny were held in common with the parent company." See *Yanosuke den,* II, 353–354, 362, and I, 191–194, esp. p. 193. Cf. *Mitsubishi Ginkōshi,* pp. 21–35. Nagasawa also notes that even organizationally the Exchange Office was not completely separate, for there was some overlap in personnel between its branches and those of the main shipping enterprise.

63. Kobayashi Masaaki, "Takashima Tankō ni okeru kanshū to haraisage," *Keizaikei* 101:107 (October 1974); and the same author's *Nihon no kōgyōka,* pp. 161–192, esp. pp. 179–180, 184.

64. Yasuoka Shigeaki has made this point in an essay which emphasized the cautious, conservative nature of zaibatsu investment. See "The Tradition of Family Business in the Strategic Decision Process and Management Structure of Zaibatsu Business: Mitsui, Sumitomo, and Mitsubishi," in Nakagawa, ed., *Strategy and Structure,* pp. 88–91.

65. Hatade, *Mitsubishi,* p. 42.

66. Yasuoka, "Family Business," pp. 86–87; Kobayashi, "Kindai sangyō no keisei to kangyō haraisage," p. 341; Yasuoka Shigeaki, *Zaibatsu no keieishi* (Nihon Keizai Shinbunsha, 1978), pp. 51–53. For some cases of Mitsubishi's early diversification, which are exceptions to this generalization, see Chapter 6, n. 48.

PART TWO: FORMATION OF THE N.Y.K. 1880–1894

1. Iwai Ryōtarō, *Mitsui Mitsubishi monogatari* (Chikura Shobō, 2d ed., 1936), p. 241; Yamamura, "The Founding of Mitsubishi," p. 154.

2. See, for example, *Yamamoto Tatsuo,* p. 123; *JWM,* March 28, 1908, p. 348, compares the 2 brothers.

3. Miwa Ryōichi, "Nippon Yūsen no setsuritsu to Mitsubishi no tenkan: umi no Mitsubishi kara riku no Mitsubishi e," Nakagawa et al., *Keieishi no kiso chishiki,* pp. 70–71; and Chapter 1 of *Yanosuke den,* II.

4. THE ATTACK ON MITSUBISHI: 1880–1882

1. Shiroyanagi, *Zaikai taiheiki*, p. 88.
2. If we include the head office in Tokyo, Hokkaido branches made up 17% of the Exchange Office's capital, which in 1882 was ¥1,965,000. Compiled from figures in *Mitsubishi Ginkōshi*, pp. 35–36. The Exchange Office provided a specified amount of capital to each of its branches, which paid 12% annual interest on this to the head office and received in turn considerable financial autonomy. Mishima, ed., *Mitsubishi zaibatsu*, p. 126; Nagasawa, "Shoki Mitsubishi no . . . kaiungyō," pp. 45–46.
3. Quoted in *Mitsubishi Ginkōshi*, p. 32.
4. *Mitsubishi Ginkōshi*, pp. 45–46. This transaction has an indirect bearing on the origins of the Mitsubishi Bank. It will be referred to again in Chapter 5.
5. *SEDS*, XVIII, 377. On Mitsubishi's Hokkaido operations, see the comments of Shōda Heigorō. *SEDS*, XVIII, 362–363, 368–370. Cf. *Yanosuke den*, I, 209; and *Hakodate kaiunshi* (Hakodate-shiyakusho, 1958), pp. 208–210, 238–240.
6. The contract is in OM, A1061. See also Nakamura, *Ōkuma zaisei*, pp. 76–77, 81. Rice, other agricultural crops, and Hokkaido marine products still constituted the overwhelming bulk of Mitsubishi's freight shipments.
7. This was hardly surprising, for some of the medium-sized European shipping firms on the East Asian run made the full transition from sail to steam only in the mid-1870s. See George Blake, *The Ben Line, 1825–1955* (Thomas Nelson & Sons Ltd., 1956), pp. 36–58.
8. Miwa, "Kaijō yusō," p. 396.
9. Shiroyanagi, *Zaikai taiheiki*, pp. 73–74. While the number of ships in the country was increasing rapidly, Mitsubishi's steamships had declined from a high of 41 in 1876 to 32 by February 1882. The fact that net tonnage (24,126 in 1882) had not similarly declined may be attributed to improvements in ship hulls—to increase cargo volume and hence net tonnage—or to Mitsubishi padding of measurements to meet a government minimum of 22,000 NT set in 1882. Compare *M Sha shi*, IX, 213–215; and *Yanosuke den*, I, 154–161.
10. For exchange rates during these years, see Table 2.45 in Andō Yoshio, ed., *Kindai Nihon keizaishi yōran* (Tokyo Daigaku Shuppankai, 1975), p. 60. For Mitsubishi's charges, see *M Sha shi*, VIII, 208–210; XI, 452–453; XII, 703–704; and *YD*, p. 495. In the early 1880s Mitsubishi expressed its accounts solely in paper currency, but in 1884 and 1885 it kept accounts for paper currency and silver yen separately. (The silver yen was the official "trade dollar," tied in value to the Mexican dollar).
11. *Yokohama-shi shi*, series 4, vol. 1 (Dōhen, 1965), p. 538. (All subse-

quent references to this work are from the volume cited here.) Rice constituted 42% of the value of all commodities handled by Mitsui Bussan in the few months after its establishment in 1876, as compiled from the table in *Mitsui Senpaku Kabushiki Kaisha sōgyō 80 nenshi* (Dōshahen, 1958), p. 21.

12. For the connection between the Miike Coal Mine and Mitsui shipping, see ibid., pp. 22–39; Sasaki Seiji, "Mitsui kaiungyō no seisei," *Kokusai keizai kenkyū* 9:187–205 (1959); Saitō Yoshihisa, "Mitsui Bussan Kaisha ni okeru kaiungyō," in Yasuoka Shigeaki, ed., *Zaibatsushi kenkyū* (Nihon Keizai Shinbunsha, 1979), pp. 105–145; and Shibagaki, *Nihon kin'yū shihon*, p. 139. See also the articles on Mitsui's Shanghai Branch, "Mitsui Bussan Kaisha to Ueda Yasusaburō," in *Mitsui bunko ronsō* 7 (November 1973).

13. The ¥700,000 figure appears in many sources, but the earliest I have found is Shiroyanagi, *Zaikai taiheiki*, p. 77. Mitsui share of foreign trade is estimated from the table in Togai, p. 45. In 1897 the figure was 10.7%; in 1912, 20.1%.

14. Masuda, p. 251. The company is usually known as the Tokyo Fūhansen Kaisha, but the "Tokyo" did not become part of the name until early 1882. See *SEDS*, pp. 10–15; and Wray, p. 223 n17.

15. Some of the company's promoters who became important in shipping affairs later in the 1880s were Fujii Nōzō, from Fushiki port in Ishikawa Prefecture, Moroto Seiroku, from Ise, a rice merchant, landowner, and later a major stockholder in N.Y.K., and Miyaji Sukesaburō, a shipping expert serving the Hokkaido Colonization Office in Hakodate. See *SEDS*, p. 9; and Wray, pp. 223–224. On Fujii, see *Fushiki-kōshi* (Dō Kaiun Shinkōkai, 1973), pp. 228–236.

16. Kawasaki Shōzō responded to the latter offer by leasing 3 small ships to the company. *Kawasaki Kisen 50 nenshi* (Kobe, Dōshahen, 1969), p. 6.

17. Obata, p. 119.

18. *SEDS*, p. 17. Hirschmeier, "Shibusawa," p. 234. The Dai Ichi Bank referred to here is the same bank as the previously mentioned Dai Ichi Kokuritsu Ginkō (First National Bank). The name was changed following revisions in the banking law.

19. Shiroyanagi, *Zaikai taiheiki*, pp. 79–80. Andrew Fraser, "The Expulsion of Ōkuma from the Government in 1881," *Journal of Asian Studies* 26.2:227 (February 1967), mentions Mitsubishi "payments to supporters in local assemblies," and Iwai, *Mitsui Mitsubishi monogatari*, p. 272, comments on widespread bribes to government officials. Though the Fūhansen Kaisha was a private company, its president, Tōtake Hideyuki, was a navy captain. Masuda, p. 251.

20. *SEDS*, pp. 15–16.

21. Shiroyanagi, *Zaikai taiheiki,* pp. 80–81. This work assumes that Kawada and Ono promoted the Niigata Bussan Kaisha, but Mitsubishi's contract with the firm had been signed in 1879 by Mitsubishi's Niigata branch manager, Hama Masahiro. See OM, A1061. On the Etchū company, see *Fushiki-kōshi,* pp. 244–247.

22. In 1882 virtually all Miike exports went to Shanghai. By 1891 on a scale of 100 the distribution was: Shanghai (28), Hong Kong (57), and other ports (15). A full table is in "Mitsui Bussan Kaisha to Ueda Yasusaburō," pp. 318–319; and Wray, p. 227. For background see Sugiyama Shin'ya, "Bakumatsu – Meiji shoki ni okeru sekitan yushutsu no dōkō to Shanhai sekitan shijō," *Shakai keizai shigaku* 43.6:19–41 (1978); and for later trends, see Yamashita Naotō, "Nihon teikokushugi seiritsuki no Higashi Ajia sekitan shijō to Mitsui Bussan: Shanhai shijō o chūshin ni," in *Enerugī to keizai hatten,* ed., Shakai Keizai Shigakkai (Fukuoka, 1979), pp. 255–306.

23. Andō, ed., *Keizaishi yōran,* pp. 51, 60.

24. Smith, pp. 86–103; Kobayashi, *Nihon no kōgyōka;* Tamaki Hajime, *Gendai Nihon sangyō hattatsushi,* vol. 29, *Sōron,* I (Gendai Nihon Sangyō Hattatsushi Kenkyūkai, 1967), pp. 353–364. See Chapter 6, n. 43.

25. Untitled memorandum by Ōkuma Shigenobu and Itō Hirobumi, November 1880, *Ōkuma Shigenobu kankei monjo* (Waseda Daigaku, 1934), IV, 180–183.

26. *Ekitei-kyoku nenpō* 10:2 (1881); Okutani Matsuji, *Shinagawa Yajirō den* (Kōyō Shoin, 1940), pp. 164–167.

27. Enomoto Morie and Kimi Nobuhiko, *Hokkaidō no rekishi* (Yamakawa Shuppansha, 1970), pp. 136–137. The total includes expenses of all kinds, not just the original government investment. It is higher than a commonly used figure of ¥14 million but is consistent with a contemporary estimate given in the *Japan Gazette,* August 13, 1881. According to this, expenditures had reached ¥18,527,306 by June 30, 1881.

28. Nakamura, *Ōkuma zaisei,* pp. 79–80, 254.

29. Fraser, "The Expulsion of Ōkuma," pp. 215–217.

30. *Godai Tomoatsu denki shiryō,* (Tōyō Keizai Shinpōsha, 1971–1974), IV, #173–176, pp. 169–176; *YD,* pp. 464–465; *Yanosuke den,* I, 208.

31. *YD,* p. 477.

32. William Davis Hoover, "Godai Tomoatsu (1836–1885): An Economic Statesman of Early Modern Japan," PhD dissertation, University of Michigan, 1973, closely parallels Hirschmeier's interpretation of Shibusawa in downplaying the desire for profit.

33. The company's early planning documents stress this point heavily. See *Godai shiryō,* III, #182–183, pp. 369–371; cf. Godai's April 9, 1881, letter to Ōkuma in ibid., I, #448, p. 368. The idea of exporting Hokkaido

products to China appeared frequently in the early Meiji period. For a Foreign Ministry proposal of November 1871, see Ōkuma monjo, IV, 57–58.

34. See *Godai shiryō*, III, 389; and for the petition, #189, pp. 392–393.
35. Hoover, p. 311. This is not necessarily Hoover's opinion. He presents both views and does not explicitly commit himself, but he leans toward the separate-company hypothesis.
36. *Godai shiryō*, I, #452, pp. 371–373.
37. *YD*, pp. 466–467.
38. *Godai shiryō*, IV, 239.
39. For this interpretation, see ibid., pp. 239–240; for Hirose's letter, see ibid., III, #188, pp. 389–392. Hoover, p. 314, presents a different view which I have criticized. Wray, p. 236 n 45.
40. Enomoto and Kimi, p. 138.
41. *Japan Gazette*, August 4, 1881.
42. Nakamura, *Ōkuma zaisei*, p. 255. For the *Mainichi* editorials, see *Godai shiryō*, IV, #177, p. 176–181.
43. As reported by Lebra, p. 48.
44. *Godai shiryō*, I, #453, p. 373. Cf. *Yanosuke den*, I, 209; and Enomoto and Kimi, pp. 138–139.
45. *Godai shiryō*, I, #448, p. 368.
46. *YD*, p. 465. The semi-official newspaper which had criticized the government sale, the *Tokyo nichinichi*, was largely dominated by Choshu interests. Andrew Fraser, "Komuro Shinobu (1839–1898): A Meiji Politician and Businessman," *Papers on Far Eastern History*, 3:73 (March 1971). For a popular account which discusses the individuals of the various factions and their threat to Mitsubishi, see Shiroyanagi Shūko, *Nihon fugō hasseigaku* (Chikura Shobō, 1931), pp. 356–393.
47. *Godai shiryō*, III, 373. For a fuller list of stockholders, see Wray, p. 297.
48. Fraser, "The Expulsion of Ōkuma," pp. 217–218, 231.
49. The largest potential anti-Mitsubishi alignment of two major concerns in 1881, that between Mitsui and the Kansai shipping interests connected with Sumitomo, did not occur until 1964 (in the form of the Mitsui-O.S.K. Line) and then partly through government prompting.
50. *YD*, pp. 470–472, 474–475.
51. For a list of the 15 officials, see *YD*, p. 484.
52. *YD*, pp. 486–491. *Yamamoto Tatsuo*, pp. 96–97.
53. Nishino Kiyosaku, *Hanseiki zaikai sokumenshi* (Tōyō Keizai Shuppanbu, 1932), p. 149.
54. *Tokyo keizai zasshi*, November 19 to December 17, 1881, in *KS*, I, 95–130. For a serialized pro-Mitsubishi reply, see *Meiji nippō*, February 10, 17, and 22, 1882, in *KS*, I, 139–146. For summaries, see *YD*, pp. 491–495.

55. Two important outside interests of Yatarō criticized in these articles which I have not yet discussed were Shibusawa's Dai Ichi Bank, in which Yatarō was the eighth largest stockholder with shares worth ¥38,000, and the Japan Railway Company. The latter had been established on November 11, 1881, just before Taguchi began his series. Mitsubishi soon held 8% of the company's stock. See Wray, p. 242n64.

56. Okutani, pp. 164-166. On June 13, 1882, Shinagawa was promoted from junior vice-minister to vice-minister.

57. This account of the negotiations is taken from a March 4, 1882, "Memorandum for the record" (*shuki*) by Okazaki Koremoto, a Mitsubishi secretary. See Shukuri, pp. 428-430. Portions of this memorandum are quoted without acknowledgment and with several crucial omissions in *YD*, pp. 496-498.

58. For the Third Directive and 3 earlier drafts, see *M Sha shi*, IX, 198-213. See also *Yokohama-shi shi*, p. 542; and Sasaki, *Nihon kaiun kyōsōshi*, p. 239.

59. Enomoto and Kimi, p. 139; *Yokohama-shi shi*, pp. 540-543.

60. Noda Nobuo, "Nihon zaibatsushi e no kiyo," *Keiei shigaku*, 5.1:102 (October 1970).

61. *Yamamoto Tatsuo*, pp. 97-98.

62. *SEDS*, p. 38; *Yamamoto Tatsuo*, p. 118; and *Segai Inoue kō den*, (Hara Shobō, 1968), III, 552, 557-559.

63. Masuda, pp. 251-252.

64. Fraser, "Komuro," pp. 61-83; *Zaikai bukko ketsubutsu den*, I, 517-518; *SEDS*, p. 40; and *Segai Inoue*, III, 555-556.

65. *Tsukahara*, pp. 70-71; Wray, pp. 248-249 n74 and 75.

66. Tokutomi Iichirō, *Kōshaku Matsukata Masayoshi den* (Dō Denki Hakkōjo, 1935), I, 1135, provides details of the July 12 decision. For an earlier plan, see *Godai shiryō*, III, #211, pp. 462-471. For the May 30 plan, see *Yokohama-shi shi*, pp. 543-544. Also, in an earlier plan, the company's name was designated the Imperial Mail Steamship Company (Teikoku Yūsen Kaisha).

67. For Shinagawa's speech and the directive, see *SEDS*, pp. 42-45, 49-50.

68. On this drive, see *Tsukahara*, pp. 71-74.

69. Hoover, p. 267.

70. Nishino, pp. 141-142, 423. In 1895 Moroto's 1,600 shares placed him fifth among all N.Y.K. stockholders. *NYK-KNS*, October 31, 1895.

71. November 24, 1882, *SEDS*, p. 40.

72. *SEDS*, pp. 58-61; *KS*, I, 191-198; *NYK 50 nenshi*, pp. 38-41.

73. Okutani, pp. 187, 189-190; Seoka Makoto, "Kindai Sumitomo no keiei rinen," in Miyamoto Mataji and Sakudō Yōtarō, eds., *Sumitomo no keiei shiteki kenkyū* (Jikkyō, 1979), pp. 398-399.

74. Okutani, pp. 187–188; *KS*, I, 219–223.
75. Nishino, p. 152.
76. *Yokohama-shi shi*, p. 548; *YD*, pp. 545–546; Fraser, "Komuro," pp. 63–66, 73; Masuda, p. 252; *SEDS*, pp. 40–41; Nishino, pp. 150–152; *Yamamoto Tatsuo*, pp. 120–121. Baba and Ōishi will reappear in the KUK's General Meeting of August 15, 1885.
77. Okutani, p. 190; *Yokohama-shi shi*, p. 550. For Hoshi's activity in the KUK General Meeting of April 30, 1883, see *SEDS*, p. 53.
78. Sasaki, *Nihon kaiun kyōsōshi*, p. 193.
79. Calculated from figures in Kondō Tetsuo, "Shokusan kōgyō to zairai sangyō," *Iwanami kōza, Nihon rekishi*, vol. 14, *Kindai* I (Iwanami Shoten, 1975), p. 242.
80. Smith, pp. 98–99.
81. For the circumstances in which these 2 documents were written, see *YD*, pp. 520, 540; and *Yanosuke den*, I, 223. For the *ikensho*, I have used the text in *YD*, pp. 521–538; for the *benmōsho*, *Yanosuke den*, I, 547–577.
82. This charge was accurate. Much of Yatarō's stock was held in the name of Asabuki Eiji, a former Mitsubishi employee who, with Yatarō's backing, had left the company in 1880 to join a trading company in Yokohama, the Bōeki Shōkai. He later continued to perform useful tasks for Mitsubishi. Nishino, p. 136; *Asabuki Eiji kun den* (Dō Shi Denki Hensankai, 1928).
83. *SEDS*, p. 40; Masuda, p. 252.
84. *SEDS*, p. 45. This 2% figure, equivalent to ¥52,000, is referred to as a "dividend" in the KUK directive but as a "repayment" in a company pamphlet. In the latter sense the government's ¥2.6 million investment in company shares can be interpreted as a long-term loan to be repaid in annual installments at no interest over 50 years—the same terms Yatarō received after his *myōgakin* petition of 1877. See "Kyōdō Un'yu Kaisha sōritsu gaikyō" (undated pamphlet), pp. 7–8. Internal evidence suggests this was written in June 1883. See n. 105 of this chapter.
85. Roger F. Hackett, *Yamagata Aritomo in the Rise of Modern Japan* (Harvard, 1971), pp. 87–88; *YD*, p. 512.
86. For background on this incident, see Hilary Conroy, *The Japanese Seizure of Korea, 1868–1910* (University of Pennsylvania, 1960), pp. 78–168, esp. pp. 101–103. See also *YD*, p. 511; and *M Sha shi*, IX, 341–371, 548–549.
87. *Yanosuke den*, I, 571.
88. July 14 speech to KUK promoters, *SEDS*, pp. 43–44.
89. *Yanosuke den*, I, 574–575; Utsumi memorandum, November 2, 1880, OM, A2950.

90. Sasaki, *Nihon kaiun kyōsōshi*, pp. 198–199.

91. *SEDS*, p. 59; *NYK 50 nenshi*, pp. 44–46.

92. *Godai shiryō*, I, #456, p. 375; Fraser, "The Expulsion of Ōkuma," p. 225.

93. Conroy, p. 99. On the Vladivostok and Korean lines, see *M Sha shi*, VIII, 35–41; and Wray, pp. 267–269.

94. Ōe, pp. 124–125.

95. The quotations and summary of Shinagawa's agricultural thought come from Thomas R. H. Havens, *Farm and Nation in Modern Japan, Agrarian Nationalism, 1870–1940* (Princeton, 1974), pp. 64, 65, 69. See also Okutani, p. 189.

96. *SEDS*, pp. 47–48.

97. *SEDS*, pp. 48–49. On Shinagawa and Nōkai, see Havens, pp. 39–40.

98. Okutani, p. 188; Hackett, p. 101; *Yanosuke den*, I, 222; Inoue to Itō, December 9, 1882, in *Segai Inoue*, III, 556–567.

99. Correspondence in *M Sha shi*, IX, 466–469.

100. *Yanosuke den*, I, 217; Nishino, pp. 136–137.

101. The following analysis is based on Sasaki, *Nihon kaiun kyōsōshi*, pp.205, 211–212; and on my own interpretation of the directives.

102. For the KUK's articles of association of October 19, 1882, see *SEDS*, pp. 51–56; and *NYK 50 nenshi*, pp. 29–37.

103. *M Sha shi*, X, 57–58, 70–73.

104. *YD*, pp. 554–555.

105. Ignoring the need for retained earnings, this pamphlet stated that after subtracting the government's share, the ¥600,000 would leave a 16% dividend for the private stockholders, Even this was considered a low estimate, and if profits were higher, the dividend would be raised to 25%. "Kyōdō Un'yu Kaisha sōritsu gaikyō," pp. 7–8. Large dividends were common in the early Meiji period. Company owners felt obligated to provide dividends even when business was bad. Not to do so was considered a serious breach of faith.

106. *SEDS*, pp. 29–31; *Yokohama-shi shi*, p. 547; Nishino, pp. 145–146; *YD*, pp. 474–475; Lebra, pp. 64–65.

107. *KS*, I, 165.

5. *COMPETITION AND MERGER: 1883–1885*

1. Fairbank, Reischauer, and Craig, p. 260.

2. Noda Kazuo, *Zaibatsu* (Chūō Kōronsha, 1967), p. 34; Ōe, pp. 140–141; Shibagaki, *Nihon kin'yū shihon*, p. 72.

3. The variety of interests participating in these 3 companies calls into question another generalization implicit in Reischauer's quotation—that a merger between Mitsubishi and Mitsui interests would have been typical

of the kind of grouping and consolidation going on in the 1880s. This grouping was occurring among smaller concerns, and the KUK, rather than the N.Y.K., was the typical merger.

4. The vote totals come from the *Tokyo keizai zasshi,* May 5, 1883, in *SEDS,* pp. 82–83.

5. For the debate over the number of directors, see *SEDS,* p. 83; for the list of promoters, ibid., p. 57; and *KS,* I, 180. Mitsui Takenosuke was not a Mitsui family head. Roberts, pp. 10–11, discusses the unique relationship between Mitsui Bussan and the Mitsui family. On Kimura and Magoshi, see Shiroyanagi, *Nihon fugō,* pp. 151–152; and Ōtsuka Eizō, *Magoshi Kyōhei ō den* (Dō Denki Hensankai, 1935), pp. 65–104; on Amamiya, see Morikawa, *Nihongata keiei no genryū,* pp. 74–81.

6. "Kyōdō Un'yu Kaisha sōritsu gaikyō," p. 10.

7. *SEDS,* pp. 62–63; Wray, p. 291.

8. Noda Masaho, "Corporate Finance of Railroad Companies in Meiji Japan," in Nakagawa Keiichirō, ed., *Marketing and Finance in the Course of Industrialization* (Tokyo University, 1978), pp. 89–92. This installment payment system was legal in Japan until 1948.

9. *KS,* III, 173. The *Chōya shinbun,* August 17, 1885, dates this ¥30 price as late 1884. *KS,* III, 161. There is also a widely accepted theory that Mitsubishi was buying KUK shares at this time. For discussion, see Chapter 6.

10. *SEDS,* p. 57. For the mid-1880s, see *Mitsui Ginkō 80 nenshi* (Dō Hensan Iinkai, 1957), pp. 100–106.

11. Noda, "Nihon zaibatsushi e no kiyo," p. 103.

12. Nishino, pp. 159, 426. (*Jūyaku* technically meant president, vice-president, and board of directors: *teikan,* article 37). This information came to Nishino in conversation with Oda Shōjirō, who had heard it personally from Katō. When Nishino was writing his book, Oda was a large individual stockholder in the N.Y.K. See also Wray, pp. 293–294.

13. Only 1 of the 37 non-Mitsui KUK promoters appears as a claimant on this debt certificate list. The list contains only 27 people (minus Hisaya), but at the time of the merger the KUK had 4,614 private stockholders. The full list is in *NYK–H* 2, 1887, pp. 18–20. A shorter version containing only those with 20 or more claims appears in *SEDS,* p. 149. For the liquidation of accounts and dividend payments, see pp. 118–119; and especially Takatera, *Meiji genka shōkyakushi,* p. 156.

14. *YD,* p. 516; *Yanosuke den,* I, 220.

15. *Godai shiryō,* III, 372–373; Wray, pp. 297–298.

16. Obata, p. 121; Itō, p. 15.

17. *Yanosuke den,* I, 160–161; *NYK 70 nenshi,* p. 18.

18. For the arrival of the ships, see *SEDS,* p. 64; "Kyōdō Un'yu Kaisha

sōritsu gaikyō," pp. 5-6. KUK sailing times are given in KUK, Kaisō-bu, "Fūhansen kōkai nissū mikomi," Matsuo [Shigeyoshi] ke monjo, vol. 78, no. 9, n.d., For steamships, see *Chūō-kushi*, ed., Tokyo-to Chūō-kuya-kusho (1958), III, 417-420.

19. For the lines, see *NYK 50 nenshi*, pp. 44-46; *Yokohama-shi shi*, pp. 551-552; for the slogan, *KD*, p. 134; and for administration, Nagasawa, "Shoki Mitsubishi no . . . kaiungyō," p. 36. In 1884 Fukuzawa commented on the weaknesses of the 2 companies, as expressed in the above slogan, but he hoped that the competition would enable them to overcome these problems and make both firms stronger. See *Fukuzawa Yukichi zenshū* (Iwanami Shoten, 1960), IX, 417-439.

20. *YD*, p. 557; *KS*, III, 261; Sasaki, *Nihon kaiun kyōsōshi*, pp. 232-233. See Wray, pp. 301-304, for a fuller list of rates.

21. Sasaki, *Nihon kaiun kyōsōshi*, pp. 220, 231-232, derived from *KS*, III, 263-264. Cf. Yamamura, *Samurai Income and Entrepreneurship*, p. 221.

22. *M Sha shi*, IX, 259-262, 321-322; XI, 137-139, 239-240; *KS*, III, 73-81; *YD*, p. 555.

23. Sasaki, *Nihon kaiun kyōsōshi*, pp. 216-217; Wray, pp. 306-307.

24. Percentages computed from the budget in *M Sha shi*, X, 213-214.

25. For figures on depreciation, see the sources for Table 21 and Takatera, *Meiji genka shōkyakushi*, pp. 121, 135-162. For Mitsubishi subsidy figures, see Table 10. The KUK figures appear in the company's accounts in *SEDS*, pp. 100, 118. Mitsubishi's depreciation had been higher than normal in 1882 and 1883 because it stopped insuring its ships and transferred insurance expense (previously included in ship expenditures) to depreciation. See *M Sha shi*, X, 215; XI, 401-402; and Wray, pp. 312-313n26.

26. *OSK 80 nenshi*, pp. 9-13, 402, 789-803; *OSK 50 nenshi*, pp. 1-36; Nishino, pp. 163-166; *Tsukahara*, pp. 84-86.

27. *OSK 50 nenshi*, pp. 10-11; *Tsukahara*, facing p. 84.

28. For the OSK promoters, see *OSK 50 nenshi*, pp. 11, 484-485; and Wray, pp. 314-316.

29. Calculated on the basis of 11.5 years in view of the accounting change in 1885. See Shibagaki, *Nihon kin'yū shihon*, p. 83.

30. *YD*, pp. 387-396; Kobayashi, *Nihon no kōgyōka*, p. 247. In the last 6 months of 1884 the shipyard showed a profit of ¥40,576 and in 1885, ¥51,066.

31. Kobayashi Masaaki, "Takashima Tankō ni okeru Mitsubishi baishū no igi," *Keizaikei* 102 & 103:124, 129 (March 10, 1975).

32. Ibid., p. 130. Mitsubishi's use of prisoners as laborers in the Takashima Mine led to a sensational exposé in the late 1880s about "slavery" in the mine, where "human beings are dealt with as cattle" and "are whipped

on until their skins are inflamed." See Kosaka Masaaki, ed., *Japanese Thought in the Meiji Era*, tr., David Abosch (Tōyō Bunko Reprint Edition, 1969), p. 216.

33. *Mitsubishi Ginkōshi*, pp. 35–39; *YD*, p. 561; Wray, pp. 320–321n35. Despite this decision to close the Exchange Office, some of its individual branches continued to operate until later in 1885. See also n.88 of this chapter.

34. A Mitsubishi move into banking in 1885 was not related to the kind of exchange and financing service to shippers carried out by the Exchange Office. It was not the revival of the office after a temporary retreat. Cf. Wray, pp. 320–322. Mitsubishi made one more move in mid-1885 in relation to the defunct business of the Exchange Office. In June 1885 it set up a small warehouse operation. This, too, was not an attempt to revive the office. Warehousing was only one of several functions performed by the office, and the small concern started by Mitsubishi in June was run together with banks independent of Mitsubishi. Mitsubishi seems to have intended to enter the warehouse business regardless of who was managing the shipping enterprise, and though it transferred its warehouses to the N.Y.K. as part of the merger, in April 1887 it set up its own company, the Tokyo Sōko Kaisha (Tokyo Warehouse Company) with a capital of ¥500,000. For a slightly different emphasis, see *Yanosuke den*, II, 388–390.

35. Yatarō, letter to Godai, April 12, 1884, *YD*, pp. 572–573; cf. Hoover, pp. 268–269. On the KUK, see the *Mainichi shinbun*, December 12, 1884, in *KS*, III, 18; and Sasaki, *Nihon kaiun kyōsōshi*, p. 222.

36. "Ko shachō jiseki shiryō," in *YD*, pp. 563–564. Hijikata was a member of the neutral Tosa faction in the government.

37. Shibusawa to Inoue Kaoru, February 2, 1885, *SEDS*, p. 82 (my emphasis).

38. *SEDS*, p. 99. Cf. *KS*, III, 88–89, 160.

39. Especially useful on the interplay of domestic politics, the Korean incident, and shipping policy is Shiroyanagi, *Zaikai taiheiki*, pp. 218–223.

40. Although this agreement was dated February 5, it appeared in the government gazette on February 1. See *M Sha shi*, XII, 75–78, for other points of the agreement.

41. For the contract, see *M Sha shi*, XII, 79–80; for a useful chronology of the January negotiations, pp. 93–97; and for the cessation order, pp. 108–109.

42. *M Sha shi*, XII, 89, 96–97; *Yokohama-shi shi*, p. 556; Tanaka, pp. 284–285.

43. This letter was carried to KUK Executive Director Komuro Shinobu on

April 5 by Mitsubishi Assistant Manager Okazaki Koremoto, who made further verbal protests. *M Sha shi*, XII, 133-134.

44. See Itō's letter to Yanosuke of April 7 and a portion of an April 15 KUK report to Tsukahara Shūzō, head of the Shipping Bureau. *M Sha shi*, XII, 135-139.

45. *M Sha shi*, XII, 127-129.

46. *M Sha shi*, XII, 134, 137.

47. April 8 letter of Mitsubishi Business Manager Uchida Kōsaku to Hakodate Branch Manager Funamoto Ryūnosuke and company telegrams, *M Sha shi*, XII, 129-132.

48. Sasaki's comments on Mitsubishi stock buying and selling are taken largely from the *Mainichi shinbun*, December 12, 1884; and the *Tokyo keizai zasshi*, September 5, 1885, *KS*, III, 18, 170-171. In the remainder of this chapter I have frequently criticized Sasaki's views, because (1) his is perhaps the most detailed secondary account in Japanese of the competition; and (2) most subsequent scholars have followed his interpretation rather uncritically. I am therefore not simply criticizing Sasaki as an individual scholar; rather, I am using him as a convenient strawman, a "code word" for most Japanese historiography on the competition and merger. The major exception to Sasaki is Mishima Yasuo, *Mitsubishi zaibatsushi: Meiji hen* (Kyōikusha, 1979), pp. 96-112, which is the clearest, most straightforward account in Japanese of the 1885 competition. Mishima's views agree basically with mine. But he has not had room to show explicitly how they differ from earlier interpretations.

49. *Yanosuke den*, I, 236-238.

50. In the original repayment agreement of 1883 Mitsubishi had received an interest elimination (*ribiki*) provision calculated at 6%. These terms were eased to 10% through renegotiations in February 1885, and Mitsubishi was able to pay off a ¥1,325,675 debt with ¥632,694. Shukuri, pp. 444-446; *Yanosuke den*, I, 234-236; *M Sha shi*, XII, 53-59. Cf. Chapter 4, n.103. At the time Mitsubishi was making these repayments, the government was lending the KUK ¥160,000. One might say that money formerly in the possession of Mitsubishi was being used to pay the KUK dividend. For Sasaki's arguments summarized here, see *Nihon kaiun kyōsōshi*, pp. 220, 225-228.

51. *SEDS*, p. 106.

52. Okutani, p. 191; Shiroyanagi, *Zaikai taiheiki*, pp. 92, 98. Shiroyanagi's is the earliest reference to this ¥400,000 figure, but Okutani, who gives the same figure, provides more detail. Thus there may be an independent source. It was an astonishingly large sum, though, and must remain open to doubt.

53. *YD*, pp. 561–562; Roberts, pp. 121–122.
54. For the former view, see Okutani, p. 191; for the latter, Nishino, pp. 154–155. For comments on estrangement between Saigō and Inoue, see Shiroyanagi, *Zaikai taiheiki*, p. 98; and the same author's *Nihon fugō*, p. 60.
55. Yanosuke's memorial to Minister of Agriculture and Commerce Matsukata, March 18, 1885, *YD*, pp. 566–569.
56. These official views are found most explicitly in *YD*, pp. 565, 574, 580.
57. *SEDS*, p. 38; *Yamamoto Tatsuo*, p. 118.
58. *Zaikai bukko ketsubutsu den*, II, 517–519; Nishino, p. 155; "Nippon Yūsen Kabushiki Kaisha," in *Jinteki jigyō taikei 5, Kaiun bōeki hen* (Chūgai Sangyō Chōsakai, 1940), pp. 6–7. Morioka was one of the Satsuma swordsmen who killed 6 imperial loyalists in the Teradaya Incident of 1862.
59. *Godai shiryō*, III, 488, 514–521; Hoover, pp. 274–276.
60. *Tsukahara*, facing p. 86; *KS*, III, 308–313; *SEDS*, pp. 106, 117.
61. Yatarō's biographer, who rejects this "offensive strategy" interpretation, made no use of the early April correspondence, with the exception of Yanosuke's April 6 letter to Matsukata, which appears in many sources. The other letters and telegrams are printed only in *M Sha shi*.
62. Okutani, pp. 178, 193.
63. *KD*, p. 140. The fact that Saigō was in China from early March to late April contradicts those sources which identify him as appointing Morioka. Conroy, pp. 169–170; Nishino, pp. 154–155; Wray, pp. 337–338.
64. Morioka's report appears in *M Sha shi*, XII, 132–142, as an appendix to Mitsubishi's telegrams.
65. *KS*, III, 99–106; Sasaki, *Nihon kaiun kyōsōshi*, p. 226. For the KUK tea-union contract and the passenger competition at Kobe, see the *Tokyo keizai zasshi*, April 25, 1885, pp. 528–529, and June 13, 1885, pp. 770–771. There seems to have been a "lull before the storm" between the repudiation of the accords in April and the extreme competition beginning in late May.
66. Sasaki, *Nihon kaiun kyōsōshi*, p. 237; *KS*, III, 149; Wray, p. 340 n 69.
67. Sasaki, *Nihon kaiun kyōsōshi*, p. 225.
68. See Chapter 4, n.4.
69. The government approval of this merger is of fundamental significance. I have noted in Part One that Mitsubishi could not obtain government approval in 1878 for its own bank and had to settle for the Exchange Bureau instead. By approving a bank owned by Mitsubishi in the heart of the 1885 competition the government in effect modified article one of the Third Directive defining Mitsubishi's business status. As in the case of the Nagasaki Shipyard in 1884, by this bank approval the govern-

ment acknowledged the growing interests of Mitsubishi outside shipping. For the bank purchase, see *Mitsubishi Ginkōshi*, pp. 46-49; *M Sha shi*, XII, 165-212; and *Yanosuke den*, II, 358-361.

70. Sasaki weakens his argument by not taking into account Mitsubishi's outside payments. He does not even mention the bank purchase and gives no figure for the repayment of government loans. The source with which he footnoted his reference to the repayment also contains no figure. (See Sasaki, *Nihon kaiun kyōsōshi*, pp. 227-228; and *KS*, III, 92-93.) His study is based almost exclusively on the newspaper accounts in *KS*. Since he did not use the *Mitsubishi Sha shi*, he did not have access to the KUK-Mitsubishi correspondence of early April.

71. Sasaki, *Nihon kaiun kyōsōshi*, pp. 225-229; for the ¥5.5 rate at the start of the competition, see *KS*, III, 107, 114, 349; and the *Tokyo keizai zasshi*, June 27, 1885, p. 835. For freight rates, see *Yokohama-shi shi*, p. 556; *KS*, III, 131. In a 1910 speech Kondō Renpei, Mitsubishi's Yokohama branch manager in 1885, stated that passenger rates on the Kobe-Yokohama run fell as low as 25 *sen*. I have been unable to confirm this from contemporary sources, which give 55 *sen* as the lowest figure. See *KD*, p. 138.

72. *KD*, pp. 138-139; *NYK 70 nenshi*, p. 20.

73. Nishino, p. 156; *Zaikai bukko ketsubutsu den*, I, 324-327. Despite its growing deficit, the KUK seems to have performed better than Mitsubishi on the Japan Sea coast. See *Fushiki-kōshi*, pp. 249-250.

74. *SEDS*, pp. 107-108.

75. Knowledge of this meeting comes primarily from the diary of Yamamoto Tatsuo in *Yamamoto Tatsuo*, pp. 126-128; and Hirohata Tadataka, *Kaiun yawa* (Nihon Kaiji Gakkai Shuppanbu, 1932), pp. 9-11. See also *SEDS*, p. 106; and *YD*, pp. 575-576.

76. In July 1885 the Emperor Meiji went on an imperial tour through western Japan, and in this "moment of truth" the government chose to use Mitsubishi ships for the imperial party. Yatarō's biographer suggests that "patrons of Mitsubishi in the Imperial Household Ministry" may have been responsible for this decision. *YD*, p. 571.

77. He had also brought the exchange rate of paper currency to silver yen down from 1.70 in 1881 to 1.05 in 1885.

78. *Yamamoto Tatsuo*, p. 128.

79. *KD*, pp. 141-143. This conversation was recorded by Katō Masayoshi. See also Asahara Jōhei, *Nihon kaiun hattenshi* (Chōryūsha, 1978), p. 36. A *mon* was a small copper coin used during the Tokugawa period.

80. *KD*, pp. 143-144. This information, as well as the conversation cited in the previous note, came to Suehiro, the author of Kondō's biography,

in an interview with Katō Masayoshi. *SEDS*, p. 111. At this time the KUK directors were the same 5 elected in April 1883.

81. *SEDS*, pp. 110–111; *Yokohama-shi shi*, p. 558.
82. As recorded in *KD*, p. 144. On Saigō's administrative posts, which are listed incorrectly in many official records, see Wray, p. 353 n 88; and *Yamamoto Tatsuo*, p. 123.
83. *SEDS*, p. 108; *NYK 70 nenshi*, p. 21.
84. *Meiji un'yushi*, p. 47; Segawa, pp. 242–243.
85. Yanosuke to Saigō, letter dated August 1, 1885; *SEDS*, pp. 108–109; *Yanosuke den*, I, 246–249. For questions regarding the dating of this letter, see Wray, p. 354 n 91; and *YD*, p. 757.
86. See *SEDS*, XVIII, 359–376, esp. pp. 376–380. In his study of business ideology, *Capitalism and Nationalism in Prewar Japan: The Ideology of of the Business Elite, 1868–1941* (Stanford, 1967), pp. 27–29, Byron Marshall has utilized this debate to illustrate business attitudes toward government intervention. The debate serves as an excellent source for a study of business attitudes, but as an event in the tortuous path toward merger it was inconsequential.
87. *KS*, III, 163.
88. *M Sha shi*, XII, 358–362; *Mitsubishi Ginkōshi*, p. 39; *Yanosuke den*, II, 388–389. Shibusawa at the time was president of the Dai Ichi Bank.
89. Morioka's speech is in *SEDS*, pp. 112–114.
90. For comment on statistics used in this speech, see Wray, p. 358.
91. For a description of *sōkaiya*, used recently to keep stockholders meetings under control, see Frank Baldwin, "The Idioms of Contemporary Japan VII: Sōkaiya," *Japan Interpreter* 8.4:502–509 (Winter 1974).
92. Nishino, pp. 158–159. Asabuki tried to disguise his real motives and instead of asking for a specific number of shares, he approached the matter indirectly, stating that if someone had shares to sell, he wanted to buy. This tactic apparently created the mistaken impression that Mitsubishi was buying up whole blocs of KUK shares.
93. Ibid., pp. 158–160, 426. Nishino obtained this account of the meeting from Oda Shōjirō, who had heard it from Katō. See n. 12 of this chapter.
94. See *KS*, III, 178–192; and for a short summary, *SEDS*, p. 115. For other accounts of the General Meeting, see *KS*, III, 154–164.
95. *YD*, p. 581, mistakenly assumes that these votes are equivalent to shares. The two are quite different. See Wray, p. 361. Also, Table 27 suggests that Takanashi's survey omitted government shares. The government's full support for the merger made the outcome of the General Meeting a fait accompli, despite the messy details. Morioka's actions were not necessarily illegal, for despite the KUK regulations, no commercial law yet governed the procedures of General Meetings, and the government's

late July order effectively overrode the KUK voting system. Takanashi's report, then, may well be statistically accurate, but it is less valuable as a legal scorecard than as a measure of discontent, an indication that the government had to follow procedures to allow the small stockholders to express their opposition even if these procedures invited disruption.

96. *KD*, pp. 144-145; Nishino, p. 160.

97. I have followed Nishino, p. 161, in this interpretation. See also *YD*, pp. 580-581.

98. Letter in *Tsukahara*, facing p. 78; and *SEDS*, p. 112.

99. *Segai Inoue*, III, 561-562.

100. Summary of Morioka report in ibid., pp. 563-564.

101. *NYK 70 nenshi*, p. 21.

102. Petition from Mitsubishi to the Ministry of Agriculture and Commerce, September 15, 1885, *YD*, pp. 757-759. For controversy regarding the dating of this petition, see Wray, p. 365 n109. Such petitions may seem petty, but they are a good illustration of the Japanese habit of obscuring the source of decisions. They provide parallels to the *ringi* system, n. 22, Chapter 2. Also, for a century Mitsubishi has used the surface rhetoric (*tatemae*) of this petition to propagate its official line that it "lost the shipping industry." *Mitsubishi Fact Book '82* (Mitsubishi Kōhō Iinkai, 1982), p. 9. This serves to obscure Mitsubishi's victory and its extremely successful underlying strategy of exploiting public funds and the merger process.

103. Apropos of these comments, it is said that in the 1880s when dividends "were not paid out because business was bad, the conservative and timid capital suppliers often demanded scrapping of the enterprise." Hirschmeier and Yui, p. 113.

104. Fraser, "Komuro," pp. 76-77.

105. *Yanosuke den*, I, 253; Yamamura, *Samurai Income and Entrepreneurship*, p. 162.

106. Terai Hisanobu, *Shio no michihi* (Gotō Shoten, 1953), pp. 27-29. An analysis of the ships kept by the N.Y.K. supports Terai's argument. In 1885 Mitsubishi had 18 ships over 1,000 tons, but in 1900 only 7 of these remained with the N.Y.K. On the other hand, the KUK had 12 such ships in 1885, and the N.Y.K. still had 10 in 1900. Calculated from *NYK 70 nenshi*, pp. 676-677.

107. See Wray, p. 371, esp. n. 114; and Takatera, *Meiji genka shōkyakushi*, p. 156.

108. *NYK 70 nenshi*, pp. 21-22; *SEDS*, p. 127; Mishima, ed., *Mitsubishi zaibatsu*, pp. 330-331; Nishikawa Yoshirō, "Nippon Yūsen Kabushiki Kaisha kyūchōbo shiryō oboegaki," *Hitotsubashi daigaku kenkyū nenpō shōgaku kenkyū* 21:85-158 (1979).

109. Takatera Sadao, "Introduction and Diffusion of Depreciation Accounting in Japan, 1875-1903," in Nakagawa, ed., *Marketing and Finance*, pp. 109-111; Takatera, *Meiji genka shōkyakushi*, p. 121; *M Sha shi*, XI, 401-403.

110. *SEDS*, pp. 119-120.

111. *M Sha shi*, XI, 404-405; XII, 389-390, 394-401; Takatera, *Meiji genka shōkyakushi*, pp. 156, 158. Takatera's figures (e.g., ¥1.86 million for March) are slightly low because some ships were valued in silver yen and he has not converted their value to paper currency.

112. "[NYK] no josei narabi kyūsaisaku," Matsuo ke monjo, vol. 78, no. 8, p. 1; *KD*, p. 147; Takatera, *Meiji genka shōkyakushi*, pp. 149-162; *JWM*, November 29, 1890.

113. See the section on stockholding, Chapter 6.

114. *NYK 50 nenshi*, pp. 63-79; *SEDS*, pp. 127-137.

115. Memorial of August 11, 1885, *YD*, pp. 579-580.

116. For the recent history of this company form, see Chalmers Johnson, *Japan's Public Policy Companies* (American Enterprise Institute, 1978). One further provocative parallel with the KUK was the new company's name. The government first planned to call the KUK the Teikoku Yūsen Kaisha (Imperial Mail Steamship Company). The N.Y.K. (Nippon Yūsen Kaisha) substituted "Japan" for "Imperial." The crucial term, *yūsen*—referring to mail, but implying a broader government-company relationship—remained the same.

117. Shiroyanagi, *Zaikai taiheiki*, pp. 100-101.

118. That the first N.Y.K. president was a former official executioner should not surprise readers familiar with the diverse experiences of Meiji leaders. For humorous examples, see Albert M. Craig, "Kido Kōin and Ōkubo Toshimichi: A Psychohistorical Analysis," in Craig and Shively, pp. 264-265.

6. SHAPING A CORPORATE IDENTITY: 1886-1894

1. Noda, "Nihon zaibatsushi e no kiyo," p. 107; cf. Inoue Yōichirō, "Meiji kōki no kaiji seisaku," in Andō, ed., *Nihon keizai seisaku shiron*, I, 187.

2. Personnel data comes from *NYK 70 nenshi*, pp. 617-658; *NYK 50 nenshi*, pp. 771-786; *NYK-H* 1, 1887, p. 21. Identifications can be made from *Yanosuke den*, I, 260-269; and *KD*, pp. 133, 146.

3. *Tokyo keizai zasshi*, December 26, 1885, pp. 1702-1703; also in *Yanosuke den*, I, 270-272.

4. *KD*, pp. 147-148. See also *Fukuzawa zenshū*, X, 483-487.

5. *Yanosuke den*, II, 512; *NYK-H* 1, 1887, p. 22.

6. *Zaikai bukko ketsubutsu den,* II, 613–615; *KD,* p. 148. Yoshikawa, the son of a Shinto priest, was born in Nara.

7. Nakagawa Keiichirō, "Business Strategy and Industrial Structure in Pre-World War II Japan," in Nakagawa, ed., *Strategy and Structure,* p. 24. On Mitsubishi's revenue, see Table 38.

8. *M Sha shi,* XIII, 21; *Yanosuke den,* I, 272. Stock was also given to former employees who became N.Y.K. executives. Kondō Renpei, for example, received 600 shares from the Iwasaki family. See *KD,* p. 147; and Table 37 in this section.

9. There is some indirect and puzzling evidence on this issue that this was Mitsubishi's motive. Table 30 showed that 36 votes could be cast for shares held in excess of 5,000. These 36 votes could be secured by an additional 7,200 shares. The maximum number of shares eligible for voting purposes would thus be 5,000 + 7,200 = 12,200—the same number given to Mitsubishi employees. These matching totals can hardly be dismissed as coincidence, but their real significance is not clear.

10. Okutani, p. 191; Hirschmeier and Yui, p. 141; Nakagawa, "Business Strategy and Industrial Structure," p. 5; Teratani Takeaki, "Japanese Business and Government in the Takeoff Stage," in Nakagawa Keiichirō, ed., *Government and Business* (Tokyo University, 1980), pp. 60–61.

11. See n. 3 of this chapter. Shibagaki, *Mitsui, Mitsubishi,* p. 26, used a shorter excerpt from this article in Tanaka, pp. 299–300 (personal communication). The Iwasaki biographer, Nakano Tadaaki, views Taguchi's assertion as a "complete fabrication" (*mattaku no netsuzō*). *YD,* p. 581.

12. *KS,* III, 161, 171.

13. *KS,* III, 173.

14. Nishino, pp. 158, 425–426. For an explanation of this misdating, see Wray, pp. 397–398. See also Mishima, *Mitsubishi zaibatsushi,* p. 111. For the 1887 lists, see *SEDS,* pp. 148–149; and *NYK 50 nenshi,* pp. 550–553. Nishino used the list in the *SEDS,* which contains the names of a number of peers who received N.Y.K. stock only in September 1887. Nakamura Masanori has used the government gazette to determine the precise dates when several of these peers were awarded shares. (Personal communication).

15. *Yanosuke den,* II, 402–403; letter from Yanosuke to Shōda, September 3, 1887, ibid., p. 571. A common argument that nominal holdings by its personnel enabled Mitsubishi to control N.Y.K. stock is flawed because (1) employees generally sold substantial portions of their stock received in the March 1886 gift (see, for example, Table 37), and (2) the amount given to employees was small relative to Mitsubishi's sales which began in 1887. An N.Y.K. stockholders list for late 1885 (unearthed in the

Mitsubishi General Research Institute in December 1983) suggests strongly that Mitsubishi held less than half the N.Y.K. stock. I can identify roughly 91,000 shares of the Iwasaki family (80,917) and Mitsubishi personnel. Doubt remains about the identity of small holders and the dating (in pencil and hence suspect).

16. Hirschmeier, "Shibusawa," p. 235; *SEDS,* p. 149. The most Shibusawa ever had subsequent to 1899 was 650 shares in 1903–1905, *NYK–KNS.* Shibusawa's influence, more precisely defined, is that he was not a large stockholder, either in the N.Y.K. or in most of the companies with which he had close dealings. His role (in the KUK, in the merger, and in the N.Y.K. after 1893) was more as a powerful adviser, a "fixer," a liaison with the government or other business interests. (In 1885 he ranked 25th with 572 shares.)

17. *NYK–KNS,* October 31, 1892. The 1899 rankings come from Nakamura Masanori, "Nihon burujoajī no kōsei," in Ōishi Kaichirō, ed., *Nihon sangyō kakumei no kenkyū* (Tokyo Daigaku Shuppankai, 1975), II, 116–119. The 1885 list has only 5 KUK promoters in the top 125.

18. At ¥70.9, about the average market value of N.Y.K. shares in 1886–1887, the ¥978,250 Mitsubishi repaid the government (see p. 219) would have purchased 13,800 shares. In effect, then, the Finance Ministry obtained these shares in return for favors done earlier for Mitsubishi.

19. For this proposal, see *Iwakura kō jikki* (Iwakura Kō Kyūseki Hozonkai, 1927), III, 821–825.

20. Matsukata to Sanjō, November 18, 1884, in "Matsukata haku zaisei ronsakushū," in Tsuchiya and Ōuchi, comps., *Meiji zenki zaisei keizai shiryō shūsei* (1931), I, 535–536; Tokutomi, I, 1121–1122; see II, 201 for commentary. See also David Anson Titus, *Palace and Politics in Prewar Japan* (Columbia, 1974), pp. 64–66.

21. Matsukata to Prime Minister Itō Hirobumi, March 24, 1887, in Tokutomi, II, 201–202; and "Matsukata haku zaisei ronsakushū," p. 540.

22. This order, dated July 22, 1887, appears in NYK–KSG, December 15, 1887, p. 27. When the cabinet system was adopted on December 22, 1885, the Shipping Bureau was moved from the Ministry of Agriculture and Commerce to the newly established Ministry of Communications (Teishinshō).

23. Titus, pp. 71–74. For a statistical breakdown of the peers created in 1884 and a partial list of members, see Walter W. McLaren, ed., "Japanese Government Documents, 1867–1889," *Transactions of the Asiatic Society of Japan,* 42.1:88 (1914). McLaren gives a total of 500—12 princes, 24 marquises, 74 counts, 321 viscounts, and 69 barons.

24. *NYK 50 nenshi,* pp. 550–553; cf. Wray, p. 405n31.

25. *Yanosuke den,* I, 444–450; Craig, "Kido and Ōkubo," p. 304.

26. The quotation is from Titus, pp. 64–74. For other discussion of the Im-

perial Household Ministry and the peers, see Ōe, pp. 139-142; and Nakamura, "Nihon burujoajī," pp. 65-128.

27. *NYK 50 nenshi,* pp. 93-95, 542; *NYK 70 nenshi,* pp. 35; *KD,* pp. 153-
155; NYK-KSG, December 15, 1887, p. 44; *NYK-H* 3, 1888, p. 5; 7,
1892, pp. 7-8. Because the N.Y.K. stock price was high (normally a
measure of the market value of company assets), from the viewpoint of
modern accounting there seems no compelling reason why the N.Y.K.
had to decrease its capital. According to the accounting precepts of the
1880s, however, it seems clear that stock price was not necessarily accepted as a measure of "actual value." The prevailing view assumed that
N.Y.K. property was still below its "nominal [that is, book] value," a
"state of affairs" regarded as "unwelcome to businessmen." *JWM,*
November 29, 1890. The N.Y.K. explained the measure as "solidifying
the basis of the company's finances." (NYK), Ketsugi yōkenroku, Kaikei-
ka, September 8, 1892. Other motives are possible. Decreasing the capital
stock meant lessening the stockholder liability as well as reducing the
company's total dividend obligation. Of course, to decrease its capital the
N.Y.K. had to issue bonds, but the obligations to bond holders was fixed.
They would not share in future growth, the benefits of which would
accrue exclusively to the stockholders. Nevertheless, orthodox accounting views which frowned upon inflated book values seem a stronger explanation of company motives, for the original decision in 1886 to
decrease the capital stock was made without reference to bonds. Inagaki
Sumio, general manager of the N.Y.K.'s Accounting Division, agreed
with this explanation.

28. Over three and a quarter years the N.Y.K. would have earned ¥156,370
on this deposit. HK, March 25, 1896, and March 16, 1899. In 1895 the
Imperial House held ¥340,000 worth of N.Y.K. bonds, compared to
Hisaya's ¥439,000. Other leading bond holders in an 1895 list, which
totals ¥2.13 million, were (in units of ¥1,000): Tamura Rishichi, 215;
Yasuda Zenjirō, 190; Mitsui Bank, 146; Yamamoto Sugunari, 137; the
Mitsubishi-affiliated Meiji Life Insurance Company, 120; Teikoku Shō-
gyō Bank, 100; Odaka Kōgorō, 95; and Tokio Marine, 70. (NYK),
Ketsugi roku, September 1895. Also, interest rates had been much
higher in the 1870s and early 1880s, before the effects of the Matsukata
deflation.

29. "[N.Y.K.] no josei narabi kyūsaisaku," 1886, Matsuo ke monjo, vol. 78,
no. 8. This richly informative handwritten draft is the most useful early
document on the N.Y.K. Many notes are scribbled upon it, frequently
disputing points made in the main text. Its main value lies in its explicit
comments about the reasons behind government policies. The author may
have been Matsuo Shigeyoshi who was then in both the Cashier's and
Budget Bureau of the Finance Ministry. He was later president of the
Bank of Japan (1903-1911). On the Finance Ministry's shares, see *NYK*

70 nenshi, p. 559; and *NYK-KNS,* October 31, 1892, and October 31, 1895.

30. In 1892, before it amortized its shares, the N.Y.K. was briefly its own largest stockholder. In the capital stock increase, the N.Y.K. utilized the installment payment system described in Chapter 5 in connection with the KUK. Subscribers paid in 4 installments. The company's shares had a par value of ¥50, and on each installment the subscriber paid ¥12.5 for every share. For cases of companies using more installments, see Noda, "Corporate Finance of Railroad Companies," pp. 89-92; *Hokkaidō Tankō Kisen Kabushiki Kaisha 50 nenshi* (Dōsha, 1939), pp. 144-146.

31. NYK-TG#136, July 29, 1896. In a similar case in 1900 the N.Y.K. replied through the Imperial Household Ministry to questions from the peers about the effect on their interests of government-imposed accounting reforms. HK, August 18, 1900. For further discussion of the auditor, see Chapter 10. See also *JWM,* December 7, 1895, p. 608; NYK-KSG, November 26, 1900; and n. 44 of this chapter.

32. Table 34 shows that these percentages would give more weight to banking if expressed in par value. In the holdings surveyed, the Imperial House had 231,266 shares, with a market value of ¥41,970,000. Nakamura, "Nihon burujoajī," p. 112; Murakami, p. 302.

33. Tokutomi, II, 201-203.

34. Roberts, pp. 139-140, completely contradicts the facts. For Nakamigawa, see *Nakamigawa Hikojirō denki shiryō,* ed., Nihon Keieishi Kenkyūjo (Tōyō Keizai Shinpōsha, 1969).

35. For their other holdings, see Nakamura, "Nihon burujoajī," pp. 116-117.

36. The number of N.Y.K. holders had increased from 2,890 to 3,627 (with the figure for shares per holder growing from 76.1 to 121.3). This was still well below the number of KUK stockholders (4,614) at the time of the merger. See Wray, pp. 420-421.

37. Miwa, "Kaijō yusō," p. 392; *Yokohama-shi shi,* p. 573.

38. Teratani Takeaki, *Nihon kōwan shiron josetsu* (Jichōsha, 1972), pp. 17-42; Furuta, pp. 624-627.

39. Some have called this shift to mining "backward integration" in that Mitsubishi was moving into an industry (coal mining) that had previously supplied its major enterprise (shipping). This characterization of Mitsubishi strategy is too narrow, for it overlooks Mitsubishi's substantial investments in metal mines, which were unrelated to shipping.

40. *M Sha shi,* XIII, 27-30; *Yanosuke den,* I, 274-291; Mishima, ed., *Mitsubishi zaibatsu,* pp. 68-79.

41. This was the bank which Mitsubishi had taken over in 1885 (see Chapter 5). The government did not permit it to be included in the new Mitsubishi Company. See n. 50 below.

42. *Katō Kōmei den* (Dō Kankōkai, 1928), pp. 17–20; Fraser, "The Expulsion of Ōkuma," p. 226; *Yamamoto Tatsuo*, pp. 95–162.

43. Whereas government enterprises were sold in the early and mid-1880s for bargain prices, the Miike sale represents a new stage in the divestiture policy. This involved (1) a government attempt to recover initial investment costs and (2) a preference for private operation; hence the sale even of profitable enterprises. The ¥4.6 million paid for the Miike Mine was almost as much as the combined cost of all other government enterprises sold between 1874 and 1896. All these enterprises were sold for ¥4.8 million, a total which includes ¥1.73 million for two mines sold to Mitsubishi in 1896. (See the next note). Kobayashi, "Nihon no kōgyōka," p. 80; Kobayashi, *Nihon no kōgyōka*, pp. 309–336; Hirschmeier and Yui, p. 137. On the Miike Mine, see Kōzuma Yukihide, *Miike Tankōshi* (Kyōikusha, 1980), esp. pp. 62–73; and for a summary of the stages in the government's policy of selling its enterprises, see Kobayashi Masaaki, "Seishō to kangyō haraisage," in *Kōgyōka to kigyōsha katsudō*, ed., Yui Tsunehiko (Nihon Keizai Shinbunsha, 1976), pp. 85–117.

44. *Yanosuke den*, II, 99–243, esp. p. 178; *Iwasaki Hisaya den*, pp. 334–382. On the sale of Mitsubishi securities, see *JWM*, June 19, 1897, pp. 611–612; and on the controversy surrounding the purchase of mines from the Imperial House, which, in its favoritism to Mitsubishi, recalled for some the Hokkaido Colonization scandal of 1881, see Kobayashi, *Nihon no kōgyōka*, pp. 337–362. Kobayashi provides a good account of government leaders' involvement in the financial affairs of the Imperial House. Fukuzawa responded to this controversy by arguing that the Imperial House should sell its shares in companies lest its voting rights lead it into conflict with private interests, thereby causing a loss of respect for the emperor. See *Fukuzawa zenshū*, XV, 435–437. Also on Mitsubishi coal mining, see Kobayashi Masaaki, "Zaibatsu to tankōgyō: Mitsubishi o chūshin ni," in *Enerugī to keizai hatten*, pp. 189–215.

45. *Yanosuke den*, II, 423–470.

46. For a contrasting form of investment in land, see Feuerwerker, *China's Early Industrialization*, pp. 183–188; and Wray, pp. 430–432.

47. Shukuri, pp. 463–477; *Yanosuke den*, II, 400–415. Compare the purchase price of Marunouchi with the ¥2 million in N.Y.K. shares Mitsubishi gained by appreciating its assets in 1885.

48. Morikawa Hidemasa, *Zaibatsu no keiei shiteki kenkyū* (Tōyō Keizai Shinpōsha, 1980), pp. 26–31; and "Iwasaki Yanosuke jidai no Mitsubishi no toppu manejimento," in Tsuchiya Moriaki and Morikawa Hidemasa, eds., *Kigyōsha katsudō no shiteki kenkyū* (Nihon Keizai Shinbunsha, 1981), pp. 52–56. The Iwasaki family, separately from Mitsubishi as a company, had begun investing in other industrial projects, such as the

Kobe Paper Mill Co. This was important in the long run; (today the Mitsubishi company into which it grew is a leading maker of computer paper). But in the period under study such ventures were small relative to Mitsubishi's main enterprises and they did not have the "trigger" impact on the firm as a whole that shipbuilding had.

49. Kobayashi, "Nihon no kōgyōka," p. 80. Asset percentages calculated from Tatematsu Kiyoshi, "Nihon shihonshugi kakuritsuki no Mitsubishi zaibatsu," *Hitotsubashi kenkyū* 25:88–90 (July 1973); see also Ishii Kanji, "Nisshin sengo keiei," *Iwanami kōza, Nihon rekishi,* vol. 16, *Kindai* III (Iwanami Shoten, 1976), pp. 73–78.

50. Morikawa, "The Organizational Structure of Mitsubishi and Mitsui," p. 67; *Mitsubishi Ginkōshi,* pp. 64–68; *Yanosuke den,* II, 369–372.

51. The N.Y.K. had petitioned the government to recognize this interpretation. "[N.Y.K.] no josei narabi kyūsaisaku," Matsuo ke monjo, vol. 78, no. 8, p. 4.

52. Matsukata to Sanjō, November 4 and December 5, 1885, in "Matsukata haku zaisei ronsakushū," pp. 537–538.

53. For the 1886 business year it was able to pay in only 2.56% for the insurance reserve and 1.58% for the repair reserve. Calculated from *NYK-H* 1, 1887.

54. Based on ship values in its 1887 accounts, for the 2 reserve funds alone the N.Y.K. would still have been ¥282,952 short of the 17% requirement. For 1886 decisions on the 17% standard, see *NYK 50 nenshi,* p. 93; and "[N.Y.K.] no josei narabi kyūsaisaku," Matsuo ke monjo, vol. 78, no. 8, p. 7. For the late 1887 study, see "Nippon Yūsen Kaisha hoshō nenkan fusokukin yosan setsumei," Matsukata ke monjo, vol. 61, Kōtsū, no. 27, n.d. We can date this in October or November. See Wray, p. 437n63.

55. To compensate for the 1886 shortages the N.Y.K. added to the funds at the new percentages. See Wray, p. 438.

56. In negotiations the company had proposed ¥1.6 per mile. "[N.Y.K.] no josei narabi kyūsaisaku," Matsuo ke monjo, vol. 78, no. 4, pp. 5, 11.

57. Ibid., pp. 5–6.

58. *NYK 70 nenshi,* pp. 36, 678; NYK-KSG, December 15, 1887, pp. 40–41; December 1, 1892, p. 6; *NYK-H* 3, 1888, p. 4.

59. *NYK 70 nenshi,* pp. 28–29.

60. *NYK 50 nenshi,* pp. 92–93.

61. Figures taken from *NYK 70 nenshi,* p. 55.

62. Budget figures calculated from *NYK-H* 1–7. See also *NYK 70 nenshi,* pp. 56, 696 (for distance traveled); and *KD,* pp. 151–153.

63. *NYK-H* 6, 1891, p. 6.

64. *NYK-H* 7, 1892, pp. 4-6. In speaking to the 1892 General Meeting, Morioka also blamed competition from railways. NYK-KSG, December 1, 1892.

65. Ibid.

66. Akira Iriye, *Pacific Estrangement: Japanese and American Expansion, 1897-1911* (Harvard, 1972), pp. 36-43. *KD*, p. 180, suggests that Ōishi's writings were prompted by the N.Y.K. as part of a campaign to influence the Diet to provide subsidies for overseas lines.

67. For emigrant statistics, see *NYK 50 nenshi*, pp. 98-99; and Wray, p. 448.

68. See Chapter 2, n. 79.

69. Macdonald to George Stephen (C.P.R. president), July 28, 1884, in Joseph Pope, ed., *Correspondence of Sir John Macdonald* (Toronto, 1921), pp. 315-316. See also Charles J. Woodsworth, *Canada and the Orient* (Toronto, 1941), pp. 212-215; and *Tsukahara*, pp. 70-71. Internal evidence in a letter from Shinagawa to Tsukahara suggests that in late 1884 Tsukahara was again preparing to visit Canada.

70. A copy of this agreement is in GN President's Subject file 162#1. See also *Fukuzawa zenshū*, XI, 511-514.

71. Matsukata ke monjo, vol. 61, Kōtsū, no. 32. The full petition is dated January 1889. See also no. 33, March 5, 1889, which is either a second petition or a summary of the earlier one dated January. On the O. & O., see Norman E. Tutorow, "Leland Stanford, President of the Occidental and Oriental Steamship Company," *American Neptune* 31.2:120-129 (April 1971).

72. For the negotiations, see *NYK 50 nenshi*, p. 88; and *Yokohama-shi shi*, pp. 574-575, which also comments on negotiations with Mexico.

73. In the 1899 revision of the incorporation procedure in the Commercial Law, a system of compliance with government regulations replaced this licensing system. Noda, "Corporate Finance of Railroad Companies," p. 89.

74. This summary is taken from Masaki Hisashi, "Zaibatsu no seiritsu to sono heisateki kin'yū," *Dōshisha shōgaku* 24.1:56-60 (July 1972); Maeda Kazutoshi, "Kaisha-hō seitei to kaisha soshiki seibi," Nakagawa et al., *Keieishi no kiso chishiki*, pp. 113-114; Noda Masaho, "Kabushiki kaisha seido no hatten to kabunushisō," ibid., pp. 151-152; Tamaki, pp. 391-399.

75. The best account of this meeting was written by Itō Yonejirō for the *Ryūmon zasshi* 481 (October 1928), in *SEDS*, pp. 168-171. Itō Hirobumi may have had more than a statesmanlike interest in the new articles, for the last N.Y.K. stockholders list available before this meeting records his ownership of 800 shares. *NYK-KNS*, October 31, 1892.

76. NYK-TG#1, December 2, 1893. "N.Y.K." soon became an abbreviation of convenience, adopted in imitation of Western companies like the P. & O. which used initials. "N.Y.K. LINE" was used as a service mark and advertising logo. Today, NYK, NYK Line, or Nippon Yusen Kaisha are all used as service marks. After World War II the periods were officially dropped, though customarily they still appear, even in company architecture. The official foreign name is Nippon Yusen Kabushiki Kaisha.

77. For the new articles, dated December 1, 1893, see *NYK 50 nenshi,* pp. 105–110; and *SEDS,* pp. 178–181.

78. Article 8. Another revision was the elimination of most of the proportional voting system. Henceforth 1 share would equal 1 vote up to 10 shares. In excess of 10 shares, 5 shares would exercise 1 vote. There was no limit to the number of votes (article 22).

79. NYK-KSG, December 1, 1893; *NYK-JH* 9, 1894, pp. 13, 42; 10/1, March, 1895, p. 35.

80. Sonoda was president of the Yokohama Specie Bank (1890–1898) and in 1898 became president of the Fifteenth Bank. *Mitsui Ginkōshi 80 nenshi,* p. 564. On the directors, see *SEDS,* p. 170; cf. *KD,* pp. 160, 247.

81. Shiroyanagi, *Zaikai taiheiki,* pp. 101–107; *Tokyo nichinichi shinbun,* March 27, 1908, *SEDS,* pp. 122–123. See also Wray, pp. 459–460.

82. *KD,* pp. 157–159, 162; NYK-TG#18, March 21, 1894. On Asada, who retained his N.Y.K. directorship until 1911, see *Zaikai bukko ketsubutsu den,* I, 62–65. Yanosuke and Kawada schemed to have Uchida appointed to the Bank of Japan, thereby providing him with an "honorable exit" from the N.Y.K. Wray, p. 463.

83. On Haruta's role in 1885, see *Yamamoto Tatsuo,* p. 127.

84. NYK-TG#21, April 11, 1894. "*Zuiji*" is an ambiguous word which could also mean "at all times."

85. *Zaikai bukko ketsubutsu den,* II, 616; *KD,* p. 175.

86. Kondō held the presidency until 1921, but the "managerial calm" began to vanish after Iwanaga's departure in 1911. See Chapter 10.

87. That is, vessels operating without a regular schedule or fixed route.

88. *OSK 80 nenshi,* pp. 14–18, 266. Overseas, by the early 1890s the O.S.K. was operating a line to the Ryukyus and an Osaka-Inch'ŏn line (via Pusan) as well as Korean coastal services.

89. See, for example, Noda, "Nihon zaibatsushi e no kiyo," pp. 106–107.

90. *OSK 80 nenshi,* pp. 19, 762–763, 789–799, 810–811; *NYK 70 nenshi,* p. 675; and Table 39 above.

91. Yoshiya Satō, "Architects of Japan's Economy (61)," *Daily Yomiuri,* October 30, 1974.

92. *OSK 50 nenshi,* pp. 41–51; *OSK 80 nenshi,* p. 28; *Tsukahara,* pp. 84–86.

93. *Tōyō Kisen Kabushiki Kaisha 64 nen no ayumi* (Nakano Hideo, publisher, 1964), pp. 5-7; *Yokohama-shi shi,* pp. 568-569.

94. Matsukata ke monjo, vol. 61, Kōtsū, no. 32, p. 18. Cf. Nippon Yusen Kaisha, *Golden Jubilee History of Nippon Yusen Kaisha, 1885-1935* (1935), pp. 36-37.

95. *NYK-JH* 9, 1894; figures from *M Sha shi,* in Tatematsu, p. 88. For comparative figures for 1896, see Sangyō Seisakushi Kenkyūjo, *Wagakuni dai kigyō no keisei hatten katei* (Tsūshō Sangyō Chōsakai Toranomon Bun-. shitsu, 1976), pp. 6, 62.

96. Uda, pp. 126-127.

97. Most of these Mitsubishi shares were held by Hisaya, though Yanosuke also had substantial holdings in the Chikuhō Railway. *Nakamigawa denki shiryō,* pp. 170-173; for statistics on later years and discussion, see Sugiyama Kazuo, "Kigyō no zaimu: tōshi katsudō to bunkateki haikei: Meijiki no tetsudōgyō, menbōsekigyō o jirei to shite," *Keiei shigaku* 10.1:66-71 (August 1975). See also Nakanishi Ken'ichi, *Nihon shiyū tetsudōshi kenkyū* (Nihon Hyōronsha, 1963), pp. 66-67. In 1897 the Kyushu and Chikuhō railways merged to become the Kyushu Railway.

98. NYK-KSG, December 15, 1887, pp. 48-49.

99. Sugiyama, "Kigyō no zaimu," p. 57; *Yanosuke den,* II, 454-470.

100. Nakanishi, p. 80. For Mitsubishi's investment in the Sanyō Railway, which was less connected with its business interests, see Shiroyanagi Shūko, *Zoku zaikai taiheiki* (Nihon Hyōronsha, 1930), pp. 58-61; and Wray, pp. 478-479.

101. *Hokkaido Tankō Kisen 50 nenshi,* pp. 18, 133, 138.

102. Furuta, pp. 626-627.

103. Noda, "Corporate Finance of Railroad Companies," p. 87; Tamaki, p. 409.

104. Uda, pp. 127-130; Steven J. Ericson, "Railways in Crisis: The Financing and Management of Japanese Railway Companies during the Panic of 1890," unpublished paper prepared for the Japanese Business History Workshop (June 1983), pp. 75-78.

105. Byron Marshall has discussed Mitsubishi's opposition to railway nationalization, as expressed by Shōda Heigorō, as an example of laissez-faire business ideology, but he does not mention that Mitsubishi was Japan's second largest stockholder in railways (the Fifteenth Bank being the largest). Marshall, pp. 22-24, 28; Ericson, pp. 15-28.

106. For two persuasive arguments against the view that government aid to the cotton spinning indsutry in the 1870s helped establish the private firms in the 1880s, see Yamamura, *Samurai Income and Entrepreneurship,* pp. 179-183; and Saxonhouse, "A Tale of Japanese Technological Diffusion," pp. 150-153.

107. Takamura Naosuke, *Nihon bōsekigyōshi josetsu* (Hanawa Shobō, 1971), I, 115–128, 247–264; Sugiyama, "Kigyō no zaimu," pp. 80–93.

108. Nakamura, "Nihon burujoajī," p. 81; Wray, p. 482.

109. *The 100 Year History of Mitsui & Co. Ltd., 1876–1976* (Tokyo, 1977), pp. 68–72.

110. Takamura, *Nihon bōsekigyō*, pp. 175–188; and Sugiyama Kazuo, "Trade Credit and the Development of the Cotton Spinning Industry: Its Role and Background," in Nakagawa, ed., *Marketing and Finance*, pp. 59–82.

PART THREE: THE ERA OF EXPANSION: 1893–1914

7. INTERNATIONAL LINES: COMMERCIAL DIPLOMACY,
1893–1902

1. Mitsui's integrated functions gave it a degree of control over the cotton spinning industry. For example, it often sold raw cotton to a firm on the condition that it also purchase Mitsui-imported machines and use Mitsui's sales network. See Sugiyama, "Trade Credit"; Kang Chao, *The Development of Cotton Textile Production in China* (Harvard, 1977), pp. 93–105, 115–120.

2. See Takamura, *Nihon bōsekigyō*, pp. 226–243; *SEDS*, pp. 151–168, 185–213; *SEDS*, X, 395–447; Miwa Ryōichi, "Bonbei kōro kaisetsu," *Ekonomisuto*, January 17, 1967, pp. 84–89; Sasaki, *Nihon kaiun kyōsōshi*, pp. 241–268; *KD*, pp. 226–229, 233; and *Wagasha kakukōro*, pp. 131–143. The statistical material is from Miwa, p. 88; and Takamura, p. 235.

3. The N.Y.K. official histories assume that these various agreements from a tentative one in August to the final October contract were essentially the same. On the contrary, the N.Y.K. had guaranteed 50,000 bales in the September 9 contract but was able to reduce this to 30,000 in the final agreement. The August, September, and October agreements are respectively in *SEDS*, X, 410–412; *SEDS*, pp. 163–165; and Sasaki, *Nihon kaiun kyōsōshi*, pp. 259–261. On the Tata firm, see Hirota Isamu, "Tātā zaibatsu no takakuka katei," in Yasuoka, ed., *Zaibatsushi kenkyū*, pp. 227–256.

4. *KD*, pp. 227–228; *SEDS*, pp. 195–200.

5. *JWM*, January 20, 1894, p. 71.

6. NYK–TG#4, December 20, 1893; #11, February 7, 1894; and #15, March 6, 1894. P&O 3/14, March 30, 1894.

7. P&O 3/15, October 5 and December 21, 1894. This underestimate of the strength of the Japanese union should not mask the fact that the cotton spinners' relations with the N.Y.K. were strained, especially when

the N.Y.K. refused their requests for further rate reductions. NYK–TG#16, March 27, 1894, and #47, October 10, 1894.

8. Nakagawa Keiichirō, "Nihon no kōgyōka katei ni okeru soshikika sareta kigyōsha katsudō," *Keiei shigaku* 2.3:26–28 (November 1967); Takamura, *Nihon bōsekigyō,* pp. 228–229.

9. NYK–TG#42, September 5, 1894; (NYK), Gian, September 19, 1894. Despite a February 1895 contract under which the N.Y.K. retained Tata as its agent, agreeing to pay it 2.5% of net freight receipts from its Bombay exports for 5 years, in 1896 the N.Y.K. decided to establish its own branch in Bombay. (NYK), Torishimariyakukai gian, July 22, 1896.

10. *SEDS,* pp. 202–207. The N.Y.K. did not abandon the shipment of Indian yarn to China. Rather, it extended the starting point of its Shanghai-Vladivostok line to Hong Kong, which linked up with the return voyage of the Bombay steamers. Cotton yarn was transshipped there to Shanghai-bound steamers.

11. Katō to the Foreign Ministry, November 5, 1895, and Kondō Renpei to the Shipping Bureau, January 9, 1896, *SEDS,* pp. 207–210; NYK–TG#109, January 8, 1896.

12. NYK–TG#24–26, May 2, 9, and 14, 1894; Nagata, p. 280; *Yokohama-shi shi,* pp. 584–585.

13. *KD,* pp. 231–233; *SEDS,* p. 210; P. & O. Minute Book #15, May 8 and 22, 1896, pp. 43–44, 49. Before the N.Y.K. entry the pool "points" had been divided as follows: P. & O., 38; the other two firms, 11 each. *NYK 70 nenshi,* p. 45.

14. P&O 3/15, March 6, 1896; and P&O 3/16, August 21, 1896. These shipments were measured at 400 pounds per bale.

15. Statistics are from Takamura, *Nihon bōsekigyō,* pp. 227, 237. On the China market, see Ōe, pp. 227–252; and Takamura Naosuke, *Kindai Nihon mengyō to Chūgoku* (Tokyo Daigaku Shuppankai, 1982), pp. 36–96.

16. Yasuba Yasukichi, "Freight Rates and Productivity in Ocean Transportation for Japan, 1875–1943," *Explorations in Economic History* 15.1:11–39 (January 1978).

17. Takamura, *Nihon bōsekigyō,* p. 229. Between December 1895 and May 1896, the N.Y.K. rebate to the cotton spinners was ¥129,149. HK, June 23, 1896. For further argument on this point, see Nakagawa, "Nihon no kōgyōka katei," p. 27.

18. There are numerous reports of the N.Y.K. mistreating Chinese. Also, in 1888 Chinese merchants in Korea had cooperated with the China Merchants Steam Navigation Co. in the establishment of a regular line to Korea. A successful boycott of Japanese ships which followed cut deeply into N.Y.K. business in Korea. *Hara Kei nikki* (Fukumura Shuppan,

1965), I, October 27, 1892, p. 202; C.I. Eugene Kim and Han-kyo Kim, *Korea and the Politics of Imperialism, 1876–1910* (California, 1967), pp. 69–70.

19. For the official attitude see Ian H. Nish, *The Anglo-Japanese Alliance, 1894–1907* (Athlone Press, 1966), p. 26 n 1; Swire's comment is quoted in Charles Drage, *Taikoo* (Constable, 1970), p. 30, from JSSI 1/11, August 3, 1894, pp. 472–473.

20. P&O 3/15, February 15, 1895.

21. Kozo Yamamura's remark that "The Sino-Japanese War . . . was basically within Japan's military capacity in 1894, and thus it did no more than strain her technological and productive abilities," certainly cannot apply to ships. See Yamamura, "Success Illgotten? The Role of Meiji Militarism in Japan's Technological Progress," *Journal of Economic History* 37.1:120 (March 1977). For a list of ships used in the Battle of the Yalu, see John C. Perry, "The Battle off the Tayang, 17 September 1894," *Mariner's Mirror* 50.4:245 (1964).

22. The N.Y.K. began a line to Taiwan in 1896, though this and connecting South China routes were less important to the N.Y.K. than to the O.S.K. For the ship figures, see *NYK 70 nenshi*, pp. 52–54.

23. Shōda Heigorō, "Kaiun shinchō hōhō torishirabesho, fuenzetsu hikki," (February 6, 1895), pp. 51–52.

24. JSSI 2/8, October 7, 1896. For the indemnity planning, see Nagaoka Shinkichi, "Nisshin sengo no zaisei seisaku to baishōkin," in Andō, ed., *Nihon keizai seisaku shiron*, pp. 111–158.

25. For the early subsidy movement, see Inoue, "Meiji kōki no kaiji seisaku," pp. 159–167; Nagata, pp. 316–322; and *SEDS*, pp. 213–236.

26. Shōda, "Kaiun shinchō."

27. NYK-TG#92, September 4, 1895. The Tokyo Chamber of Commerce memorial (August 17, 1895) is in Matsuo ke monjo, vol. 37, no. 36. For a summary see *JWM*, August 31, 1895, p. 222. For debate on the Navigation Law, see *Dai Nihon teikoku gikai shi* (Dō Kankōkai, 1926), III, 1570–1571, 1611–1613 (Lower House); and pp. 1051–1052, 1117–1120, 1196–1201 (Upper House). See also *Teikoku gikai shi* (Shugiin and Sangiin, ed., 1962), I, 176, in *Gikai seido 70 nenshi*. For the 1896 laws, see *Teishin jigyōshi*, VI, 810–821; *JWM*, March 4, 1899, pp. 217–218; U.S. Department of Commerce, *Government Aid to Merchant Shipping*, pp. 211–216; and on shipping subsidies, see Tominaga, pp. 126–163; and *Shuyōkoku senzen kaiun joseishi* (Kaiji Sangyō Kenkyūjo, 1969), pp. 1–58.

28. Shōda, "Kaiun shinchō," pp. 44–53; *JWM*, July 27, 1895, p. 88.

29. Asano Sōichirō's newly formed Tōyō Kisen developed a grandiose scheme to route a projected European service (which did not materialize) round

the Cape of Good Hope rather than through the Suez Canal because the extra subsidies based on the greater distance would make the Cape route cheaper! *JWM*, June 6, 1896, p. 634. The N.Y.K. temporarily considered routing its Seattle line, started in August 1896, through Hawaii to take advantage of the law. NYK–TG#207, December 8, 1897.

30. Tiedemann, "Big Business," p. 269.
31. Calculated from *NYK–EH,* 1896–1914.
32. Teratani, "Japanese Business and Government," pp. 62–71.
33. NYK–TG#11, February 7, 1894 and #14, February 28, 1894.
34. NYK–TG#24, May 2, 1894.
35. Some consultations about the line may have taken place in August 1894 between the N.Y.K. and the Tata firm. P&O 3/15, October 5, 1894.
36. The account showing requisitioned ships with a profit of ¥4.6 million does not begin until October 1, 1894, whereas ships were requisitioned as early as June. *NYK–EH* 10/1, 1895 to 11/1, 1896.
37. The ¥924,000 is calculated from *NYK–EH* 11/1, March 1896, p. 37; and *NYK 70 nenshi*, p. 705. NYK–TG#97, October 9, 1895; and *NYK 70 nenshi*, p. 56, identify the ¥2.25 million as earmarked for new lines. See also *NYK–EH* 11/2, September 1896, p. 41; and *JWM*, June 13, 1896, p. 652, December 5, 1896, p. 630, and June 5, 1897, p. 559. For further comment on the "accounting procedure," see Chapter 10, n.32.
38. Calculations based on *NYK 70 nenshi*, pp. 58–60, 678–679; and *Wagasha kakukōro*, pp. 391–393.
39. In this work I use the terms shipping conference, freight conference, and liner conference interchangeably. Today the conference operating between Europe and East Asia is known as the Far Eastern Freight Conference. When it was first formed in 1879 it was the China Conference, and, after the 1890s, the China and Japan Conference. I have adopted a more descriptive term, such as European–Far East Conference. The starting point for the study of pre-World War I conferences is the *Royal Commission on Shipping Rings*, British Parliamentary Papers, vols. 47 and 48, 1909. For a general study, see Daniel Marx, Jr., *International Shipping Cartels* (Princeton, 1953). Useful for material on East Asia are Kojima Shōtarō, *Kaiun dōmeiron* (Yūhikaku, 1926), which contains helpful documentation; B. M. Deakin, *Shipping Conferences: A Study of Their Origins, Development and Economic Practices* (Cambridge University, 1973), a theoretical analysis with a succinct survey on the "Far Eastern Trades," pp. 29–36; Miyamoto Seishirō, *Kaiun dōmei seidoron* (Kaibundō, 1978), a handy guide to conference rules and agreements which contains some historical material; Sheila Marriner and F. E. Hyde, *The Senior: John Samuel Swire, 1825–1898* (Liverpool, 1967), pp. 135–184; and *Report from the Select Committee on Steamship Subsidies,*

British Parliamentary Papers. vol. 8, 1901, and vol. 9, 1902. See also Hyde, *Blue Funnel;* and Hyde, *Far Eastern Trade.* Hyde's works are useful for the early history of the conference but unfortunately most come to an end in the late 1890s just when the N.Y.K. was becoming involved. Robert Greenhill, "Shipping, 1850–1914," in D.C.M. Platt, ed., *Business Imperialism, 1840–1930: An Inquiry Based on British Experience in Latin America* (Oxford, 1977), pp. 119–155, is a well-documented study mostly of conferences.

40. *China Mail,* November 22, 1879. Copy in possession of the Far Eastern Freight Conference, Head Office, London.

41. JSSI 1/13, Swire to China and Japan Conference, October 29, 1898, p. 84.

42. For a list of core members, see *Wagasha kakukōro,* pp. 398–402, 408. Other members appear in a Rebate Circular, April 1, 1897, China and Japan Homeward Conference, Far Eastern Freight Conference.

43. For Swire's early Yangtze pool agreements, see Marriner and Hyde, pp. 58–97; and K.C. Liu, "British-Chinese Steamship Rivalry in China, 1873–85," in C. D. Cowan, ed., *The Economic Development of China and Japan* (Allen & Unwin, 1964), pp. 49–78.

44. *Yokohama-shi shi,* p. 588; *The 100 Year History of Mitsui & Co.,* pp. 69–72.

45. Deakin, p. 21; Greenhill, pp. 128, 150; Yasuba; Douglass North, "Ocean Freight Rates and Economic Development, 1750–1913," *Journal of Economic History* 18.4:537–555 (December 1958).

46. For background on conference rates prior to the N.Y.K.'s first sailing, see P&O 3/15 and 3/16; Hyde, *Blue Funnel,* pp. 86–90; (NYK), Torishimariyakukai gian, June 20, 1894; and *Royal Commission on Shipping Rings,* vol. 48, p. 165, q. 16765. Evidence of Richard Holt. On the N.Y.K.'s entry, see P&O 3/15, April 24, 1896; 3/16, May 8, 1896; and 3/16, May 22, 1896.

47. *Wagasha kakukōro,* pp. 393–394.

48. On April 23 the company had proposed that conference members use a rate of 35s. alongside an N.Y.K. rate of 30s. The conference rejected this, considering the margin too great. NYK–KSG, June 10, 1896, pp. 19–21; *Tokyo keizai zasshi,* September 5, 1896, p. 419; P&O 3/16, May 29 and July 31, 1896; *SEDS,* p. 211; NYK–TG#117, March 11, 1896 and #124, April 29, 1896.

49. Rebate Circular, April 1, 1897, Far Eastern Freight Conference; Deakin, p. 32; JSSI 1/13, November 18, 1898, p. 102.

50. JSSI 1/13, December 7, 1898, p. 116.

51. *KD,* pp. 231–233; P. & O. Minute Book #16, p. 49.

52. For a well-documented study of the Straits Conference, see Chiang Hai

Ding, "The Early Shipping Conference System of Singapore, 1897–1911," *Journal of South East Asian History* 10.1:50–68 (March 1969).

53. NYK–TG#159, December 29, 1896; #171, March 31, 1897; *JWM*, March 27, 1897, p. 300.

54. Calculations on Lower House sessions are based on Tōyama Shigeki and Adachi Shizuko, eds., *Kindai Nihon seijishi hikkei* (Iwanami Shoten, 1968), pp. 225–226. For pending economic legislation, see Banno Junji, *Meiji kenpō taisei no kakuritsu* (Tokyo Daigaku Shuppankai, 1971), pp. 146–239; and George Akita, *The Foundations of Constitutional Government in Modern Japan, 1868–1900* (Harvard, 1967), pp. 124–146. Kondō's remarks are in NYK–KSG, May 27, 1897, pp. 20–24. See also *Tokyo keizai zasshi,* July 10, 1897, p. 71.

55. *NYK–EH* 12/1, March 1897, p. 4 and 12/2 September 1897, pp. 4–5; P&O 3/17, August 26, 1898; D. A. Farnie, *East and West of Suez: The Suez Canal in History, 1854–1956* (Oxford, 1969), p. 453; *Tokyo keizai zasshi,* July 3, 1897.

56. P&O 3/15, January 24, 1896.

57. On this point the *Japan Weekly Mail,* in arguing that the government had a "moral obligation" to provide the N.Y.K. with line subsidies, stated that had the company "simply consulted the financial interests of the shareholders, they would never have embarked upon vast enterprises . . . In order to furnish and equip steamers for these services, the shareholders had to abstain from pocketing several millions of *yen* which had been fairly earned by their vessels during the war." *JWM,* January 14, 1899, p. 33.

58. The above is from NYK–KSG, November 29, 1897, and December 22, 1897.

59. Farnie, p. 457; Lamar Cecil, *Albert Ballin: Business and Politics in Imperial Germany, 1888–1918* (Princeton, 1967), p. 67; *70 Years North German Lloyd Bremen, 1857–1927* (Berlin, n.d.), p. 52; NYK–KSG, May 27, 1898, pp. 10–11.

60. P&O 3/17, August 26, 1898; NYK–TG#206, December 1, 1897 and #207, December 8, 1897.

61. Woolley was later trusted as a secret go-between with the P. & O. prior to the Russo-Japanese War. See Chapter 8.

62. NYK–TG#211, January 25, 1898 and #225, May 4, 1898.

63. NYK–TG#215, February 23, 1898; JSSI 2/8, February 25, 1898; P&O 3/17, July 1, 1898.

64. Lessons from Japanese commercial diplomacy may also be found in Michael Blaker, *Japanese International Negotiating Style* (Columbia, 1977).

65. JSSI 1/13, November 18, 1898, p. 102 and Swire to A. Holt, November 11, 1898, p. 96. Military share calculated by prorating figures in TH–KG, June 3, 1901, in comparison with Appendix C–2. The navy contributed 71% of this cargo; the army, 29%.

66. JSSI 1/13, November 22, 1898, p. 106.

67. NYK–TG#248, November 24, 1898.

68. NYK–TG#249, November 29, 1898.

69. JSSI 1/13, December 7, 1898, p. 116. The following discussion of the N.Y.K.'s entry to the London berth is taken from JSSI 1/13, pp. 115–193, 441–548.

70. JSSI 1/13, John Swire & Sons to Wm. Thomson & Co., December 21, 1898, pp. 141–143.

71. JSSI 1/13, January 10, 1899, p. 167.

72. JSSI 1/13, January 11, 1899, p. 168.

73. For an account of the Ben Line which touches on its relations with the conference, see T. E. Milne, "British Shipping in the 19th Century: A Study of the Ben Line," in Peter L. Payne, ed., *Studies in Scottish Business History* (Frank Cass & Co., 1967), pp. 345–366.

74. Matsuo ke monjo, vol. 37, no. 36, pp. 26–27. On Liverpool, see Francis E. Hyde, *Liverpool and the Mersey: An Economic History of a Port, 1700–1970* (Newton Abbot, 1971).

75. JSSI 1/13, December 7, 1898, p. 116.

76. P&O 3/17, February 10, 1899.

77. Testimony of Richard Holt, *Royal Commission on Shipping Rings,* vol. 48, p. 165, q. 16765.

78. JSSI 1/13, December 15, 1898, p. 133.

79. JSSI 1/13, February 6, 1899, p. 189; *Wagasha kakukōro,* pp. 409–410. The relatively small share of the P. & O. is explained by the fact that the Liverpool lines, because of their location, were the principal carriers of Fine Goods. The N.Y.K. continued to load Fine Goods at Middlesbrough. See Marriner and Hyde, pp. 162–166; and the evidence of Samuel Samuel, *Report on Steamship Subsidies,* vol. 8, p. 193, q. 3473. In a 1911 L. & Y. Agreement, out of 116 points the Blue Funnel received 71, the P. & O., 17.5, and the N.Y.K., 16. Ocean Transport & Trading Limited, Archives, OA 1954/1.

80. JSSI 1/13, December 21, 1898, p. 142.

81. P&O 3/17, February 10, 1899.

82. JSSI 1/13, December 21, 1898, p. 141.

83. *SEDS,* p. 237.

84. On the debate in the Diet, see *Dai Nihon teikoku gikai shi,* IV, 2088–2092; and *Teikoku gikai shi,* I, 264. The Yamagata-Liberal Party agreement was reached on November 26, 1898, just as the N.Y.K. sent word

to James to give notice to the conference. See Akita, *Foundations,* pp. 142-143. Also, the N.Y.K.'s fortunes were now hitched to the Liberal Party, in contrast to the relation between Mitsubishi and the Progressive Party in the 1880s. This public debate over subsidies has suggestive connections with imperialism. The loudest opponents of special overseas line subsidies were "liberals" like Taguchi Ukichi who, like Shimada in the Diet debate, favored support for lines that would connect Japan with other East Asian countries—where they would have more obvious relevance for imperialism. In contrast, it was the government that wanted to establish the transoceanic lines on a secure financial basis.

85. For the European portion of the subsidy law, see *SEDS,* pp. 239-242; and *Wagasha kakukōro,* p. 487. The N.Y.K. failed to get the government's approval to substitute ships which did not meet the requirements of the Navigation Law. This was an important matter when charters were placed on the line in wartime. NYK-TG#260, March 1, 1899; #264, April 29, 1899; #269, June 7, 1899; and #273, July 12, 1899.

86. Henry Rosovsky's comment on subsidies, though made in a slightly different context, is relevant here: "How can one evaluate the effect of a subsidy . . . ? If it is taken only at face value, an understatement will almost certainly result. A subsidy is an official vote of confidence in an enterprise." Henry Rosovsky, *Capital Formation in Japan: 1868-1940* (Glencoe, 1961), p. 22.

87. Evidence of Richard Holt, *Royal Commission on Shipping Rings,* vol. 48, p. 173, q. 16951 and p. 175, q. 17022-17025.

88. JSSI 1/13, pp. 441-467. The geographic advantage of the Ocean Steam Ship Co. was reinforced by economic considerations, for unlike Germany and the United States, Britain did not employ through rates for its railways and shipping services.

89. NYK-TG#165, February 17, 1897. For other examples of general trading company operations, see Kozo Yamamura, "General Trading Companies in Japan: Their Origins and Growth," in Hugh Patrick, ed., *Japanese Industrialization and Its Social Consequences* (California, 1976), pp. 161-199; Miyamoto Mataji et al., eds., *Sōgō shōsha no keieishi* (Tōyō Keizai Shinpōsha, 1976); and Yoshihara, pp. 14-27.

90. A book could be written on the early relations between Samuel's firm and Japan. As the predecessor of Shell Oil it originated oil tankers. See Robert Henriques, *Marcus Samuel* (Barrie and Rockliff, 1960); Anthony Sampson, *The Seven Sisters* (Bantam Books, 1976), pp. 53-59; Farnie, pp. 431-449. Farnie asserts that the N.Y.K. had a close relationship with Samuel (p. 453). I have been unable to substantiate this. The Samuel firm was, however, an agent for the O.S.K. prior to World War I and had financial ties with Asano's Tōyō Kisen Kaisha. FO 371/2010, May 30,

1914; GN President's Subject file 3476#2, Griffiths to Hill, January 25, 1899; *JWM*, June 13, 1914, p. XI.

91. *Report on Steamship Subsidies,* vol. 8, evidence of Henry Bonar, pp. 153–159; evidence of Samuel Samuel, p. 196, q. 3530; evidence of Thomas Sutherland, p. 246, q. 4441.

92. JSSI 1/13, April 27, 1900, p. 671.

93. *NYK–EH* 16/1, March 1901, pp. 4–5. In 1908 Richard Holt of the Ocean Steam Ship Co. stated that "broadly speaking, the regular steamers on the berth do not get a third full on the homeward voyage between China and Japan." *Royal Commission on Shipping Rings,* vol. 48, p. 175, q. 17031. See also Miwa, "Kaijō yusō," p. 392; Baruch Boxer, *Ocean Shipping in the Evolution of Hong Kong* (Chicago, 1961), pp. 1–24; and for a breakdown of imports from Europe, see Takamura Naosuke, "Sangyō bōeki kōzō," in Ōishi, ed., *Nihon sangyō kakumei,* I, 68. On China's export trade, see G. C. Allen and Audrey G. Donnithorne, *Western Enterprise in Far Eastern Economic Development: China and Japan* (Allen & Unwin, 1954), pp. 52–89, 257–269. I am grateful to my colleague Ed Wickberg for discussion of these points.

94. JSSI 1/12, February 11, 1898, p. 862. See also JSSI 1/12, August 17, 1897, p. 661; May 6, 1898, p. 936; and JSSI 1/13, February 19, 1900, p. 612.

95. *Wagasha kakukōro,* p. 487.

96. TH–KG, February 12, March 12, and May 6, 1901; NYK–TG#338, June 5, 1901.

97. TH–KG, October 29, 1901; NYK–TG#359, January 15, 1902.

98. NYK–TG#359, January 15, 1902; TH–KG, December 11, 1901 and January 28, 1902.

99. TH–KG, January 28, March 11, May 12 and 19, 1902; JSSI 2/10, December 5, 1902.

100. JSSI 2/10, September 12, 1905.

101. *Tokyo keizai zasshi,* July 29, 1899, p. 258; NYK–KSG, May 25, 1903, pp. 10–11, in *JWM,* June 6, 1903, p. 615. On the growth of national fleets, see Derek H. Aldcroft, "The Mercantile Marine," in Aldcroft, ed., *The Development of British Industry and Foreign Competition, 1875–1914* (Allen & Unwin, 1968), pp. 326–363. Cf. n. 45 of this chapter.

102. Kondō report to the board on East Asian lines, NYK–TG#344, July 31, 1901; he expanded on this theme for the stockholders as well. NYK–KSG, May 29, 1901, pp. 14–31.

103. NYK–TG#344, July 31, 1901. The "opportunity" did come in 1903. For the difficulty in implementing it, see Chapter 8.

8. CHINA AND THE ISSUE OF IMPERIALISM, 1896–1904

1. "Ikō," in *KD*, pp. 10–34.
2. Telegram of September 29, 1899, NYK–TG#279, October 2, 1899.
3. *OSK 50 nenshi*, pp. 56–66, 258–261; *OSK 80 nenshi*, pp. 22–33; and *Nakahashi Tokugorō* (Dō ō Denki Hensankai, 1944), II, pp. 70–88, 121–133, 138–140.
4. In the Tientsin trade, N.Y.K. loans to the Taku Lighter Co. gave it first rights to new lighters and an advantage over both the O.S.K. and competing British firms. *NYK–EH* 13/1, September 1898, p. 3; Drage, p. 86; JSSII 1/15f, December 16 and December 23, 1899.
5. Nakahashi to Itō, December 19, 1899 and Nakahashi to Matsukata, December 20, 1899, in *Nakahashi*, II, 127–129.
6. *KD*, pp. 181–184; *OSK 50 nenshi*, pp. 258–260; and *Nakahashi*, II, 129, 139. Hoshi had been a subject of controversy earlier in the year when he allegedly made a remark to the effect that "members of the Diet should take as many bribes as are offered to them." *JWM*, April 22, 1899, p. 388. For additional comments on Hoshi's attempt to develop closer ties between businessmen and the Liberal Party, see Tiedemann, "Big Business," pp. 274–276.
7. *NYK–EH* 17/1, March 1902, p. 3 and 17/2, September 1902, p. 4; *Wagasha kakukōro*, p. 70; NYK–TG#284, November 15, 1899; NYK–KSG, November 27, 1899, pp. 12–15. See Chapter 6, n. 70.
8. Drage, p. 21; Albert Feuerwerker, *The Foreign Establishment in China in the Early Twentieth Century* (Michigan, 1976), pp. 81–83, 93–95.
9. Murase Shin'ya, "The Most-Favored-Nation Treatment in Japan's Treaty Practice During the Period 1854–1905," *American Journal of International Law* 70.2:284–288 (April 1976); John V. A. MacMurray, comp. and ed., *Treaties and Agreements with and Concerning China, 1894–1919*, vol. 1, *Manchu Period, 1894–1911* (Oxford, 1921), pp. 68–74, 91–92, 159–171; Institute of Pacific Relations, ed., *Problems of the Pacific, 1931* (Chicago, 1932), pp. 341–360; E. M. Gull, *British Economic Interests in the Far East* (Institute of Pacific Relations, 1943), pp. 49–103; L. K. Young, *British Policy in China, 1895–1902* (Oxford, 1970), pp. 77–99.
10. The Daitō Kisen Kaisha was the first Japanese firm to operate inland under the postwar treaty system, but its services were limited to the Yangtze delta region. *Nisshin Kisen Kabushiki Kaisha 30 nenshi oyobi tsuiho* (Dōshahen, 1941), pp. 17–21; Nakamura Tadashi, "Chōsha kaikō zengo: Nihon shihonshugi to Konanshō," *Rekishigaku kenkyū* 425: 1–2 (October 1975).
11. *Nakahashi*, II, 89–103.

12. *Nakahashi,* II, 104–106; *Nisshin Kisen,* pp. 21–25; *OSK 50 nenshi,* pp. 254–256, 262–263; *Teishin jigyōshi,* VI, 820.

13. Cecil, pp. 71–72; NYK–KSG, November 27, 1901, p. 23; JSSI 1/13, October 2, 1901, pp. 973–975 and October 30, 1901, pp. 986–988; JSSI 4/3, January 20, 1902; JSSI 2/22, January 22, 1902; *Nisshin Kisen,* pp. 14–15; *Nakahashi,* II, 103. For the German agreement with Britain regarding the Yangtze, see Nish, pp. 104–107.

14. JSSXI 2/1, May 1, 1902. Reference to O.S.K. is in Jardine, Matheson Archive, Press Copy Letter Book 16, #7, October 11, 1901.

15. Nakamura, "Chōsha kaikō," pp. 1–3; *Nisshin Kisen,* pp. 27–32.

16. Nakamura, "Chōsha kaikō," p. 5; MacMurray, I, pp. 411–417.

17. Kondō speech, as translated in *JWM,* June 7, 1902, p. 615, with slight modifications based on NYK–KSG, May 28, 1902, pp. 22–29.

18. Some secondary N.Y.K. sources use a figure of ¥2.5 million for the purchase. See *NYK 70 nenshi,* p. 77; and *Wagasha kakukōro,* p. 84. However, the figure ¥1,531,528 in *NYK–EH* 18/2, September 1903, p. 40, is consistent with contemporary British estimates which range from 1.2 to 1.5 million taels. (In 1903, the average exchange rate for ¥100 was 86.5 Shanghai taels).

19. *KD,* pp. 237–238; *JWM,* June 6, 1903, p. 614 and June 13, 1903, p. 641; JSSI 1/13, March 15, 1901, p. 898; *Nakahashi,* II, 96.

20. *JWM,* June 13, 1903, p. 641; NYK–KSG, November 28, 1906, pp. 13–15, in *JWM,* December 22, 1906, pp. 780–781. For a description of the economic geography of the Hankow area, see Joseph W. Esherick, *Reform and Revolution in China: The 1911 Revolution in Hunan and Hubei* (California, 1976), pp. 3–7. Also on McBain there is Jardine, Matheson Archive, Press Copy Letter Book 16, #7, June 12, 1903; GN President's Subject file 3970#14, comment by G. W. Sutherland to J.D. Farrell, November 17, 1903, p. 10.

21. Nish, pp. 216, 233, 235. Cf. pp. 253–256 for financial benefits derived by Japan from the alliance.

22. For legal arguments, see JSSXI 2/1, August 4, 1903.

23. Jardine, Matheson Archive, Press Copy Letter Book 16, #7, June 24 and July 13, 1903; JSSI 4/3, August 9, 1903.

24. JSSXI 2/1, March 1, 1904.

25. The "legal maneuvering," complicated by McBain's death, involved the N.Y.K.'s incorporation of the McBain steamers in Hong Kong on March 23, 1904, as a British firm called the Yangtsze Shipping Company. "Yōsukō Kisen Kaisha Teikan," unsorted material in N.Y.K. Company History Office. Cf. TH–KG, March 11, April 6, and August 3, 1904. For the Foreign Office decision, see JSSXI 2/1, July 13 and October 4, 1904. The N.Y.K. appealed for help from the Japanese Foreign Ministry, but by this

time Japan was embroiled in the Russo-Japanese War, and the Foreign Ministry found it impossible to press the case forcefully to the British government. *KD,* pp. 237–239.

26. NYK–KSG, November 28, 1906, pp. 15–16; *JWM,* December 22, 1906, p. 781 and June 23, 1906, p. 650; Jardine, Matheson Archive, Press Copy Letter Book 16, #7, July 13, 1903; Ishii, pp. 66–67.

27. NYK–TG#464, March 7, 1906; *JWM,* September 5, 1903, p. 243.

28. Kondō comment in *JWM,* December 22, 1906, p. 781 (cf. p. 775); from NYK–KSG, November 28, 1906, p. 16. See also Drage, p. 194.

29. I have used the term "business imperialism" partly because I am dealing with a particular business enterprise and partly to distinguish between specific business activity and more impersonal general economic forces. For a similar use of the term, see Platt, ed., *Business Imperialism.*

30. For discussion, see John Gallagher and Ronald Robinson, "The Imperialism of Free Trade," in Wm. Roger Louis, ed., *Imperialism: The Robinson and Gallagher Controversy* (New Viewpoints, 1976), p. 53–72.

31. NYK–TG#27, May 23, 1894.

32. Kondō, "Japanese Communications," p. 461.

33. In the historiography of imperialism this dependence on China can be regarded as a "push factor" from the metropolis.

34. This network and Japan's penetration of the China market in cotton cloths are expertly described in Chao, pp. 93–105, 115–120. See also Ishii, pp. 66–71; and Togai, pp. 260–288.

35. See Matsumoto Hiroshi, "Nihon teikokushugi seiritsuki ni okeru zaibatsu shihon no keisei," *Rekishigaku kenkyū,* Special Supplement: 117–128 (November 1973), most of which is reprinted in the same author's *Mitsui zaibatsu no kenkyū* (Yoshikawa Kōbunkan, 1979), pp. 369–397. The 15% figure is calculated from Peter Duus, "The Economic Bases of Meiji Imperialism: The Case of Korea, 1895–1910," unpublished paper, Table 2. Most Japanese scholars who study imperialism write within a Marxist framework and do not address the subject of business strategy as it is used in this work. On the other hand, most Japanese business historians ignore the issue of imperialism.

36. The Twenty-One Demands are beyond the chronological scope of this study, but for some background to them relevant to N.Y.K. activity in shipping and resources, see Chapter 9. For Mitsubishi's connection, see Chapter 10.

37. Many historians of expansion define imperialism too exclusively from the perspective of the imperial power. In European history, Ronald Robinson, well known for his emphasis on collaboration from indigenous forces as an explanation for imperialism, argues that "free trade imperialism enabled European merchants in the treaty ports, in

partnership with Chinese merchants, to take over the exposed riverine and maritime branches of Chinese domestic trade." Ronald Robinson, "Non-European Foundations of European Imperialism: Sketch for a Theory of Collaboration," in Roger Owen and Bob Sutcliffe, eds., *Studies in the Theory of Imperialism* (Longman, 1972), pp. 127–128. The "partnership" referred to here is what Robinson usually calls the "collaborative mechanism." The main problem with the term "free trade imperialism" is that it essentially characterizes only the activity of imperial powers but not its impact on the country being controlled. Perhaps the historian of Japan who most closely follows Robinson's ideas is Akira Iriye. His concept of peaceful economic expansion is similar to Robinson's free trade imperialism, though unlike Robinson, Iriye generally avoids the term "informal imperialism" for such expansion, at least prior to World War I. His principal focus is on Japanese attitudes toward expansion rather than on the impact of imperialism on China's capacity to follow autonomous economic policies. See Akira Iriye, "Robinson and Gallagher in the Far East: Japanese Imperialism," in Wm. Roger Louis, ed., *Imperialism*, pp. 222–225; and the same author's *Pacific Estrangement.*

38. Both parts of this definition of imperialism (the manner of acquiring the privilege and the impact) must be used in any assessment. Japan was subject to unequal treaties signed under the threat of force in the late Tokugawa period. It thereby lost some of its autonomy but did not become a serious victim of imperialism for three reasons: (1) The West did not demand as much from Japan as it had from China. (2) The Japanese state was stronger and very quickly consolidated its capacity to act. (3) Collaborative tendencies were weaker in Japan than in China.

39. Chi-ming Hou, *Foreign Investment and Economic Development in China, 1840–1937* (Harvard, 1965), p. 59.

40. Nakamura, "Chōsha kaikō," p. 7. For further comment, see Chapter 9.

41. On junk shipping, see Andrew Watson, tr., *Transport in Transition: The Evolution of Traditional Shipping in China* (Michigan, Center for Chinese Studies, 1972).

42. See Robinson's comments on China: "Britain's political hold upon China failed to break down Chinese economic self-sufficiency," in Gallagher and Robinson, p. 65. This emphasis on the continued strength of the traditional sector, like much Western historiography on China, ignores the impact of imperialism on China's autonomy and capacity to act. My argument assumes that autonomy was a necessary, though not sufficient, prerequisite for long-term development. There were many factors besides imperialism, including China's own policies and war-torn conditions, that

retarded development. Feuerwerker, *The Foreign Establishment*, pp. 97–98, comments on the issue of causation.

43. Esherick, p. 81; *Nisshin Kisen*, pp. 30–31. Cf. Yen-p'ing Hao, *The Comprador in Nineteenth Century China* (Harvard, 1970), pp. 149–153.

44. Some may say that N.Y.K. dependence on China as a feeder was more perceived than real because of the slower than expected growth of China trade. I would argue that the Japanese, especially after the Russo-Japanese War, were much more effective than the British in linking China freight with transoceanic lines. See Chapter 9.

45. Conroy, pp. 442–491.

46. Duus, "The Economic Bases," p. 14.

47. Duus has given more attention to business strategy in the cotton spinning industry in the Inter-War Years in Peter Duus, "Nihon Menbōsekigyō to Chūgoku," in Nakamura Takafusa, ed., *Senkanki no Nihon keizai bunseki* (Yamakawa Shuppansha, 1981), pp. 189–216.

48. D. C. M. Platt, "Economic Imperialism and the Businessman: Britain and Latin America before 1914," in Owen and Sutcliffe, eds., *Imperialism*, p. 310; Greenhill, p. 125. Another case study of business strategy is Robert V. Kubicek, *Economic Imperialism in Theory and Practice: The Case of South African Gold Mining Finance, 1886–1914* (Duke, 1979). This details the reluctance of gold mining entrepreneurs to become involved in wars and suggests that the international financial interests of the companies were in conflict both with government and the interests of sound mining developments in South Africa. These are interesting analogies to both Mitsubishi's withdrawal from shipping in the 1880s and the N.Y.K.'s preference for maintaining international lines over war service.

49. Besides the profits and subsidies analyzed in Chapter 7, the stock price shot up to a record high of ¥117 in late 1895. Gentler rewards included a ¥1,000 government bonus for N.Y.K. President Yoshikawa. The N.Y.K. reciprocated by presenting an offertory box to Yasukuni Shrine to comfort the souls claimed by the war. Okaniwa, p. 96; *Asabuki*, p. 136; *Zaikai bukko ketsubutsu den*, II, 616; NYK-TG#107, December 18, 1895.

50. *KD*, pp. 164–173.

51. *NYK 70 nenshi*, p. 51.

52. Quoted in Drage, p. 29. I say "seem" because the identification of Mitsui Bussan appears to have been made from the initials MB. But the normal abbreviation for Mitsui Bussan in English correspondence was MBK (Mitsui Bussan Kaisha). On the other hand, the English spelled Mitsubishi with two words, "Mitsu Bishi." Could this have been a case of the interchange

of names with the N.Y.K.? In view of the N.Y.K.'s behavior before the Russo-Japanese War (see below), there are at least grounds for suspicion. Unlike Japanese business commentators, however, foreigners did not usually mistake Mitsubishi for the N.Y.K.

53. JSSI 1/11, August 3, 1894, pp. 472–473, August 24, 1894, p. 478, and September 4, 1894, pp. 485–486.

54. Because the N.Y.K. was still subject to the 1885 directive from the government, its requisitioned ships received only ¥4.5 per ton per month. In contrast Mitsui, being free from government directive, was able to obtain a rate of at least ¥6 to ¥7. This is estimated from figures in *JWM*, July 28, 1894, p. 93. On income, see *Mitsui Senpaku 80 nenshi*, p. 52.

55. NYK–TG#306, June 25, 1900.

56. Ibid.; and NYK–KSG, November 26, 1900, p. 2. See n. 54.

57. NYK–EH 15/1, March 1900, p. 3, and 15/2, September 1900, pp. 3–4.

58. *KD*, pp. 193–196. Since the actual cost of the war was ¥1.73 billion, one wonders whether Kodama's estimate was recorded in retrospect. See Shumpei Okamoto, *The Japanese Oligarchy and the Russo-Japanese War* (Columbia, 1970), pp. 127–128; and Ohkawa Masazo, "The Armaments Expansion Budgets and the Japanese Economy after the Russo-Japanese War," *Hitotsubashi Journal of Economics* 5.2:68–83 (January 1965).

59. P. & O. Minute Book #17, pp. 241–242, 244–245.

60. The following is based on FO 46/568, pp. 65–69, 241–254. See the reference in Nish, p. 268, which led me to this file.

61. *KD*, p. 196, gives the meeting date as October 21. This is confirmed by NYK–TG#404, October 21, 1903, which records the decision to send the special letter to the government. This presents us with four events all on the same *date* in both countries: Woolley's telegram from Kobe to the head office in London, the head office reply to Woolley in Kobe, Woolley notifying the N.Y.K., and finally the directors meeting. All four events could have occurred on the same day in that order only if either the telegram from England was sent during the night or if the N.Y.K. board meeting was held in the evening. The more likely possibility, as suggested in my text, is that the sequence was different, namely, that Woolley sent his urgent telegram, omitting the words "if necessary," *after* the N.Y.K. directors meeting. This interpretation seems consistent with the wording of Woolley's telegram, which hints at some N.Y.K. movement between October 16 and October 21 in the direction of evasion of government demands. It also suggests that the N.Y.K. continued to hope for P. & O. cooperation (or that of Jardine, Matheson) even *after* its decision to promise support for the government.

62. *KD*, pp. 196–198; NYK–TG#405, October 28, 1903; *NYK 50 nenshi*, pp. 192–193. Kondō's argument was that with the pace of Russian rail-

way development the longer Japan waited, the greater would be its disadvantage. Others at the meeting, such as Shibusawa and Ōishi Masami, the publicist, supported Kondō's views and Kodama went away satisfied.

63. It is hard to imagine such a transformation in 1903, but in fact by 1909 some N.Y.K. officials considered the option of foregoing subsidies. See Chapter 10. For the government's right to requisition ships in wartime, see the 1899 government directive on the specified line subsidies in *SEDS*, p. 240. For a somewhat analogous issue involving Britain, see Francis E. Hyde, *Cunard and the North Atlantic, 1840–1973* (Macmillan, 1975), p. 138. Although the American conglomerate of J. P. Morgan had purchased Britain's White Star line, the British government, in an agreement of 1903, retained the right to use White Star ships.

64. An unidentified notation in the margin reads, "This is so." FO 46/568, pp. 247–248. It is ironic that, while Lansdowne considered helping the N.Y.K. in this predicament, at the same time he was denying the N.Y.K. berthing rights in Hankow (which were offered instead by the Russians). See n. 26 of this chapter.

65. TH-KG, November 11, 1903; NYK-KSG, November 26, 1903, pp. 3–5. The Singapore branch had dispatched a warning about insurance as early as August 29. The situation was less serious on the U.S. line, but through Mitsui Bussan's mediation Japanese importers of American raw cotton paid war risk insurance premiums from October 23 to November 15.

66. NYK-TG#411, January 13, 1904.

67. NYK-TG#414, February 17, 1904.

68. TH-KG, March 1, 1904.

69. (NYK), Gian tsuzurikomi, March 4 and 11, 1904.

70. See n. 67 above. For a case in the early 1930s when Japan's Yamashita Steamship Co. registered ships in Britain and received subsidies from the British government, see Okazaki Yukihisa, *Waga kaiun 40 nen no tsuisō* (Nihon Kaiun Shūkaijonai, 1955), pp. 151–153; and Nakagawa Keiichirō, *Ryōtaisenkan no Nihon kaiungyō* (Nihon Keizai Shinbunsha, 1980), p. 207.

71. The China Merchants' fleet was transferred to the American firm of Russell and Co. during the Sino-French War. See Feuerwerker, *China's Early Industrialization*, pp. 114, 133; and Liu, "British-Chinese Steamship Rivalry", pp. 73–76. These works do not mention the "sale" to Jardine, Matheson in 1894. See n. 53 of this chapter.

72. Of somewhat less importance is the contrast between Kondō's vow to Kawakami not to leak information before the Sino-Japanese War and the N.Y.K.'s contingency planning at this time before the Russo-Japanese War.

9. NATIONALISM AND REGIONAL STRATEGIES, 1904-1914

1. Figures vary greatly according to whether they are totals for a whole business period or the amount requisitioned at a given time. Some secondary accounts give highly inflated figures by adding army and navy totals together, but some ships were used by both services. *OSK 50 nenshi,* p. 68; *JWM,* November 5, 1904, p. 499; *Teishin jigyōshi,* VI, 954–955. For the American line in 1905, see *The Tokio Marine & Fire Insurance: The First Century, 1879-1979,* ed., Japan Business History Institute (Tokyo, The Company, 1980), pp. 53–55.

2. NYK-TG#122, April 15, 1896, #123, April 22, 1896, and #410, December 23, 1903; *JWM,* February 18, 1905, p. 182.

3. The N.Y.K. turned down the British offer because it did not have enough ships. "Ikō," in *KD,* pp. 39–40; *JWM,* January 9, 1904, p. 31, and February 18, 1905, p. 181.

4. Ocean Transport & Trading Limited, Archives, OA 1815/9; NYK-TG#420, May 11, 1904; *NYK-EH* 20/1, March 1905, p. 4, and 20/2, September 1905, p. 4; and *JWM,* January 30, 1904, p. 118. Also on the war, see Asahara, *Nihon kaiun,* pp. 73–80.

5. For example, Okamoto, pp. 268–269n18.

6. *Yokohama-shi shi,* p. 607; *NYK 70 nenshi,* p. 675; and *OSK 80 nenshi,* p. 763.

7. Takahashi to Prime Minister Saionji, Finance Minister Sakatani Yoshirō, and Minister of Communications Yamagata Isaburō, January 3, 1907, Mizumachi [Kesaroku] ke monjo, vol. 8, no. 8, Finance Ministry Archives. On the P. & O. and Antwerp, see *JWM,* January 11, 1908, p. 41.

8. Derek H. Aldcroft, "The Depression in British Shipping, 1901-1911," *Journal of Transport History* 7.1:14-23 (May 1965); Aldcroft, "The Mercantile Marine," p. 354; Greenhill, p. 150; Maejima Shōzō, *Meiji chūmatsuki no kanryō seiji* (Kyoto, Chōbunsha, 1964), p. 247; Okaniwa, p. 96; Takamura Naosuke, "Kyōkō," in Ōishi, ed., *Nihon sangyō kakumei,* II, 209–224; *Royal Commission on Shipping Rings,* vol. 47, Appendix XVII, p. 102. See my Appendix C-7.

9. *Wagasha kakukōro,* pp. 461–462; *NYK-EH,* 1907-1909.

10. NYK-TG#338, June 5, 1901.

11. This payoff was received in installments of £2,500 over 6 years. NYK-TG#503, January 15, 1908. The North German Lloyd was involved in a similar settlement in 1909 in the Caribbean, though as a recipient of money. Greenhill, p. 132; cf. Hyde, *Cunard,* p. 102, for additional examples of this practice. On the competition, see Hyde, *Blue Funnel,* p. 158; P&O 3/17, April 21, 1899; K. G. Tregonning, *Home Port Singapore: A History of Straits Steamship Co. Ltd., 1860-1965* (Oxford,

1967), pp. 11, 33; *JWM*, June 30, 1906, p. 675; NYK–TG#501, December 4, 1907; JSSI 2/10, August 10 and 26, 1907; and *KD*, pp. 240–241.

12. Ōtani Noboru nikki, January 3, 1913, Shiryō shitsu, Economics Library, Tokyo University; and numerous trade reports by Ōtani in the author's private collection (with gratitude to Tōritsu Shobō). For O.S.K. Southeast Asian plans, see Katayama Kunio, "Osaka Shōsen Nanyōsen no zenshi: Shisatsu fukumeisho o chūshin to shite," *Tōnan Ajia kenkyū* 19.4: 388–411 (March 1982).

13. NYK–TG#455, November 1, 1905; *JWM*, June 9, 1906, p. 598, June 16, 1906, p. 620, and June 30, 1906, p. 675. Quotation is from JSSI 2/10, July 22, 1907. The two firms did come to an accord in September 1907. This regulated freight rates and departures. Butterfield & Swire had sought a discount to compensate for its smaller ships and fewer departures, but at the N.Y.K.'s insistence it accepted equal rates. JSSI 2/22, September 20, 1907.

14. NYK–TG#530, May 19, 1909; JSSI 1/15, June 15, 1912, p. 827.

15. The *Japan Weekly Mail* tried to soften the impact by changing "deadly blow" to "crushing blow"! *JWM*, June 23, 1906, p. 650.

16. NYK–KSG, May 29, 1907, pp. 11–12, 17–21; *JWM*, June 15, 1907, pp. 653–654; JSSI 4/4, Iwanaga to James, July 17, 1906, enclosed with James to J. H. Scott, August 15, 1906.

17. NYK–TG#448, July 12, 1905. On the Daitō firm, see Chapter 8, n. 10.

18. NYK–TG#461, January 10, 1906; Nakamura, "Chōsha kaikō," p. 7.

19. NYK–TG#464, March 7, 1906; *Nisshin Kisen*, p. 33; *JWM*, July 14, 1906, p. 34.

20. *JWM*, August 25, 1906, p. 183, and December 15, 1906, p. 741. For its services as agent for the O.S.K., the N.Y.K. had received ¥12,000 annually. NYK–TG#191, August 7, 1897; NYK–KSG, May 28, 1902, pp. 22–29; *JWM*, June 7, 1902, p. 615.

21. NYK–TG#464, March 7, 1906. The first N.Y.K.–O.S.K. freight rate agreement covering coastal and near-seas lines was signed in June 1907. See Asahara, *Nihon kaiun*, pp. 87–88.

22. The dating of the N.Y.K. acquisition of its berth in the French settlement is made from internal evidence of 2 board meetings. NYK–TG#464, March 7, 1906, and #469, May 9, 1906. See also #472, July 4, 1906; and *JWM*, October 6, 1906, p. 461.

23. In accordance with an N.Y.K. proposal the authorized capital stock of the company had tentatively been set at ¥10 million, with the additional ¥2 million to be subscribed to by the public. There is no precise record of why the N.Y.K. preferred this larger total, but a plausible explanation would be that its greater financial resources, combined with those of Mitsubishi, would enable the N.Y.K. to obtain a majority position in the

new company. An earlier N.Y.K. proposal for ¥16 million had been rejected as excessive by Kondō and Katō, who were traveling abroad at the time. NYK–TG#476, September 12, 1906, and #478, October 24, 1906.

24. *Nisshin Kisen,* pp. 263–265, 302–303.

25. Ibid., pp. 37, 56–67; NYK–TG#489, April 10, 1907, and #490, May 1, 1907.

26. JSSI 1/15, January 13, 1911, p. 228. The Nisshin Kisen's subsidy was reduced to ¥760,000 in 1912. Its contract of March 25, 1908, with the N.Y.K. is in Nippon Yūsen Kabushiki Kaisha, *Shaki ruisan,* I, 687–689.

27. For the above account, see the report prepared by Neilage S. Brown for Butterfield & Swire in JSSI 2/23, November 19, 1910. Regarding the Hankow trade, approximately 15 piculs were equal to 1 ton. On the Japanese firm's finances, see the charts in *Nisshin Kisen* between pp. 386 and 387.

28. JSSI 2/23, Butterfield & Swire to John Swire & Sons, November 30, 1910.

29. JSSI 2/23, Butterfield & Swire to John Swire & Sons, December 21, 1910.

30. Marriner and Hyde, pp. 198–199; Aldcroft, "Depression," p. 17 (my calculation).

31. See JSSI 1/15, 2/22, and 2/23. Cf. *JWM,* April 26, 1913, p. 517, for a breakdown of trips per company; and Allen and Donnithorne, p. 125.

32. *NYK 50 nenshi,* pp. 908–913; NYK–TG#575, June 7, 1911, and #576, June 28, 1911. It is difficult to measure the impact on Japanese society in the East Asian treaty ports of the myriad minor donations given by the N.Y.K. These went for Japanese schools, libraries, hospitals, shrines, churches, building funds for police stations, "Japan Clubs," newspapers, and even field days. Most were small, some as low as ¥15; rarely were they more than ¥1,000. On the average by 1903 about 10 overseas donations were being given annually. This represents roughly a quarter of all minor donations listed in the minutes of the board meetings. Such gift-giving served to institutionalize the Japanese presence in the ports.

33. See Chapter 10, n. 64.

34. Kobayashi Masaaki, *Yawata Seitetsujo* (Kyōikusha, 1977), pp. 198–228, esp. pp. 206–207; Albert Feuerwerker, "China's Nineteenth-Century Industrialization: The Case of the Hanyehping Coal and Iron Company, Limited," in Cowan, p. 80; Marius B. Jansen, "Yawata, Hanyehping, and the Twenty-One Demands," *Pacific Historical Review* 23:34–36 (February 1954); *Nihon kōgyō ginkō 50 nenshi* (Dō Rinji Shiryō Shitsu, 1957), pp. 15–21, 83–86. *Yanosuke den,* II, 260 states (without citation) that the N.Y.K.'s ¥1 million investment in the Tayeh mines was made in 1906 and lists it separately from the Industrial Bank loan to the mine. There is

nothing in the N.Y.K. accounts to suggest a direct investment in the Tayeh mines, however, and the company purchased no additional Industrial Bank debentures until 1911. For further discussion, see Chapter 10.

35. Marius B. Jansen, *The Japanese and Sun Yat-sen* (Stanford paperback, 1970), p. 142; Iriye, *Pacific Estrangement,* pp. 182–183; *Nisshin Kisen,* pp. 299–300, 391–393; Esherick, pp. 135–136, 282n140.

36. FO 371/1312, Hong Kong and Shanghai Banking Corporation to Foreign Office, January 30, 1912, p. 87 and February 1, 1912, p. 82. JSSI 2/23, February 3, 1912, describes the stockholders meeting. See also FO 371/ 1311, MacDonald to Grey, January 26, 1912, p. 439, and FO 371/1312, Grey to Bryce, February 7, 1912, p. 90; Peter Lowe, *Great Britain and Japan, 1911–1915* (Macmillan, 1969), pp. 84–85; and Jansen, *Sun,* p. 256n40.

37. Drage, pp. 180–183; JSSI 2/23, July 18, 1912; FO 371/1939, Greene to Grey, January 4, 1914, and memorandum by E. F. Crowe, December 29, 1913, pp. 310–311; FO 371/1939, Jordan to Grey, February 6, 1914, and Grey to Greene, March 9, 1914, pp. 322–323; Lowe, pp. 160–161 (to which I am indebted for these references).

38. NYK–KSG, November 28, 1906, pp. 18–23; *NYK–EH* 23/1, March 1908, p. 4.

39. NYK–TG#615, June 27, 1913. On the bean trade, see *Mitsui Bussan shōshi* (1965 reprint), pp. 60–62; and on the economy in general, see Herbert P. Bix, "Japanese Imperialism and the Manchurian Economy, 1900–31," *China Quarterly* 51:425–443 (July/September 1972).

40. *JWM,* September 2, 1905, p. 260.

41. *Chōsen Yūsen Kabushiki Kaisha 25 nenshi* (Seoul, Dōshahen, 1937), pp. 195–198, 245–253, 268; *NYK 70 nenshi,* pp. 622, 632, 643; *JWM,* January 20, 1912, p. 66.

42. Calculated from the *Report on Steamship Subsidies,* Appendix 7, p. 267. See also *SEDS,* X, 462.

43. NYK–TG#366, April 2, 1902.

44. *Wagasha kakukōro,* p. 144; HG, March 27, 1912; *JWM,* December 21, 1907, pp. 687–688, 693, and January 11, 1908, p. 41; and my Appendix C-6.

45. HK, June 23, 1896; HG, May 1 and December 11, 1912, January 17 and September 27, 1913, and February 3, 1914.

46. *JWM,* July 13, 1912, p. I; NYK–TG#578, July 26, 1911.

47. *JWM,* October 19, 1912, p. 456, June 13, 1914, p. X, March 2, 1912, p. 253, and September 21, 1912, p. 327.

48. *JWM,* August 24, 1912, p. 197; my Appendixes C-6, C-7.

49. The gist of Inchcape's letter to the P. & O., translated here from Japanese, is in HG, July 10, 1912. Except where otherwise noted, this discussion

of the British India Line's tactics is taken from FO 371/2010, which includes material from December 1913 to October 1914. Cf. Lowe, pp. 289-292.

50. British Cabinet papers, Cab. 37/119, 1914, no. 21, memorandum of January 30, 1914.

51. FO 371/2010, Inchcape to Langley, May 18, 1914.

52. Cab. 37/119, memorandum on Indian coastal trade, p. 4. (see n. 50 above).

53. P. & O. Minute Book #18, October 30, 1912, p. 487; *JWM*, September 21, 1912, p. 327; Farnie, pp. 522-525.

54. *NYK-EH* 23/2, September 1908, pp. 4-5; Gary Dean Best, "James J. Hill's 'Lost Opportunity on the Pacific,'" *Pacific Northwest Quarterly* 64.1:8-11 (January 1973); TH-KG, May 4, 1910; HG, October 24, 1912, March 5, 1913, and June 3, 1914.

55. *JWM*, November 1, 1913, p. IV, November 29, 1913, p. II, and January 17, 1914, p. I.

56. N.Y.K. management under Kondō's presidency has been so characterized in Nakagawa Keiichirō, "Ryōtaisenkan no Nihon kaiun," in Nakamura, ed., *Senkanki*, p. 255.

57. NYK-TG#621, November 19, 1913, #623-626, January 24 through February 3, 1914; *JWM*, January 3, 1914, p. 6, February 28, 1914, p. 245, and March 7, 1914, p. VII.

58. NYK-TG#626, February 3, 1914; *JWM*, March 14, 1914, p. 312. On the role of the subsidy bill in the downfall of the cabinet, see *Hara nikki*, III, March 23, 1914, pp. 408-409; and for background, see Tetsuo Najita, *Hara Kei in the Politics of Compromise, 1905-1915* (Harvard, 1967), pp. 188-191.

59. *Japan Advertiser*, May 30, 1914, enclosed in FO 371/2010, June 23, 1914; *JWM*, May 30, 1914, p. 596, June 6, 1914, p. III, June 13, 1914, p. 650, and July 11, 1914, p. VIII.

60. *JWM*, November 29, 1913, p. II, and January 17, 1914, p. I.

61. NYK-KSG, May 28, 1912, pp. 27-30.

62. The additional ¥600,000 making up the 1914 subsidy demand for ¥1.97 million was to cover interest payments on ship purchases. NYK-TG #624, January 26, 1914.

10. EXPANSION: A FINANCIAL AND INSTITUTIONAL ANALYSIS, 1893-1914

1. The European line's profits exceeded 100% of operating profit because of huge deficits in other services. These profit figures are estimates, as there is no breakdown for 1907/2. See Appendixes C-5, C-7.

2. The N.Y.K. had planned to abolish the westward Kobe-Otaru line but after protests from shippers decided instead to downgrade it to an irregular service. (NYK), Torishimariyakukai gian, July 24, 1907. An important feature of this line during its subsidized period up to 1906 was that its rebates as a percentage of freight income were at the same level as those on the European line. (See Appendix C-3). This implies close ties between shippers and shipping firms in domestic trade. The fact that Tokugawa shipping had also been characterized by close shipper-transporter ties (albeit in a different institutional context) may help to explain the ease with which Japanese traders entered the international rebate system in the 1890s.

3. NYK-TG#490, May 1, 1907, #492, June 12, 1907, #493, July 3, 1907, #502, December 25, 1907, #507, March 18, 1908. Unfortunately, since SKS places near-seas and domestic lines in one category, it is impossible to measure precisely the extent of N.Y.K. withdrawal from coastal services. I infer that it was substantial because of the cutbacks mentioned here and the strategic lines to China and South Manchuria, which increased the near-seas portion of this category.

4. NYK-KSG, May 27, 1908, pp. 8–9.

5. *NYK-EH* 23/1, March 1908, pp. 8–9. The deliberations of this committee seem to have been behind the decision to withdraw in December 1907 from the Southeast Asian line where the company was competing with the North German Lloyd. If the German firm had known that the withdrawal was part of a new strategy, perhaps it might not have paid its £15,000 bribe! See Chapter 9, n. 11.

6. Regarding the South American line, in 1908 the N.Y.K. had rejected a proposal from the Brazilian shipping firm Lloyd Brazileiro for a joint service to be subsidized by both the Brazilian and Japanese governments. Kondō argued that the line would not be profitable. In 1905 Tōyō Kisen had opened a Hong Kong–South American westcoast line. Annual deficits of almost ¥400,000 soon forced the company to suspend this operation, but it revived the service following the passage of the 1909 subsidy law. See Nobuya Tsuchida, *The Japanese in Brazil, 1908–1941* (PhD dissertation, UCLA, 1978), pp. 112–119; and *Tōyō Kisen,* pp. 80–83, 106, 108–109. For a copy of the 1909 law and general accounts of it, see *Teishin jigyōshi,* VI, 823–828; Teratani, "Japanese Business and Government," pp. 69–70; U.S. Department of Commerce, *Government Aid to Merchant Shipping,* pp. 216–218; Asahara, *Nihon kaiun,* pp. 97–101. On policy questions, see Tsurumi Yūsuke, *Gotō Shinpei* (Keisō Shobō, 1966), III, 63–70; *Teikoku gikai shi,* I, 576–577; and especially the Lower House debate of February 2, 1909 in *Dai Nihon teikoku gikai shi,* VII, 812–817. For the policy context, see Kokaze Hidemasa, "Meiji

kōki ni okeru kaiun seisaku no tenkai: Enyō kōro hojosaku o chūshin ni,"
Shakai keizai shigaku 48.3:262–285 (August 1982). Besides the N.Y.K.,
subsidies were also given to the O.S.K. for its Tacoma line and to Tōyō
Kisen for its lines to San Francisco and South America. Although the
Navigation Encouragement Law was abolished when the new law came
into effect on January 1, 1910, ships which were certified for aid under
the old law prior to the end of 1909 continued to receive bounties under
its provisions until the end of 1914. Also, the subsidy program for the
near-seas and remaining coastal lines continued.

7. The law gave the government certain powers over personnel as well, prohibiting employment of foreigners in overseas branch offices. In a revision
in March 1910, the Ministry of Communications also gained the right to
approve appointments of directors in companies subsidized under the
law. *JWM*, March 5, 1910, p. 403; *NYK 70 nenshi*, p. 107.

8. NYK–TG#520–525, January 18, 1909 through March 3, 1909. See also
JWM, January to March 1909.

9. NYK–TG#527, April 21, 1909.

10. NYK–TG#530, May 19, 1909, #535, September 15, 1909, #537,
October 20, 1909, and #538, October 27, 1909; NYK–KSG, November
26, 1909, pp. 9–17; *JWM*, December 4, 1909, p. 713. The N.Y.K. "submission" was for the European and American lines. The Australia line,
the contract for which was renewed for 5 years in 1908, was allowed to
stay under the old law.

11. Takamura, "Sangyō bōeki kōzō," pp. 48, 60n9.

12. Ranking by tonnage, *NYK 70 nenshi*, p. 93; NYK–KSG, May 28, 1913,
pp. 6–7.

13. In Japanese shipping parlance the N.Y.K., O.S.K., and Tōyō Kisen, along
with Nisshin Kisen, were usually known as *shasen* ("mainline companies").
They were contrasted with *shagaisen* (roughly, "nonmainline companies"), a term originally used for independents opposing N.Y.K. and
O.S.K. coastal liner services in the early 1890s. The distinction between
shasen and *shagaisen* as it developed was more popular than substantive.
The *shasen* were the large, subsidized firms concerned exclusively with
shipping. The *shagaisen* were independents who were often engaged in
other business, Mitsui Bussan being the most famous example. The distinction was not between liner and tramp, however, for some of the *shagaisen* operated liner services, and serveral of the larger ones even received
government subsidies. See Nakagawa, *Ryōtaisenkan*, pp. 47–55.

14. See Nakagawa, *Ryōtaisenkan*, pp. 111–117.

15. Estimated from figures on freight distribution in *OSK 80 nenshi*, p. 712.

16. Nakagawa, *Ryōtaisenkan*, p. 112.

17. NYK–TG#390, March 25, 1903.

18. *Report on Steamship Subsidies,* vol. 8, p. 99, q. 1605, p. 241, q. 4343.

19. *JWM,* April 18, 1914, p. viii. For a study of a liner company that was dependent primarily on passenger traffic, see Hyde, *Cunard,* esp. pp. 58–158.

20. For the comparative growth rates, see S. G. Sturmey, *British Shipping and World Competition* (The Athlone Press, 1962), p. 392. The world shares are from Lloyds Register courtesy of Mr. Yonesato Masaaki of the N.Y.K. Company History Office.

21. Nakagawa Keiichirō, "Japanese Shipping in the Interwar Period," unpublished paper, p. 32. HG, February 14, 1912; SKS (cf. my Appendixes C-2, C-7); *NYK-EH* 28/2, September 1913, p. 4; (NYK), Torishimariyakukai gian, May 11, 1896.

22. Hyde, *Blue Funnel,* p. 148; *Royal Commission on Shipping Rings,* vol. 48, p. 175, q. 17014.

23. Greenhill, pp. 135–136; see also Aldcroft, "Depression," pp. 21–22; and Sturmey, pp. 364–382.

24. The petition appears in *JWM,* April 13, 1912, p. 440.

25. NYK-KGS, November 29, 1911, p. 5; *JWM,* April 27, 1912, p. 495.

26. *JWM,* May 11, 1912, p. 557.

27. The quotation is from a Ministry of Communications statement reproduced in *JWM,* June 29, 1912.

28. HG, July 10, 1912. At the time the rate per ton on general cargo for London was 50s. For other freights, see the charts in *Wagasha kakukōro,* pp. 475–484. The government had accepted the N.Y.K. request for a rate increase of 2s.6d.–5s. on imports. See also Kokaze, pp. 278–280.

29. HG, December 11 and 28, 1912.

30. HG, March 11, April 22, and June 3, 1914; NYK-KSG, May 28, 1914, pp. 2–5. In 1914 the American line had a slightly different problem. Because of a poor harvest, wheat and flour shipments were well below expectations. Tramps, some of them Japanese, had canvassed for cargo at west coast ports and taken away what remained of these shipments. N.Y.K. liners had to return to Japan virtually in ballast. *JWM,* April 18, 1914, p. viii.

31. Gabriel Kolko, *Railroads and Regulation, 1877–1916* (Princeton, 1965); Alfred D. Chandler, Jr., *The Visible Hand: The Managerial Revolution in American Business* (Harvard, 1977), p. 544n76.

32. According to the original agreement the N.Y.K. was to pay 5% of the ¥3.6 million each year for 20 years. See *NYK-EH* 10/2, September 1895, pp. 7–9. The initial payment, however, was not made until late 1901. Also, in the "mysterious accounting procedure" I referred to in Chapter 7, the value of these ships was written down in company accounts before it officially purchased them. Without this procedure the amount of the

long-term loan would have been closer to ¥5 million. See *NYK–EH* 11/1, March 1896, p. 37, for the writing down of value and 12/1, March 1897, p. 38, for their first appearance as a liability in company accounts. The N.Y.K. also tried unsuccessfully to have the payments stretch out over 50 years. NYK–TG#207, December 8, 1897. See also OM, A2951.

33. John Swire to Butterfield & Swire, JSSI 1/11, September 27, 1894, p. 510.

34. This is the conclusion of Okaniwa, pp. 108–110. My views are similar, but are presented in a slightly different format and time span. I have started in 1897 to avoid any financial entanglements with the Sino-Japanese War, and I conclude in 1914.

35. *JWM,* November 29, 1902, p. 590.

36. NYK–TG#472, July 4, 1906.

37. These ships were expected to produce an annual net revenue of 12.5 to 15.5% of their purchase price. NYK–TG#574, May 31, 1911. See also *Wagasha kakukōro,* pp. 433–435; and Asahara, *Nihon kaiun,* pp. 90–94, 103–106.

38. Calculated from *NYK–EH.* By "net purchase price" I mean the book value of purchases minus the book value of ships that were either transferred to subsidiaries in exchange for stock or sold. Also, I have no evidence that this 1.8% (a ¥975,000 loan) was used for ships. I have still used it in my calculations because I am primarily concerned with *all* sources of capital, and this was the *only* loan taken out by the N.Y.K. between the Sino-Japanese War and 1914.

39. In Figure 13 I have added to current liabilities payments made during the following year (e.g., 1915 for the 1914 figures) for insurance and repairs and I have subtracted an equivalent amount from the insurance and repair reserves that make up the bulk of long-term liabilities. This last device does not adhere to strict accounting practice, but I am most concerned with the ratio between the various categories in the figure.

40. Beginning in 1901 yearly contributions to depreciation and the main reserves were fixed in the following way: to the insurance reserve went 2.5% of gross ship cost; to the repair reserve 1.25% of ship construction cost; and to depreciation 2% of ship construction cost. *NYK–EH* 16/2, September 1901, p. 12.

41. Assets equal capital plus liabilities. *OSK 80 nenshi,* pp. 31, 812; *OSK 50 nenshi,* p. 528. Gross income includes subsidy.

42. Yamamura, "Japan, 1868-1930," pp. 168–198, esp. pp. 179–186. An exception to this generalization was Tōyō Kisen, which relied heavily on both domestic and foreign loans. It had ties with Kuhn, Loeb & Co. in the United States and Westminster's Bank in Britain. Okaniwa, pp. 105–107. Tōyō Kisen, however, was not a successful firm, and only World

War I temporarily saved it from going under. Ericson has also argued that Yamamura underestimated the role of banks in railway investment.

43. U.S. Department of Commerce, *Government Aid to Merchant Shipping*, p. 25; Teratani, "Japanese Business and Government," p. 71. In the above data, subsidies are included in operating profit but not in operating income. See Appendixes C–5, C–8, C–9.

44. Takamura Naosuke, "Dokusen shihonshugi no kakuritsu to chūshō kigyō," *Iwanami kōza, Nihon rekishi*, vol. 18, *Kindai* V (Iwanami Shoten, 1975), p. 58.

45. With the same method of calculation used for the N.Y.K. in Table 55, O.S.K. costs per owned ton in 1903 would also have been just over ¥50 (*OSK 80 nenshi*, pp. 763, 800–802). In that year, however, ships chartered in by the O.S.K. accounted for 18% of tonnage employed (*OSK 50 nenshi*, p. 840). Since expenses incurred in operating these chartered vessels are included in my calculations, they distort the figures for comparison of owned tonnage. Data are unavailable on the amount of tonnage chartered in by the N.Y.K. The expenses for such tonnage included in Table 55 obviously create distortion, though less so than would be the case for the O.S.K. In relative terms (charter fees as a percentage of ship costs—see Table 56) it was roughly 2 to 3 times more active as a charter operator than the N.Y.K. Table 55, then, while not a precise measurement, is useful for showing trends, since abnormal years like 1904–1905 (wartime) and 1909–1911 (minimal N.Y.K. chartering) are avoided.

46. Report based on the *Japan Gazette*. The "mutinies" had delayed the departure of some steamers from Seattle. This brought the following ironic suggestion to Great Northern Railway President James Hill: "I think the management in Japan should know that in this country [the U.S.A.] it is of the utmost importance to keep all business moving on the time advertised." GN President's Subject file 2956#1, October 31, 1896.

47. *NYK 70 nenshi*, p. 83.

48. *JWM*, April 27, 1912, p. 490, and May 4, 1912, p. 522; NYK–TG#594, May 1, 1912.

49. Masayoshi Chūbachi and Koji Taira, "Poverty in Modern Japan: Perceptions and Realities," in Patrick, ed., *Japanese Industrialization*, p. 418; Kobayashi Masaaki, *Kaiungyō no rōdō mondai*, vol. 2 of *Nihon kaiun keieishi*, 1980, pp. 11–69, esp. pp. 64–69; and George O. Totten, "Collective Bargaining and Works Councils as Innovations in Industrial Relations in Japan during the 1920s," in R. P. Dore, ed., *Aspects of Social Change in Modern Japan* (Princeton, 1967), pp. 233–239.

50. NYK–TG#492, June 12, 1907, and #594, May 1, 1912.

51. *Royal Commission on Shipping Rings*, vol. 48, p. 272, q. 20528. On London strikes, see HG, June 14, July 10, and September 19, 1912.

52. Calculations made from *NYK 70 nenshi*, pp. 675, 696–698; and *NYK-EH*. See also Yasuba, p. 19; and Yasuba Yasukichi, "Gaikō kaiun to keizai hatten: sekitan to no kanren o chūshin ni," in *Enerugī to keizai hatten,* 1979, pp. 223–248.

53. NYK-TG#519, December 23, 1908, and #243, October 12, 1898.

54. Nomura Jiichirō, *Waga kaiun 60 nen* (Kokusai Kaiun Shinbunsha, 1955), pp. 37–39; NYK-TG#460, December 27, 1905. On market shares of leading coal mining firms, see Kobayashi Masaaki, *Kindai Nihon keizaishi* (Sekai Shoin, 1983), p. 122.

55. Hyde, *Cunard*, pp. 125–129; Aldcroft, "The Mercantile Marine," pp. 340–342; Yasuba, p. 18. Exchange rates are calculated at £ = ¥10. These cost figures are more useful for showing trends than precise comparisons, for it is hard to determine whether all categories of expense are parallel. Hyde gives "aggregate costs" for Cunard, but it is not clear if this includes depreciation.

56. N.Y.K. estimates calculated from *NYK-EH*. Inagaki Sumio, general manager of the N.Y.K.'s Accounting Division, kindly confirmed that N.Y.K. accounts listed after-tax profits. The payment rates (which are not tax "rates") are calculated by adding the tax, which was listed as an expense, to the stated profit to obtain the pretax profit, and then dividing the tax by this pretax profit. The figures for Cunard and the P. & O. are calculated in the same manner from U.S. Department of Commerce, *Government Aid to Merchant Shipping*, p. 61. The arrangement of the accounts there is similar enough to N.Y.K. procedure to be useful for general comparative estimates. For further discussion, see my Conclusion. On the tax dispute involving the N.Y.K., see Takatera, *Meiji genka shōkyakushi*, pp. 289–303. The bureau chief was Hamaguchi Yūkō, prime minister in an allegedly Mitsubishi-supported cabinet (1929–1931).

57. On the match industry, see Yamashita Naotō, "Keiseiki Nihon shihon-shugi ni okeru matchi kōgyō to Mitsui Bussan," *Mitsui bunko ronsō* 6:93–166 (1972); and Kumiko Terazawa, "Mitsui Bussan Kaisha: Its Growth and Effects on the Japanese Economy (1876–1930)," *Stone Lion Review* 3:41–42 (Spring 1979).

58. Yasuba, p. 15.

59. *Wagasha kakukōro*, pp. 184–186.

60. *JWM*, January 7, 1911, p. 6; NYK-KSG, May 26, 1910, pp. 2–3; *NYK-EH* 28/1, March 1913, p. 4. The above argument on rates assumes that the N.Y.K. could not have operated a competitive, regular line outside the conference without much larger subsidies.

61. NYK-KSG, November 26, 1903, pp. 25–26.

62. NYK-KSG, May 25, 1903, pp. 10–11, in *JWM*, June 6, 1903, p. 615.

63. The quotation on "net welfare effect" is from Yasuba, p. 16. The remarks

on the economic value of shipping and on military considerations are from Yasuba's "Comments" on Teratani, "Japanese Business and Government," pp. 79–80.

64. NYK–TG#499, October 30, 1907; #539, November 5, 1909; #548, May 4, 1910; *NYK–EH* 24/2, September 1909, p. 35, and 25/1, March 1910, p. 36. This maneuver was not prompted by problems with Nisshin Kisen's business performance, which was improving during these years, as profits rose as a percentage of subsidy from 17.6 in 1908 to 116.7 in 1913. Okaniwa, p. 113. Also, for one integrated investment project, see HK, November 18, 1902.

65. NYK–TG#551, June 8, 1910. Similar decision-making on other investments is recorded in NYK–TG#553, July 4, 1910, and #558, September 28, 1910. For background on the stock market and bond market during this period, see Shimura, pp. 29–48.

66. See *Yanosuke den,* II, 309–312; Morikawa Hidemasa, "Iwasaki Yanosuke jidai," pp. 56–60; "The Organizational Structure of Mitsubishi and Mitsui," p. 68; Inoue Yōichirō, "Nihon kindai zōsengyō kakuritsuki ni okeru Mitsubishi Nagasaki Zōsenjo," *Keiei shigaku* 3.1.33–50 (March 1968). In November 1896 Yanosuke replaced Kawada Koichirō as president of the Bank of Japan. In 1893 he had left the presidency of Mitsubishi to Hisaya.

67. Import tariffs applied in 1911 were also important, though less so than the shipbuilding subsidy. See Yasuba Yasukichi, "Comments" on Teratani, "Japanese Business and Government," p. 80. For assessments of the shipbuilding law, see Inoue, "Mieji kōki no kaiji seisaku," pp. 201–205; and Teratani Takeaki, *Nihon kindai zōsenshi josetsu* (Gannandō Shoten, 1979), pp. 75–79.

68. Figures on N.Y.K. total new purchases are calculated from *NYK 70 nenshi,* pp. 679–682. Secondhand ships are not included in the calculations. For the purchases under the Shipbuilding Law, see Inoue, "Meiji kōki no kaiji seisaku," p. 186. From 1899 to 1912 Mitsubishi built 12 ships for the navy totaling 37,139 tons, or about one-fifth the tonnage for commercial vessels. Mishima, *Mitsubishi zaibatsushi,* pp. 184–190. Between 1898 and 1912 Japan's share of the world's shipbuilding market grew from 0.58 to 2.00%. Calculated from Sidney Pollard and Paul Robertson, *The British Shipbuilding Industry, 1870–1914* (Harvard, 1979), p. 249.

69. Asset figures for 1896 and 1904 are calculated from Tatematsu, p. 88. Figures for 1914 are calculated from *Mitsubishi Gōshi Kaisha: Sha shi,* in *Mitsubishi Sha shi,* ed., Mitsubishi Sha Shi Kankōkai (Tokyo Daigaku Shuppankai, 1980), vol. 23, XXI, 1914, pp. 2361–2363.

70. On mining and the risk-avoidance strategy, see Kobayashi, *Nihon no*

kōgyōka, pp. 374-375, who criticizes Hirschmeier's view that national-ism motivated entrepreneurs to accept risk and endure low profits. Kobayashi argues instead that diversification occurred because it was a means of avoiding risk. On Mitsubishi's move into shipbuilding and the crucial role of the N.Y.K. as the basis for Mitsubishi's diversification into heavy industry, see Mishima, ed., *Mitsubishi zaibatsu,* pp. 194-201, esp. pp. 334-337. On the Kobe shipyard, see *Yanosuke den,* II, 326-340.

71. Yasuba, "Comments" on Teratani, "Japanese Business and Government," pp. 79-80.

72. Sanuki, pp. 43-49.

73. P&O 3/15, February 21, 1896. The shipbuilding subsidy made up some of this extra cost. See *JWM,* March 4, 1899, p. 217.

74. NYK-TG#216, March 2, 1898.

75. NYK-TG#217, March 9, 1898, #218, March 16, 1898, and #219, March 23, 1898. The account of this delay in *Yanosuke den,* II, 312-317 is erroneous in several respects. It blames the delay on Lloyds' inspector who refused to register the *Hitachi Maru* (he was supported in his opinion by N.Y.K. technical advisers); it downplays the degree of Mitsubishi's commitment to the second ship; and it exaggerates the eventual compensa-tion, giving an inflated figure of "over ¥260,000."

76. NYK-TG#531, June 16, 1909.

77. Interview with Harada Kenjirō, former N.Y.K. director, June 14, 1974. See also Terai Hisanobu, *Kaiun no saiken* (Shichiyōsha, 1948), p. 91.

78. The Business Department was the precursor of Mitsubishi Shōji, today Japan's largest trading company. On Mitsubishi's shipping, see the follow-ing articles by Mishima Yasuo: "Mitsubishi Shōji: zaibatsugata shōsha no keisei," *Keiei shigaku* 8.1:16-17 (August 1973); "Sōgō shōsha: sengo ni okeru kenkyūshi," in *Nihon no zaibatsu,* ed., Yasuoka Shigeaki (Nihon Keizai Shinbunsha, 1976), pp. 246-249; and "Sekitan yushutsu shōsha kara sōgō shōsha e: Mitsubishi Shōji," in Miyamoto, *Sōgō shōsha,* pp. 122-135. On Mitsui, see *Mitsui Senpaku 80 nenshi,* pp. 59-60; and Ma-tsumoto, *Mitsui zaibatsu,* p. 476. Ship purchasing figures are calculated from *Teishin jigyōshi,* VI, 829-830; and Tatematsu, p. 93.

79. Mitsubishi Shōji Kabushiki Kaisha, ed., *Ritsugyō bōeki roku* (Dōsha, 1958), pp. 878-880; *Yanosuke den,* I, 400, and II, 259-263; Mishima, "Sōgō shōsha: sengo ni okeru kenkyūshi," pp. 248-249, and "Sekitan yushutsu shōsha," pp. 123-125; Nakagawa, "Business Strategy," pp. 18-21; Kobayashi, *Yawata,* pp. 220-223; *KD,* p. 8; Hatade, *Mitsubishi,* pp. 131-143.

80. Nakagawa, "Japanese Shipping," p. 31.

81. *NYK-KNS;* Yamashita Kamesaburō, *Shizumitsu ukitsu* (Yamashita

Kabushiki Kaisha Hisho-bu, 1943), II, 129. On N.Y.K. bank deposits, see Appendix D.

82. It is appropriate to mention that Mitsubishi's own investment policy became more expansionist during World War I partly because of the growing influence of Koyata (Yanosuke's son), who took over the presidency from Hisaya in 1916. See *Iwasaki Koyata den* (Dō Hensan Iinkai, 1957).

83. Nomura, pp. 22–23; *NYK 70 nenshi*, p. 81; *KD*, p. 187.

84. NYK–TG#617, August 6, 1913, #629, April 30, 1914; *Terai*, p. 45.

85. For an analysis of Kondō's failures which begins with World War I, see Terai, *Shio no michihi*, pp. 58–62.

86. JSSI 2/22, March 12, 1909 and September 20, 1907. There are summaries of Iwanaga's early career in GN President's Subject file 2956#2: see the *New York Tribune*, July 23, 1896; and *The Trade Register* (Seattle), August 29, 1896, pp. 5–6.

87. *KD*, pp. 254–255; Asahara Jōhei, "Taishō jidai no kabunushi sōkai," in *Yūsen no omoide* (comp., N.Y.K. nai Yūsenkai, 1962), p. 3.

88. Sawai Kenkichi, "Hayashi Tamio sensei," in *Yūsen no omoide*, p. 155. Hayashi had returned from Shanghai in 1906 because the climate did not suit his health. NYK–TG#473, July 18, 1906. Suda had earlier become head of the company's Supervisory Department, a post responsible for navigation and engineering which had been held by a foreigner until 1899. In 1881 Suda graduated from the Imperial College of Engineering (Kōgakuryō), a forerunner of Tokyo University. For the next 6 years he worked in the Ministry of Industry and the Shipping Bureau. Before A. R. Brown went to England in March 1887 on behalf of the N.Y.K., the company had been "vainly looking for a Japanese engineer to accompany him." In February of that year Suda joined the N.Y.K., went to England with Brown, and remained there for over 4 years conducting specialized research. When he returned to Japan in mid-1891 he went to the N.Y.K.'s Yokohama branch and gradually worked his way up until he became head of the Supervisory Department in April 1900. See D. Matsushita, comp., *Marine Transport and Foreign Trade* (Chūgai Sangyō Chōsakai, 1919), pp. 265–266; and *Zaikai bukko ketsubutsu den*, I, 638–639.

89. NYK–TG#175, April 22, 1897, and #586, December 5, 1911; *NYK 70 nenshi*, p. 119. On N.Y.K. managers, see Morikawa Hidemasa, *Nihon keieishi* (Nihon Keizai Shinbunsha, 1981), pp. 51–54, 77–82, 89–92.

90. Yamashita Naotō, "Nisshin-Nichirō senkanki ni okeru zaibatsu burujoajī no seisaku shikō: Yūrakukai no dōkō o chūshin ni," *Rekishigaku kenkyū* 450:12–26 (November 1977); NYK–TG#101. November 2, 1895; *Machida Chūji ō* (Dō Denki Kankōkai, 1950), pp. 62–74.

91. *Hara Kei nikki,* III, June 4, 1910, pp. 30–31; Yamashita, *Shizumitsu ukitsu,* II, 48.

92. *JWM,* February 20, 1909, p. 222, February 27, 1909, p. 253, March 6, 1909, p. 292.

93. NYK–TG#523, February 17, 1909. For the public statement, see *JWM,* February 13, 1909, p. 192.

94. NYK–TG#524, February 22, 1909.

95. NYK–TG#525, March 3, 1909; *Hara Kei nikki,* II, March 17–20, 1909, pp. 345–346.

96. NYK–KSG, May 28, 1914, pp. 11–22; Asahara, "Taishō jidai," pp. 3–4; Najita, p. 113. Also, as an N.Y.K. bondholder in 1906, Hara Kei had received a repayment installment of ¥2,000. HK, September 19, 1906.

97. Shimura, pp. 29–42; and conversations with Professor Nakagawa Kei-ichirō.

98. *JWM,* May 30, 1908, p. 604.

99. NYK–KSG, November 25, 1898, pp. 13–31.

100. *JWM,* August 3, 1901, p. 112; NYK–KSG, November 30, 1895, pp. 2–5; *JWM,* December 7, 1895, p. 608; *NYK–KNS,* October 31, 1900. The debate is from NYK–KSG, November 25, 1900, pp. 45–51. The attack on Watanabe omitted the honorific from his name.

101. As paraphrased in *JWM,* April 6, 1901, p. 363.

102. *JWM,* December 1, 1900, p. 570.

103. NYK–KSG, May 29, 1901, pp. 39–48; *JWM,* June 15, 1901, p. 640, February 13, 20, and 27, 1909, pp. 195, 222, 253; Teratani, "Japanese Business and Government," pp. 65, 68.

104. *JWM,* July 13, 1912, p. 41. Technically these shares were not "free," since they were part of assets already owned by stockholders. "Free share," in the English parlance of the time, is a rendering of the Japanese *mushō kabu,* today translated as "stock dividend," that is, a dividend received in the form of stock rather than cash. Though the term "free share" is thus a misnomer from the stockholders' viewpoint, it does perhaps convey the distinction between reserves and capital stock that existed in the eyes of pre-World War I management. Managers sought to control reserves and to keep a lid on the capital stock to limit the amount of money going out of the company in the form of dividends.

105. NYK–KSG, May 28, 1914, pp. 16–39.

106. *OSK 80 nenshi,* pp. 812, 827–828; *NYK–EH.*

107. As paraphrased in *JWM,* January 10, 1914.

CONCLUSION

1. Johnson, *MITI*, p. 23.
2. For a view of government policy in this period which emphasizes its concern with exploiting comparative advantage in products like tea, raw silk, and cotton goods, see Ichirou Inukai and Arlon R. Tussing, "*Kōgyō Iken*: Japan's Ten Year Plan, 1884," *Economic Development and Cultural Change* 16.1:51–71 (October 1967).
3. Terai, *Shio no michihi*, p. 59.
4. Feuerwerker, *China's Early Industrialization*, pp. 124–137, 168–172, 183. In 1893, ¥100 was equivalent to 72 Shanghai taels. Exchange rates are given in The Bank of Japan, Statistics Department, *Hundred-Year Statistics of the Japanese Economy* (July 1966), pp. 318–319.
5. John H. Kemble, "A Hundred Years of the Pacific Mail," *American Neptune* 10.2:135–139 (April 1950); Chandler, *Visible Hand*, pp. 191–192.
6. P. & O. figures are calculated from U.S. Department of Commerce, *Government Aid to Merchant Shipping*, p. 53. The subsidy-per-ton calculations here are not given for their precise accuracy but rather for their comparative purposes. They are based on the following rates: £1 = ¥10; $1 = ¥2; and DM 2.1 = ¥1. Some of my German calculations come from accounts expressed in dollars. See ibid., pp. 82–84. The total North German Lloyd tonnage (867,000) is from early 1914 and includes vessels under construction. *JWM*, May 16, 1914, p. 556. I have used 1913 as the sample year for the whole fleet comparison because the North German Lloyd subsidy was cut in half in 1914. See also Asahara, *Nihon kaiun*, pp. 109–117, esp. pp. 113–115, which contains yen figures and tonnage statistics on the North German Lloyd's East Asia line for 1914 (before the subsidy reduction). His N.Y.K. figures, which he uses for comparison, do not bear a precise date, but the evidence on ship size suggests that they refer to 1910–1912. The tonnage figures for the N.Y.K.'s European line include only its 11 regular ships.
7. For a representative view, see Aldcroft, "The Mercantile Marine."
8. For a summary of the 1898 contract, see *Report on Steamship Subsidies*, vol. 8, Appendix 11, pp. 275–277.
9. Cecil, p. 67; *70 Years North German Lloyd*, p. 52.
10. Hyde, *Blue Funnel*, pp. 41–42, 143–149.
11. *JWM*, January 10, 1903, p. 30, identifies these national figures as being for 1901. See also *JWM*, October 17, 1903; and U.S. Department of Commerce, *Government Aid to Merchant Shipping*, pp. 59, 223, and pp. 135–165 for the French program. Aldcroft, "The Mercantile Marine," p. 333, has slightly different figures based on net tonnage. In these it appears as if the French subsidy rate may be even higher, but the overall proportions

among national totals is similar to the estimates included here. All figures are for owned tonnage. If charters were included, the O.S.K.'s subsidization rate would have been slightly lower than the N.Y.K.'s.

12. I have calculated the Cunard figure as follows: ¥600,000 from a postal subvention, ¥1.5 million from an Admiralty subsidy, and ¥585,000 from the government loan. This loan figure represents the average annual interest saved by the difference between the government interest rate of 2.75% and the market rate of 5%. Obviously this is only a gross approximation. See U.S. Department of Commerce, *Government Aid to Merchant Shipping,* pp. 51–61, 165.

13. Hyde, *Cunard,* pp. 71, 105–108.

14. Aldcroft, "The Mercantile Marine," p. 336.

15. Takamura, "Dokusen shihonshugi," p. 87n37.

16. *JWM,* November 30, 1912, p. 643.

17. The relative tonnage was P. & O., 1.45; N.Y.K., 1.00; Cunard 0.83. U.S. Department of Commerce, *Government Aid to Merchant Shipping,* pp. 60–61.

18. Some qualification of these reserve totals must be made because of different accounting procedures. The Cunard had placed close to ¥10 million in a repair reserve between 1912 and 1914. However, the company apparently used most of these funds and therefore they cannot be thought of as a long-term liability like the N.Y.K. repair reserve from which the N.Y.K. drew next to nothing from the viewpoint of these gross comparisons. If we interpreted Cunard's accounts more in accordance with N.Y.K. procedure, at most its reserves would be around ¥15 million. That is higher than the figure given here, but beside the N.Y.K.'s ¥42 million, it does not alter the overall proportions we are concerned with. See Hyde, *Cunard,* pp. 133, 153; and U.S. Department of Commerce, *Government Aid to Merchant Shipping,* p. 61.

19. The Messageries Maritimes contract appears in U.S. Department of Commerce, *Government Aid to Merchant Shipping,* pp. 156–157, 242–248.

20. Dividends were not a significant factor in explaining the difference in the size of these firms' reserves. Only the P. & O., at 15%, had a higher rate than the N.Y.K. Cunard's was about the same; German firms' were slightly lower.

21. *Dai Nihon teikoku gikai shi,* VII, 815.

22. *JWM,* January 14, 1899, p. 33.

23. Pascale and Athos, p. 316.

24. For a list of these options, see Terai, *Shio no michihi,* pp. 58–59.

25. John P. McKay, *Pioneers for Profit: Foreign Entrepreneurship and Russian Industrialization, 1885–1913* (Chicago, 1970); and Hao.

26. JSSI 1/13, April 11, 1901, p. 908.

27. Henriques, pp. 13–88.
28. Aldcroft, "The Mercantile Marine," p. 358; Nakagawa, *Ryōtaisenkan*, p. 38.
29. Sturmey, p. 32.
30. *Report on Steamship Subsidies*, vol. 8, p. 250, q. 4530.

Bibliography

The place of publication is not given for Japanese works published in Tokyo.

Most official biographies and company histories published in Japan are edited and privately published by committees bearing the name of the person or firm concerned. To avoid repetition I have followed the Japanese editorial practice of indicating the editor and publisher by the word *Dō* ("the same").

Akita, George. *The Foundations of Constitutional Government in Modern Japan, 1868-1900.* Cambridge, Harvard University Press, 1967.

Aldcroft, Derek H. "The Depression in British Shipping, 1901-1911," *Journal of Transport History* 7.1:14-23 (May 1965).

——. "The Mercantile Marine," in Aldcroft, ed., *The Development of British Industry and Foreign Competition, 1875-1914.* London, Allen & Unwin, 1968, pp. 326-363.

Allen, G. C. *A Short Economic History of Modern Japan.* 2d rev. ed. London, Unwin University Books, 1962.

—— and A. G. Donnithorne. *Western Enterprise in Far Eastern Economic Development: China and Japan.* London, Allen & Unwin, 1954.

Andō Yoshio. *Burujowajī no gunzō* (Business groups). Vol. 28 of *Nihon no rekishi* (History of Japan). Shōgakukan, 1977.

——, ed. *Nihon keizai seisaku shiron* (Essays on the history of Japanese economic policy), vol. 1. Tokyo Daigaku Shuppankai, 1973.

——, ed. *Kindai Nihon keizaishi yōran* (A handbook of modern Japanese economic history). Tokyo Daigaku Shuppankai, 1975.

Araki Nobuyoshi. *En no rekishi* (A history of the yen). Kyōikusha, 1979.

Arisawa Hiromi, comp. *Nihon sangyō 100 nenshi* (One hundred years of Japanese industry). Nihon Keizai Shinbunsha, 1966.

Asabuki Eiji kun den (A biography of Asabuki Eiji). Dō Shi Denki Hensankai, 1928.

Asahara Jōhei. "Taishō jidai no kabunushi sōkai" (Stockholders General Meetings in the Taishō period), in *Yūsen no omoide*, pp. 3–16.

——. *Nihon kaiun hattenshi* (History of the development of Japanese shipping). Chōryūsha, 1978.

Baldwin, Frank. "The Idioms of Contemporary Japan VII: *Sōkaiya*," *Japan Interpreter* 8.4:502–509 (Winter 1974).

Bank of Japan, Statistics Department. *Hundred-Year Statistics of the Japanese Economy*. July 1966.

Banno Junji. *Meiji kenpō taisei no kakuritsu* (The establishment of the Meiji constitutional structure). Tokyo Daigaku Shuppankai, 1971.

Best, Gary Dean. "James J. Hill's 'Lost Opportunity on the Pacific'," *Pacific Northwest Quarterly* 64.1:8–11 (January 1973).

Bix, Herbert P. "Japanese Imperialism and the Manchurian Economy, 1900–31," *China Quarterly* 51:425–443 (July–September 1972).

Black, John R. *Young Japan: Yokohama and Yedo, 1858–1879*. 2 vols. 1883. Reprint. Oxford University Press, 1969.

Blake, George. *The Ben Line: The History of Wm. Thomson & Co. 1825–1955*. London, Thomas Nelson & Sons, 1956.

Boxer, Baruch. *Ocean Shipping in the Evolution of Hong Kong*. Chicago, University of Chicago, Department of Geography, Research Paper no. 72, 1961.

Branch, Alan E. *The Elements of Shipping*. 3d ed. London, Chapman and Hall, 1975.

Brown, Sidney Devere. "Ōkubo Toshimichi: His Political and Economic Policies in Early Meiji Japan," *Journal of Asian Studies* 21.2:183–197 (February 1962).

——. "Ōkubo Toshimichi and the First Home Ministry Bureaucracy," in Bernard Silberman and Harry D. Harootunian, eds., *Modern Japanese Leadership: Transition and Change*. Tucson, University of Arizona Press, 1966, pp. 195–227.

Bush, Lewis. *The Life and Times of the Illustrious Captain Brown*. Tokyo, Voyageurs Press, 1970.

Cabinet Papers. Public Record Office, London.

Cecil, Lamar. *Albert Ballin: Business and Politics in Imperial Germany, 1888–1918*. Princeton, Princeton University Press, 1967.

Chandler, Alfred D., Jr. *Strategy and Structure: Chapters in the History of the Industrial Enterprise*. New York, Doubleday & Co., Anchor Books, 1966.

——. "Institutional Integration: An Approach to Comparative Studies on the History of Large-Scale Business Enterprises," in Nakagawa Keiichirō, ed., *Strategy and Structure of Big Business*, 1976, pp. 121–147.

——. *The Visible Hand: The Managerial Revolution in American Business.* Cambridge, Harvard University Press, 1977.

Chao Kang. *The Development of Cotton Textile Production in China.* Cambridge, East Asian Research Center, Harvard University, 1977.

Chiang Hai Ding. "The Early Shipping Conference System of Singapore, 1897-1911," *Journal of South East Asian History* 10.1:50-68 (March 1969).

Chō Yukio and Sumiya Kazuhiko, eds. *Kindai Nihon keizai shisōshi* (A history of modern Japanese economic thought), vol. 1. Yūhikaku, 1969.

Chōsen Yūsen Kabushiki Kaisha 25 nenshi (A 25-year history of the Korean Mail Steamship Company). Seoul, Dōshahen, 1937.

Chūō-kushi (A history of Chūō ward). Edited by Tokyo-to Chūō-kuyakusho, vol. 3. 1958.

Clark, Rodney C. *The Japanese Company.* New Haven, Yale University Press, 1979.

Conroy, Hilary. *The Japanese Seizure of Korea, 1868-1910.* Philadelphia, University of Pennsylvania Press, 1960.

Cowan, C. D., ed. *The Economic Development of China and Japan.* London, Allen & Unwin, 1964.

Craig, Albert M. *Chōshū in the Meiji Restoration.* Cambridge, Harvard University Press, 1961.

——. "Kido Kōin and Ōkubo Toshimichi: A Psychohistorical Analysis," in Craig and Donald H. Shively, eds., *Personality in Japanese History.* Berkeley, University of California Press, 1970, pp. 264-308.

Dai Nihon teikoku gikai shi (The history of the Imperial Japanese Diet). 18 vols. Dō Kankōkai, 1926-1930.

Deakin, B. M. *Shipping Conferences: A Study of Their Origins, Development and Economic Practices.* Cambridge, Cambridge University, 1973.

Drage, Charles. *Taikoo.* London, Constable, 1970.

Duus, Peter. "The Economic Bases of Meiji Imperialism: The Case of Korea, 1895-1910," unpublished paper.

Ekitei-kyoku nenpō (Annual report of the Bureau of Posts and Communications), nos. 6-11 (1876-1882).

Ekitei-ryō nenpō (Annual report of the Bureau of Posts and Communications), nos. 1-5 (1872-1876).

Enerugī to keizai hatten (Energy and economic development). Edited by Shakai Keizai Shigakkai. Fukuoka, Nishi Nihon Bunka Kyōkai, 1979.

Enomoto Morie and Kimi Nobuhiko. *Hokkaidō no rekishi* (A history of Hokkaido). Yamakawa Shuppansha, 1970.

Ericson, Steven J. "Railways in Crisis: The Financing and Management of

Japanese Railway Companies during the Panic of 1890." Unpublished paper, June 1983.

Esherick, Joseph W. *Reform and Revolution in China: The 1911 Revolution in Hunan and Hubei.* Berkeley, University of California Press, 1976.

Fairbank, John K., Edwin O. Reischauer, and Albert M. Craig. *East Asia: The Modern Transformation.* Boston, Houghton Mifflin, 1965.

Far Eastern Freight Conference. Documents. Head Office, London.

Farnie, D. A. *East and West of Suez: The Suez Canal in History, 1854–1956.* Oxford University, 1969.

Feuerwerker, Albert. *China's Early Industrialization: Sheng Hsuan-huai (1844–1916) and Mandarin Enterprise.* Cambridge, Harvard University Press, 1958.

——. "China's Nineteenth-Century Industrialization: The Case of the Hanyehping Coal and Iron Company, Limited," in C. D. Cowan, ed., *The Economic Development of China and Japan,* 1964, pp. 70–110.

——. *The Foreign Establishment in China in the Early Twentieth Century.* Michigan Papers in Chinese Studies, no. 29. Ann Arbor, University of Michigan, 1976.

Foreign Office. Records. Great Britain, Public Record Office. [FO].

Fox, Grace. *Britain and Japan, 1858–1883.* Oxford University, 1969.

Fraser, Andrew. "The Expulsion of Ōkuma from the Government in 1881," *Journal of Asian Studies* 26.2:213–236 (February 1967).

——. "Komuro Shinobu (1839–1898): A Meiji Politician and Businessman," *Papers on Far Eastern History* 3:61–83 (March 1971).

Fujimura Michio. *Nisshin sensō – Higashi Ajia kindaishi no tenkanten* (The Sino-Japanese War: Turning point in modern East Asian history). Iwanami Shoten, 1973.

Fukuzawa Yukichi zenshū (Complete works of Fukuzawa Yukichi), vols. 9–11 and 15. Iwanami Shoten, 1960–1961.

Furuta Ryōichi. "Kaijō kōtsūshi" (The history of sea transportation), in *Miyagi kenshi* (History of Miyagi prefecture), vol. 5. Sendai, Zaidan Hōjin Kankōkai, 1960, pp. 595–628.

—— and Hirai Yoshikazu. *A Short History of Japanese Merchant Shipping.* Translated by Duncan MacFarlane. Tokyo, Tokyo News Service, 1967.

Fushiki-kōshi (A history of the port of Fushiki). Dō Kaiun Shinkōkai, 1973.

Gallagher, John and Ronald Robinson. "The Imperialism of Free Trade," in Wm. Roger Louis, ed., *Imperialism: The Robinson and Gallagher Controversy,* 1976, pp. 53–72.

Godai Tomoatsu denki shiryō (Biographical materials on Godai Tomoatsu). Edited by Nihon Keieishi Kenkyūjo, 4 vols. Tōyō Keizai Shinpōsha, 1971–1974.

Great Northern Railway Company Records. Minnesota Historical Society. [GN].

Greenhill, Robert. "Shipping, 1850-1914," in D. C. M. Platt, ed., *Business Imperialism, 1840-1930: An Inquiry Based on British Experience in Latin America.* Oxford University, 1977, pp. 119-155.

Gull, E. M. *British Economic Interests in the Far East.* London, Institute of Pacific Relations, 1943.

Hackett, Roger F. *Yamagata Aritomo in the Rise of Modern Japan, 1838-1922.* Cambridge, Harvard University Press, 1971.

Hakodate kaiunshi (The history of Hakodate shipping). Hakodate-shiyakusho, 1958.

Halliday, Jon. *A Political History of Japanese Capitalism.* New York, Pantheon Books, 1975.

Hao Yen-p'ing. *The Comprador in Nineteenth Century China: Bridge Between East and West.* Cambridge, Harvard University Press, 1970.

Hara Kei nikki (The diary of Hara Kei). 6 vols. Fukumura Shuppan, 1965.

Hatade Isao. "Mitsubishi seiseiki ni okeru shihon chikuseki to tochi shoyū" (Capital accumulation and land ownership in Mitsubishi's formative period), *Rekishigaku kenkyū* 325:16-31 (June 1967); and 326:47-53 (July 1967).

———. *Nihon no zaibatsu to Mitsubishi* (Japan's zaibatsu and Mitsubishi). Rakuyū Shobō, 1978.

Havens, Thomas R. H. *Farm and Nation in Modern Japan, Agrarian Nationalism, 1870-1940.* Princeton, Princeton University Press, 1974.

Henderson, W. O. *The Rise of German Industrial Power, 1834-1914.* Berkeley, University of California Press, 1975.

Henriques, Robert. *Marcus Samuel: First Viscount Bearsted and Founder of the 'Shell' Transport and Trading Company, 1853-1927.* London, Barrie and Rockliff, 1960.

Hidemura Senzō et al., eds. *Kindai keizai no rekishiteki kiban* (The historical basis of the modern economy). Kyoto, Mineruba Shobō, 1977.

Hirohata Tadataka. *Kaiun yawa* (Evening conversations on shipping). Nihon Kaiji Gakkai Shuppanbu, 1932.

Hirota Isamu. "Tatā zaibatsu no takakuka katei" (The diversification process in the Tata Industrial Group), in Yasuoka Shigeaki, ed., *Zaibatsushi kenkyū*, 1979, pp. 227-256.

Hirschmeier, Johannes. *The Origins of Entrepreneurship in Meiji Japan.* Cambridge, Harvard University Press, 1964.

———. "Shibusawa Eiichi: Industrial Pioneer," in William W. Lockwood, ed., *The State and Economic Enterprise in Japan.* Princeton, Princeton University Press, 1965, pp. 209-247.

——— and Yui Tsunehiko. *The Development of Japanese Business, 1600–1973.* Cambridge, Harvard University Press, 1975.

Hitotsubashi Daigaku Sangyō Keiei Kenkyūjo (Hitotsubashi University, Industrial Management Research Institute). *Nippon Yūsen Kabushiki Kaisha kaikei chōbo mokuroku: Meiji 18 nen – Shōwa 19 nen* (A catalog of the N.Y.K. account books, 1885–1944). Kunitachi, 1978.

Hokkaido Tankō Kisen Kabushiki Kaisha 50 nenshi (A 50-year history of the Hokkaido Colliery & Steamship Company). Dōsha, 1939.

Hook, Elizabeth. *A Guide to the Papers of John Swire and Sons Ltd.* London, School of Oriental and African Studies, 1977.

Hoover, William Davis. "Godai Tomoatsu (1836–1885): An Economic Statesman of Early Meiji Japan." PhD dissertation, University of Michigan, 1973.

Hou Chi-ming. *Foreign Investment and Economic Development in China, 1840–1937.* Cambridge, Harvard University Press, 1965.

Hutchins, John G. B. *The American Maritime Industries and Public Policy, 1789–1914.* Cambridge, Harvard University Press, 1941.

Hyde, Francis E. *Blue Funnel: A History of Alfred Holt and Company of Liverpool from 1865 to 1914.* Liverpool, Liverpool University Press, 1957.

———. *Liverpool and the Mersey: An Economic History of a Port, 1700–1970.* Newton Abbot, David & Charles, 1971.

———. *Far Eastern Trade, 1860–1914.* London, A. & C. Black, 1973.

———. *Cunard and the North Atlantic, 1840–1973: A History of Shipping and Financial Management.* London, Macmillan, 1975.

Inagaki Sumio, "'Jigyō hōkokusho': seiritsu katei ni okeru kigyō jōhō no kaishi" (The business report [NYK] : Disclosure of business information at the time of the company's establishment), *Keiei zaimu* (Zeimu Kenkyūkai), Nos. 1485–1487, June 2, 9, and 16, 1980, pp. 15–21, 11–16, 12–17.

Inoue Yōichirō. "Nihon kindai zōsengyō kakuritsuki ni okeru Mitsubishi Nagasaki Zōsenjo" (The Mitsubishi Nagasaki Shipyard during the period of the establishment of the modern Japanese shipbuilding industry), *Keiei shigaku* 3.1:33–50 (March 1968).

———. "Meiji kōki no kaiji seisaku" (Maritime policy in the late Meiji period), in Andō Yoshio, ed., *Nihon keizai seisaku shiron*, 1973, pp. 159–205.

Institute of Pacific Relations, ed. *Problems of the Pacific, 1931.* Chicago, University of Chicago Press, 1932.

Irimajiri Yoshinaga. *Iwasaki Yatarō* (Biography). Yoshikawa Kōbunkan, 1960.

Iriye, Akira. *Pacific Estrangement: Japanese and American Expansion, 1897–1911.* Cambridge, Harvard University Press, 1972.

———. "Robinson and Gallagher in the Far East: Japanese Imperialism," in Wm. Roger Louis, ed., *Imperialism*, 1976, pp. 222–225.

Ishii Kanji. "Nisshin sengo keiei" (Business after the Sino-Japanese War),

Iwanami kōza, Nihon rekishi, vol. 16, *Kindai* III. Iwanami Shoten, 1976, pp. 47–94.

Itō Yonejirō. *Nihon no kaiun* (Japanese shipping). Hōbunkan, 1922.

Iwai Ryōtarō. *Mitsui Mitsubishi monogatari* (Stories of Mitsui and Mitsubishi). Chikura Shobō, 1934.

———. *Kagami Kenkichi den Katō Takeo den* (Biographies of Kagami Kenkichi and Katō Takeo). Tōyō Shokan, 1955.

Iwakura kō jikki (Authentic records of Prince Iwakura). Edited by Iwakura Kō Kyūseki Hozonkai, 3 vols., 1927.

Iwasaki Hisaya den (Biography of Iwasaki Hisaya). Dō Hensan Iinkai, 1961.

Iwasaki Koyata den (Biography of Iwasaki Koyata). Dō Hensan Iinkai, 1957.

Iwasaki Yanosuke den (Biography of Iwasaki Yanosuke). Iwasaki Yatarō-Iwasaki Yanosuke Denki Hensankai, 2 vols., 1971.

Iwasaki Yatarō den (Biography of Iwasaki Yatarō). Iwasaki Yatarō-Iwasaki Yanosuke Denki Hensankai, 2 vols., 1967.

Iwasaki Yatarō nikki (The diary of Iwasaki Yatarō). Iwasaki Yatarō-Iwasaki Yanosuke Denki Hensankai, 1975.

Iwata, Masakazu. *Ōkubo Toshimichi: The Bismarck of Japan.* Berkeley, University of California Press, 1964.

Jansen, Marius B. "Yawata, Hanyehping, and the Twenty-One Demands," *Pacific Historical Review* 23:31–48 (February 1954).

———. *Sakamoto Ryōma and the Meiji Restoration.* Princeton, Princeton University Press, 1961.

———. *The Japanese and Sun Yat-sen.* Stanford Paperback, 1970.

Japan Gazette. July and August, 1881.

Japan Weekly Mail [JWM].

Jardine, Matheson & Co. Ltd. Archives, Cambridge University.

Jennings, Eric. *Cargoes: A Centenary Story of the Far Eastern Freight Conference.* Singapore, Meridian Communications, 1980.

Jinteki jigyō taikei (Businesses and their leaders) 5 *Kaiun bōeki hen* (Shipping and trade volume). Chūgai Sangyō Chōsakai, 1940.

John Swire and Sons Ltd. Archives, School of Oriental and African Studies, University of London. [JSS].

Johnson, Chalmers. *Japan's Public Policy Companies.* Washington, D.C., American Enterprise Institute for Public Policy Research, 1978.

———. *MITI and the Japanese Miracle: The Growth of Industrial Policy, 1925–1975.* Stanford, Stanford University Press, 1982.

Kaiun shiryō (Historical materials on sea transport). Edited by Koshino Kiyone, 3 vols., 1886. [KS].

Kaji Teruyoshi. "Meiji shoki ni okeru kaiun seisaku tenkan" (The change in shipping policy in the early Meiji period), *Shōdai ronshū*. Kobe Shōka Daigaku. 24.4:78–93 (November 1972).

——. "Mitsubishi zaibatsu no seisei to kaiun" (The formation of the Mitsubishi zaibatsu and shipping), *Shōdai ronshū* 25.1–3:137–163 (September 1974).

——. "Kyōdō Un'yu Kaisha no setsuritsu" (The establishment of the KUK), *Kaiun keizai kenkyū*. Nihon Kaiun Keizai Gakkai. 8:1–25 (1974).

Kajinishi Mitsuhaya. *Seishō* (Political merchants). Chikuma Shobō, 1963.

Kamachi, Noriko. "The Chinese in Meiji Japan: Their Interaction with the Japanese before the Sino-Japanese War," in Akira Iriye, ed., *The Chinese and the Japanese: Essays in Political and Cultural Interactions*. Princeton, Princeton University Press, 1980, pp. 58–73.

Kaplan, Eugene J. *Japan: The Government-Business Relationship*. Washington, D.C., U.S. Department of Commerce, Bureau of International Commerce, 1972.

Katayama Kunio. "Osaka Shōsen Nanyōsen no zenshi: shisatsu fukumeisho o chūshin to shite" (O.S.K. research reports on Southeast Asia prior to the opening of its Java line), *Tōnan Ajia kenkyū* 19.4:388–411 (March 1982).

Katō Kōmei den (Biography of Katō Kōmei). Dō Kankōkai, 1928.

Katsuta Magoya. *Ōkubo Toshimichi den* (Biography of Ōkubo Toshimichi). 3 vols. Dōbunkan, 1910.

Kawabe Nobuo. "Japanese Business in the United States before World War II: The Case of Mitsubishi Shoji Kaisha, The San Francisco and Seattle Branches." PhD dissertation, The Ohio State University, 1980.

Kawasaki Kisen 50 nenshi (A 50-year history of the Kawasaki Steamship Company). Kobe, Dōshahen, 1969.

Keene, Donald. *The Japanese Discovery of Europe, 1720–1830*. Rev. ed. Stanford, Stanford University Press, 1969.

Kemble, John Haskell. "A Hundred Years of the Pacific Mail," *American Neptune* 10.2:123–143 (April 1950).

Kim, C. I, and Han-kyo Kim. *Korea and the Politics of Imperialism, 1876–1910*. Berkeley, University of California Press, 1967.

Kobayashi Masaaki. "'Kindai sangyō no keisei to kangyō haraisage" (The formation of modern industry and the sale of government enterprises), in Kajinishi Mitsuhaya, ed., *Nihon keizaishi taikei* (A general outline of Japanese economic history), vol. 5, *Kindai* I. Tokyo Daigaku Shuppankai, 1965, pp. 291–355.

——. "Nagasaki Zōsenjo no haraisage" (The government sale of the Nagasaki Shipyard), *Keizaikei*. Kantō Gakuin Daigaku. 73:13–29 (June 1967).

——. "Nihon no kōgyōka to kangyō haraisage" (Japan's early industrialization and the sale of government enterprises), *Keiei shigaku* 6.1:69–90 (September 1971).

——. "Takashima Tankō ni okeru kanshū to haraisage" (The acquisition and sale of government enterprise: The case of the Takashima Coal Mine), *Keizaikei.* Kantō Gakuin Daigaku. 101:90–107 (October 1974).

——. "Takashima Tankō ni okeru Mitsubishi baishū no igi" (The significance of Mitsubishi's purchase of the Takashima Coal Mine), *Keizaikei.* Kantō Gakuin Daigaku. 102 & 103:113–130 (March 10, 1975).

——. "Seishō to kangyō haraisage" (Political merchants and the sale of government enterprises), in *Kōgyōka to kigyōsha katsudō* (Industrialization and entrepreneurship). Edited by Yui Tsunehiko, vol. 2 of *Nihon keieishi kōza.* Nihon Keizai Shinbunsha, 1976, pp. 85–117.

——. *Nihon no kōgyōka to kangyō haraisage: seifu to kigyō* (The industrialization of Japan and the sale of government enterprises: Government and business). Tōyō Keizai Shinpōsha, 1977.

——. *Yawata Seitetsujo* (The Yawata Iron and Steel Works). Kyōikusha, 1977.

——. "Zaibatsu to tankōgyō: Mitsubishi o chūshin ni" (The zaibatsu and coal mining: The case of Mitsubishi), in *Enerugi to keizai hatten,* 1979, pp. 189–215.

——. *Kaiungyō no rōdō mondai* (Labor problems in the shipping industry). Vol. 2 of *Nihon kaiun keieishi,* 1980.

——. *Kindai Nihon keizaishi* (Modern Japanese economic history). Sekai Shoin, 1983.

Kokaze Hidemasa. "Meiji kōki ni okeru kaiun seisaku no tenkai: Enyō kōro hojosaku o chūshin ni" (The development of shipping policy in late Meiji: Subsidization of transoceanic lines), *Shakai keizai shigaku* 48.3:262–285 (August 1982).

Kojima Shōtarō. *Kaiun dōmeiron* (A discussion of shipping conferences). Yūhikaku, 1926.

Kondō Renpei. "Japanese Communications: The Mercantile Marine," in Ōkuma Shigenobu, ed., *Fifty Years of New Japan,* vol. 1, pp. 447–464.

Kondō Tetsuo. "Shokusan kōgyō to zairai sangyō" (Industrial promotion and traditional industries), *Iwanami kōza, Nihon rekishi,* vol. 14, *Kindai* I. Iwanami Shoten, 1975, pp. 209–254.

Kōzuma Yukihide. *Miike Tankōshi* (A history of the Miike Coal Mine). Kyōikusha, 1980.

Kubicek, Robert V. *Economic Imperialism in Theory and Practice: The Case of South African Gold Mining Finance, 1886–1914.* Durham, N.C., Duke University Press, 1979.

"Kyōdō Un'yu Kaisha sōritsu gaikyō" (The general situation of the establishment of the Union Transport Company). Pamphlet. N.d.

Lebra, Joyce C. *Ōkuma Shigenobu: Statesman of Meiji Japan.* Canberra, Australian National University Press, 1973.

Liu, Kwang-Ching. *Anglo-American Steamship Rivalry in China, 1862–1874.* Cambridge, Harvard University Press, 1962.

——. "British-Chinese Steamship Rivalry in China, 1873–85," in C. D. Cowan, ed., *The Economic Development of China and Japan,* 1964, pp. 49–78.

Lockwood, William W. *The Economic Development of Japan: Growth and Structural Change, 1868–1938.* Princeton, Princeton University Press, 1954.

Louis, Wm. Roger, ed. *Imperialism: The Robinson and Gallagher Controversy.* New York, New Viewpoints, 1976.

Lowe, Peter. *Great Britain and Japan, 1911–1915: A Study of British Far Eastern Policy.* London, Macmillan, 1969.

Lu, David John. *Sources of Japanese History,* vol. 2. New York, McGraw-Hill, 1973.

McKay, John P. *Pioneers for Profit: Foreign Enterpreneurship and Russian Industrialization, 1885–1913.* Chicago, University of Chicago Press, 1970.

MacMurray, John V. A., comp. *Treaties and Agreements with and Concerning China, 1894–1919.* Vol. 1, *Manchu Period, 1894–1911.* 2 vols. New York, Oxford University Press, 1921.

Maejima Hisoka. *Jijoden* (Autobiography). Dō Denki Kankōkai, 1956.

Maejima Hisoka: yūbin sōgyōdan (Maejima Hisoka: Stories of the establishment of the postal service). Dō Denki Kankōkai, 1956.

Maejima Shōzō. *Meiji chūmatsuki no kanryō seiji* (Bureaucratic politics of middle and late Meiji). Kyoto, Chōbunsha, 1964.

Marriner, Sheila and F. E. Hyde. *The Senior: John Samuel Swire, 1825–1898.* Liverpool, Liverpool University Press, 1967.

Marshall, Byron K. *Capitalism and Nationalism in Prewar Japan: The Ideology of the Business Elite, 1868–1941.* Stanford, Stanford University Press, 1967.

Marx, Daniel, Jr. *International Shipping Cartels: A Study of Industrial Self-Regulation by Shipping Conferences.* Princeton, Princeton University Press, 1953.

Masaki Hisashi. "Zaibatsu no seiritsu to sono heisateki kin'yū" (The formation of the zaibatsu and their closed finance), *Dōshisha shōgaku* 24.1:45–75 (July 1972).

Masuda Takashi. *Jijo Masuda Takashi ō den* (The autobiography of Masuda Takashi). Uchida Rōkakuho, 1939.

Mathias, P. and A. W. H. Pearsall. *Shipping: A Survey of Historical Records.* Newton Abbot, David & Charles, 1971.

"Matsukata haku zaisei ronsakushū" (Collected financial memoranda of Count Matsukata), in Tsuchiya Takao and Ōuchi Hyōe, comps., *Meiji zenki zaisei keizai shiryō shūsei,* vol. 1 (1931), pp. 257–655.

Matsukata ke monjo (Papers of Matsukata Masayoshi). In the Finance Ministry Archives.

Matsumoto Hiroshi. *Mitsui zaibatsu no kenkyū* (Studies of the Mitsui zaibatsu). Yoshikawa Kōbunkan, 1979.

Matsuo [Shigeyoshi] ke monjo [Papers of Matsuo Shigeyoshi]. In the Finance Ministry Archives.

Matsushita, D., comp. *Marine Transport and Foreign Trade*. Chūgai Sangyō Chōsakai, 1919.

Meiji Japan Through Contemporary Sources, vol. 3, *1869-1894*. Tokyo, The Centre for East Asian Cultural Studies, 1972.

Meiji un'yushi (A history of Meiji transport). Nippōsha, 1913.

Meiji zaiseishi (Meiji financial history). Edited by Ōkurashōnai Dō Hensankai. 15 vols. 1904-1905. Reprint. Yoshikawa Kōbunkan, 1971.

Milne, T. E. "British Shipping in the 19th Century: A Study of the Ben Line," in Peter L. Payne, ed., *Studies in Scottish Business History*. London, Frank Cass & Co., 1967, pp. 345-366.

Mishima Yasuo. "Mitsubishi Shōji: zaibatsugata shōsha no keisei" (The formation of a zaibatsu-type general trading company: The case of Mitsubishi Shōji), *Keiei shigaku* 8.1:8-25 (August 1973).

———. "Sōgō shōsha: sengo ni okeru kenkyūshi" (General trading companies: Historical research in the postwar period), in *Nihon no zaibatsu* (Japan's zaibatsu). Edited by Yasuoka Shigeaki. Vol. 3 of *Nihon keieishi kōza*. Nihon Keizai Shinbunsha, 1976, pp. 225-254.

———. "Sekitan yushutsu shōsha kara sōgō shōsha e: Mitsubishi Shōji" (Mitsubishi Shōji: From coal exporter to general trading company), in Miyamoto Mataji et al., eds., *Sōgō shōsha no keieishi*, 1976, pp. 121-174.

———. "Kawasaki Shōzō no zaisan chikuseki katei" (The accumulation process in Kawasaki Shōzō's fortune), *Keiei shigaku* 12.3:1-21 (June 1978).

———. *Mitsubishi zaibatsushi: Meiji hen* (The history of the Mitsubishi zaibatsu: The Meiji period). Kyōikusha, 1979.

———, ed. *Mitsubishi zaibatsu* (The Mitsubishi zaibatsu), in *Nihon zaibatsu keieishi* (The business history of the Japanese zaibatsu). Nihon Keizai Shinbunsha, 1982.

Mitsubishi Fact Book '82 [in Japanese]. Mitsubishi Kōhō Iinkai, 1982.

Mitsubishi Ginkōshi (A history of the Mitsubishi Bank). Dō Hensan Iinkai. Special ed., 1959.

Mitsubishi Gōshi Kaisha: Sha shi (1894-1914) (Mitsubishi limited partnership: Company records). Reissued as part of *Mitsubishi Sha shi* (Records of the Mitsubishi Company). Edited by Mitsubishi Sha Shi Kankokai. Tokyo Daigaku Shuppankai, 1980-1982.

Mitsubishi Sha shi (1870-1893) (Records of the Mitsubishi Company).

Edited by Mitsubishi Gōshi Kaisha Sōmu-bu Chōsa-ka. 1910–1919. [M Sha shi].

Mitsubishi Shōji Kabushiki Kaisha, ed. *Ritsugyō bōeki roku* (Records of trading enterprises). Dōsha, 1958.

Mitsubishi zaibatsu ni okeru shikin chōtatsu to shihai (Fund acquisition and control in the Mitsubishi zaibatsu). Edited by Mitsubishi Keizai Kenkyūjo. Prepared for the Keizai Kikakuchō Chōsa-kyoku Chōsa-ka, no. 6 (April 12, 1959).

"Mitsui Bussan Kaisha to Ueda Yasusaburō," (The Mitsui Trading Company and Ueda Yasusaburō), *Mitsui bunko ronsō* 7:201–319 (1973).

Mitsui Bussan shōshi (A short history of Mitsui Trading Company). The Company, reprint, 1965.

Mitsui Ginkō 80 nenshi (An 80-year history of the Mitsui Bank). Dō Hensan Iinkai, 1957.

Mitsui Senpaku Kabushiki Kaisha sōgyō 80 nenshi (A history of the Mitsui Shipping Company through 80 years of business). Dōshahen, 1958.

Miwa Ryōichi. "Bonbei kōro kaisetsu" (The opening of the Bombay line), *Ekonomisuto*, January 17, 1967, pp. 84–89.

———. "Suijō kōtsū" (Water transportation), in Toyoda Takeshi and Kodama Kōta, eds., *Kōtsūshi*, 1970, pp. 477–488.

———. "Kaijō yusō" (Maritime transport), in Andō Yoshio and Matsuyoshi Sadao, eds., *Nihon yusōshi* (A history of Japanese transport). Nihon Hyōronsha, 1971, pp. 385–474.

Miyamoto Mataji. "Kaisō Kaisha no kōhai" (The rise and fall of the Marine Transportation Company), in *Uozumi sensei koki kinen ronsō* (Essays to commemorate Professor Uozumi's 70th birthday). Suitashi, Kansai Daigaku, 1959, pp. 645–668.

———. "Nihon Seifu Yūbin Jōkisen Kaisha ni tsuite" (The Japanese Government Mail Steamship Company). *Osaka Daigaku keizaigaku* 9.1:1–32 (July 1959).

———. *Onogumi no kenkyū* (A study of the Onogumi). 4 vols. Ōhara Shinseisha, 1970.

———. *Meiji zenki keizaishi no kenkyū* (Studies in early Meiji economic history). Osaka, Seibundō, 1971.

——— and Sakudō Yōtarō, eds. *Sumitomo no keiei shiteki kenkyū* (Historical studies of Sumitomo business). Jikkyō, 1979.

——— et al., eds. *Sōgō shōsha no keieishi* (The business history of general trading companies). Tōyō Keizai Shinpōsha, 1976.

Miyamoto Seishirō. *Kaiun dōmei seidoron* (An examination of the shipping conference system). Kaibundō, 1978.

Mizumachi [Kesaroku] ke monjo (The Mizumachi family papers). Finance Ministry Archives.

Morikawa Hidemasa. "The Organizational Structure of the Mitsubishi and

Mitsui Zaibatsu, 1868–1922: A Comparative Study," *Business History Review* 44.1: 62–83 (Spring 1970).

——. *Nihongata keiei no genryū* (The origins of Japanese-style management). Tōyō Keizai Shinpōsha, 1973.

——. *Nihon zaibatsushi* (A history of the Japanese zaibatsu). Kyōikusha, 1978.

——. "Nihon zaibatsu no keiei senryaku: ishi kettei katei o chūshin ni" (Zaibatsu business strategy: The decision-making process), *Keiei shigaku* 13.1:30–51 (October 1978).

——. *Zaibatsu no keiei shiteki kenkyū* (Historical studies of zaibatsu management). Tōyō Keizai Shinpōsha, 1980.

——. *Nihon keieishi* (Japanese management history). Nihon Keizai Shinbunsha, 1981.

——. "Iwasaki Yanosuke jidai no Mitsubishi no toppu manejimento" (Mitsubishi's top management during the period of Iwasaki Yanosuke), in Tsuchiya Moriaki and Morikawa Hidemasa, eds., *Kigyōsha katsudō no shiteki kenkyū*, 1981, pp. 49–66.

Murakami Katsuhiko. "Shokuminchi" (Colonies), in Ōishi Kaichiro, ed., *Nihon sangyō kakumei no kenkyū*, vol. 2, 1975, pp. 229–314.

Murase Shin'ya. "The Most-Favored-Nation Treatment in Japan's Treaty Practice During the Period 1854–1905," *American Journal of International Law* 70.2:273–297 (April 1976).

Nagaoka Shinkichi. "Nisshin sengo no zaisei seisaku to baishōkin" (Financial policy after the Sino-Japanese War and the indemnity), in Andō Yoshio, ed., *Nihon keizai seisaku shiron*, vol. 1, 1973, pp. 111–158.

Nagasawa Yasuaki. "Iwasaki Yatarō to Mitsubishi no hasshō" (Iwasaki Yatarō and the origins of Mitsubishi), in Miyamoto Mataji, ed., *Kamigata no kenkyū* (Studies of the Osaka area). Osaka, Seibundō, 1976.

——. "Shoki Mitsubishi no keiei soshiki: kaiungyō o chūshin ni shite" (Mitsubishi's early management organization: The shipping industry), *Keiei shigaku* 11.3:26–49 (March 1977).

——. "Shoki Mitsubishi no keiei soshiki: kōzan, tankō o chūshin to shite" (Mitsubishi's early management organization: Metal and coal mining), in Hidemura Senzō et al., eds., *Kindai keizai no rekishiteki kiban*, 1977, pp. 418–434.

——. "Meijiki Mitsubishi no toppu manejimento soshiki" (Mitsubishi's top management organization during the Meiji period), *Keiei shigaku* 14.1: 28–45 (September 1979).

Nagata Masaomi. *Meijiki keizai dantai no kenkyū* (Studies of economic organizations in the Meiji period). Nikkan Rōdō Tsūshinsha, 1967.

Najita, Tetsuo. *Hara Kei and the Politics of Compromise, 1905–1915.* Cambridge, Harvard University Press, 1967.

Nakagawa Keiichirō. "P. & O. Kisen Kaisha no seiritsu" (The formation of the P. & O.), *Keizaigaku ronshū* 26.1 & 2:276–301 (March 1959).

——. "Nihon no kōgyōka katei ni okeru soshikika sareta kigyōsha katsudō" (Organized entrepreneurship in the process of Japan's industrialization), *Keiei shigaku* 2.3:8–37 (November 1967).

——. "Business Strategy and Industrial Structure in Pre-World War II Japan," in Nakagawa, ed., *Strategy and Structure of Big Business*, 1976, pp. 3–38.

——. "Japanese Shipping in the Interwar Period." Unpublished paper.

——. *Ryōtaisenkan no Nihon kaiungyō* (Japanese Shipping in the Inter-War Period). Vol. 1 of *Nihon kaiun keieishi*. 1980.

——. "Ryōtaisenkan no Nihon kaiun" (Japanese shipping in the Inter-War Period), in Nakamura Takafusa, ed., *Senkanki no Nihon keizai bunseki* (Analyses of the Japanese economy during the Inter-War Years). Yamakawa Shuppansha, 1981, pp. 251–280.

——, ed. *Strategy and Structure of Big Business*. Vol. 1 of *International Conference on Business History*. Tokyo University, n.d. [1976].

——, ed. *Marketing and Finance in the Course of Industrialization*. Vol. 3 of *International Conference on Business History*. Tokyo University, n.d. [1978].

——, ed. *Government and Business*. Vol. 5 of *International Conference on Business History*, Tokyo University, 1980.

—— and Yui Tsunehiko, eds. *Keiei tetsugaku, keiei rinen: Meiji-Taishō* (Business philosophy: Ideas on management in the Meiji and Taishō periods). Daiyamondosha, 1969.

—— et al., eds. *Kindai Nihon keieishi no kiso chishiki* (Basic information on modern Japanese business history). Yūhikaku, 1974.

Nakahashi Tokugorō (Biography). 2 vols. Dō ō Denki Hensankai, 1944.

Nakamigawa Hikojirō denki shiryō (Biographical materials on Nakamigawa Hikojirō). Edited by Nihon Keieishi Kenkyūjo. Tōyō Keizai Shinpōsha, 1969.

Nakamura Masanori. "Nihon burujoaji no kōsei" (The composition of Japan's bourgeoisie), in Ōishi Kaichirō, ed., *Nihon sangyō kakumei no kenkyū*, vol. 2, 1975, pp. 65–128.

Nakamura Naomi. *Ōkuma Shigenobu* (Biography). Yoshikawa Kōbunkan, 1961.

——. *Ōkuma zaisei no kenkyū* (Studies of Ōkuma's finance). Azekura Shobō, 1968.

Nakamura Tadashi. "Chōsha kaikō zengo: Nihon shihonshugi to Konanshō" (The context of the opening of Changsha: Japanese capitalism and Hunan province), *Rekishigaku kenkyū* 425:1–13 (October 1975).

Nakamura Takafusa, ed. *Senkanki no Nihon keizai bunseki* (Analyses of the Japanese economy during the Inter-War Years). Yamakawa Shuppansha, 1981.

Nakanishi Ken'ichi. *Nihon shiyū tetsudōshi kenkyū* (Studies in the history of Japan's private railways). Nihon Hyōronsha, 1963.

Nichimen 70 nenshi (A 70-year history of Nichimen). Dō Shashi Hensan Iinkai, 1962.

Nihon Ginkō 80 nenshi (An 80-year history of the Bank of Japan). Edited by Nihon Ginkō Shiryō Chōsa Shitsu, 1962.

Nihon kaiun keieishi (History of the Japanese shipping business). 6 vols. Edited by Kaiji Sangyō Kenkyūjo. Nihon Keizai Shinbunsha, 1980-1984.

Nihon keieishi kōza (Japanese business history series). Edited by Miyamoto Mataji and Nakagawa Keiichirō. Nihon Keizai Shinbunsha, 1976-1977.

Nihon kōgyō ginkō 50 nenshi (A 50-year history of the Japan Industrial Bank). Dō Rinji Shiryō Shitsu, 1957.

Nippon Yūsen Kabushiki Kaisha 50 nenshi (A 50-year history of the N.Y.K.). Dōshahen, 1935.

Nippon Yūsen Kabushiki Kaisha 70 nenshi (A 70-year history of the N.Y.K.). Dōshahen, 1956.

Nippon Yūsen Kabushiki Kaisha eigyō hōkokusho (N.Y.K. business report). 1899-1914. [NYK-EH].

Nippon Yūsen Kabushiki Kaisha jigyō hōkokusho (N.Y.K. business report). 1894-1899. [NYK-JH].

Nippon Yūsen Kabushiki Kaisha kabunushi seimeibo (N.Y.K. stockholders list). 1895-1914. [NYK-KNS].

Nippon Yūsen Kabushiki Kaisha kabunushi sōkai gijiroku (Minutes of the N.Y.K. stockholders meetings). 1894-1914. [NYK-KSG].

Nippon Yūsen Kabushiki Kaisha Otaru Shiten (N.Y.K. Otaru Branch Office). Hokkaidō ni okeru Nippon Yūsen shōshi (A short history of the N.Y.K. in Hokkaido). October, 1962.

Nippon Yūsen Kabushiki Kaisha. *Shaki ruisan* (Collected company regulations). N.d.

Nippon Yūsen Kabushiki Kaisha torishimariyakukai gijiroku (Minutes of the N.Y.K. directors meetings). 1893-1914. [NYK-TG].

Nippon Yūsen Kaisha hōkoku (N.Y.K. business report). 1887-1893. [NYK-H].

Nippon Yūsen Kaisha kabunushi seimeibo (N.Y.K. stockholders list). 1892. [NYK-KNS].

Nippon Yūsen Kaisha kabunushi sōkai gijiroku (Minutes of the N.Y.K. stockholders meetings). 1887-1893. [NYK-KSG].

Nippon Yusen Kaisha. *Golden Jubilee History of the Nippon Yusen Kaisha, 1885-1935*. 1935.

(NYK). Miscellaneous material in the Sha Shi Hensan Shitsu (Company History Office):

——. Gian (Measures). Keikei-ka (Accounting Department). 1894-1902 and 1909-1914.

——. Gian tsuzurikomi (A file on measures). Kaikei-ka (Accounting Department). 1903–1908.

——. Hōkoku (Reports). Gaikō-ka no bu (Foreign Lines Department). 1912–1914. [HG].

——. Hōkoku (Reports). Kaikei no bu and Kaikei-ka no bu (Accounting Department). 1893–1914. [HK].

——. Ketsugi roku (Records of decisions). Kaikei-ka (Accounting Department). 1895–1914.

——. Ketsugi yōkenroku (Important records of decisions). Kaikei-ka and Kaikei-kakari (Accounting Department and Section). 1886–1896.

——. Sho kanjō setsumeisho (Explanations of various accounts). 1899–1913. [SKS].

——. Teishutsu shiryō (Submitted material). [Unsorted documents used for *NYK 50 nenshi*].

——. Torishimariyakukai gian (Measures of the Board of Directors). 1893–1914.

——. Torishimariyakukai hōkoku (Report to the Board of Directors). Kamotsu-ka Gaikō (Freight Department, Foreign Lines). 1898–1911. [TH-KG].

——. Torishimariyakukai hōkoku (Report to the Board of Directors). Kamotsu-ka Naikō (Freight Department, Domestic Lines). 1901–1908.

Nish, Ian H. *The Anglo-Japanese Alliance: The Diplomacy of Two Island Empires, 1894–1907.* London, The Athlone Press, 1966.

Nishikawa Yoshirō. "Nippon Yūsen Kabushiki Kaisha kyūchōbo shiryō oboegaki" (Notes on the N.Y.K.'s old ledger books), *Hitotsubashi Daigaku kenkyū nenpō shōgaku kenkyū* 21:85–158 (1979).

Nishino Kiyosaku. *Hanseiki zaikai sokumenshi* (Half a century of the business world: A side view of its annals). Tōyō Keizai Shuppanbu, 1932.

Nisshin Kisen Kabushiki Kaisha 30 nenshi oyobi tsuiho (A 30-year history of the Japan-China Steamship Company [with appendixes]). Dōshahen, 1941.

Noda Kazuo. *Zaibatsu* (The zaibatsu). Chūō Kōronsha, 1967.

Noda Masaho. "Corporate Finance of Railroad Companies in Meiji Japan," in Nakagawa Keiichirō, ed., *Marketing and Finance in the Course of Industrialization,* 1978, pp. 87–101.

Noda Nobuo. "Nihon zaibatsushi e no kiyo" (Some comments on the history of the Japanese zaibatsu), *Keiei shigaku* 5.1:94–113 (October 1970).

Nomura Jiichirō. *Waga kaiun 60 nen.* (Sixty years of our shipping). Kokusai Kaiun Shinbunsha, 1955.

North, Douglass. "Ocean Freight Rates and Economic Development, 1750–1913," *Journal of Economic History* 18.4:537–555 (December 1958).

Obata Kyugoro. *An Interpretation of the Life of Viscount Shibusawa.* Tokyo, Shibusawa Seien ō Kinenkai, 1939.

Ocean Transport & Trading Limited. Archives, Liverpool.

Ōe Shinobu. *Nihon no sangyō kakumei.* (Japan's industrial revolution). Iwanami Shoten, 1968.

Ōishi Kaichirō, ed. *Nihon sangyō kakumei no kenkyū* (Studies of Japan's industrial revolution), vol. 2. Tokyo Daigaku Shuppankai, 1975.

Okamoto, Shumpei. *The Japanese Oligarchy and the Russo-Japanese War.* New York, Columbia University Press, 1970.

Okaniwa Hiroshi. *Nihon kaiun kin'yū hattatsushi* (The historical development of shipping finance in Japan). Privately printed. December 1959.

Okazaki Yukihisa. *Waga kaiun 40 nen no tsuisō* (Reminiscences on 40 years of our shipping). Kobe, Nihon Kaiun Shūkaijonai, 1955.

Ōkubo Toshimichi monjo (Papers of Ōkubo Toshimichi). Edited by Nihon Shiseki Kyōkai. 10 vols., 1927–1929.

Ōkuma monjo (Papers of Ōkuma Shigenobu). In Waseda University. [OM].

Ōkuma monjo (Papers of Ōkuma Shigenobu). 5 vols. Waseda Daigaku Shakai Kagaku Kenkyūjo, 1958–1962.

Ōkuma monjo mokuroku (A catalog of the Ōkuma papers). Edited by Waseda Daigaku Ōkuma Kenkyū Shitsu, 1952.

Ōkuma Shigenobu, ed. *Fifty Years of New Japan,* vol. 1. 1910. Reprint. New York, Kraus Reprint Co., 1970.

Ōkuma Shigenobu kankei monjo (Papers related to Ōkuma Shigenobu). Edited by Watanabe Ikujirō. 6 vols. Waseda Daigaku, 1932–1935.

"Ōkurashō enkakushi" (Records of the development of the Finance Ministry). 2 vols., in Tsuchiya Takao and Ōuchi Hyōe, comps., *Meiji zenki zaisei keizai shiryō shūsei.* Vols. 2 and 3 (1934).

Okutani Matsuji. *Shinagawa Yajirō den* (Biography of Shinagawa Yajirō). Kōyō Shoin, 1940.

Osaka Shōsen Kabushiki Kaisha 50 nenshi (A 50-year history of the O.S.K.). Osaka, Dōshahen, 1934.

—— *80 nenshi* (An 80-year history of the O.S.K.). Osaka, Osaka Shōsen Mitsui Senpaku Kabushiki Kaisha, 1966.

Ōta Shume. "Bakumatsu no Nagasaki to Iwasaki Yatarō" (Nagasaki during the Bakumatsu and Iwasaki Yatarō), *Nagasaki dansō* 44:1–26 (February 25, 1966).

Owen, Roger and Bob Sutcliffe, eds. *Studies in the Theory of Imperialism.* London, Longman, 1972.

P. & O. Management Report to the Board. P. &. O. Archives. National Maritime Museum. Greenwich. [P&O].

P. & O. Minute Book. P. & O. Library, Head Office, London.

Pascale, Richard Tanner and Anthony G. Athos. *The Art of Japanese Management: Applications for American Executives.* New York, Warner Books, 1982.

Patrick, Hugh T. "Japan, 1868–1914," in Rondo Cameron, ed., *Banking in the Early Stages of Industrialization.* Oxford University, 1967, pp. 239–289.

Platt, D. C.M. "Economic Imperialism and the Businessman: Britain and Latin America before 1914," in Roger Owen and Bob Sutcliffe, eds., *Studies in the Theory of Imperialism.* 1972, pp. 295–311.

——, ed. *Business Imperialism, 1840–1930: An Inquiry Based on British Experience in Latin America.* Oxford University, 1977.

Pollard, Sidney and Paul Robertson. *The British Shipbuilding Industry, 1870–1914.* Cambridge, Harvard University Press, 1979.

Report from the Select Committee on Steamship Subsidies. British Parliamentary Papers, vol. 8, 1901 and vol. 9, 1902.

Roberts, John G. *Mitsui: Three Centuries of Japanese Business.* Tokyo, Weatherhill, 1973.

Robinson, Ronald. "Non-European Foundations of European Imperialism: Sketch for a Theory of Collaboration," in Roger Owen and Bob Sutcliffe, eds., *Studies in the Theory of Imperialism,* 1972, pp. 117–142.

Rosovsky, Henry. *Capital Formation in Japan: 1868–1940.* Glencoe, Free Press, 1961.

Royal Commission on Shipping Rings. British Parliamentary Papers, vols. 47–49, 1909.

Saitō Yoshihisa. "Meiji shonen no kaiun seisaku" (Japanese shipping policy in the early Meiji period), *Dōshisha shōgaku* 22.5–6:60–86 (March 1971).

——. "Mitsui Bussan Kaisha ni okeru kaiungyō" (The shipping enterprise of the Mitsui Trading Company), in Yasuoka Shigeaki, ed., *Zaibatsushi kenkyū,* 1979, pp. 105–145.

Sampson, Anthony. *The Seven Sisters: The Great Oil Companies & the World They Shaped.* New York, Bantam Books, 1976.

Sangyō Seisakushi Kenkyūjo. *Wagakuni dai kigyō no keisei hatten katei* (Japanese large enterprises: Their process of formation and development). Tsūshō Sangyō Chōsakai Toranomon Bunshitsu, 1976. [Prepared by Nakamura Seishi].

Sanuki Toshio. *Sangyō kōzō* (Industrial structure). Nihon Keizai Shinbunsha, 1981.

Sasaki Seiji. *Nihon kaiun kyōsōshi josetsu* (An introduction to the history of Japanese shipping competition). Kobe, Kaiji Kenkyūkai, 1954.

——. "Mitsui kaiungyō no seisei" (The inception of the Mitsui shipping business), *Kokusai keizai kenkyū* 9:187–205 (1959).

——. *Nihon kaiungyō no kindaika* (The modernization of Japan's shipping industry). Kobe, Kaibundō, 1961.

——. "Sensō to Nihon kindai kaiungyō" (War and Japan's modern shipping industry), *Kaiun keizai kenkyū*. Nihon Kaiun Keizai Gakkai. 14:19–36 (1980).

——. "Kindai kaiungyō no hatten to zaibatsu" (The development of the modern shipping industry and the zaibatsu), *Keizai keiei kenkyū* 32.1:1–28 (1982).

Saugstad, Jesse E. *Shipping and Shipbuilding Subsidies*. U.S. Department of Commerce. Trade Promotion Series, no. 129. Washington, D.C., 1932.

Saxonhouse, Gary. "A Tale of Japanese Technological Diffusion in the Meiji Period," *Journal of Economic History* 34.1:149–165 (March 1974).

Segai Inoue kō den (Biography of Marquis Inoue), vol. 3. 1933–1934. Reprint. Hara Shobō, 1968.

Segawa Shizuo. *Kaiun kōkokushi* (Shipping and our prosperous nation: Its history). Kaiji Ihōsha, 1927.

70 Years North German Lloyd Bremen, 1857–1927. Berlin, Atlantic-Verlag G.M.B.H. (n.d.).

Shibagaki Kazuo. *Nihon kin'yū shihon bunseki* (An analysis of Japanese finance capital). Tokyo Daigaku Shuppankai, 1965.

——. "The Early History of the Zaibatsu," *Developing Economies* 4:535–566 (December 1966).

——. *Mitsui, Mitsubishi no hyakunen* (A hundred years of Mitsui and Mitsubishi). Chūō Kōronsha, 1968.

Shibusawa Eiichi denki shiryō (Biographical materials on Shibusawa Eiichi), vols. 2, 8, 10, 18, and 51, ed., Shibusawa Seien kinen zaidan ryūmonsha. 1957–1958. [SEDS].

Shibusawa Yeiichi. "Joint-Stock Enterprise in Japan," in Ōkuma Shigenobu, ed., *Fifty Years of New Japan*, vol. 1, pp. 465–485.

Shimura Kaichi. *Nihon shihon shijō bunseki* (An analysis of Japan's capital market). Tokyo Daigaku Shuppankai, 1969.

Shinjo Hiroshi. *History of the Yen*. Tokyo, Kinokuniya, 1962.

Shiroyanagi Shūko. *Zaikai taiheiki* (Records of the tranquil world of business). Nihon Hyōronsha, 1929.

——. *Zoku Zaikai taiheiki* (Additional records of the tranquil world of business). Nihon Hyōronsha, 1930.

——. *Nihon fugō hasseigaku* (The embryology of Japan's plutocracy). Chikura Shobō, 1931.

——. *Iwasaki Yatarō den* (Biography of Iwasaki Yatarō). Kaizōsha, 1932.

——. *Nihon kaiun no kensetsusha, Iwasaki Yatarō* (The builder of Japanese shipping: Iwasaki Yatarō). Chōbunkaku, 1942.

Shōda Heigorō. "Kaiun shinchō hōhō torishirabesho, fuenzetsu hikki" (Documents on investigating methods of shipping promotion, with attached speech). (February 6, 1895). Pamphlet.

Shukuri Shigeichi. *Shōda Heigorō* (Biography). 1932.

Shuyōkoku senzen kaiun joseishi (A history of prewar shipping subsidies of major countries). Edited by Kaiji Sangyō Kenkyūjo, Chōsa Shiriizu 69-12, 1969.

Smith, Thomas C. *Political Change and Industrial Development in Japan: Government Enterprise, 1868-1880*. Stanford, Stanford University Press, 1955.

Sturmey, S. G. *British Shipping and World Competition*. The University of London, The Athlone Press, 1962.

Suehiro Kazuo. *Danshaku Kondō Renpei den narabi ikō* (The life and posthumous papers of Baron Kondō Renpei). 1932. [KD].

Sugii Rokurō. "Meiji seifu no kaiun seisaku" (The shipping policy of the Meiji government), *Geirin* 7.5:2-38 (1956).

———. "Jōyaku kaiseishijō no engan bōeki" (Coastal trade from the standpoint of the history of treaty revision), *Bunka shigaku* 13:44-63 (July 1957) and 14:34-46 (September 1958).

Sugiyama Kazuo. "Kigyō no zaimu: tōshi katsudō to bunkateki haikei: Meijiki no tetsudōgyō, menbōsekigyō o jirei to shite" (Business finance: Investment activity and its cultural background, the case of the railway and cotton spinning industries in the Meiji period), *Keiei shigaku* 10.1:54-86 (August 1975).

———. "Trade Credit and the Development of the Cotton Spinning Industry: Its Role and Background," in Nakagawa Keiichirō, ed., *Marketing and Finance in the Course of Industrialization*, 1978, pp. 59-82.

———. *Kaiungyō to kin'yū* (The shipping industry and finance). Vol. 4 of *Nihon kaiun keieishi*, 1981.

Sugiyama Shin'ya. "Bakumatsu – Meiji shoki ni okeru sekitan yushutsu no dōkō to Shanhai sekitan shijō" (Trends in Japan's coal exports and the Shanghai coal market in the Bakumatsu and early Meiji periods), *Shakai keizai shigaku* 43.6:19-41 (1978).

Sumiya Mikio and Koji Taira, eds. *An Outline of Japanese Economic History, 1603-1940: Major Works and Research Findings*. University of Tokyo, 1979.

Sutiagina, M. V. *Mitsubishi – kono kyodai kigyō shūdan* (Mitsubishi: The giant enterprise group). Translated from Russian by Nakamura Heihachi and Nihei Takeo. Aoki Shoten, 1975.

Takamura Naosuke. *Nihon bōsekigyōshi josetsu* (An introduction to the history of the cotton spinning industry in Japan). 2 vols. Hanawa Shobō, 1971.

———. "Sangyō bōeki kōzō" (The structure of industry and trade), in Ōishi Kaichirō, ed., *Nihon sangyō kakumei no kenkyū*, vol. 1, 1975, pp. 43-78.

———. "Kyōkō" (Financial panics), in Ōishi Kaichirō, ed., *Nihon sangyō kakumei no kenkyū*, vol. 2, 1975, pp. 185-228.

——. "Dokusen shihonshugi no kakuritsu to chūshō kigyō" (The establishment of monopoly capitalism and small and medium enterprises), *Iwanami kōza, Nihon rekishi*, vol. 18, *Kindai* V. Iwanami Shoten, 1975, pp. 43-92.

——. *Kindai Nihon mengyō to Chūgoku* (The modern Japanese cotton industry and China). Tokyo Daigaku Shuppankai, 1982.

Takatera Sadao. *Meiji genka shōkyakushi no kenkyū* (Studies in the history of Meiji depreciation accounting). Miraisha, 1974.

——. "Introduction and Diffusion of Depreciation Accounting in Japan, 1875-1903," in Nakagawa Keiichirō, ed., *Marketing and Finance in the Course of Industrialization*, 1978, pp. 105-115.

Takaura Tadahiko. "Mitsubishi no 'shasoku' ni tsuite" (On the Mitsubishi company code), *Keizaikei*. Kantō Gakuin Daigaku. 101:108-123 (October 1974).

Tamaki Hajime. *Gendai Nihon sangyō hattatsushi* (The historical development of modern Japanese industry), vol. 29, *Sōron* (Introduction) I. Edited by Dō Kenkyūkai, 1967.

Tanaka Sōgorō. *Iwasaki Yatarō den* (Biography of Iwasaki Yatarō). Tōyō Shokan, 1955.

Tatematsu Kiyoshi. "Nihon shihonshugi kakuritsuki no Mitsubishi zaibatsu" (The Mitsubishi zaibatsu during the period of the establishment of Japanese capitalism), *Hitotsubashi kenkyū* 25:83-101 (July 1973).

Teikoku gikai shi (The history of the Imperial Diet). Vol. 1 of *Gikai seido 70 nenshi* (A 70-year history of parliamentary institution). Edited by Shūgiin and Sangiin. 12 vols., 1962.

Teishin jigyōshi (The history of communications industries), vol. 6. Teishinshō, 1940.

Teishinshō 50 nen ryakushi (A brief 50-year history of the Ministry of Communications). Dōhen, 1936.

Terai Hisanobu. *Kaiun no saiken* (The reconstruction of shipping). Shichiyōsha, 1948.

——. *Shio no michihi* (The ebb and flow of the tide). Gotō Shoten, 1953.

Terai Hisanobu (Biography). N.Y.K. nai Denki Hensan Iinkai, 1965.

Teratani Takeaki. *Nihon kōwan shiron josetsu* (An introductory discussion of the history of Japanese ports). Jichōsha, 1972.

——. *Nihon kindai zōsenshi josetsu* (An introduction to the history of modern Japanese shipbuilding). Gannandō Shoten, 1979.

——. "Japanese Business and Government in the Takeoff Stage," in Nakagawa Keiichirō, ed., *Government and Business*, 1980, pp. 57-78.

Terazawa, Kumiko. "Mitsui Bussan Kaisha: Its Growth and Effects on the Japanese Economy (1876-1930)," *Stone Lion Review* 3:39-50 (Spring 1979). Harvard University. East Asian Graduate Students' Colloquium.

The 100 Year History of Mitsui & Co. Ltd., 1876-1976. Translated by

T. I. Elliott and edited by Japan Business History Institute. Tokyo, The Company, 1977.

The Tokio Marine & Fire Insurance: The First Century, 1879–1979. Edited by Japan Business History Institute. Tokyo, The Company, 1980.

Tiedemann, Arthur E. "Big Business and Politics in Prewar Japan," in James W. Morley, ed., *Dilemmas of Growth in Prewar Japan.* Princeton, Princeton University Press, 1971, pp. 267–316.

——. "Japan's Economic Foreign Policies, 1868–1893," in James W. Morley, ed., *Japan's Foreign Policy, 1868–1941, A Research Guide.* New York, Columbia University Press, 1974, pp. 118–152.

Titus, David Anson. *Palace and Politics in Prewar Japan.* New York, Columbia University Press, 1974.

Togai Yoshio. *Mitsui Bussan Kaisha no keiei shiteki kenkyū* (Historical studies of Mitsui Bussan's management). Tōyō Keizai Shinpōsha, 1974.

Tokutomi Iichirō. *Kōshaku Matsukata Masayoshi den* (Biography of Prince Matsukata Masayoshi). 2 vols. Dō Denki Hakkōjo, 1935.

Tokyo Kaijō Kasai Hoken Kabushiki Kaisha 100 nenshi (A 100-year history of the Tokio Marine & Fire Insurance Company). I. Edited by Nihon Keieishi Kenkyūjo. Dōsha, 1979.

Tokyo keizai zasshi (The Tokyo Economic Journal).

Tominaga Yūji. *Kōtsū ni okeru shihonshugi no hatten* (Capitalistic development in the transportation industry). Iwanami Shoten, 1953.

Tōyō Kisen Kabushiki Kaisha 64 nen no ayumi (The 64-year course of the Oriental Shipping Company). Comp. Nakano Hideo. 1964.

Toyoda Takeshi and Kodama Kōta, eds. *Kōtsūshi* (A history of transportation). Vol. 24 of *Taikei Nihonshi sōsho* (The library of Japanese history). Yamakawa Shuppansha, 1970.

Tregonning, K. G. *Home Port Singapore: A History of Straits Steamship Co. Ltd., 1860–1965.* Singapore, Oxford University Press, 1967.

Tsuchida, Nobuya. *The Japanese in Brazil, 1908–1941.* PhD dissertation, University of California, Los Angeles, 1978.

Tsuchiya Moriaki and Morikawa Hidemasa, eds. *Kigyōsha katsudō no shiteki kenkyū: Nakagawa Keiichirō sensei kanreki kinen* (Historical studies in entrepreneurship in honor of Professor Nakagawa Keiichirō's 60th birthday). Nihon Keizai Shinbunsha, 1981.

Tsuchiya Takao and Ōuchi Hyōe, comps. *Meiji zenki zaisei keizai shiryō shūsei* (Collected materials on the financial and economic history of the early Meiji period), vols. 1–3. Kaizōsha, 1931–1934.

Tsukahara Mushū ō (Biography of the Venerable Tsukahara Shūzō). Edited by Tsukahara Shūzō Shi Kaiji Kankei 50 Nen Kinen Shukugakai Iin, 1925.

Tsurumi Yūsuke. *Gotō Shinpei* (Biography), vol. 3. Keishō Shobō, 1966.

Tuturow, Norman E. "Leland Stanford, President of the Occidental and

Oriental Steamship Company: A Study in the Rhetoric and Reality of Competition," *American Neptune* 31.2:120-129 (April 1971).

Uda Tadashi. "Wagakuni tetsudō jigyō keieishi ni okeru seifu to kigyō: 'tetsudō seiryaku' no tenkai kōzō" (Government and business in the history of the Japanese railway industry: The development structure of railway strategy), *Keiei shigaku* 6.1:124-139 (September 1971).

U.S. Department of Commerce. *Government Aid to Merchant Shipping.* Special Agent Series, No. 119, 1919. Rev. ed. August 1, 1923. Washington, D.C., 1925.

Wagasha kakukōro no enkaku (The history of our company's shipping lines). Edited by N.Y.K. Kamotsu-Ka. 1932.

Watson, Andrew, tr. *Transport in Transition: The Evolution of Traditional Shipping in China.* Ann Arbor, University of Michigan, Center for Chinese Studies, 1972.

Woodsworth, Charles J. *Canada and the Orient.* Toronto, Macmillan, 1941.

Wray, William D. "Mitsubishi and the N.Y.K. Line, 1870-1894: The Beginnings of the Modern Japanese Shipping Industry." PhD dissertation, Harvard University, 1976. (Harvard Archives: HU90/11197B; Tōdai Economics Library: 27-A/97). [Abbreviated as Wray].

——. "Nippon Yūsen Kaisha no Ōshū kōro ni okeru keiei senryaku to unchin dōmei, 1896-1907" (Business strategy and the freight conference on the N.Y.K.'s European line), in Tsuchiya Moriaki and Morikawa Hidemasa, eds., *Kigyōsha katsudō no shiteki kenkyū,* 1981, pp. 67-84.

——. "Senkanki ni okeru kigyō no jishusei to Yūshō teikei mondai" (Company autonomy and N.Y.K.-O.S.K. cooperation in the Inter-War Years), *Keiei shigaku* 18.2:1-22 (July 1983).

——. "The NYK and the Commercial Diplomacy of the Far Eastern Freight Conference, 1896-1956," forthcoming in a volume on shipping, Tokyo University Press.

——. "Shipping: From Sail to Steam," in Marius Jansen and Gilbert Rozman, eds., *Japan in Transition: From Tokugawa to Meiji,* forthcoming from Princeton University Press.

Yamaguchi Kazuo. "Meiji shoki no gaikoku kaiun to Mitsubishi Kaisha" (Foreign shipping in the early Meiji period and the Mitsubishi Company), in *Sekai keizai bunseki - Wakimura Yoshitarō kyōju kanreki kinen ronbunshū* (Analysis of the world economy: Essays in honor of Professor Wakimura Yoshitarō). Iwanami Shoten, 1962, pp. 120-157.

——. "Kaiun" (Shipping), in Arisawa Hiromi, comp., *Nihon sangyō 100 nenshi,* 1966, pp. 81-87.

Yamamoto Hirobumi. "Shoki shokusan seisaku to sono shūsei" (Industrial promotion policy in the early Meiji period and its revision), in Andō Yoshio, ed., *Nihon keizai seisaku shiron*, vol. 1, 1973, pp. 3-54.

Yamamoto Mitsuhiko. *Kawasaki Shōzō* (Biography). 1918.

Yamamoto Tatsuo (Biography). Dō Sensei Denki Hensankai, 1951.

Yamamura, Kozo. "The Founding of Mitsubishi: A Case Study in Japanese Business History," *Business History Review* 41.2:141-160 (Summer 1967).

———. "Japan, 1868-1930: A Revised View," in Rondo Cameron, ed., *Banking and Economic Development*. Oxford University, 1972, pp. 168-198.

———. *A Study of Samurai Income and Entrepreneurship*. Cambridge, Harvard University Press, 1974.

———. "General Trading Companies in Japan: Their Origins and Growth," in Hugh Patrick, ed., *Japanese Industrialization and its Social Consequences*. Berkeley, University of California, 1976, pp. 161-199.

———. "Success Illgotten? The Role of Meiji Militarism in Japan's Technological Progress," *Journal of Economic History* 37.1:113-135 (March 1977).

———. "Entrepreneurship, Ownership, and Management in Japan," in Peter Mathias and M. M. Postan, eds., *The Cambridge Economic History of Europe*, vol. vii, pt. 2. Cambridge, Cambridge University Press, 1978, pp. 215-264.

Yamashita Kamesaburō. *Shizumitsu ukitsu* (Sinking and floating: The vicissitudes of life). 2 vols. Yamashita Kabushiki Kaisha Hisho-bu, 1943.

Yamashita Naotō. "Keiseiki Nihon shihonshugi ni okeru matchi kōgyō to Mitsui Bussan" (The match industry and Mitsui Bussan in the formative period of Japanese capitalism), *Mitsui bunko ronsō* 6:93-166 (1972).

———. "Nisshin-Nichiro senkanki ni okeru zaibatsu burujoajī no seisaku shikō: Yūrakukai no dōkō o chūshin ni" (Policy aims of the zaibatsu bourgeoisie between the Sino- and Russo-Japanese Wars: The attitude of the Yūrakukai), *Rekishigaku kenkyū* 450:12-26 (November 1977).

———. "Nihon teikokushugi seiritsuki no Higashi Ajia sekitan shijō to Mitsui Bussan: Shanhai shijō o chūshin ni" (The East Asian coal market and Mitsui Bussan during the period of the formation of Japanese imperialism: The case of the Shanghai market), in *Enerugī to keizai hatten*, 1979, pp. 255-306.

Yasuba Yasukichi. "Kaijō unsō to kōgyōka: josetsu" (Ocean transportation and industrialization: An introduction), in Hidemura Senzō et al., eds., *Kindai keizai no rekishiteki kiban*, 1977, pp. 262-276.

———. "Freight Rates and Productivity in Ocean Transportation for Japan, 1875-1943," *Explorations in Economic History* 15.1:11-39 (January 1978). [Abbreviated as Yasuba].

———. "Gaikō kaiun to keizai hatten: sekitan to no kanren o chūshin ni"

(Ocean shipping and economic development: The connection with coal), in *Enerugi to keizai hatten,* 1979, pp. 223–248.

Yasuoka Shigeaki. "The Tradition of Family Business in the Strategic Decision Process and Management Structure of Zaibatsu Business: Mitsui, Sumitomo, and Mitsubishi," in Nakagawa Keiichirō, ed., *Strategy and Structure of Big Business,* 1976, pp. 81–101.

———. *Zaibatsu no keieishi* (Zaibatsu business history). Nihon Keizai Shinbunsha, 1978.

———, ed. *Zaibatsushi kenkyū* (Studies in zaibatsu history). Nihon Keizai Shinbunsha, 1979.

Yokohama-shi shi (The history of Yokohama city). Series 4, vol. 1. Dōhen, 1965.

Yokohama Shōkin Ginkōshi (The history of the Yokohama Specie Bank). Internal publication, 1920.

Yoneda Fujio. *Gendai Nihon kaiun shikan* (A historical view of contemporary Japanese shipping). Kaiji Sangyō Kenkyūjo, 1978.

Yoshihara Kunio. *Sogo Shosha: The Vanguard of the Japanese Economy.* Tokyo, Oxford University Press, 1982.

Yoshino, M. Y. *Japan's Managerial System: Tradition and Innovation.* Cambridge, MIT Press, 1968.

Yoshino Toshihiko. *Nihon Ginkō* (The Bank of Japan). Iwanami Shoten, 1963.

Young, L. K. *British Policy in China, 1895–1902.* Oxford University, 1970.

Yui Tsunehiko. "Kaijō hokengyō no sōgyō to kakuritsu: Tōkyō Kaijō Hoken Kaisha no baai" (The initiation and establishment of the marine insurance industry: The case of the Tokio Marine Insurance Company), *Keiei shigaku* 3.1:54–66 (March 1968).

Yunoki Manabu. *Kinsei kaiunshi no kenkyū* (Studies of early modern shipping history). Hōsei Daigaku Shuppankyoku, 1979.

Yūsen no omoide (Reminiscences of the N.Y.K.). Edited by N.Y.K. nai Yūsenkai, 1962.

Zaikai bukko ketsubutsu den (Biographies of former great business leaders). 2 vols. Jitsugyō no Sekaisha, 1936.

Index

Abe Taizō, 270, 478

Administration: structure of Mitsubishi, 73, 117; centralization of, 74–76; weakness of KUK, 215–217; changes in N.Y.K., 269–275, 469; main personnel of N.Y.K., 466–469; N.Y.K. board, 469–471; structure in outline, 472; terminology of, 521–522. *See also* Management

Agricultural products: transported by Mitsubishi, 100; transported from China to Europe, 335; from S. Manchuria, 398; rate war on, 429, 609n30

Agriculture, Shinagawa's emphasis on, 160

Agriculture and Commerce, Ministry of (Nōshōmushō), 136–138; on founding of KUK, 147–148

Akai Zenpei, 179

Akira Iriye, 359, 360, 598n37

Akita Prefecture, 134

Akkeshi forests, 139

Alt & Company, 41

Amagasaki Cotton Spinning Company, 281

Amamiya Keijirō, 171, 235

American line, N.Y.K.: ships for, 310; subsidy for, 320; place of Shanghai in, 344; in wartime, 374; strategies for, 400, 408, 419; obstacles to, 408–409; tonnage in, 414; profits of, 441

Anglo-Japanese Alliance, 352, 354, 382; attempts to broaden, 397

Antwerp, 513; terminus of N.Y.K. European line, 317, 325; competition with Hamburg, 377–378

Aomori Prefecture, 284

Arishima Takeo, 478–479

Arisugawa, State Minister, 191

Arnhold Karberg & Company, 349, 392

Article 12 of First Directive, 79–80

Asabuki Eiji, 211, 234, 566n82, 574n92

Asada Masabumi, 179, 508; in N.Y.K., 228, 229, 231, 268; resignation of, 271

Asahi Glass, 464

Asano Kaisōbu (Asano Marine Transportation Office), 278

Asano Sōichirō, 171; and Tōyō Kisen Kaisha, 277–278, 374; on European service, 588n29

Assets, Mitsubishi: revaluation of, 221–222; and Marunouchi, 581n47

Assets, N.Y.K.: types of, 433; relation to ship purchases, 435; and current ratio, 435–436

Audit, of N.Y.K., 223, 243, 269, 270; stockholders on, 478

Australia, 263, 289

Australian line, N.Y.K., 344, 608n10; subsidy for, 305; ships for, 310; tonnage on, 414

Austrian Lloyd, on Bombay-Kobe line, 295–296, 300, 402–403

Autonomy: as management strategy, 5, 7–9, 11, 12; recognition of by Ōkubo, 70–71; lack of in KUK, 165–166; and subsidies, 307–308, 441; government restrictions on, 383; limited, in N.Y.K., 504–508, 516; erosion of Chinese, 514; and imperialism, 598n42

Baba Kinsuke, 246

Baba Tatsui, 150, 211

Balance of trade, 58; Japan-China, 61

Harvard East Asian Monographs

21. Kwang-Ching Liu, ed., *American Missionaries in China: Papers from Harvard Seminars*

22. George Moseley, *A Sino-Soviet Cultural Frontier: The Ili Kazakh Autonomous Chou*

23. Carl F. Nathan, *Plague Prevention and Politics in Manchuria, 1910–1931*

24. Adrian Arthur Bennett, *John Fryer: The Introduction of Western Science and Technology into Nineteenth-Century China*

25. Donald J. Friedman, *The Road from Isolation: The Campaign of the American Committee for Non-Participation in Japanese Aggression, 1938–1941*

26. Edward Le Fevour, *Western Enterprise in Late Ch'ing China: A Selective Survey of Jardine, Matheson and Company's Operations, 1842–1895*

27. Charles Neuhauser, *Third World Politics: China and the Afro-Asian People's Solidarity Organization, 1957–1967*

28. Kungtu C. Sun, assisted by Ralph W. Huenemann, *The Economic Development of Manchuria in the First Half of the Twentieth Century*

29. Shahid Javed Burki, *A Study of Chinese Communes, 1965*

30. John Carter Vincent, *The Extraterritorial System in China: Final Phase*

31. Madeleine Chi, *China Diplomacy, 1914–1918*

32. Clifton Jackson Phillips, *Protestant America and the Pagan World: The First Half Century of the American Board of Commissioners for Foreign Missions, 1810–1860*

33. James Pusey, *Wu Han: Attacking the Present through the Past*

34. Ying-wan Cheng, *Postal Communication in China and Its Modernization, 1860–1896*

35. Tuvia Blumenthal, *Saving in Postwar Japan*

36. Peter Frost, *The Bakumatsu Currency Crisis*

37. Stephen C. Lockwood, *Augustine Heard and Company, 1858–1862*

38. Robert R. Campbell, *James Duncan Campbell: A Memoir by His Son*

39. Jerome Alan Cohen, ed., *The Dynamics of China's Foreign Relations*

40. V. V. Vishnyakova-Akimova, *Two Years in Revolutionary China, 1925–1927*, tr. Steven I. Levine

41. Meron Medzini, *French Policy in Japan during the Closing Years of the Tokugawa Regime*

42. *The Cultural Revolution in the Provinces*

43. Sidney A. Forsythe, *An American Missionary Community in China, 1895–1905*

44. Benjamin I. Schwartz, ed., *Reflections on the May Fourth Movement: A Symposium*

45. Ching Young Choe, *The Rule of the Taewŏn'gun, 1864–1873: Restoration in Yi Korea*

STUDIES IN THE MODERNIZATION OF THE
REPUBLIC OF KOREA: 1945–1975

90. Noel F. McGinn, Donald R. Snodgrass, Yung Bong Kim, Shin-Bok Kim, and Quee-Young Kim, *Education and Development in Korea*

91. Leroy P. Jones and Il SaKong, *Government, Business and Entrepreneurship in Economic Development: The Korean Case*

92. Edward S. Mason, Dwight H. Perkins, Kwang Suk Kim, David C. Cole, Mahn Je Kim, et al., *The Economic and Social Modernization of the Republic of Korea*

93. Robert Repetto, Tai Hwan Kwon, Son-Ung Kim, Dae Young Kim, John E. Sloboda, and Peter J. Donaldson, *Economic Development, Population Policy, and Demographic Transition in the Republic of Korea*

106. David C. Cole and Yung Chul Park, *Financial Development in Korea, 1945-1978*

94. Parks M. Coble, *The Shanghai Capitalists and the Nationalist Government, 1927-1937*

95. Noriko Kamachi, *Reform in China: Huang Tsun-hsien and the Japanese Model*

96. Richard Wich, *Sino-Soviet Crisis Politics: A Study of Political Change and Communication*

97. Lillian M. Li, *China's Silk Trade: Traditional Industry in the Modern World, 1842-1937*

98. R. David Arkush, *Fei Xiaotong and Sociology in Revolutionary China*

99. Kenneth Alan Grossberg, *Japan's Renaissance: The Politics of the Muromachi Bakufu*

100. James Reeve Pusey, *China and Charles Darwin*

101. Hoyt Cleveland Tillman, *Utilitarian Confucianism: Ch'en Liang's Challenge to Chu Hsi*

102. Thomas A. Stanley, *Ōsugi Sakae, Anarchist in Taishō Japan: The Creativity of the Ego*

103. Jonathan K. Ocko, *Bureaucratic Reform in Provincial China: Ting Jih-ch'ang in Restoration Kiangsu, 1867-1870*

104. James Reed, *The Missionary Mind and American East Asia Policy, 1911-1915*

105. Neil L. Waters, *Japan's Local Pragmatists: The Transition from Bakumatsu to Meiji in the Kawasaki Region*

108. William D. Wray, *Mitsubishi and the N.Y.K., 1870-1914: Business Strategy in the Japanese Shipping Industry*

109. Ralph William Huenemann, *The Dragon and the Iron Horse: The Economics of Railroads in China, 1876-1937*

110. Benjamin A. Elman, *From Philosophy to Philology: Intellectual and Social Aspects of Change in Late Imperial China*

111. Jane Kate Leonard, *Wei Yuan and China's Rediscovery of the Maritime World*

112. Luke S. K. Kwong, *A Mosaic of the Hundred Days: Personalities, Politics, and Ideas of 1898*